D0934967

THE EURO AS A STABILIZER IN THE INTERNATIONAL ECONOMIC SYSTEM

THE EURO AS A STABILIZER IN THE INTERNATIONAL ECONOMIC SYSTEM

Edited by

Robert Mundell
and
Armand Clesse

KLUWER ACADEMIC PUBLISHERS

Boston / Dordrecht / London

Distributors for North, Central and South America:
Kluwer Academic Publishers
101 Philip Drive
Assinippi Park
Norwell, Massachusetts 02061 USA
Telephone (781) 871-6600
Fax (781) 681-9045
E-Mail <kluwer@wkap.com>

Distributors for all other countries:
Kluwer Academic Publishers Group
Distribution Centre
Post Office Box 322
3300 AH Dordrecht, THE NETHERLANDS
Telephone 31 78 6392 392
Fax 31 78 6546 474
E-Mail <services@wkap.nl>

    Electronic Services <http://www.wkap.nl>

Library of Congress Cataloging-in-Publication Data

The Euro as a stabilizer in the international economic system/edited by Robert
Mundell and Armand Clesse.
        p.cm.
    Includes bibliographical references.
    ISBN 0-7923-7755-9(alk.paper)
    .I.Euro. 2.Monetary policy--European Union countries. 3.International finance.I.
    Mundell, Robert A. II. Clesse, Armand.

    HG925 .E8678 2000
    332.4'94--dc21

                                                                00-020396

Printed on acid-free paper.

Printed in the United States of America

*To Charles P. Kindleberger and Pierre Werner,
pioneers in the theory and practice of the European
and international economic and monetary system*

Contents

Contributors   xi

Preface   xv

Acknowledgments   xvii

Introduction   xix

PART I: THE VIABILITY OF THE EURO

1. **A New Bi-Polarity?**   3
   Charles P. Kindleberger

2. **The Theoretical and Historical Perspectives on the Emergence of the Euro**   21
   Robert Skidelsky and Kalin Nikolov

3. **External Relations of the Euro Area**   35
   C. Randall Henning

4. **The International Political Implications of the Euro**   47
   Richard Rosecrance

5. **The Euro and the Stability of the International Monetary System**   57
   Robert Mundell

PART II: MANAGEMENT OF THE EURO

6. **The Euro and Its Consequences for Global Capital Markets**   87
   Norbert Walter

7. **Impact of the Euro on Members and Non-**   93
    Members
    Jeffrey A. Frankel

✕ 8. **Exchange Rate Policy-Making in the Euro Area:**   111
      Lessons From Trade?
      Klaus Günter Deutsch

9. **Reinforcing European Integration to Promote the**   135
    Euro: A Range of Policy Options
    Pierre Maillet

10. **Currency Crises and Capital Controls in**   157
    Emerging Countries: The Case of the African
    CFA Franc and Its Euro Future
    Emil-Maria Claassen

PART III: THE EURO IN THE INTERNATIONAL ECONOMY

⨍11. **Key Currencies After the Euro**   177
      Richard N. Cooper

⅄ 12. **The Political Economy of the Euro as an**   203
       International Currency
       Jeffry A. Frieden

13. **The Prospect for Global Monetary Bilingualism**   215
    Gerhard Michael Ambrosi

14. **The Euro and the Outsiders: The Case of the**   231
    Swiss Franc
    Jörg Baumberger

15. **The Euro and the Dollar: Currency Competition,**   251
    Competitiveness and Policy Coordination
    Christian de Boissieu

16. **The Impact of the Euro on the International Stability: A Chinese Perspective** 261
   Mingqi Xu

PART IV: CONFERENCE SESSIONS 271

Session 1: **Monetary Leadership and Economic Stability: The Lessons of the Pound and the Dollar** 273

Session 2: **Monetary Leadership and Economic Stability in a Globalizing World** 291

Session 3: **The Emergence of the Euro and Its Future Position vis-à-vis Other Leading Currencies** 309

Session 4: **The Impact of the Euro on International Stability** 335

Session 5: **The Institutional Implications of the Euro** 359

Session 6: **What Should Be the Euro's International Role?** 375

PART V: KEYNOTE SESSION 391

Conference Participants 433

Pictures Taken at the Conference 437

Index of Contributors 441

Contributors

(professional positions at the time of the conference)

Gerhard Michael Ambrosi is Professor of European Economic Policy at the University of Trier, Germany. His publications include *Systemtransformation und Zahlungsunion* [Systemic Transformation and Payments Union], Pfaffenweiler, 1993. He is publishing 'Economic Policy Coordination and the Euro', in *European Integration and the Euro*, Brussels (Euro Institute), in November 1999.

Jörg Baumberger is Professor of Economics at the University of St. Gallen, Switzerland, where he teaches public finance and public economics, financial intermediation and real estate economics. His latest publication is *Real Estate and Property*, Geneva, 1999. He is currently working on a book on the economics of real estate markets.

Christian de Boissieu is Professor of Economics at the University of Paris-I (Panthéon-Sorbonne). Consultant to the World Bank and to the European Commission, he is also a member of the Council of Economic Analysis created by the French Prime Minister Lionel Jospin in 1997. His recent publications include *Les mutations de l'économie française*, Paris, 1997, and *Monnaie et Economie*, Paris, 1998.

Emil-Maria Claassen holds the Chair of International Economics at the University of Paris-Dauphine. Previously he taught at the Free University of Berlin from 1989 to 1991. His work for the World Bank, the UN and the IMF has focused on macroeconomic issues like the impact of financial liberalization on stabilization policies. His most recent publication is *Global Monetary Economics*, Oxford, 1997.

Richard N. Cooper is the Maurits C. Boas Professor of International Economics at Harvard University. He has served on several occasions in the US Government, most recently as Chairman of the National Intelligence Council. His recent writings include 'Should Capital Controls Be Banished?' (*Brookings Papers on Economic Activity*, no. 1, 1999) and *Exchange Rate Choices* for the Federal Reserve Bank of Boston.

Klaus Günter Deutsch is a senior economist at the Division of Economic and Banking Policy, European Integration, Deutsche Bank Research. He has written on trade policy-making in Europe, EMU, various G-7 issues, banking and capital markets, corporate governance and pension issues.

Jeffrey A. Frankel is a member of the Council of Economic Advisers at the Executive Office of the President, Washington, D.C. In 1988 and 1989, he was a Visiting Professor of Public Policy at Harvard University. His most recent publications include *Regional Trading Blocs in the World Economic System*, Washington, D.C., 1997, and (with R. Caves and R. Jones) *World Trade and Payments: An Introduction* (8th ed.), New York, 1999.

Jeffry A. Frieden is Professor of Government at Harvard University. He specializes in the politics of international monetary and financial relations. He is the co-editor (with B. Eichengreen) of *Forging an Integrated Europe*, Michigan, 1998, and (with D. Gros and E. Jones) of *The New Political Economy of EMU*, Oxford, 1998.

C. Randall Henning is Associate Professor at the School of International Service of American University and Visiting Fellow at the Institute for International Economics, Washington, D.C. His publications include *Cooperating with Europe's Monetary Union*, Washington D.C., 1997, and *Transatlantic Perspectives on the Euro*, Washington, D.C., forthcoming.

Charles P. Kindleberger is the Ford International Professor of Economics, emer., at the Massachusetts Institute of Technology. His numerous publications include *The World in Depression, 1929-1939*, Berkeley, 1973, *A Financial History of Western Europe*, New York, 1984, and *World Economic Primacy: 1500-1990*, Oxford, 1996.

Pierre Maillet is Professor of Economics, emer., and a honorary Director General of the European Commission. Between 1973 and 1991, he held the Jean Monnet Chair at the University of Lille 1 in France. He is the co-author (with D. Velo) of *L'Europe à géométrie variable*, Paris, 1994, and (with W. Kösters) of *Une Europe plus favorable à l'emploi*, Paris, 1996.

Robert Mundell is the C. Lowell Harriss Professor of Economics at Columbia University, New York. The author of numerous articles and several books, he is known for his contributions to the theory of optimum currency areas, international macroeconomic equilibrium, supply-side economics and studies in the theory and history of the international monetary system.

Kalin Nikolov is a Research Officer at the Center for Post-Collective Studies at The Social Market Foundation in London. He published in 1999 *Russia: the 1998 crisis and beyond.*

Richard Rosecrance is Professor at the University of California, Los Angeles, and Director of the Center for International Relations at UCLA. His publications include *America's Economic Resurgence: A Bold New Strategy*, New York, 1990. He is currently working on *The Rise of the Virtual State: Wealth and Power in the Coming Century.*

Robert Skidelsky is Professor of Political Economy at Warwick University in the UK and Chairman of The Social Market Foundation in London. His publications include *The road from serfdom: the economic and political consequences of the end of communism*, New York, 1996, and a biography of John Maynard Keynes.

Nobert Walter has been Chief Economist at the Deutsche Bank Group since 1992. He is the Managing Director of Deutsche Bank Research, covering a wide spectrum of issues ranging from country rating to company analysis. He is the author of *On the New Wealth of the Nation*, Washington, D.C., 1993.

Mingqi Xu is a Research Professor at the Shanghai Academy of Social Sciences and an Assistant Director of the Institute of World Economy at SASS. He is also the editor in chief of the *Journal of Social Sciences* and of *Shanghai Academy of Social Sciences Quarterly*. His most recent publication is *Contemporary World Economy and Politics.*

Preface

The introduction of the euro was an important event for the world economy and the international political system. For the first time in history, a substantial group of European countries—eleven of the fifteen members of the European Union including three members of the G-7—have voluntarily agreed to replace their national currencies with a single currency. The euro area has already become established as the second largest currency area in the world and will therefore become a major player in the international monetary system.

The creation of the euro poses a number of interesting questions. Will the euro be a strong or a weak currency? Will the euro challenge the leading position hitherto held by the United States dollar and would sharing of the burdens and advantages of reserve currency status improve or worsen the stability of the international monetary system? How will the euro affect US relations with Europe? Does the formation of the euro intensify European integration in other fields? Is a bi-polar international monetary system viable?

These and other issues motivated the Luxembourg Institute for European and International Studies and the Pierre Werner Foundation to organize an international conference in Luxembourg on December 3-4, 1998, on the eve of the birth of the euro. At the outset we were aware that the issue of the euro went far beyond pure economics. Money, after all, is too important a subject to be left to economists. We therefore planned a multi-disciplinary conference, inviting as participants, besides economists, bankers, political economists, economic historians and politicians. This book offers to the general reader the proceedings of the conference together with papers written by participants before or after the meeting.

The conference was organized in honor of Charles P. Kindleberger and Pierre Werner. Professor Kindleberger has devoted a major part of his work to the inquiry into the conditions for achieving stability in the international system. Pierre Werner chaired the group of experts which came up, in the early 70s, with the report requested by the European Summit of The Hague for the creation of a European monetary union.

R. Mundell   A. Clesse

Acknowledgments

The topic of the conference, namely the creation of a new common currency for a major part of Europe, and the importance of the two men in whose honor the meeting was organized, Charles P. Kindleberger and Pierre Werner, led the organizers to give the event a special luster and to invite some of the finest experts on international monetary issues. This however meant that the whole event, including this book, was bound to become expensive. It was only with the generous support of sponsors from the private as well as the public sphere, together with the contributions of the Pierre Werner Foundation and the Luxembourg Institute for European and International Studies, that we were able to achieve our ambition.

We would therefore like to thank the following banks, corporations, organizations and newspapers for their support: ABN AMRO Bank (Luxembourg) S.A.; AGF/Assubel Vie Luxembourg S.A.; ARBED S.A.; Artesia Bank Luxembourg S.A.; Association des Banques et Banquiers Luxembourg; Banque Colbert (Luxembourg) S.A.; Banque Continentale du Luxembourg S.A.; Banque et Caisse d'Epargne de l'Etat Luxembourg; Banque Générale du Luxembourg S.A.; Banque Internationale à Luxembourg S.A.; Banque de Luxembourg S.A.; Banque Nationale de Paris (Luxembourg) S.A.; Cariplo Bank International S.A.; Chambre de Commerce du Luxembourg; Crédit Européen Luxembourg; European Investment Bank; F. van Lanschot Bankiers (Luxembourg) S.A.; Fortis Bank Luxembourg S.A.; HypoVereinsbank Luxembourg S.A.; IKB International; KBC Bank Luxembourg S.A.; Kredietbank S.A. Luxembourgeoise; Le Jeudi; Luxemburger Wort; Norddeutsche Landesbank Luxembourg S.A.; Représentation de la Commission Européenne à Luxembourg; SGZ-Bank International S.A.; Société Européenne de Banque Luxembourg S.A.; Société Générale Bank & Trust; Swiss Life (Luxembourg) S.A.; Tageblatt. The Luxembourg Government kindly offered the conference facilities at the European Conference Center in Luxembourg-Kirchberg—the room for the working sessions and the hemicycle for the keynote session.

Finally, I would like to thank all those who through their active involvement in the organization of the conference and the preparation of the book contributed to a successful outcome of the whole endeavor, above all the Pierre Werner Foundation and its president, Charles Ruppert, its vice-president, Guy de Muyser, and Pascale Cloos, secretary of Charles Ruppert.

Of the staff of my Institute I would like to thank Antti Kunnas, who played an important role in the preparation of the conference; Françoise Lentz and Aline Palige for their part in the practical organization; Anemone Thomas for coordinating the publication of the book; Abey Hailu Senbeta, who did the camera-ready copy; Vicky de la Concha, Antoine Kremer, Adrian Pabst, Joep de Roo, Tania Tennina, Tim Wilson and Yael Zucker.

Thanks go also to Michael Palmer for his proofreading of the conference proceedings, Elizabeth Murry from Kluwer, and Denise Schauls for the final proofreading and quality control of the volume. Special thanks to my co-editor Robert Mundell.

A. Clesse

Introduction

Robert Mundell

International monetary history has witnessed a number of important turning points in the international monetary system over the past century and a half. One such turning point was in 1873 when the bimetallic system gave way to an expanding gold bloc and a rapidly declining silver bloc. Two wars played a part in that breakdown as the currencies of the two major bimetallic countries, the United States and France, became inconvertible in the US Civil War, and the Franco-Prussian War, respectively. The sequel to that turning point was the movement to the gold standard by all the major countries excepting China.

Another turning point came with the outbreak of World War I. The belligerent countries engaging in deficit spending went off the gold standard and most of their gold arrived in the United States. This gold was monetized by the newly-created Federal Reserve System and doubled the US price level. Despite a postwar deflation, the dollar price level in the 1920s was still about 30 percent higher than before 1914. When, therefore, Germany, Britain and France, and most of the rest of the world restored the gold standard in the 1920s, the price level was too high relative to gold and an international scramble for reserves, commencing with French conversion of sterling balances, led to the deflation and currency chaos of the 1930s.

Another turning point came with the rise in the dollar price of gold in 1934 and the Tripartite Agreement among the United States, Britain and France in 1936. This agreement inaugurated a new system of fixed exchange rates anchored to the externally-convertible gold dollar. But again war intervened and World War II, Korean War and Vietnam War inflation made gold undervalued, leading once more to a breakdown of the system in 1971, when President Richard M. Nixon took the dollar off gold, removing the last vestiges of the convertibility discipline from US monetary policy. By 1973, the international monetary system had disintegrated into national currency areas separated by fluctuating exchange rates with no currency anchored to gold.

The 1970s saw an outbreak of inflation on a scale never before witnessed in the world economy in war or peacetime. The removal of constraints increased the role of the US dollar in the international monetary economy and inflation raised the seigniorage-inflation tax on dollar balances held in official reserves by central banks outside the United States. The arrangements were by no means congenial to the rest of the world and particularly to Europeans who needed fixed intra-European exchange rates to get the full benefit of their common market in goods, services and investment. The decisions made at the Hague Summit in 1969 to advance European integration into the monetary sphere were given impetus by US inflation and the falling dollar of the late 1970s.

The European Monetary System established in 1978 was an important step along the route to monetary union. The exchange rate mechanism that resulted evolved into what was in fact a DM area, which was an effective system for stabilizing many exchange rates and establishing an independent rate of inflation in Europe but it had the political disadvantage of putting monetary decision-making in the hands of a single national central bank, the Bundesbank, instead of a European body. The only way to correct this asymmetry was to take the big step of creating a single currency that would replace the national currencies. The Delors Report, completed in 1989, made a three-stage plan for European Monetary Union (EMU) based on a single currency.

German reunification in 1990 now introduced a new political element into the policy equation and accelerated interest in monetary and indeed political union. The Treaty of Maastricht signed in December 1991 reflected the growing belief that monetary union was the best next step along the integration road and the safest way to move toward a prosperous European Union with power shared widely among all its members. Largely at the urging of the Bundesbank, detailed convergence requirements were established to ensure that monetary stability would not be upset by fiscal imprudence. A deadline was imposed to inhibit back-sliding and it was therefore agreed that monetary union of at least some of the major countries would take place no later than 1999.

Completion of the earlier stages was by no means assured. Political problems had to be met in all the countries. The crisis of the exchange rate mechanism in 1992-93 raised questions about the ability of a large number of the countries to conform to the same monetary and fiscal targets. Nevertheless, by May 1998, eleven countries had both elected for—and accepted—the union, constituting an area with a GDP smaller than that of the United States but significantly larger than that of Japan. On January 1, 1999, the euro came into being and created a currency area second only to that of the dollar area.

It is not obvious when turning points have been reached. Events that assume significance much later are often missed at the time, and some current events are accorded significance, which does not materialize. Only in hindsight can it be determined definitively that a new era was reached with the introduction of the euro. In hindsight it may turn out to be just another marking point on the road to European integration. But there is a chance that it will turn out to be more fundamental in the sense that it alters in a basic way the character of the international monetary system. That has been a basic theme—or rather query—of the conference on 'The Euro as a Stabilizer in the International Economic System'.

***

This introduction will summarize the views expressed in the papers prepared for publication. The papers have been divided for publication into three distinct but overlapping parts. The papers in Part I provide an overview of the general issues thrown up by the introduction of the euro, including the viability of a bi-polar currency system and the potential of the euro as a supplement or rival to the dollar in the international monetary system. The papers in Part II concern aspects of the management of the euro after its introduction and prospects for changes in both internal and external policies of the euro area. The papers in Part III deal with the euro in the key-currency system, the impact of the euro on countries outside the euro area, and the international implications and importance of the dollar-euro exchange rate.

Part I includes papers by Charles P. Kindleberger, Robert Skidelsky and Kalin Nikolov, C. Randall Henning, Richard Rosecrance, and Robert Mundell.

Charles P. Kindleberger in his paper entitled 'A New Bi-Polarity?' draws on themes he had addressed earlier in his books, *The World in Depression, 1929-1939*, published in 1973, and *World Economic Primacy, 1500-1990*, published in 1996, and on ideas of 'dominance' developed by François Perroux. Dominance is here defined in the sense that one country dominates others when they have to respond to its initiative, but does not in turn have to react to theirs. Perroux applied this argument to the United States, and its relevance in a 'dollar-dominated' world is obvious. Kindleberger's earlier writings, he notes, had not furnished any examples of economic bi-polarity.

The issue turns partly on the costs and benefits of leadership. Leadership often involves disproportionate contributions to an alliance, and leadership, in the wake of free-rider occurrences, may become unpalatable. As the United States considers its world position, looking across the Atlantic at a rising superpower in Europe, will the 'special relationship' become one of partnership or rivalry? Before addressing this question directly, Kindleberger considers some aspects of the history of cost-sharing in alliances, and raises the question whether rivalry in trade, finance and culture with the United States will serve to forge European unity and if so how quickly.

Kindleberger believes that, despite the US comeback in the 1990s, the world role of the United States is slipping, just as the economic, financial and perhaps cultural identity of the European Union is growing. What kind of equilibrium can be established if the United States is not likely to continue as a cheap hegemon? He first considers, without great hope, the possible alternatives of world government, regionalism, 'regimes', and leadership with responsibility. World government he dismisses as premature and utopian. The second alternative, regionalism, is simplistic because channels of commerce are not primarily geographical. The 'regimes' idea consists of 'principles, norms, rules and decision-making procedures around which actors' expectations converge', an idea perhaps closely linked to 'functional federalism', i.e., tackling different problems with separate institutions designed for particular purposes; it usually requires, however, some form of leadership by one or a few countries. The next idea, a resurgence of US leadership, has to confront US domestic problems—drugs, racism, the ghettos, the breakdown of the family and the like—which undermine its prestige, and would not in any case be a cheap solution.

From that perspective, therefore, Kindleberger concludes his paper with the following observations, already alluded to in his earlier works: (1) A world in which one nation is in decline and no other has risen to take its place in ensuring peace and stability is likely to encounter trouble; (2) bi-polarity may work well if the world escapes crises, but leadership is needed in crises like war, famine, depression and financial breakdown; (3) primacy in the world economy has moved from one country to another as nations pass through a 'life-cycle' not unlike that of a human being, including great vitality in youth and middle age and loss as the aging process unfolds. His final remark adds the hope that 'the coming new bi-polarity between the European Union and the United States will rest on consensus and endure for a long period of time, though historical economics fails to make that hope strong and confident'.

The paper by **Robert Skidelsky and Kalin Nikolov** starts off by noting that the gold standard and the Bretton Woods System were both associated with 'leader' currencies. Under both systems powerful national currencies were linked to a gold base. They did most of the work gold was supposed to do. Did the two systems work because they had leader currencies, or did they just happen to have them? This is the question posed by Professor Kindleberger whose answer was that the gold standard was not self-equilibrating; it worked because Britain managed it. The Bretton Woods system also worked because the United States managed it. Without management, or leadership as he calls it, countries would not have accepted the rules of the game. A corollary of the argument is there where there exist several top currencies, they will compete for mastery, centralized management becomes impossible, and a global monetary system will break down.

Skidelsky and Nikolov, however, argue that the pre-war gold standard was not a centrally managed one. Before 1914 there was already a shadowy 'sterling area' of countries affiliated to Britain, which conducted most of its trade in pounds. Germany was the economic locomotive of continental Europe, supplying its neighbors with much of their manufactured goods and capital, and taking most of their imports. France supplied Russia with much of its development capital, for political reasons. Even though London can be described as 'lender of last resort' for the system, the Bank of England needed support from France and Russia in the Baring Crisis of 1890. The economic order is best described as cosmopolitan. It was dominated by bankers and traders, not governments. Cooperation between central banks was *ad hoc*, but it was real none the less. It was broken up by political, not monetary, competition.

Sterling should not be considered a hegemonic currency before World War I. Implicit in the idea of hegemony is the power to exact tribute, in this case seigniorage. England could do so with respect to its empire but was not able to do so to any great extent outside it. After World War I, the pound and the dollar were hegemonic currencies, their role as reserve currencies being acknowledged by the Genoa Conference of 1922. Britain now exploited the privileged position of sterling 'to borrow short and lend long' and this played a role in upholding the restored gold standard for a few years. The system collapsed in 1931 not through competition between the co-hegemons—there was plenty of cooperation between the Bank of England and the Federal Reserve System in the late 1920s—but because of the profound disturbance to trade and capital flows caused by World War I, and, secondly, because France, which had never accepted the gold exchange standard set up in Genoa, started exchanging its sterling holdings for gold.

The years 1931 to 1936 resemble to some extent the years following 1971, when the Bretton Woods system broke down and failed to be restored. In the 1930s there were still two dominant currencies, the pound and the dollar. Twenty or so countries, mostly in the British Empire, pegged their currencies to sterling and held a large part of their monetary reserves in sterling, for reasons of history and trade. The relationship between the dollar and sterling was conflictual until 1936. The currency war was only ended with the Tripartite Monetary Agreement of 1936, by which Britain, the United States and France agreed to support each other's currencies, at an agreed exchange rate in the foreign exchange markets. But this currency war resulted from the breakdown of the gold standard; it did not cause it. If there was a real seigniorial currency in the 1930s, it was the German mark which enabled Germany, under the Schachtian system of bilateralism in Eastern Europe, to pile up mark balances or debts in the bilateral clearings.

The postwar or Bretton Woods system was much more obviously a Kindlebergian hegemonic system. The dollar alone was convertible into gold and, therefore, the major reserve currency of the system. The build-up of dollar balances—acceptable because of their convenience—led to the Triffin paradox which, however, became the motive force of the system. It collapsed when US foreign liabilities exceeded its gold reserves.

The hegemonic thesis thus needs considerable modification. The gold standard and Bretton Woods were not the same kind of system. We need to distinguish between pre-eminent and hegemonic currencies. The collapse of 1931 was not due mainly to the war of currencies: that followed after the restored gold standard had collapsed.

The lessons of history give a modest comfort to those who now look at an emerging global economy with two or possibly three pre-eminent currencies: the dollar, the euro and the yen. The situation does not have to be a recipe for currency wars. Indeed, it is quite likely that it will lead, in due course, to another Tripartite Monetary Agreement. This would be a formal recognition that the world is, in fact, divided into major, but overlapping currency zones, as was the world before 1914.

C. Randall Henning starts his paper with a review of Kindleberger's theories on the important role of hegemonic powers in the international monetary system. Thus, the economic disaster of the 1930s was laid at the feet of lost hegemony as Great Britain relinquished its position at the top at a time when the United States was not prepared to lead. Kindleberger's theory, now referred to as structural realism or neorealism, embodies the notion that a stable, liberal international economic order requires hegemonic leadership.

The logic of neorealism suggests that international cooperation will decline, leading to a widespread expectation among economists that the United States and the euro area will pursue policies of 'mutual benign neglect' with regard to exchange rates and perhaps international financial crises as well. This would imply that crises that should be confronted will not be addressed in a timely manner or will go unattended entirely.

Counterpoised to neorealism has been a school of thought attaching primary importance to the institutionalization of cooperation in international regimes, labeled 'neoliberal institutionalism'. The quality of international cooperation relies in substantial measure on the robustness of international institutions, such as the G-7 and IMF, and the domestic institutions for making external monetary policy in the EU and US. Henning, however, argues that such an approach would not predict strong cooperation either owing to relative weakness of these institutions insofar as monetary relations among major states and the euro area are concerned. Further institutional development, at both the European and international levels, would be required to justify optimism for the future of international monetary cooperation.

Henning's chapter broadly reviews the history of transatlantic monetary relations, particularly as it related to European monetary integration, examines recent US-EU conflicts, addresses euro-area exchange rate policy-making and the adaptation of international institutions, and offers a number of conclusions. To be avoided are the scenarios, sketched by Kindleberger in 1973, where the US and EU vie for leadership, or where one is unable and the other unwilling to lead, while each retains a veto over system strengthening. Preferred scenarios were (1) revived US leadership, (2) assertion of leadership by Europe, and (3) cession of sovereignty to international institutions, but it is not yet clear which scenario is most apt. It should not be assumed too readily that the euro will have a stabilizing impact on the global monetary system. The bi-polar structure of the system would suggest less rather than more cooperation. It would help if the EU clarified the institutions and procedures through which external monetary policy will be made, moved toward greater transparency in decision-making, and went ahead with needed structural reforms, particularly in the labor market, which hold the key to reducing the chronically high rate of unemployment. With progress along these lines, the European economy would become more flexible and dynamic as well as a coherent partner in international monetary and financial cooperation with the United States, Japan and other countries.

Richard Rosecrance in his paper 'The International Political Implications of the Euro' contends that the use of the euro will not rival that of the US dollar any time soon, that a low-valued euro might improve European competitiveness and avoid deflation in European countries riddled by unemployment, but that in the longer term Europe will opt for a high-valued euro in part to put the new currency in other countries' hands. This could have advantages for the international monetary and economic system as a whole because it would permit Europe to perform some of the tasks of economic stabilization (such as serving as a market for or lender of last resort) that are presently too large for the United States to handle.

Competitive relations between the dollar, the euro and the yen, however, could theoretically raise problems analogous to those presented by dollar, franc, and sterling rivalries in the early 1930s. These were very serious and led to exchange control and to the collapse of capital mobility. In the 1930s, with the League of Nations faltering, trade and monetary clubs were 'underlapping' and conflictual in character, and bloc conflict ultimately broke out into war. A similar phenomenon occurred before World War I. After

Bismarck's fall in 1890, alliances similarly took on an exclusive and non-overlapping character, eventuating in the Triple Alliance and Triple Entente which led directly to World War I.

Overlapping club memberships are a means both to solve collective goods problems and also knit disparate units together. Clubs with a small number of members may be able to create collective goods that larger organizations could not. Links between clubs provide the needed cement to hold institutions together.

Since the end of the Cold War (which itself led to underlapping clubs and the threat of hot war) a new pattern of geographic (both political and economic) rivalry has been averted, with North America, Asia and Europe participating in each other's organizations. But as the EU broadens its membership in Europe and gains strength, NATO (which is in the wrong functional field) will prove to be insufficient. There will be a need to fashion a new North American relationship with Europe, probably including both commercial and monetary issues, extending another overlapping link that may in time be broadened to include Japan.

Robert Mundell starts his paper with the suggestion that the introduction of the euro will mark a turning point in the international monetary system perhaps more important than the breakdown of the system in the early 1970s. Before and after that breakdown the dollar was the dominant currency. On the other hand, the euro has the chance that it will alter the power configuration, creating a partner or rival to the dollar that could challenge US supremacy.

In the first sections of the paper, Mundell discusses the characteristics of great international currencies from a historical point of view. He lists five important elements: the size of transactions domain, the stability of monetary policy, the absence of controls, the 'fall-back' factor, and the strength and continuity of the central state. From the standpoint of the first four elements, Mundell concludes that the euro can stand up to the dollar: the EU economy will eventually exceed the US economy in size; the Maastricht rules and the culture of stability in Frankfurt will work toward stability; EU controls are not likely to be more onerous than US controls; and, although, unlike earlier monetary leaders, the euro has no metallic fall-back value, the European System of Central Banks has access to gold and foreign exchange reserves vastly exceeding those of the United States. A possible danger for the euro lies in the political weakness of the European Union, a factor which, however, is less of a defect if the alliance with the United States is maintained and the intentions expressed at Maastricht of developing a closer political union can be made a reality.

Mundell then proceeds to examine the liquidity effects from introducing the euro, which he divides into seven parts. Five factors—efficiency effect, level and stability of the money multiplier, redundant reserves from pooling, and automatic credit as the euro is readily accepted as a means of payment—are liquidity-creating factors that are bearish for the exchange value of the euro, whereas two other factors—the international demand for euros and diversification out of dollars into euros—will be bullish factors. Because the former factors come about quickly whereas the latter factors are delayed, the euro is likely to be weak in the short run but strong in the long run.

The next sections discuss the probable expansion of the euro area, first to the other members of EU that did not enter the process in 1999, then to other members invited to join the EU, and finally, to the remaining members of Central and Eastern Europe that are candidates for admission. Mundell argues that the best approach to monetary union for these countries is to establish currency boards, noting that if a country cannot handle the discipline of a currency board it is not ready to handle monetary union.

The paper concludes with a discussion of international reactions to the euro, the probability that international competition and countervailing power considerations will lead to an extension of the dollar area, and the need for some kind of cooperation to manage the euro-dollar rate.

***

Part II includes papers by Norbert Walter, Jeffrey A. Frankel, Klaus Günter Deutsch, Pierre Maillet and Emil-Maria Claassen.

Norbert Walter argues that the euro will soon emerge as an important international currency, and its introduction is certain to have profound implications for global capital markets and financial policies. Because of its sheer size, EMU will create the second-largest bond market in the world, with German government debt establishing itself as the likely benchmark product. It will have a volume equivalent to about one half of the dollar-denominated component.

EMU will also give birth to the world's second-largest equity market. Currently, the US is well ahead with a total volume of approximately US$ 10.9 trillion, as compared to Euroland's US$ 2.7 trillion, and the ratio of market capitalization to GDP in the eleven member states, on average about 44 percent in 1997, was still far below the corresponding figure of 139 percent for the US. Yet the focus of asset allocation in the euro equity market has already shifted from a national orientation to relative performance in the euro zone, and a great boost will be felt when the UK joins Euroland, a distinct possibility after the general elections expected to be called in 2001.

Given the size of the financial markets and of the Euroland economy, the euro will be widely used in international financial markets from the very beginning. Right from the start it will become the only good alternative to using the US dollar in foreign trade invoicing, in foreign exchange interventions, as an investment currency, and as an anchor for the exchange arrangements of other countries. Unlike the DM, which, despite making significant inroads into the dollar's domain as a world currency, was dwarfed by the huge and dynamic US capital market, the euro will begin life as an international currency and could pose a challenge to the dollar in a number of areas. For many countries Euroland will be by far the most important trading partner, and outside Euroland itself it will become a kind of parallel currency for the large multinationals in Europe. Walter expects the euro's share in international trade invoicing to rise to roughly 35 percent over the next decade and its share in world foreign exchange reserves to rise to 25-30 percent over the medium term.

EMU will also give Europe, Walter argues, greater clout in international monetary affairs. As there will be no changes to the *status quo* of flexible exchange rates among the world's major currencies for the foreseeable future, the risk of exchange volatility among the dollar, euro and yen will continue to exist in the future and may even increase. At the same time, however, it is not at all clear whether the ECB and the Euroland governments will be prepared to bear a greater share of the burden of global leadership in monetary affairs and help to stabilize global capital markets and those currencies that have become subject to speculative attacks. In sum, Euroland may have to learn the lesson that domestic stabilization policy cannot be separated as neatly from global financial instability as many in Europe wish or think possible and that getting Europe's monetary house in order may simply not suffice.

Jeffrey A. Frankel discusses the impact of the euro on members and non-members in the monetary union. His paper starts with a definition of an optimum currency area as 'a region that is neither so small and open that it would be better off pegging its currency to a neighbor, nor so large that it would be better off splitting into subregions with different currencies'. He argues that regional units are more likely to benefit, on balance, from joining together to form a monetary union if (1) they trade a lot with each other; (2) there is a high degree of labor mobility among them; (3) the economic shocks they face are highly correlated; and (4) there exists a federal fiscal system to transfer funds to regions that suffer adverse shocks. By all four criteria, he argues, the European Union is less well suited for a monetary union than the United States. Nevertheless, Frankel recognizes that the degree of integration in Europe is increasing over time and no doubt realizes that monetary union will itself accelerate closer conformity to the criteria.

Frankel goes on to discuss the impact of EMU on other countries. If the UK, Sweden or others decided to join, he argues, there is always the danger that shocks will occur in the interim that result in exchange rate crises, a manifestation of imperfect qualifications on the OCA criteria. With respect to the United States, he believes that the latter will benefit to the extent that it contributes to European prosperity, and makes the important point that US firms will benefit from savings in transactions costs 'perhaps more than European firms because they are already used to operating in large markets'.

Frankel then discusses the euro and the dollar as international currencies and concludes: 'The odds are against the euro rapidly supplanting the dollar as the world's premier currency. The dollar will probably continue to be the world's favorite currency for holding reserves, pegging minor currencies, invoicing imports and exports, and denominating bonds and lending.' This despite the fact that the United States is a debtor country with a large current account deficit.

Frankel continues with an evaluation of the advantages to the home country of being a reserve center, including (1) convenience for residents; (2) more business for the country's banks and financial institutions; (3) seigniorage; and (4) political power and prestige. Against these advantages he lists two 'costs': larger fluctuations in demand for the currency; and an increase in the average demand for the currency. He believes that 'some Europeans seem to worry that international currency status for the euro might lead to a loss of export competitiveness for European firms'.

Frankel also asks: Which is more efficient for the world monetary system, a single reserve currency, or two, three, or more? On the one hand, there are clear efficiencies in having a single international currency; on the other hand, a multiple-reserve currency system, some argue, could give the world protection against the abuse of responsibility by a reserve country that ran deficits at the expense of others. A healthy rivalry would therefore keep both governments in line.

Frankel concludes that there is no reason to expect the euro to surpass the dollar anytime soon, nor for the costs from the US viewpoint to outweigh the substantial political and economic advantages of a successful EMU.

In his paper on 'Exchange rate policy-making in the euro area: Lessons from trade?', **Klaus Günter Deutsch** puts forward the following hypothesis: The quality and effectiveness of external policy-making depends on three factors: the effective delegation of powers on the basis of a clear constitutional mandate; the political authority of negotiators which can only originate in shared objectives of their principals; and flexibility in negotiations with other nations. In the common commercial policy of the EU, these needs have only been partly met in the past four decades. In external monetary policy, functional delegation has taken place, but the allocation of political authority is still being contested and objectives are not shared by all participants. The drawback of this situation is that policy flexibility might be severely limited under difficult circumstances. Dealing with Europe will not become much easier just for the reason that EMU has come into being; rather it will become more complex.

The constitutional set-up of the ECB for internal monetary policy is excellent and the capacity of the ECB to make decisions is well developed. This is in sharp contrast, however, to the external monetary policy of the euro area. Although the Treaty lays down price level stability as the single objective of the ECB's monetary policy, conflicts of interest arise, of course, between internal and external monetary policies. The terms of the Maastricht Treaty leave room for political wrangling in some of these areas. Responsibilities in exchange rate policy were split into fundamental and day-to-day decisions. For the former, the governments would retain ultimate responsibility, while the ECB would be in charge of the latter. According to the Treaty, the Council of Ministers, acting unanimously on a recommendation from the ECB or from the Commission, and after consulting the ECB and then the European Parliament, may conclude formal agreements on the exchange rate system for the euro in relation to other currencies. Denmark and Greece were the first countries to participate, from January 1, 1999, in the Exchange Rate Mechanism II, which was set up according to this procedure. It is also laid down in the Treaty that the ECB is responsible for day-to-day foreign-exchange operations and intervention. If no formal exchange rate system exists in relations with non-EU countries, the Council, acting by a qualified majority, may formulate general orientations for exchange rate policy.

Pierre Maillet argues that Europe created a single currency in order to boost the functioning of the single market but now needs to speed up and reinforce the process in order to make the euro function effectively. Specifically, what needs to be organized now is the budgetary part of macroeconomic policy. A differentiated Europe has been created in the monetary domain, raising the question of whether a similar approach should not be applied to other domains also. There are several dimensions in which deeper integration is needed.

In the area of taxation, as far as direct taxation is concerned, only if taxation on the income of capital, the most mobile factor, is harmonized will there be a functioning of capital markets that is favorable to economic efficiency. In the legal field, the absence of a European legal framework creates difficult problems for the restructuring across borders of the European productive system, as exemplified in the joint ventures with branches in the two participating countries. In research and development policies, the apparently high level of spending is rendered much less effective by the fact that national efforts are to a large extent duplicated. In the regions with different levels of economic development, it is likely that growth will accentuate the need for regional policies to help laggard regions in catching up. Environmental policy needs greater harmonization, especially with regard to irreversible, as opposed to correctable, conditions. In the field of labor-management relations, because the common currency will impose a common inflation rate, it may be necessary to place the mechanisms for collective negotiation between unions and management at a level that represents the entire EMU area. In the field of fiscal policy, some national flexibility will be required in order to allow adjustment to asymmetric shocks, given the inability to use individualistic monetary policies, but coordination will be needed to ensure compatibility of policies in the interest of the area as a whole.

It would be desirable in the course of the next few years, Maillet argues, to have a marked operation of budgetary confrontation, which would translate itself into a search for jointly agreed compromises in order to achieve a convergence of national economic developments in the framework of the monetary union. The first phases of this process have already been initiated but not all member states seem prepared to take the final leap. If the more reluctant states do not in time see their way clear to move toward common policies in general, it would be necessary to accept the need for a more diversified Europe.

Emil-Maria Claassen begins his paper by posing the need to study the implications of the euro for exchange rate policy, not only with respect to the major currencies or future members of the monetary union, but also 'Emerging Countries' that want to fix their currencies to the dollar or the euro. Claassen's paper concentrates on euro exchange rate policies with reference to the thirteen countries of the African Franc Zone.

The African Franc Zone is divided into two currency areas, the West African Zone (Benin, Burkina Faso, Côte d'Ivoire, Mali, Niger, Senegal, Togo) and the Central African Zone (Cameroon, Central African Republic, Chad, Congo-Brazzaville, Gabon, Guinea), with a total population of 90 million, a GDP of roughly 3 percent of French GDP and a quantity of money equal to about 1 percent of the French money supply. The substitution of the French franc by the euro is not seriously contested in Africa. But the change does not simply mean a shift of 'numéraire'. There is also a question of monetary sovereignty in connection with choice of exchange rate regime and whether or not devaluation is an option. Until January 1994, when the CFA franc was devalued from 50 to 100 French francs, the exchange rate tool had been eschewed by both the African members and by France. It will have to be left to future historians to determine whether the French government had exercised a de facto veto right against any devaluation. But when the shift in pegs from the franc to the euro takes place, how will sovereignty be distributed?

Claassen suggests three possibilities. One is that the monetary policy of the union could remain dependent, not anymore on the Banque de France or the Bundesbank as in the past, but now on the new ECB. Another possibility would be an association of the African CFA Zone to the remaining countries of the former EMS, which would devolve any necessary change in the parity value to an outcome of 'collective' decisions between the African 'Group of Thirteen' and the European Council of Ministers (as prescribed by the Maastricht Treaty), and in addition require, as entry conditions to the Euro club, full capital-account convertibility of the former CFA franc (which does not exist now despite the 1994 devaluation).

The most pessimistic possibility, in Claassen's view, would be the collapse of the French Franc Zone, perhaps as a result of maintaining exchange controls, giving rise to different exchange rates, at least between the Central and West African Zones. Under this scenario, the emergence of a currency board for each individual zone, Central and West, may become a valuable solution of last resort. The fixed peg for each currency board could be related again to the euro, but it could only be a 'unilateral' peg, since a consensus for a 'bilateral' exchange rate mechanism (in the form of the former EMS) by the European Council of Finance Ministers seems to be improbable.

***

The book concludes with Part III, which includes papers by Richard N. Cooper, Jeffry A. Frieden, Gerhard Michael Ambrosi, Jörg Baumberger, Christian de Boissieu and Mingqi Xu.

Richard N. Cooper reviews the forms of, and reasons for, the international use of national currencies. He concludes that while the creation of EMU with its own currency, the euro, will mark a major event in the annals of monetary history, and will require major changes within Europe, for many decades it is not likely to affect much the international monetary system outside Europe, and in particular the international uses of the dollar. The main reasons have to do, first, with the deeply entrenched network externalities associated with convenience, familiarity, and widespread use of the dollar by others; and second, with the fact that the euro by itself is only a unit of account, not an instrument in which investments can take place. It will be many years, even decades, before Europe has a financial instrument that can rival the US Treasury Bill in its universality of acceptance and in its liquidity. Unless economic and financial developments in the United States take such a disastrous turn that they cast doubt on the reliability of the T-bill, the dollar is likely to retain its pre-eminence as an internationally recognized short-term store of value and a transactions currency for decades to come. In time the euro will no doubt become an important international currency, but the process is likely to be gradual. Moreover, in the context of a growing world economy, the euro will supplement, rather than directly displace, the dollar in its diverse international roles.

The creation of EMU will have important implications for the world economy. But they lie more in the uncertainties concerning intra-EMU balance-of-payments adjustment and the implications for international cooperation of the awkward division of responsibilities under the Maastricht Treaty than in the likely displacement of the dollar in its major international uses.

Jeffry A. Frieden notes that EMU brings a new monetary authority to the playing field of international monetary policy-making. The euro zone will face potential conflicts, at the core of which is the potential trade-off between the pursuit of international and domestic (EMU-specific) objectives. Policies aimed to ensure the euro's international role, or to secure EMU policy-makers' international bargaining influence, require reducing the priority placed on some domestic targets. For example, a strong euro may conflict with the desire of European exporters for a 'competitive' currency. The development of a consistent EMU-area international economic negotiating position may have to ignore the concerns of a troubled region. All this is complicated by the institutional complexity—and confusion—of currency EMU arrangements. Such potential conflicts of interest will have a powerful effect on the constraints imposed on euro policy-makers, and it is important to understand what conflicts may develop and whom they may implicate.

Whether the international goal is to make the euro a leading international currency or to catapult the EMU authorities into a position as one of two leaders in a bi-polar monetary system, three sets of potential areas of conflict can be anticipated: short-term exchange rate policy; the longer-term monetary stance of the euro authorities; and the character of the EMU financial system. The European Central Bank, the monetary authority *per se,* is a central bank without a country, and international monetary and financial politics are still organized around countries. To make matters even more complicated, the Maastricht Treaty appears to reserve the making of explicit exchange rate arrangements on the part of the Economic and Monetary Union to the Council of Ministers, and not the ECB. It is unthinkable that such exchange rate agreements could be made and sustained without the cooperation of the ECB, but the nature of collaboration between the ECB and other EU policy-making institutions is still being developed. For these and other reasons there remains a great deal of uncertainty about the overall bias to be expected from ECB monetary policy.

There also remains great uncertainty about the future of Europe's financial systems. Some national financial systems are still quite backward and the euro zone is far from being a serious competitor to the United States as a major financial market. Much of the problem is regulatory: there is no single set of European financial regulations, and it is not clear how the regulatory environment for European finance will evolve over the coming decade. At the same time the division of authority for lender of last resort facilities in EMU is extremely ambiguous. Officially, national governments retain sole responsibility for 'their' financial institutions. Unofficially, it is widely recognized that serious financial problems in one EMU member would spill over to the rest of the members, to one degree or another. In this context, the ECB would probably be required to adjust policy to take a local financial crisis into account; and *in extremis*, it might be called upon to act as an unofficial lender of last resort. An additional problem is that neither Europe's central bankers nor other national policy-makers are eager to be explicit about how they see the evolution of the regulatory and crisis-management functions of the euro zone, partly out of fear of creating moral hazard problems.

Frieden recognizes that there are powerful pressures for European governments and EU institutions to resolve the problems that stand in the way of the euro's realization of its global potential. But the future of the euro is complicated by the fact that these political forces, as well as these policy-making authorities, operate in an environment of great institutional novelty and uncertainty, in which it is not always clear who the relevant forces and authorities are.

The paper by **Gerhard Michael Ambrosi**, 'The Prospect for Global Monetary Bilingualism', draws his theme from the frequently observed link between money and language. He analyzes several of the effects of introducing the euro into the global configuration and seeks to draw conclusions about the relationship of the dollar and the euro. In contrast to the assertion of Eichengreen and others—that the transition to a world in which the euro rivals the dollar as a reserve currency will be slow (or never occur)—he advances several reasons why the euro's importance may be accelerated. One factor is the effect of the financial crises of the 1990s in alerting investors all over the world of the need for diversification, which, because the euro is the only major alternative to the dollar, will result in an increased demand for euro-denominated assets. Another factor involves the abolition of national currencies in conjunction with the creation of the euro, with two technical consequences: one is a considerable overhang of dollar reserves in Europe; the other is the disappearance of the unique status of the dollar as the main financial basis for the creation of ECUs through revolving swap operations by national central banks.

A third factor relates to the conditions which prevailed in the United States at the time when that country became a major reserve supplier. At the time of the setting up of the Bretton Woods arrangements, the United States was a major creditor country with a chronic export surplus and massive gold reserves. Today, it is Europe, not the United States, that is in that position, and this leads to the prospect that the euro area will be in a better position to provide for reserve growth in the rest of the world. The paper concludes with the observation that it takes a long time to implement monetary blueprints and therefore endorses (former Federal Reserve Chairman) Paul Volcker's appeal for world monetary cooperation, specifically to 'start the intellectual process now [rather] than wait for the crisis and conflict that, if not inevitable, are all too possible'. This process should start from the working hypothesis that the monetary 'language' of the future is spelled in terms of dollars *and* euros.

Jörg Baumberger starts his paper on 'The Euro and the Outsiders: The Case of the Swiss Franc' with a list of the benefits to monetary union members from the euro: (a) to take advantage of various economies of scale and networks related to the size of a currency area; (b) to simplify accounting, bureaucratic reporting, and statistics; (c) to preclude all temptations for competitive devaluation in the European Union; (d) to break the primacy of the dollar, at least in Europe; (e) to strengthen politically the union and make it safe for permanent peace in Europe; and (f) hopefully to increase the aggregate cake of seigniorage of the EU. These benefits were deemed to exceed the following possible costs: (a) loss of the money instrument for absorbing macroeconomic shocks; (b) loss of options for diversification; (c) loss of benefits of international currency competition; (d) loss of a national lender of last resort; and (e) net loss of seigniorage for at least some countries. Given this decision, what can be said about the position of the outsiders, of which the 'oddest of them no doubt is Switzerland'. Switzerland opted to stay out not only of EMU but the EU itself. Baumberger's paper explores the meaning, risks, benefits and costs of not joining the union.

One factor that makes Switzerland special is that since 1945 its currency has appreciated against all other currencies in the world, including the DM. Switzerland has a substantial share of international asset management, and employment and value-added by the banking insurance industries account for 5.4 and 12.1 percent respectively, giving Switzerland a heavy stake in finance. The Swiss role as an alternative asset and liability denomination may well be enhanced by the monetary unification of Europe.

Switzerland's unique set-up has produced one truly unique result: what has been called an *interest rate island*. The Swiss franc has been a strong currency for almost a century. No currency, in or out, save the Swiss franc, has a long-run record of interest rates consistently lower than the DM rates. Unlike the other members, if Swiss interest rates had to converge, they would converge from *below*. Curiously, this differential cannot be explained by differences in inflation which, statistically, is no better in Switzerland than in Germany. The nominal difference on average of 200 basis points reflects a difference in *real* interest rates. The differential has, however, declined in recent years, casting some doubt on the viability of the island hypothesis.

Will the introduction of the euro sink the island? The answer requires an understanding of why it existed in the first place. It could possibly arise because the island's records are *a posteriori* whereas interest rates are a function of expectations, particularly of exchange rate developments. It is possible that Swiss interest rates were lower because of a continuing expectation that, with its long uninterrupted history of stability—vastly exceeding the DM which was introduced only in 1948—it would appreciate against the DM; but this explanation is hard to swallow given he impressive performance of German monetary policy in the postwar period. Another possibility may have something to do with Swiss aloofness from international armed conflicts, economic sanctions (signaled by, *inter alia,* non-membership in the UN), cross-border tax investigation, banking secrecy, or even large gold reserves. Another possibility is the high net creditor position of Switzerland, built up as a result of high savings and persistent net capital exports. Yet another possibility is that the interest discount reflects the price international investors are willing to pay for an alternative currency denomination in a world where the alternatives are legion but where most of them are relatively shaky. All of these explanations may play a role and it is difficult to isolate the key factor.

The paper concludes with a discussion of the possibility that the euro may become a parallel currency in Switzerland, a possibility that cannot be excluded but is not likely to be a serious problem if the Swiss National Bank maintains its strict policy of price stability.

The paper by **Christian de Boissieu** discusses some aspects of the competition between the dollar and the euro, addressing the issue of currency competition and the competitiveness of the euro in both the short and the long run, as well as the market shares of the euro concerning financial and commercial transactions. He starts by noting that the euro will, like the dollar, fluctuate according to growth and interest differentials and other cyclical factors. What is crucial for the medium and long term, however, is the role of the euro as an international reserve currency and its credibility as the single currency of Europe.

Currency competition and competitiveness appeal to the 'quality' theory of money. He quotes Hayek who underlined two 'not wholly unrelated dimensions': the expected behavior of the value of the currency, and its acceptability, equivalent to its degree of liquidity. Stability depends on monetary policy, while acceptability or liquidity depends on the presence of fully deregulated, deep, resilient and sophisticated capital markets. The credibility of the euro, both inside and outside Europe, will be conditioned by the average growth record of the zone and particularly by the record of the most important and strategic countries (Germany, France, Italy...). Continued unemployment in Europe, a chronic problem of the last two decades, would tend to undermine credibility, so structural reforms to reduce the overall cost of labor (especially for unskilled workers) is urgently needed. The large current account surplus posted by Europe could be a positive factor for the credibility of the euro at the start, but in the long run, deficits pose the only means by which the rest of the world could acquire euro balances. At some point there could be a trade-off between liquidity and credibility considerations such as occurred with the dollar in the 1950s and 1960s. Europe is now, of course, far from facing Triffinesque problems, but they must be kept in mind when looking at the long-term credibility of the single currency.

De Boissieu continues with a discussion of the main challenges. These are legion. They include: tax harmonization; progress in economic coordination and the quality of the policy mix; implementing structural reforms in the spheres of social security and pension schemes, labor market flexibility, and educational systems; making the ECB more accountable, perhaps drawing on the experience of the United States (the Humphrey-Hawkins procedure, publication of the FOMC minutes with the usual lag...); organization of the lender-of-last-resort function for the ECB in the case of systemic crisis; and progress toward political harmonization (common defense, conditions for EU enlargement).

The paper concludes with a discussion of the relation between exchange rates and market shares, currency competition and policy coordination. De Boissieu thinks that we will continue to live in a world in which the degree of policy coordination (monetary, budgetary...) is going to lag much behind the degree of financial integration. 'The outcome, namely financial instability and systemic risks, is somewhat unavoidable.' Nevertheless, more effective coordination in the G-7 would be a complement to the tough currency competition that will keep developing.

The last paper in the volume, by **Mingqi Xu**, discusses the significance of the introduction of the euro from a Chinese perspective. He starts his paper by noting that most observers in international economics see the euro as a stabilizer in the international economic system. The fact that the Asian financial crisis left the euro zone practically unscathed reinforced this belief. The euro will become the second biggest international currency and many people, especially Europeans, believe that it will become a competitor to the US dollar. Xu, however, believes that there is a potential instability in the two-polar monetary system without well-designed international management and policy coordination.

Suppose the euro and the dollar become equals in the international financial sphere, taking into account international reserves and world trade. Will there be a stable equilibrium? The answer is probably not, because there will always be differences in growth rates, balances of payments, interest rates and inflation, which will be reflected in exchange rates. Portfolio shifts can lead to large swings. Everyone will become speculators! In today's markets, institutional investors possess huge amounts of funds which are invested for short-term profit, and under the two-polar system speculative disturbances by these players will only be more severe, assuming they are not combated by measures taken by the international authorities and governments.

It is doubtful, as many people have hoped, that international monetary reform will be speeded up by the euro and that the current unstable financial situation can be changed in the near future. Since the launch of the euro, the US government has repeatedly refused the appeal of quick reform of the international monetary system and denied the need for international management of exchange rates. Many Americans, Xu believes, think that the birth of the euro will not change much of the pattern of the current system and that in the near future the dollar will still hold its dominant position. So they do not care about the need for coordination and cooperation in managing exchange rates. Europeans, by contrast, indicate their desire to coordinate more closely with the US. But the US government insists on its traditional exchange rate policy of benign neglect. Therefore, over the short-term horizon, international management of the euro-dollar exchange rate is not likely to happen.

For China, the development of a two-polar system has important implications. Being a big developing country with an open economic policy, China is very sensitive to the international economic situation. Exchange rate turbulence will mean that China will have to be more cautious. The euro creates a new opportunity for diversifying Chinese foreign exchange reserves, but it is not the most important issue for China. If China shifts its $145 billions of foreign exchange reserves according to the market movements and expectations, it will add to the instability of the foreign exchange market. If it does not do so, fluctuations could cause huge losses. If all countries in the world take the same attitude and wait for the right time to switch reserve assets, turbulence in the international capital and foreign exchange markets will be unavoidable.

Whatever the outcome of the two-polar system, Xu thinks that China is going to anchor its currency RMB to a basket of currencies in which the dollar and the euro will have decisive weight. Under the two-polar system it would be costly to stick to dollar-pegging, which is the present system. But fixing to two currencies or a more general basket does not change the essence of the matter. At present China sticks to the dollar to maintain economic stability at home and also for Asia. If double pegging does not provide stability, countries may have to choose between the dollar and the euro as the object of their pegging. But without a stabilizing mechanism between the two polarities, the two-polar system is not necessarily a good thing for developing countries' exchange rate management. If the euro-dollar rate fluctuates frequently, developing countries may be forced to adopt a more flexible exchange rate regime. No one can be sure whether it is stabilizing or destabilizing to the international economic system.

The euro is still in its adolescence. It will eventually become an adult. But in its adolescent period, it will be a source of instability. To move toward adulthood, Europe needs to take some important steps. One is to learn how to take initiatives in the Group of Seven and other international forums. If the EU is going to be a power and the euro is going to be a key international currency, the EU must act like a leader from now on at least in the international economic domain. It cannot ignore the exchange rate with the dollar and it should create an internal mechanism to let the ECB use monetary policy to adjust the exchange rate when needed. The EU needs also to speed up the integration of its internal capital market, the defects of which make it inferior to that of the dollar. It also needs to adjust its attitude to the balance of payments, because it is impossible for the euro to become an important international key currency without running either a trade deficit or a currency account deficit. China hopes that in the long run the EU will take steps to limit speculative international capital flows, strengthen its internal capital market, take upon itself some leadership in the international economy, and enhance its demand for reform of the international monetary system.

PART I
THE VIABILITY OF THE EURO

1. A NEW BI-POLARITY?

Charles P. Kindleberger

Introduction

1989 brought an end to a world system of bi-polarity in which the poles were the United States and the Union of Socialist Soviet Republics. The question addressed in this paper is whether that system will be followed by a new bi-polarity between the United States and the European Union (EU). It leaves aside a number of problems which the writer is not competent to discuss: the possibility put forward by Samuel Huntington (1993) that the world will encounter a clash of civilizations, including eruptions in the Middle East and South Asia, and the rise of China to the world-power status. It focuses on economic issues, whereas the US-USSR confrontation was mainly military and diplomatic. The central issue is whether the new bi-polarity, if it takes form, will be stable.

The writer has addressed a similar topic in the past. In *The World in Depression, 1929-1939* (1986), he contended that the great depression was so wide, deep and so long because no country acted to stabilize the world economy. The United Kingdom had passed the zenith of its power and responsibility; the United States was only slowly moving out of isolationism. A later book, *World Economic Primacy, 1500-1990* (1996) traces the economic and financial leadership of the largely western world from the Italian city-states to Spain, Brugge, Antwerp, Amsterdam, London and New York, invoking five economic functions that needed to be filled: maintaining a market for distress goods; providing counter-cyclical, or at least stable, long-term lending; policing a relatively stable system of exchanges rates; ensuring the coordination of national macroeconomic policies; and service as a lender of last resort in financial crisis, abroad as well as at home. Political scientists interpreted this economic leadership in a wider sense of hegemony, extending it from the economic to the political, military and cultural areas. Even before this, a French economist, François Perroux (1948) developed a theory of 'dominance' which he applied to the United States. One country dominated others when they had to respond to its initiative, but it did not have to react to theirs. The later book suggested that economic primacy inheres in a single country brimming with energy and vitality which ultimately loses them in a life-cycle that includes aging. It furnished no examples of economic bi-polarity.

Dominance and hegemony do not appeal to me as rhetoric, implying, as they do, the use of force rather than example, persuasion, even subsidies. A pair of political scientists, Norman Froelich and Joe A. Oppenheimer (1970), and a distinguished economist, the late Mancur Olson (1966), have noted that a leading country typically pays more than its proportionate share of joint venture like a war fought by allies, or a program of foreign aid, because it is rewarded in a different coin than economic return, income or avoidance of loss, such as prestige, or, the French obsession, *gloire*. The need to overprovide arises from the presence of 'free riders', who share in the consumption of public goods, including peace, freedom from aggression, economic stability and the like, but hold back from contributing to their cost. Disproportionate payment by the leader conflicts with the theory of the 'public-choice' school which holds that all action is directed to economic income or its complement, leisure. There have been numerous historical examples of leading countries which have taken on costly burdens in the public interest. In the Napoleonic Wars, Britain subsidized the armies of Austria, Prussia and Spain against the French (Sherwig, 1969). Prussia in the Zollverein of 1834 agreed to the division of customs receipts according to the populations of the various kingdoms, duchies, principalities, etc., rather than by the source of their collection. It had more and busier ports and places of entry into the tariff union, but giving up this source of potential income induced, or seduced, the other units to join up (Dumke, 1974). United States settlements under Lend-lease, contributions to the United Nations Relief and Rehabilitation Agency (UNRRA), interim aid and the European Recovery Program (Marshall Plan) can also be cited. On the opposite side is Count Camilio Cavour who engineered the unification of Italy from its position as premier of the kingdom of Sardinia (which included Piedmont), but managed to weigh down the new kingdom with the debt he had piled up in the 1850's in building up the infrastructure of Piedmont (Kindleberger, 1979, p.63).

One reason to dwell on the costs of leadership is that the United States appears to be less and less willing to bear even a proportionate share of the expenses to justify the more-than-proportionate share it wants of decision-making in international institutions. In an unpublished memorandum, Allan Meltzer (1991) makes this point and adds that if other countries pay more, they will want more say in decisions. Decline in US foreign aid, delay in paying its dues to the United Nations, and slowness in voting for expansion of the International Monetary Fund and World Bank are sharp indications. A columnist for the *Boston Globe,* William Pfaff, has written that as the

American century comes to an end, there is little evidence that the United States will support the costs of a global hegemony (July 6, 1998).

As the United States considers its world position, across the Atlantic the rising European Union is in train of becoming a superpower. An Italian diplomat raised the question whether the United States will be the EU's partner, and concluded that the Union's needs deserve attention and equal status with the United States (Massari, April 12, 1998). Needs and status hinge in part on the relationship of the euro to the dollar, and whether the euro will be a rival of the dollar or a complement, though what exactly is meant by a complement is unclear. Writing in a European number of *The New Yorker* with the title of his article 'Europe Re-Invented', John Cassidy states that 'Eurosclerosis' is a thing of the past, that Europe is changing rapidly and could easily emerge as the world's dominant power (April/May, 1998).

As in the 'special relationship' between the United States and the United Kingdom, and a bi-polarity between the United States and the USSR, the key issue is whether partnership, especially equal partnership but also that between a senior and a junior partner, and continuing confrontation is stable. The issue is general. In the United States, a number of partnerships of firms of lawyers and accountants, as reported in the press, have broken up and reformed with different persons because the younger members are dissatisfied with the treatment—largely the division of the earnings of the firm—from the older.

My summer reading happens to include Tolstoy's *War and Peace* (1869)—a standard assignment of summer reading of the last years of secondary school, but well worth the repetition. Among the generals preparing to defend Russian territory, Smolensk and Moscow against the French invaders, there is a great question whether the two armies under the generals, Barclay de Tolly and Prince Bagration, should be brought together under one command, led by Kutzukov. A similar issue arose in response to the German offensive in the Ardennes in December 1944, whether General Eisenhower should or should not assign the British armies under Field Marshal Montgomery, and the 12th US Army group under General Omar N. Bradley, to one commander, who proved to be Montgomery. 'Shared responsibility is no responsibility' claimed Ludwig Bamberger, the German banker-economist-politician responsible for the statutes of the Reichsbank in 1875 (Zucker, 1975, pp. 38, 78).

I proceed to discuss cost-sharing, trade, finance, and the strength of the European unity before returning to the possible bi-polarity and its alternatives. As above, moreover, economic and financial history are used to an extent in the hope that they will be suggestive.

Cost-Sharing

Examples of the disproportionate shares of cost taken by a leader (or hegemon) have been given above in the cases of Britain in the Napoleonic Wars, the Zollverein and US aid to Europe and Japan after World War II, along with the counter-example of Count Cavour of Piedmont in Italian unification. I am not informed whether the United States share of the failed attempts in peacekeeping in Yugoslavia was disproportionate to those of European countries on some basis, as surely was that of the action against Iraq when it attacked Kuwait. But the question arises whether the European Union has the built-in mechanism for burden-sharing that national governments with substantial budgets and at least mildly progressive taxation have. If economic relations among the members of the EU are to be converted from international to interregional, something more than the allocations of costs and expenditures in the Commission's budget, and the perverse sharing under the Common Agricultural Policy are needed. In a forgotten paper of 1949, Penelope Hartland made clear that balances of payments among regions in a single country were kept in more or less equilibrium not only by movements of capital and labor, as postulated in international trade theory, but also by sharing through central taxes and spending. A region that suffers an adverse movement will be relieved through the reduction of income and other taxes, and helped by inward transfers in social programs. In the Common Market, a European Social Fund was established to assist poor regions, and the European Investment Bank to assist in their growth. These institutions, however, fall short of the automatic regional stabilizers of sizable budgets with progressive taxation and social welfare programs. Moreover, the insistence of France on the *juste retour*, that the value of any French contribution to a joint project, such as the Airbus, should be matched by an equal expenditure in France, is the antithesis of burden-sharing as well as a violation of the economic principle of buying in the cheapest market and selling in the dearest.

Whether the European Union enjoys the social cohesion or consensus necessary to achieve cost- and burden-sharing is as yet unclear. C.A. Ciampi, the Italian minister for treasury, budget and planning, believes it does as he writes of 'a general consensus throughout Italian society that European integration was necessary and fully consistent with national interest' (1998, p. 3). Among the smaller countries of Europe, Belgium, the Netherlands and Austria, but not Denmark, appear to be ready to put Europe first and their patriotism second. I have a hard time believing Eugen Weber when he writes, *à propos* of nationalism, that he defines himself as a historian first, a Californian second and an American third (1996, p. 295). Small countries aside, the success of the Union depends upon whether the larger like Italy, according to Ciampi, are capable of submerging their nationalism or patriotism within an overarching European consensus and creating a European 'identity'.

Social cohesion has been defined in one attempt in terms of the proportion of gross domestic product (GDP) spent on 'social protection', the metric being sought to develop a numerical variable to enter econometrically into the determination of price stability (Prast, 1998). The writer observes that taxation, unionization, minimum-wage legislation and the system of social benefit are also relevant. From an American perspective, social cohesion involves a long series of less measurable issues such as abortion, teen-age pregnancy, racial, gender and age discrimination, family values, even religious fundamentalism in which various groups within the country hold views that are deeply different and divisive.

In an issue devoted to nationalism, which can perhaps be transformed to apply to European integration, a number of authors in *Critical Review* (Spring 1996) make a sharp distinction between civic and ethnic nationalism. Civic nationalism is constructed or chosen by free will; ethnic is one a people acquire by birth and inheritance. Civic nations are exemplified by France, Canada and the United States, ethnic by Germany, Japan and Eastern countries. (The United Kingdom of Great Britain and Northern Ireland is not categorized).

In the strongest formulation, nationalism is xenophobic and exclusive, whereas patriotism is about attachment (Weber, 1996, p. 292). A usual point is said to have been made by Eric Hobsbawm that countries unite by being against others (ibid., p. 294). But it is generally agreed by the participants that neither choice nor birth can create the necessary attachment alone. There must be a common language—exceptions being made for Switzerland and Belgium—and shared experience and memories. That a civic nation is created only by choice, or an ethnic one only by the accident of birth is a myth (Yack, 1996). Weber, who has written on the 70 years it took peasants to become Frenchmen (1976), stresses the need for schools, literacy, education and printing. He quotes Ernest Renan: 'Common glories in the past, a common will in the present, having done great things together and wanting to do more, these are the essential conditions of a People' (Weber, 1996, p. 289).

The European Union has the advantage, according to *The Economist* (July 1998) of starting as an economic entity, rather than a military or diplomatic one. But European memories of 1870, 1914, 1939 and the current Yugoslav quagmire may not serve to produce the transfer of fundamental loyalties from the nation to the Union which political scientists and philosophers believe to be necessary.

Will rivalry with the United States serve to forge European unity, and if so, slowly or quickly? This issue is explored for trade, finance and culture, but stays clear of questions of political rivalry in Asia and the Middle East.

Trade

The experience of the Common Market in trade has been outstanding. Tariffs have been removed internally, lowered vis-à-vis the outside world. Trade creation has been impressive, trade diversion limited. European trade grew faster than gross national product and in turn stimulated growth, though the latter was held back to a degree by structural problems. One is tempted to find a parallel between the European Union today and the Zollverein as the precursor of German reunification, along with the reduction in Italian state tariffs in 1847-48 as performing a similar function for the formation of the Kingdom of Italy in 1860. One could reason that the British move to free trade, peaking in the repeal of the Corn Laws in 1846, and the example it set for other European countries until 1879, rested on its understanding of the proper behavior for a leader of the world economy.

There is trouble, however, in deciding whether free or freer trade follows from rational choice, like the unqualified version of civic nationalism, whether it responded to the political rise of the industrial middle class over the landed aristocracy, signified by the Reform Bill of 1832, or was primarily an attempt to slow down industrialization on the continent in what has been called 'free-trade imperialism' (Semmel, 1970). One can perhaps find a parallel free-trade imperialism in US pressures in the Atlantic Charter, Lend-lease settlements, the aborted International Trade Organization (ITO), the successful General Agreements on Tariffs and Trade (GATT) and World Trade Organization (WTO), all designed to pressure the world to eliminate quotas and reduce tariffs so as to stimulate exports of US goods and services. Adam Smith's intellectual justification for free trade, qualified as it was by support of the Navigation Acts to foster the production of sailors for national defense, was written 70 years before the repeal of the Corn Laws, though it doubtless influenced the free-trade ideas and early actions of William Huskisson. It should be recalled, however, that Adam Smith was strongly influenced by the ideas of the French Physiocrats, farming nobility who wanted freedom to export grain. John Stuart Mill asserted, 'A good cause seldom triumphs unless someone's interest is bound up in it' (quoted in Semmel, 1970, p. 207). Manchester wanted free trade to promote its export of cotton textiles, but for a long time defended the embargo on the export of textile machinery that might assist competitors abroad (Redford, 1934). In addition, the manufacturing interest of Manchester persuaded the Colonial

Office to forbid British India putting a tariff on British cotton goods 150 years after the British industry got its start with the tariffs on muslin and calico, not to mention British restrictions on imports from the Dutch Republic in the successful effort to take over the position of world trade leader (de Vries and van der Woude, 1997, chaps 7, 8). Board of Trade officials, notably John Bowring, William Jacobs and John McGregor, urged the importation of more grain from the Continent, especially Germany, in order to divert that country's efforts away from industry to agriculture. Friedrich List, the German nationalist, described free trade as the 'hypocrisy of the export interest, the clever device of the climber who kicks the ladder away when he has attained the summit of greatness' (cited by Fielden, 1969, p. 85).

It can be argued that the United States promotes tariff reductions worldwide with a similar purpose of free trade imperialism. The pressures go back to Cordell Hull and the Reciprocal Trade Agreement Act of 1934, followed by renewals and rounds of reciprocal reductions, the last of which, in Uruguay, added services to commodities for easier entry. The British Board of Trade was only mildly interested in reciprocity, except in the Cobden-Chevalier treaty with the French in 1860, given the hold in its thought of David Hume's 'law' that imports quasi-automatically beget exports. In the present Asian crisis Japan, Indonesia and other countries have expressed irritation at the efforts of the IMF and World Bank, thought to be pushed by the United States, to opening up their economies to imports. Free trade imperialism? Early in the recovery efforts in Europe, however, the United States accepted discrimination against US exports at the same time as it favored more intra-European trade through such programs as the European Payments Union.

Particular problems may arise in the field of US-European trade, as in the cases of the 1950's 'chicken war' and US objections to subsidies for the Airbus, or the worry in Europe over US monopolies such as Microsoft. On the whole, however, it seems likely that the European Union and the United States can live comfortably in the trade area, with the possible exception of services with strong cultural overtones.

Finance

The relationship of the euro to the dollar poses more difficult issues. Many economists, for example David Currie (1997), think that the establishment of the euro as a world currency will lead central banks and international traders outside the Continent to shift reserves and working balances from dollars to euros in significant amounts, thereby leading to a depreciation of the dollar against the euro. A possible offsetting factor has been pointed out by Robert

McCauley (1997) in the widening and deepening of European capital markets, or a single market. This would lead countries outside to shift some borrowing from New York to Europe for expenditure elsewhere. What the net effect on the exchange rate would be in the long run remains a guess. While the location of a single EMU capital market, if one, will be decided in the long run by a Darwinian process, the current plans of the Frankfurt and London exchanges to merge, and the agitation it created in Paris, now planning a rival all-European center, makes forecasting risky.

These long-run considerations lie beyond a series of immediate steps, which are also difficult to discuss with any assurance. Bank mergers are taking place in the major financial countries of Europe, including Britain, Switzerland and Scandinavia. Some observers expect the merger movement to end with two or no more than three large banks in each country. It is likely, moreover, that the separate financial centers in Europe will gradually form into a hierarchical pattern, such as occurred in the separate countries of Europe in the 18th and 19th centuries when London, Paris, Berlin, Zurich, Milan, Vienna etc. emerged as the financial center of the country after competitive struggles of money, banking and capital markets (Kindleberger, 1974). This question rests in some suspense pending the British decision whether or not to join EMU and the euro. With London absent, Frankfurt— the seat of the European Central Bank—is the likely winner in the competition for pride of place, but Paris and perhaps Brussels have not been completely eliminated.

Meanwhile, a host of innovations is under way: deregulation, disintermediation, securization, more mergers and acquisitions, including those of banks with non-monetary financial institutions such as mortgage and insurance companies (Steinherr, 1990). If London joins the Monetary Union after the next election in 2002, what then? London was the leading trading center in Eurodollar and other euro currencies. It has skills, experience and tradition, but only a limited flow of savings from local sources. In the return to gold in 1925, London dominated British decision-making and industry was not even consulted (Boyce, 1988). With the Labor Party in power for the next years it is unclear whether London will carry the same clout as three-quarters of a century ago.

Apart from developments within the EMU, and the flow of money and capital across the Atlantic, the press is full of discussion of the mutual roles of the euro and the dollar in coming years. Some writers call for equal partnership (Massari, 1998), others for the dollar as first among equals (Chan, 1998). Klaus Friederich, chief economist of the Dresdner Bank, states that the euro will not be a substitute for the dollar but a complement, and in the long run will give the dollar 'a run for its money' (1998). Richard Portes, a British economist, is quoted in *The New York Times* as saying, 'Ultimately, we're going to have a more cooperative and less US-led process in things like international financial crisis, where clearly the European voice is much less than its weight in the world economy' (April 28, 1998, 1st Business Page). In the same article, C. Fred Bergsten of the Institute for International Economics in Washington, DC states that 'we will move from a purely dollar centered world to a bi-polar monetary world'.... and 'the euro will move up alongside the dollar as a second key currency and will attain market share pretty close to the dollar within three to five years' (ibid.)

'Second key currency' and 'market share' are clear concepts. The Annual Reports of the Bank for International Settlements record the volume trade and security issues denominated in various currencies. 'Partnership' and 'equal voice' are more elusive. In a financial crisis such as that in East Asia since July 1997 should the United States and the EMU coordinate policy before taking action as lenders of last resort? Should the weights of voting be equal, the designation of high officials by nationality, and even the location of international financial institutions be re-examined and altered? One observer noted that since the start of the Asian crisis, the 15 members of the European Union have collectively contributed through the IMF a total of $20.7 billions,—that is more than the $18 billion provided by the United States (Massari, 1998). It is not evident how these figures were compiled or what they mean since 'through the IMF' may refer to IMF quotas, bilateral commitments from governments or from banks persuaded by the IMF to extend existing loans or make new loans.[1]

As long as the IMF and the World Bank are located in Washington (and the United Nations headquarters with the Security Council and General Assembly in New York) it is hard to see how the EMU in Frankfurt (and the Commission in Brussels) can have an equal voice or equal partnership with the US Treasury in the world financial institutions. The Fund and the Bank were established in Washington at the Bretton Woods Conference in 1944 in an effort to commit the United States to an active role in world financial affairs. The leading officials of the institutions were established by custom— the managing director of the Fund to go to a European, the president of the Bank to an American.

These arrangements could be changed only with great difficulty because of what economic historians call 'path dependency', the hold that the past has over the present even when changed circumstances call for a new direction.[2] Will the EMU speak with one voice on financial issues, especially on issues where one member has had views which differed from those of others, for example, France on the role of gold in international payments?

In the economic crisis of 1931, following especially the collapse of the Austrian Creditanstalt, first the newly formed Bank of International Settlements put together a rescue package; it was small and failed. A second amount was called for: France held back on political grounds, insisting that Germany abandon building a pocket battleship (the *Panzerkreuzer*) and the Austrian-German customs union; the United States contented itself with the Hoover moratorium on war debts an reparations. Britain followed the failure of the second B.I.S effort with a loan of its own: 50 million Austrian schilling ($7 million) for one week, an offer verging on pathos.

The Asian financial crisis of 1997-98 (and perhaps longer) was tackled by IMF with US leadership, it appears and, according to the unclear account above, with somewhat more European than American money. The extent of the troubles of Thailand, Indonesia and South Korea, plus perhaps Malaysia, plus commitments to Russia and Ukraine, appear to have reduced the moneys available for further last-resort lending to small amounts, and encountered the resistance of the US Congress to contribute its share to their expansion. Some voices have been raised in the Congress calling for the refusal of rescue operations to countries that tolerate legal abortion, putting one in mind of French political conditions of 1931.

In short there is a danger that a new bi-polarity with equal sharing of power may create an unstable equilibrium, like that of the balance of power in general, or, in philosophical terms, like Bouridon's ass which starved to death equidistant between two bales of hay, unable to decide which one to tackle first.

Culture

The writer lacks the knowledge or the credentials to discuss culture, but was struck by an account in *The New York Times* (July 1, 1998) of a meeting in Ottawa among cultural ministers of nineteen countries which regard the United States as a threat to their cultural independence. Cultural imperialism may differ from free-trade imperialism in that it is largely unintentional, although various industries, such as motion pictures, publishers and multi-national corporations such as Coca-Cola, Disney and McDonald's may from time to time pressure the US government to resist foreign steps to limit their penetration of foreign markets. Canada in particular has been troubled by American magazines and television stations which compete with domestic efforts, has abandoned some efforts to limit the publication of special Canadian editions of US periodicals, but has retained a prohibition of Canadian advertisers buying advertisement in such 'split-runs' (*The New York Times*, July 30, 1998, p. D7).

Writing on 'globalization', H.W. Arndt concludes an economic discussion by mentioning social globalization: the spread of pop music, standardized fast food, pornography and drugs, and sets against them the benefits of globalization in modern medicine, literature and access to other cultures. He concludes that the subject lies outside the bounds of economic discourse and that answers must be left to subjective judgment (1998, p. 87).

Culture can be brought into the realm of economics, however, by regarding it as a public good. In the 1960's, Harry Johnson and Albert Breton, born in Canada, wrote of nationalism as a public good which the populace of a country might demand even at some cost in income. Two other economists of Canadian origin developed the concept of an 'optimum currency area', one that can function effectively with a single money (Mundell, 1961; McKinnon, 1963). The notion can be extended from money to economics in general, and an optimum economic area which under free trade can be the world. The political optimum area is large for aggressive countries, small for those that want to get by without trouble. The optimum social area, I suggest, though I trespass on foreign territory, is smaller than the economic one, and one in which the individual has a sense of identification or belonging in the scheme of things. The criterion for full globalization in economic terms is factor-price equalization; in social terms intermarriage. The integration between Christians and people of Jewish origin in the United States today is indicated by a rising rate of intermarriage, now covering more than half of young people born to Jewish parents, by the collapse of exclusion of Jewish families from upper-class suburbs of American towns, and of discrimination against Jewish individuals in politics, the professions, business and the academy. Many, but by no means all Jewish thinkers are concerned over the potential loss of Jewish identity and tradition in the United States.

In the 18th and 19th centuries, European cultural integration was maintained at the aristocratic level where the high and lesser nobility of various countries spoke French, intermarried, congregated in cultural capitals and resorts. With the aristocracy dispossessed, a new elite consists of the stars of the entertainment world, top officials of multinational corporations and café society. In many instances, the heads of corporations reached the pinnacle only after service in foreign subsidiaries where they acquired some cosmopolitanism. With international mergers and acquisitions, social integration between the United States and western (and northern Europe) may exceed that within Europe itself, especially in the publishing field, central to culture, where Pearson, P.L.C. of Britain, Bertelsmann of Germany, Elsevier of the Netherlands and Hachette of France have staked out large positions in the United States.

The United States today has one cultural advantage that Britain held in the 19th century; its ignorance of foreign languages, requiring Europeans to communicate within the Union to a considerable degree in English, or American. It is even said that Germanophone Switzerland and the

Francophone counterpart learn English as a second language, rather than that of their other countrymen, because of the scale-economy, English is spoken outside the continent of Europe. It is understood that Helmut Schmidt, one time chancellor of the Federal Republic of Germany, and Valéry Giscard d'Estaing, President of France, spoke English together. Foreign-language requirements in social science in the United States have given way in higher education to more mathematics, a retrograde step at a time when more and more scholarship, much of which had converted to English, is moving back to German and perhaps Italian. The French never left. Moreover Spanish is appearing more and more in newspapers and on television in the United States, although there is a semi-isolationist movement in California to give up bilingual education.

Despite the Ottawa conference on culture and the Canadian anxiety to fend off American folkways and their reinforcing media, to an amateurish observer there would seem to be an equal or even greater likelihood of cultural integration between the United States and separate members of the EU than among the countries of the Union itself. Young people are readier to explore the world today than was the generation after World War II. American youth seeks college terms or years abroad; European students are inclined in many cases to extend their higher education after the baccalaureate in an American university. Residual xenophobic patriotism may well give way, along with a regress from the cultural imperialism of blue jeans, gangsta' rap and television sit-coms designed for the 18-24 year old. One can hope.

Alternatives to US or European Hegemony, Leadership and to Bi-Polarity

A strong likelihood exists that despite the US comeback in the 1990s, the world role of the United States is slipping, as the economic, financial and perhaps cultural identity of the European Union is growing. Is the United States likely to continue as a cheap hegemon, a concept which flies in the face of political science, or can it, with Europe, establish a stable bi-polar system? I first consider a list of alternative bases for ordering the world policy and economy, none in my offhand judgment of much promise. They are world government, regionalism, regimes, including 'functional federalism' which I am not sure I understand, and leadership with responsibility. After them comes bi-polarity.

a) *World Government* I dismiss as premature and utopian. It may evolve in the years, decades, centuries to come. It would be daring to predict. It has been pushed by many, including Wendell Wilkie, the lawyer who ran for president against Franklin Roosevelt in 1940 on a 'One World' ticket, and by World Federalists, but in these and every other case quickly lost impetus.

b) *Regionalism* is a system under which large geographic areas of the world are called upon to develop political organization, much like the European Union, though on the whole somewhat looser. One in embryo is the Association of East Asian Nations (ASEAN), another is the North American Free Trade Area (NAFTA). An early enthusiast in the United States was William Yandall Elliott, professor of government at Harvard University, who recommended regional bodies for Europe, Asia, North and South America and possibly the Middle East and Africa (1955). Like the European Union, these might start with economic commissions, free-trade areas, development banks, such as the Inter-American and Asian ones. The notion rests, however, on a fallacy that economic relations are universally stronger among neighboring countries than with those at greater distances. It is significant that Australia and New Zealand originally had very close ties with the United Kingdom and have gradually, but only slightly, shifted the weight of their dealings to the United States and the Far East. Argentina was closely linked to Great Britain and Spain, Brazil to the United States, but both are gradually increasing their mutual relations.

But transoceanic connections are often as vital as those with contiguous countries, as meetings of the Pacific Rim countries and the proposal of a North Atlantic Free Trade Area, linking the United Kingdom to Canada and the United States, imply. The subject of this paper, relations between the United States and Europe, transcends a world organized on regional lines. Regionalism is simplistic and fails to meet fully the challenges of a complex world.

c) *Regimes* are a political concept put forward principally by Stephen Krasner of Stanford University (1983) and seconded by Robert Keohane in *After Hegemony* (1984). Regimes consist of 'principles, norms, rules and decision-making procedures around which actors' expectations converge,' in Krasner's definition. They should probably also include institutions and habits of international dealing inherited from a hegemonic period that set them in motion. I suspect that this is more or less what Richard Cooper, professor of economics of Harvard, means by 'functional federalism', implying tackling different problems separately in institutions established for particular purposes: the Organization for Economic Cooperation and Development (OECD) among developed countries, the United Nations Commission for Trade and Development (UNCTAD) among developing nations, the G-5, G-7, G-10, alongside the IMF and IBRD, in finance, continental development banks, and similar organizations in trade (World Trade Organization or WTO), health (WHO), air travel (ICAO), food

(FAO), education (UNESCO) among others. Such organizations function best, however, when some country or two or three countries push hard. For lack of enthusiastic support, they subside into quietude as the careers of WHO, FAO and UNESCO in recent years seem to indicate.

d) *A Resurgence of US leadership:* Even before the sharp recovery in the economic and American optimism in the 1990s, a series of books appeared maintaining that the United States was *Bound to Lead* (Nye, 1990), that it would recover from its malaise of the 1980s, that its decline was a myth, with the book's subtitle: *Leading the World Economy into the 1990s* (Nau, 1990). I confess I was wrong, or at least premature in anticipating a loss of US economic vitality and the slippage of the dollar as international money (Kindleberger, 1996, chap. 10). In the latter case, the dollar retained its role for lack of alternative, as neither the Deutschmark nor the yen challenged the dollar as a matter of German or Japanese policy. That challenge came with Maastricht and the estimated time of arrival of the euro.

In his latest book, Walt W. Rostow adopted a position midway between loss of leadership by the United States and its recovered role in the van (1998). He recommends that the United States provide the 'critical margin' to international political and economic efforts. It is not completely clear what this means, whether the United States should initiate action when other countries hold back, or wait for another to point the way and follow in close support. In an op-ed piece in the *Boston Globe,* Ronnie C. Chan, observing from Hong Kong, writes that the question is not whether the United States leads in the next century, but how, and suggests that it should not lead from the front of the parade but from behind, serving as first among equals, expressions that are not without ambiguity. Both Rostow and Chan are worried over US domestic problems: drugs, racism, the ghetto, the breakdown of the family and the like, and their impact on American capacity to lead from the front or rear, or provide a critical margin.

These notions come close to a shift from one kind of responsibility, the active, to another, the passive. Active responsibility outlines solutions, leads in applying them, persuades others to follow; passive responsibility, on the other hand, involves mainly a support role, as Germany and Japan played in the golden era from 1950 to 1973, contributing but refraining from acting independently, as, for example, France and Russia have lately done in selling arms to Iran or Iraq. In a passive responsible role the United States would stay up with Sweden and Canada in contributing per capita to foreign aid and UN peace-keeping efforts, pay its past dues to the UN and its contribution to the enlargement of the IMF. *Noblesse oblige* calls at a minimum for discharging obligations and on most interpretations for more. Cheap hegemony, as indicated earlier, is an oxymoron. It is also a path to chaos.

Conclusion

At an advanced age, one cannot be expected to produce original ideas. I end then on two or three that I have expressed before.

a) A world in which one nation is in decline and no other has risen to take its place in ensuring peace and stability is likely to encounter trouble (1986).

b) Bi-polarity may work well if the world escapes crises. In crises such as war, famine, depression, financial breakdown, however, leadership is needed. This conclusion is not only inconvenient as Walter Bagehot held about the lender of the last resort, but frustrating. Shifting from pluralism to central authority when crises arise is difficult because of path dependence, and sometimes impossible. For a canonical example, see the Dutch Republic in the 18th century (1996, esp. chapter 2).

c) Primacy in the world economy over the years has moved inexorably from one country to another, as nations pass through a 'life-cycle' not unlike that of a human being. Successful ones have great vitality in youth and middle age, but lose much of it as the aging process unfolds. There can be resurgence, but it seems foolish to count on its performance (1997).

To these I would add a hope that the coming new bi-polarity between the European Union and the United States will rest on consensus and endure for a long period of time, though historical economics fails to make that hope strong and confident.

Notes

1. For a statement of official financing commitments for Thailand, Indonesia and South Korea by the IMF ($35 billion), the World Bank ($16.1 billion), the Asian Development Bank ($9.7 billion) and 'Bilateral Commitments' excluding a $5 billion Indonesian currency reserve, but otherwise undesignated by geographic origin ($50.1 billion), see Bank of International Settlements, 1998, p. 134

2. An analogous case is the composition of the Security Council of the UN with five permanent members with vetos over resolutions: China, France, the USSR, the United Kingdom and the United States. The rise of Japan and Germany in economic strength failed to alter the original structure; it seems unlikely that France and the United Kingdom, if it joined the Union, would accept replacement by the European Union with its new (as of January 1999) 'high representative' for foreign policy, the *PESC Politique Etrangère et Sécurité Commune (The Economist,* July 18, 1998, p. 16)

References

Arndt H.W. 1998. 'Globalisation.' Banca Nazionale del Lavoro *Quarterly Review,* vol. 51, no. 204 (March), pp. 73-89.

Bank for International Settlements. 1998. *68th Annual Report,* 1 April 1997-31 March 1998 (June 8). Basle.

Boyce R. 1988. 'Creating the myth of consensus: public opinion and Britain's return to the gold standard.' In P.L. Cottrell and D.E. Moggridge, eds., *Money and Power.* London: Macmillan, pp. 173-197.

Breton, Albert. 1964. 'The Economics of Nationalism.' *Journal of Political Economy,* vol. 72 (August), pp. 376-386.

Cassidy, John. 1997. 'Europe Re-invented: Why America still thinks the Continent as economically backward.' *The New Yorker,* April 27 and May 4, pp. 13-14.

Ciampi, C. A. 1998. 'Price Stability and Balanced Public Accounts as a Condition for Sustainable Development.' Banca Nazionale del Lavoro *Quarterly Review,* vol. 51, no. 204 (March), pp. 3-16.

Cooper, Richard N. 1974. 'Economic Mobility and National Economic Policy.' *Wicksell Lectures.* Stockholm: Almquist and Wicksell.

Currie, David. 1997. 'The pros and cons of EMU.' *Research Report.* London: *The Economist* Intelligence Unit, pp. 1-102.

de Vries, Jan, and Ad van der Woude. 1997. *The First Modern Economy: Success, Failure and Perseverance of the Dutch Economy, 1500-1815.* Cambridge: Cambridge University Press.

Dumke, Rolf H. 1976. 'The Political Economy of German Unification: Tariffs, Trade and Politics of the Zollverein.' Doctoral dissertation in economic history. University of Wisconsin, Madison.

The Economist, various issues.

Fielden, Kenneth. 1969. 'The Rise and Fall of Free Trade.' In C.J. Bartlett, ed., *Britain Pre-eminent: Studies in British World Influence in the Nineteenth Century.* London: Macmillan, pp. 76-100.

Gallagher, John, and Ronald Robinson. 1965. 'The Imperialism of Free Trade.' *Economic History Review,* ser. 2, vol. 6, pp. 1-15.

Gellner, Ernest. 1983. *Nations and Nationalism.* Oxford: Blackwell.

Hobsbawm, Eric. 1992. *Nations and Nationalism since 1780.* 2nd ed. Cambridge: Cambridge University Press.

Huntington, Samuel P. 1993. 'The Clash of Civilizations.' *Foreign Affairs,* vol. 72 (Summer), pp. 22-49.

Johnson, Harry G. 1963. *The Canadian Quandary: Economic Problems and Policies.* Toronto: McGraw-Hill.

Keohane, Robert O. 1984. *After Hegemony: Cooperation and Discord in the World Political Economy.* Princeton: Princeton University Press.

Kindleberger, Charles P. 1986. *The World in Depression, 1929-1939.* Rev. ed. Berkeley: University of California Press.

Kindleberger, Charles P. 1996. *Centralization vs Pluralism: A Historical Examination of Political-Economic Struggles and Swings within some Leading Nations.* Copenhagen: Handelshøjskolens Forlag.

Kindleberger, Charles P. 1996. *World Economic Primacy, 1500-1990.* New York: Oxford University Press.

Krasner, Stephen D. 1983. 'Structural Causes and Regime Consequences: Regimes as Intervening Variables.' In Krasner, ed., *International Regimes.* Ithaca: Cornell University Press, pp. 1ff.

Massari, Maurizio. 1998. 'Europe is a rising superpower, will the US be its partner?' *The Boston Globe,* April 12, p. D-7.

McCauley, Robert N. 1997. 'The Euro and the Dollar.' Bank for International Settlements. Working Paper, no. 50 (November). Basle.

McKinnon, Ronald I. 1963. 'Optimum Currency Areas.' *American Economic Review,* vol. 53, no. 4 (September), pp. 717-725.

Meltzer, Allan H. 1981. 'US Leadership and Postwar Progress.' Unpublished paper, revised July.

Mundell, Robert A. 1961. 'A Theory of Optimum Currency Areas.' *American Economic Review,* vol. 51 (November), pp. 509-517.

Nau, Henry R. 1990. *The Myth of America's Decline: Leading the World Economy into the Nineties.* New York: Oxford University Press.

The New York Times, various issues.

Nye, Joseph S. Jr. 1990. *Bound to Lead: The Changing Nature of American Power.* New York: Basic Books.

Olson, Mancur, and Richard Zeckhauser. 1966. 'An Economic Theory of Alliances.' *Review of Economics and Statistics,* vol. 42 (August), pp. 266-279.

Perroux, François. 1948. 'Esquisse d'une théorie de l'économie dominante.' *Economie Appliquée,* nos. 2-3.

Pfaff, William. 1998. 'As the American Century ends, a debate on the future.' *The Boston Globe,* July 6, p. A-15.

Prast, H. 1998. 'Inflation, Distortionary Taxation and the Design of Monetary Policy.' Banca Nazionale del Lavoro *Quarterly Review,* vol. 51, no. 204 (March), pp. 37-53.

Redford, Arthur. 1934. *Manchester Merchants and Foreign Trade, 1794-1858.* Manchester: University Press.

Rostow, W. W. 1998. *The Great Population Spike and After: Reflections on the 21st Century.* New York: Oxford University Press.

Semmel, Bernard. 1970. *The Rise of Free Trade Imperialism: Classical Political Economy, the Empire of Free Trade, and Imperialism, 1750-1850.* Cambridge: Cambridge University Press.

Sherwig, John M. 1969. *Guineas and Gunpowder: British Foreign Aid in the Wars with France, 1793-1813.* Cambridge: Harvard University Press.

Smith, Adam. 1776 (1937). *An Inquiry into the Nature and Causes of the Wealth of Nations.* New York: Modern Library.

Steinherr, Alfred. 1990. 'Financial Innovation, Internationalization, Deregulation and Market Integration in Europe: Why does it All Happen Now?' In Donald

E. Fair and Christian de Boissieu, eds., *Financial Institutions in Europe under Competitive Conditions.* Dordrecht: Kluwer Academic Publishers, pp. 49 ff.

Weber, Eugen. 1976. *From Peasants into Frenchmen: The Modernization of Rural France, 1870-1914.* Stanford: Stanford University Press.

Weber, Eugen. 1998. 'What Rough Beast?' Review essay of E.J. Hobsbawm, 'Nations and Nationalism since 1780.' *Critical Review,* vol. 10, no. 2 (Spring), pp. 285-298.

Yack, Bernard. 1998. 'The Myth of the Civic Nation.' *Critical Review,* vol. 10, no. 2 (Spring), pp. 193-221.

Zucker, Stanley. 1975. *Bamberger: German Liberal Politician and Social Critic, 1823-1899.* Pittsburgh: University of Pittsburgh Press.

2. THE THEORETICAL AND HISTORICAL PERSPECTIVES ON THE EMERGENCE OF THE EURO

Robert Skidelsky and Kalin Nikolov

The main question to be asked in this paper is whether the emergence of two (and possibly three or four) leading currencies will make the world economy more or less stable than it now is in a dollar-led global system. Interest in this question has obviously been sharpened by the launch of the 'euro' at the beginning of 1999. The question of stability is also pertinent in the light of the succession of financial and currency crises, as well as the greater volatility of economies, which have followed the breakdown of the Bretton Woods system in 1971.

In neo-classical theory, the question makes little sense in a world of freely floating exchange rates. Rational speculators will quickly drive the value of the currency to its equilibrium level. Bubbles, crashes and currency crises will not occur and any attempt by policy-makers to manipulate their exchange rates in pursuit of policy goals will be self-defeating in the long run.

However, it has been argued by Professor Kindleberger that a fixed exchange rate system is superior to an unmanaged float. Indeed, experience has to some extent proved him right. Although 'floating' should, in theory, remove the adjustment issues which plague fixed-exchange rate systems, experience has shown that a floating exchange rate system does not, in itself, quickly ensure balance of payments equilibrium. Massive speculative capital flows can have serious and prolonged real effects.

The recent turmoil in world financial markets (including the sustained overvaluation of the pound) has reawakened interest in Kindleberger's theory of what makes a global system of fixed exchange rates possible. He has argued that such world monetary arrangements are only possible if one of the fixed currencies is 'hegemonic'. This paper will first survey the main theories of financial instability, and show that financial instability can occur—and has historically occurred—in both floating and fixed-exchange rate systems. It will then take up Kindleberger's contention that the two historic fixed-exchange rate systems—the pre-1914 gold standard and the post-1945 Bretton Woods system—only worked because they had a 'hegemonic' currency. We will then consider the implications of these discussions for the future of a world in which there are two or more leading currencies.

It would be useful to remind ourselves what financial crises are and how they come about. Broadly speaking there are two types of financial crises: currency/balance of payments crises in which an imbalance on the external account (current and capital) forces the country to abandon its fixed exchange rate system, and far more seriously, banking crises, which arise when the financial system is unable to meet its obligations and the nation's payments and credit provision system grinds to a halt.

Under the classical gold standard system financial crises were predominantly of the second kind. Typically, after a credit boom the collapse of several overextended banks led to a widespread liquidity crunch. Boom turned into recession as loans were called in and debtors forced into insolvency. Occasionally, depositor panic would set in bringing down healthy as well as unhealthy banks. But the exchange rate almost always held firm. The link to gold was the cornerstone of the pre-World War I economy and the consensus among the few who had the vote was that unemployment was an individual rather than social responsibility. The resulting swings in aggregate demand led to substantial volatility of output and employment, but the gold standard had the necessary credibility to withstand speculative attacks and these seldom occurred.

After World War I, and particularly after the Great Depression, fixed exchange rate systems became much less credible, as the 'lender of last resort' function of central banks became more prominent. As a result banking crises began to spill over into currency crises. The main lesson that policy-makers drew from the failure of central banks to act quickly in 1930 and lend to affected banks was that an effective 'lender of last resort' was needed in times of financial crisis to bail out the banking system. A potentially unlimited discount window was institutionalized in virtually all countries' central banks. After World War II, systemic financial collapses in the developed world became a thing of the past but the readiness of central banks to expand reserve money and consequently to abandon exchange rate pegs led to an erosion of the latter's credibility.

The troubles of the 1990s produced a new crop of models of bubbles, manias, and crashes, centered on the interaction between vulnerable banking systems and the exchange rate. Countries with high growth rates and sound budgets attract creditors like bees. Banks all round the world were falling over themselves to lend dollars to the East Asian tigers. When crisis hit, the foreign exchange liabilities of the banking systems turned out to be too large.

When the reserves ran out, the exchange rate collapsed. The interaction between debt contracts denominated in dollars and a collapsing exchange rate made much of the banking system insolvent. The role of foreign currency loans was to make an 'orderly devaluation' impossible.

Today, there are two basic approaches in the academic literature to analyzing currency crises.

In the first, a structural budget deficit is magnetized by the Central Bank or leads to the build-up of unsustainable debt. Either can produce a loss of reserves and a 'flight of capital' out of domestic into foreign currencies. This was the 'canonical' explanation of the Latin American crises of the 1980s. One can easily assimilate the banking system analysis into the 'canonical framework'. Implicit government guarantees for the banking system can be thought of as contingent implicit government liabilities—expenditure commitments not explicitly laid out by law which the state would have to honor if the banks failed. Thus the debts of a weak financial system can quickly become government debts which are covered by central bank credit. Capital flight then rationally ensues bringing down the peg.

A theory of self-fulfilling speculative attacks was developed to explain the ERM crisis of 1992. Here the fundamentals are assumed to be sound. There is an equilibrium in which agents have confidence in the country's commitment to the peg, and no speculative attacks take place and another equilibrium which involves a loss of investor confidence in the commitment which triggers off a speculative attack, thus validating itself by bringing the peg down. But the idea that the pound fell just because Soros thought it would is far fetched. Investor doubts about Britain's commitment to the peg reflected real economic and political problems in Britain.

The gold standard and the Bretton Woods System were both associated with pre-eminent currencies. Under both systems powerful national currencies were linked to a gold base. Did the two systems work because they had leader currencies, or did they just happen to have them?

This is the question posed by Professor Kindleberger. To him we owe the analysis of monetary systems in terms of structural characteristics. It is interesting that though thousands of students still write essays on Kindleberger's 'hegemonic' thesis, he nowhere explains what he means by a 'hegemonic' currency. For the purposes of this discussion, we need two definitions. We will define a 'leading currency' as one in which foreign nationals find it convenient to conduct their international payments and which they hold in their foreign exchange reserves. A country whose currency possesses these characteristics will stand out from the rest in a number of other ways: in its share in world trade, in the sophistication of its financial and banking institutions, and in the soundness of its fundamentals, which include political stability. We will define the Kindlebergian notion of a 'hegemonic currency' as a single leading currency. A world which has a number of leading currencies is, by definition, one without a hegemonic currency. Agents have a choice in which currency to trade and in which to invest.

Kindleberger rightly disposes of the argument that the gold standard was self-equilibrating. Monetary historians today agree that it lacked an automatic adjustment mechanism between creditors and debtors, since surplus countries could 'hoard' their surpluses, and debtor countries could (and did) suspend convertibility of their currencies into gold rather than deflate their economies. But there is much less agreement on what made it 'work'. Kindleberger argues that it worked because Britain managed it; the Bretton Woods system also worked because the United States managed it—managed in the sense that the top currency in both systems, the pound for the gold standard and the dollar for Bretton Woods, lubricated the adjustment mechanism. Without this management, or leadership as he calls it, countries would not have accepted the 'rules of the game' of both systems. A corollary of the argument is that where there exist several leading currencies, they will compete for custom, centralized control of monetary flows is impossible, and a global system of fixed exchange rates will break down. Kindleberger thinks the notion of a 'consensual hegemony' is an oxymoron.

According to Kindleberger the hegemonic currency—it should more accurately be called the hegemonic country—supplies the public goods of a global economy, in the sense of providing members of the system 'inducements' to maintain stable exchange rates and free trade policies. These inducements are an open market for imports, a flow of investment capital and emergency finance for short-term balance of payments disturbances. Only a country with the characteristics described is likely to have the ability and incentive to provide such services. Countries with a large share of world trade are likely to have internationally acceptable currencies and to develop financial facilities and domestic conditions geared to maintaining and expanding trade relations.

For Kindleberger a world of floating exchange rates is inferior to one of stable exchange rates. Historically it is associated with trade and currency wars, and greater economic volatility. Such a world is likely to break up into trade blocs, with a greater risk of war. His thesis is thus rooted in a Keynesian, or non-classical, model of non-market adjustment.

The leader country supplies on a global scale the economic services which, in Keynesian theory, domestic governments need to provide to maintain a high level of aggregate demand. The domestic counterparts of Kindleberger's leadership function are a high level of government consumption, a high level of government investment, and counter-cyclical policy. Without these domestic public goods, Kindleberger argues, following Keynes, a 'free' economy is liable to deflationary pressures, which destroy its domestic support.

Why should the 'leader' country provide these services? The brief answer is that it is in its enlightened self-interest to do so. Here Kindleberger's argument needs to be supplemented by Mancur Olson's classic study, *The Logic of Collective Action*. A collective good is one which every member of a 'group' wants to 'consume', but which no individual member of the group has an incentive to supply. Where the group is the whole population of a state—in Olson's terminology 'all encompassing'—one gets the standard argument for compulsory contribution, or taxation. Where the group interest is narrower, members can be got to contribute voluntarily to the good's provision by being offered inducements or 'special incentives' by the organization promoting their interest—ranging from intimidation to membership privileges. Olson's main examples are producer groups—groups of firms interested, say, in protection, or trade unions which aim to establish a system of collective bargaining. Where the group is small enough, an individual may have a special incentive of his own for supplying the collective good—to gain prestige, for example—even though no one else contributes.

This model can be readily applied to the international system, where the number of actors (states) is small. It is clearly in the self-interest of countries heavily involved in world finance and trade to secure conditions in which these activities can be profitably maximized. However, there is a crucial implication that the inducements they offer to maintain a suitable external environment come at disproportionate cost to their long-run economic vitality. In Britain's case these costs have been exhaustively documented by historians: the maintenance of free imports long after the rest of the world had started to put up tariffs against British exports, the 'costs of empire' and the privileged position of an institution (the City of London) which existed to channel domestic savings into foreign investment rather than in domestic manufacturing. Similar critiques were made of US 'over-extension' in the 1970s and 1980s. (Little has been heard of such 'declinist' theses in the 1990s.) The rise and fall of financial hegemonies is the motor of Kindleberger's economic history. The transition from one hegemony to another ushers in the period of economic disturbances. Thus, according to Kindleberger, the Great Depression was so severe because Britain no longer could and the United States wouldn't 'manage' the global financial system. Today, he suggests, we are in another of these transition periods, with the euro and the yen rising up to challenge the formerly almighty dollar.

Kindleberger's concept of hegemonic and leading currencies bears more than a passing relation to the more tightly specified concept of a 'vehicle' currency introduced by Paul Krugman in his seminal 1980 paper. He argues that we can rationalize the widespread use of the dollar in world payments by appealing to the highly liquid US financial markets which lower transactions costs in trades involving the US currency. Thus a Chilean who wants to trade pesos for Spanish pesetas will find it cheaper to first trade pesos for dollars and then dollars for pesetas rather than simply go to the peso-peseta market. The liquidity afforded by large US financial markets and America's importance in world trade determined its leading position as the global reserve and payment currency.

But how does this concept relate to Kindleberger's own notion of a 'hegemonic' currency? A hegemonic currency according to our definition is simply a single vehicle currency. The distinguishing feature of Kindleberger's theory is, although he does not state it explicitly, that when a hegemonic world political and military power combines with a single vehicle currency then a global system of fixed exchange rates and financial stability is possible. One way we can make sense of this argument is to think of it in terms of the cost advantages that a hegemonic currency affords to the hegemonic power in its interventions to offer financial support to countries in difficulties.

Investors look for several essential characteristics in their financial portfolios. A high return, low variation of returns, and, very importantly, high liquidity (the ability to easily convert their holdings into cash at a low cost). A single vehicle currency which provides all three features will then attract most of the world's capital and would be able to mobilize resources at very little cost in terms of higher interest rates. If investors have little choice of whom to lend to, the hegemonic country will be able to borrow as much as it needs without having to pay over the odds for it.[1] In economic terms, if there are no close substitutes to the leading country's financial assets then it will be able to derive financial advantages from its monopoly position in world debt markets. The arrival of other leading currencies is likely to change this. Now investors have a choice and the resulting competition for world loanable funds will result in higher interest rates, which makes it more expensive to hand out loans and aid to other nations in order to preserve world financial and political stability.

Does the economic history of the 20th century bear out the Kindleberger thesis?

Was it true that the pre-1914 gold standard system 'worked' because it was managed by Britain? Is it true that it collapsed in 1931 because of a Darwinian war of currencies? Is it true that a non-hegemonic system is much less stable than a hegemonic one? Economic historians now challenge all these elegant, but simplistic notions. This suggests that the 'thesis' may not offer much of a guide to what is likely to happen in the future.

The first thing which strikes one about the pre-1914 world is that the 'services' or 'inducements' which Kindleberger specifies as necessary for a liberal world economy were provided by Germany and France as well as by Britain, though Britain was the major provider. But the three centers were not overly competitive. You can describe the prevailing state of affairs as 'consensual hegemony', but the 'sharing out' of leadership functions was much more the result of the division of the world into informal, though overlapping, spheres of influence based on both economics and politics.

Before 1914, there was already a shadowy 'sterling area' of countries affiliated to Britain, which conducted most of its trade in pounds, was the main recipient of British loans, and held its national reserves in sterling. Germany was the economic locomotive of continental Europe, supplying its neighbors with much of their manufactured goods and capital, and taking most of their imports. France supplied Russia with much of its development capital, for political reasons. Even though London was the main source of emergency finance, the Bank of England needed support from the central banks of both France and Russia in the Barings Crisis of 1890. The economic order is best described as cosmopolitan. It was dominated by bankers and traders, not by governments. Cooperation between central banks was *ad hoc,* but it was real none the less. It was broken up by political, not monetary, competition.

We can approach the historical issue by asking a different kind of question: was sterling a hegemonic currency? Was it privileged above others in the sense of being the favorite store of value (for instance as a reserve currency) and means of payment throughout the world? Implicit in the idea of hegemony is the power to exact tribute. In financial terms, this means the ability to derive seigniorage—income from printing money. In the simplest case one gets goods by paying with money rather than by giving equivalent goods in return.

It is not clear that sterling had any such privilege before 1914. None of the core gold standard countries held each other's currencies as reserves before 1914. On the other hand, the peripheries of the system were linked to the core currencies through currency boards. There was a possibility of *seigniorage* in these arrangements, and there has been much dispute about whether Britain, even before 1914, was accumulating 'sterling balances' or debts to its trading partners. There is no evidence that sterling in general was being over-supplied. Britain was able to manipulate its imperial position in India to force on it unwanted goods and services, while using India's foreign currency earnings to offset its deficits with North America and elsewhere. But the limits of sterling's hegemony were set by the bounds of Britain's colonial empire.

After the First World War, there were two leading currencies, the pound and the dollar. Their role as reserve currencies was acknowledged by the Genoa Conference of 1922. Britain now exploited the privileged position of sterling to 'borrow short and lend long' before 1931. This played a part in upholding the restored gold standard for a few years. Much more important was the overseas lending of the United States which was financed by a large trade surplus. The system collapsed in 1931 not because the United States was 'unwilling' to take Britain's place, but because the deflationary forces unleashed by the US collapse in 1929, and the interaction between this and the unsustainable debt build-up in Central Europe and Latin America, were far too strong to be checked by any counter-cyclical measures, whether in the United States or globally, with the instruments and ideas then available.

The years 1931 to 1936 resemble to some extent those following 1971, when the Bretton Woods system broke down and failed to be restored. In the 1930s there were still two dominant currencies, the pound and the dollar. Twenty or so countries, mostly in the British Empire, though not including Canada, but with some others, pegged their currencies to sterling—we may call it a sterling exchange standard—and held a large part of their monetary reserves in sterling, for reasons of history and trade. There was some build-up of sterling balances in the late 1930s, but they were more or less covered by Britain's gold and dollar reserves.

The relationship between the dollar and sterling was conflictual till 1936. The US refused to sanction sterling's depreciation in 1931. The dollar was on gold. When the pound depreciated against the dollar in 1931, America raised the price of gold from $20 to $35 dollars an ounce, thereby restoring the '5 dollar pound'. The currency war was ended with the Tripartite Monetary Agreement of 1936, by which Britain, the United States and France agreed to support each other's currencies, at an agreed exchange rate, in the foreign exchange markets. But this currency war resulted from the breakdown of the gold standard: it did not cause it. Insofar as successive sterling and dollar depreciations helped both Britain and the United States recover from the slump, they contributed to world recovery.

The postwar or Bretton Woods system of fixed but adjustable exchange rates was much more obviously a Kindlebergian hegemonic system. The dollar alone was convertible into gold, and was therefore the major reserve currency of the system—though the sterling area lingered on. Because it was convenient to all, the US was able to get its major allies Germany, France and Japan to accept increasing quantities of dollars in payment for goods. This led to the Triffin paradox: but in this paradox was to be found the source of the system's liquidity. It collapsed when US foreign liabilities exceeded its gold reserves.

Did Bretton Woods work solely because of the privileged position of the dollar? This is an interesting counter-factual question. In 1944, only the United States was on the gold standard. As originally drafted, the Agreement envisaged that most of the leading powers would resume specie payments. It did not turn out like that, and the dollar was left as the only important reserve currency. Again, with the exception of a small German revaluation in the late 1960s, none of the surplus countries contemplated revaluing their currencies or resuming long-term lending, so the adjustment mechanism depended solely on dollar outflows.

There also is no simple Kindlebergian explanation for the end of the Bretton Woods system. Unlike in 1931, there was no obvious 'successor' to the dollar. The United States remained the mightiest economy in the world. One could say that it abused its right of seigniorage to pay for the Vietnam war, thereby failing to provide one of the essential public goods that a hegemonic currency must—its store of value function. A link between the collapses of 1931 and 1971 was the role of France. On both occasions the Bank of France started converting foreign currency into gold. But in each case France was a spoiler, not a challenger.

The hegemonic thesis thus needs considerable modification. The gold standard and Bretton Woods were not the same kind of system. We need to distinguish between pre-eminent and hegemonic currencies. The collapse of 1931 was, no more than that of 1971, caused by the competition between currencies. After 1971 neither the DM, the yen, or the franc replaced the dollar as payment or reserve currencies.

Our discussion so far has raised two separate albeit related questions: (a) is economic and financial stability more or less likely under a fixed exchange or a free floating system? (b) is a world which has *several* leading currencies likely to be more or less stable *whatever* the exchange rate regime?

The answer to the first question is still subject to much debate. Since the end of Bretton Woods the world has moved to a system of floating exchange rates, less restrictions on capital mobility and increased importance of other currencies such as the Deutschmark and the Japanese yen in world trade and payments. Crucially commodities such as gold have ceased to play any significant role in providing a nominal anchor and countries have now moved to a system based exclusively on paper money. Has this significantly contributed to financial instability?

1973 marked a watershed in the world monetary system. Never before had we seen such large and persistent exchange rate movements or such sustained jumps in the world inflation rate as the ones which occurred in the aftermath of the two oil shocks. The monetary authorities and their associated political systems took almost 20 years to adjust to the 'freedom', which their ability to print money had afforded them. With the link to gold severed, governments could ignore the impact of their fiscal and monetary policies on the exchange rate and pursue political objectives. This imparted significant instabilities into the world economy. The high US interest rates and the associated dollar rise during the early 1980s were a contributing factor to the Latin American debt crisis. Similarly the strength of the Deutschmark in 1992 forced a number of countries including the UK off the ERM. In both cases tight monetary policies and loose fiscal stances were propagated through fixed exchange rate systems leading to recessions, which became politically unsustainable.

In the 1990s fiscal and monetary disturbances seem to have declined in importance as the new economic and political consensus favors 'sensible' economic policies. Central banks have finally succeeded in anchoring their economies in an equilibrium with low inflationary expectations and stable monetary conditions, perhaps with the help of the microchip revolution which has been exerting downward pressure on prices. The relative macroeconomic stability has also contributed to a decline in developed country currency volatility compared to the situation of the 1970s and 1980s.

Hence, to the extent that domestic factors are the primary causes of economic and financial instability, we can expect that the world will be a less volatile place whatever the exchange rate regime. So the question of fixing versus floating is less salient than it once was.

An important caveat, however, concerns the growing openness of capital accounts which has given rise to a much more serious form of foreign and domestic shocks whose origins lie in the financial system. With such considerations in mind, it seems likely that floating will be the better system in the coming years, even though some exchange rate volatility will continue.

What about our second question? The world now has three leading currencies—the dollar, the euro and the yen (in order of their importance), and all three of them have big ambitions to be a 'hegemonic currency'. In so far as this quest for pre-eminence has resulted in deflationary policies and overvaluation, it has had adverse effects for financial stability in many parts of the globe and especially in Europe and Japan. Excessively tight Japanese monetary policy has often been cited as a cause of the lead-up to the current depression the country finds itself in. In the early 1990s the reflation of the Japanese economy was thought to be at odds with the country's ambition of replacing the dollar as the hegemonic currency of the 21st century.

The rise of economic powers such as Japan and their growing importance in world trade has led to other sorts of problems. One reason for the vulnerability of the South East Asian economies was that they conducted most of their trade with Japan but pegged their currencies to the dollar. Thus when the dollar rose sharply against the yen in the mid-1990s their loss of competitiveness in vital export markets contributed significantly to the build-up of external imbalances that eventually brought ruin to the region. Most countries however have learned from this experience and now target a much wider basket in order to hedge themselves against the volatility in the exchange rates of the major countries. Provided that policy-makers remember the lessons of 1997-1998 such mistakes should be less likely.

Far more seriously, the rapid trade liberalization that took place during the exchange rate stability of the Bretton Woods years has ground to a halt in the face of the persistent currency misalignments that have been taking place. Almost every year there is a trade dispute involving two of the three major trading blocs (with the advent of the euro these are now the three major currencies)—the US, Japan and the EU. The dollar/yen rate is a major political issue for reasons of domestic trade protectionism. In a situation of a few big players in the world economy it is much easier for protectionist lobbies to identify target countries and push their own interests forward. There is ample evidence that they have been doing so in recent years.

A superficial look at the historical evidence indeed suggests one somewhat paradoxical observation, namely that countries are more willing to liberalize their trade regimes under a system of fixed exchange rates. But how likely is such a system now that we have three trading and currency blocs that are increasingly ambitious about their position in the world economy? Who fixes to whom then becomes a sensitive and difficult political issue? The dollar's predominance makes it the obvious choice of leading currency. But will Europe and Japan agree to play second fiddle? Probably not. Currently all three are relatively self-sufficient economies which export only around 10-15 percent of GDP. The consensus is that benign neglect of their currencies has few significant macroeconomic consequences and all of them practice it under one guise or another. In any case an agreement by Tokyo and Frankfurt to follow Fed monetary policy would have much more severe political consequences than an exchange rate of 1 euro/$1 or 200 yen/$1. All this may well change, however, if for example a collapse in the US Stock Market plunges the world into renewed financial turmoil.

In the final analysis Kindleberger's thesis needs strong qualification. Financial crises are a function of domestic monetary and fiscal policies in individual economies as well as of the way the world financial arrangements (fixed, floating systems, etc.) transmit the policies of the leading countries to the rest of the global economy. In the 1930s excessively tight US monetary policy was transmitted through the fixed exchange rates of the gold standard to plunge the world into the Great Depression. In the 1960s it was the opposite—excessively loose US monetary policy was imparting inflationary pressure through the Bretton Woods 'par value' system. In the 1980s US fiscal laxity led to large interest rate and exchange rate swings.

However, we accept the main point of what we take to be Professor Kindleberger's approach, which is to focus on the structural characteristics of monetary systems, rather than on their supposedly self-equilibrating properties; or to put it another way, to concentrate not on the rules of the game, but on system characteristics which made particular rules of the game possible.

The lessons of history give a modest comfort to those who now look at an emerging global economy with two or possibly three pre-eminent currencies: the dollar, the euro, and the yen. This situation does not have to be a recipe for currency wars. Indeed, it is quite likely that if there develops closer co-ordination in the economic policies of the world's superpowers (for example as a result of a major financial calamity), this will eventually result in greater convergence in business cycles. Hence, in due course, another Tripartite Monetary Agreement will become more likely. As in the world before 1914, good economic policies and greater international cooperation will ensure world financial stability regardless of the number of leading currencies.

Note

1. Portes and Rey (1998) estimate that the US pays between 50 and 75 basis points less on its national debt due to its position as the world vehicle currency.

References

Calvo, G. 1995. 'Varieties of Capital-Market Crises.' University of Maryland. Working Paper, no. 15.

Flemming, J., 1999. 'Bubbles, exchange rates and capital flows.' In *Capital Regulation: For and Against.* London: The Social Market Foundation.

Frenkel, J., and A. Razin. 1996. *Fiscal Policies and Growth in the World Economy.* Third edition. Cambridge: MIT Press.

Krugman, P. 1979. 'A model of balance of payments crises.' *Journal of Political Economy.*

Krugman, P. 1980. 'Vehicle currencies and the structure of international exchange.' *Journal of Money, Credit and Banking.* Columbus: Ohio University Press, pp. 513-526.

Obstfeld, M. 1986. 'Rational and Self-Fulfilling Balance of Payments Crises.' *American Economic Review,* no. 76, pp. 72-81.

Obstfeld, M., and K. Rogoff. 1996. *Foundations of International Macroeconomics.* Cambridge: MIT Press.

Olson, M. 1965. *The Logic of Collective Action.* Cambridge: Harvard University Press.

Portes, R., and H. Rey. 1998. 'The Emergence of the Euro as an International Currency.' *Economic Policy,* no. 26, pp. 307-343.

Skidelsky, R. 1999. 'Historical reflections on capital movements.' In *Capital Regulation: For and Against.* London: The Social Market Foundation.

Skidelsky, R. 1999. 'Two Stories of Investment: Risk versus Uncertainty.' Conference Paper (April). Moscow.

3. EXTERNAL RELATIONS OF THE EURO AREA

C. Randall Henning

Charles Kindleberger's work provides a particularly useful starting point for examining the external relations of the euro area and the prospects for the international monetary system. In *The World in Depression, 1929-1939*, he laid the lion's share of responsibility for the economic disaster of the 1930s at the feet of hegemony lost. Great Britain had lost its position as international economic hegemon and the United States was as yet unwilling to fill the vacuum. This left no major power both willing and able to serve as lender of last resort, maintain a stable flow of investment capital and absorb distress exports (Kindleberger, 1973).

Professor Kindleberger's thesis inspired a generation of international political economists in their analyses and debates over what is called within the discipline 'structural realism' and 'neorealism', which embody among other things the notion that a stable, liberal international economic order requires hegemonic leadership. The creation of the euro represents the most important test of the thesis for the monetary area since *The World in Depression* was published in 1973.

The logic of neorealism suggests that international cooperation will decline. (Professor Kindleberger's formulation was less deterministic.) Indeed, there is a widespread expectation among economists that the United States and the euro area will pursue policies of 'mutual benign neglect' with regard to exchange rates and perhaps international financial crises as well. This would imply that crises that should be confronted will not be addressed in a timely manner or will go unattended entirely.

Counterpoised to neorealism has been a school of thought attaching primary importance to the institutionalization of cooperation in international regimes, labeled 'neoliberal institutionalism'. The quality of international cooperation relies in substantial measure on the robustness of international institutions, such as the G-7 and IMF, and the domestic institutions for making external monetary policy in the EU and US. However, I argue that such an approach would not predict strong cooperation either, owing to the relative weakness of these institutions insofar as monetary relations among major states and the euro area are concerned. Substantial, further institutional development, at both the European and international levels, would be required to justify optimism for the future of international monetary cooperation.

The present chapter briefly reviews the history of transatlantic monetary relations, particularly as it relates to European monetary integration, examines recent US-EU conflicts, addresses euro-area exchange rate policy-making and the adaptation of international institutions, and offers conclusions.

Transatlantic Relations and European Integration

Several conditions contributed to monetary integration in Europe over the decades. Monetary instability in the global system, I argue, is ranked highly among them. Often caused by benign neglect of the dollar or transatlantic conflict over macroeconomic policy and the balance of payments, instability in the international system provided compelling incentives for European states to pursue monetary integration at the regional level (Henning, 1998).

Severe transatlantic conflicts were followed in nearly every case by a tightening of regional integration in Europe. When the United States supported the Bretton Woods regime in the 1950s, monetary integration was excluded from the European agenda. Monetary stability was thought to be achievable within Europe through adherence to the multilateral regime, centered on the International Monetary Fund and its Articles of Agreement. But, when the United States began running balance of payments deficits in the early 1960s and the D-mark was revalued for the first time, intra-European trade and payments were disrupted and Walter Hallstein oversaw the preparation of the first Commission report on monetary integration. When the United States ignored the weakness of the dollar and then jettisoned the Bretton Woods regime in 1971, the European Community commissioned the report by the committee chaired by former Luxembourg Prime Minister Pierre Werner. The EC officially adopted the plan laid out in the report, the 'Werner Plan', and then created the Snake. Although monetary union was not implemented under the timetable foreseen in the Werner Plan, when the United States and Germany conflicted over the locomotive theory in 1977-78, German Chancellor Helmut Schmidt and French President Valéry Giscard d'Estaing launched negotiations that led to the creation of the European Monetary System. When the United States and Europe clashed over current account adjustment in the mid-1980s, the EC tightened monetary cooperation (the Basle-Nyborg agreement) and later committed itself to monetary union (Maastricht Treaty).

When systemic instability destabilized intra-European economic relations, regional monetary integration advanced several objectives. First, it advanced exchange rate stability on a regional basis. Second, regional monetary cooperation softened the impact of fluctuations against the dollar and deflected American pressure for policy adjustments. Third, monetary integration, if it were profound, offered the promise of exercising countervailing pressure on the United States, establishing greater symmetry in US-European monetary relations.

Thus, EMU is in part a defensive reaction against US monetary diplomacy, as it unfolded over the postwar decades. EMU shields the euro area from some of the disruptive effects of dollar fluctuations and might thus predispose European monetary authorities toward a policy of 'benign neglect' of its own of the exchange rate for the euro—producing, when combined with a similar stance on the part of US policy-makers, 'mutual benign neglect'. Such policies could well be accompanied by substantial volatility in, and misalignments of, the exchange rate. Because other contributors to this volume consider these economic effects at length (see also Henning forthcoming), the following section concentrates on a number of important institutional questions raised by EMU.

Policy-Making Institutions and Cooperation

The quality of international cooperation depends on the new institutions and processes for making external monetary policy of the euro area and the adaptation of international institutions to the presence of the monetary union. Transatlantic monetary cooperation depends as well on policy-making in the United States, of course. The European side is the main focus of this paper, however, because the US side has been examined elsewhere (Destler and Henning, 1989; Henning, 1994; Henning, 1999), US institutions are not directly affected by EMU, and the European arrangements are particularly obscure at the moment.

Consider first the experience of the international community in dealing with the European Union in the trade field. The members of the GATT and WTO have more than four decades of experience in bargaining with the Community on trade matters. Consensus decision-making, at least among the large member states, has posed a considerably greater problem than the greater collective power of Europe in such negotiations. The internal decision rule spawned minimalist liberalization offers that could be rendered flexible only with transatlantic brinkmanship (to which US policy-making of course made its own inimitable contribution). Agriculture during the Uruguay Round comes most prominently to mind. While this process allowed regional and multilateral trade liberalization to progress over the decades, this pattern of bargaining would be disastrous in the monetary and financial field, where the markets are so much more sensitive to policy conflict and new information.

In the monetary area, as in the trade arena, the higher the threshold required for making decisions within the Council of Ministers on exchange rate policy or international monetary agreements, the narrower will be the range of agreements that are also ratifiable internally. (Putnam, 1988; Evans, Jacobson, and Putnam, 1993) A high ratification threshold in Europe would reduce the likelihood of US-EU agreement, for example, and skew any agreements that are concluded toward European preferences. Non-Europeans should thus, of course, prefer a lower rather than a higher threshold within the monetary union.

The mechanisms by which exchange rate policy could actually be formulated are incomplete and untested. The ECB will conduct foreign exchange operations, but some of the operational details have been quite obscure. Key officials have also been vague on how a decision to intervene in the foreign exchange markets would be made. More importantly, the ECB cannot act alone in many important contingencies. Effective and accountable policies require a coherent political partner to share responsibility with the central bank for the common external monetary policy. Under the Maastricht Treaty (Article 109 in particular), however, the Council will have to act by unanimity on matters concerning the international monetary regime and by qualified majority when issuing 'general orientations' regarding exchange rate policy. Council decisions on the representation of the monetary union at the international level must be taken by unanimity. The European Commission must initiate all of these decisions, and the ECB must be consulted in the course of making them (Henning, 1997). These requirements impose a high decision-making threshold and could well predispose the Council against action.

Officials outside of Europe also naturally prefer transparency to opaqueness in decision-making in the Council. Of course, transparency within the Council in general, and Ecofin in particular, is remarkably low. Opaqueness has helped states to shield themselves from societal pressures when instituting reforms, but comes at the cost of democratic accountability. With transparency of decision-making within Ecofin, American, Japanese and other non-European negotiators could mold their proposals to enhance ratifiability within the EU, or even broker bargains among the Europeans.

Consider, now, the adaptation of the meetings of the G-7 finance ministers and central bank governors and the International Monetary Fund to the presence of the monetary union. I favor a consolidation of European representation in these bodies over time. For example, a 'G-3', composed of the United States, Japan, and euro area, could discuss monetary and exchange rate issues and then expand the meeting to the traditional 'G-7' when considering a broader set of questions. Other adaptations could also be envisioned (Alogoskoufis and Portes, 1991; Begg, Giavazzi and Wyplosz, 1997; Eichengreen and Ghironi, 1998; Kenen, 1998), but this arrangement would have the virtue of respecting the treaty commitment of the EU member states to adhere to a common external monetary policy and speak with one voice, while also accommodating the relative decentralization of fiscal, financial and other economic policies within the EU.

On these matters, the international community faces a serious dilemma: The rest of the world would be better off with consolidated EU representation only if the EU moves toward majority voting and transparency. Consolidated representation leaves the rest of the world *worse* off if instead decision-making were based on consensus and remains opaque. Much hinges, therefore, on institutional reform within the European Union. The Treaty of Amsterdam mandates greater openness in EU institutions and the IGC that is scheduled to convene in 2000 will address institutional matters again.

How have transatlantic negotiations over common institutions developed in practice? In December 1998, the EU proposed that a tripartite delegation composed of the EU presidency (or chair of the Euro-11 Council), the Commission, and ECB represent the euro area in the International Monetary Fund (IMF) and the meetings of finance ministers and central bank governors from the Group of Seven, 'finance G-7'. The United States Treasury rejected this proposal on the grounds that (1) a disproportionate number of Europeans would attend, (2) the Commission would lack sufficient authority in the monetary area, and (3) the presidency would lack continuity. As would be expected, the smaller member states of the euro area were particularly intent on representation by the chair of the Euro-11 Council in these meetings. The United States and European Union negotiated for six months over this matter.

The group finally agreed, at a meeting in Frankfurt in June 1999, that its meetings would be split into two parts with different configurations. During the first part, in which the world economic outlook, multilateral surveillance and exchange rates are discussed, the ECB president and the chair of the Euro-11 Council (usually, but not always, the presidency of Ecofin) would attend along with the finance ministers and central bank governors of the United States, Japan, United Kingdom and Canada (this configuration was anticipated by Alogoskoufis and Portes, 1991, p. 233). The national central bank governors of the euro-area member states would be excluded, however, until the second part of the meeting, devoted to the broader set of issues relating to the international financial system, at which point the ECB president and Euro-11 chair might be asked to leave. The Commission would be allowed to take part on specific issues, such as assistance for Russia.

These arrangements would apply for an indefinite period of time (*Financial Times*, June 15, 1999).

The European Union and the international community face a similar set of issues in the International Monetary Fund. A representative of the ECB now attends many, though not all, meetings of the Executive Board. But monetary union raises more far-reaching questions: How should the IMF best conduct multilateral surveillance of the member states of the monetary union? Can euro-area members articulate and adhere to a common external monetary policy, particularly in light of the fact that several of them represent non-European countries in the 'constituency system'? Should European representation be consolidated? Should the European Union itself be given membership status? European states have avoided many difficult questions by defining their obligation to pursue a common external policy narrowly, so as to exclude many of the matters that come before the Executive Board. But it will become increasingly difficult to avoid these matters of reorganization over the long run.

As of mid-1999, Ecofin's treatment of external representation had been limited to the question of which officials should go to international meetings. It has said little about what the euro-area representatives should say at those meetings, how that message should be prepared (presumably the Economic and Financial Committee and Commission will play roles here), what the latitude of the delegation would be in responding to proposals from non-Europeans, and how any agreement would be ratified. In particular, it would be *un*acceptable for the Euro-11 presidency to read a prepared statement in the name of the monetary union and be unable to respond to proposals for joint action.

Moreover, Ecofin had arrived at no explicit agreement for how the euro area should represent itself in *bilateral* negotiations with the United States directly. The EU has not provided an answer to Henry Kissinger's famous question rephrased: Whom in Europe should the Secretary of the Treasury telephone when he or she wants to rescue a currency or a country? Although it might be unrealistic to expect that the euro area would provide a single telephone number, the Secretary should know which three or four numbers to use, and should know whose telephone calls to answer.

Recent Policy Issues and Conflicts

The risks of not having tried and proven policy-making procedures in place within the euro area for external monetary policy are accentuated by the present economic environment. The financial crisis that began in Asia in mid-1997 and spread to Russia and Latin America in 1998 necessitated a global adjustment of current account balances. As the stricken countries experienced a halt to capital inflows, depreciation of their currencies and severe recessions, the industrialized countries had to accept more imports. Japan, suffering its own prolonged recession, was not in a position to do so, and in fact aggravated the global adjustment problem substantially by running increased current account surpluses itself. This left primarily the United States and European Union as sources of demand in the world economy. The United States current account deficit rose by almost $100 billion from 1996 to 1998. American policy-makers were clear about their desire for Europe to join in this process. (Gore, 1998; Summers, 1998; Daley, 1998; Truman, 1999). But rather than contributing to the adjustment, the euro area *increased* its surplus over the same period. While Europeans might argue that in the absence of the global financial crisis their surplus would have increased even more, such reasoning provides little comfort to the US Congress and policy-makers.

The euro area's current account position reflected its choice of the mix of monetary and fiscal policies. Member governments succeeded in maintaining discipline in fiscal policy at the outset of the monetary union, enabling the ECB to pursue a monetary policy that was more relaxed than would otherwise have been the case. Interest rate reductions in December 1998 and April 1999 were premised largely on the maintenance of governments' fiscal discipline. The monetary union thus pursued, in the words of French Finance Minister Dominique Strauss-Kahn, the 'Clinton-Greenspan' rather than the 'Reagan-Volcker' policy mix. As the theory of open economy macroeconomics pioneered by Robert Mundell (1963) and Marcus Fleming (1962) anticipates, this mix led, through lower European interest rates, to steady depreciation of the euro during the first several months of the monetary union. The initial weakness of the euro was reinforced by continued strength in the US economy and the expectation of a tightening by the Federal Reserve. These currency movements compounded the current account adjustment problem.

US officials faced a dilemma when confronting less-than-desirable demand within the euro area. A further easing of monetary policy would stimulate demand, but would also further weaken the euro against the dollar, with ambiguous effects on the current account, at best. A fiscal expansion in the euro area would have the desired impact on the current account balances in the short to medium term. Indeed, American policy-makers have pressed European governments to undertake fiscal stimuli in previous episodes of current account conflict, such as during 1977-78 and 1985-87 (Putnam and Henning, 1989; Destler and Henning, 1989). Such a stimulus would violate the Stability and Growth Pact of the euro area, however, and threaten to reverse the remarkable improvement in fiscal and debt positions achieved during the convergence process prior to the creation of the monetary union. Any sustained increase in European fiscal deficits would worsen an already formidable fiscal challenge for Europe in the coming decades and potentially increase American borrowing costs as well over the long term.

US officials resolved this dilemma by recommending structural reforms in the European economies. Assistant Secretary of the Treasury for International Affairs Edwin M. Truman was particularly direct in a Spring 1999 speech when, amplifying Treasury Secretary Lawrence H. Summers's previous statements, he inveighed against 'persistent low levels of domestic European investment' and 'Europe's reliance on export-led growth'. Changes in policies and regulations that gave more flexibility to the markets for labor, goods, and capital, and the advancement of privatization programs, among other measures, would boost internal investment (Truman, 1999; Summers, 1997a and 1997b). Not only would these measures stimulate growth and employment within Europe, they would also shift the savings-investment balance of the euro area, reducing net capital outflows, placing upward pressure on the euro, and reducing the current account surplus of the monetary union. Although structural reforms usually take a long period of time to implement, particularly compared to the macroeconomic instruments, a credible commitment to substantial reforms could affect investment behavior and financial markets over a shorter period of time.

The importance that American officials attach to the policies of the monetary union derives from the politics of economic openness within the United States. Proposals to secure fast-track trade negotiating authority failed twice in the 105th Congress. The membership of the WTO is now defining the agenda for the next round of multilateral trade negotiations. Forward progress on regional trade liberalization, such as the Free Trade Area of the Americas, depends on maintaining favorable economic conditions and creating more favorable political conditions. Meanwhile, the steel industry filed for protection under anti-dumping statutes, received substantial relief, and continued to press for more in the political arena. Other industries could well follow. Presidential candidates are gearing up for the primary season in early 2000 and elections in November of that year.

These conditions render US economic policies vulnerable to backsliding on openness. Defenders of economic openness and peaceable transatlantic economic relations in the United States would not want to superimpose upon this picture a deteriorating American trade and current account position, particularly where the United States were the only major source of net demand for the world economy. But this is precisely what officials in the administration and Congress observed during 1998 and early 1999. The buoyant domestic economy and the low rate of unemployment have contained the backlash to 'globalization' in the United States. But the favorable domestic economic situation will not continue without setbacks indefinitely.

The prevailing economic and political environment calls for an active presence for international policy cooperation. A *laissez-faire* posture by the leading governments and central banks would be particularly dangerous at this juncture. But international institutions and internal policy mechanisms that would be needed to buttress even minimalist *ad hoc* cooperation between the United States, Japan, and international community in general, on the one hand, and the euro area, on the other hand, are not robust, to say the least.

Conclusions

Professor Kindleberger concluded his 1973 book by sketching six scenarios for the future. The scenarios to be avoided were (1) the United States and Europe vying for leadership of the world economy, (2) one unable to lead and the other unwilling, as during the 1930s, and (3) each wielding a veto over system strengthening without pursuing constructive programs of its own. The preferred scenarios were (1) revived US leadership, (2) assertion of leadership by Europe, and (3) cession of sovereignty to international institutions (Kindleberger, 1973). Although originally intended to apply to the 1970s, this description of alternative pathways also applies to the future of the international monetary system after the completion of the monetary union. But it remains unclear which scenario is most apt.

In particular, it would be premature to conclude that the euro will have a stabilizing impact on the global monetary system. Several additional factors will determine whether the monetary union will have such an effect. The new system will contain two large, relatively closed monetary areas that are jointly dominant but potentially competing. The structure of the international system alone would suggest less rather than more cooperation. The initial policy record of the euro area suggests a *laissez-faire* posture toward the euro as far as foreign exchange intervention and declaratory policies are concerned and is thus at least consistent with the neorealist expectation.

Institutional development and elaboration could counteract these potentially destabilizing features of the structure of the international system. The June 1999 G-7 agreement whereby the United States accepted the ECB president and Euro-11 Council chair and the Europeans accepted the expulsion of the national central bank governors from the first half of the meeting, represents forward movement. But, for reasons discussed above, this solution is incomplete and provisional. Further reforms of euro-area policy-making, the G-7 and international institutions such as the IMF will be necessary over the longer term.

The European Union must clarify the institutions and procedures through which external monetary policy will be made, international monetary agreements will be negotiated and ratified, and policy within international financial institutions will be represented. In particular, Ecofin must establish itself as the effective political 'pole' for external monetary policy, working with the ECB and European Commission. Consensus decision-making must be resisted; majority voting must be the effective decision rule when that is allowed under the treaties. The Council should set down in advance arrangements by which international agreements could be reached on short notice, should a foreign exchange or financial crisis require the participation of the euro area in concerted action by the international community. Such arrangements would include designating a representative for negotiations with the United States and in the G-7, conferring a mandate to negotiate agreements on the designated official, and specifying in advance the procedures for quickly ratifying (or rejecting) any agreement that the representative negotiates. Within the framework of the decisions made by Ecofin and the European Council in December 1998 and the finance G-7 in June 1999, this representative would be the chair of the Euro-11 Council, who would have the assistance of the Commission and work in close consultation with the ECB.

It is also desirable for the European Union, and the Council of Ministers in particular, to move toward greater transparency in decision-making. The EU is advancing the transparency agenda set down in the Amsterdam treaty. More remains to be done, however, and the agenda of the upcoming IGC, intended to complete the work on institutional reform that was left unfinished at Amsterdam, should include this important item.

In terms of economic policy, Europe faces the formidable challenge of structural reform. Such reforms, particularly in the labor market, hold the key to reducing the chronically high rate of unemployment while maintaining discipline in macroeconomic policy. These policy changes also hold the key to stimulating European investment, reducing current account surpluses, and providing a boost to growth in the rest of the world.

With substantial progress on these institutional and structural reforms, the formation of the monetary union will enable Europe itself to draw the full benefit from the euro and will benefit the international community. The European economy would become more flexible and dynamic, as well as a coherent partner in international monetary and financial cooperation with the United States, Japan and other countries. Without institutional and structural reforms, the European economy could stagnate and frustrate international cooperation. In that case, the net benefit to the stability of the international monetary system and the international community in general would have to be reconsidered.

References

Alogoskoufis, George, and Richard Portes. 1991. 'International Costs and Benefits of EMU.' *European Economy*, special edition, no. 1, pp. 231-245.

Begg, David K., Francesco Giavazzi, and Charles Wyplosz. 1997. 'Options for the Future Exchange Rate Policy of the EMU.' Occasional Paper, no. 17. London: Centre for Economic Policy Research.

Daley, William M. 1998. Remarks at the 4th Annual Transatlantic Business Dialogue Meeting. Charlotte, N. C., November 6.

Destler, I. M., and C. Randall Henning. 1989. *Dollar Politics: Exchange Rate Policymaking in the United States.* Washington, D.C.: Institute for International Economics.

Eichengreen, Barry, and Fabio Ghironi. 1998. 'European Unification and International Monetary Cooperation.' In Barry Eichengreen, ed., *Transatlantic Economic Relations in the Post-Cold War Era.* New York: Council on Foreign Relations.

Evans, Peter B., Harold K. Jacobson, and Robert D. Putnam, eds. 1993. *Double-Edged Diplomacy: International Bargaining and Domestic Politics.* Berkeley: University of California Press.

Fleming, J.M. 1962. 'Domestic Financial Policies under Fixed and under Floating Exchange Rates.' *IMF Staff Papers,* 9, pp. 369-379.

Gore, Al. 1998. Remarks on the Transatlantic Business Dialogue. Charlotte, N.C., November 6. Washington, D.C.: Office of the Vice-President.

Henning, C. Randall. 1994. *Currencies and Politics in the United States, Germany, and Japan.* Washington, D.C.: Institute for International Economics.

Henning, C. Randall. 1997. *Cooperation with Europe's Monetary Union.* Policy Analyses in International Economics, no. 49. Washington, D.C.: Institute for International Economics.

Henning, C. Randall. 1998. 'Systemic Conflict and Regional Monetary Integration: The Case of Europe.' *International Organization*, no. 52 (Summer), pp. 537-573.

Henning, C. Randall. 1999. *The Exchange Stabilization Fund: Slush Money or War Chest?* Policy Analyses in International Economics, no. 57. Washington, D.C.: Institute for International Economics.

Henning, C. Randall. Forthcoming. 'United States-European Union Relations after the Inception of the Monetary Union: Cooperation or Rivalry?' In C. Randall Henning and Pier Carlo Padoan, *Transatlantic Perspectives on the Euro.* Washington, D.C.: Brookings Institution.

Kenen, Peter B. 1998. 'EMU and Transatlantic Economic Relations.' HWWA Discussion Paper, no. 60. Hamburg.

Kindleberger, Charles P. 1973. *The World in Depression, 1929-1939.* London: Penguin Press.

Mundell, Robert. 1963. 'Capital Mobility and Stabilization Policy under Fixed and Flexible Exchange Rates.' *Canadian Journal of Economics and Political Science* (November), pp. 475-485.

Putnam, Robert D. 1988. 'Diplomacy and Domestic Politics: The Logic of Two-Level Games.' *International Organization,* no. 42 (Summer), pp. 427-460.

Putnam, Robert D., and C. Randall Henning. 1989. 'The Bonn Summit of 1978: A Case Study in Coordination.' In Richard N. Cooper, Barry Eichengreen, C. Randall Henning, Gerald Holtham, and Robert D. Putnam, *Can Nations Agree? Issues in International Economic Cooperation.* Washington, D.C.: Brookings Institution.

Summers, Lawrence H. 1997a. 'EMU: An American View of Europe.' Remarks delivered at the Euromoney Conference, April 30.

Summers, Larry. 1997b. 'American Eyes on EMU.' *Financial Times,* October 22.

Summers, Lawrence H. 1998. 'Transatlantic Implications of the Euro and Global Financial Stability.' Remarks on the Transatlantic Business Dialogue. Charlotte, N.C., November 6. Washington, D.C.: Treasury Department.

Truman, Edwin M. 1999. 'The Single Currency and Europe's Role in the World Economy.' Remarks on the World Affairs Council. Press release, April 6. Washington, D.C.: Treasury Department.

4. THE INTERNATIONAL POLITICAL IMPLICATIONS OF THE EURO

Richard Rosecrance

The euro was created on January 1, 1999. Even though it depreciated afterwards, the prospects are for a stronger euro as time passes. More countries will join Euroland, increasing the Euro-11 to Euro-15 and probably in time to at least Euro-26. That total will include only two countries previously belonging to the old Soviet Union (Estonia and Latvia), and thus additional members are likely to join. New members will contribute to greater demand for euros, pushing the currency to higher values.

At the same time, countries which previously held European reserves (the DM, the franc and the pound sterling) will automatically transfer their holdings to euros, and other trading countries, blocs, and international organizations will buy euros to reduce their exposure to the US dollar. China, Japan, Southeast Asia, Latin America, and the Middle East will add euros to their stock of reserve assets, probably selling dollars in the process.

Some of these changes will merely be substitutive (changing in European currency reserves for euros, for example) and some will be permanent additions to the European share of the world's reserve stock. Again these movements will favor appreciation of the euro.

As Richard Cooper shows, however, the demand for euros will not automatically bring forth an increase in supply. The reserve role of the US dollar was reflective of conscious US monetary policy to put the dollar in hands of foreign traders and investors by running deficits in the US balance of payments. The United States also borrowed abroad in large amounts, selling US government bonds to foreign lenders. Foreign demands for liquidity were thus accommodated, and the use of the dollar as a reserve and trading currency increased in London's Eurodollar market, Latin America, and East Asia.[1]

It is thus uncertain whether the role of the euro will rise to rival that of the US dollar quite as rapidly as Robert Mundell and Richard Portes expect.[2] The year 2010 seems a little early to achieve equality in worldwide holdings of the two primary reserve currencies. As Mundell explains, this change would require a $100 billion transfer from dollars to euros for each of the next twelve years.[3&4]

The mechanisms to achieve such a transfer are not straightforward. Mundell observes: 'Unless this massive shift were offset by increasing lending by Europe and increased borrowing by the United States, it would mean a massive shift in current account balances, with that of Europe's turning strongly negative, and that of the United States moving in a positive direction.'[5] Richard Cooper notes, 'this [shift] will require (other things equal) a current account deficit by the EMU-countries on a continuing basis, achieved by an appreciation of the euro relative to the dollar and other foreign currencies...'[6] Cooper then observes, however, that the result could stem from the provision of 'exports of long-term financial capital from Europe'[7] putting euros in the hands of foreigners as the United States put dollars in the hands of foreigners through its investments abroad in the 1950s and 1960s.[8]

In the 1960s the United States ran a balance of trade surplus, but a balance of payments deficit, caused by American military aid and US investment abroad. The dollar was still fixed to gold, but dollar holdings outside the United States rapidly rose to exceed the value of the American gold stock.[9] This ultimately forced a US devaluation, severing the link with gold, and also after the Kingston agreement, the establishment of freely floating exchange rates. The dollar fell in value relative to the yen and the DM.

Euro investments abroad are recorded on the negative side of the balance of payments, and they have to be financed by exports from receiving countries to Europe. A high-valued euro would make these transactions possible. European borrowing is on the positive side, but the loans have to be repaid by European exports to lender countries. A lower-valued euro would be consistent with this outcome. But the problem is that European domestic deficits would increase with European foreign borrowing, possibly violating the terms of the Stability Pact. For this reason, it is unlikely that European countries will borrow abroad in large amounts—issuing short-term euro-bills in return.[10] How then does Europe get its currency into foreign hands? Essentially by running a deficit in the balance of trade or by lending abroad. Both of these involve foreigners selling net exports to Europe.

A high-valued euro would produce this result. But a high-valued euro presents complications for weaker Euroland countries: Portugal, Spain, and Italy to say nothing of the probable new central and eastern European members of the group. As Jeffry Frieden points out, exporters or producers of import-competing goods will find this difficult, possibly increasing the already large unemployment in these countries.[11] The problem would accentuate with Greece, as well as Romania and Bulgaria joining EMU.

There will therefore be countervailing pressures within Euroland. Producers of non-tradable goods and financial investors will prefer a high-valued euro. The reverse will be true for exporters and import-competing industries.[12] A high-valued euro would compete effectively with the US dollar, but it would have significant European domestic consequences. A low-valued euro would ease the plight of marginal European producers, but would be less attractive to foreigners as a reserve currency alternative to the dollar.

A Low-Valued Euro?

From an external standpoint, a high-valued euro would be preferable to a lower-valued alternative. There is, however, a considerable prospect of a European currency which is set to maintain or even increase European surpluses with the rest of the world.

Economists and political scientists remember the tension between the franc, the pound, and the dollar in the 1930s.[13] While the monetary authorities of two currencies could probably have reached agreement, (franc and dollar, pound and franc, dollar and pound), the game theoretic core was too small to accommodate the requirements of all three of them.[14] Thus competitive devaluation followed, and agreement to stop the vicious cycle was not reached until 1936—too late to prevent a devastating collapse in worldwide capital flows.

In the first decade of the next century, there might be a similar competition between the euro, the dollar, and the yen, each striving to undercut the others. This competition would be particularly difficult for the United States which is already facing balance of payments deficits in the neighborhood of $300 billion per year. As a result, the United States could scarcely stand by while the euro was pushed downward by the European Central Bank, or the yen devalued by Japanese monetary authorities. The only advantage of this scenario from an American standpoint would be that capital flows into the United States would offset trading losses. US interest rates would probably remain higher than those in either Europe or Japan, and the dollar would stay as a key currency. Even then, however, the financial advantages of holding dollars could be cancelled by a sudden run on the dollar stemming from larger and larger trading deficits.[15] In sum, strategies of competitive devaluation would not be beneficial to the world economy, to say nothing of the United States.

A High-Valued Euro?

Some believe that Europe is not an optimum currency area[16] and perhaps that the euro should not have been created.[17] There seems little doubt that a high-valued euro will put pressure on marginal producers of traded goods and exports. Unemployment rates in less competitive countries may rise as imports flow into European markets.

Internationally, however, a high-valued euro would gain adherents and prestige. The higher its value, the more rapidly, *ceteris paribus*, other countries can run surpluses in the European market, gaining supplies of euros. This could have a very beneficial result for the United States, as the erstwhile key currency country in the system. For many years the United States has served as the market and lender of last resort in the international financial system, providing 'hegemonic stability' to the system.[18] The result in recent years at least has been heavy American balance of payments deficits. For a considerable period of time, US officials hoped that Japan might perform some of the stabilization task. While Japan has invested abroad and has helped Thailand in the recent financial crisis, it has not generally served as a market of last resort for any country, certainly not for developing nations. It runs a surplus with every East Asian country except for China, Indonesia and Brunei.

Table 1: Japanese Trade Balances with Asian Countries in Yen, 1997

	Exports	Imports
Hong Kong	3.3m	202t
Singapore	2.4m	700t
Thailand	1.7m	1.1m
Malaysia	1.7m	1.3m
Philippines	1.8m	506t
S. Korea	3.1m	1.7m
Taiwan	3.3m	1.5m
Cambodia	7.0t	1.5t
Asian NICs	12m	4.2m
China	2.6m	5.0m
Indonesia	1.2m	1.7m
Brunei	18t	169t

Source: JETRO, 1998

In addition, its own domestic stagnation has sapped its foreign buying power. Also, as John Ravenhill shows, the expectations of 'product life-cycle theory' are not met by Japanese behavior.[19]

When Raymond Vernon originated the product-cycle theory at Harvard Business School in the 1960s, it was assumed that the 'pioneers' of any new product would (1) initially produce the good for their own market and then export it abroad. (2) Ultimately they would confront late-coming competitors who would first regain their own markets and then begin to export to the pioneer country. (3) In the third and final stage, both pioneer and late-coming countries would produce abroad and then import the product back into their own home markets. This chronology roughly fitted the case of the television set, and the United States ended up importing its televisions from low cost producers abroad.[20]

In the Japanese case, however, while Tokyo has produced new products in low cost locations abroad, few or none of them have been reimported back into the Japanese market. *Keiretsu* restrictions have dictated that the products be sent to the US market, further increasing the American trade deficit. This has caused a continuing imbalance in East Asian trade. Partly for political reasons, the Japanese surplus with the United States has now been denominated as an East Asian surplus. Despite hopes that Japan would in time adopt the role of a financial stabilizer,[21] the promise has not been fulfilled. The Japanese government's inability to stimulate the economy has made this prospect even more remote.

Japanese behavior reflects a short-sightedness that has been modeled in the 'Sharks and Fishes' computer game.[22] The objective of the game is to maintain ecological balance among the two species. In the game, the fish live on abundant plankton, and the sharks live on the fish. Obviously if the sharks eat up all the fish, they also die. For balance to occur, the sharks must eat the fish slowly, enabling them to feed and reproduce. Japan is now in the somewhat unenviable position of 'shark' in the international trading system. If it eats up all the fish (that is saturates the world with its goods, undercutting foreign industry), it runs the risk of ultimate loss. As foreign consumption falls, there may be no one to buy its products. This no doubt overly dramatic example at least underscores the point that the failure of Japan to act as a 'hegemonic stabilizer' generates a need for others to fill that role, assisting the United States.

A high-valued euro would permit the European Union to share the long-standing American stabilizing role as both a market and lender of last resort. Europe would invest extensively abroad, putting the euro in the hands of East Asians and Latin Americans. It would also buy the products of developing nations and NICs, thereby increasing the market for rising nations, lessening the instabilities generated by the recent financial crisis. While such a role would generate domestic pressures in some Euroland countries, it is already implicit in the requirements for joining the EMU. Nations of the European fringe have decided to join, convinced that the returns in capital inflows will more than offset the deflationary aspects of membership.

Relations Between the Euro, Dollar and Yen

The current international exchange rate regime is not one of freely fluctuating rates. Most countries' currencies are linked to one of the major currencies, heretofore the dollar, the DM, and the yen. Only major currencies have fluctuated in respect of each other. Nonetheless, the fluctuations have been quite large, and had to be restrained in the 1985 Plaza Agreement. Much more recently, the dollar and the yen have risen (declined) as much as 50 percent against one another. Despite the availability of hedging mechanisms, these large fluctuations have hampered trade, and, more important, capital flows.[23] Uncertainties in currency values have constrained international investment.

In recent years, American financial leaders have declined to seek a relationship to the new euro, apparently preferring values dictated by market outcomes. In the short term, this is quite understandable. In the longer term, however, recessionary conditions may tempt one or more of the major currency areas to seek an advantage vis-à-vis the others through devaluation. This could lead to competitive reactions not unlike those of the period 1930-36 and to a collapse of international confidence. Capital flows could then be restricted. With a pool of international capital in the tens of trillions of dollars, the result could be catastrophic.

The entire history of international monetary relations since World War II has been written in terms of permitting deficit countries to regain their feet through devaluation and new inflows of capital to restore confidence. France, Britain, Mexico, Brazil, and the United States have all undergone major currency crises. When these occurred, major competitors alleviated, they did not accentuate the problem. They gave the affected nation leeway, credit, and time to solve its problem. Thus, a British devaluation did not suddenly precipitate a French counter-depreciation. The Japanese and the Germans acknowledged the US devaluation in 1971-73 without seeking to offset the American gain. This stabilizing behavior was even more characteristic of the treatment of developing countries, particularly Mexico and Brazil.

To be sure, there have been some negative portents. Under inflationary pressure, Britain faced a currency crisis in September, 1992. It then asked for help from the German Bundesbank and sought to maintain the value of the pound sterling by raising interest rates up to 15 percent. The Bundesbank, however, only lowered its own interest rates by ¼-½ percent. Speculation then forced Britain out of the ERM, and the value of sterling plummeted. The

French franc also suffered. It depreciated against the DM and could remain within the ERM only when the ERM countries agreed to increase the bands of fluctuation to 15 percent.[24]

This example is perhaps the exception that proves the rule: surplus countries normally allow countries in trouble to devalue without retaliation. They provide liquidity and time for the nation in difficulty to adjust.[25] The financial crisis in Asia and Latin America also underscored the demands of international lending agencies for domestic contraction prior to international assistance. Brazil, Thailand, and Indonesia were forced through swinging contractions prior to IMF bailouts. Viewed from an international perspective, however, these countries were not principal players in the system.

Paul Volcker (along with Jacques Chirac) has recently called for establishing some relationship between the euro, the dollar and the yen to reduce the impact of speculative overshooting. Yen and dollar relationships varied over the past two years between 147 and 105, nearly a 50 percent fluctuation. If one includes values as far back as 1995, the changes have been of the order of 160 percent.

The Theory of Overlapping Clubs

The call for some linkage between currency areas raises anew a perennial problem of international relations. Once a new bloc or grouping is created, conflict is likely to rise unless a connection is forged with other regional or functional groups. The world is not likely to see a single effective and legitimate worldwide international government established in the next few decades. Despite the existence of the United Nations organization, authoritative decisions cannot be made by either the General Assembly or the Security Council. The UN General Assembly's resolutions are only recommendatory, and in any event majorities in that body do not possess the national resources needed to carry them out. The Security Council is hamstrung by the veto.

In the 1930s de facto economic and political groupings governed world politics. A Japanese sphere in Asia was paralleled by a Nazi German sphere in Central and Eastern Europe.[26] In the Western Hemisphere, the United States had its own little de facto club. With the League of Nations faltering, the dominant regional blocs were underlapping. Thus bloc conflict and maneuvering became the characteristic of international politics. That bloc conflict ultimately broke out into war.

The world has rarely experienced the creation of major overlapping clubs. Usually, as with traditional alliances, these have been starkly limited in geographic focus. The Three Emperor's League (1873) did not include

France or England. The Dual Alliance (1879) left out Russia as well as Britain and France. It is true that Germany's Otto von Bismarck participated in connections with all European countries but France, even though no single alignment or alliance included the whole group. When Bismarck negotiated the Reinsurance Treaty with Russia in 1887, critics questioned the overlapping (and partly conflicting) obligations which Germany then undertook to Austria and Russia. After Bismarck's fall in 1890, alliances took on an exclusive and non-overlapping character, eventuating in the Triple Alliance and Triple Entente which led directly to World War I.

One can in part discern the background tenor of events by determining the degree to which military alliances are overlapping in character. Today, Russia remains a member of one NATO Council, but not the other. There is yet no geographically exclusive Warsaw Pact opposing NATO. What is true of military relationships also holds for economics. If these are exclusive and underlapping, economic conflict is likely to rise. And there was a period in the 1960s and 1970s when it appeared that economic bloc conflict would once again determine major outcomes. The Soviet bloc linked Eastern Europe and a few countries in the Middle East, Africa and Asia. The Western bloc comprised most of Latin America, Western Europe and some states in Asia and the Middle East. Some Middle Eastern, African and Asian countries stood aside from this conflict and pursued a neutralist course. In the 1970s, the 'new international economic order' encouraged decoupling of the South from the North. Once again the prospect of distinct and opposed 'underlapping' clubs emerged. This did not happen because Soviet Communism collapsed, and Western capitalist models became more attractive.

Since the end of the Cold War in 1989, a new pattern of geographic (both political and economic) rivalry has been averted. We do not now face Asia v. North America v. Europe. The United States is an important participant in European affairs through NATO, OECD, and G-7(8). While ASEAN is a narrow geographic group in Southeast Asia, APEC brings in Japan, the United States and Canada, as well as Australia and New Zealand. NAFTA is now being broadened to include other countries in Central and South America. EU is broadening its membership in Europe. While NATO provides a link between the two hemispheres, it is in the wrong functional field. Ultimately, as the euro moves forward and gains strength, there will be a need to fashion a new North American relationship with Europe, probably including both commercial and monetary issues—extending another overlapping link, between the EU and North America. In time this may be broadened to include Japan.

Overlapping club memberships are a means both to solve collective goods problems and also knit disparate units together.

Clubs with a small number of members may be able to create collective goods that larger organizations could not.[27] Club goods are not entirely public in that outsiders may not be allowed to share their benefits, though inside the club there is non-rivalry in supply. It is therefore unnecessary to provide public goods for the entire world. Links between clubs provide the needed cement to hold institutions together.[28]

Conclusion

The creation of the euro could raise difficult problems for both the yen and the dollar. It seems likely that the euro will be high-valued rather than low-valued. If so, Europe will share some of the stabilizing features of hegemonic countries in providing markets and lenders of last resort to the rest of the world. On the other hand, three major currencies could engage in rivalries not unlike those of the 1930s unless a relationship is forged among them. New and more effective institutional and monetary linkages between Europe, North America and Japan—along lines advocated by Paul Volcker—will be necessary to avoid this outcome.

Notes

1. See Richard Cooper, 'Key Currencies After the Euro', Weatherhead Center for International Affairs, Working Paper 98-3 (Harvard University, 1998).
2. See particularly Robert Mundell, 'The Euro and the Stability of the International Monetary System' (Columbia University, January 1999) and the essay by George Alogoskoufis and Richard Portes in Paul Masson, Thomas Krueger, and Bart Turtelboom, eds., *EMU and the International Monetary System* (Washington, D.C.: International Monetary Fund, 1997).
3. See Mundell, p. 11.
4. See also C. Fred Bergsten, 'The Dollar and the Euro', *Foreign Affairs* (July-August 1997).
5. Mundell, p. 11.
6. Cooper, p. 11.
7. Cooper, p. 11.
8. In this case, as Cooper points out, Europe would be 'in effect purchasing long-term assets for short-term liabilities' (Cooper, p. 11).
9. See Joanne Gowa, *Closing the Gold Window: Domestic Politics and the End of Bretton Woods* (Ithaca: Cornell University Press, 1983).
10. See Cooper, p. 13, and Mundell, pp. 11-12.
11. See Jeffry Frieden, 'The Euro: Who Wins? Who Loses?', *Foreign Policy*, no. 112 (Fall 1998).
12. Ibid.

13. See Kenneth Oye, *Economic Discrimination and Political Exchange: World Political Economy in the 1930s and 1980s* (Princeton: Princeton University Press, 1992).
14. See William Robinson, 'Interwar Financial Discord' (Cornell University, 1981).
15. See Lester C. Thurow, *The Future of Capitalism* (New York: William Morrow, 1996), p. 230. Thurow writes: 'When a run against the dollar starts, there are enormous amounts of money that can, and will, move into appreciating currencies. Sixty percent of official reserves and 50 percent of private reserves are currently held in dollars. Those funds will certainly move, but they will be a small fraction of the total funds avalanching down the slope.'
16. See J. A. Frankel and A. K. Rose, 'The Endogeneity of the Optimum Currency Area Criteria', *Economic Journal,* vol. 108, no. 449 (July 1998).
17. See also Deepak Lal, 'The Euro', *Intercom,* vol. 21, no. 3, 1999.
18. See Charles P. Kindleberger, *The World in Depression, 1929-1939* (Berkeley: University of California Press, 1986), Robert Keohane, 'The Theory of Hegemonic Stability and Changes in International Economic Regimes', in Ole Holsti, Randolph Siverson, and Alexander George, eds., *Change in the International System* (Boulder: Westview, 1980), and Stephen Krasner, 'State Power and the Structure of International Trade', *World Politics* (April 1976).
19. M. Bernard and J. Ravenhill, 'Beyond Product Cycles and Flying Geese: Regionalization, Hierarchy, and the Industrialization of East Asia', *World Politics,* vol. 47, no. 2 (January 1995).
20. See Raymond Vernon, 'International Investment and International Trade in the Product Cycle', *Quarterly Journal of Economics,* vol. 80, pp. 190-207.
21. See R. Rosecrance and J. Taw, 'Japan and the Theory of International Leadership', *World Politics* (January 1990), pp. 184-209.
22. See A. K. Dewdney, 'Computer Recreations', *Scientific American,* vol. 251, no. 6 (December 1984), pp. 14-22.
23. See Paul Volcker, 'The Art of Central Banking: How It Can Solve Financial Crises', Harberger Lecture, February 19, 1999, UCLA.
24. See Stephen Solomon, *The Confidence Game* (New York: Simon and Schuster, 1995), pp. 477-480.
25. Although Beth Simmons, *Who Adjusts* (Princeton: Princeton University Press, 1996) provides contradictory evidence of national behavior in the 1930s on this score.
26. See Albert Hirschman, *National Power and Foreign Trade* (Berkeley: University of California Press, 1980).
27. See Mancur Olson, *The Logic of Collective Action* (Cambridge: Harvard University Press, 1965).
28. See R. Rosecrance and A. Stein, 'The Theory of Overlapping Clubs', in R. Rosecrance, ed., *Creating an Encompassing Coalition to Prevent Deadly Conflict* (Carnegie Corporation of New York, Spring 1999).

5. THE EURO AND THE STABILITY OF THE INTERNATIONAL MONETARY SYSTEM

Robert Mundell

An Epoch-Making Event

The introduction of the euro at the beginning of 1999 promises to mark a turning point in the international monetary system. It is often compared with the transformation of the international monetary system in the early 1970s from the system of fixed exchange rates endorsed at the Bretton Woods conference to the regime of managed flexible exchange rates. But in fact its significance is deeper. The collapse of the Bretton Woods arrangements did not alter the power configuration of the international system. Both before and after the breakdown, the dollar was the dominant currency. The introduction of the euro, on the other hand, will challenge the status of the dollar and alter the power configuration of the system. For this reason the introduction of the euro may be the most important development in the international monetary system since the dollar replaced the pound sterling as the dominant international currency soon after the outbreak of World War I.[1]

If it is true that the euro will challenge the dollar in the system, will the new international monetary system be more or less unstable? The answer to this question depends in part on the meaning attached to stability. The word as defined in the dictionary has at least three relevant meanings: (a) the state or quality of being stable, or fixed; (b) resistance to change, or permanence; or (c) the tendency of an equilibrium position to be restored after an initial displacement. All three of these meanings have relevance to the euro, as indicated by the following three questions:

(a) Will economic variables, say exchange rates, fluctuate more or less as a result of the introduction of the euro?

(b) Will the euro create a new configuration of currency areas that will last for, say, several decades in the 2000s?

(c) Will the euro alter the convergence conditions of exchange rate dynamics: will it turn a stable system into an unstable one or aggravate any instability of the existing system?

These issues will be addressed in this paper. First, however, we shall try to see what history and theory say about how well the euro will stack up against the dollar. We begin by discussing the characteristics of currencies that have in the past become successful 'dominant' international currencies.

Great International Currencies

From among the thousands of currencies ever struck or issued, economists can achieve a grand simplification by distinguishing those currencies that have had a critical systemic significance for the international economy. Today we would be able to count on the toes of one foot the currencies besides the dollar that are in some meaningful sense critical to the functioning of the international monetary system. So it has been in every age in history since money, or at least coinage, was invented. The dollars of the 20th century, the pounds of the 19th century and the livres of the 18th century all have their counterparts in earlier centuries. Without attempting to seek generality or completeness, Table 1 lists some of the main international currencies of earlier eras with the great powers that produced them.

A currency is 'international' when it is used outside the domain in which it is legal tender, or when its fractions or multiples are imitated elsewhere. Typically even great currencies have piggybacked on the prestige of predecessors, only to usurp the latter's role. The practices of derivation and imitation have almost inadvertently provided a virtually-universal continuity to currency areas in the history of the international monetary system.

The Persian daric and the Greek stater were virtually the same coin. The Persian sigloi was modeled on the Babylonian shekel as was the Greek drachma. The Roman denarius was patterned on the drachma. The Islamic dinar was an imitation of the Roman aureus, solidus or besant; while the Islamic dirham was modeled on the Greek (and Sasanian) drachma. The Carolingian denier was modeled after the Islamic half-dirhem. The florins of Florence and sequins of Genoa were simply 'light' or degraded aureii. The Dutch gulden was modeled on the Arabian maravedi. The US dollar was modeled on the Spanish dollar. Originality is not the stuff of what great international currencies are designed.

Table 1: Great Currencies and Great Powers

	Period	Gold	Silver	Paper
Greece	7th-3rd C. BC	stater	drachma	
Persia	6th-4th C. BC	daric	shekel	
Macedonia	4th-2nd C. BC	stater		
Rome	2nd C. BC-4th C.	aureus	denarius, sesterce	
Byzantium	5th-13th C.	solidus (bezant)	siliqua	
Islam	7th-13th C.	dinar	dirhem	
Franks	8th-11th C.		denier	
Italian City States	13th-16th C.	florin, sequin, ducat	grosso	
France	13th-18th C.	denier	livre, louis d'or	
Holland	17th-18th C.	guilder (gulden)	stiver	stivers, 1573
Germany	14th-19th C.		thaler	
France	1803-1870	20-francs, 40-francs	franc	
Britain	1820-1914	pound or sovereign	shilling	paper pound
US	1915-	eagle	dollar	greenback
EU	1999-			paper euro

Features of Great International Currencies

What makes a currency important internationally? Obviously, confidence in its stability is a key characteristic. But stability depends on several factors: size of transactions domain; stability of monetary policy; absence of controls; strength and continuity of the issuing state; and fall-back value.

Size of Transactions Domain

Size in the sense of depth and breadth of the market is a measure of the degree to which a currency can exploit the economies of scale and scope inherent in money as a public good. The larger the transactions domain, the more capable a currency can act as a cushion against shocks. The larger the single-currency area, the better it can act as a cushion against shocks. If you consider a shock such as German unification, manifested in a debt-financed increase in annual government spending and transfers east of more than 150 billion DM, close to destabilizing the German economy, then think of the effect of the same shock on a smaller economy. Alternatively, think how much more easily the shock would have been handled had there been in 1992 a stable European currency!

Size feeds on itself because it produces stability and stability increases its attractiveness. The larger is the transactions domain, the more liquid the currency because the less any particular shock will depress the price. The size of a single-currency area determines its liquidity. A currency that is money for 100 million people is ten times more liquid than a currency that is money for 10 million. The most direct measure of the transactions domain is the money supply itself, but alternative surrogates, such as the GDP or magnitude of the capital market are also relevant.

Size is relative. How the euro will survive depends on the competition. Its two rivals are obviously the dollar and the yen. How such a tri-currency world would work out depends importantly on relative market sizes. From this standpoint, the outlook for the euro is very favorable. The EU-15 has a population of 375 million, and the EU-11, which includes those countries that entered EMU on the first round, contains 292 million, somewhat larger than the United States; by comparison, Japan has 125 million. At current exchange rates, the GDP of the EU-15 is running at the rate of $8.4 trillion, that of the EU-11, at $6.6 trillion. These compare to US GDP running at $8.5 trillion and Japanese GDP at $4.1 trillion. All of a sudden, with or without the four countries that will not proceed to EMU on the first round, the EU becomes a player on the same scale as the United States and Japan. Over time, as the other countries join, as the per capita incomes of the poorer members of EU catch up, and as the EU expands into the rest of Central Europe, the euro will have a substantially larger transactions domain than the dollar.

Openness also plays a role because it affects dependence. The less open, the more self-sufficient. As measured by the ratios of exports or imports to GDP, the 'G-3' economies are about equally open. Of course the percentage of current exports to GDP in Europe is now around 30 percent, but when intra-European exports and imports are netted out, the openness figures are remarkably similar. It makes a difference of course whether openness is measured by exports or imports; economies with trade deficits will have higher import than export ratios. The US ratio of imports to GDP is the highest, at nearly 11 percent; the EU-15 and Japan's import ratios are substantially lower, at around 8 percent. With openness measured by exports, on the other hand, Japan's and the EU-15's ratios are around 9 percent, while the US's is a little over 8 percent. What emerges from these numbers is the significant fact that the three giant economies are all relatively closed, creating the risk that the monetary authorities may tend to underestimate the importance of the exchange rate and by neglect condemn the system to undesirable volatility.

Stability of Monetary Policy

The importance of the monetary policy stance scheduled for the EMU countries can hardly be underestimated. No currency has ever survived as an international currency with a high rate of inflation. Historically, the countries producing the great currencies have avoided inflation by maintaining the gold or silver content, with devaluation or debasement a comparatively infrequent phenomenon. The lower the rate of inflation, the lower the cost of holding money balances, and the more of them will be held. In addition to a low rate of inflation, a *stable* rate is also desirable; because inflation and variance go hand in hand.

Additional considerations are predictability and consistency in monetary policy. In a democracy, both are abetted by *transparency*. If the monetary authorities openly state their targets and their strategies for achieving them, the market and the critical public will be able to make its own judgement about inflation outcomes. It cannot be said, however, that policy at the ECB will be any more transparent than it is at the Federal Reserve.

From the standpoint of sound monetary policy, however, the outlook for the euro is very favorable. The Maastricht Treaty is unambiguous in making price stability the target of monetary policy. Although the European System of Central Banks (ESCB) can and should assist the monetary union in carrying out its other objectives, it is forbidden to do so if such assistance would conflict with price stability. Monetary policy will not be used to reduce unemployment by 'surprise inflation' or to inflate away embarrassing public debts.

There remains considerable discretion for the independent European Central Bank (ECB). It will have to determine how price stability can best be achieved. The problem is complicated by lags in the effect of monetary policy. Because of lags, it is never certain whether price stability can best be achieved by inflation, monetary, or exchange rate (or price-of-gold) targeting.

The case for exchange rate targeting is very strong for a small open economy near a very large and stable neighbor (as Austria, the Netherlands and Belgium were to Germany) but it is not so strong for the EU-11 as a whole. The only candidate for the EU-11 to target would be the US dollar, a currency with a transactions area only somewhat larger than Europe's.[2]

Monetary targeting, however, suffers from the defect that in the early stages of the transition, the liquidity properties of the euro will be subject to a wide range of error. We shall need to address this issue explicitly in a later section. In the meantime, we can anticipate a conclusion by stating that the best approach for a large economy like the EU is to target the inflation rate, formulating monetary policy actions on forecasts of inflationary pressures. Leading indicators that should always be taken into account include gold prices, other commodity prices, rates of change in the different monetary aggregates, the growth rate and bond prices. The most successful central bankers have been pragmatists. But there is no reason why an independent ECB, modeled partly after the Bundesbank, cannot be as effective a body as the Federal Reserve System in the United States or the Bank of Japan. As Otto Pöhl once said, 'credibility is the capital stock of any central bank' and there is no reason why the management of the ECB should not be able to establish credibility at the outset.

Absence of Controls

It would be bad news for a would-be international currency if payments were subjected to exchange controls. The modern climate in that respect is far worse than the situation only a few centuries ago when, in the heady days of the American Revolution, George Washington, despite his position as Commander of the Revolutionary Armies, was said to be able to maintain his account at the Bank of England. That is a far cry from the modern world when, whenever sanctions are contemplated, the accounts of errant governments are blocked. In the twilight of the pound as an international currency, exchange controls in Britain were rampant and the 'sterling area' came to be defined as a zone of currency controls. The threat of inconvertibility and exchange controls is a factor further undermining the fall-back value of a currency.

Even the United States has used controls as an instrument of its foreign policy. From 1933 until 1975, US citizens were forbidden to hold gold despite the fact that, for most of that period, the dollar was supposed to be 'freely convertible into gold' along the lines of the IMF Statute, Article IV-4-b of the Bretton Woods Agreement. In the 1960s the United States restricted capital movements in the form of an 'interest-equalization-tax', by imitation of the long-debunked 'scientific tariff'. In subsequent years, accounts of 'erring' foreign governments have been blocked as part of US or international sanctions. There is no question of course that the United States has a right to impose such sanctions over the use of its own currency. By the same token, however, the competition from a new European currency that is an alternative to the dollar has a chance of restoring some of the earlier laudable tenets of international economic liberalism if the current trend toward dirigism can be resisted.

Strength and Continuity of the Central State

Monetary stability depends of course on monetary policy. But monetary policy is in turn affected by its sine qua non, political stability. Strong international currencies have always been linked to strong central states in the period of their ascendancy. The reason is not far to seek. When a state collapses, so does the stability of the currency. Examples include the hyperinflations of the defeated powers after World War I, the collapse of the rouble after the October 1917 Revolution; the hyperinflation of Kuomintang China after the communist forces of Mao-Tse-Tung crossed the Yang-Tse; and the hyperinflations in the former Yugoslavia in the 1990s. It does not bode well for its currency if a state is not powerful enough to defend itself against enemies from outside and within.

What about the euro? Is the EU a strong central state? It is here that one can see a *potential* weakness in the euro. The decision-making power of the government in Brussels is a pale shadow of that in Washington or in the capitals of the EU members. Rarely up to now has the EU been able to forge a common foreign or defense policy. The problems arising from the weakness of the central state in the EU cannot be swept under the rug. However, it should be realized that there are strong mitigating factors. The end of the Cold War and the collapse of the Soviet Union put aside what was in the postwar years the most dangerous threat to European security. A closely connected factor is NATO, the most successful alliance in history. As long as the EU is tied to NATO and the military alliance with the United States, the EU will be able to fend off enemies from without even if it is not a strong central state.

What about instability from within? Nothing can be taken completely for granted. Monetary union is supposed to be irrevocable. But it might not be in the face of a violent economic crisis. A real test would be its ability to hold itself together in the face of a drastic terms-of-trade shock such as that experienced in the 1970s when oil prices quadrupled. Dealing with a major economic crisis would probably require further deepening of the integration process. At the same time, however, the process of monetary union will itself be a catalyst for closer political union, quickly bringing to common attention the most fissiparous issues. These factors will greatly mitigate what would otherwise be a dangerous weakness.

The Fall-Back Factor

Modern currencies differ from the great currencies of the past, which were all either gold or silver or convertible into one or both of those metals. These currencies had a fall-back value if the state collapsed. If enemies approached the walls of the great Italian city-states that coined the sequins, florins or ducats of the Middle Ages, the 3.5-gram gold content would still maintain its value. Metallic currencies frequently outlive the state issuing them, as the flourishing of Macedonian staters in the centuries after Alexander's death attest. A more recent example is the Maria Theresa thaler which continued to circulate in Eastern Africa long after that lady and the Austro-Hungarian Empire were no more. That does not hold for a paper currency. After the Battle of Gettysburg in the United States, Confederate notes became worthless.

Until the advent of the dollar, there is no historical record of any fiat currency achieving great international significance. Before the 20th century all the great international currencies were metallic. The predecessor of the dollar, the pound sterling, achieved its great luster as a metallic currency. But it was phased out when it ceased to be convertible into gold and even freely convertible into its successor, the dollar. Even so, inertia hovers over international currencies and the international stretch of the pound continued long after Britain had ceased to be a dominant power and the biggest international trader.

The dollar achieved its international importance as a gold currency. When it was selected as the unofficial anchor at Bretton Woods, it had ceased to be internally redeemable, but was still externally convertible into gold, the only such currency (apart from the Swiss franc). If the dollar is now a fiat currency, as a 'ghost of gold' it is the exception that makes the rule.

The introduction of the SDR provides an illustration of the importance of the fall-back factor. When first distributed in 1970, it had a gold weight guarantee confirmed in the first Amendment to the Articles of Agreement of the IMF. The gold guarantee made it a substitute for gold rather than the dollar and, at a time when gold was underpriced, a coveted asset that was in great demand. After the dollar was taken off gold, however, the international monetary authorities reneged on the gold guarantee, and the SDR went through a series of transformations, ultimately turning into, with the birth of the euro, a four-currency basket. Had its gold guarantee been maintained, however, the SDR would have been much more important in the international monetary system and qualified as an infinitely more useful supranational unit of account. Lacking both a commodity fall-back value and the backing of a strong state, the SDR fell by the wayside on the scrapheap of bureaucratic timidity.

There is in this a lesson for the euro. In any great political emergency, and especially one that threatened the durability of the EU, there would be a run on the euro that would not be mitigated by any fall-back value. A run or even the risk of a run would make it difficult to float long-term securities in euros. The same strictures hold for the risks of exchange control.

It might be argued against this, that economies like Germany's thrived even when it was on the front line of the Cold War. Yet two factors need to be understood. The first was the existence of NATO, which kept Germany under the security umbrella of the United States. The second was that Germany, like most of the other countries on the European continent, did not—or only rarely—issued debt exceeding 10-15 years. The substantial quantities of really long-term securities issued in Europe have been phenomena of the post-Cold War world.

It is true that such an emergency might also weaken the dollar. Total political and military security can never be assumed. Nevertheless, the US situation differs in that the dollar has an established reputation. Though a federation, the United States has a strong central government; and is a military superpower. The lesson in this for the euro is that the ESCB will need larger holdings of external reserves than otherwise or than the United States, at least at first. Fortunately, the EU countries have dollars and gold in abundance and will therefore be able to meet any foreseeable contingency.

Liquidity Effects

There has been rather little discussion of the impact of EMU on liquidity. My own view has been that it will be substantial. It will be convenient to break the liquidity impact into six different factors: (1) the efficiency effect of the euro; (2) the change in the money multiplier; (3) excess reserves arising from reserve pooling; (4) the 'exorbitant privilege' implications of the euro becoming a reserve currency; (5) foreign demand for euros; and (6) diversification from the dollar into the euro. The first four of these effects are 'inflationary' whereas the last two are 'deflationary'.

Efficiency Effect

When the currencies of the EU-11 or EU-15 are phased out and replaced by the euro, there will be a once-for-all liquidity effect that will be the same as a sudden, once-for-all increase in the European money supply, with proportionate inflationary effects. This is because the liquidity of the euro is greater than the liquidity of the sum of its parts. When, say, 500 billion euros worth of national currencies are replaced by 500 billion euros, European liquidity will be increased just as if there had been a sudden increase in the European money supply.

A similar effect will be experienced in the bond market. Like all assets, bonds have a liquidity dimension. Liquidity is measured by the ease with which an asset can be turned into cash without loss; it is inversely related to the cost of turning a bond into cash and then requiring it. Bonds with a large market are more liquid than bonds with a small market. The redenomination of national debts and corporate bonds from local currencies to euros will all of a sudden create a vast single market in euro-denominated bonds, a bond market of the same massive scale as that of the United States. The liquidity of this debt will be much larger than the liquidity of the combined public and corporate debts now denominated in national currencies. The redenomination of these national debts is bound to have a revolutionary effect on world capital markets.

How important is this liquidity effect likely to be? Some indication can be got by comparing the degree of securitization in Europe with that of the United States and Japan, the two countries in the world with the largest bond market. Outstanding government and corporate bonds in the Big Three markets—taking the EU-15 as a single entity—amounted to just short of $40 trillion in 1995. Of this total, $12.5 trillion was accounted for by the EU-15, and the remainder of $27 trillion by the US and Japan together. The liquidity of the EU-15 debt will be greatly enhanced by the adoption of the single currency.

There is a related issue. The superiority of the new facility—the ability to issue euro-denominated debt—will make it attractive to increase the aggregate outstanding. But by how much? One heroic (or crude) way to estimating the potential increase is to compare ratios of outstanding bonds to GDP—securitization ratios—in different countries. Using the outstanding-debt figures cited above for 1995, and taking the 1995 GDPs of the EU-15, the US and Japan as $8422 trillion, $7265 trillion and $5135 trillion respectively (remember these are translated into dollars at 1995 exchange rates), the securitization ratios in the EU and the US + Japan come to, respectively, 1.5 and 2.18. This is a remarkable difference and at least part of it can be attributed to the disadvantage the EU countries have up until now faced in their national-currency bond markets. No doubt there will be some shift from the other markets to the European markets and also an increase in total outstanding issues in Europe. Outstanding bonds in the EU-15 in 1995 would have had to have been an additional $6 trillion to equal the ratio in the United States and Japan. The euro will create magnificent new openings until the market reaches maturity.

Money Multiplier: Level

Another liquidity effect concerns the money multiplier. The new money multiplier will be the EU-15 money supply divided by the total supply of euro currency outstanding, with an adjustment for the proportion of currency held outside banks. One coordination problem is likely to arise because of different legal or practical reserve ratios in the different member countries. But a more serious problem is the creation of euro substitutes. Because the replacement of a national currency by the euro transfers seigniorage to the ECB, each country has an incentive to minimize the need for euros. This incentive exists even though it is weakened by the redistribution of ECB profits to the national central banks (NCBs).[3]

What if one or more of the NCBs created a lender-of-last resort facility that enabled the banks to get by on a far smaller ratio of euros to deposit liabilities? The incentive for NCBs to do so may be eliminated for the most part by the provision by which their money incomes are earmarked for the general account and then 'allocated to the national central banks in proportion to their paid-up shares in the capital of the ECB'.[4] There nevertheless remain opportunities for the private sector or another branch of the government to perform functions previously performed by the NCBs. The EU's money multiplier will have to be watched closely.

The ratio of reserve money to money in the EU countries, and the reciprocal of its money multiplier, has been falling since the early 1990s. The ratios for the EU-11 and EU-15 countries were, respectively, 39.5 and 31.7 in 1990, but had fallen to 31.5 and 25.8 by 1996. The latter figure contrasts with the higher ratio in the United States in 1996 of 38.4. The decline in these ratios, and the corresponding increases in the money multiplier, can be expected to increase with the introduction of the euro.

Money Multiplier: Stability

There is, however, considerable potential uncertainty about the aggregate multiplier arising because of differential multipliers in individual countries.

The EU at present is still a collection of national monetary systems that have very different characteristics. One measure of different national structures is the ratio of reserve money to money plus quasi-money (a broad definition of money somewhat larger than M2). See Table 2.

Table 2: Reserve Money / Money + Quasi-money (Percentage)

	1990	1996
Austria	10.5	10.2
Belgium	14.3	7.1
Denmark	9.2	15.4
Finland	11.4	12.6
France	8.4	5.8
Germany	16.4	13.9
Greece	16.4	13.9
Ireland	21.8	14.3
Italy	23.2	16.2
Luxembourg	0.9	1.1
Netherlands	10.8	8.8
Portugal	32.9	10.2
Spain	16.9	15.9
Sweden	15.2	14.2
United Kingdom	4.2	3.6
United States	16.2	15.5
Japan	9.7	10.3

Source: Calculated from *IMF International Financial Statistics* and national sources.

Two observations can be made from this table. First, leaving aside the special cases of Luxembourg,[5] and Greece,[6] the reserve ratios differ radically, from a low of 3.6 percent in the UK to a high of 16.2 percent in Spain. This means that the EU money multiplier will tend to increase or decrease respectively as balance of payments surpluses accrue to low-reserve or high-reserve countries. The other observation is that the national reserves ratios have been declining, but at very different rates. A potentially varying money multiplier will make it riskier to rely on monetary targeting in the transition period when banking systems and reserve ratios have not yet been harmonized.

Redundant Reserves from Pooling

More well-known liquidity effects arise from the centralization of international reserves. It is convenient to divide these reserves into three types: (a) foreign exchange held in European currencies, ECU's, IMF reserve positions and SDRs; (b) foreign exchange held in non-European currencies; and (c) gold. The first category of assets (a) 'may' be held and managed by the ECB. The ECB will also receive 'up to an amount equivalent to' 50 billion euros. The contributions of each member state will be fixed in proportion to its share in the subscribed capital of the ECB.[7]

Reserve needs will be lower in Europe on two counts. First, with the formation of the EMU, intra-union deficits and surpluses will be netted out and reserve needs for the union as a whole will be considerably smaller than the sum of the reserve needs of individual members. If external (mainly dollar) reserves were at an appropriate level before the union, they would be excessive after it. The same holds for gold reserves, of which the EU countries account for almost half the world's monetary stock—although here gold reserves could partially compensate for the weakness created by the absence of a strong central state. Any immediate action to dispose of the part of these reserves that are considered excessive would be damaging to exchange rate stability

Second, and in the long run much more important, the ESCB's need for foreign exchange reserves will decline drastically once the euro is successfully launched. The euro will then become a reserve currency of choice for many countries around the world. Reserve currencies have less need for reserves—especially if there is confidence in its monetary policy—because its own currency is liquid internationally; reserve currency status is a widow's cruse that keeps the owner in perpetual liquidity.

Apart from IMF positions and SDRs, EU-15 reserves at the end of 1996 amounted to 350.6 million ounces of gold (to which could be added 92.0 million held by the EMI). The other big holders were the United States with 261.7 million ounces, Switzerland with 83.3 million ounces, and the IMF with 103.4 million. These countries and institutions thus hold 891 million ounces or 80 percent of the world total of 1,108.1 million ounces. Pooling all foreign exchange would give the ECB $387 billion, or 25.9 percent of the world total of $1,498 at the end of 1996. This compared with the holdings of $209 billion in foreign exchange in Japan or about $300 billion in 'Greater China' (China, Taiwan and Hong Kong).

Automatic Credit

The foreign exchange reserves would not seem so excessive (at least compared to the Asian holdings) were it not for the fact that the euro, as already mentioned, will itself become a widely-used international currency, conferring on the EU the 'exorbitant privilege' to run a 'deficit without tears'—to use the phrases of Charles de Gaulle and Jacques Rueff in their pungent attacks on the role of the dollar as a reserve currency in the 1960s. Non-reserve currency countries have a 'hard' balance of payments constraint. Reserve currency countries, by contrast, have a 'soft' balance of payments constraint insofar as they can allow euro liabilities to accumulate rather than use gold or foreign exchange assets. The importance of this factor can easily be assessed by noting the extremely low level of foreign exchange holdings of the principal reserve center, the United States, which is the largest economy in the world and its largest importer and exporter.

International Demand for Euros

How large will the international demand for euros be? Some guesses can be made based on the growth of demand for reserves as a whole. World GDP figures are notoriously subject to error due to factors arising from imperfect measurement and the variability of exchange rates. Nevertheless, in round numbers let us assume that nominal GDP grows over the next dozen years at a 6 percent per annum. In this case, world GDP will double in the twelve years between 1998 and 2010, proportioned among the US, the EU and the rest of the world as follows:

Table 3: US, EU, and World GDPs, 1998 and 2010, Trillions of US Dollars

	1998	2010
United States	9	18
European Union	9	18
Rest of the World	12	24
Total	30	60

Holdings of international reserves, including foreign exchange, gold valued at market prices, and IMF Drawing Rights, totaled about $2.0 trillion in 1998, about 1/15 of GDP. The situation for 1998 and that assumed for 2010 is shown in Table 4.

World holdings of foreign exchange reserves, measured in dollars, quadrupled over the last dozen years, from $382.1 billion at the end of 1985 to $1,599.9 at the end of 1997,[8] an increase which exaggerates the real increase because of the high dollar in 1985. I shall assume that world reserves between 1998 and 2010 will only double, taking into account an assumed lower rate of inflation and reduced need for reserves in Europe. The estimates for reserve holdings will thus probably err on the conservative side (and therefore reinforce rather than weaken my conclusions).

Table 4: Reserves and GDP, 1998 and 2010, Trillions of US Dollars

	1998	2010
GDP	30.0	60.0
Reserves	2.0	4.0
Foreign Exchange	1.6	3.2
Gold	0.3 ($300/oz.)	0.6 ($600/oz.)
IMF Money	0.1	0.2
Ratio	1/15	1/15

Taking foreign exchange holdings at $1.6 trillion in 1998, of which perhaps three-quarters are in dollars, world reserves in 2010 will be $3.2 trillion. I shall assume that by this date the world community will want to divide its foreign exchange reserves equally between dollars and euros.

Table 5: Foreign Exchange Holdings, 1998-2010, Trillions of US Dollars

	1998	2010	Change
Dollar Balances	1.2	1.2	-
Euros	-	1.2	1.2
Other	0.4	0.8	0.4
Total	1.6	3.2	1.6

As a consequence, demand for dollar reserves will stagnate, while the demand for euro reserves will increase by as much as $1.2 trillion, an annual average of $100 billion a year. Unless this massive shift were offset by increasing lending by Europe and increased borrowing by the United States, it would mean a massive shift in current account balances, with that of Europe's turning strongly negative and that of the United States moving in a positive direction. The 'exorbitant privilege' effect represents in the short run a tremendous increase in power but in the long run it presents the temptation, if it is not accompanied by fiscal discipline, that it will be used as a way of building up in the long run a substantial increase in indebtedness.

Diversification Problem

One of the problems associated with the movement toward an international monetary system dominated by euros as well as dollars lies in the difficulty of the transition. Weakness in the euro would imply appreciation of the dollar. More probably, however, the main danger is in a prospective appreciation of the euro. If we assume, as we did in the previous section, that steady-state equilibrium growth will involve approximately equal demand for euros and dollars on the part of central banks by the year 2010, the best solution would be for a steady increase in euro holdings as increased reserves are needed without any direct diversification from the dollar. However, it is much more likely that once confidence has been established in the euro, several countries will want to exchange euros for dollars, threatening sweeping changes in the dollar-euro rate. The mere expectation that other countries were considering diversification would provoke expectations of dollar weakness and massive shifts of the type that occurred in the late 1970s.

The danger point will come when US growth slows and the US expansion ends. The pattern over two centuries of recessions in the United States is for the balance of payments to worsen under the gold standard or fixed exchange rates, and for the dollar to depreciate against foreign currencies when it is flexible. This is because the net capital outflow during recessions typically exceeds the improvement in the trade balance arising from falling imports. There is no reason to think that any weakening of growth in the US economy in 1999 or 2000 will be any different. The dollar will therefore depreciate. What will be different, however, is the existence of the euro. In the past when the dollar has depreciated, there has been diversification out of the dollar. But the thinness of the markets for 'strong' currencies like the yen, mark and the Swiss franc quickly puts a floor to the falling dollar. The situation with the euro will be quite different, taking into account both the large size of its transactions domain and the reserve demand for it and for eurobonds as a new investment vehicle. Some degree of management of the rate will become imperative.

Expansion of the Euro Area

Eleven members of the EU entered monetary union on January 1, 1999. Bilateral exchange rates among these countries were locked on July 1, 1998, and rates against the ecu were fixed on January 1, 1999. The replacement of currency notes and coins will commence on January 1, 2002 and must be completed by June 30 of that year, after which the EMU will have been completed. What are the prospects for expansion of the EU-11?

The EU-4

The four members of the EU that did not enter in 1999 are the UK, Sweden, Denmark and Greece. Greece failed to make the convergence requirements but, after a 14 percent devaluation of the drachma in May 1998, is on track to enter by 2002 at a rate against it of 357 drachmas. The three northern countries satisfied the convergence requirements but their populations were not yet prepared to take the plunge. Of crucial importance is the UK, partly because it has the largest economy but also because its example would most likely be followed by the other two.

Britain's hesitation is no surprise. European integration has always posed a problem for Britain which, historically, has seen its political role in keeping the Continent divided on balance of power grounds. With the emergence of the US as a superpower, however, that role became obsolete. Britain's reluctance to join the Economic Community in the late 1950s put Britain on the periphery of the integration movement and her hesitation about EMU threatens to repeat the situation. Two questions might be separated: (1) Has Britain benefited or is it weakened by EMU? And (2) given EMU, is Britain better off in or out?

The first question is difficult to answer because it involves the scrapping of the pound, a currency of great international importance in the 19th century, and also in effect the end of the 'balance of power game' that Britain has played in Europe since the 12th century. Britain was a late and reluctant entrant into the EU and the factors that have fed Britain's resistance to increased deepening of integration continue to exist.

Nevertheless, given the *fait accompli* of EMU and the euro, there are high costs to Britain staying out. One is the loss of sovereignty. Macroeconomic policy will increasingly be in the hands of the EU-11. The non-members will be subject to Europe-wide decisions in which they play no or little part. More important perhaps are some practical reasons. EMU will foster the reorganization of the money and banking industry in Europe, which will give an advantage to countries in EMU. It is true that Britain has in the past managed to use outside currencies like the Eurodollar and could do the same for the euro. But the fact will become more and more clear that the pound sterling will become increasingly unnecessary. London can certainly expect to remain perhaps one of the two or three most important financial centers in the world, but its position would be enhanced if Britain entered EMU and somewhat diminished if it did not join. All the arguments for a European country joining EMU apply to Britain in the long run.

Britain's entry will depend on the outcome of a referendum. The Labor Party will probably support it; and the Conservative Party, will be split, with its leader leading the opposition. Whatever the opinion at the moment, my own view is that British opinion will swing toward a pro-EMU position, and that Britain, as well as Sweden and Denmark will be committed to join EMU by the year 2002, as indicated in Table 6.

Table 6: Timetable for Expansion of the EU Area

Group	Probable Date of Entry	Country	Recent Population (millions)	1998 GDP (billions of US dollars)
EU-11	1999	Austria	8.0	209.8
		Belgium	10.2	253.9
		Finland	5.2	119.3
		France	58.7	1,420.8
		Germany	82.4	2,125.8
		Ireland	3.6	76.0
		Italy	57.4	1,171.2
		Luxembourg	0.4	17.3
		Netherlands	15.7	371.7
		Portugal	10.0	100.2
		Spain	39.3	548.7
		Total	290.9	6,414.7
EU-3	2002	Britain	59.2	1,325.1
		Sweden	9.0	233.4
		Denmark	5.3	177.3
EU-1	2002	Greece	10.5	110.0
		Cumulative Total	374.9	8,260.5
CEEEC-5	2005	Slovenia	2.0	15.0
		Czech Republic	10.3	54.0
		Poland	38.7	140.0
		Hungary	10.2	50.0
		Estonia	1.5	7.0
		Cumulative Total	437.6	8,526.5
CEEEC-6	2010	Slovakia	5.4	20.0
		Croatia	4.8	20.0
		Lithuania	3.7	11.0
		Latvia	2.5	5.0
		Romania	22.6	38.0
		Bulgaria	8.3	10.0
		Cumulative Total	484.9	8,630.5

Sources: IMF International Financial Statistics; WEFA World Outlook, 1998; WEFA EURASIA 1998.

The CEEEC-5

Five Central European and Eastern European countries—the CEEEC-5—were invited to make an application to join the EU in 1998. There were no surprises in the choice of Slovenia, the Czech Republic, Hungary or Poland, but Estonia was a surprise, the only Baltic state. Apart from the political support of Sweden, Estonia had the advantage of a currency-board type monetary policy linked to the mark. If these countries all established early currency boards, and thus chose the best alternative route to convergence, there is every possibility that they could be admitted to EU membership by the year 2005.

The CEEEC-6

Other candidates in Central and Eastern Europe include Slovakia, Croatia, Lithuania, Latvia, Romania and Bulgaria. In some of these countries the main problem is political: poor records on human and civil rights; in others it is economic; and in a few it is both economic and political. There is nevertheless a possibility that many of these countries would be ready for admittance in 2010.

The euro area, however, will certainly extend beyond Europe. The CFA franc countries, which currently fix the CFA franc to the French franc at 100 CFA F = 1 FF, have transferred to the euro at the corresponding FF rate. Countries in the north of Africa and the Middle East are likely to find their interests in stabilizing to the euro bloc. The more countries that enter it, the more attractive it will be. Success snowballs.

International Reactions and the Euro-Dollar Rate

It should not be thought that a change as momentous as the introduction of the euro will leave 'other things constant'. The only constant is the law of change, governed by competition and self-interest. After the euro is launched, it will be adopted, as already argued, by the remaining four members of the EU, including, importantly, Britain. It may further be assumed that it will be adopted as a kind of currency-board peg by several of the states lining up for entry into EU. When that occurs, the 'weight' of the euro-bloc will exceed that of the dollar area. It would be an illusion to suppose that the expansion of the euro area will not provoke a countervailing expansion of the dollar area. Bigness begets bigness.

Expansion of the dollar area is likely in Latin America. After decades of monetary instability, a growing number of countries in Latin America are perceiving the benefits of stable prices and exchange rates. If there were a large stable country in Latin America, it might be attractive to envisage a system of stable exchange rates anchored on that country. There is not, however, and at the present time the most attractive anchor for stability is the dollar. Among the larger countries, Argentina has taken the lead with a new (and weaker) variant on the currency board idea. It is conceivable that Mexico, at last on the road to recovery from its 1994-95 fiasco, and Brazil, also seeking stability after a devaluation, will see a solution along the same lines as Argentina. If so, we could see in the next decade an expansion of the dollar area throughout much of Latin America.

What about Asia? It is tempting to think that Asia might go the way of Europe, with its own currency area. However, this widely-held view misses a fundamental point. Europe's currency area would have been dead in the water in the inter-war period or even before 1914 when the Franco-German conflict was unresolved. It is unlikely that an Asian currency area could contain simultaneously powers with such diverse interests as Japan and China. It seems much more likely that for the next two decades the dollar will be the main default international currency. Under certain circumstances, one could even imagine the formation of a yen-dollar bloc.

Whatever the currency area formation, one thing is certain. The dollar-euro rate will become a matter of great concern to Europe, the United States and the rest of the world. Diversification from the dollar into the euro would create the threat of a soaring euro and play havoc with the sensitive issues of competitiveness and unemployment in Europe. The alternative of a falling euro on the other hand would raise the specter of an outbreak of inflation that would necessitate deflationary policies. It would be a grave mistake to believe that the closed nature of the three big blocs would make exchange rates less important or that the dollar-euro rate can be treated with 'benign neglect'.

The most urgent focus for management will be on the dollar-euro rate. As the world moves from monetary unilateralism to bilateralism, policy coordination will become more important. Under unilateralism, other countries were comparatively free to fix or change their currencies against the dollar, with a kind of benign neglect of exchange rate on the part of the United States. That will no longer be possible with the euro. If intervention is required it will have to be cooperative. In view of the long period of transition from a mainly dollar world to a world in which the dollar and euro vie on equal terms, it may be necessary to develop the infrastructure capable of dealing with the problem.

International management of the dollar-euro rate will not be easy. Suppose the dollar is depreciating against the euro and it is agreed that intervention is desirable. Where should the responsibility for intervention lie? Should the US support the dollar by selling reserves, or should Europe support the dollar by buying reserves? Action by the US, taken alone, without sterilization, is deflationary for the world economy; action by Europe is inflationary. Obviously action by the US would be desirable if there were excess inflation in the world economy, whereas action by Europe would be desirable if there were excess deflation. The division of responsibility would have to be determined by an inflation index for the world economy.[9] If gold were stable in terms of commodities the price of gold would itself serve as a satisfactory index.[10]

The 'Stability' of the International Monetary System

The ground has now been prepared for a discussion of the questions posed about the stability of the international monetary system. We shall take up the subject in terms of the three concepts of the word stability noted in the introduction.

Exchange Rate Volatility

The first is whether variables in the system will fluctuate more or less as a result of the introduction of the euro. Will exchange rate or balance-of-payments fluctuations be larger or smaller as a result of the introduction of the euro? The initial presumption must be that they will be smaller. Exchange rate fluctuations among the EU-11 will disappear completely as the eleven currencies are replaced by the euro. As long as the union is considered to be irrevocable, forward margins will also disappear and interest rates will converge completely, except for residual tax differences or differentials in default risk. The EU-11 will represent a new and large zone of exchange stability of a size only somewhat smaller than the dollar itself. As more countries enter EMU the zone of exchange rate stability will represent a larger economic area than the United States.

Will balance-of-payments fluctuations be increased or diminished as a result of the single-currency EU? The answer here is not completely unambiguous but there is a strong presumption that balances of payments are smaller and fluctuate less under a common currency than under flexible exchange rates? Two sources of instability will be removed. The first is that with the removal of exchange rate fluctuations as an incentive for capital flows, speculative capital movements will be eliminated or reduced. The second source of instability is monetary policy, especially the disequilibrium practice of sterilizing the monetary effects of capital flows. Under a common currency capital movements will conform to those that would prevail under a well-functioning currency board. 'The money goes where the action is.' Rapidly-growing regions will have surpluses and slow-growing smaller surpluses or deficits.[11] Surpluses greater or less than desired levels will be automatically corrected by the expenditure-specie-flow mechanism of the balance of payments. Intra-EU balances of payments will continue to exist, correction of excess balances will become automatic and unobservable if not relatively painless.

Another issue concerns the volatility of the euro against other currencies. A case could be made that the erection of a zone of stability in Europe will increase the volatility of the exchange rates of those countries that did not enter EMU, including the pound sterling, the Swiss franc, and the Swedish and Danish crowns. That instability could be reduced or eliminated if those countries joined the new ERM or adopted ERM-like policies. The drachma-euro rate, for example, can be expected to hover around its central parity against the euro as long as its economic reform package proceeds on schedule. A similar argument holds for the prospective members of EU in Central and Eastern Europe.

What about the dollar-euro rate? This will become the most important price in the world. It might be thought that because the EU economy is more closed than its national components, the dollar-euro rate will fluctuate more than its most important predecessor, the dollar-DM rate. This proposition, however, is not strictly correct. Long before the introduction of the euro, the ERM of the EMS already exhibited many of the monetary characteristics of a common currency. It is not the ratio of imports or exports to GDP that determines exchange rates but the whole pattern of the balance of payments including especially capital movements. Once speculation over entry into EMU is settled, there will no longer be destabilizing shifts from the 'weaker' members into the stronger currencies.

Nevertheless instability could arise from another source. The mark-dollar has gone from an average of DM 4.0 in 1968 to DM 1.82 in 1980 to DM 2.94 in 1985 to DM 1.56 in 1992 to DM 1.43 in 1995 to DM 1.73 in 1997. Under equilibrium circumstances, it is hard to imagine that the dollar-euro rate will be more unstable than the dollar-mark rate has been. However, once the euro has been established the reserve-configuration of the payments system will no longer be in equilibrium. Diversification will mean a tendency for the euro to appreciate against the dollar. There is no reason to expect that the appreciation would be steady and smooth. More likely it would be erratic. This seems to be a case where international management of the rate will become necessary.

Stability of Currency Areas

Will the euro create a new equilibrium configuration of currency areas that will be quasi-permanent, in the sense that they will survive for, say several decades? The answer, I believe, is yes. The creation of the euro will automatically carry with it the development of a substantial euro area, comprising countries that elect to stabilize their currencies to the euro and use the EU capital markets. The Mecca for the euro will be in Africa and Eastern Europe. At the same time, the expanding euro area will provoke explicit attention to the dollar area, involving most of Latin America and perhaps a considerable part of Asia. The competing dollar and euro areas will be features of the international monetary landscape for a long time to come—barring another great war or unforeseeable acts of God, perhaps another century. The great uncertainty lies not with these two currency areas, but the nature of the structure that will develop in Asia. As already noted, unlike Europe, Asia does not have the political structure to create a unified currency area. For the next few decades, it seems likely that the dollar will remain the dominant outside currency in Asia with the yen independently floating or attaching itself, depending partly on political considerations, more to the dollar or the euro area.

Dynamic Stability

Will the euro create a situation that will alter the convergence conditions of exchange rate dynamics, i.e., will it turn a stable system into an unstable one or aggravate any instability of the existing exchange rate system? The answer to this question requires a comparison of the stability conditions of a decentralized currency system with that of a system in which some of the countries combine into a new currency area. There is implicit in this question a general mathematical problem: How are convergence conditions of dynamic stability altered by collapsing several balance of payments equations into one. How is the stability of a system altered by economic union? More generally how is the dynamic stability of an equilibrium affected by choices of currency area?

There is not to my knowledge any answer to this question in the economics literature.[12] One could presume that integration in special cases would work in one way or another. For example, the integration of a small unstable country with a large stable one would probably improve the stability characteristics of the system as a whole. It seems on balance likely that the removal of the currencies of formerly weak economies from the European system, assuming that they are not large enough to destabilize the large stable countries, will tend to strengthen rather than weaken the stability characteristics of the system.

It is also true that the elimination of intra-European exchange rate fluctuations should reduce the frequently-reversible capital flows that have been a source of instability in the past.

Conclusions

The euro should stand up very well. It has two great strengths: a large and expanding transactions size; and a culture of stability surrounding the ECB in Frankfurt. Initially, the EU-11 will be smaller than the dollar area, but as three northern members enter, as the EU expands, and as the poorer countries catch up, the euro area will eventually be larger than the dollar area. From the standpoint of monetary policies, there is also not much to choose between the two areas. Information is globally mobile and there is no reason why the ECB should not become as efficient as the Federal Reserve System in the United States.

The euro also has two weaknesses: it is not backed by a central state, and it has no fall-back value. In an unstable world, these weaknesses would be fatal. But the present environment is far from unstable. The Pax Americana has been just as efficient in preventing major conflicts as the Pax Britannica and the Pax Romana of earlier eras. If, as one should expect, NATO survives in a post-euro world, the stability of the next decades should be as assured as that of the past four decades. Coupled with very substantial EU gold and currency reserves, which could be centralized or ear-marked for the ECB if the need arises, membership in NATO suffices to mitigate the weakness of the EU central government. Provided political coordination proceeds in the direction of integration, and important conflicts of conceit and nationalism are resolved, the euro should be able to maintain itself on an even keel with the dollar.

Changes can be expected in the liquidity position of Europe when the euro is introduced. Four effects can be expected to aggravate inflationary pressure: the replacement of national currencies with a more efficient euro; the increase in the money multiplier (it will also be more unstable); the pooling of reserves; and the reduction of fiscal discipline arising from the general acceptance of the euro as a means of payment. These tendencies will have to be carefully monitored in the early stages of the transition.

Against these potentially inflationary effects, there will be two not unrelated factors that will promote an appreciation of the euro and hence be potentially deflationary. One is the fact that the rest of the world (including the United States) will want to hold part of its reserves in euros. On the assumption that after twelve years the world will want to hold half its reserves in dollars and half in euros, there would be a build-up of euros averaging $100 billion a year, leading to a massive change in either trade balances and capital movements. To the extent that this demand materializes, the ECB will have to follow a looser monetary policy to provide the high-powered reserves that will be needed to back up these euro balances (most of which will be held in bank deposits). The other factor is that which will arise from diversification. The build-up of euros is not likely to be smooth. Once a cycle starts in which the dollar starts to depreciate against the euro, speculation will make the cycle self-reinforcing. This presents a potential danger point for the international monetary system which will have to be managed internationally.

The EU-11 or even the EU-15 will not be the end of the euro area. It is highly probable that if the euro is successful in the early stages, the other members will see it in their interest to join. Expansion will also proceed to several of the countries in Central and Eastern Europe, with as many as five new entrants by 2005 and eleven by 2010. The CFA franc countries will also be associated directly with the euro, and their example will probably be followed by other countries in Africa or the Middle East. The best approach to convergence for these countries is to establish currency boards with the euro—or alternatively an ERM solution with very small or zero exchange rate margins and the cessation of changes in holdings of domestic assets. Because a currency board mimics the monetary policy that is automatic under a common currency, it is the best mechanism for establishing convergence. If a country cannot do a currency board, it cannot do monetary union!

It should not be thought that a change as momentous as the introduction of the euro promises to be will leave 'other things constant'. The only thing that will remain constant are the laws of change, which include competition and expansion. By 2010 if not before the euro area will be larger than the transactions area of the United States and competition will probably provoke policy reactions in the United States and other countries. It may further be assumed—because it is in their self-interest—that the euro will be adopted as a kind of currency-board anchor by several of the states lining up for entry into the EU. When that occurs, the 'weight' of the euro-bloc will begin to exceed that of the dollar area. Countervailing steps will then be taken by the United States, including perhaps an expansion of the dollar area into Latin America and/or Asia, and even the formation of a yen-dollar bloc, a G-2 counterpoise to the euro-bloc.

Whatever the prognosis, the dollar-euro rate will become a matter of great concern to Europe, the United States and the rest of the world. Diversification from the dollar into the euro would create the threat of a soaring euro which would play havoc with the sensitive issue of unemployment in Europe. The alternative of a falling euro would raise the specter of an outbreak of inflation that would necessitate deflationary policies. It would be a grave mistake to believe that the closed nature of the three big blocs would make exchange rates less important.

The most urgent focus of management will be on the dollar-euro rate. As the world moves from monetary unilateralism to monetary bilateralism, policy coordination will become more important. Under unilateralism, other countries were comparatively free to fix or change their currencies against the dollar, with a kind of benign neglect of exchange rate on the part of the United States. That will no longer be possible with the euro. If intervention is required it will have to be cooperative. In view of the long period of transition from a mainly dollar world to a world in which the dollar and euro are quasi-equal partners, it will be necessary to develop new institutions capable of dealing with the problem.

Notes

1. It could be argued that replacement of the pound sterling by the dollar after 1914 was not a fundamental change in the system insofar as the US had already become the largest economy in the world with a GDP more than thrice its rivals in Britain and Germany; the future of the dollar as the principal international currency of the 20th century was therefore already assured. If so, the introduction of the euro could have more lasting importance than any event since the breakdown of bimetallism and the transition to the international gold standard in the early 1870s.
2. Whereas a small country can target the currency of a large country without seriously disrupting the latter's policy, the same cannot be said of two areas of comparable size. A one-side arrangement would run into prestige problems, and a shared arrangement presents complications that would make it difficult to negotiate.
3. Article 33 (1.b) of the Protocols and Declarations annexed to the Treaty provides for the transfer of ECB's net profits (except for a maximum of 20 percent transferred to the general reserve fund) to the shareholders of the ECB (i.e., the NCBs) in proportion to their paid-up shares.
4. Article 32.5 of *Protocols and Declarations...*
5. Luxembourg is a special case because of its monetary union with Belgium; the Belgian franc provides the bulk of the reserve money in Luxembourg.
6. Greece is a special case because it is still a low-income developing country and has only recently made serious attempts to establish monetary stability. Generally speaking the reserve ratio in question will be lowest in countries that have a history of monetary stability and a high level of financial development, a factor closely associated with per capita income.
7. See Compilation of Community Legislation

8. *IMF International Financial Statistics Yearbook*, 1998; pp. 66-67. The IMF calculates reserves in US dollars, then translates them into SDRs at the official exchange rate for publication in the *IFS*. The above figures for foreign exchange reserves were 347.9 billion SDRs in 1985 and 1,185.7 billion SDRs in 1997 which, converted at the $/SDR exchange rate of $1.0984 at the end of 1985 and 1.3493 at the end of 1997, gives the figures used above.

9. This was the situation arrived at the June 1987 G-7 summit meeting following the Louvre Accord, when it was judged desirable to prevent further depreciation of the dollar against the yen and European currencies. The stumbling block was creating the appropriate index. Quite a furor was created when, at the September 1997 IMF meetings, Secretary James Baker III announced that the index should 'include gold'. Search for the appropriate index ended shortly after the stock market crash in October of that year and the strained relations between the United States and West Germany as a consequence of disagreement over the dollar/DM rate.

10. Gold has unfortunately been rendered more unstable as a consequence of drastic fluctuations in the rate of inflation and the tendency of central banks and the international institutions to sell when the market is declining. The decisions announced in September 1999 to limit gold sales by the ESCB, however, will serve to remove one potentially destabilizing element hanging over the gold market.

11. The conventional definition of the balance of payments, reflected in inflows or outflows of outside money, is not well adapted to growing economies. Under a well-functioning monetary union (like that of the United States) in which all countries are growing, all regions may experience 'balance of payments surpluses' and in general there will be an excess of surpluses over deficits by the amount of the increase in the money supply of the union as a whole. In a growing economy it would be more meaningful, if more complicated and less operational, to define the balance of payments surplus as reserve inflows in excess of the desired amount, as suggested in Mundell (1965).

12. Metzler (1951) analyzed the question of stability in his study of the multiple-country transfer problem and considered the question of integration in the matrix-multiplier model but with no reference to exchange rates or monetary conditions. In Mundell (1968) I analyzed the dynamics of currency markets in a general equilibrium system and paid special attention to the formation of alternative currency areas and the stability of systems with different pivot currencies.

References

Metzler, Lloyd A. 1951. 'A Multiple-Country Theory of Income Transfers.' *Journal of Political Economy,* no. 59 (February), pp. 14-29.

Mundell, Robert A. 1961. 'A Theory of Optimum Currency Areas.' *American Economic Review,* vol. 51 (November), pp. 509-517.

Mundell, Robert A. 1965. *The International Monetary System: Conflict and Reform*. Montreal: Private Planning Association of Canada.

Mundell, Robert A. 1968. 'Hicksian Stability, Currency Markets and the Theory of Economic Policy.' In J. N. Wolfe, ed., *Value, Capital and Growth*. Chicago: Edinburgh University Press, pp. 445-466.

Mundell, Robert A. 1997. 'Updating the Agenda for Monetary Reform.' In Mario I. Blejer, Jacob A. Frenkel, Leonardo Leiderman, and Assaf Razin, in cooperation with David M. Cheney, eds., *Optimum Currency Areas*. Washington, D.C.: International Monetary Fund, pp. 29-48. Proceedings of a Festschrift Conference Sponsored by the IMF, the Central Bank of Israel, Tel Aviv University and the Hebrew University in honor of R. A. Mundell.

Mundell, Robert A. 1998. 'The Euro and International Monetary Reform.' In Ullrich Heilemann, Dietmar Kath, and Norbert Kloten, eds., *Entgrenzung als Erkenntnis und Gestaltungsaufgabe: Festschrift für Reimut Jochimsen zum 65. Geburtstag*. Berlin: Duncker & Humblot, pp. 331-344.

PART II
MANAGEMENT OF THE EURO

6.   THE EURO AND ITS CONSEQUENCES FOR GLOBAL CAPITAL MARKETS[1]

Norbert Walter

The euro will soon emerge as an important international currency, and its introduction is certain to have profound implications for global capital markets and financial policies. While the shape of the currency itself has become clearly visible, a considerable degree of uncertainty surrounds its ultimate impact on investment and financing decisions.

Birth of a Financial Titan

The decisions on the timely start of the European Monetary Union (EMU) and the selection of participating states have already been made by the European Council. Following its agreement in early May 1998, the euro will be introduced in three stages during the period between January 1999 and mid-2002. The new year will mark the start of the currency union itself, for which the council has selected, as widely expected, eleven founding members: Austria, Belgium, Finland, France, Germany, Ireland, Italy, Luxembourg, the Netherlands, Portugal, and Spain. The European Union's other members— Denmark, Greece, Sweden, and the UK—will, for various reasons, not participate from the start.

Following the United States, Euroland will be the second-largest economic area with a single currency. Nearly 30 percent of the OECD's aggregate GDP is generated within its borders, and it will undoubtedly play a major role in world trade. With imports from and exports to non-EMU members amounting to more than 11 percent and 12 percent, respectively, Euroland will be slightly more dependent on foreign trade than are the United States. Its emerging economy will be less vulnerable to exchange rate swings than have been the individual members of the Exchange Rate Mechanism (ERM)—meaning that the European Central Bank (ECB) will be able to concentrate on internal stabilization policies rather than having to give its attention to exchange rate issues. The ECB has started its operations in a rather benign monetary environment, which supports the expectation that Europe will benefit from a stable euro. To date, impressive progress has been made, especially in regards to monetary convergence: Euroland's inflation, at 1.7 percent in 1997, stood at its lowest level in more than thirty years and is now expected to drop even further to a level as low as about 1.3 percent in 1998. The outlook for stabilization is good, thus pushing to the background the foremost worry of many of EMU's various opponents

The euro will bring about numerous changes in the European—and global—financial markets. Beyond creating a single, centrally steered money market, it will lead to the disappearance of the foreign exchange markets among the participating currencies, while, at the same time, creating enormous markets for the dollar-euro and yen-euro rates. In addition, EMU will foster the integration of the members' national bond markets (stock markets, on the other hand, may well remain under the influence of purely national developments and their particular microeconomic factors, such as taxes, regulations, and accounting rules). On balance, the emerging euro financial market will represent a considerable improvement when compared to the national markets of the past. There will be plenty of new opportunities for debtors and investors alike.

First Steps and a Large Response

The euro market will have far-reaching international implications, both because of its sheer size and the structural adjustments that will be precipitated by its introduction. EMU will create the second-largest bond market in the world, with German government debt establishing itself as the likely benchmark product. It will have a volume equivalent to about one half of the dollar-denominated counterpart. This euro bond market will offer a great variety of investment and financing opportunities for private and public entities from all over the world. Growth of the overall market may slow as the participating countries continue to reduce their budget deficits, but it could be stimulated by the development of the market for corporate bonds. In short, the euro bond market will become the first real alternative to the dollar bond market.

EMU will also give birth to the world's second-largest equity market. In terms of market capitalization, the United States is well ahead with a total volume of approximately US$10.9 trillion, as compared to the Euroland's US$2.7 trillion. The ratio of market capitalization to GDP in the eleven member states, on average about 44 percent at end-1997, was still far below the corresponding figure in the US (139 percent). The number of listed companies in the EMU area is fairly low as well. Yet, the focus of asset allocation in the euro equity market has already shifted from a national orientation to the relative performance of individual stocks within the respective industry in the euro zone. Also, new European stock indices will guide investors through the new universe of opportunities. A further boost to the Euroland equity market will likely be felt in a couple of years when the UK joins Euroland. This is a distinct possibility after the general elections expected to be called in 2001.

Given the size of the financial markets and of the Euroland economy, the euro will be widely used in international financial markets from the very beginning. Right from the start, it will become the only good alternative to using the US dollar in foreign trade invoicing, in foreign exchange interventions, as an investment currency, and as an anchor for the exchange arrangements of other countries. In the past 25 years, the D-mark has admittedly made inroads into the dollar's domain as a world currency, both as a key currency in the central banks' reserve holdings and as the ERM's main anchor, but it never proved quite as attractive as the dollar in many other respects, largely because the German financial market was dwarfed by the huge and dynamic US capital market. There was no rival to the dollar in the international realm, including the yen.

Born to Be Strong

The euro is of a different caliber. It will begin life as an international currency notwithstanding the widely published fears of inherent euro anemia. Size does matter! That said, this new status as the world's unrivalled number-2 currency will, however, entail both economic advantages and disadvantages. On the benefit side, the inherent consequence of being able to use one's own currency as an international contract and reserve currency will minimize exchange-rate risks, whether one borrows or issues bonds in the international financial market. Foreign investors are attracted by a large financial market, because they imply lower interest rates and, consequently, improved financing conditions for investment purposes. If foreign trade can be settled in one's currency, both exporters and importers will enjoy greater planning certainty as exchange rate risks and hedging costs are eliminated. Moreover, a central bank takes in additional profits, if its banknotes are also used abroad. Annual seigniorage profits from euro notes circulated outside the euro zone may amount to roughly 0.05 percent of GDP in the EU. On the other hand, the use of a currency for international transactions may entail a higher degree of vulnerability to exogenous factors, for instance, via the exchange rate, and a weakening of central bank control over the supply of money.

How will the euro live up to its international role? The euro may pose a challenge to the dollar in a number of areas. In trade invoicing, for example, the greenback—used in just under 50 percent of world exports—is the predominant invoicing currency. By comparison, the EU currencies' share amounts to roughly a third, mainly due to the large volume in intra-regional trade within the EU. For many countries, Euroland will be, by far, the most important trading partner. Given the close economic ties between Euroland and the non-participating EU member states (as well as EFTA and Eastern European countries), the euro will become a kind of 'parallel' currency, above all for the large multinationals in Europe. In Asia and Latin America, the US dollar's predominance will likely persist in the foreseeable future because of its vehicle function and the region's close trade links with the US. Even though the oil price should continue to be quoted in US dollars on the international commodity markets, bilateral contracts for oil deliveries invoiced in euros are conceivable. The euro's share in trade in Euroland will no longer be regarded as foreign trade, though inner-European trade will soon begin to grow markedly. I expect the euro's share in international trade invoicing to rise to roughly 35 percent over the next decade.

The euro's growing significance as an invoicing currency in world trade will also have an impact on central bank's exchange rate policies and the composition of their reserve portfolios. The vast majority of Euroland's European trade partners will seek to keep their exchange rates stable versus the euro. It will become the official exchange rate anchor for many of them. This applies to the future ERM-II members, possibly Switzerland, and also to some countries in Eastern Europe, the Middle East, and Northern Africa and irrespective of whether or not they will join the EU. All these countries will hold a substantial part of their currency reserves in euros to be able to cushion undesirable exchange rate fluctuations by means of foreign exchange interventions.

Ultimately, the euro's significance as a reserve currency will critically depend on the policies pursued by Asia's central banks, as these hold just over 40 percent of the world's official currency reserves (more than US$600 billion, mostly denominated in US dollars). Even though Asia's future exchange rate policy is difficult to forecast, it is fairly clear that there is still greater scope for the use of the euro as reserve currency, mainly for reasons of portfolio diversification. I think it is possible that the euro's share in world foreign exchange reserves will rise to 25-30 percent over the medium term.

For the evolution of the euro's international role, its function as a store of value in international portfolios is, of course, of crucial importance. This, however, is anything but certain. There are many factors impacting on the currency preferences of asset holders all over the world that cannot be judged with any degree of confidence. Let me just make some simplified assumptions about the performance of the euro. First, it may take some years until the community of investors fully accepts the euro as the successor to the D-mark and other European currencies. Second, the outlook for the inflation performance is good. Third, the ECB will gain credibility not only in Europe but also in global markets within a few years' time. In essence, there will not be a major crisis of confidence in the euro at the start of monetary union.

Given the economic potential and the depth of euro capital markets, many private investors may want to better diversify the current composition of their holdings. Clearly, portfolios of international investors around the world are not optimally diversified. The euro financial market should, at least, provide the pre-conditions as both short-term, liquid instruments as well as long-term ones will be available, at a significant scale, in a stable currency from 1999 onwards. However, returns on Euroland and US assets are likely to remain strongly correlated, in particular in the fixed-income markets. Also, share price movements on European and US stock exchanges are only gradually becoming more diverse. Wall Street is still the leading exchange.

The New Kid on the Block

On balance, I would expect gradual portfolio adjustments by private investors over a period of five to ten years. The US dollar's share in global portfolios will likely exceed the euro's, but the euro may gain some market share at the expense of the dollar. A global re-balancing of portfolios, both of central banks and the private sector, in the range of 10-15 percent seems to be within reach. That alone would require net capital flows into Euroland in the order of some US$600-800 billion. Yet, before hasty conclusions about likely exchange rate effects are drawn, a look at the financing side seems appropriate.

The euro will also gain importance as a financing currency, at least as the interest rate environment remains favorable. For many countries in Eastern Europe and Asia, tapping the euro market and thereby diversifying the currency exposure of their foreign debt may well make sense. Russia, for example, has successfully launched a DM-denominated euro bond recently. Many more debtors from emerging markets will follow suit. It is very difficult to estimate the potential of the global re-balancing transactions that will be undertaken by debt managers, but they are likely to be considerable.

Of course, debt and asset managers will not only respond to the new currency, but also to the risks and returns in the different financial markets. These are influenced by the business cycle, by interest and exchange rates. It is hard to say, at this juncture, how much of the expected adjustments will be due to the new currency universe itself. As neither the potential scale nor the speed of the re-balancing activities, by both debt and asset managers, can be predicted with any degree of accuracy, the net effect of EMU on global capital markets is open to anybody's guess. To me, it seems that the combination of situational factors, stronger growth in Euroland and a slackening US economy, a rather strong dollar bound to depreciate, the huge US current-account deficit, the flight to quality in response to the emerging market financial crisis, and expectations of price stability in Euroland and an appreciating euro will lead to a net inflow of capital into euro-denominated securities and to a modest appreciation of the euro against the dollar over the course of the next two years.

If this process evolves as laid out, the euro will enter the foreign exchange market as a strong currency, strengthening the credibility of the ECB. Hence, further portfolio adjustments by Asian central banks and private investors from abroad may take place. This process, from a European perspective, could turn into a virtuous circle leading to a strengthening of the euro. All this, however, assumes that the Asian crisis does not continue to worsen considerably, which, in turn, would lead to very sluggish global demand and investment.

A Possible Co-Leadership Role

No doubt, EMU will give Europe greater clout in international monetary affairs. That does not mean, however, that international policy coordination among the three major economic regions of the world will become any easier. As there will be no changes to the status quo of flexible exchange rates among the world's major currencies for the foreseeable future, the risk of exchange rate volatility among the dollar, euro, and yen will continue to exist in the future, it may even increase. Policy-making, particularly in monetary affairs, will even become more strongly oriented towards domestic concerns, as the Euroland and US economies are not highly dependent on exchange rate movements. Moreover, it is, by no means, clear whether the ECB and the Euroland governments will be prepared to bear a greater share of the burden of global leadership in monetary affairs and help to stabilize global capital markets and those currencies that have become subject to speculative attacks. If the Asian situation deteriorates further, Euroland may feel the full impact of globalization and may have to learn the lesson that domestic stabilization policy cannot be separated as neatly from global financial instability as many in Europe wish possible. Getting Europe's monetary house in order may simply not suffice.

Note

1.   This article was published in *World Economic Affairs*, November 1998.

7.   IMPACT OF THE EURO ON MEMBERS AND NON-MEMBERS

Jeffrey A. Frankel

It may be late in the game to debate the merits of EMU for its members. But I begin with a review of the pros and cons. The UK, Sweden and others have yet to decide whether to join, so for them the evaluation is still relevant. The second half of these notes will turn to the implications of the euro as a new international currency. Impacts on countries outside EMU are discussed in addition to countries inside.

Impact of EMU Per Se on the Members

The two big advantages of fixing the exchange rate, for any country, are: (1) to reduce transactions costs and exchange rate risk, which can discourage trade and investment, and (2) to provide a credible nominal anchor for monetary policy. The big advantage of a floating exchange rate, on the other hand, is the ability to pursue an independent monetary policy.[1]

Which factors are likely to dominate, the advantages of fixed exchange rates or the advantages of floating? The answer must depend, in large part, on characteristics of the country in question. There is no one right answer for all countries or all times. Many of the country characteristics that are most important in this context are closely related to the size and openness of the country. This observation brings us to the theory of the Optimum Currency Area.

Definition of an Optimum Currency Area

Countries that are highly integrated with each other, with respect to trade and other economic relationships, are more likely to constitute an optimum currency area. We define an optimum currency area as a region for which it is optimal to have its own currency and its own monetary policy.[2] This definition can be given some more content by assuming that smaller units tend to be more open and integrated than larger units. Then an OCA can be defined as *a region that is neither so small and open that it would be better off pegging its currency to a neighbor, nor so large that it would be better off splitting into subregions with different currencies*.[3]

Why does the OCA criterion depend on openness? The advantages of fixed exchange rates increase with the degree of economic integration, while the advantages of flexible exchange rates diminish. Recall the two big advantages of fixing the exchange rate that we just identified: (1) to reduce transactions costs and exchange rate risk that can discourage trade and investment, and (2) to provide a credible nominal anchor for monetary policy. If traded goods constitute a large proportion of the economy, then exchange rate uncertainty is a more serious issue for the country in the aggregate. Such an economy may be too small and too open to have an independently floating currency. At the same time, because fixing the exchange rate in such a country goes further toward fixing the entire price level, an exchange rate peg is more likely to be credible, and thus more likely to succeed in reducing inflationary expectations.[4]

Furthermore, the chief advantage of a floating exchange rate, the ability to pursue an independent monetary policy, is in many ways weaker for an economy that is highly integrated with its neighbors. This is because there are ways that such a country or region can cope with an adverse shock even in the absence of discretionary changes in macroeconomic policy.

The Trade Criterion

Consider first, as the criterion for openness, the marginal propensity to import. Variability in output under a fixed exchange rate is relatively low when the marginal propensity to import is high. Openness can act as an automatic stabilizer.

The Labor Mobility Criterion

Consider next, as the criterion of openness the ease of labor movement between the country in question and its neighbors. If the economy is highly integrated with its neighbors by this criterion, then workers may be able to respond to a local recession by moving across the border to get jobs, so there is less need for a local monetary expansion or devaluation.

The Symmetry of Shocks Criterion

Of course the neighbor may be in recession too. *To the extent that shocks to the two economies are correlated,* however, *monetary independence is not needed in any case: the two can share a monetary expansion in tandem.* There is less need for a flexible exchange rate between them to accommodate differences.

The Fiscal Transfer Criterion

Consider, finally, a rather special kind of integration: the existence of a federal fiscal system to transfer funds to regions that suffer adverse shocks. The existence of such a system, like the existence of high labor mobility or high correlation of shocks, makes monetary independence less necessary.

The EU vs. the US, Judged by the Four OCA Criteria ✗

We have just seen that regional units are more likely to benefit, on net, from joining together to form a monetary union if: (1) they trade a lot with each other, (2) there is high degree of labor mobility among them, (3) the economic shocks they face are highly correlated, or (4) there exists a federal fiscal system to transfer funds to regions that suffer adverse shocks.

Each of these criteria can be quantified, but it is very difficult to know what is the critical level of integration at which the advantages of belonging to a currency area outweigh the disadvantages. The states of the United States constitute a possible standard of comparison. It seems quite clear that the degree of openness of the states, and the degree of economic integration among them, are sufficiently high to justify their use of a common currency. How do the members of the European Union compare to the states in this regard? US states appear to be more open than European countries, by both the trade and labor mobility criteria. It appears that when an adverse shock hits a region of the US such as New England or the oil states of the South, out-migration of workers is the most important mechanism whereby unemployment rates and wages are eventually re-equilibrated across regions.[5]

Labor mobility among European countries is much lower than in the United States. In some parts, the geographical radius within which many people live their entire lives is smaller than the distance over which Los Angelenos commute to work on a daily basis.[6] Americans are three to two times as likely to move between states as are Germans to move between their Länder, or the French to move between their Départements.[7] Europeans are presumably even less inclined to move across national boundaries within the European Union than they are to move within their own countries. Thus, by the labor mobility criterion, European countries are less well-suited to a common currency than are American states.[8]

The other two criteria are also better satisfied within the United States than within Europe. Disturbances across US regions have a relatively high correlation, compared to members of the European Union.[9]

When disparities in income do arise in the United States, federal fiscal policy helps to narrow them. One recent estimate suggests that when a region's per capita income falls by one dollar, the final reduction in its disposable income is only 70 cents. The difference, a 30 percent federal cushioning effect, includes both an automatic decrease in federal tax receipts plus an automatic increase in unemployment compensation and other transfers. The cushioning effect has been estimated at 17 percent in the case of Canada. European countries have greater scope for domestic fiscal stabilization than do American states (and will retain at least some of this scope despite the fiscal constraints that the EMU process is imposing on them). Furthermore there are some cross-country fiscal transfer mechanisms. Nevertheless, neither the fiscal transfer mechanisms that are already in place within the European Union nor those that are contemplated under EMU—so-called 'structural funds'—are as large as those in the US (or Canadian) federal fiscal system.[10]

Judged by these optimum currency area criteria, the European Union is not as good a candidate for a monetary union as is the United States. But the extent of European integration is increasing over time, partly as a result of such measures as the removal of barriers to trade and labor mobility in 1992. Even if EU members such as Italy and the UK in 1992 did not satisfy the criteria for joining the optimum currency area in the 1990s, perhaps they will in the future. This point is especially acute for new members such as Sweden. The effect of EU accession in 1995 will be to promote Sweden's trade with other European countries. Statistical estimates using the gravity model of bilateral trade suggest that membership in the EU increases trade with its members by roughly 50 percent or more.[11] Thus it is more likely that Sweden will satisfy the OCA criterion in the future than in the past.

The Endogeneity of the Income Correlation Criterion

What about the other parameter, the degree of income correlation among members? We come now to a key point. *Income correlation surely depends on trade integration.*

Our hypothesis is that this relationship is positive: the more Sweden trades with the EU, the more will Swedish income be correlated with EU income. We think it evident that the incomes of US states, for example, are highly correlated with each other because their economies are highly integrated. The result would be immediate in a demand-driven model (where the correlation of income depends in a simple way on the marginal propensities of the two countries to import from each other), but it could also follow in a variety of other models (e.g., productivity shocks spilling over via trade).

Now consider what happens when Sweden decides to join EMU (European Economic and Monetary Union). The elimination of exchange rate uncertainty and currency transaction costs stimulates trade with other EU members. Integration and correlation rise further. (Based on the statistical evidence, we believe that the stimulus to trade from stabilizing the exchange rate is rather small, though positive.[12] The advantages to eliminating different currencies altogether probably adds something, beyond the reduction in exchange rate variability to zero.)

To identify the effect of bilateral trade patterns on income correlations, we need exogenous determinants of bilateral trade patterns. Rose and I (1998) have used the exogenous variable of the gravity model: bilateral distance, common border dummy, common language dummy, the product of sizes, the product of incomes per capita. In this way we hope to see whether an exogenous increase in trade between two countries raises or lowers the correlation between their incomes. Our finding is that an increase in trade raises the correlation. Thus countries are more likely to satisfy the OCA criterion ex post than ex ante.

Impact of EMU on Other Countries

So much for the implications of monetary integration on members of the euro area. What about the implications for other countries?

Impact on Other European Countries

If the UK, Sweden or others decide to enter into a transition to membership in EMU, there is always the danger that shocks will occur in the interim that result in exchange rate crises of the sort experienced in 1992-93 (or East Asia 1997). This would be one manifestation of imperfect qualifications under the OCA criteria.

Impact on the Rest of the World

Perhaps, to the extent EMU reduces transactions costs for intra-European trade, it will engender some trade-diversion at the expense of other trading partners. But, overall, I see grounds for hope that there will be enough trade creation so that other countries are not harmed economically. This is even leaving aside the political advantages from having a stable and integrated European continent. EMU is an inspiring adventure/achievement/experiment. Like earlier stages of European integration, it was born out of a desire to banish permanently the possibility of another European war and as such is to be applauded.

Impact on the United States

The main effect is that, to whatever extent EMU contributes to European prosperity, it will also contribute to American prosperity, through trade and other channels. This is true in particular if European growth is led by domestic demand. US firms should benefit from savings in transactions costs, perhaps even more than European firms because they are already used to operating in large markets.

Will the Euro Challenge the Dollar as International Currency?

While the 'euro' has become shorthand in Europe for the advent of the monetary union, it is important to distinguish the question of the international currency role of the euro from the question of the dollar-euro exchange rate or other aspects of EMU.

What Is an International Currency?

An international currency is one that is used outside its home country. This includes uses by countries' monetary authorities, as well as in the private sector.

Official uses of international currencies include:
- the pegging of minor currencies, and
- the holding of foreign exchange reserves by central banks. (This function is called 'reserve currency' status.)

Private-sector uses of international currencies include:
- invoicing and payment for imports and exports,
- denominating financial transactions, and
- a medium for foreign exchange trading. (The international medium-of-exchange function is called 'vehicle currency' status.)

How Does the Dollar Currently Rank Against Other International Currencies?

Most measures show a gradual decline in international use of the dollar. Reserve currency use, perhaps the most important measure, is shown in Figure 1.

The dollar's share of central bank reserve holdings declined from 76.1 percent in 1973, to 56.0 percent in 1990. Central banks gradually shifted their portfolio shares into marks and yen. But the dollar's share in reserve holdings has been relatively flat in the 1990s, even rising.

Other major measures of international currency status are shown in Table 1. Overall, they tend to show the same thing: the dollar still on top, despite a gradual decline in its use versus the mark and yen over the last twenty years. The dollar is still more important than its three or four rivals combined.

- The first column reports the popularity of major currencies among smaller countries choosing a peg for their currencies. It is still the case that no currencies anywhere are pegged to the yen. Three currencies [Estonia, Bulgaria, Bosnia] are now pegged to the mark, however. Elsewhere (Africa) the French franc is still the most common choice as a peg [29 percent of peggers], after the dollar [39 percent]. If one broadens the test to include countries that peg to a weighted basket, whether tightly or loosely, one again gets the conclusion that the dollar remains dominant. [Even among East Asian countries, where the yen occasionally has a statistically significant weight, the weight placed on the dollar is always far higher.][13]
- In the past, almost all trades in the foreign exchange market involved the dollar, as the currency either bought or sold. These days, the firm would be a bit more likely than before to be able to go directly from pounds to marks.[14] But as of April 1998, 87 percent of foreign exchange transactions still involved the dollar. The figures are reported in the third column of the tables (divided by two so that the total does not exceed 100 percent).
- The various measures of use of currencies to denominate private international financial transactions—loans, bonds, and deposits—still show the dollar as the dominant currency.

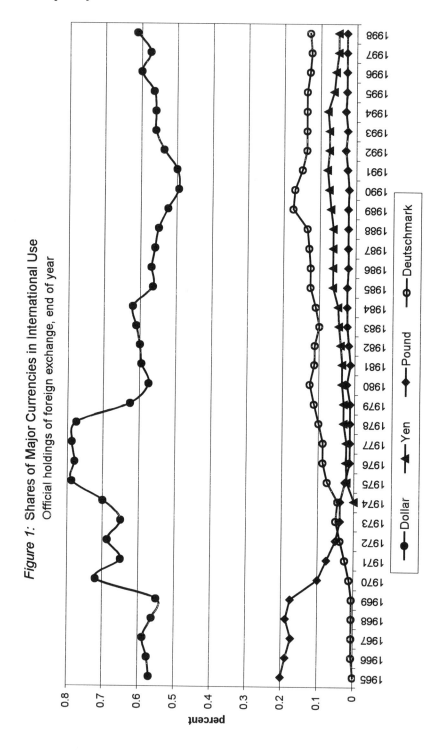

Figure 1: Shares of Major Currencies in International Use
Official holdings of foreign exchange, end of year

- Figures on the use of international currencies as substitutes in local cash transactions, are not generally available. The two leaders are certainly the dollar, for which internationally circulating cash has been estimated by the Fed at 60 percent of US currency outstanding, and the mark, for which international circulation has been estimated by the Bundesbank at 35-40 percent of German currency outstanding. The implication is that dollars circulating abroad are more than four times greater than marks.

Table 1: The Importance of Major Currencies (shares in international use)

	Official use of currencies		Currency of denomination in private transactions			
	Pegging of minor currencies[15]	Foreign exchange reserves held by central banks[16]	Foreign exchange trading in world markets[17]	International capital markets[18]	International trade[19]	Cash held outside home country[20]
US dollar	.39	.61	.44	.54	.48	.78
Deutsch-mark	.06	.13	.15	.11	.16	.22
Japanese yen	.00	.05	.11	.08	.05	NA
pound sterling	.00	.04	.06	.08		.00
French franc	.29	.01	.03	.06	} .15	.00
other EMS currencies	.04	}NA	}.09	NA		.00
ECU[21]	.00			.01	.00	.00
other/un-specified	.22	.11	.15	.12	.16	NA

What Are the Determinants of International Currency Status?

Will the dollar in the future maintain its global role? There are four major sorts of conditions that determine whether a currency is an international currency.[22]

1. *Patterns of output and trade*. The currency of a country that has a large share in international output, trade and finance has a natural advantage. The US economy is still the world's largest, in terms of output and trade, and will be larger than the 11 economies of Euroland aggregated together. If the

United Kingdom and the rest of the four non-member EU countries join in the future, however, the area will be virtually equal in economic size to the United States.

[If the measure of being a vehicle currency is how often it is used in the invoicing and financing of international trade, then other aspects of the pattern of trade may also be relevant. The fact that much of Japan's imports are oil and other raw materials and that much of its exports go to the Western Hemisphere, for example, helps explain why a disproportionately small share of trade is invoiced in yen as opposed to dollars. Raw materials still tend heavily to be priced in dollars.]

2. *History.* There is a strong inertial bias, in favor of using whatever currency has been the vehicle currency in the past. An individual (exporter, importer, borrower, lender, or currency trader) is more likely to use a given currency in his or her transactions if everyone else is doing so. For this reason, the world's choice of international currency is characterized by multiple stable equilibria.[23] The pound remained an important international currency even after the United Kingdom lost its position as an economic superpower early in the century. In the present context, the inertial bias favors the continued central role of the dollar.

3. *The country's financial markets.* Capital and money markets must be not only open and free of controls, but also well-developed, deep and liquid. The large financial marketplaces of New York and London clearly benefit the dollar and pound relative to the Deutschmark and yen.

4. *Confidence in the value of the currency.* Even if a key currency were used only as a unit of account, a necessary qualification would be that its value not fluctuate erratically. As it is, a key currency is also used as a form in which to hold assets (firms hold working balances of the currencies in which they invoice, investors hold bonds issued internationally, and central banks hold currency reserves). Here confidence that the value of the currency will be stable, and particularly that it will not be inflated away in the future, is critical.

The monetary authorities in Japan, Germany and Switzerland, in the 1970s established a better track record of low inflation than did the United States, which helped their bids for international currency status. Given the good US inflation performance more recently, this is no longer much of a concern.

A more important negative aspect for the dollar is the fact that the United States is now a large-scale debtor country. Indeed, 1997 was the first year when the country actually paid out more in interests, dividends, and repatriated profits to foreigners, on their past US investments, than it received on its own past investments abroad. Even if the Federal Reserve never succumbs to the temptations or pressures to inflate away the US debt, the continuing US current account deficit is always a possible source of downward pressure on the dollar. Such fears work to make dollars less attractive.[24]

What Is the Prognosis for the Dollar and the Euro?

In light of these desiderata for a would-be international currency, is it likely that the euro will rival the dollar as leading international currency? EMU will automatically give the new currency a share roughly equal to the sum of those currently held by the ecu, DM, French franc, and other EMS currencies, by most measures. [By the measure of currency pegging, the euro will have a greater share, because all 11 EMU members will be added in. By the measure of reserve holdings, it will have a smaller share, because members' holdings of each other's currencies will disappear. The same is true of foreign exchange trading.] Subsequently, the euro's share will probably gradually rise, to move in the direction of 'Euroland' share of output, which is similar to the size of the US economy.

The odds are against the euro rapidly supplanting the dollar as the world's premier currency. The dollar will probably continue to be the world's favorite currency for holding reserves, pegging minor currencies, invoicing imports and exports, and denominating bonds and lending. It is not that the dollar is ideally suited for this role. At least one characteristic mars its appeal: The United States is a debtor country with a large current account deficit. But an international currency is one that people use because everyone else is using it.

Two of the four determinants of reserve currency status—developed financial markets and historical inertia—support the dollar over the euro. The third, economic size, is a tie. The fourth determinant could in principle disqualify the dollar, if the Federal Reserve launched a high-inflation strategy, but this is unlikely to happen. The new European Central Bank, for its part, will have to 'earn its spurs'.

Over the period 1970-1992, US GDP fell from 24 percent of Gross World Product, evaluated at PPP rates, to 20 percent. It is possible that one can explain much of the downward trend in the dollar's share of world reserve holdings over the last 25 years, and the upward trends in the yen and mark shares, by the falling share of US GDP in the world economy, and the rising share of the Japanese and German GDPs. A careful econometric study of the determinants of central bank reserve holdings is beyond the scope of this article. But an analysis of the role of relative growth rates suggests that the currency shares adjust only very slowly.

Is It Good or Bad for the Euro to Rival the Dollar as Lead International Currency?

Does it matter whether the dollar remains the leading international currency? Of course central banks' reserve currency holdings have important implications for the determination of the exchange rate. But this is another question. What about the global role of the dollar per se?

Advantages to the Home Country

One can think of four advantages to a country of having its currency used internationally.

1. *Convenience for residents.* It is certainly more convenient for a country's exporters, importers, borrowers and lenders to be able to deal in their own currency than foreign currencies. The global use of the dollar, as with the global use of the English language, is a natural advantage that American businessmen tend to take for granted.[25]

2. *More business for the country's banks and other financial institutions.* There need be no firm connection from the currency in which banking is conducted to the nationality of the banks (nor from the nationalities of the savers and borrowers to the nationality of the intermediating bank). British banks, for example, continued to do well in the Eurodollar market after the pound lost its international role. Nevertheless, it stands to reason that US banks have a comparative advantage at dealing in dollars. Only US banks have access to the safety net provided by US regulatory authorities (access to the discount window, and so forth).

3. *Seigniorage.* This is thought by some to be perhaps the most important advantage of having other countries hold one's currency. They must give up real goods and services, or ownership of the real capital stock, in order to add to the currency balances that they use. Just as American Express reaps profits whenever people hold its travelers' checks, which they are willing to do without receiving interest, so the United States profits whenever people in Argentina or Russia hold dollars that do not pay interest. Wherever hyperinflation or social disorder undermine the public's faith in the local currency, the American dollar is the preferred alternative. (The drug trade and other illegal activities is another source of demand, of course.)

[There is an another (smaller) component of seigniorage in addition to the currency component. Most foreign central banks and other investors hold their dollars in the form of interest-paying treasury bills. To the extent that the reserve currency role of the dollar allows the US Treasury to pay a lower interest rate on its liabilities than must other borrowers, the difference is a further source of seigniorage.[26] Some argue that the US would have a harder time financing its current account deficit if the dollar were not an internationally accepted reserve currency.]

4. *Political power and prestige.* The benefits of 'power and prestige' are decidedly nebulous. Nevertheless, the loss of key currency status and the loss of international creditor status have sometimes been associated, along with such non-economic factors as the loss of colonies and military power, in discussions of the historical decline of great powers.

Disadvantages to the Home Country

One can think of two disadvantages from the viewpoint of a key-currency country. They explain why Japan, Germany and Switzerland have in the past been reluctant to have its currency held and used widely.

1. *Larger fluctuations in demand for the currency.* It is not automatically clear that having one's currency held by a wide variety of people around the world will result in greater variability of demand. Perhaps such instability is more likely to follow from the increase in the degree of capital mobility, than from key currency status per se. In any case, central banks are particularly concerned that internationalization will make it more difficult to control the money stock. This problem need not arise if they do not intervene in the foreign exchange market. But the central bank may view letting fluctuations in demand for the currency be reflected in the exchange rate as being just as undesirable as letting them be reflected in the money supply.

2. *An increase in the average demand for the currency.* This is the other side of seigniorage. In the 1960s and 1970s, the Japanese and German governments were particularly worried about the possibility that if assets were made available to foreign residents, an inflow of capital would cause the currency to appreciate and render exporters uncompetitive on world markets. In 1998, some Europeans seem to worry that international currency status for the euro might lead to a loss in export competitiveness for European firms.

Impact on the Rest of the World

Which is more efficient for the world monetary system, a single reserve currency, or two, three or more? On the one hand, there are clear efficiencies in having a single international currency. These 'network externalities' stem from the reason we have money in the first place—to avoid a 'double coincidence of wants'.

On the other hand, there are some who argue that a multiple-reserve currency system would be more stable than a system that relied on a single currency like the dollar. One rationale for this position would be that when an international currency has no rivals, its home government might be tempted to abuse its responsibility and run deficits at the expense of others. In this view, the existence of a second international currency creates a healthy rivalry that keeps both governments in line.

The introduction of the euro in January 1999 will instantly create an international currency that potentially rivals the dollar. The standard measures of international currency use will show a euro that inherits roughly the roles of its constituent currencies. Subsequently the dollar will probably lose share gradually, as it lost share in the 70s and 80s to the mark and yen. There will be some small associated costs for the US. But from the viewpoint of the United States government, maintaining the international role of the dollar will be just one more reason, on the list of reasons that already exist, to pursue sound macroeconomic policies. There is no reason to expect the euro to surpass the dollar anytime soon, nor for the costs from the US viewpoint to outweigh the substantial political and economic advantages to a successful EMU.

Notes

1. To be sure, other factors enter as well. Another advantage of fixed exchange rates, for example, is that they prevent competitive depreciation or competitive appreciation. Another advantage of having an independent currency is that the government retains seigniorage. Most of the important factors, however, can be lumped into the major arguments presented in the text.

2. Stretching the definition of integration even further, another kind of integration, more political in nature, can help reduce the need for monetary independence: to the extent that domestic residents have economic priorities, especially on fighting inflation versus unemployment, that are similar to those of their neighbors, there will be less need for a differentiated response to common shocks (Corden, 1972; Alesina and Grilli, 1991). Finally, to the extent that individuals think of themselves as citizens of Europe more than citizens of their own country, they may be willing on political grounds to forego discretionary monetary responses even to disturbances that are so large that a national policy response would be in their economic advantage.

3. The classic references are Mundell (1961) and McKinnon (1963). A recent survey is Tavlas (1992). The issues are also reviewed by Bayoumi and Eichengreen (1994).

4. Romer (1993).

5. Blanchard and Katz (1992).

6. While economists and demographers may have their own ways of measuring labor mobility, anthropologists/archaeologists recently produced an extreme illustration of low mobility in the UK. Excavation near the town of Cheddar, England, uncovered a 6,000-year old skeleton. Scientists, having obtained a sample of DNA from 'Cheddar Man', set off to see if they could find a match among any of the residents of the nearby town. Before long, they were able to verify that a local schoolteacher was a direct relation [perhaps a direct descendant of a sibling of Cheddar Man]. The schoolteacher lived only one-half mile from his forbearer's cave. Evidently, in this one English family at least, successive generations do not like to move far from their ancestral home.

7. Eichengreen (1993).

8. Decressin, Jorg, and Antonio Fatas (1995).

9. Bayoumi and Eichengreen (1993).

10. We are using Bayoumi and Masson, rather than earlier estimates by Sala-i-Martin and Sachs (1991) or lower estimates as suggested by von Hagen.

11. The Frankel and Wei papers cited above provide estimates, and other citations to the literature.

12. Small effects are estimated, for example, in Frankel and Wei (1995a,b; 1997).

13. Frankel and Wei (1993).

14. Bank of England (1992) or Bank for International Settlements (1993).

15. Source: IMF, *International Financial Statistics*. Data pertain to 3/31/98. None of the EMS countries was officially classified as pegging to the Deutschmark or ECU. ('Other' includes SDR and South African rand, at .08 and .06 respectively.)

16. Source: IMF, Annual Report 1998, Table I.2. Data pertain to end-1997. ('Other' includes Swiss franc at .01.)

17. Source: Bank for International Settlements, Basle, 1998. Data pertain to April 1998. All figures have been divided by 2, so that total adds to 100 percent even though there are two currencies in each transaction. ('Other' includes Swiss franc at .04.)

18. Total funds raised in 1996, including international bond issues, medium- and long-term syndicated bank loans, and other debt facilities. Source: N. Funke and M. Kennedy, 'International Implications of European Economic and Monetary Union', *Economics Department Working Paper,* no. 174, OECD, Paris, 1997.

19. Source: ibid. Data pertain to 1992. ('Other EMS currencies' are Italian lira and Dutch guilder.)

20. Data pertain to 1995. Source: Calculated from US and German central banks' estimates (B. Eichengreen and J. Frankel, 'The SDR, Reserve Currencies, and the Future of the International Monetary System', in *The Future of the SDR in Light of Changes in the International Financial System*, edited by M. Mussa, J. Boughton, and P. Isard, International Monetary Fund, 1996). Shares of the yen and Swiss franc are set at zero for lack of data, even though they are thought to be greater than that (K. Rogoff, 'Large Banknotes: Will the Euro Go Underground?', *Economic Policy* (April 1998).

21. From January 1999, the ECU becomes the euro. The mark, French franc, and nine other EU currencies are to be irrevocably fixed to the euro, and to disappear entirely by 2002.
22. Bergsten (1975), Tavlas and Ozeki (1991), Frankel (1992), and Hale (1995).
23. Krugman (1984).
24. A contrary viewpoint is possible. As argued by Triffin, *only if a country like the United States does run a deficit* will other countries be able to run a surplus and thereby earn the dollars they need to match reserve growth with real economic growth.
25. One had to wonder what the reaction of American manufacturers and farmers would be in 1984 when Treasury Secretary Don Regan berated the members of the Keidanren for paying their imports in dollars rather than yen.
26. This was the basis of European resentment against the dollar standard and against the US basic balance deficit in the 1960s, to the extent that the European need to acquire dollars was the fundamental origin of that deficit.

References

Alesina, Alberto, and Vittorio Grilli. 1991. 'The European Central Bank: Reshaping Monetary Politics in Europe.' In M. Canzoneri, V. Grilli, and P. Masson, eds., *Establishing a Central Bank: Issues in Europe and Lessons from the US.* London: CEPR. Cambridge: Cambridge University Press.

Bayoumi, Tamim, and Barry Eichengreen. 1993a. 'Shocking Aspects of European Monetary Unification.' In F. Giavazzi and F. Torres, eds., *The Transition to Economic and Monetary Union in Europe.* New York: Cambridge University Press.

Bayoumi, Tamim, and Barry Eichengreen. 1993b. 'Is There a Conflict Between EC Enlargement and European Monetary Unification?' *Greek Economic Review,* 15, no. 1 (Autumn), pp. 131-154.

Bayoumi, Tamim, and Barry Eichengreen. 1993c. 'Monetary and Exchange Rate Arrangements for NAFTA.' IMF Discussion Paper, no. WP/93/20 (March).

Bayoumi, Tamim, and Barry Eichengreen. 1994. 'One Money or Many? Analyzing the Prospects for Monetary Unification in Various Parts of the World.' *Princeton Studies in International Finance,* no. 76 (September). International Finance Section, Princeton University.

Blanchard, Olivier, and Lawrence Katz. 1992 'Regional Evolutions.' *Brookings Papers on Economic Activity*, no. 1, pp. 1-61.

Cohen, Daniel, and Charles Wyplosz. 1989. 'The European Monetary Union: An Agnostic Evaluation.' In R. Bryant, D. Currie, J. Frenkel, P. Masson, and R. Portes, eds., *Macroeconomic Policies in an Interdependent World.* Washington, D.C.: Brookings, pp. 311-337.

Corden, W. Max. 1972. 'Monetary Integration.' *Princeton Studies in International Finance,* no. 93 (April). International Finance Section, Princeton University.

De Grauwe, Paul, and Wim Vanhaverbeke, 1991. 'Is Europe an Optimum Currency Area? Evidence from Regional Data.' CEPR Discussion Paper, no. 555 (May). London.

Edison, Hali, and Michael Melvin. 1990. 'The Determinants and Implications of the Choice of an Exchange Rate System.' In W. Haraf and T. Willett, eds., *Monetary Policy For a Volatile Global Economy.* Washington, D.C.: American Enterprise Institute.

Eichengreen, Barry. 1988. 'Real Exchange Rate Behavior Under Alternative International Monetary Regimes: Interwar Evidence.' *European Economic Review,* no. 32, pp. 363-371.

Eichengreen, Barry. 1992. 'Should the Maastricht Treaty Be Saved?' *Princeton Studies in International Finance,* no. 74 (December). International Finance Section, Princeton University.

Frankel, Jeffrey, and Andrew Rose. 1998. 'The Endogeneity of the Optimum Currency Area Criterion.' *The Economic Journal,* vol. 108, no. 449 (July), pp. 1009-1025.

Frankel, Jeffrey, and Shang-Jin Wei. 1995a. 'Emerging Currency Blocs.' In H. Genberg, ed., *The International Monetary System: Its Institutions and its Future.* Berlin: Springer, pp. 111-143.

Frankel, Jeffrey, and Shang-Jin Wei. 1995b. 'European Integration and the Regionalization of World Trade and Currencies: The Economics and the Politics.' In Barry Eichengreen, Jeffry Frieden, and Jürgen von Hagen, eds., *Monetary and Fiscal Policy in an Integrated Europe.* New York and Heidelberg: Springer-Verlag Press.

Frankel, Jeffrey, and Shang-Jin Wei. 1997. 'Regionalization of World Trade and Currencies: Economics and Politics.' In Frankel, ed., *The Regionalization of the World Economy.* Chicago: University of Chicago Press.

Kenen, Peter. 1969. 'The Theory of Optimum Currency Areas: An Eclectic View.' In R. Mundell and A. Swoboda, eds., *Monetary Problems in the International Economy.* Chicago: University of Chicago Press.

Krugman, Paul. 1993. 'Lessons of Massachusetts for EMU.' In F. Giavazzi and F. Torres, eds., *The Transition to Economic and Monetary Union in Europe.* New York: Cambridge University Press, pp. 241-261.

McKinnon, Ronald I. 1963. 'Optimum Currency Areas.' *American Economic Review,* vol. 53 (September), pp. 717-725.

Mundell, Robert A. 1961. 'A Theory of Optimum Currency Areas.' *American Economic Review,* vol. 51 (November), pp. 509-517.

Romer, David. 1993. 'Openness and Inflation: Theory and Evidence.' *Quarterly Journal of Economics,* vol. 108, no. 4 (November), pp. 869-903.

Sala-i-Martin, Xavier, and Jeffrey Sachs. 1991. 'Fiscal Federalism and Optimum Currency Areas.' In M. Canzoneri, V. Grilli, and P. Masson, eds., *Establishing a Central Bank: Issues in Europe and Lessons from the US.* London: CEPR. Cambridge: Cambridge University Press, pp. 195-219.

Tavlas, George. 1992. 'The "New" Theory of Optimal Currency Areas.' Washington, D.C.: International Monetary Fund.

8. EXCHANGE RATE POLICY-MAKING IN THE EURO AREA: LESSONS FROM TRADE?[1]

Klaus Günter Deutsch

National interests of the governments of Germany and France concerning European monetary integration converged in 1986/87, when a dispute over German monetary policy led to French calls for monetary union and to German proposals for the establishment of an independent European central bank in the European Communities. The Maastricht Treaty represented a compromise between Germany and France on a European central bank along the lines of the Bundesbank model in exchange for granting France (as well as all the other EU member states) a say in monetary policy. Today, in the spring of 1999, EMU is in place, and the euro is being traded on foreign exchanges around the globe. Initially, internal and external stability have not gone together, a scenario not widely expected. Whereas consumer prices in the euro area are forecast to rise by only about one percent in 1999, the euro depreciated by eight percent during the first three months of its existence. The euro's start showed both internal strength and external weakness (Deutsche Bank Research, 1999).

Resolving the conflict over European monetary policy was but one underlying interest of the European governments. A shared objective— sometimes admitted in public, sometimes not—was to enhance the collective policy autonomy of the European nations in international monetary affairs. In a world of highly mobile financial capital and macroeconomic interdependence, the asymmetry in the transatlantic monetary relationship favoring the US over 'Europe' (Germany) was to be reduced through the creation of EMU. Fluctuations in the exchange rate of the US dollar vis-à-vis the D-mark had created tensions within the European Monetary System time and again (Gros and Thygesen, 1992). In the euro area, this can no longer happen. Thus, EU member states decided to pool monetary sovereignty, to delegate the execution of monetary policy to the European Central Bank

(ECB), and to deepen macroeconomic policy coordination (Moravcsik, 1998; McNamara, 1997).

Although international considerations played a considerable, yet not very visible role in the path-breaking decisions on EMU, the future external monetary policy of the euro area was contentious from the start and has remained so ever since.

Given the traditional French preference for managing exchange rates globally and the opposite preference of the various coalition governments under Chancellor Kohl (1982-1998) in Germany for floating exchange rates in the trilateral relationship with the US and Japan, the Maastricht Treaty reflected a compromise not fully worked out at the time of the negotiations. Since then, the constitutional, institutional, and policy dimensions of the external monetary policy of the euro area have created tensions within the EU and in relations with partners all over the globe.

In this study (based on Deutsch, 1999b), I will reflect on the issues and try to deduce some highly abstract and subjective lessons from the only other external economic policy of the European Union, namely the trade policy (Deutsch, 1999a; von Schöppenthau, 1999; see also Hayes, 1994; Schuknecht, 1992).

To put in a nutshell, the hypothesis is the following: The quality and effectiveness of external policy-making depends on three factors: on the effective delegation of powers on the basis of a clear constitutional mandate; on political authority of negotiators which can only originate in shared objectives of their principals; and on flexibility in negotiations with other nations. In the Common Commercial Policy of the EU, these needs have only been partly met in the past four decades. In external monetary policy, functional delegation has taken place, but the allocation of political authority is still being contested and objectives are not yet shared by all participants. The drawback of that situation is that policy flexibility might be severely limited under difficult circumstances. Dealing with Europe will not become much easier just for the reason that EMU has come into being; rather, it will become more complex (Kahler, 1995).

I will briefly reflect upon the rules laid down in the Treaty on European Union and on the first-round players. I will also provide a short comment on the external representation of the euro area. Then, I will draw some conclusions from decision-making in the Common Commercial Policy and finally argue that the external monetary policy of the euro area will continue to be a half-way house for many years to come.

The Constitutional Set-Up

The founding fathers of EMU agreed to establish a common central bank and grant it independence in all monetary policy, personnel, budgetary, and legal matters. It was deemed necessary not only by the German government and its close stability-conscious allies, but also by the vast majority of governments and central banks that direct government interference in interest rate policy would threaten the ECB's ability to safeguard price stability. The Treaty of Maastricht left no doubt that the institution would have all the necessary independence and the means to effectively conduct monetary policy, generally assumed to be an indispensable precondition for meeting the price stability objective. Decisions on monetary policy strategy and instruments were made in the final run-up to stage three, and there can be no doubt that the constitutional set-up is excellent and the capability of the ECB to make decisions well developed.

Unfortunately, the same cannot be said of the external monetary policy of the euro area (see Deutsch, 1999b; Henning, 1997; Kenen, 1998, 1995). Although the Treaty lays down price level stability as the single objective of the ECB's monetary policy, conflicts of interest may, of course, arise between internal and external monetary policies. The terms of the Maastricht Treaty leave room for political wrangling in some of these areas. Responsibilities in exchange rate policy were split into fundamental and day-to-day decisions. For the former, the governments would retain ultimate responsibility, while the ECB would be in charge of the latter.

According to the Treaty, the Council of Ministers, acting unanimously on a recommendation from the ECB or from the Commission, and after consulting the ECB and then the European Parliament, may conclude formal agreements on an exchange rate system for the euro in relation to other currencies. Denmark and Greece were the first countries to participate, from January 1, 1999, in the Exchange Rate Mechanism II, which was set up according to this procedure. It is also laid down in the Treaty that the ECB is responsible for day-to-day foreign-exchange operations and intervention.

If no formal exchange rate system exists in relations with non-EU currencies, the Council, acting by a qualified majority, may formulate general orientations for exchange rate policy (Art. 111, §2 Treaty of Amsterdam on European Union, respectively Art. 109, §2 Maastricht Treaty). This can be enacted either after having received a recommendation from the Commission and having consulted the ECB, or after having received a recommendation from the ECB. In December 1997, the European Council at its meeting in Luxembourg passed a resolution that the Council will only consider announcing 'general orientations' in exceptional circumstances, for instance in case of massive exchange rate distortions vis-à-vis third currencies.

However, it was not resolved who would determine the nature and extent of the misalignment and what would happen in case of divergent views of the ECB, the European Commission, and the majority of governments represented on the Council. Also, as only the full Council can make binding decisions, it remained open whether the four non-participating states will vote on it or not.

As any 'general orientation' would finally have to affect day-to-day decisions on forex interventions and/or the ECB's interest rate policy, it is unclear what the Executive Board of the ECB would do, if the Council and the ECB failed to agree. My interpretation of the institutional set-up is that the ECB could disregard 'general orientations', if it saw risks to price stability. The hierarchy of objectives leaves no room for doubts in that regard; the priority of the internal objective is explicitly mentioned in Art. 111 §2 Treaty of Amsterdam itself and can also be derived from the general mandate of the ECB (see also Bognar, 1997, on legal interpretations).

The constitutional set-up of the ECB is considerably stronger than that of the Bundesbank, even though it became known in retrospect that former Bundesbank President Otmar Emminger, who served from 1977 to 1979, had found agreement with the government that in case of a conflict with price stability—an issue, on which the government would ultimately decide—forex interventions required to comply with a commitment to the 'narrow' exchange rate mechanism (ERM I) of the European Monetary System (March 1979-August 1993) would be suspended (Emminger, 1986, p. 361; Henning, 1994, pp. 188-189; Ungerer, 1997, p. 154, n. 8). Politically, however, the situation may be more difficult for the ECB, as it would have to decide on a cooperative or confrontational position vis-à-vis the Council. This decision might have to reflect broader concerns of support of public opinion and governments. Quite distinct from the Bundesbank's traditional reliance on public support, the ECB cannot yet fully rely on strong support from the public in the euro area.

There can be no doubt, however, that some governments in the euro area will at any given time consider exchange rate developments and policy issues to be too important to be left to the ECB or to market forces. Ignoring exchange rates is no usual policy stance for democratic governments in Europe. If there is need for a proof of this assumption, the recent debate on the future order for international monetary relations has provided ample evidence. It is thus appropriate to consider the players at the outset of exchange rate policy-making in the euro area.

The Players and the Process at the Start

The transition to the euro in financial markets was smooth, even though some problems creeped up in payment systems. This was not the case, though, at the political level. A public controversy arose between key governments and the ECB on interest and exchange rate policies for the euro area. German and French government officials called for further interest rate cuts, even after the coordinated surprise rate cut by the national central banks of ten of the eleven participating countries in December 1998 (the Banca d'Italia followed later). Also, these governments argued strongly in favor of exchange rate management. As the euro has depreciated versus the dollar in foreign exchange markets during the first three months of its existence (rather than appreciating as had been widely expected), concern about a euro that could prove too strong for the sluggish economies in the euro area has subsided somewhat.

The Euro Area Governments

The center-left governments of euro area countries have worried quite a lot about interest and exchange rates since they have come to power. Given the very low level of inflation in the core countries and slower growth due to the economic and financial crises in many developing countries and Japan, France and Germany in particular have pressed for macroeconomic policies fostering growth and employment. They have stressed the need to cut interest rates further and to stabilize exchange rates (read: to prevent an appreciation of the euro that might dampen economic activity). French Finance Minister Dominique Strauss-Kahn has repeatedly argued that the euro area should pursue a Clinton/Greenspan policy-mix of tight fiscal policy and loose monetary policy and avoid a Volcker/Reagan policy-mix of large budget deficits and tight monetary policy, a view which was shared by the then German Minister of Finance, Oskar Lafontaine, who held the position until March 11, 1999. Also, arguments about potential net portfolio diversification into euro-denominated securities by global institutional investors and current account developments, particularly the widening US deficit, seemed to indicate an appreciation of the euro against the dollar. Also, Lafontaine and his aides demanded far-reaching changes in the international monetary and financial system, in particular with respect to the establishment of a target zone system.

Target zones in the trilateral relationship have not been tried in practice, at least not in the sense of explicitly setting central and intervention rates known to the public. The intensive cooperation among governments and central banks in the brief phase between the Plaza and Louvre Accords (September 1985 to February 1987) was mainly due to their shared interest in an orderly depreciation of the overvalued dollar (Plaza) and avoiding a hard landing (Louvre) in the absence of strong domestic policy adjustment. To some extent, international cooperation was a substitute for domestic paralysis. Policy coordination took place, because US diplomacy skillfully used the leverage of dollar politics (the story is told by Funabashi, 1988; see also Destler and Henning, 1989; Nau, 1990; Dobson, 1991; Gyothen and Volcker, 1992; Henning, 1994; Bergsten and Henning, 1996). Since then, cooperation has been somewhat sporadic. The most recent example of coordinated intervention in the foreign-exchange market appears to have been in summer 1995, to strengthen the dollar, especially against the yen, which was overvalued at the time (Bergsten and Henning, 1996, p. 32f.).

The idea of target zones was originally developed by the British economist John Williamson in the early 1980s and refined later on (Williamson, 1982, 1985 and 1994). It has been promoted by the former Chairman of the US Federal Reserve System, Paul A. Volcker, in particular, and had been studied by the Bretton Woods Commission, which he chaired, in the early 1990s. The latter had already proposed closer cooperation in international monetary policy under the auspices of the IMF (Bretton Woods Commission 1994). Volcker himself advocated, in a 1995 speech, a model based on target zones with the following features: Central rates based on equilibrium values for the currencies; intervention rates expressed as a fairly wide range of values, say of plus or minus ten percent, around these central rates, and willingness to intervene at or near the margins and to modify monetary policies in support of the exchange rate objective. The IMF should be involved in reaching consensus on the equilibrium values and be prepared to propose adjustments at its own initiative (Volcker, 1995). Also, the Bretton Woods Commission hoped that if the central banks established the credibility of their intentions, international capital flows would have a stabilizing effect.

Many economists, however, have voiced doubts as to whether credible commitments would be possible at all, given the domestic preoccupations of governments; whether knowledge was sufficient to reach agreement on the fundamental equilibrium value of exchange rates, given that no consensus exists regarding the factors that determine a country's permanent savings-investment balance; and whether such a system could be viable or whether it would probably be instable due to destabilizing capital flows and speculative attacks in a world of very high capital mobility.

The German government has evidently been influenced by the target zone idea. In late February 1999, the 'T-word' was dropped from German official rhetoric, and with the resignation of Oskar Lafontaine from public office, the main proponent left the scene. The French government expressed similar, but less far-reaching views. Whereas Mr. Strauss-Kahn echoed the call for more exchange rate stability in the trilateral relationship, he did not call for a formal target-zone system, but for strengthened multilateral surveillance under the auspices of the IMF, whose Managing Director Michel Camdessus has also supported changes to the exchange rate system. French President Jacques Chirac, however, on a trip to the United States in February 1999, supported the establishment of some formal system to manage the dollar and the euro. The German and French government's initial elan, however, has been considerably dampened, as not much backing was forthcoming from other EU countries. Of course, the response from central bankers in the ESCB and the Fed has been negative. Japanese government officials, however, made several statements supporting changes to the system. Both the British government and the Bank of England remained cool on these ideas.

Obviously, the stance of the Clinton administration has been of great importance, and Secretary of the Treasury Robert Rubin has argued in public that establishing a formal exchange rate system for the dollar, the euro, and the yen is not seen as being desirable for the USA. As the US government is opposed to any changes to the system of floating exchange rates, Uncle Sam finally had to say no to Europe's center-left governments. In a way not seen since the breakdown of the Bretton Woods system, governments from the US, Europe, and Japan have been divided over principles of global exchange rate policy.

The European Central Bank

ECB President Wim Duisenberg explained in public the policy stance of the ECB on international monetary policy issues. He stressed that the exchange of views on financial issues at the global level should be simplified by having just three major currency blocs. Target zones, however, could conflict with the maintenance of price stability and could, therefore, not be sustainable. He said that exchange rate flexibility among the major currency blocs was important as business cycles in the United States and the euro area were not necessarily fully synchronized. Furthermore, global capital mobility would probably render any attempt at setting target zones ineffective and, moreover, could potentially lead to a situation in which the ECB would have to raise interest rates in order to support the exchange rate of a depreciating euro even though this would conflict with a growth objective. Mr. Duisenberg explained, however, that the ECB would not ignore the external value of the euro; it certainly would not want an overvalued currency. He also emphasized that the ECB will take a neutral stance towards an international role of the euro. Maintaining price level stability in EMU was a necessary condition for the international recognition and use of the euro, Mr. Duisenberg emphasized (Duisenberg, 1998, 1999). Other members of the Board of the ECB have expressed very similar views on the subject matter (see Deutsch, 1999b).

The European Commission

Commensurate with its contested role in external monetary affairs of the euro area, the European Commission so far has restrained itself in the debate on global monetary issues. In publications, it has argued that the creation of EMU facilitate international policy coordination and global stability (European Commission, 1997, 1990). The Commission also began in 1998 to consult governments of the prospective euro area on methods of assessing exchange rate developments in order to create consensus on fair values. The Commission's role in decision-making on international monetary matters is still unclear. Probably, it will continue to monitor the macroeconomic policies and performances of the member states and comment on foreign exchange-related matters, but it is unlikely that the Commission will risk adopting a high profile or provoke a conflict with the ECB or key governments, as its mandate is too limited in this field.

Private-Sector Interests

The external value of the euro as well as the exchange rate system are of obvious interest to producers of tradeables, non-tradeables, and financial firms in the euro area (see Frieden, in this volume, and Henning, 1994). Producers of tradeables typically favor a currency with a good record in terms of price level stability and a fair or undervalued exchange rate, while financial firms typically favor both price stability and a strong currency. Producers of non-tradeables, by contrast, tend to favor a strong exchange rate and macroeconomic expansion, even if the goal of price stability has to be compromised. Private-sector groups tend not to be too concerned with the choice of exchange rate systems, and there is considerable evidence that even with respect to EMU itself, support of big firms and banks was as much political as inspired by economic self-interest (Moravcsik, 1998, chapter 6).

As long as the euro-dollar exchange rate does not seem to be severely misaligned, producers of tradeables will probably abstain from the policy debate on trilateral monetary issues. If a substantial appreciation of the euro against the dollar occurs in 1999 or 2000, some export-oriented groups, however, can be expected to lobby for changes. As German exporters, which—among euro area companies—have a substantial share in extra-

European exports, have often had to cope with an appreciating domestic currency and have only very rarely put severe pressure on the Bundesbank, it is unlikely, however, that the exchange rate of the euro will become heavily politicized.

Policy Issues in 1999

At the start of EMU, participating governments had to decide how they should be represented in international fora, in particular in the G-7 and the International Monetary Fund.

Representation in the Group of Seven (G-7)

The regulations in the Treaty on representation of the countries participating in Stage 3 of EMU are restricted to only a few remarks regarding decision-making, laid down in Article 111 (109), § 4 (Treaty of Amsterdam on European Union). The latter stipulates that '[...], the Council shall, on a proposal from the Commission and after consulting the ECB, acting by a qualified majority decide on the position of the Community at international level as regards issues of particular relevance to economic and monetary union and, acting unanimously, decide its representation [...]'.

Not all EU member states have taken part in Stage 3 from the outset so it was necessary to agree on interim rules. The EU Commission recently submitted to the European Council a proposal for this transition, which was approved by the Euro-11 group of ministers of economics and finance at a meeting on November 30, 1998. The proposal was officially adopted at the Vienna summit on December 12, 1998, and has in the meantime been submitted to the relevant international bodies since then (see Table 1).

The following procedure has been decided: Meetings of the G-7 Finance Ministers' and Governors' Group will, additionally, be attended by the president of the Council or the president of the Euro-11 Council (if the president is a national of a member country not participating in EMU). In that case, the president of the Euro-11 group will come from the country holding the EU presidency in the following six months. In a transition phase, one of the three ministers of the euro area countries permanently represented in the G-7—Germany, France and Italy—will provide support for the president of the Euro-11 Council for the sake of greater continuity. The ECB president as well as a Commission representative is also to act as consultant in G-7 meetings. It has not been laid down whether the Commission will be represented by its president or a commissioner. This decision will be taken independently by the Commission. Apparently, the central bank governors of Germany, France and Italy will continue to participate. They did not waive their right to take part. Generally speaking, it should be noted that the Euro-11 group may only coordinate positions but may not take decisions for the entire European Union in international talks.

Table 1: Presidency of the European Council and Euro-11 Group

		First half year	Second half year
1999	Ecofin	Germany	Finland
	Euro-11	Germany	Finland
2000	Ecofin	Portugal	France
	Euro-11	Portugal	France
2001	Ecofin	Sweden	Belgium
	Euro-11	Belgium	Belgium
2002	Ecofin	Spain	Denmark
	Euro-11	Spain	Greece (1) or Denmark (2) or Italy (3)
2003	Ecofin	Greece	Italy
	Euro-11	Greece or Italy	Italy

1) Greece joins EMU, Denmark does not; 2) if Denmark joins; 3) neither Greece nor Denmark joins EMU.
Source: European Council

The non-EU partners have already agreed to ECB President Wim Duisenberg attending G-7 Ministers' and Governors' meetings. He will be able to comment on issues regarding, for example, multilateral surveillance in the framework of the IMF and on exchange rate issues. The governments of the USA, Canada, and Japan, at the time of the writing (March 1999), had not publicly commented on the other proposals. However, the participation of a Commission representative seems to be a controversial issue. The G-7 meetings below the top level will thus include five European central bank governors, four or five finance ministers, possibly one Commission representative, and the US, Canadian and Japanese central bank governors and finance ministers. This means a widening of the circle of participants by up to three persons. A maximum of eleven Europeans could be present, compared with six non-Europeans. EMU has evidently not led to simpler representation but to a more complicated structure. Even though this is unlikely to obstruct the G-7's ability to function, it has already induced the other countries to object to such 'overrepresentation' of the Europeans. Participation by the EMU central bank governors could be reviewed and possibly suspended, reducing the 'European delegation' by three persons initially (four once the UK has joined). However, there is no indication as to who could bring about such a decision—apart from the three EMU central bank governors themselves. Ultimately, the Commission representative also seems dispensable. In the run-up to a G-7 meeting on February 20, 1999, the German government respected the US government's opposition to participation of a Commission official in the meeting and did not invite him for the full meeting. This would have been in full compliance with the Vienna declaration of the euro area governments, in which a participation of the Commission in G-7 meetings as a consultant was proposed to non-euro area partners. The Commission declined to participate at all under these circumstances. It remains to be seen whether the G-7 partners can agree on a working role for the Commission.

The Council has sought to keep the transition regulation as closely as possible to the status quo. A permanent solution will have to be found, at the latest, once the four pre-ins have joined. This solution will have to aim more strongly at the functioning of the G-7, at efficient representation, and at subsidiarity. In the medium to long run, national central bank governors from the four European G-7 states as well as a Commission representative may not need to participate any longer.

All these institutional issues are not as important as the substantive matters. In the final economic analysis, the fiscal policy stance of the large economies in the euro area, the monetary policy stance and the exchange rate policy of the ECB are essential. On monetary and exchange rate policies, the ECB president can be expected to speak at international meetings, on fiscal policies the respective national ministers of finance. Widely diverging fiscal policy stances of the governments of the large economies, a serious conflict between expansionary fiscal and restrictive monetary policies, or a conflict between some governments and the ECB over the external value of the euro or the global exchange rate system would undermine any attempt at a coherent representation of the euro area's interests. The European Commission and the ECB will, of course, continue to provide macroeconomic surveillance of participating countries and inform governments of potential divergence problems. As long as an appropriate policy-mix is pursued and the euro does not seem to be severely misaligned, external representation will not cause headaches for euro area's monetary diplomats. It may, however, create some internal conflicts between those governments who are represented in the G-7 and those who are not.

Representation of the Euro Area at the IMF

At the Vienna meeting of the European Council, agreement was also reached on proposals as to how EMU should be represented in the IMF. The ECB had already been granted an observer position at the Executive Board and has nominated Robert Raymond, a long-time former French and ECB monetary official, to represent the euro area in all discussions in the IMF of relevance to the euro area. The views of the EU or EMU are to be presented there by the Executive Director of the country holding the Euro-11 presidency, assisted by a Commission representative. The much more fundamental issue, i.e. whether euro area governments would even start to consider to work on a common approach towards IMF policy issues and make use of their combined voting power, which even surpasses that of the US—Euro-11 members have 22.15 percent of votes, the US has 17.85 percent—has not been addressed so far. Nor have the euro area's IMF members seriously considered to go for a consolidation of national quotas into a European one (Henning, 1997; Thygesen, 1997; Polak, 1997).

External Trade Policy-Making: Experiences and Lessons

As recent policy episodes do not provide much insight into the factors that may shape the institutional structure of exchange rate policy-making of the euro area, it may be useful to reconsider the experience in trade policy in a highly abstract fashion (based on Deutsch, 1999a). However, a caveat has to be made at the beginning. The most significant difference between trade and monetary policy is speed. Markets for goods and services do not react very fast to trade policy decisions, and trade negotiations typically go on for a couple of years until a major breakthrough is achieved and markets are liberalized. Financial markets are very dynamic and fast. Therefore, in international monetary policy the capacity to act, organizational clarity, and very quick interaction between markets and policies are all very important. Nevertheless, some general aspects have to be considered in both fields, namely the extent of delegation, the allocation of political power and authority, and the flexibility of external negotiators (see for a similar analysis Kahler, 1995).

The politics of trade policy in the history of European integration has always been a three-level bargaining game (Putnam, 1988; Evans et al., 1993) that typically resulted in managed trade liberalization. National domestic lobbying of pressure groups, complex intergovernmental bargaining in Brussels with a significant role to play for the Commission, and international talks had to be managed by the trade commissioner and key governments. Germany and France have been the leaders of the two camps of 'open regionalists' and 'closed regionalists' among member states, i.e. those favoring both internal and external liberalization and those supporting common market projects but not necessarily also external liberalization. In that three-level bargaining game, the Commission would act as a broker mediating the demands of foreign governments for market opening or rule making, the distributional conflicts within the Community, and the interests of the private sectors involved. Constraints originating in domestic politics often could only be resolved by finding complex distributional formula in international negotiations.

Depending on the overall policy orientation of governments and EC bureaucrats, policy was either brought consistently onto an inward-orientated track, as in the mid-1970s, or directed towards market economics and external opening, as in the 1980s and 1990s.

Institutional structures played an important role in the evolution of trade policy in Brussels. As member states had already formally delegated powers to the Commission in the Treaty of Rome, the extent of effective delegation has been contested between the principals and the agent ever since. Also, it has been questioned how the shared authority of governments and the Commission could be brought to full use, and how flexibility in international negotiations could be assured. I will consider each issue in turn.

Delegation

The founding fathers of the EC envisaged a community which would evolve into a customs union and thus have a common trade policy towards third countries. In Articles 110-116 of the Treaty of Rome, the set-up of the Common Commercial Policy of the EEC was laid down. In practice, functional delegation of negotiating powers to the Commission actually occurred as long ago as in the Kennedy Round of the GATT (1963-67) even in advance of the full transition to the customs union as much by design as by default (Preeg, 1970). As the Commission representative effectively came to speak on behalf of the Community in these years, a system evolved that put governments closely behind the Commission. A special machinery developed, the Article 111- or 113-Committee (referring to Article 111, later 113, Treaty of Rome) comprising national representatives who consult on the matters and bring national preferences to bear on a Community stance. In large international negotiations, in particular in the multilateral trade negotiations under the auspices of the GATT, the member states would initially give a broad mandate to the Commission and prioritize issues. They would typically leave it to the Commission to work on specific concepts, to negotiate with trading partners, and to reach agreements that could be ratified at home as well as abroad. However, the Commission was never granted much leeway or came close to complete autonomy, which the ECB enjoys at least in internal monetary policy, if not in exchange rate matters. Rather, the governments tried to influence the process and the substance as much as possible. The power of the Commission, in turn, resulted from its good knowledge of preferences of trading partners, of governments and private sector groups as well as from its ability to broker compromises when distributional conflicts threatened to prevent efficient agreements.

Authority

The authority of Commission representatives and of the European Communities in international trade fora was questioned by foreign governments more than once in the course of forty years of policy-making in the context of the Common Commercial Policy, which was supposed to work along the principle of qualified majority voting but in essence relied on consensus in important matters. Often, a single government could block significant moves at the international table and undermine the authority of trade negotiators who were unable to reach mutually beneficial agreements in international talks. In difficult trade policy fields subject to exclusive Community powers (mixed agreements are another political matter), the Commission negotiators often had to act without the clear guidance of a substantive mandate of their principals, the governments, and risked to interpret their freedom of maneuver too generously. If trade commissioners could not marshal the internal support of key governments or important lobbies, trade partners had to learn that the Community had not arrived at a joint position at all, or that agreements reached at the international table would later be broken in the capitals of the member states. The experience of the Community trade negotiators in the farm trade talks in the Uruguay Round of the GATT may serve as an example in that regard (see Deutsch, 1999a: Chapter V for a detailed political history). Usually, however, governments could not themselves readily substitute for Commission leadership in international negotiations. In these cases, 'Europe' was short on authority, and stalemate prevailed.

Flexibility

Closely related to the issue of political authority is policy and bargaining flexibility. In the course of international negotiations, which often span a period of several years, flexibility in adjusting policy positions to new information or changed circumstances is essential. There are two ways of achieving policy flexibility under conditions of functional delegation and shared political authority. Either, principals must be able and willing to change mandates of the agent quite often and thereby adjust tasks to circumstances, or functional delegation must be strengthened up to a point where agents, on the basis of constitutionally clarified mandates, can react flexibly to new information, to changing positions by negotiation partners, or to radical changes in economic circumstances. In the trade policy-making of the European Communities, governments, largely for reasons of domestic politics, often preferred to give a circumscribed mandate to the Commission and to manage the institution on a short leash rather than to extend a broad mandate and let policy evolve from the center. The serious backdrop of that approach, however, was that the Council more than once proved unable to solve internal distributional problems and to up-date mandates and instructions as deemed appropriate or necessary from a Community point of view. As a consequence, Commission negotiators often had their hands tied and could not engage in give-and-take bargaining with foreign governments.

The machinery for foreign trade policy-making, therefore, worked only well under conditions of great consensus or in the absence of distributional conflicts among member states, or their proto-coalitions. Then, the Commission was given a meaningful mandate. Governments were willing to support Community negotiators and share political responsibility. And, the Commission negotiators could strike beneficial bargains with diplomats of third countries. At times, particularly in the mid-1990s, the European Union could even provide trade policy leadership and help to bring negotiations on post-Uruguay Round trade issues such as financial services or telecommunications equipment to a successful conclusion (Deutsch and Speyer, 1998). Under conditions of internal political conflicts, which may originate from domestic concerns in large member states or from intergovernmental distributional concerns, external trade policy-making often became a very difficult endeavor.

Implications for External Monetary Policy-Making

Insufficient delegation, political authority more often divided rather than shared, and limited flexibility in responding to new opportunities or challenges did not prevent trade policy from scoring some big points for European welfare and foreign policy, but repeatedly undermined the credibility and reliability of the European Union or its institutional predecessors in world trade negotiations and international affairs in general.

What are the lessons to be learnt from trade policy-making in external monetary policy-making? I will again proceed in the same logical order.

Delegation

In exchange rate policy, things are somewhat different because governments have de facto transferred wide powers to the ECB and only retained powers on formal exchange rate systems and intermediate-range policy matters such as providing 'general orientations'. In practice, the ECB will enjoy almost full freedom to act. Functional delegation of powers to the common institution is ensured. It is also very unlikely that governments will be able to reach a consensus on changing the Treaty in that regard, as unanimity would be required. The German and French governments' desire to have a say in the setting of exchange rate policy of the euro area vis-à-vis the USA and Japan cannot distract from the fact that they are demandeurs in this regard. They would need to muster 62 votes out of a total of 87 votes in the Council for establishing 'general orientations', a very high threshold. As the representatives of the ECB seem to be inclined to interpret their mandate of safeguarding price level stability as implying non-interference of governments on exchange rates, a compromise between the ECB and governments on exchange rate management does not seem to be in the offing. For believers in central bank independence, the strength of the ECB should be a good sign. However, in the long run the ECB must take the broader notion of political support into account. In case of sustained criticism of exchange rate policy and/or developments by constituent governments, the ECB may find it difficult to garner public support for its stance.

In my personal view, the Luxembourg Council compromise provides a good political basis for strengthening functional delegation. As the governments will not suddenly stop worrying about exchange rates—nor should they do so!—it is essential that the Commission, the ECB, the euro area governments and the IMF work hard and closely together so as to better model and forecast fundamental exchange rates, agree on fair values within rather broad boundaries, given the limited state of economic knowledge, and help to de-politicize the matter in normal times. There is no need to publish the results, but a clear need to avoid highly controversial public discussions that might unsettle the financial markets and create problems for the ECB's monetary policy.

In the long run, changes to the floating rate system may deserve serious reconsideration. European governments will have to play a prominent role in setting up a global exchange rate system that better bridges the conflicting needs of systemic stability and exchange rate adjustment. In the current political and economic environment, fundamental changes do not seem to lie in the interest of the USA and are therefore not likely to be enacted. Also, a demanding formal system does not seem to be feasible right now.

Authority

Political authority of the euro area representatives will be essential for the standing of the euro area in international monetary diplomacy, in public opinion and financial markets. Also, it will determine the credibility of the ECB's monetary policy as well as of that institution itself. Given functional delegation but also the contested mandate of the ECB in international monetary policy, political authority will have to be shared among governments and the central bank, in particular its president. Whereas the personal standing of the ECB president has not been in doubt at any time since he assumed responsibility, a serious gap in intergovernmental coordination on the matter has come to the surface. If governments cannot reach agreement on common positions in international monetary affairs, they cannot achieve political authority. It is unlikely that a German-French compromise position will be a workable substitute for a common position which has been reached at least by qualified majority voting, if not by consensus. Coordination only among Germany and France will not be very effective, because other governments might object to such behavior and the ECB would find it difficult to deal with a politically prominent minority position of governments. If (some) governments and the ECB cannot reach a common view—as for example in the debate on target zones—the ECB will have to bear the entire burden, and its president must invest his personal authority.

In the Group of Seven, there is also the problem that not all representatives of the euro area will be sufficiently empowered to take decisions. The question as to who can authoritatively represent the position of the single currency area in G-7 meetings has been solved only formally. Initially, the ECB will enjoy the authority resulting from its responsibilities, provided a majority can be found on the ECB Governing Council for a certain position. By contrast, the Euro-11 finance ministers, who may shape national fiscal policies but cannot formulate a binding Community position on internal and external monetary matters, or the Euro-11 president, will be no more than the euro area's ambassadors. Decisions may only be taken by the complete Council. Political authority in issues relating to EMU's external representation will remain fragmented for the time being.

Nor will political authority result from formal arrangements such as the Vienna proposal for external representation. The fact that governments agreed to have the president of the Euro-11 group represent the euro area in international fora but, in case of a member state not participating in G-7 meetings, only with the assistance of France, Germany, or Italy, speaks for itself. It is obvious that formal structures should not diverge too drastically from underlying power structures. As governments have openly acknowledged, providing political authority in external affairs will necessitate the close coordination of key governments as well as the accommodation of the interests of smaller or less influential member states. Also, it is unlikely that formal qualified majority voting on international monetary matters will be tried at all. Rather, the functional equivalent of a 113 Committee in trade policy will have to be created among finance officials in international monetary policy as well. In the Vienna declaration, the heads of government and state openly acknowledged the need to create a new machinery.

Flexibility

If an international financial emergency or an exchange rate policy issue requires rapid and coordinated action on the part of the euro area policy-makers, the flexibility of the euro area authorities in reacting to such challenges will be crucial. A major financial crisis or a strong and sudden misalignment of the euro's external value may then prompt immediate foreign exchange interventions, interest rate changes, or at least public rhetoric signaling to the markets that the ECB is about to act. Financial markets are very dynamic and fast. Often, there is little time for political authorities to conduct protracted negotiations on what to do and how to react. The ECB will not always have the time to wait for governments to come up with a view, but will have to take immediate action.

It cannot be taken for granted that the governments will always accept that fact of life but will try to bring their influence to bear on decision-making in the ECB. In that case, it is conceivable that the Commission and a large number of member states, which do not necessarily have to form the required majority in the Council, will push for action or for the formulation of 'orientations', while a minority in the Council and the ECB do not see any need to do so. Hence, political conflicts between the governments over the euro's external value or internal monetary policy to affect it cannot be ruled out.

International coordination of fiscal policies may also seem desirable, as both fiscal and monetary policies affect the exchange rate. Thus, the governments of the euro area face the task of adjusting policies in light of the combined impact of these actions on the euro-dollar exchange rate. The governments of the large economies will then have to work closely together.

The evolution of the relationship of monetary and fiscal policy of the euro area, and of national governments and the ECB, will in no small part determine the overall success of the EMU endeavor as well as the journey of the euro on foreign exchange markets. The making of exchange rate policy for the euro area will be only one important role in that unfolding drama that has to be learned from scratch, both by the ECB and by the participating governments.

It must be assumed that the euro area's decision-making bodies will only be able to agree on fast, internationally coordinated measures if a broad consensus is reached on exchange rate policy among the member states and the ECB. In view of the history of controversy between France and Germany it is unlikely that the two countries will be of one mind on fundamental issues, even though they have drawn much closer together in the recent past. The flexibility of the euro area's representatives is thus likely to be severely limited. Given the complex internal coordination requirements, a flexible position of these representatives in G-7 talks or other fora can only be expected (for the transition phase and afterwards) if all indicators call for rapid action and no serious internal conflict has to be solved. As a consequence, the G-7 will likely become even less attractive as a forum for trilateral policy coordination, particularly for the non-European participants.

Conclusions

At least at the outset of EMU, its external monetary policy—like the Common Commercial Policy of the EU—suffers from insufficient functional delegation, divided political authority, and limited flexibility. For a politically and economically heterogeneous entity, this is hardly a surprising diagnosis. Nor is it necessarily all to the disadvantage of the euro area. Standard bargaining theory offers some insights in that regard (Raiffa 1982). Insufficient delegation and limited flexibility will enhance the 'distributive' bargaining power of the euro area, but reduce the 'integrative' bargaining power and the ability to act. Whether this is 'good' or 'bad' from an economic or political point of view, depends on the circumstances. The euro area's representatives will, for example, find it even easier than in the past to ignore US demands for fiscal expansion, a course which they often do not want to follow. In hard times, however, the drawbacks may well make themselves felt early on.

However, the trade policy experience provides for some comfort. EC trade negotiators and their principals have managed to sustain an open world trading system despite their internal institutional shortcomings. To some extent, the rigid institutional set-up has also helped to prevent far-reaching policy reversals toward protectionism. Politically, however, negotiating on trade was often more treacherous for partners in the world economy than trading itself. Similarly, it will not be particularly easy to deal with 'Europe' in international monetary affairs. Again, as long as the ECB, with the help of member states' economic policies, manages to control inflation in the euro area, the internal pre-conditions for international monetary and exchange rate stability can be met. As is well known, this is only a necessary, but not a sufficient condition. Foreign exchange markets may in the long run reflect economic and monetary fundamentals, in the short run serious over—or undershooting of exchange rates can and does occur. Often, this seriously disrupts economic activity, sets perverse incentives, and creates conflicts.

On balance, the prospects for international monetary cooperation are not as bad as analysis of the institutional short-comings of the euro area's external monetary policy-making machinery would suggest. Trilateral macroeconomic cooperation may receive a boost from coordination efforts on the part of the Federal Reserve, the ECB, and, possibly, also the Bank of Japan. This form of quiet cooperation could become increasingly effective. The three central bank governors will be able to tackle questions such as the 'appropriate' euro-dollar exchange rate in a more pragmatic manner, away from the public eye and uninhibited by political disputes and official parlance. However, the process of central bank cooperation will not always reflect the preferences or compromise positions of European governments or their partners. Moreover, the dollar-yen exchange rate may remain subject to more intense political pressures and economic fluctuations. It may turn out that the political influence of the US Treasury Secretary or the Japanese Finance Minister on their respective central banks regarding exchange rate policy may even exceed the combined influence of the ministers on the ECB.

In rather clear cases of misalignment, Europe's monetary authorities—the ECB as well as EMU-11 governments—may well have to come to grips with responses that might even have to be coordinated with the United States or Japan. The specter of a rapid substantial appreciation of the euro is still there, for example. In these circumstances, the euro area authorities may well surprise their partners with a common position and a readiness for joint action. The set of interest rate cuts in the US and in Europe in the autumn of 1998 was partly geared to the business cycle in the US and to the required convergence of interest rates in the states participating in EMU, but also partly a response to heightened financial uncertainty. In Europe, this was even achieved prior to EMU and to common monetary policy-making in the ECB. Moreover, the ECB lowered rates on April 8, 1999—the refinancing rate was cut by 50 basis points to 2.5 percent and the deposit and marginal lending facilities were lowered as well—as the euro area's economy showed little inflationary pressures and slower growth, even though some depreciation of the euro against the dollar had already taken place. The ECB demonstrated its resolve to act in accordance with domestic priorities, but not on fears of external weakness.

There is no particularly good reason why the ECB should not be able to cooperate with the Fed and the Bank of Japan, or others, if required. Neither does EMU put an end to international policy coordination, nor is it a fresh start to global governance of exchange rates. Economic cooperation and mutual policy adjustment will continue to be in the occasional interest of governments in the US, Japan, and Europe, but institutional structures in the euro area are not yet designed for effective international coordination. If a lesson can be learnt from forty years of trade policy-making, it is this: The way to more complete functional delegation, to joint political authority, and to full-scale flexibility in the international monetary policy will be a very, very long one. It will require political unification to a far greater extent than envisaged anywhere in Europe at present, but that does not mean that it will not eventually evolve.

Note

1. The views of the author do not necessarily reflect views of Deutsche Bank Research.
   I am indebted to Bernhard Speyer for comments and to Claudia Frenzel for correcting my English.

References

Bergsten, Fred C., and C. Randall Henning. 1996. *Global Economic Leadership and the Group of Seven.* Washington, D.C.: Institute for International Economics.

Bognar, Zoltan. 1997. *Europäische Währungsintegration und Außenwirtschaftsbeziehungen.* Baden-Baden: Nomos.

Bretton Woods Commission. 1994. *Bretton Woods: Looking to the Future.* Washington, D.C.

Deutsch, Klaus Günter. 1999a. *The Politics of Freer Trade in Europe. Three-level Games in the Common Commercial Policy of the EU, 1985-1997.* Münster and Hamburg: Lit. New York: St. Martin's Press.

Deutsch, Klaus Günter. 1999b. 'External Representation and Exchange-Rate Policy of the Euro Area.' *EMU Watch,* no. 64. Frankfurt/M.: Deutsche Bank Research.

Deutsch, Klaus Günter, and Axel Siedenberg. 1999. 'Der Euro im internationalen Finanz- und Währungssystem.' In Rolf Caesar and Hans-Eckart Scharrer, eds., *Die Europäische Währungsunion. Regionale und globale Herausforderungen.* Bonn, pp. 304-324.

Deutsch, Klaus Günter, and Bernhard Speyer. 1998. 'Multilateral Trade Policy: A Post-Millenium Agenda.' *Bulletin,* no. 4, Frankfurt/M.: Deutsche Bank Research.

Deutsche Bank Research. 1998. *Europe's New Currency.* Frankfurt/M.

Deutsche Bank Research. 1999. 'ECB Interest Rate Outlook.' *EMU Watch,* no. 66. Frankfurt/M.

Destler, I.M., and C. Randall Henning. 1989. *Dollar Politics. Exchange Rate Policymaking in the United States.* Washington, D.C.: Institute for International Economics.

Dobson, Wendy. 1991. *Economic Policy Coordination: Requiem or Prologue?* Washington, D.C.: Institute for International Economics.

Duisenberg, Willem F. 1998. *The International Role of the Euro and the ESCB's Monetary Policy.* Speech, November 20.

Duisenberg, Willem F. 1999. *The Single European Monetary Policy.* Speech, University Hohenheim, February 9.

Emminger, Otmar. 1986. *D-Mark, Dollar, Währungskrisen.* Stuttgart: DVA.

European Commission, Directorate General Economic and Financial Affairs. 1990. 'One Market, One Money.' *European Economy,* no. 44.

European Commission, Directorate General Economic and Financial Affairs. 1997. 'External Aspects of Economic and Monetary Union.' Euro Papers, no. 1, July, SEK (97) 803.

Evans, Peter B., Harold K. Jacobsen, and Robert D. Putnam, eds. 1993. *Double-Edged Diplomacy. International Bargaining and Domestic Politics.* Berkeley, Los Angeles, London: University of California Press.

Funabashi, Yoichi. 1988. *Managing the Dollar: From the Plaza to the Louvre.* Washington, D.C.: Institute for International Economics.

Gros, Daniel, and Niels Thygesen. 1992. *European Monetary Integration. From the European Monetary System to the European Monetary Union.* London: Longman.

Hartmann, Philipp. 1998. *Currency Competition and Foreign Exchange Markets.* Cambridge: Cambridge University Press.

Hayes, J. P. 1993. *Making Trade Policy in the European Community.* New York: St. Martin's Press.

Henning, C. Randall. 1994. *Currencies and Politics in the United States, Germany, and Japan.* Washington, D.C.: Institute for International Economics.

Henning, C. Randall. 1997. *Cooperating with Europe's Monetary Union.* Washington, DC: Institute for International Economics.

Kahler, Miles. 1995. *Regional Futures and Transatlantic Economic Relations.* New York: Council on Foreign Relations Press for the ECSA.

Kenen, Peter B. 1995. *Economic and Monetary Union in Europe. Moving Beyond Maastricht.* Cambridge: Cambridge University Press.

Kenen, Peter B. 1998. 'EMU and Transatlantic Economic Relations.' HWWA-Diskussionspapier 60. Hamburg.

McNamara, Kathleen R. 1998. *The Currency of Ideas. Monetary Politics in the European Union.* Ithaca and New York: Cornell University Press.

Moravcsik, Andrew. 1998. *The Choice for Europe. Social Purpose and State Power from Messina to Maastricht.* Ithaca and New York: Cornell University Press.

Nau, Henry R. 1990. *The Myth of America's Decline. Leading the World Economy into the 1990s.* Oxford, New York: Oxford University Press.

Polak, Jacques. 1997. 'The IMF and Its EMU Members.' In Paul R. Masson, Thomas H. Krueger, and Bart G. Turtelboom, eds., *EMU and the International Monetary System.* Washington, D.C.: IMF, pp. 491-511.

Preeg, Ernest H. 1970. *Traders and Diplomats. An Analysis of the Kennedy Round of Negotiations under the General Agreement on Tariffs and Trade.* Washington, D.C.: The Brookings Institution.

Putnam, Robert D. 1988. 'Diplomacy and Domestic Politics: The Logic of Two-Level Games.' *International Organization,* 42, 3, pp. 427-460.

Raiffa, Howard. 1982. *The Art and Science of Negotiation.* Cambridge: Harvard University Press.

Schöppenthau, Philipp von. 1999. *Die Europäische Union als handelspolitischer Akteur. Die Textilverhandlungen der GATT-Uruguay Runde.* Wiesbaden: Gabler.

Schuknecht, Ludger. 1992. *Trade Protection in the European Community.* Chur: Harwood Academic Publishers.

Thiel, Elke. 1999. 'WWU und transatlantische Beziehungen.' In Rolf Caesar and Hans-Eckart Scharrer, eds., *Die Europäische Währungsunion. Regionale und globale Herausforderungen.* Bonn, pp. 356-370.

Thygesen, Niels. 1997. 'Relations Among the IMF, the ECB, and the IMF's EMU Members.' In Paul R. Masson, Thomas H. Krueger, and Bart G. Turtelboom, eds., *EMU and the International Monetary System.* Washington, D.C.: IMF, pp. 512-530.

Ungerer, Horst. 1997. *A Concise History of European Monetary Integration. From EPU to EMU.* Westport, Connecticut and London: Quorum.

Williamson, John. 1982. 'Exchange Rates and Trade Policy.' In C. Fred Bergsten and William R. Cline, *Trade Policy in the 1980s.* Washington, D.C.: Institute for International Economics.

Williamson, John. 1985. *The Exchange Rate System.* Rev. ed. Washington, D.C.: Institute for International Economics.

Williamson, John. 1994. *Estimating Equilibrium Exchange Rates.* Washington, D.C.: Institute for International Economics.

Volcker, Paul A. 1995. The Quest for Exchange Rate Stability: Realistic or Quixotic? Speech, London, November 29.

9. REINFORCING EUROPEAN INTEGRATION TO PROMOTE THE EURO: A RANGE OF POLICY OPTIONS[1]

Pierre Maillet

Introduction

The theme of this conference is the euro as a stabilizing force in the international economic system. The subject can be approached from the outside, that is, the point of view of other currencies as well as the links with a new organization of the International Monetary System (IMS). This is effectively the approach chosen by the majority of the contributions. Or else one could take an internal perspective by examining how the organization and the functioning of the European Union (EU) could help fostering the international role of the euro given that the latter benefits from the strength of the European economy as well as from the external strategy of the European political union. This is the approach adopted here.

In terms of the activities and the proper functioning of the EU, the creation of the euro—unlike many previous innovations—is by no means a marginal operation. This time we are dealing with a real revolution that affects the citizens of the Union as a whole as much as the economic agents—business—as well as policy- and decision-makers, governments and the civil service. This observation is frequent, but rarely has anyone presented the totality of consequences in terms of a series of actions to be taken or patterns of behavior to be modified in order to enable the euro to function in the best possible way and generate all the benefits that one might expect from it.

In a stylized fashion, particular attention is being directed at the following points:

- to prevent this currency from being rejected by the social group whose customs and, more importantly, whose symbols it modifies;

- to ensure that all economic policy measures other than those of monetary policy are compatible and, where possible, synergetic with the existence of a single currency and a common monetary policy;
- to create and ensure the functioning of the political instruments or procedures that are necessary for this comprehensive European strategy in all its internal aspects.

The future role of the euro has both an internal and an external dimension. These two aspects will be dealt with in turn.

Initially, in the wake of the Werner Plan of 1971, the internal aspect was predominant because the objective was to put in place in an integral manner the single market, which was considered to be a source of more economic efficiency and thus higher living standards. To this end, one would have to induce the economic agents to consider the single market as their playing field and to take into account the whole European economic area for all decisions with medium- to long-term consequences (investment, important commercial orientations, cross-border partnerships). For all this it was vital to reduce or eliminate the exchange rate risk, either through a monetary union or preferably through a single currency.

Integration and the euro: two symmetric chains of cause and effect:

1. monetary union → good functioning of the single market
   → integration → economic advantages
2. single market → adaptations towards OCA (Optimum Currency Area) → good functioning of the euro → economic and political advantages

---

The aim was therefore to use the euro in the interest of European integration in terms of the first chain of cause and effect. However, it was gradually becoming clear that—in particular as a consequence of successive rounds of enlargement—the European territory did not as yet constitute an OCA, and that therefore there may occur asymmetric shocks in different countries or regions to which one can no longer react with differentiated monetary policies. Hence, one will have to resort to other instruments of economic policy, notably budgetary ones, if one really wants to avoid adjustments via the reduction of activity and therefore of employment, while at the same time ensuring the compatibility of these actions with monetary policy *per se*. But it is also desirable to speed up the transformation of the European economy towards an OCA by means of further integration (in the interest of the euro), according to the second chain of cause and effect.

Finally, for the euro to be fully accepted by the people and not to be considered as a scapegoat for economic failures, notably unemployment, there is now a need for a big effort in information and technical preparation, but in addition to these immediate tasks, there is above all a need—and without losing time—to balance the panoply of primary objectives and give economic union the same importance as monetary union.

Preparing the internal role of the euro thus necessitates comprehensive progress in the integration of the European economy. Section I analyses the possible structural actions: fiscality, the legal status of European business, coordination of Community or national measures and contrasting different national actions, which are deemed to be a large field for experiment.

In terms of macroeconomics (section II), it will be suggested to improve the search for compatibility of all elements of the policy mix, but also to commit to new paths, like the creation of a detailed coordination procedure for public budgets throughout the EU. This would combine budgetary reflections with reflections on the definition and implementation of structural policies.

The external aspect of a European currency is in relative terms more recent. For the last few decades, Europe has opened up to the rest of the world while this external environment simultaneously underwent a fundamental transformation, namely globalization.

For Europe, this means that it has become much more vulnerable to the technical, economic and political transformations of the rest of the world. Europe needs to learn how to resist these transformations but also how to influence them in a favorable way for both its population and those of third countries, thereby steering a course towards stability and peace. To this end, the euro will occupy the role of one of the major currencies in the world. For this role to be as important as the European ambitions, there is an obvious need for the conduct of monetary policy to be well adapted—as mentioned in many contributions—but there is also the need, perhaps most importantly, that a united Europe endows itself with a true foreign policy capacity and that it pays a great deal of attention to using its internal economic advantages in the interest of this foreign policy capacity. Section III is concerned with this.

The external economic openness as much as a world currency at Europe's disposal make the European economy more sensitive to world market forces, especially financial markets, which are very sensitive to real or apparent political action. This confers a particular importance upon a number of institutional aspects and the discipline on the part of the politicians of the EU in their speeches with an 'announcing effect' by which they have to exhibit a 'European spirit' so as to ensure a coherent impression that Europe exhibits to the outside world as for its own willingness and determination (section IV).

Finally, section V examines a highly delicate but crucial issue, which is frequently mentioned but perhaps in too discreet a manner. In the context of temporary differentiation in Europe, we will explore the possibilities of 'closer cooperation' that have been opened up by the Treaty of Amsterdam: to what extent should the EU progress temporarily in this direction?

Section I: A Panoply of Structural Actions Conducive to Integration

Three action paths can be envisaged:

- completion or, at least, progress towards realizing the transformations aimed at creating a genuine single market in the classical sense of the term;
- reinforcing the coordination of different structural action programs;
- taking better advantage of various policy experiments.

Completing the Single Market

The Convergence of Fiscal Policies

The general aim is to avoid different economic actions being modified by fiscal divergences in a way that would prevent maximum economic efficiency.

With regard to *indirect taxation*, keeping VAT rates at different levels prevents a shift to a principle of taxation rather than of production, which would make the single market identical in its fiscal nature relative to all the national markets, thereby eliminating—in the eyes of the economic agents—an important geographical differentiation between national territories, and thus facilitating the integration of productive systems. This explains the renewed efforts on the part of the European Commission towards further tax harmonization. The principle has been well established but periodically one shies away from implementing it.

Member state governments are certainly reticent for two reasons: first, since the beginning, some governments have feared that this operation would lead to a reduction in tax revenues due to the unequal extent of trade relations with their European partners. Second, and more seriously, the majority of governments are hardly enthusiastic in the face of yet further budgetary constraints.

The new constraints—without a proper economic justification[2]—introduced by the Stability Pact, which is now firmly part of EMU, reinforce the hesitation on the part of potential members to give up definitely all room for maneuver relative to that which constitutes the essential part of their tax revenues and which allows the maintenance of public expenditure at a level deemed politically necessary, while respecting the upper limits of public debt.

As for *direct taxation*, only if taxation on capital revenue is harmonized will there be a functioning of capital markets that is wholly favorable to economic efficiency via the appropriation of funds where it is economically most beneficial apart from taxation. This harmonization is also championed by politicians who wish to maintain in their countries substantial levels of taxation on this kind of revenue in the pursuit of social justice, and who do not want to be prevented from doing so by other countries that have lower tax rates, thus attracting funds. Agreement seems far from achieved but the Council of Ministers in its Ecofin form seems to become aware of the intensity of the problem.

In these two fields, the urgency for progress is manifest. It is also necessary for new approaches to figure in the *acquis communautaire* before enlargement, so that the candidate countries know exactly what they will be committed to and so that they prepare for the realities of tomorrow rather than for today's.

The Legal Rights of Business

The restructuring across borders of the European productive system has been hampered ever since the beginning of the single market by the absence of a European legal framework, which would allow mergers and restructuring to operate in a legally simple manner without having to resort to the expensive and discouraging solution of the joint creation of branches in the two countries of the mother companies. But the creation of a legal status for European business, which has been discussed for more than 25 years, is contentious regarding the question of how the employees' participation in decision-making is dealt with (whether to introduce a legal obligation of co-decision—*Mitbestimmung*); the obstacle is important, because it is the result of cultural differences between the various countries.

As this absence of legislation constitutes a serious hindrance to genuine economic integration, would it not be possible to take advantage of the stimulus provided by the euro in terms of attempts of cross-border restructuring in order to re-launch vigorously the idea of a legal status for European business?

Policy Coordination and Shaping of Structural Developments

The aim is two-fold: first of all, it seems appropriate to promote the compatibility and synergy of different public policy measures that take place at the supranational, national and sometimes regional levels, in order to strengthen the general competitiveness of the economy and, more specifically, to foster the development of production and of activities that play a key part in satisfying those needs that are deemed to have priority (e.g. in matters of health care) or in the evolution of technology. Second, it is also appropriate to strengthen the political independence of the EU in its geopolitical dialogue by making it less dependant upon external provisions for goods that play a strategic role; it is in this area that the implementation of a voluntary Common Foreign and Security Policy (CFSP) could make a decisive contribution, by making the potential power of the EU serve the interests of its external ambitions (including an important role for the euro).

It is certain that these very different elements are essentially the product of decisions made by business itself, under the influence of the market mechanisms, and the main task of public power in a market economy is to see to the unimpeded functioning of competition; but it would be naive to forget that in the current geopolitical situation, those governments that want to conduct a genuine foreign policy can ignore this orientation of the productive system; the existence of two-way relations between, on the one hand, the State Department and the Pentagon, and, on the other, several big American companies is well known, as well as the scope of reciprocal influence between MITI and a number of large conglomerates in Japan.

Europe for its part cannot abstain from behavioral practices analogous to those of its big competitors and thus to foster the development of strategic sectors. This is of course particularly valid for the entire defense industry, but also for a number of commodities that are of prime importance in the economic and technological development or that exert a decisive influence upon societal organization. Reinforcing coordination with a view to enhancing coherence should take place in three main areas.

R&D Policies

Even if statistically, Europe seems to make a big effort, one must be aware of the fact that the 30 percent of world spending on R&D activities are the sum of $8 + 7 + 5 + 3 + 2 + \ldots$ percent, which correspond to the national efforts that are, for a large part, duplicated. An improved coordination strategy is necessary to mitigate these duplications, to reinforce synergies, to devote to a number of fields or research areas a global effort allowing to overcome the minimum threshold that enables competitiveness vis-à-vis our big competitors. Reinforcing and coordinating multiple actions to the benefit of innovation (intense and rapid use of the fruits of research) is also necessary. Of course, this coordination has to be limited to the essential areas and topics.

Coordinating Physical Public Investment

Even if the limitedness of the Community budget rules out for a long time to come that it contributes substantially to financing physical public investment (with an economic aim like transport or communications infrastructure or with a social aim like hospital equipment), an improved coordination of national or regional programs, which are involved over the long term in certain areas, would without additional cost strengthen the efficiency of some of those investment projects to a considerable extent.

A Closer Coordination of Regional Policies

The aim of economic and social cohesion has priority in the eyes of the people concerned; this regionally balanced development is translated by an economic catching-up process of the 'laggard' regions and can contribute to the overall efficiency of the EU as well as to reducing the frequency of asymmetric shocks (cf. section II).

By now it is unanimously recognized that the single market and the four freedoms do not automatically foster the geographical convergence of levels of economic development, of income levels and of living standards. Yet the advent of the euro does not reduce these requirements. In terms of choice of location, the single currency will facilitate the comparison of costs and market potential of alternative locations, but it is difficult to say what the effect will be on the willingness to concentrate business in order to take advantage of economies of scale, on the expected role of the closeness of important markets, on the search to delocalize services by taking advantage of the possibilities offered by telecommunications. While it is debatable, *a priori* one can imagine a favorable effect on underdeveloped regions which lag behind but which are already experiencing some growth, and a disadvantageous effect for others in stagnation—in other words quite a varied impact. Regional policy in Europe must therefore be strengthened.

However, there is coexistence between regional policy conceived and implemented at the EU level, of which the main instrument is the Structural Fund, and regional policies conceived and implemented by member states, or at least some of them; to these have to be added development strategies if these have both strong competencies (as is the case with the German Länder, the three regions of the Kingdom of Belgium, and the Spanish autonomous provinces) and a certain budgetary autonomy.

It thus seems indispensable and indeed a priority (for it does not involve extra costs) to reinforce via a better coordination the synergy of the regional policies that are conducted at various geographical levels. The advent of the single currency could be an opportunity to improve (or to create) this kind of coordination between different decisional levels, at least via a strongly structured dialogue, in which the Regional Committee (that still seeks a role) could participate.

Comparing Experiments by Member States

This third path brings together all those actions that at first sight could seem very interesting in reinforcing economic integration in the EU, such as harmonizing legislation on social matters or communitarizing the negotiations of the social partners, the implementation of which clashes with the presence of strong social, political or cultural differences of the member states and therefore seems unrealistic (at least for some years), or even in contradiction with the willingness to maintain this diversity, which is one source of wealth of Europe. This juxtaposition of national actions should thus continue. It would even be interesting to consider this as a rich source of experimentation in strongly complex areas and to seek to extract value from it by comparing systematically the modalities and effects of national implementation, by taking due account of the psychological and sociological differences between member states, which have to be very prudent in attempts of transposition from one country to another.

We will thus present on two issues that are taken as examples some reflections which will be generalized thereafter.

Negotiations Between the Social Partners: Is a Communitarization Possible?

Negotiations between the social partners are a key element in determining income levels and therefore, indirectly, in achieving stable prices. In view of the objective pursued by the EU concerning inflation, the question arises whether it is not desirable that mechanisms for collective negotiations be put in place between two entities, on the one hand, trade unions that are able to speak for, and negotiate on behalf of, workers, and, on the other hand, employers' associations that are able to speak for, and negotiate on behalf of, business for the whole of the EU (or at least, for the members of Euroland).

Moreover, these two entities could engage in dialogue with the two public bodies that are responsible for public macroeconomic policy—the ECB and the Ecofin Council (or the Euro Council). This would be in some ways a slightly extended transposition of what happens more or less in a number of member states.

Although this idea is *a priori* attractive, it is hardly sociologically realistic because organizing negotiations between the social partners is in each country the product of a long historical evolution and a reflection of national culture. To this first difficulty must be added a second, more economic one. If the objective is to render the evolution of incomes more compatible with that of productivity, the reaction will be that the latter is not identical across member states, and that this is a good thing because it is the differences that—if they go in the right direction—will allow the gradual reduction of levels of differential development.

The idea to conduct at the European level income negotiations therefore seems totally premature. Instead, one has to consider positively the above-mentioned idea that a quadripartite dialogue is introduced institutionally or informally, between UNICE, ETUC, the Ecofin Council and the ECB. This would enrich the content and quality of debates and would introduce into the fundamental decision-making additional transparency, which the EU so desperately needs.

Protecting the Environment: Largely Decentralized Actions But Systematic Comparisons

The rules agreed upon in this area have an influence on the economic conditions for production in numerous sectors, notably in agriculture and industry, with concrete effects that can differ significantly across countries or regions, as a function of natural features, such as orography or population density. Does this entail a need for harmonization? Two considerations have to be weighed: first, in terms of environmental perturbations, one has to distinguish carefully between the irreversible effects and those that can be corrected on the one hand, and between localized and cross-border effects on the other hand. Second, the importance that is attached to these forms of degradation varies according to the population, as a function of national physical realities, but also according to the psychological attitude of the population vis-à-vis the environment.

If a common attitude is applied with respect to perturbations with irreversible and/or cross-border effects, in the other cases it is reasonable to accept a diversity of reactions in order to make actions acceptable (provided this reaction is not used as a voluntarist and indirect means to distort competition). It would also be necessary to cease to resort exclusively to public action, and to push for the development of concerted sectionalized patterns of behavior at the initiative of companies pertaining to that sector.

But if these initiatives are free to express themselves (public initiatives at the national or regional levels, or private initiatives across borders), it is important to verify the compatibility (and to ascertain that they are not used indirectly to distort competition), and, above all, to take advantage of the richness of knowledge that could be extracted from this abundance of experience by comparing it systematically.

The Systematic Resort to Conflictual Experience Rather than to Encouraged Harmonization in Europe

The preceding rationale can be extended to many other cases. Two cases will be reported here:

- in Europe, there is general agreement on the need for a *significant overhaul of the welfare state*. Even if the problems are the same across countries, the ways of tackling them are profoundly different. It thus seems wise to respect the diversity of national action, under the condition of preventing serious incompatibilities (in the spirit of Art. 100), and to consider this diversity as an experiment of different formulae.

- harmonizing labor-related legislation is systematically demanded by the trade unions (upwards harmonization, to be defined), and sometimes also by business as a condition for completing the single market. To me, this does seem neither a priority nor really practicable, while the current diversity regarding as much the content of this legislation as the evolution in each country can be as an enriching *source of experimentation*, at a moment when, on issues as urgent as working time, even the experts with the most balanced judgement do not reach agreement.

Generally speaking, everything relating to the development of a legislative and regulatory framework, a lot of subsidiarity and the respect of diversity seem necessary in order to respond to the expectations of the populations, but the comparative presentation of national implementation records, which is already being done, could go much further by organizing a systematic confrontation of the content and the effects of national developments of labor-related legislation, by paying close attention to distinguishing what points to national specificities (of a psychological and sociological nature) and what could have more general significance.

Section II: Macroeconomic Coherence

Progress would be particularly interesting in two areas: coherence of the various elements of the policy mix, and enhanced budgetary coordination.

The Internal Coherence of the Policy Mix

If the need for coherence between the various elements of the policy mix, especially the monetary and budgetary components, is by now largely recognized, the modalities to achieve this are widely debated and give rise to vigorous conceptual and institutional opposition. Some defend the idea that the fundamental objective consists in stable prices (a key condition for economic efficiency, including to reduce unemployment) and that the content of the policy mix should prepare for this. Pushing this argument to the extreme, it would mean that the ECB would have to define the macroeconomic strategy (hence the importance of its independence) and that the important budgetary orientations would have to derive from it (this is the idea underlying the Stability Pact).

Without underestimating the importance of tendential stability of prices, others remind us that the socio-political balance of the member states of the EU requires a strong reduction of unemployment and that therefore the two objectives of employment and prices must be targeted simultaneously and in a balanced fashion. To this end, to the extent that achieving these two objectives resides with different institutions, their powers should be balanced; hence the idea of an economic government beside the ECB. Some also add that such a coordination would avoid the risk that the ECB turns into a scapegoat for most of the economic problems of the euro zone.

Finally, some would like to associate closely the European Parliament with determining the 'goal mix' (and, at least in some speeches, to confer more power upon the European Parliament than most national parliaments have). These oppositions are expressed clearly by experts in each countries, but they also manifest themselves as a function of the countries' experience over the last decades (the extreme case being Germany, which is satisfied with the substantial—yet not exclusive let alone predominant role—of the Bundesbank, in contrast, it is France that argues most vigorously in favor of a powerful economic government, and is wary of more parliamentary power). If on the political level the debates continue in a non-systematic fashion, it is nevertheless the case that this is one of the main issues in defining the new institutional architecture of the EU (which the Amsterdam Treaty has left open) and in obtaining a genuine macroeconomic coherence that appears to be a decisive condition for a full condition of the euro in its internal and external aspects. Only this coherence will allow an efficient coordination of employment policies envisaged by the Amsterdam Treaty (Art. 3).

Enhanced Budgetary Coordination

The *classical set of arguments* in favor of budgetary supervision in Europe is based on four points:

- as the European economy is not as yet fully integrated, the member states may experience asymmetric shocks to which they cannot react anymore by the use of monetary policy. The only remaining instrument is of a budgetary nature and member states should be able to resort to it if it is to be avoided that adjustments are made by a reduction in production levels and thus to the detriment of employment;

- budgetary behavior of member states should not impede the search for stable prices; community supervision is therefore necessary;

- between countries with important commercial and financial relations, *a fortiori* in a partially integrated economic area, national budgetary policy exerts a noticeable influence upon the economy of partner countries, at the same time as its national impact is influenced by the budgetary strategy of its neighbors; national budgetary management cannot be independent anymore;

- the three preceding points taken together lead us to recognize that there is a need to ensure coherent national budgetary policies, in order to make them compatible with one another, and, if possible, synergetic; this is not ensured spontaneously but requires a coordination mechanism, of which the Stability Pact is considered to be the main instrument (even a sufficient one in the eyes of many).

This classical set of arguments is totally valid but exhibits *four important weaknesses*:

- it confers excessive importance upon stable prices, to the possible detriment of other objectives of macroeconomic policy; effectively, member states put the budgetary strategy at the service of a vast panoply of economic objectives, and efforts of coordination must take this into account;

- it confers excessive importance upon an instrument that is conducive to very rigid coherence, that is, the respect of the rules laid down by the Stability Pact, defined once and for all, while the EU is immersed in a profoundly evolutionary environment; it is unreasonable to deprive oneself of flexibility, which is hailed after all when it comes to the functioning of markets;

- it focuses on a single budgetary characteristic, that is, the negative surplus (expenditure-tax revenues), without paying any attention to the structure of revenues (fiscal structures) or to that of expenditure, whose impact on the economy is also a determinant; a more complete view of budgets is necessary;

- it fails to take account of the multiplicity of public budgets, of which national budgets constitute only one element, besides those of territorial collectivities and that of social security; it is necessary to take account of this multiplicity of budgetary decisions.[3]

The conclusion of this overview is therefore clear. Coordinating budgetary policies has to be done by responding to a two-fold concern:

- a classical macroeconomic concern, aiming at a global compatibility between budgets, and paying particularly close attention to the negative surplus;

- a more original, more detailed concern, of a meso- (sometimes even micro-)economic character, aiming essentially at a better coherence of structural policies (construed widely, e.g. sectoral structures, public investment, regional policies), which have budgetary implications.

This implies that this coordination concerns the totality of public budgets at all geographical levels and that it is done in close relation to all Community policies. The implementation of such a conclusion implies a serious change in the usual Community management. Budgetary coordination to be put in place in the near future thus differs significantly from the classical concept: the latter is based on the scope and the development of the negative surplus, as well as, if there is a deficit (which is generally the case), on the modalities of covering it. The concept put forward here is much larger, for it is concerned with *coupling budgetary considerations with considerations of implementing all the structural policies* with budgetary implications, at whatever decisional level (Community, national, regional). It is then possible to speak of a genuinely European budgetary strategy.

Finally, one could point to an interesting socio-cultural consequence of such an extended budgetary coordination. A political Europe will not be realized unless the Europeans feel a sense of common belonging—a European identity is frequently evoked; associating national representatives, at a geographically limited level, to the discussions on a European budget could be an opportunity to reflect together as much on the ends of the European construction as on the means to respond to the current, concrete problems; the comparison of responses at the national and infra-national levels could also be an opportunity for better mutual understanding and to overcome the national realm in preparing a better response to modernity and to the development of the world. If this is supported by a preceding wide social and cultural debate, such a confrontation could constitute a *pedagogical instrument* of prime importance in order to help the populations progress on the path towards a European Union.

Section III: EMU and CFSP

Creating a monetary union will modify quite significantly the ways in which the European economy will insert itself into the world economy:

- a global balance of payments will replace 15 national balances of payments. The issue of external competitiveness will have to be considered globally and not nationally, though with less intensity, for the relation between GNP and exports or imports will only be approximately 12 percent (a figure close to that of the US or Japan), whereas it used to be between 25 percent and 30 percent for the largest member countries, and reached 60 percent or 70 percent for others;

- the euro will gradually acquire a growing role on the world markets, to the detriment of the dollar (and maybe the yen), insofar as it possesses the qualities of an international currency; this role will be enhanced, first, by the scope of trade of the EU with the rest of the world (currently 15 percent of world trade, against also 15 percent for the US and 8 percent for Japan), second, by the success of stable prices in the EU, and, finally, by the intensity of efforts on the part of European economic agents to request pricing and billing in euros (notably for petrol);

- finally, putting in place EMU will require a definition of relations between the euro and other important currencies, and of the relations between the European authorities and their counterparts, above all the Americans and the Japanese. According to the treaty provisions, the choice of exchange rate mechanisms with third currencies belongs to the Council of Ministers, but the everyday management is the ECB's task; the two have to coordinate and this reveals yet again the blurred relations between them. These blurred relations extend to the macroeconomic dialogue between the great powers within the G-7.

Responding to these changes has to take account of the fact—insufficiently dealt with by the economic literature, but abundantly proved by experience—that the relations between the important currencies cannot occur on an exclusively monetary basis by a dialogue conducted only between central banks and devoting most attention to exchange and interest rates. Effectively, this would prolong either antagonism on the basis of competition, or thwart efforts for a partnership, which reflect relations of power that are not only economic but also at least as much political. There is thus a subtle but real link between the currency and foreign policy.

There is not, nor can there be, complete independence between managing monetary and organizing commercial relations, for the latter exerts a direct influence on the scope of exchange flows and on the size of the negative surplus of the external balance. Yet this organization is to some extent a reflection of foreign policy, itself the expression of important political choices. The importance of the themes to be dealt with over the next years within the WTO exceeds considerably that of more sectoral issues of recent years: the underlying philosophy of liberalizing the exchange of services, putting in place a world competition policy, treating more specifically everything relating to culture. So many issues, the dealing of which could have a substantial impact upon things as important as the development of big sectors (such as aerospace or telecommunications) and even the way of life. Europe has to see to ensuring its future.

It is also noticeable that it is only by means of discussions between the great powers that a definition can hopefully be attained of modalities for an institutional framework of the world capital markets, which would enable to reap benefits of economic efficiency generated by the free flow of medium-term capital, without suffering the malign influences of short-term capital movements on the volatile exchange rates. Suggestions have been advanced, but their adoption is still missing; a Europe that speaks with a single voice could play a role of prime importance. In preparing these discussions, the central banks play a crucial role, which is justified by their competence, and by the role they will have to play within this framework. But it is at government and EU levels that the decisions will be taken, and it is desirable that they will be in conformity with the fundamental outlook of the EU's external strategy.[4]

The external monetary policy and the foreign policy therefore exert mutual effects on one another and must be closely coordinated. Two kinds of progress are therefore necessary: first, as much as internally it is widely required not to leave the ECB determine on its own (or predominantly) the hierarchy of the important economic objectives, as much as externally one cannot leave the ECB wholly autonomous in taking directions or in conducting actions that have a decisive influence on the EU's external strategy. There is an important ground for coordination between the Council of Ministers (in its Ecofin or plenary composition) and the ECB, whose competencies well exceed the rules of exchange rates. But for this to function, the EU needs a proper CFSP. If the members of the EU take EMU seriously, they also have to take seriously at the same time the rapid application of the provisions on CFSP in the Maastricht and Amsterdam Treaties.

Section IV: The Quest for a Comprehensive European Strategy: Aiming at Less for Better Achievements and More Coherence

The general idea that constitutes the framework of the preceding sections is three-fold. In order to progress, there has to be simultaneous
- extension of applying the principle of subsidiarity so as to reduce the scope and the variety of Community tasks and to promote a re-focus on what is indispensable;
- as a counterweight, as subsidiarity in many areas leads to the coexistence of actions carried out at different geographical levels, reinforcing the procedures of contrasting and coordinating different decisional levels;
- take advantage of Europe's cultural diversity, and therefore of the variety of behaviors and actions, in order to enable diverse experience to flourish and to make most use of the results via rigorous comparisons, without systematic harmonization.

There are three groups of key terms: simplify and re-focus, contrast and coordinate, experiment and compare. It is in this spirit that we chose a small number of action fields that have priority, some of which are well-known, others are novel. Can such a strategy be achieved? Its implementation requires three conditions: elaborate intellectually a synthetic approach to the problems and their solutions, manifest politically more ambition and more modesty, reinforce institutionally a more marked responsibility and better policies. Let us specify these three elements.

The Need for Synthetic Visions

Several countries object to a number of actions that have been mentioned. This reluctance derives for most of them from a partial view of things, that focuses either on the difficulties related to implementation, or on the inconvenience or on direct losses, while the indirect advantages of a better functioning of the whole European economy are most frequently ignored or grossly understated. If, as is desirable, most governments or some lobbying groups were to conduct cost-benefit analyses of various suggestions for action, these analyses are confined to direct effects and therefore neglect completely indirect effects; the best example is the ambition to the 'just budgetary return', which neglects completely the general economic advantages that a country can reap from more integration. It is rare that studies of the impact of integration are concerned with locating derived advantages within a comprehensive view of the integration process, and this myopia can also be observed as much in nationally conducted analyses (whether by governments or by lobbying groups) as in presentations and arguments by the Commission, the European Parliament or the Economic and Social Committee. The result is that when new action is suggested, a number of countries are opposed and most frequently a positive decision is only reached in the form of a compromise that takes up only partially the benefits that can be expected from the sort of action that is envisaged.

The answer is evident: each suggested decision should be systematically placed within a global and concrete vision of the European construction: global in order to identify the impact of interdependencies, concrete in order to go beyond theoretical formulae, such as 'respecting the principle of an open market economy where there is free competition' (Art. 3a) or 'the principle of subsidiarity' (Art. 3b or Art. 5 of the revised treaties) and to inquire about the best current (and future) modalities of integrating the European economy into the world economy, which is evolving significantly.[5]

Practically speaking, it is on the level of a central Community institution that this could be organized: it never has been.[6] Let's wait with some optimism for the next Commission to take up and implement this idea, against all expected opposition (as comprehensive knowledge is the source of power), in order to better fulfil one of its tasks—perhaps the main one—, which is to convince all Europeans that a well-conceived European construction can be a positive-sum game.

Re-Focusing Community Actions: More Willingness and More Modesty

This synthetic view should help the Community in focusing on the essential. After having restricted the latter for too long to the single market (indispensable, but insufficient) and after taking almost 30 years to put in place EMU, the Community has been taken by a frenzy of activism in all respects. This change occurred about 1990, at the initiative of the then incumbent Commission, which considered itself too readily as a genuine European government (at a time when national governments were pushed by their populations to limit the scope of their activities), under the impulse or with the blessing of the European Parliament and with the more or less tacit approval by the Council (or sometimes even in response to demands by particular governments motivated by requests from certain national pressure groups). Yet these two budgetary authorities do not have the necessary human and financial resources at their disposal, as the recent report by the Reflection Group clearly shows.

'Qui trop embrasse mal étreint.' *Nolens volens*, national governments tend towards reducing the scope of their interventions, and therefore the

European institutions should not move into the opposite direction. Concretely speaking, the people expect from their leaders that the latter do not get involved into everything—and thereby manifest more modesty—but that they also make more efforts to progress in certain areas, above all the Common Foreign and Security Policy, and that they exhibit more willingness in the interest of a re-focused and reinforced ambition. To this end, changes in conduct are necessary.

Adapted Institutions and Political Attitudes

The issue of overhauling the Community institutions, which functioned well with six member states, but which have become less and less adapted, has been on the table for several years: the IGC that prepared the Amsterdam Treaty has been guilty in failing to act on its main tasks, which was precisely to organize this overhaul. The trouble that the institutions have experienced recently could be the opportunity to restore order in their functioning and to proceed with the re-focusing that is advocated above, if one wants to reflect in depth on the organization of the various responsibilities (that go significantly beyond the Commission). A new Parliament will perhaps help the Council, consisting of governments that currently enjoy a certain life expectancy and whose members could exhibit courage; the matter is therefore mainly in the hands of current and future politicians.

In the market economy as we know it, where international financial markets play a crucial role, the strength of a currency derives obviously from the cleverness with which the monetary authorities manage monetary policy, but also as much from less objective factors, among which speeches by politicians have an important role: sudden rises or falls, apparently unrelated to economic fundamentals, have been observed in recent years following spectacular speeches—or small sentences that had been wisely pondered... with a view to the impact on domestic politics.

In the light of the existence of a single European currency, it will become essential that national politicians are concerned by the impact that their speeches—even if they are intended exclusively for internal use—could have on international agents; with the creation of a common monetary policy defined by the ECB, they will have to be careful not to make statements that are contradictory with the ECB until they have thoroughly reflected upon the possible effects of such a dissonance.

There will have to be a significant change in political behavior in Europe, at least for the tenors of political life, be they in office or in opposition. It is fundamental for the external role of the euro that the rest of the world has the impression that there is a single European position, possibly after a debate, officially within the monetary committee, or, informally, between the monetary authority and the government, and this is fundamental for the external role of the euro; any cacophony has to be avoided.[7]

Section V: A Final Question: Strengthening Integration With How Many?

The marked diversity of points of view among European countries on the future of Europe has led for some years to conceiving a differentiated participation of the member states in the integration process. If the debates on this idea were a bit too abstract in the beginning, three events have given much more consistency to a new possible shape of Europe's institutional architecture. The Treaty of Maastricht has envisaged explicitly the possibility of a coexistence among the member states of two subgroups, one comprising the participants of EMU, and the other the countries that remain outside it, and a decision by the Council of Ministers envisaged organizing the relations between the two in the form of an ERM II. Subsequently the German memorandum by Schäuble and Lamers advocating a 'hard core' put this issue on the agenda of national governments. Finally, the Treaty of Amsterdam has opened up an institutional path by means of the formula of 'closer cooperation'. This issue has passed from the academic realm to that of the decision-makers, and the creation of the euro has made the shift to an economically differentiated Europe more concrete.

All the actions considered above, which are aimed at completing the single market or have a structural character, evidently have to include all member states because they correspond to a minimal vision of economic integration. In contrast, realism forces us to ask ourselves if it is possible in a few years' time to make all countries participate in a marked operation of budgetary confrontation, which would translate itself by the search for jointly agreed compromise; in fact, this would be a genuine revolution relative to current practices. For sure, the functioning of the ERM required from all participants the willingness to attain a convergence of national economic developments, and if one hopes for convergence, one has to accept more mutual information on projects, a detailed examination of their compatibility, accepting alterations to the initial projects after a comprehensive, jointly conducted debate. The first phases of this process have been initiated, practice is more discrete regarding the last phase, and not all the member states seem prepared to make this final leap.

Is it thus necessary to continue to align oneself to those who wish to preserve as much as possible their autonomy (even if in reality, due to growing interdependencies, this autonomy becomes increasingly formal or virtual) or is it possible, by relying on the provisions of the Amsterdam Treaty that open the door for 'closer cooperation', to proceed temporarily in a group with limited membership, in the hope that, once the example has been conclusive, the others will rejoin more or less rapidly? There are three insights to this question.

If for different reasons (national prestige, the myth of independence, benign neglect vis-à-vis geopolitics, etc.) all 15 member states do not wish to see the strongly structured common foreign policy dispose of means for action of which the EU has an urgent need, should one not at least begin with those that are open to this idea?

On the other hand, the getting under way of the operation that leads to the next enlargement is imminent, even if the transitory period will last several years. For quite a long time, these new partners will hardly desire, nor be capable of, participating in a comprehensive budgetary coordination (as much as they will not be ready to become full members of EMU). It would thus probably be inappropriate to create—and to operationalize—with 15 members a procedure that would be part of the *acquis communautaire*, which we ask the candidate countries to accept fully.[8]

Economically, the launching of the euro has entailed the creation of an economically differentiated Europe in monetary matters. Is it necessary to adopt the same attitude in budgetary matters, or, on the contrary, to attempt to maintain the unity of the EU at 15 in this field? More specifically, is it necessary to organize budgetary coherence at the level of the 15, of the Euroland (today standing at 11), at the level of the participants in closer cooperation that will perhaps differ? On the one hand, coupling budgetary coordination with examining structural policies is a means of prioritizing the convergence towards an OCA, which is particularly interesting for a number of countries outside the euro zone whose characteristics discard them most from this zone; it would therefore be desirable to associate them closely to such a budgetary procedure. But, on the other hand, budgetary coordination has to be closely tied to the elaboration of monetary policy in order to define the best policy mix, and, for this to occur, there is a need for better operation at the level of the euro zone (currently standing at 11). Here as well, the answer is far from obvious.

In the face of these divergent considerations, the conclusion is not clear, but there are a number of powerful arguments in favor of a diversified Europe according to experimental modalities, under the condition that these are presented as a formula for a transition period, at the end of which the countries that do not participate in the closer cooperation will state their positions unambiguously.

The preceding propositions are not entirely novel (several have been formulated as part of the work within the network of Jean Monnet Chairs), but all of them are innovative and their adoption would constitute in some respects minor revolutions. Is it reasonable to formulate them, or is it unequivocally foolish? A couple of months ago one could have hesitated.

After serious turmoil that the Community has just experienced, which shed light on the necessity of a significant overhaul of Community practices, perhaps it is not useless to seek to contribute to the content itself of the Community's tasks and competencies.

Notes

1. In a deliberately succinct way, this chapter uses some reflections that have been presented by the author more comprehensively in recent times at various conferences. The ensuing papers will be published soon:
   - 'L'Euro, achèvement et point de départ', Colloque Jean Monnet 'L'Euro et le monde', Coïmbra Lisbonne, 1-4 juillet 1998. Actes diffusés par l'Action Jean Monnet, DG X Commission européenne, Bruxelles.
   - 'Actions communautaires en faveur des ajustements nécessaires du système productif européen.' Colloque ECSA-World, Bruxelles, 17-18 septembre 1998. Actes disponibles début 1999 à l'Action Jean Monnet, DG X Commission européenne, Bruxelles.
   - 'Une vision élargie de la coordination budgétaire dans l'Union européenne.' 4A Conferenza annuale della Facolta di Economia: Il governo dell'Economia in Europa et in Italia, Pavia, 9-10 octobre 1998, à paraître dans *The European Union Review*, début 1999.
2. Cf. Luigi Pasinetti, 'The myth (or folly) of the 3 % deficit/GDP Maastricht parameter', *Cambridge Journal of Economics*, 22 (1998), pp. 117-136.
3. Finally one can add that in the set of arguments most widely expressed, the distrust on the part of the monetary authorities vis-à-vis budgetary autonomy is based on a partial vision of the causes underlying inflation; the emphasis is essentially put on 'demand-induced inflation', and the literature of the recent years—contrary to that of earlier decades—tends to relegate 'cost-push inflation' to secondary importance.
4. Without exhausting the issue, far from it, two elements could be mentioned:
   - the debates around the notion of sustainable development correspond to real problems, even if they are approached in a confused manner. A certain reorientation of the style of development policy in developed countries seems indispensable at some point, which can only be realized under the pressure of governments that act in concert.
   - if, generally speaking, the choice of the modalities of the competition among the poor countries of the globe is done or should be done on the basis of economic considerations, the scope of this competition and the choice of countries in question cannot but be done on the basis of political choices.

5. This idea is less far-fetched or unrealistic than could seem to certain readers, for Art. 130R envisages that 'requirements in the domain of environmental protection should be integrated in the definition and implementation of other Community policies'. What seems possible for an important, yet not decisive, area should *a fortiori* be possible for an area of high priority, like employment.

6. Thirty years ago, the Commission had sketched such an institution by suggesting that a medium-term program be elaborated. During this period, the choice of this term collided sufficiently with a member state for the project to stop at that stage. Then, the creation of a forward studies unit within the Commission seemed to be a promising step, yet the correspondence of its studies and the operational reflections of the Commission has never been done. Neither the Parliament (which has financial resources) nor the Economic and Social Committee (that brings together numerous experts and political actors) have ever taken up this issue. The European University Institute in Florence has always preferred to remain quite recluse and specialized.

7. One can add that the legitimate concern with transparency of Community debates is to be treated carefully: the public debates within the Council do not always have the best effect. Thus it will be noted that recent rows between the 'partners' on the CAP certainly do not promote the adoption of a common position and its external credibility during the future negotiations within the WTO.

8. However, in the opposite sense, one can observe that a well-organized procedure of vast budgetary coordination, which leads to examine jointly the main aspects of the medium-term development of the EU, could constitute a valuable pedagogical instrument in favor of integration that would benefit as much the more reticent member states as the candidate countries; it would therefore be a shame to deprive oneself of it.

10. CURRENCY CRISES AND CAPITAL CONTROLS IN EMERGING COUNTRIES: THE CASE OF THE AFRICAN CFA FRANC AND ITS EURO FUTURE

Emil-Maria Claassen

The 'traditional' currency crises over the past years occurred in those countries which had adopted the regime of a fixed exchange rate. This statement should not be interpreted as if any fixed-foreign-exchange-rate regime is crisis-prone. Two examples may be mentioned which are comparable with each other and which have performed extremely well.

On the one hand, there have been Austria (8.1 millions of inhabitants) and Switzerland (7.1 millions). Since the mid-1970s and early 1980s, Austria followed a fixed peg (which had never been modified) with respect to the Deutschmark (seven schillings for one German mark) with a band of $\pm$ 0.11 percent around the par value (instead of $\pm$ 2.25 percent within the European Monetary System since January 1979 and of $\pm$ 15 percent since August 1993). In contrast, Switzerland followed steadily a floating exchange rate (as Germany did) and succeeded in a higher record of price stability than Germany (and, consequently, than Austria).

The other comparable examples are Hong Kong (6.3 millions of inhabitants) and Singapore (3.7 millions). The currency board of Hong Kong had been implemented since 1983 (7.78 HK dollar equal to one US dollar). Singapore pursued the policy of floating (except for the period of 1981-85 when the US dollar was highly appreciating). Again, Singapore had been more successful than Hong Kong in terms of price stability.

By looking at the world economy during the 1990s, floating exchange rates have become the generalized exchange rate regime among industrialized economies (including the euro). In contrast, there is still a number of emerging countries (Table 1) which maintained fixed exchange rates or shifted recently to them in terms of the implementation of a currency board. Compared to the recent currency crises in large countries (Mexico,

Table 1: Fixed-Exchange-Rate Regimes: Cross-Section of Small Emerging Economies with Long-Run Currency Peg

---

I. Small economies with no domestic paper currencies ('dollarized' economies)

Panama (US dollar since 1934 and 1 balboa = 1 US dollar).The *Pacific islands* using the Australian dollar: Nauru since 1968, Kiribati since 1979, and Tuvalu since 1979. The Pacific islands using the US dollar since 1986: Marshall Islands and Micronesia.[1]

II. Currency-board economies

Brunei with peg to Singapore dollar (1 Brunei dollar = 1 Singapore dollar) since 1967. *Djibouti* with peg to the US dollar since February 1973 (1.72 Djibouti franc = 1 US dollar). Six Caribbean islands sharing a common currency (the *East Caribbean* dollar where 2.70 EC dollar = 1 US dollar), namely Antigua & Barbuda, Dominica, Grenada, St Kitts & Nevis, St Lucia, and St Vincent & Grenadines, since May 1976. *Hong Kong* with peg to the US dollar (1.78 HK dollar = 1 US dollar with $\pm$ 1 percent band) since October 1983. *Argentina* (1 peso = 1 Argentine dollar = 1 US dollar) since 1992. *Estonia* with peg to the German currency (8 croons = 1 DM) since June 1992. *Lithuania* with peg to the dollar (4 litai = 1 US dollar) since 1994. *Bulgaria* (1 leva = 1 DM) since July 1997.

III. Small economies with long-run currency peg (full or limited capital-account convertibility)

1. Caribbean countries with peg to the US dollar ($\pm$ 1 percent band):[2] *Bahamas* since 1949. *Barbados* since July 1975. *Belize* since January 1977.
2. Gulf states with peg to the US dollar ($\pm$ 1 percent band): *Oman* since 1973. *Bahrein* since July 1979. *Quatar* since November 1979. *United Arab Emirates* since January 1980. *Saudi Arabia* since June 1986.
3. African countries: When some *South African homelands* became independent, namely Lesotho in 1979, Swaziland in 1986, and Namibia in 1990, they introduced their own currencies which had been pegged at par with the rand (1 loti = 1 lilangeni = 1 Nambia dollar = 1 rand).
Thirteen African countries (belonging to the *French Franc Zone*) at par with the French franc, 50 F CFA = 1 FF since 1948 and 100 F CFA = 1 FF since January 1994 (with an enforcement of capital controls). The 'fourteenth' country of the CFA franc is the Federal Islamic Republic of the *Comoro Islands*; in January 1994, the Comoro franc had been devalued less, namely by 33 percent (instead of 50 percent).

Sources: IMF, *International Financial Statistics*. Maurice Obstfeld and Kenneth Rogoff, 'The Mirage of Fixed Exchange Rates', *Journal of Economic Perspectives,* Fall 1995. Atish R. Gosh, Anne-Marie Gould, and Holger C. Wolf, 'Currency Boards: The Ultimate Fix?', IMF Working Paper, 1998, no. 8.

Thailand, Indonesia, Russia, and Brazil), the fixed-exchange-rate regime of the remaining small emerging countries seems to belong to an 'endangered species'.

Among the emerging economies, there are three currency areas which have pegged their common currency either to the US dollar (East Caribbean countries) or to the rand (South African area) or to the French franc (French Franc Zone). The latter is the largest one (94 millions of inhabitants). In addition, it has a long history of capital controls. They had been enforced since the devaluation of the CFA franc in January 1994 and they have been maintained in January 1999 when the French franc was replaced by the euro as the new 'numéraire'.

The theoretical base for capital controls is summarized in section I. Their justification could be derived from 'self-fulfilling' expectations dominating the foreign exchange market and disconnected with any fundamentals. Section II describes the hybrid form of a currency area with capital controls which is the CFA-Franc Zone. In practice, it does not use the traditional 'unilateral' form of a fixed-exchange-rate regime but the 'bilateral' one with respect to the anchor currency.

Self-Fulfilling Expectations and Capital Controls

In the recent literature on financial crises, 'self-fulfilling' expectations, under the regime of fixed exchange rates, can lead to a currency crisis, even if the macroeconomic 'fundamentals' would exclude any abrupt change in the foreign exchange rate.[3] To a certain degree, these expectations resemble Milton Friedman's 'destabilizing speculation' in his 'Case for Flexible Exchange Rates' published in 1953.

Convertibility Tests: Banking versus Currency Crisis

Self-fulfilling expectations pay an important role in the traditional theoretical literature on the explanation of banking crises. Their ultimate cause consists of the a-priory fragility of the banking system in terms of the maturity mismatch between bank assets (loans) and bank liabilities (deposits). Bank loans belong to the category of 'non-tradable' assets. The distinction between tradable and non-tradable credit claims refers to their liquidity or to their marketability on short notice.[4] Bonds and shares (direct finance) can be sold on the stock market at any moment, even though their market prices are fluctuating daily. In contrast, bank loans, even if they are of first quality in terms of the non-existence of any default risk, are not traded on open markets—a phenomenon which explains precisely the well-known 'liquidity mismatch' between bank loans and bank deposits.

The banking fragility can give rise to bank runs, even if each bank remains fully solvent. If depositors become uncertain about the solvency of their banks, they may queue up to withdraw their deposits. The convertibility constraint, under which each bank operates, namely the conversion of deposits into cash on a first-come, first-served basis, may invite other depositors to 'run'. According to Diamond and Dybvig (1983), this scenario is even conceivable if the 'fundamentals' of the concerned bank—a well-diversified portfolio without any 'lemons'—would exclude a priori any convertibility test. Since banks are linked together by the interbank market, withdrawals from one bank can undermine the liquidity of other banks with the subsequent herd behavior on the banking sector. Thus, bank runs are conceivable under 'self-fulfilling' expectations.[5]

Currency crises under a fixed-exchange-rate system are explained by a similar formal framework as the causal links of a banking crisis. Either the 'fundamentals' (foreign-debt overhang, current-account deficit, budget deficits, level of international reserves, real appreciation of the domestic currency...) do not reflect any longer the present level of the exchange rate (the so-called 'first generation' models of speculative attacks) or self-fulfilling expectations lead to a 'currency run' ('second generation' models).

'The analogy of national currency to a bank is pretty clear. The central bank has promised to buy back its own currency with external currency at an announced price, and for that purpose holds reserves of hard currency. In the benign equilibrium [our first generation model mentioned above], expectations in currency markets around the world support behaviors that validate the expectations and sustain the pegged exchange rate. The second, pessimistic equilibrium [the second-generation model] is that the central bank defaults on its commitment. Like bank depositors worried about what other depositors will do, holders of a pegged currency fear that they will act too late to save their assets. Potential claims on central bank reserves include not only the external liabilities of the central bank and the government but all those of private banks, businesses, and households, domestic and foreign.'[6]

The first type of currency crises, derived from the change in the underlying *fundamentals* of a fixed exchange rate, is represented in Figure 1. In contrast to most other macro models in this field,[7] we shall operate with the real exchange rate defined as the relative price (q) between tradable and non-tradable goods. The line P_0 represents a given general price level which can be the result of various combinations for the price level of tradable goods (P_T) and the price level of non-tradable goods (P_N).[8] P_0 should be the general price level which equilibrates the demand and supply

of money. The schedule P_0 implies a given quantity of money. The initial
real exchange rate (q_0) is indicated by the slope of the ray $0q_0$. The nominal
exchange rate is fixed at the level E_0 such that the price level of P_T is given
by $E_0P^*_T$ where P^*_T is the foreign price level of tradable goods. The initial
macro equilibrium—or Tobin's benign equilibrium—is at point A.

Figure 1: Real Depreciation under Fixed and Floating Exchange Rates

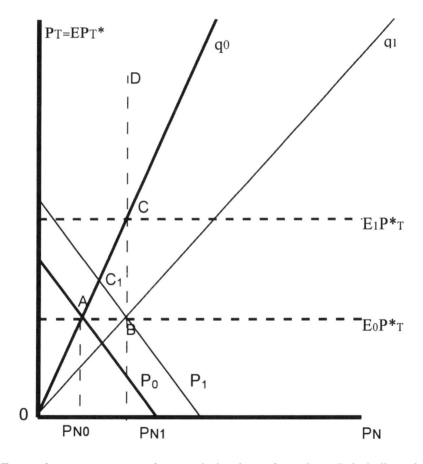

For various reasons, a real appreciation has taken place. It is indicated
by the rotation of the ray $0q_0$ toward $0q_1$. One 'classical' case for the real
appreciation (at least, in developing countries with an open financial
economy) are net capital inflows (capital balance surplus exceeding the
current account deficit) such that the increase in international reserves
(balance of payments surplus) had not been fully sterilized by the monetary
authorities. The quantity of money increases and the higher price level is
indicated by the new schedule P_1. Since the exchange rate remains fixed, the
higher price level has been brought about only by the rise of P_{N0} to P_{N1} and

the economy moves from point A to point B. The real exchange rate has 'declined' from $q_0 = E_0P^*_T/P_{N0}$ to $q_1 = E_0P^*_T/P_{N1}$.

At point B, the value of the exchange rates—the nominal rate E_0 and the real rate q_1—is at a level of 'fundamental disequilibrium'. If politicians maintain the nominal exchange rate at the level E_0, the price level of tradable goods is not modifiable and it remains at the horizontal dotted line $E_0P^*_T$.

The only chance of bringing about the real depreciation is a deflationary monetary policy which shifts the P_1 schedule back toward P_0. This deflationary policy will induce a fall in P_N since P_T remains constant (point A).[9] If, on the other hand, a nominal devaluation is envisaged, one possible solution would be point C with the higher price level for tradable goods equal to $E_1P^*_T$. It will have an 'inflationary' impact (a once-and-for-all increase in P_T) and the new LM schedule (our P-schedule) has to pass through point C.[10]

Box 1: Real Depreciation Under Price Stability (the q-line and P-line of Figure 1)

The real exchange rate is measured by the slope of the q-line, namely by P_T/P_N. A real depreciation rotates the q-line from q_1 toward q_0.

At first sight, some justified confusion may emerge with the interpretation of the P-line. Its slope (even though negative) also is equal to the ratio P_T/P_N and for that reason, it could be confounded with the real exchange rate (q). But it is not the real exchange rate or, more precisely, the P_1-line 'indicates' *various* real exchange rates (derived from various q-lines) for which the stability of the general price level (P_1) is maintained.

By moving upward on the P_1-line—for instance, from point B to point C_1 in Figure A (being similar to Figure 1)—P_T increases and P_N decreases. Both changes—the first is positive and the second negative—indicate 'evidently' a real depreciation. But this special type of real depreciation (P_T rises and, simultaneously, P_N declines) is traced under the *additional constraint* of a constant general price level, namely P_1: the real depreciation q_0 is realized under the special condition of price stability indicated by the P_1-line.

Thus, a nominal devaluation of ΔE giving rise to $\Delta P_T = \Delta E \times P^*_T$ has to be accompanied by a *decline* in P_N in order to maintain a constant general price level. It is for that 'monetary' reason that the slope of the P_1-line (representing the 'LM-sector' for a given money supply) is negative.

The price level is measured as a weighted arithmetical average:

$$P = a\,P_T + b\,P_N$$

A constant price level implies that

$$a \, \Delta P_T + b \, \Delta P_N = \Delta P = 0$$

where the weight coefficients, a and b, are assumed to be constant (with $a + b = 1$). The slope of the P_1-line is equal to

$$(\Delta P_T / \Delta P_N) = - (b / a)$$

Figure A: General price level (P_1): equal weights for tradables and non-tradables

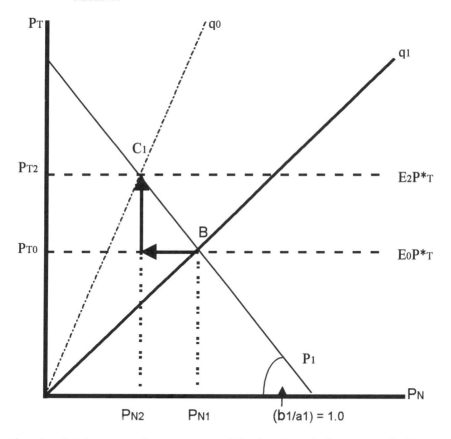

If $a = b = 0.5$ (corresponding to a non-weighted arithmetical average), the P_1-line has the negative slope of 45°. A fifty-percent increase in P_T would imply a fifty-percent decrease in P_N (see point C_1 in Figure A) in order to realize the constant price level P_1, even though that example would signify a real depreciation rate of 100 percent: the nominal devaluation (in terms of P_T) amounts to 50 percent and the real depreciation (in terms of P_T *and* P_N) to 100 percent.

Figure B: General price level (P'1): higher weight (a) for tradables and lower weight (b) for non-tradables

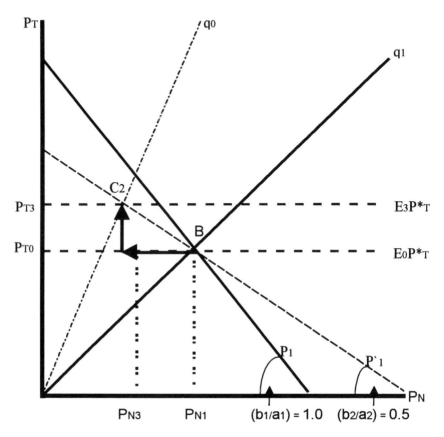

If one assumes a different weight combination for T and N as in Figure B (where a = 0.66 and b = 0.33 such that b/a = 0.5), tradable goods play a more important role for the general price level than non-tradable goods. For the same *real* depreciation (q_0), represented now by point C_2, the increase in E and P_T will be lower and the decline in P_N stronger where both movements will maintain the general price level at P'$_1$ (equivalent to P$_1$).

If one envisages a float, the position of 'multiple equilibria'—or Tobin's pessimistic equilibrium—could be a possible outcome for a crisis-prone country opting for a floating rate, if one follows the 'theorem of self-fulfilling expectations'. Thus, the exchange rate E_1 can move to any situation above point C, say to point D, because people expect that the domestic currency depreciates to the level D. The basis of the 'speculative attack' can occur randomly or it is triggered by bad news about the economy (crash of the stock market, excess government debt, the fragility of the banking system, and social unrest). However, this latter view could admit that economic agents do not attack at random, but they assess a wide spectrum of possible bad fundamentals leading to a 'fire sale' price of the domestic currency. In this sense, expectations can be 'destabilizing' (as in the old literature on flexible exchange rates) or 'self-fulfilling' (as in the recent literature).

Capital Controls for Coping With Currency Crises

With respect to the limitation of financial crises and, in particular, of currency crises, the proposal of capital controls has often been advanced. The most famous one, suggested again by Tobin in 1972 during his lectures in honor of Joseph Schumpeter at Princeton, was to 'draw sand in the wheels' of capital flows by a tax on short-term capital movements. At that time, capital controls were not unusual. Before 1973, the United States discouraged capital outflows by the interest-rate equalization tax on American residents when they invested their funds in foreign deposits (Eurodollars), and Germany discouraged capital inflows by imposing required reserves (the 'Bardepot'—deposit in cash—of 40 percent) on bank deposits held by foreigners. In 1996, Tobin proposed a tax of 0.2 percent (instead of 1 percent in 1972) on financial round trips to another currency which would be equivalent to a yearly tax rate of 2.4 percent, if capital flows take place every month. In recent time (1998), he referred to another device being used in Chile (until September 1998). Instead of an explicit tax, extra reserve requirements on foreigners' bank deposits would deter capital inflows.[11]

Bank runs or their liquidity crises stand for the case of negative externalities or, in more fashionable terms, for systemic risks. They can be prevented by the central bank in its function of lender of last resort or by a compulsory insurance agency in insuring deposits against bank failures. In contrast, central banks cannot act as lenders of last resort with foreign currencies since the volume of their international reserves is limited. Their ultimate option for avoiding an imminent currency crisis consists of the choice between a freely floating rate or capital controls. The critical objection against a floating rate concerns the timing of its implementation. Its introduction should occur long before the 'predictable' arrival of the currency crisis, since otherwise the floating exchange rate could provoke the 'overshooting' phenomenon (see point D in Figure 1).

For advocates of fixed exchange rates, the option could consist of a policy mix between devaluation *and* the implementation of capital controls, or between devaluation *and* the enforcement of existing capital controls as it had been the case for the African CFA-Franc since January 1994.

The Exchange Rate Regime of the CFA-Franc Zone

The last French monetary crisis within the EMS ended on 2 August 1993 when the fluctuation around the central parity value was enlarged from + 2.25 to + 15 percent. At the same date, the Banque de France strengthened foreign exchange controls for the African CFA franc within France. These controls were a prelude to the devaluation of the CFA franc by 50 percent taking place five months later, namely on 12 January 1994 (from 1 F CFA = 0.02 FF to 1 F CFA = 0.01 FF). The heavy exchange controls on capital account-transactions had been maintained until now.

For the reader who is unfamiliar with the example of African monetary integration, some rough data may be chosen to illustrate the size of this single currency area. The African Franc Zone consists of 13 African countries and they are divided into two currency areas, the West African Zone (Benin, Burkina Faso, Côte d'Ivoire, Mali, Niger, Senegal, Togo) and the Central African Zone (Cameroon, Central African Republic, Chad, Congo-Brazzaville, Equatorial Guinea, Gabon). Their population amounts to 94 million inhabitants. In 1997, their GDP was roughly 3 percent of French GDP and their quantity of money about 1 percent of the French money supply.[12]

Two Recent Customs Unions Within the French Franc Zone

Whether it had been pure historical coincidence or a long-term project, the Treaty of the Westafrican *Economic* Union was signed for the Westafrican monetary zone at the moment of the devaluation around January 1994 and a similar treaty was established two months later for the Centralafrican monetary union. Both treaties of a customs union imply the implementation of a 'Common Market' (and of a 'Commission' of the Brussels type) for each of both areas. At first sight, one gets the impression that the European model represents the welfare key for all other regions of the world.

This critical remark concerns the sequencing of integration, that means in the African sense, first monetary integration (existing already for more than forty years) and second commercial integration in terms of a customs union (for each area and including the 'harmonization' of economic policies). However, one could admit that, in any case, despite a needless discussion about optimal sequencing, the establishment of a customs union (the gradual elimination of any 'internal' duties and the equalization of the 'external' tariff) is nevertheless welfare-increasing.

The emergence of 'trade blocs' within the world economy over the last thirty years has occurred simultaneously with the appearance of a great number of small economies. Thus, during the second half of this century, the number of countries has increased from 74 to 193 which is mainly due to the end of colonialism and to the collapse of the Soviet Union. Among this spectacular increase in the number of countries, 87 of them have a population lower than 5 millions, 58 have less than 2.5 millions, and 35 are with less than 500,000 inhabitants. Thus, among the thirteen countries of the French Franc Zone, Côte d'Ivoire stands at the top (14 millions), while Equatorial Guinea having the lowest size of population (400,000).

In this context, one could rise the question what is the *optimal size* of a country? Are small countries necessarily poorer (or less rich) than big countries? Among the ten countries of the world economy with the highest population (depassing 100 millions), only the United States and Japan belong to the prosperous ones. On the other side, there are small countries which have reached the maximum level of income per capita. Thus, Luxembourg (400,000 inhabitants) has attained this maximum, namely 41,200 US dollars, while Singapore (3.7 millions) has reached an income per inhabitant of 26,700 US dollars (both in 1996).[13]

Today, we begin to understand that the prosperity of small economies is derived principally from their foreign trade, provided that international trade is liberalized. However, world trade is dominated by the 'clause of the most favored nation'. Thus, if a small African country specialized in the production of groundnuts would like to negotiate with the United States (producing equally groundnuts) about the reduction of import tariffs into the US, the United States is obliged to grant this favor of a reduced import tariff to all other nations. In this respect, the United States is less motivated to negotiate with a small country instead of a big one or of a trade bloc, since it could obtain greater trade (or tariff) concessions for its exports toward this trade bloc and, by this, toward the rest of the world. Under this aspect, the constitution of two customs unions could bring about an important improvement in foreign trade between the member countries of the French Franc Zone and other countries of the world (including the European Union).

As Table 2 indicates, the most important trade relationships of the French Franc Zone are those with the EU (about 50 percent). In this sense, the two newly constituted customs unions could obtain import trade concessions from the EU. However, the 'internal' trade within the African Franc Zone had been extremely weak in contrast to the traditional trade blocs like those of Europe or of North America where the most important trade takes place between member countries (thus, for instance, in the case of Europe, between Germany and France, and for North America, between the US and Canada). From this point of view, the 'gains from international trade' will remain rather limited for the African customs unions. It may also be for that reason that *two* customs unions (instead of a single one) had been implemented within the French Franc Zone.

Table 2:   Foreign Trade of the French Franc Zone, 1990-96 (in percentage of total foreign trade of the zone)

	Trade with member countries	Trade with France	Trade with European Union
West African zone	10.9	20.9	47.8
Central African zone	6.4	30.1	58.3
Total zone	8.9	24.3	51.6

Source: Calculated from the data published by Michael T. Hadjimichael and Michel Galy, 'The CFA Franc Zone and the EMU', IMF, Working Paper no. 97/156, November 1997.

Exchange Rate Options for the CFA Franc

Single currency with external peg. Two issues are puzzling for anybody who is concerned with the rationale of a monetary union among African independent states (beside the above-mentioned fact that the 'internal' trade within the African monetary area is extremely low). First, it seems rather astonishing that thirteen countries (where eight of them belong to the group of the least developing countries) can form a 'monetary union' with an advanced economy like France. The average (nominal) GDP of the total zone was $ 458 per capita in 1996 where at the top level was Gabon ($ 3490) and at the bottom Chad ($ 180). Second, the French Franc Zone is only a hybrid type of a currency area. Even though there is a common currency among the thirteen member countries which is the CFA franc and not the French franc, it has never opted for an 'unilateral' devaluation of the CFA Franc with respect to the French franc (what is rather 'usual' for other pegged currencies within the world economy).[14]

In this respect, the Franc Zone could resemble to a currency board (like, for instance, the monetary union of the six island-states of the East Caribbean) characterized by a fixed peg and a full backing of the outstanding currency by (gross) international reserves. But it is even not that. As Table 3 on the French Franc Zone indicates, net international reserves had been highly negative since the early 1980s, but the money supply was not decreased, except for the years 1992-93, as the monetary rules of the Zone foresee it (total net reserves should not fall below the level of 20 percent of the monetary base consisting of banknotes plus bank reserves). The trend in international reserves (in terms of negative data for net reserves) was reversed only after the devaluation of January 1994. In addition, the devaluation occurred, when the 'operation account' (65 percent of international reserves to be deposited at the French Treasury minus credits granted by the Treasury to the Zone) tended to become negative toward the end of 1993.

Table 3: CFA Franc: 13 African Countries, 1980-96

	80-90	91	92	93	94	95	96
Net international reserves over monetary base	-38.4	-26.1	-39.9	-46.4	-6.6	5.3	15.5
'Operation' account (French Treasury) over monetary base	12.3	17.1	5.6	0.6	63.3	73.5	72.4
Growth of money supply (M2)	7.6	2.5	-6.7	-8.0	41.3	9.6	6.3

Sources: Calculated from IMF, *International Financial Statistics* and from Banque de France, *La Zone Franc*, annual reports.

The euro as a simplistic 'numéraire'-issue? The substitution of the French franc by the euro as the new external 'numéraire' has not been contested seriously in Africa. Because the French franc will disappear, at least in 2002, one had to replace 1 F CFA = 0.01 FF simply by 1 F CFA = x euro units where 1 F CFA = 0.01 FF = 0.00152449 euro (or 100 CFA F = 0.15244 euro). Since there had been steadily an 'irreversibly' fixed peg with respect to the French franc (with the exception of January 1994), nothing will be changed fundamentally according to the prevailing African view, except that the fixed peg will be related to the euro instead of the French franc, while the French Treasury could continue its pooling function of international reserves owned by the countries of the 'Euro-CFA' Zone. With the presence of capital controls, the only dominating fright within the African Franc Zone consists of a new devaluation at the moment when the new euro currency (banknotes) will be in circulation.

Unfortunately, monetary economics of open economies are not all that 'simplistic' neither for the future European Monetary Union nor for the future Euro-CFA Zone. The basic question is not the numéraire aspect, but the degree of 'sovereign' monetary policy either for a single country or a currency area. The degree of monetary sovereignty is determined by the choice of the exchange rate regime.

Which monetary sovereignty for the euro CFA? The African francophone zone could follow its tradition in terms of a fixed peg, related now to the new anchor currency (euro). Until January 1994, the exchange rate tool was refused by the African members *and* by France. Whether the French government had exercised de facto a veto right against any devaluation (before January 1994) remains an open question to be discussed by economic historians. For the future, the monetary policy of the African Franc Zone could remain 'dependent', not anymore on the Banque de France or the Bundesbank as in the past, but now with respect to the new European Central Bank (or rather with respect to the European Council of the eleven finance ministers). The other extreme case, opposite to the 'unilateral' peg with respect to the euro, would be the choice of a floating rate.

An intermediate solution could be an association of the African CFA Zone to the remaining countries of the former EMS, i.e. to the 'outs' (or 'pre-ins') of EMU like Greece or Denmark. However, any necessary change in the central parity value between the euro CFA and the euro would be an outcome of 'collective' decisions between the African 'Group of Thirteen' and the European Council of Finance Ministers (see Appendix on the Maastricht Treaty, Article 109.4). In addition, the entry conditions to the euro club would be the full (capital-account) convertibility of the former CFA franc.

The most pessimistic view would be the collapse of the French Franc Zone as the result of maintaining exchange controls and of the subsequent emergence of parallel foreign exchange markets giving rise even to different exchange rates, at least between the Central and West African Zones. One historical precedent happened in January in 1994, when the Comoro franc (which is the CFA franc of the Federal Islamic Republic of the Comoro Islands with 530,000 inhabitants) was devalued less, namely by 33 percent. Under this scenario, the emergence of a currency board for each individual zone, Central and West, may become a valuable alternative of last resort. The fixed peg for each currency board could be related again to the euro, but it could only be a 'unilateral' peg, since a consensus for a 'bilateral' exchange rate mechanism (in analogy to the former EMS) managed by the European Council of Finance Ministers seems to be improbable.

Appendix: Extracts From the Maastricht Treaty

Declaration on monetary cooperation with non-Community countries. The Conference affirms that the Community shall aim to contribute to stable international relations. To this end the Community shall be prepared to cooperate with other European countries and with those non-European countries with which the Community has close economic ties.

Declaration on monetary relations with the Republic of San Marino, the Vatican City and the Principality of Monaco. The Conference agrees that the existing monetary relations between Italy and San Marino and the Vatican City and between France and Monaco remain unaffected by the Treaty establishing the European Community until the introduction of the ECU as the single currency of the Community. The Community undertakes to facilitate such renegotiations of existing arrangements as might become necessary as the result of the introduction of the ECU as a single currency.

Protocol on France. The high contracting parties, desiring to take into account a particular point relating to France, have agreed upon the following provisions, which shall be annexed to the Treaty establishing the European Community. France will keep the privilege of monetary emission in its overseas territories under the terms established by its national laws, and will be solely entitled to determine the parity of the CFP franc.

Article 109

1. By way of derogation from Article 228, the Council may, acting unanimously on a recommendation from the ECB or from the Commission, and after consulting the ECB in an endeavor to reach a consensus consistent with the objective of price stability, after consulting the European Parliament, in accordance with the procedure in paragraph 3 for determining the arrangements, conclude formal arrangements on an exchange rate system for the ECU in relation to non-Community currencies. The Council may, acting by a qualified majority on a recommendation from the ECB or from the Commission, and after consulting the ECB in an endeavor to reach a consensus consistent with the objective of price stability, adopt, adjust or abandon the central rates of the ECU within the exchange rate system. The President of the Council shall inform the European Parliament of the adoption, adjustment or abandonment of the ECU central rates.

2. In the absence of an exchange rate system in relation to one or more non-Community currencies as referred to in paragraph 1, the Council, acting by a qualified majority either on a recommendation from the Commission or after consulting the ECB or on a recommendation from the ECB, may

formulate general orientations for exchange rate policy in relation to the primary objective to maintain price stability.

3. By way of derogation from Article 228, where agreements concerning monetary or foreign exchange regime matters need to be negotiated by the Community with one or more States or international organizations, the Council, acting by a qualified majority on a recommendation from the Commission and after consulting the ECB, shall decide the arrangements for the negotiation and for the conclusions of such arrangements. These arrangements shall assure that the Community expresses a single position. The Commission shall be fully associated with the negotiations. Agreements concluded in accordance with this paragraph shall be binding on the institutions of the Community, on the ECB and on Member States.

4. Subject to paragraph 1, the Council shall, on a proposal from the Commission and after consulting the ECB, acting by a qualified majority decide on the position of the Community at international level as regards issues of particular relevance to economic and monetary union and, acting unanimously, decide its representation in compliance with the allocation of powers laid down in Articles 103 and 105.

5. Without prejudice to Community competence and Community agreements as regards economic and monetary union, Member States may negotiate in international bodies and conclude international agreements.

Notes

1. 'Dollarized' European 'countries' are *Monaco* (French franc since 1865); *San Marino* (Italian lira since 1897); *Liechtenstein* (Swiss franc since 1921); *Vatican City* (Italian lira since 1930).
2. 'Crawling peg' currencies or in more recent time 'crawling band' currencies of South America (like those of Brazil, Chile, and Mexico) have not been taken into account.
3. See, for instance, the survey in IMF, *World Economic Outlook*, May 1998, chapter 4.
4. However, this distinction is not fully comparable or even analogical with the separation between tradable and non-tradable goods. Non-tradable goods are not subject to international price competition, while bank loans are exposed to an international interest-rate competition in a financially open economy.
5. '... a bank run in our model is caused by a shift in expectations, which could depend on almost anything, consistent with the apparently irrational observed behavior of people running on banks.' Douglas W. Diamond and Philip H. Dybvig, 'Bank Runs, Deposit Insurance and Liquidity', *Journal of Political Economy*, vol. 99, June 1983, p. 404. See also Demirgüç-Kunt and Enrica Detragiache, 'The Determinants of Banking Crises in Developing and Developed Countries', *IMF Staff Papers*, vol. 45, March 1998, p. 83.

6. James Tobin, 'Financial Globalization: Can National Currencies Survive?', Annual World Bank Conference on Development Economics, Washington, D.C, April 20-21, 1998, p. 10.

7. For a survey see, for instance, Paul B. Kenen, 'Analyzing and Managing Exchange-Rate Crises', *Open Economies Review*, vol. 7, 1996, pp. 469-492.

8. The schedule P_0 should have been drawn as a rectangular hyperbola to the extent that one defines the price level as $P = P_N{}^a P_T{}^b$ where a (b) represents the weight of non-tradable (tradable) goods within total goods. For sake of simplicity, the schedule P_0 has been drawn as a straight line assuming $a = b = 0.5$ (or by using implicitly a non-weighted average between P_N and P_T). See the later Box 1.

9. Thus, the relative fall in P_N will be greater than the relative fall in P and M (the quantity of money), respectively. If non-tradable goods make up half of total goods ($a = 0.5$), and a real depreciation rate of 20 percent is required for q, the general price level has to fall by 10 percent. The rate of monetary contraction will be lower (10 percent) than the rate of the real depreciation.

10. A 'non-inflationary solution' of a nominal devaluation would be point C_1 for the price level at P_1 (compare point B with C_1). The rate of the real depreciation is higher than the rate of the nominal depreciation. It results from an increase in P_T (via E) *and* from a fall in P_N. See Box 1 and Emil-Maria Claassen, *Global Monetary Economics,* Oxford University Press, 1996, p. 105.

11. James Tobin, *The New Economics One Decade Older,* Princeton University Press, 1974, p. 89; 'Prologue', in M. Ul Haq, I. Kaul and I. Grunberg, eds., *The Tobin Tax: Coping with Financial Volatility,* Oxford University Press, 1996, p. xi, and James Tobin (1998), p. 18. See also Kunibert Raffer, 'The Tobin Tax: Reviving a Discussion', *World Development*, vol. 26, no. 3, 1998, pp. 529-538.

12. We have excluded the new member country Guinea-Bissau (1 million inhabitants) which joined the West African Monetary Union in May 1997.

13. The optimum size of a country, from an economic point of view, has been analyzed by Alberto Alesina, Enrico Spolare and Romain Wacziarg, 'Economic Integration and Political Disintegration', National Bureau of Economic Research, September 1997, and by Alberto Alesina and Enrico Spolare, 'On the Number of Size of Nations', *Quarterly Journal of Economics*, November 1997.

14. By letting out the other option of a fundamentally independent monetary policy in terms of a floating exchange rate for the CFA Franc.

PART III
THE EURO IN THE
INTERNATIONAL ECONOMY

11. KEY CURRENCIES AFTER THE EURO[1]

Richard N. Cooper

Introduction

On January 1, 1999, eleven European countries introduced a new European currency, the euro, which by mid-2002 will lead to the complete withdrawal of their existing national currencies. This change is a bold monetary experiment of unprecedented magnitude. It will require substantial changes both in the execution of day-to-day economic transactions and in the overall functioning of European economies. An enormous amount of effort has been devoted to making the change as smooth as possible and to understanding the consequences of the change within Europe.

The rest of the world is largely a bystander in this engaging process. Europeans have shown little interest in the external ramifications of their actions, and few non-Europeans until recently paid much attention to the dramatic changes taking place within Europe. What will they portend for outsiders, and in particular for the role of the US dollar and other national currencies in the world economy?

The Japanese yen, the German mark, the French franc, the British pound, the Swiss franc, and especially the US dollar are national currencies used extensively in diverse ways by non-nationals around the world. With the creation of the euro, the German mark and the French franc will disappear, and possibly, at a later date, the British pound as well. It would be natural for the euro to replace these European currencies in their international roles, although with the initial and inevitable confusions associated with the introduction of the euro that cannot be taken for granted; foreigners may take refuge from the turbulence by moving to the dollar, the yen, or other currencies. But creation of the euro raises the possibility that in the longer run it will not only replace the mark and the franc in their international roles, but will also compete more effectively with the dollar and the yen as international currencies, even to the extent of eventually displacing them as well.

Indeed, precisely this specter has been held out by Fred Bergsten (1997, and in Masson et al., 1997), and in milder form by Alogoskoufis and Portes (in Masson et al., 1997) and by Portes and Rey (1998). Bergsten suggests that within a decade as much as $1000 billion now held in foreign currency balances around the world, mainly in US dollars, may shift into euros, with profound consequences for the exchange rate between the dollar and the euro and possibly for macroeconomic performance as well.

This paper will address these various issues. It first takes up the reasons why national currencies might be used internationally, and provides some data on the international role of currencies in the mid-1990s, and on their recent evolution. It then takes up the factors suggesting that the euro will emerge as an international currency, possibly displacing the dollar. I then offer reasons for believing that a major displacement of the dollar will not take place, at least for several decades. Next it addresses the consequences if that forecast proves to be incorrect. A concluding section touches on probably more important issues that are not discussed in detail in the paper.

International Roles for National Currencies

The classical roles for money are as a unit of account, a medium of exchange, and a store of value. These roles also have applicability in the international economy. Actually, there are two quite different unit of account functions that a national currency can play. The first is as a comprehensible common standard of measurement. There are often occasions in which we want to make international economic comparisons, or even to aggregate economic magnitudes involving two or more countries. We need a common unit of measurement to do this. It could be any commonly agreed measure, even an artificial one, but it is not unnatural to use the currency of the largest national economy. It is noteworthy that the International Monetary Fund now keeps its accounts in a wholly artificial unit, the SDR (defined as a basket of the five leading currencies), but it is incomprehensible to most people outside the specialized community of IMF aficionados, and I conjecture most interested parties outside the IMF itself mentally translate SDR-measured magnitudes into dollars or some other national currency.

The second unit of account function involves denominating assets (e.g. international bonds or consortium loans) or registering trade invoice values or prices of international trade commodities—anything that requires a well-defined monetary specification. Whenever cross-border transactions are involved, at least one party must generally use a currency other than his own. For reasons to be discussed below, two parties may prefer a third currency. But the only way to avoid some international use of national currencies for this purpose would be a regime in which all sales by convention are made in the currency of the seller (or all purchases in the currency of the buyer). Such a convention would stifle much useful international trade in goods, services, and assets.

Logically units of account for invoicing or denomination could be separated from the medium of exchange, and indeed some bonds denominated in a particular currency can be purchased in a variety of currencies. But again it is natural in many cases for the unit of account, if it is a functioning money, to be used also as the medium of exchange. Thus goods invoiced in dollars are usually paid for in dollars. So the argument for some international monetary unit of account also applies to its use as a medium of exchange.

Finally, 'money' is used as a store of value, at least temporarily. Some limited international use of national currencies in this role flows naturally from their use as a medium of exchange, since parties may want to accumulate over time the currencies they will need to make payments on a specific date, e.g. on an import contract or for interest on an outstanding bond. In addition, monetary authorities accumulate 'foreign exchange reserves' to be used to intervene in foreign exchange markets should that prove desirable. It is worth noting explicitly that 'money' held as a store of value by business firms or financial institutions is not usually held in the form of money at all, but in liquid interest-bearing assets. This fact will play an important role in the argument developed below. However, many individuals around the world, for diverse reasons, find it expedient to hold monies, i.e. banknotes, from countries other than their own, and the US greenback has become overwhelmingly the favored instrument in most parts of the world.

Why do we see extensive international holdings of national currencies? In principle, people could hold only national currencies; with well-functioning foreign exchange markets they could convert into another currency only at the moment it is needed.

The reasons for holding foreign currencies are many and diverse, but for private parties they boil down to three: market barriers, transactions costs, and liquidity (which on some definitions are included in transactions costs). National exchange controls create an obstacle to currency conversions when needed, particularly if the need is not acceptable to the authorities or if it arises unexpectedly. Transactions costs inhibit transactions, especially reversible transactions or those that can enjoy some offset netting over a period of time.

Up to a point, transactions costs in financial markets are influenced by the size of the institutions participating in the market and hence, to assure competition, also by the size of the market. That is because of economies of scale in efficient financial management systems (e.g., a given software program, once written, can handle few or many transactions with indifference, but the average costs decline with number of transactions).

Many economies are too small to have highly efficient, competitive markets in foreign exchange.

But foreign exchange markets are subject to another, quite different efficiency as a function of use and scale, called network externalities. By analogy with language or the telephone, the more people who use it, the more useful it is to any single user. My ability to communicate by phone or fax beyond a circle of known acquaintances depends on how many of the parties I potentially might want to communicate with have telephones and fax machines. The value of a telephone to me depends on how many other potential respondents have phones. My ability to communicate with strangers hinges on finding a common language of communication. Polyglot Chinese use Mandarin in China; polyglot Indians and Nigerians use English within India and Nigeria.

The network externality in financial markets concerns mainly liquidity: the ability to carry out a transaction whenever I want to carry it out without incurring extra cost. Liquidity will generally be higher the higher the number of transactions—the 'thicker' the market. This phenomenon is present in foreign exchange markets—accounting for the fact that many international transactions between two countries other than the United States involve intermediation through US dollars rather than direct exchange of the two currencies involved. Transactions costs will be lower, but they will be lower mainly because of the larger number of transactions of each currency with the US dollar than between the two currencies, resulting in lower bid-ask spreads.

The phenomenon is also present in securities markets, thus influencing which securities people will want to hold as a temporary store of value to meet unpredictable needs. In particular, the market in US Treasury securities is unrivalled in this regard.

National Currencies in the World Economy

The various functions of money can all be observed in the international use of national currencies. Organized commodity markets are almost universally reported and traded in US dollars, and many off-market transactions use these market prices. Foreign trade other than commodities is often denominated in currencies other than those of the exporting country. Funke and Kennedy (1997, Table 8) report that in 1992 48 percent of world exports were denominated in dollars, down from 56 percent in 1980 (all of the drop and then some can be explained by the drop in the share of oil in world exports). This compares with a US share in world exports of 12 percent. Sixteen percent of world exports were denominated in German marks (up from 14 percent in 1980), compared with a German export share of 11 percent. The Japanese yen accounted for five percent of export invoices (up from 2 percent in 1980), compared with Japan's 9 percent share of world exports.

Funke and Kennedy (1997, Table 7) report the currency of denomination of international bonds and other international long-term lending (mainly syndicated bank loans), reproduced here as Table 1. Dollars accounted for 43 percent of the bonds in 1996, about the same as 1980, but up and down in the meantime. German marks actually declined during this period, from 22 percent to 14 percent, with yen, pounds, and French francs all showing increases. The Ecu rose to 8 percent of all new international bond issues in 1990, but then declined to less than one percent in 1996.

Globalization of patterns of investment suggest that more and more national portfolios will be diversified, both geographically and across currencies. Thus this particular use of national currencies is likely to extend to many currencies, not just those of the major countries, including for example the Australian dollar and the South African rand, and eventually the Chinese yuan and the Russian ruble. Whether the diversification takes place into national or international bonds will depend on many issues, including yield, covenants, quality of secondary markets, transparency of information, reliability of the system for settling disputes, etc. But increasing cross-currency diversification of portfolios will be a natural consequence of globalization of information and ease of transactions. The major currencies can all expect to experience a secular decline in share, within rising totals.

International lending other than bonds was 77 percent in US dollars in 1996, down from 93 percent in 1980 (a year of high dollar deposits in the banks by oil-exporting countries, the peak year of oil revenues). The DM, yen, pound, and French franc all gained in share. More dramatic by far than changes in the currency composition of international lending, however, was the growth in the total, from $116 billion in 1980 to $1059 in 1996, so all major currencies, including the dollar, experienced a rapid increase in international use. While data are not readily available, currencies used for loan transactions presumably roughly followed the currencies of denomination, although not exactly (as is evident for ECU lending). For instance, in April 1995 84 percent of global gross foreign exchange market turnover involved the US dollar on one side of the transaction, leaving only 16 percent that did not involve the US dollar. This is strong evidence for the presence of network externalities, discussed above. Runners-up were the DM at 37 percent, the yen at 24 percent, and the pound at 9 percent (BIS, 1996). Many of these transactions were undoubtedly with the dollar. Since such transactions necessarily involve two currencies, total transactions add to 200 percent.

Table 1: International Capital Markets

	Total Funds Raised[a]					
	1975	1980	1985	1990	1995	1996
Total issues in:						
US dollar equivalent: ($US billion)	40.6	116.5	259.8	361.4	841.3	1058.6
Shares of selected currencies:						
US dollar	74.3	76.2	68.8	44.6	56.0	54.4
Japanese yen	0.2	1.6	7.1	9.0	10.0	7.5
Deutschmark	9.2	8.5	4.7	7.2	10.6	10.9
Pound sterling	0.4	1.9	3.5	11.9	6.9	8.3
French franc	0.9	1.6	0.6	3.0	2.3	5.9
Ecu		0.0	3.7	7.8	2.5	0.5
	International Bonds[b]					
	1975	1980	1985	1990	1995	1996
Total issues in:						
US dollar equivalent: ($US billion)	19.9	38.3	167.8	229.9	467.3	710.6
Shares of selected currencies:						
US dollar	51.2	42.7	60.9	34.8	37.8	43.5
Japanese yen	0.4	4.8	7.2	13.4	17.7	11.1
Deutschmark	16.3	21.9	6.8	8.0	15.6	14.1
Pound sterling	0.2	3.0	4.2	9.2	4.6	7.3
French franc	1.8	3.0	0.9	4.2	2.7	6.5
Ecu		0.0	4.3	7.8	1.5	0.6

Notes

a   Total funds include international bond issues, medium- and long-term syndicated bank loans and other debt facilities.
b   International bonds include gross public and private offerings of euro-bond issues and foreign bond issues.

Source: OECD Secretariat.

A vast and vigorous euro-currency market, based in London, has evolved from small beginnings in 1957 based on British banks accepting deposits and lending in US dollars. It has spread to several other currencies, based on British law and practice, and free from domestic regulation by the countries whose currencies are being quoted. The nearly $7 trillion of assets in this market are difficult to interpret, since over 90 percent of them involve transactions among banks. Moreover, domestic de-regulation in many countries now permits local deposits in foreign currencies, confounding interpretation. It is suspected that many euro-bank liabilities in DM are actually to German residents, who hold their funds abroad to escape German taxation. At the end of 1996, at least 46 percent of all foreign deposits in the euro-currency market reported by industrial country banks were denominated in dollars, 15 percent were in DM, and 6 percent were in yen (BIS, 1997, Table 4A). Roughly the same ratios hold for the much lower deposits by non-banks: 51, 17, and 5 percent, respectively. The Italian lire and the French franc were close behind the yen. The existence of the euro-currency market reminds us that the use of a national currency can be detached from the nationality of financial institutions and even, to some extent, from national monetary authorities.

National governments or central banks held a total of $1481 billion of foreign exchange in their official reserves at the end of 1996. Of this, at least 64 percent were denominated in US dollars, 14 percent in German marks, 6 percent in yen, 3 percent in pounds, and lesser shares in other currencies (from IMF, *Annual Report, 1997*, Table I.2). The dollar share was down substantially from the 79 percent of 1975, but showed a marginal increase (especially in developing countries) over the past decade. Again, these shares must be assessed in the context of a substantial increase in reserves over time, up from $716 billion in 1989 and $373 billion in 1980. Alterations in share occurred within a rapidly rising total. Eighty percent of the increase in reserves in 1996 was in US dollars, ten percentage points of which were changes in valuation (IMF, Table I.3). The fact that US short-term interest rates were higher than those in other major countries (except for Britain) may have played a role in recent preference for the dollar.

Finally, it should be noted that national banknotes, especially the US dollar, are used extensively outside the issuing country. It is the nature of such holdings that they cannot be known with precision. But over half US currency by value is in the form of $100 bills, rarely seen within the United States. The Federal Reserve has estimated that 55-70 percent of US banknotes in circulation, $373 billion at the end of 1995, were outside the United States (Porter and Judson, 1996). German marks are much less extensively used, but are common in the former Yugoslavia.

Impact of the Euro

The previous section has provided empirical information on the state and recent trends in international use of national currencies. Creation of the euro will represent a major 'disturbance' to the international financial system. Will it affect international use of national currencies in ways beyond the obvious one, viz. the international uses of the DM and the French franc (and maybe the pound) will disappear? Some authors have argued affirmatively, that the very scale of the EMU, even at its smallest, certainly at its largest, will induce a major reassessment by traders, investors, and central banks around the world, leading to an international use of the euro under the various headings that will substantially exceed the current international use of existing EU currencies.

As noted at the outset, Bergsten foresees a major international portfolio shift of $500-1000 billion into euros during the first five to ten years of its existence; most of the shift will come out of dollars, $100-300 billion from official reserves, the remainder from private holdings. This analysis takes as its starting point the prospective economic size of the EMU and its importance in world trade. The 15-nation EU has a slightly larger GDP than the United States, and also slightly larger foreign trade (excluding intra-EU trade). Excluding Britain and Sweden reduces both to somewhat smaller than the United States, but still roughly the same magnitude. The analysis goes on to argue that while European capital markets are now generally smaller and less well developed than those of the United States, this deficiency is likely to be made up during EMU's formative years. The United States has a large current account deficit, compared with a modest surplus for the European Union, and a large net debtor position, requiring eventual depreciation of the dollar to improve the trade balance in order to service the growing external indebtedness. Table 2 (from Prati and Schinasi, in Masson et al., p. 266) offers some comparative statistics for USA, Japan, EU(15), and EU(11).

The Maastricht Treaty's emphasis on price stability assures a reasonably firm monetary policy, and a stable unit of value. Finally, Europe is likely to experience some fiscal expansion during the early years of EMU, which, combined with firm monetary policy and fiscal contraction in the United States (aimed at balancing the Federal budget by 2002), will assure a prospective appreciation of the euro against the US dollar. For all these reasons, the euro will be an attractive vehicle for third parties, and even for Americans, to acquire.

Absent major policy failure by the United States, Bergsten expects the dollar to remain a leading world currency, but he also expects the euro to come to rival it in importance, suggesting that after a decade about 40 percent of 'world finance' will be held in euros, 40 percent in dollars, and 20 percent in yen and other currencies.

Alogoskoufis and Portes (1997) also foresee that 'the euro will substitute to a large extent for the dollar as an international means of payment, unit of account and store of value', although they do not attempt to estimate the magnitude of the shift. They point out that if such a shift is to occur, euro-denominated assets will have to be provided to the rest of the world on a net basis, and this will require (other things equal) a current account deficit by the EMU-countries on a continuing basis, achieved by an appreciation of the euro relative to the dollar and other foreign currencies, such as the yen (see also Cooper, 1992).

Provision of euros through a current account deficit is possible, but not necessary. Short-term claims could also be provided through exports of long-term financial capital from Europe, in effect purchasing long-term assets for short-term liabilities to the rest of the world, much as the United States did during the 1950s and 1960s. In such an eventuality, the euro would not necessarily have to appreciate. So what occurs will depend not only on the institutional changes within Europe and on the attractiveness of the euro to the rest of the world, but also on how portfolio preferences of Europeans evolve. That, of course, will inter alia depend on relative yields; low interest rates in Europe are more likely to induce a search for higher-yield claims on the rest of the world, obviating the development of a current account deficit; by the same token, however, low interest rates on euro-denominated assets, relative to yields on alternative liquid assets, will reduce their attractiveness to foreigners.

Why the Euro Will Not Replace the Dollar Anytime Soon

As noted, it is useful to draw distinctions among the different roles that a money performs. But 'money' is only part of the story, a convenient unit of account. The terms 'dollar' and 'euro' are really short-hand, metaphors for a more complex set of phenomena. One does not hold 'dollars', but dollar-denominated assets, or banknotes (greenbacks). If substantial balances are to be held, there must be a convenient medium for holding them. The great strength of the British pound in the 19th and early 20th centuries was not only that Britain was the world's largest trading nation and that British trade was largely denominated in sterling. London was also the world's pre-eminent financial market. Within the City developed a highly liquid, highly efficient secondary market in bankers acceptances and in British Treasury bills, a short-term claim on the government. The same may be said currently of the US Treasury bill in New York and elsewhere.

Table 2: European Union (EU), Japan, and North America: Selected Indicators on the Size of the Capital Markets, 1995

	Population (in millions)	GDP	Total Reserves Minus Gold	Stock Market Capitalisation	Debt Securities[1]			Bank Assets[2]	Bonds, Equities, and Bank Assets[3]	Bonds, Equities, and Bank Assets[3] (in percent of GDP)
					Public	Private	Total			
					(in billions of US dollars)					
EU (15)[4]	369.0	8,427.0	376.3	3,778.5	4,814.4	3,858.6	8,673.0	14,818.0	27,269.5	323.60
EU (11)[5]	286.1	6,803.9	284.5	2,119.4	3,909.7	3,083.5	6,993.2	11,971.6	21,084.2	309.89
EU (8)[6]	181.8	5,054.8	199.2	1,693.8	2,330.4	2,611.0	4,941.4	9,456.0	16,091.2	318.34
North America	387.7	8,065.6	106.7	7,314.7	7,332.2	4,411.9	11,744.1	5,652.4	24,711.1	306.38
Canada	29.6	565.6	15.0	366.3	589.1	93.3	682.4	515.8	1,564.5	276.61
Mexico	94.8	246.2	16.8	90.7	30.7	23.5	54.2	136.6	281.5	114.34
United States	263.3	7,253.8	74.8	6,857.6	6,712.4	4,295.1	11,007.5	5,000.0	22,865.1	315.22
Japan	125.2	5,114.0	183.3	3,667.3	3,450.3	1,875.5	5,325.8	7,382.2	16,375.2	320.21
Memorandum items:										
EU countries										
Austria	8.1	233.3	18.7	32.5	105.9	105.4	211.3	457.7	701.6	300.66
Belgium	10.0	269.2	16.2	105.0	305.1	165.3	470.4	734.2	1,309.5	486.45
Denmark	5.2	173.3	11.0	56.2	142.1	187.8	329.9	155.5	541.6	312.55
Finland	5.1	125.0	10.0	44.1	94.0	50.2	144.2	143.5	331.9	265.54
France	57.5	1,537.9	26.9	522.1	681.9	803.6	1,485.5	2,923.0	4,930.5	320.61
Germany	81.7	2,412.5	85.0	577.4	893.6	1,286.0	2,179.6	3,752.4	6,509.3	269.82

Greece	10.5	114.3	14.8	17.1	99.7	5.8	105.5	63.9	186.4	163.06
Ireland	3.6	61.9	8.6	25.8	38.5	7.4	45.9	82.3	154.0	248.63
Italy	56.3	1,087.2	34.9	209.5	1,222.0	396.2	1,618.2	1,513.5	3,341.2	307.33
Luxembourg	0.4	19.3	0.1	30.4	1.0	15.8	16.8	555.0	602.2	3,124.56
Netherlands	15.5	395.7	33.7	356.5	210.4	177.3	387.7	808.0	1,552.2	392.28
Portugal	9.3	102.7	15.9	18.4	56.0	15.8	71.8	161.8	252.0	245.25
Spain	38.7	559.2	34.5	197.8	301.3	60.5	361.8	840.2	1,399.8	250.34
Sweden	8.8	229.2	24.1	178.0	233.0	185.7	418.7	202.8	799.5	348.84
United Kingdom	58.5	1,106.3	42.0	1,407.7	429.9	395.8	825.7	2,424.4	4,657.8	421.01

Notes:

1. Domestic and international debt securities shown by the nationality of the issuer.
2. The 1994 data are shown for all banks except for the following: commercial banks plus savings banks for Denmark; commercial banks for Canada (consolidated worldwide), Greece, Luxembourg, and Mexico; domestically licensed banks for Japan (excluding trust accounts); commercial banks plus savings banks plus cooperative banks for Sweden; and commercial banks plus savings banks plus savings and loan associations for the United States.
3. Sum of the stock market capitalization, debt securities, and bank assets.
4. Austria, Belgium, Denmark, Finland, France, Germany, Greece, Ireland, Italy, Luxembourg, the Netherlands, Portugal, Spain, Sweden, and the United Kingdom.
5. Austria, Belgium, Finland, France, Germany, Ireland, Italy, Luxembourg, the Netherlands, Portugal, Spain.
6. Austria, Belgium, Finland, France, Germany, Ireland, Luxembourg, the Netherlands.

Sources: Bank for International Settlements; Bank of England, Quarterly Bulletin (November 1995); Bank of Japan, Economic Statistics Monthly (May 1996); Central Bank of Ireland, Quarterly Bulletin (Winter 1995); International Finance Corporation, Emerging Stock Markets Factbook 1996; Organization for Economic Cooperation and Development, Bank Profitability; Financial Statements of Banks, 1985-1994; and International Monetary Fund, International Financial Statistics and World Economic Outlook databases.

Amounts measured in billions of dollars can be bought or sold readily, 24 hours a day, anonymously, without influencing the price of the outstanding bills. In effect, for large holders the US T-bill has become interest-bearing money. It can be converted into means of payment at virtually no cost. Government securities dealers had *daily* transactions in T-bills of $40-50 billion.

The liquidity of the US treasury bill market is abetted by the Federal Reserve, which carries out its open market operations largely in treasury bills or other short-dated government securities. At the end of 1996 there were $777 billion in US Treasury bills outstanding, and another $2112 billion in Treasury notes with original maturities under five years, many of which at any moment in time will mature in less than a year. The Federal Reserve during 1996 added only $17 billion to its stock of Treasury securities, but it had repurchase agreements valued at $458 billion during the year. Moreover, the Federal Reserve in effect made a perfectly liquid market for foreign official monetary authorities by buying and selling T-bills offmarket in matched transactions (mainly overnight) that totaled $3,092 billion, an average of nearly $12 billion per working day.

There is nothing comparable to this market on the European continent, or in Japan, and there is not likely to be for decades to come.[2] The German government, influenced by legal limitations, has eschewed short-term debt, which at the end of 1996 was only 4 percent of marketable Federal government securities, amounting to 27 billion DM (about $16 billion); Germany also lacks a uniform contract for futures transactions (Prati and Schinasi in Masson et al., 1997).

France has the most effective short-term financial market on the Continent, but it relies heavily on repurchase transactions by the Bank of France, thus works mainly with the knowledge and approval of the Bank of France, with respect to securities acceptable to the Bank of France. Outright Bank of France purchases of treasury bills are low. As in Germany the treasury bill market is poorly developed, although its use has grown since it was introduced in 1985. Short-term government securities amounted to the equivalent of about $50 billion at the end of 1996—8 percent of marketable government debt. The share rises to 30 percent if 2- and 5-year notes are included.

In short, the European market is now small and fragmented. Introduction of the euro will of course eliminate currency differences among the participating Europeans countries, but that alone will not create a highly liquid secondary market in securities. That will not occur without a consolidation of outstanding government debts (as of, say, end 1991) under EMU responsibility, something that seems to be prohibited by the Maastricht Treaty, and indeed would be anathema to citizens in the fiscally conservative countries. Ironically, the Stability Pact will slow the development of a highly liquid euro-denominated asset, by limiting the extent to which European governments issue debt through budget deficits. Thus national government debt will grow only slowly after the introduction of the euro. Even if Germany were to run the full three percent of GDP budget deficit normally permitted by the Stability Pact, that would increase total outstanding German government debt only five percent a year. Only a drastic shortening of the average maturity, something Germany's debt managers—and the Bundesbank—would resist strongly, would permit the emergence of a euro-based competitor to the US treasury bill market. The German government inaugurated two new debt instruments in 1996: 6-month bills and 2-year notes. Of the largest ever net public borrowing by the Federal government of 83 billion DM in 1996, 23 percent was at relatively short term. But agreement with the Bundesbank limited outstanding 'bubills', with less than one-year maturity, to a maximum of 20 billion DM (*Monthly Review*, March 1997, p. 29).

A preference by monetary authorities for marketable securities over bank deposits is suggested by the fact that DM-denominated reserves in the form of deposits fell from over half in 1990 to barely one-third in 1996, involving an absolute fall in deposits within a growing total, as marketable securities became available.

Having a common currency does not by itself assure a widely accepted and liquid store of value. America's states typically issue short-term tax anticipation notes; but the market for them is fragmented and for large transactions and for most states they are relatively illiquid on secondary markets despite their short-term maturities; their acceptability and hence liquidity is also influenced by tax considerations since, as in Europe, state taxation of interest-bearing securities is a matter left to the states, and they have quite different definitions of taxable income.

Liquidity of a financial instrument is subject to 'network externalities'— the more agents who have the security, and the more frequently they trade them, the more liquid the security is likely to be. This factor is likely to be more important than economies of scale in the choice of a currency for international use, since Europe and Japan, as well as the United States, have sufficiently large *domestic* markets to achieve any likely technical economies of scale (e.g. indivisibilities in setting up a clearing system) involved in running a monetary and financial system. Where network externalities are involved, they tend to be self-reinforcing. The product in question is very difficult to dislodge, short of a major shock to the network. The creation of the euro creates an important alternative, but by itself it is not likely to provide a shock large enough to dislodge the US Treasury bill from its international role. Its acceptability and its convenience are too great.[3]

Any holder of a financial asset has to assess several different kinds of risk: credit risk (that the issuer will fail), market risk (that interest rates will move sharply and unexpectedly), exchange rate risk (that exchange rates will move sharply and unexpectedly), liquidity risk (that the asset cannot be converted quickly to means of payment when needed). Credit risk is lowest for governments, especially those with access to a central bank. Market risk is lower at short maturities. Exchange risk is higher for a currency different from the one needed to make payments, but it can be hedged. The US Treasury bill market is low risk on all counts, except where external debt or imports are not denominated in dollars.

Similar observations might be made with respect to US banknotes—greenbacks—especially the $100 bill. They are widely recognized and widely acceptable around the world, making them deeply rooted because of the externality involved. Money traders anywhere are even adept at identifying counterfeits. Over $200 billion in US banknotes are estimated to be circulating outside the United States. This total is likely to continue to grow even after introduction of euro banknotes in 2002, except where cash expenditures by European travelers are overwhelming, as German use of DM was in the former Yugoslavia—possibly in the central and eastern European countries, all aspirants to future EU membership, and in North Africa.[4]

The willingness to hold interest-bearing assets is of course influenced inter alia by their yield. It has not hurt the role of the dollar in recent years that short-term interest rates on US securities have exceeded those on DM assets, which in turn have exceeded the all-time low yield below 0.5 percent on short-term yen assets. Economists often argue that persistent yield differences on low-risk assets of comparable maturity must reflect expected movements in exchange rates, prospectively compensating for the differences in yield. That may be so, but forward exchange rates, which typically reflect yield differentials accurately, are notoriously poor (and biased) forecasters of future spot rates. In short, exchange rates typically do not move as yield differentials would suggest. This should not be entirely surprising. As noted above, at least some private balances in foreign currencies are held for their usefulness in transactions and for their liquidity. The owners do not necessarily expect to hold their balances for long enough for expected changes in exchange rates to come into play; while aggregate totals may grow, they reflect a continual change in ownership. Moreover, while the risk of depreciation is constantly present, depreciation may not actually materialize for an indefinite period. Nonetheless, a change in relative yield would influence the aggregate holding of foreign currency balances, partly by influencing the timing of their acquisition and disposition.

In this context, the historical switch from sterling to the dollar as the leading international currency shows only that such a switch can happen, not that it is likely to happen. Bergsten (1997) has emphasized the similarities between the dollar's overtaking the British pound and the possibility of the euro's overtaking the dollar, notably the relatively larger and growing size of the emerging currency's economy in each case, and the switch from a net creditor to a net debtor position vis-à-vis the rest of the world by the incumbent currency's economy. But one can just as well, and more pertinently, emphasize the important differences between the pound-dollar switch in the 1930s and 1940s and the prospect of a dollar-euro switch in the early 21st century. First, Britain's economy and its overseas financial position had been devastated by two World Wars. Second, the large external sterling balances accumulated during and shortly after the Second World War were reluctantly held because they could not be used freely for importation, in some years even from Britain. Third, exchange controls sharply limited the use of sterling in financing third country trade (i.e. trade not involving Britain or sterling area countries). In short, sterling was highly limited in its usability. Such is not the case with the dollar today, or for the foreseeable future. There is a large difference between a currency reluctantly held and one that is voluntarily held, as the dollar is; not surprisingly, the latter is preferred to the former, and holders of sterling switched as soon as they could gracefully do so.

The creation of the euro will eliminate the current international use of those European currencies which are subsumed by the euro. Since the bulk of DM holdings are undoubtedly held by residents of member countries of the European Union, their replacement by euros, which will no longer be 'international' currency for the members of the EMU, will paradoxically increase the relative international role of the dollar and the yen. But that is a statistical artifact.

What is not a statistical artifact is that many foreign exchange reserves now held by European countries, for defense of their currencies in foreign exchange markets, will become redundant after creation of the euro. Estimates of redundancy vary, since our understanding of the official demand for reserves remains imperfect, but Leahy (1994) has produced a not-very-confidently held average redundancy of 35 percent. If EMU members were to unload these reserves, mainly dollar-denominated, that would exert a major impact on foreign exchange markets, appreciating the euro relative to the dollar. But partly for this reason, partly because central bankers hate to part with reserves once they have been acquired, EMU members are not likely to unload their redundant reserves quickly, or indeed even at all until circumstances call for their use, e.g. to prevent unwanted depreciation of the euro.

Some Remarks on the Japanese Yen

The observations about short-term markets in euro-denominated securities applies even more to yen-denominated assets. For a variety of reasons, mainly having to do with the desire to borrow at preferential interest rates, the Japanese government declined for decades to develop a market-priced treasury bill market (see Ito, 1992). It crossed that hurdle in the early 1990s, but the market remains small and relatively undeveloped. Securities transactions are plagued by both regulations and taxation. Japan traditionally has focussed its financial market around the leading banks. They issue CDs, but the secondary market is not well-developed, except for repurchase agreements. In any case, as the world has learned during the last decade, even the largest commercial banks carry some credit risk, and in the mid-1990s the large Japanese banks were down-graded in their access to the world's interbank markets. So while large bank CDs represent a possible vehicle for holding yen-denominated assets, they are less satisfactory than short-dated government securities.

The inflexibilities and limitations of the Japanese financial market are in the midst of change. The Japanese government is committed to major financial reforms during the next five years. In April 1998 the Foreign Exchange Law (placing institutional restrictions on who in Japan can deal in foreign currency) was repealed. Many other changes are envisioned, with a view to making Tokyo a financial market that can compete effectively with London and New York. It remains to be seen whether the planned changes will be fully implemented and, if implemented, whether they will be executed in the spirit of the current plans—that is, whether Ministry of Finance (MOF) officials will in fact maintain some distance from the operations of financial institutions and markets, and whether Japanese institutions can function well in the absence of continuing guidance from the Ministry of Finance.

The main impact of the financial reforms will be on residents of Japan, who will enjoy greater competition in financial markets, leading to greater choice, higher yields, and lower costs. But the increased competition and reduced regulation will make short-term transactions in Tokyo's financial market more attractive to foreigners as well.

The plans for financial reform are silent on the question of government securities, partly no doubt because the MOF badly wants to reduce the budget deficit, and is loath to relinquish its preferred position with Japanese institutional investors. And while plans acknowledge the importance of revising the tax laws as they pertain to financial transactions, no concrete plans for change have been advanced—reflecting, no doubt, a reluctance to make any changes that may reduce revenue.

Thus the international role of the yen as a temporary store of value is limited, and is likely to remain so for at least another decade. What happens beyond that depends on how successful are the ambitious plans for financial market reforms. Even then, growth of the yen's role will be limited by the network externalities associated with the dollar discussed above. Moreover, the relative size of the Japanese economy in the world economy is likely to decline slowly, because of low labor force growth in the decades ahead; Japan's relative economic importance may have reached its peak in the late 1980s. Growing Japanese investment in Asian countries, often farming out labor-intensive slices of the production process, will doubtless encourage greater international use of the yen, not only by Japanese firms operating abroad, but also by their suppliers and perhaps also their non-Japanese customers. But the growth is likely to be slow, and not much affected by the creation of the euro.

Consequences of a Euro-Based International Monetary System

The conclusion of the foregoing discussion is that the euro will not come to rival the dollar seriously in its major international roles for many years to come, perhaps decades, beyond the obvious substitution of euro-denominated assets and invoices for assets and invoices now denominated in various national European currencies.

But suppose this prognostication about an always uncertain future were wrong. What differences would it make? Try to imagine a future in which many or most of the current international roles of the dollar are played by the euro.

The first point to note is that the EMU countries together will have large interest payments to foreigners. That by itself will require some depreciation of the euro, relative to what it would be otherwise, in order to generate the trade surpluses required to make the interest payments. So long as world demand for foreign exchange assets is growing, however, the rest of the world will steadily increase its investments in euro-denominated assets, and *ceteris paribus* that will tend to appreciate the euro. The net effect of these conflicting tendencies will depend both on the level of interest rates and on the rate of growth in rest-of-world holdings of euros. So long as the growth in world demand for euros exceeds the rate of interest paid on them, the net effect will be to appreciate the euro more than otherwise.

Second, short-term interest rates in high-quality euro securities will be modestly lower than otherwise, because of the world demand for international liquidity, and short-term interest rates on dollar securities will be somewhat higher. Third, pride of French and some Brussels officials will swell, while pride of some US Treasury officials will be deflated.

Apart from these effects, however, the world will function pretty much as it does today. Some things will not be radically different. In particular, the United States will not find it markedly more difficult to finance current account imbalances, nor will Europe find financing of current imbalances markedly easier. The ease or difficulty of such financing depends above all on the size of the economies involved, on the development of their financial markets, and on public perceptions of skill in managing them, which together influence access to the world capital market. The Europeans will not have a greater voice than they now do in discussions of world economic management, although on some issues they may speak with greater coherence. Europe will not experience an improvement in its terms of trade by virtue of invoicing international trade in euros. The constantly changing dollar price of oil responds to world shifts in demand and supply of oil, not to the fact that it is denominated in dollars rather than yen or marks. Similarly for other commodities.

Europeans will probably pay less attention to the dollar exchange rate than they do today, and for that reason European monetary authorities might take a stance of benign neglect toward the exchange rate. If the US authorities continued to do the same, the result might be greater volatility in exchange rates between the dollar and the euro than has been the case between the dollar and the various European currencies. On the other hand, the US authorities, faced with a single most significant exchange rate, might take a more active view toward both the appropriate level and the variability of that exchange rate, and thus manage the rate more aggressively than they have in the past. Thus the US and the European roles would be reversed in this respect, and the United States among other changes would want to hold more foreign exchange reserves (mainly in euros) than it has done historically.

Of course, by assumption, the rest of the world would be holding most of its foreign exchange reserves in euros. This last point reminds us that to get to this state there is likely at some point to have been a substantial conversion of foreign-held dollars into euros. That process, rather than the end result, might create major disturbances for the world economy, causing, if it occurred rapidly, major changes in both exchange rates and in interest rates in the United States and Europe. Thus potential turbulence lies much more in the transition than in the final configuration.

Important Neglected Issues

The foregoing discussion has focussed on the impact of the euro on the international role of the dollar and other currencies. There are several other implications, possibly more important, arising from creation of the euro.[5] The first concerns 'balance of payments' adjustment within Europe and its implications for European attitudes toward trade protection. A second concerns the mechanics of international cooperation in exchange rate management. A third concerns the desire of the new ECB to establish its reputation in the early EMU period for being a tough inflation fighter and for being independent of government.

Adjustment to disturbances within Europe may not take place smoothly for many years after the introduction of EMU, due to incomplete price and wage flexibility and imperfect labor mobility within Europe. Indeed, this is the outcome most feared by many opponents of EMU, and even by some of its proponents (see Obstfeld, 1997, and references there cited). Monetary union postulates an adjustment mechanism that relies on price and wage flexibility, and ultimately on labor and capital mobility within the geographic domain in question. (An alternative compensating mechanism, to avoid adjustment, involves subventions from some regions to others, and is taken up below.)

The need for adjustment cannot be avoided in any dynamic economy, subject as it is to changing patterns of demand and output, driven ultimately by continuing technical change. If the adjustment process works poorly, some regions will be depressed for long periods, and others will experience booms. A regional boom will generally arise from outside demand for the region's exportable products, and that will both increase the region's imports and lead to bidding up the prices of local factors of production and non-tradable goods and services, for which import competition is limited. At the same time, regions experiencing a decline in export demand will see a decline in their incomes and imports, and downward pressure on the prices of local factors of production and non-tradable goods and services. Whether prices actually decline in response to that pressure depends on their flexibility, i.e. on the extent of nominal wage and price rigidity, something that is common in modern economies.

The effect of all this on the rest of the world depends on how economic policy-makers respond. If price increases in the booming regions are interpreted as 'inflation' (which they would seem to be if not compensated by actual price reductions in the relatively depressed regions), the monetary authorities might tighten monetary conditions, which in turn would appreciate the euro against non-member currencies. Both tighter money and a stronger currency would dampen aggregate demand, leading the members of EMU to an overall condition of stagnation (which does not exclude that a few regions are still booming, although less so than before the policy response). Effective inter-regional adjustment requires allowing the price mechanism to work, which means allowing prices of non-tradables to rise in booming regions.

If in contrast the monetary authorities ease monetary conditions to relieve the depressed regions, the EMU as a whole will experience demand-led growth, in part through real depreciation of the euro, and greater inflation—a course that the commitment to price stability would seem to rule out. Either way, the rest of the world will feel the impact of these responses to imperfect regional adjustment.

Adjustment can be mitigated or avoided altogether if depressed regions are subsidized by booming regions. Drawing on the alleged experience of the United States, it is often said that inter-regional fiscal transfers greatly cushion regional imbalances, with the implication that the European Union should greatly augment such transfers as it moves toward monetary union.[6] It is of course true that in the United States Federal government expenditures and Federal taxes are substantial, roughly 40 percent higher than the aggregate tax collections of the state and local governments. It is also true that when income in a region declines, its contribution to Federal taxes (the most important of which is income taxes) declines, while at the same time Federal expenditures in the region are not likely to decline, and through some limited programs may actually increase.[7] The reverse occurs in a booming region: Federal tax payments rise, while expenditures are not likely to rise (unless an autonomous increase in Federal government expenditures is the source of the boom). This response reflects the 'automatic stabilizer' role of modern tax systems, linked to corporate and personal income, and to employment in the form of payroll taxes.

But this automatic stabilizer exists in any modern fiscal system, even for the whole country. It is not limited to federal systems. When economic activity slackens, tax revenues fall. Unless government expenditures are consciously cut in response to the fall in revenues (as, unfortunately, might be required under Europe's Stability Pact), the budget provides an automatic cushion to a decline in activity. Of course, the government must borrow more to cover its enlarged deficit, taking on an obligation against the future income of all its citizens. For a region within a country, this obligation does not fall on its residents alone, but rather is spread over all the residents of the country. One would have to believe in a strong form of Ricardian equivalence, however, to suppose that this difference is crucial to the cushioning impact of the government sector on current income and output.[8]

While some US states are net recipients of federal funds and others are net contributors to federal funds on a continuing basis, and those net flows are to some extent related to income differentials among regions, what is relevant for inter-regional payments adjustment is the cyclically sensitive component of federal expenditures: do such (net) expenditures increase as a result of relative decline in regional activity, and do they decline in a booming region? In reality, the inter-regional transfers (taking into account both taxes and expenditures) sensitive to transitory shocks are quite low in the United States. Von Hagen (1992) estimates them at only 0.1 percent of the change in state income. Most of the substantial cushioning effect does not involve inter-regional transfers, but rather the sensitivity of tax revenues to economic activity that exists in most modern economies. Nonetheless, lower labor mobility in Europe than in the United States may warrant greater reliance on inter-regional fiscal transfers to cushion regional payments imbalances. The Union has not yet addressed this issue squarely.

A second point concerns *international cooperation in exchange rate management*. As noted above, free floating between the US dollar and the yen and the euro is likely to lead to more volatility of exchange rates than has been true under the managed floating of the past. Suppose authorities would like to damp this volatility through official action, which typically works better if the actions are undertaken cooperatively (Dominguez and Frankel, 1993), or even nudge the exchange rate back toward more acceptable levels, as has happened on occasion during the past 12 years.

Imagine sitting in Washington or Tokyo or Ottawa after 1999. With whom exactly does one consult on exchange rate policy in post-EMU Europe? Historically, discussions on exchange rate cooperation have occurred within the G-7 setting, i.e. finance ministers and their deputies. But under Maastricht the ECB will have full control over exchange rate policy (as distinguished from choice of the exchange rate regime, which remains the responsibility of governments). Ministers have responsibility for other aspects of macroeconomic policy (except of course monetary policy). But much cooperation in the past has focussed on exchange rate management. The ECB president presides over a committee in which he has only one vote, and in any case it would be anomalous for him to attend an international meeting of finance ministers. Without a clear interlocutor for exchange rate policy of the euro, international cooperation will be difficult. This has not been a problem to date, since finance ministries everywhere have responsibility for exchange rate management, with responsibility being somewhat ambiguous and a source of continuing tension in Germany.[9]

Third, once the new ESCB is created and endowed with monetary authority, it will be concerned with *establishing a reputation* for 'sound' monetary policy, especially with a skeptical German public, which will be uneasy about passing monetary authority from its respected Bundesbank to a new, untried institution. The ECB thus will be tempted to pursue a monetary policy that is tighter than economic conditions require, and than would be pursued by a monetary authority whose reputation was secure. Tight monetary policy could possibly be rationalized by the conviction that fiscal policies in the member states are too 'loose', even when governments must finance their budget deficits in the capital market rather than at national central banks, which by now will cease to have money-creating powers. This combination will for a time ensure a 'strong' euro in international markets, with corresponding depressing effects on European export competitiveness and its associated impact on the rest of the world.

Conclusions

This paper has reviewed the forms of, and reasons for, the international use of national currencies. It concludes that while the creation of an Economic and Monetary Union in Europe, with its own currency, the euro, will mark a major event in the annals of monetary history, and will require major changes within Europe, it is not likely to affect much for many decades the international monetary system outside Europe, and in particular the international uses of the US dollar. The main reasons have to do, first, with the deeply entrenched network externalities associated with convenience, familiarity, and widespread use of the dollar by others; and, second, with the fact that the euro by itself is only a unit of account, not an instrument in which investments can take place. It will be many years, even decades, before Europe has a financial instrument that can rival the US Treasury bill in its universality of acceptance and in its liquidity. Unless economic and financial developments in the United States take such a disastrous turn that they cast doubt on the reliability of the T-bill, the dollar is likely to retain its pre-eminence as an internationally recognized short-term store of value and a transactions currency for decades to come. In time, the euro will no doubt become an important international currency, but the process is likely to be gradual; moreover, in the context of a growing world economy, the euro will supplement rather than directly displace the dollar in its diverse international roles.

The creation of EMU has important implications for the world economy. But they lie more in the uncertainties concerning intra-EMU balance of payments adjustment and the implications for international cooperation of the awkward division of responsibilities under the Maastricht Treaty than in likely displacement of the dollar in its major international uses.

Notes

1. An earlier version of this paper appeared in *The World Economy*, vol. 22, January 1999.
2. On German financial markets, see various issues of the *Monthly Report* of the Bundesbank; on French financial markets, see Bruneel 1992, Banque de France 1994, and CNCT 1997; on Japanese financial markets in the early 1990s, see Ito (1992).
3. The presence of network externalities gives rise to the possibility of multiple equilibria, which if strongly stable require a major disturbance to generate a switch from one equilibrium to another. This phenomenon can be observed in many settings, such as the continuing dominance of the QWERTY keyboard for typewriters and now for computers; the continuing dominance of Microsoft's DOS operating system and its descendants in personal computers; the growing dominance of English, a relatively complicated (but tolerant) language, as the language of world commerce and diplomacy, etc. For a discussion of multiple equilibria in the context of international currencies, see Rey (1997); in the context of language (in a Canadian setting), Church and King (1993).
4. The Bundesbank has estimated 'conservatively' that about 16 billion DM (roughly $10 billion) in German banknotes are held outside Germany. Bundesbank *Monthly Report*, April 1997.
5. The subsequent discussion draws on Cooper (1992).
6. See, e.g., Eichengreen (1990); the Delors Report mentions the need for greatly increased 'structural funds' to help correct regional imbalances. At Maastricht Spain insisted on and received formal assurances on the need for a large increase in funds to go to the four poorer countries of the Community. This criterion, however, is not at all the same as that calling for centrally-allocated funds to assist in adjustment to latent regional imbalances in payments.
7. Unemployment compensation in the United States is financed by each State. If necessary, loans from the Federal government are made, but must be repaid. Under certain circumstances, usually involving a national recession, the Federal government may contribute to unemployment compensation beyond the 26 weeks normally allowed.
8. Under the extreme form of Ricardian equivalence, private savings would rise to match the future debt obligations. This rise in private saving would neutralize fully the cushioning effects of any government deficit on aggregate demand in the country as a whole, but would only reduce them for a particular depressed region which did not have to carry the entire burden of the increased debt associated with any increase in the overall budget deficit. Increased saving in other regions would reduce its exports, however, and on that account would worsen its condition. Of course, if a rise in federal tax revenues arose because of a regional boom elsewhere, there need not be any increase in its overall budget deficit.
9. Article 109(2) of the Maastricht Treaty provides that apart from formal agreements with non-member countries the Council of Ministers 'may

formulate general orientations for exchange rate policy for these currencies. These orientations shall be without prejudice to the primary objective of the ESCB to maintain price stability.' Since the ESCB will be the sole judge of what is required for price stability, any such guidelines from the Council will only be hortatory.

References

Bank for International Settlements. 1996. *Central Bank Survey of Foreign Exchange and Derivative Activity* (May). Basle.

Bank for International Settlements. 1997. *International Banking and Financial Market Developments* (May). Basle.

Bergsten, C. Fred. 1997. 'The Dollar and the Euro.' *Foreign Affairs,* no. 76 (July/August).

Banque de France. 1994. 'Les interventions de la Banque de France sur le Marché Monétaire.' Note d'Information, no. 97 (Février).

Bruneel, Didier. 1992. *La Monnaie.* Paris: La Revue Banque Editeur.

Conseil National du Crédit et des Titres. 1997. *Rapport Annuel 1996.* Paris: Banque de France.

Church, Jeffrey, and Ian King. 1993. 'Bilingualism and Network Externalities.' *Canadian Journal of Economics,* 86 (May), pp. 337-345.

Cooper, Richard N. 1992. 'Will An EC Currency Harm Outsiders?' *Orbis* 36 (Fall).

Dominguez, Kathryn M., and Jeffrey A. Frankel. 1993. *Does Foreign Exchange Intervention Work?* Washington, D.C.: Institute for International Economics.

Eichengreen, Barry. 1990. 'One Money for Europe? Lessons from the United States.' *Economic Policy* (April), pp. 118-187.

Funke, Norbert, and Mike Kennedy. 1997. 'International Implications of the European Economic and Monetary Union.' OECD Working Papers, no. 174. Paris: OECD.

Henning, C. Randall. 1994. *Currencies and Politics in the United States, Germany, and Japan.* Washington, D.C.: Institute for International Economics.

Ito, Takatoshi. 1992. *The Japanese Economy.* Cambridge: MIT Press.

Leahy, Michael P. 1994. 'The Dollar as an Official Reserve Currency under EMU.' International Finance Discussion Papers, no. 474. Washington Federal Reserve Board.

Masson, Paul R., Thomas H. Krueger, and Bart G. Turtelboom, eds. 1997. *EMU and the International Monetary System.* Washington, D.C.: International Monetary Fund.

Obstfeld, Maurice. 1997. 'Europe's Gamble.' *Brookings Papers on Economic Activity,* no. 2.

Porter, Richard D., and Ruth A. Judson. 1996. 'The Location of U.S. Currency: How Much Is Abroad?' *Federal Reserve Bulletin* (October).

Portes, Richard, and Hélène Rey. 1998. 'The Emergence of the Euro as an International Currency.' *Economic Policy* (April), pp. 307-343.

Rey, Hélène. 1997. 'International Trade and Currency Exchange.' Centre for Economic Performance Discussion Paper, no. 322 (February). London School of Economics.

Von Hagen, Jürgen. 1992. 'Fiscal Arrangements in a Monetary Union: Evidence from the U.S.' In Donald F. Fair and Christian de Boissieu, eds., *Fiscal Policy, Taxation, and the Financial System in an Increasingly Integrated Europe.* Dordrecht: Kluwer Academic Publishers.

12. THE POLITICAL ECONOMY OF THE EURO AS AN INTERNATIONAL CURRENCY

Jeffry A. Frieden

Economic and Monetary Union (EMU) in Europe will have important effects on international monetary affairs. This is true on both economic and policy-making dimensions. As for the first, the euro is a major new currency whose use in international transactions will affect global monetary and financial relations in and of itself. The euro might rival the dollar as the principal international currency, which would fundamentally alter the character of other countries' exchange rate policies. Or the euro might prove a feeble currency, of little import to countries not directly tied to it. In this sense, the euro's international economic role is of interest and importance.

On the second, policy-making, dimension, the euro zone authorities are a vital new set of interlocutors in international monetary politics. This has to do not with the financial role of the euro as a currency, but rather with the involvement of the policy-making institutions of the Economic and Monetary Union in international monetary negotiations. This role, too, will have a broad impact on the international monetary system. The EMU authorities could turn inward to focus on the zone's monetary problems, even at the expense of the euro's international 'obligations'. This might imply fragmentation and conflict in international monetary relations, even a shattering into relatively self-contained currency blocs. Alternately, the euro zone might act vigorously as one of the world's principal policy-making partners, fully engaged in working out responses to global monetary problems. In this case, the result might be substantial movement toward a new international monetary architecture. Wherever reality takes us, there is no doubt that EMU brings a new monetary authority to the playing field of international monetary policy-making.

These are broad, complex, and important issues, which I do not dare address directly in this essay. Instead, I hope to provide insights into the processes and circumstances that will affect the outcomes in question. I discuss factors that I think will determine the role of the euro, and EMU authorities, in the international monetary and financial system. I emphasize the implications of contending interests among groups in the societies that make up the euro zone. I focus on these domestic conflicts of interest both because I believe that they are important and because they have routinely been ignored in most the scholarly and popular discussions.

Determinants of the Euro's International Role

Again, there are two dimensions to the international role of the euro, that of the currency itself on international markets, and that of the EMU authorities in the corridors of international monetary and financial power. On both dimensions, we can build on substantial analyses of the sources of currency-market and policy prominence; on both dimensions, I emphasize the typically underplayed *political economy* aspects of these sources.

We can start with the international role of the euro as a currency. Most current discussions of this issue usefully dissect a variety of purely economic factors: network externalities in trade and payments, invoicing behavior, portfolio allocation decisions.[1]

Yet these exclusively economic considerations are only some of the determinants of the euro's attractiveness to international users. The role of the euro will be fundamentally affected by euro zone *policy*, both short- and long-term. The desirability of a currency depends on its expected evolution, which depends in turn on the anticipated monetary policy stance of the issuing authorities. It also depends on the financial solidity of the issuing currency's 'home base', which depends in turn on the perceived depth and stability of the domestic (in this case euro zone) financial system. Both factors are determined by *policy*, both are highly *political*, and both will be decided in the cauldron of European economic policy-making, with its rich history of conflicts of interests.

The policy prerequisites of international monetary and financial leadership are generally recognized, and have been the subject of rich scholarly analysis.[2] Generally speaking, lasting international currency status is associated with four characteristics that are directly or indirectly dependent on national policy:

1. A generally stable currency, to reduce the risk of holding assets denominated in it.

2. A generally strong exchange rate, to avoid capital losses on the part of those who hold assets denominated in it.

3. Deep and liquid financial markets, to allow holders to diversify or liquidate their positions if necessary—that is, for example, if either of the first two conditions appear to be evolving in ways not to holders' liking.

4. Strong regulatory backing to minimize the possibility of financial difficulties and crises, so as to ensure that the third condition will hold.

The international use of a currency also typically depends on the home country having a substantial share of world trade, which of course is not directly amenable to policy. All these conditions are, however, interrelated. For example, holders of a currency are more likely to accept fluctuations in its value, the deeper and more efficient is the home financial (and forward) market. And a country's share of world trade will almost certainly have an impact on the economic and political implications of its exchange rate policies.

This makes clear how important the policy stance of the home government of such a currency is to its standing. And it is worth noting that these policies—toward the exchange rate and financial regulation—are often politically contentious.

The reason for the general politicization of these policies is that they involve trade-offs, on which important socio-economic groups typically have very different interests and views. J. Lawrence Broz (1997) tells the fascinating story of how attempts to establish the US dollar as an international currency after the turn of the 20th century led to substantial political conflict. An international position for the dollar required major monetary and financial policy shifts—such as the establishment of a central bank and of new financial instruments and regulations. These changes were strongly supported by the major American banks and firms that expected to gain from the 'internationalization' of the dollar, but were just as strongly opposed by other interests in the United States. This and other historical and contemporary experiences demonstrate clearly how a currency's international status often implicates powerful interests on different sides of relevant issues.[3]

In addition to the international role of the euro as a currency, we are interested in the role EMU policy-making authorities might play in international monetary and financial relations. Certainly there is no technical barrier to the ECB becoming the principal interlocutor of other national macroeconomic authorities in international monetary and financial affairs.

The determinants of such a role—and, potentially, the barriers to such an evolution—will be political. Substantial international involvement of EMU policy-makers in the corridors of international monetary and financial diplomacy requires these authorities to be able to speak and act as one. This in turn requires that whatever conflicts of interest may persist among members of the EMU are resolved before the ECB and other euro-authorities project their influence outside the borders of the European Union. This, too, requires agreement among EMU members to subordinate their particularistic concerns to the evolution of a common policy aimed at addressing global issues.

Whether the issue in question has to do with the position of the euro or of the EMU authorities, the governments, policy-makers, and peoples of the euro zone face potential conflicts. At the core of these expected conflicts is a crucial issue: the potential trade-off between the pursuit of international and domestic (in this case, EMU-specific) objectives. Policies aimed to ensure the euro's international role, or to secure EMU policy-makers' international bargaining influence, require reducing the priority placed on some domestic targets. For example, a strong euro may conflict with the desire of European exporters for a 'competitive' currency; and the development of a consistent EMU-area international economic negotiating position may have to ignore the concerns of a troubled region. All this is complicated by the institutional complexity—and confusion—of current EMU arrangements. Such potential conflicts of interests and institutions will have a powerful effect on the constraints imposed on euro policy-makers, and it is important to understand what conflicts may develop and whom they may implicate.

Anticipated Conflicts of Interest Over Euro Policy

At the core of the controversies that will shape euro policy are the complex of interests and institutions that will determine the willingness of the EMU to make domestic sacrifices for international goals. This is true whether the goal in question is to make the euro a leading international currency, or to catapult EMU authorities into a position as one of two leaders in 'bipolar' monetary system (Fratianni and Hauskrecht 1998). Three sets of potential areas of conflict can be anticipated: short-term exchange rate policy, the longer-term monetary stance of the euro authorities, and the character of the EMU financial system. In all three cases, there are substantial differences among powerful groups in the EU, as well as substantial institutional ambiguities and complications.

Immediate exchange rate policy. By this I have in mind the euro's value over the short or medium term, whether it has been relatively strong or relatively weak. A weak euro—and one expected to weaken further—is not very likely to attract substantial international use. By the same token, policies oriented toward a weak exchange rate are not generally associated with attempts to coordinate macroeconomic policies with other countries—such international cooperation is typically the result of attempts to join forces to stabilize and defend, not drive down, currencies.

The exchange rate excites powerful interests, with diametrically opposed inclinations. Those concerned with their competitive position at home or abroad want a relatively weak currency to raise the price of foreign goods on home markets and reduce the price of home goods on foreign markets. But a depreciated exchange rate is typically unpopular with monetary hard-liners, especially in the financial community. This is because it tends to be inflationary, and because assets denominated in a weak currency tend to be less attractive to investors.[4]

The trade-off here is an age-old one in exchange rate policy, usually thought of as the choice between competitiveness and credibility. There is no clear economic argument for one or the other—too strong an exchange rate can wreak havoc with the payments balance, too weak a one can ignite inflationary embers. The issue is, however, highly political, as it implicates powerful opposing interests.

And this sort of conflict of interest can only be ignored at the peril of serious miscalculations, as in fact early experience with EMU demonstrates. Initial expectations were for a rising euro, based on expectations that the ECB would focus on proving its inflation-fighting mettle. These expectations ignored the powerful lobbies for a depreciated exchange rate, especially among Europe's exporters and import-competers. In fact, at the time of the introduction of the single currency, European manufacturers were extremely concerned about export and import competition, in the face of a wave of Asian and Brazilian devaluations and continued attempts by Eastern and Central European producers to increase their sales in Western Europe. The reality of and potential for surging imports led European manufacturers to exert powerful pressures against an appreciation of the euro, and their views seem to have carried the day—much to the surprise of many euro-watchers in early 1999.

General exchange rate policy orientation. Here I have in mind the broad character of the monetary stance of the authorities. In the case of the euro, as for all international currencies, the principal question is how the authorities weight international and domestic (euro zone) concerns. This tension is commonly expressed as being between international and domestic stability, that is, emphasis on the stability of the exchange rate as opposed to the use of monetary policy for domestic purposes. Monetary authorities, of course, are concerned about both international and domestic dimensions of their policy choices, and cannot always achieve their goals on both dimensions simultaneously—domestic stabilization may destabilize currency markets, while defending the exchange rate may weaken the domestic economy.

Over the course of time, countries' macroeconomic authorities develop a reputation with regard to the international or domestic bias of their overall monetary stance. Economic agents have long expected the Swiss government to give pride of place to the international position of the franc; before 1990 the Swedish authorities had a well-deserved reputation for using the exchange rate as an active instrument of domestic macroeconomic (especially employment and wages) policy. This reputation reflects the society's underlying socio-political and economic character. Visceral German aversion to inflation, for example, meant that no amount of concern about the strength of the Deutschmark would lead the Bundesbank to countenance a substantial increase in inflation.

In the case of the euro, it is a matter of great uncertainty what the relative importance of domestic and international goals will be to the EMU authorities. And these goals implicate contending interests. As with the shorter-term exchange rate, many in the financial community are eager to ensure that the euro challenge the dollar for use as an international vehicle, which would require clear commitments by the ECB to avoid policy changes motivated solely by domestic considerations.

Yet much of the support for EMU came precisely from groups in the European Union who wanted a zone of monetary stability—*domestic* monetary stability. The larger currency area would allow more effective attention to EU economic needs, and avoid the whipsawing of macroeconomic policy by global forces. And European labor movements and small businesses, many of which were ambivalent about EMU in any event, are intent on making sure that it does not subordinate European to international considerations. The commonly expressed view that EMU must help reduce unemployment—unrealistic as it may be, given the powerful structural factors that are the principal determinants of the region's joblessness—is emblematic of a general desire on the part of labor and others that the EMU authorities act more forcefully on the 'domestic' (European) economic front than has been possible in the contentious transition to EMU.

There are political bases for both domestic and international orientations. This is reflected in the divergences of opinion among informed analysts. Some observers, emphasizing powerful domestic factors, have argued that the transition from eleven small open economies to one large closed economy will allow (or lead) the ECB to focus on internal concerns. Others, noting the greater potential for a single currency to affect international developments, stress the prospects for a more concerted global role for the EMU authorities. Each possibility finds strong support in Europe; both cannot be pursued simultaneously.

Not only are there powerful conflicts of interest over the general course of European monetary policy, there are major institutional complications. The international position of the euro depends at least in some measure on the stance of EMU authorities in international monetary and financial forums. Yet it is very unclear who the relevant authorities are, and how they will be represented. Representatives of the European Union are often included in international meetings, but not all members of the EU are in EMU, and in any case their statutory authority over monetary policy is very limited (indeed, at least in principle, they have none). The member states of the Economic and Monetary Union are of course members of the IMF, and several are in the Group of Seven; yet, again, they are not formally (or informally) capable of making monetary or financial commitments on behalf of the euro.

The European Central Bank, the monetary authority *per se*, is a central bank without a country, and international monetary and financial politics are still organized around countries. To make matters even more complicated, the Maastricht Treaty appears to reserve the making of explicit exchange rate agreements on the part of the Economic and Monetary Union to the Council of Ministers and not the ECB. It is unthinkable that such exchange rate agreements could be made and sustained without the cooperation of the ECB, but the nature of collaboration between the ECB and other EU policy-making institutions is still being developed.

For all these reasons, there remains a great deal of uncertainty about the overall bias to be expected from ECB monetary policy. This uncertainty was, again, much in evidence in the first months of the euro. Much of the early discussion of the ECB's expected stance focused on the bank's need to establish its reputation as a tough successor to the Bundesbank. This ignored the political environment within which the ECB operates, in which member governments and their constituents are keen to ensure that monetary policy takes full account of their domestic concerns. The importance of this political environment was reinforced by the French government's willingness and ability to block the appointment of Wim Duisenberg to head the Bank until receiving an informal commitment that he would step down early in favor of a Frenchman. The centrality of the political setting was also hammered home when the new Social Democratic government in Germany began, in the person of Finance Minister Oskar Lafontaine, to exert very public pressure on the ECB to loosen monetary policy. What followed was a delicate dance in which the Bank did not want to be seen as responding too blatantly to political pressure, but also did not want to be too far from the desires of its constituents. The result was a substantially looser ECB stance than many scholars had anticipated, and a generally revised expectation that ECB policy would have to take careful account of both domestic and international pressures.

The 'home' financial system. The status of a currency on international markets, and the status of macroeconomic policy-making authorities in international negotiations, depend importantly on the breadth, depth, and reliability of the relevant financial system. The financial sources of negotiating influence are straightforward: the prominence of a nation's government in discussions of international macroeconomic concerns depends on the importance of its financial markets to the global economy. No matter how large the nation's economy may be, if it is of trivial importance to world financial and macroeconomic conditions, it will have a limited role in international macroeconomic policy forums.

Domestic financial circumstances also have a powerful impact on the international role of national currencies. Where the local financial market is underdeveloped, foreigners will be less willing to hold assets denominated in the currency. This is true both about the size of the market, and about the range of instruments available in it.

In a way, the solidity of the home financial market can substitute for other concomitants of international-currency status. For example, extremely well-developed forward markets can reduce the expected cost of the currency's volatility to potential users and holders. In the case of the United States, there is little question that the monetary authorities privilege domestic macroeconomic concerns over international ones, but American financial markets are so broad and deep that few users of dollars are particularly concerned. Of course, the longer the time horizon of the investor, the harder it is to protect against adverse policy trends, but in the short and medium run well-developed financial markets provide important reassurances to potential users of an international currency.

This also affects the use of the currency in debt and equity contracts. The fact that the dollar-based stock and bond markets are extremely well developed gives investors strong incentives to invest in dollar-denominated assets. Thin capital markets mean that potential investors take additional risks, such as finding themselves illiquid in the event of inauspicious conditions.

An important component of the financial stability that can reinforce currency use is the home regulatory environment. If investors regard the home authorities as reliable guarantors of the stability of local financial conditions, they will be more likely to hold assets in the currency. This is true both of the general regulatory setting—how financial markets are organized—and of the specific expectations that financial regulators will be able to deal effectively with a crisis, whether with lender of last resort facilities or some other similar crisis management initiatives. Inefficient and cumbersome financial regulations, and inadequate provisions for crisis containment, will reduce interest in the local markets and the local currency.

The depth and breadth of financial markets attracts further investors and borrowers, and the process is self-reinforcing. The more reliable the markets, the more they will be used; and the more they are used, the deeper and broader they become. There may also be feedback to financial regulation, as better developed markets increase the pressures on regulators to improve both general financial regulation and crisis management policies.

On the other hand, poorly developed and regulated financial systems, and uncertain lender of last resort facilities, dampen interest in a currency and assets denominated in it. And there remains great uncertainty about the future of Europe's financial systems. Certainly there has been important movement in the direction of a more consolidated and efficient financial market, and more reliable regulation. However, some of the national financial systems of the Economic and Monetary Union are still quite backward, and the euro zone as a whole is far from being a serious competitor to the United States as a major financial market. Much of the problem is regulatory: there is no single set of European financial regulations, and it is not clear how the regulatory environment for European finance will evolve over the coming decade.

At the same time, the division of authority for lender of last resort facilities in EMU is extremely ambiguous. Officially, national governments retain sole responsibility for 'their' financial institutions. Unofficially, it is widely recognized that serious financial problems in one EMU member would spill over to the rest of the members, to one degree or another. In this context, the ECB would probably be required to adjust policy to take a local financial crisis into account; and, *in extremis*, it might be called upon to act as an unofficial lender of last resort.

The problem is that both financial regulation and crisis facilities are potentially controversial. Financial market regulation has been a political minefield in the United States for decades, for it implicates extremely powerful interests, such as financial institutions with lucrative local monopolies or segmented markets. Some European countries have faced similar political obstacles to financial de-regulation and re-regulation. And while in principle few oppose lender of last resort facilities, if the issue is whether Dutch taxpayers should participate in a bailout of Spanish banks, thorny political problems are likely to arise.

In addition, neither Europe's central bankers nor other national policy-makers are eager to be explicit about how they see the evolution of the regulatory and crisis-management functions of the euro zone. Too direct a definition of expected policies would create powerful incentives for perverse behavior by investors and others. Weak banks in a weak national system could exploit a hypothetical stated willingness of the ECB to act as ultimate lender of last resort for all of the EMU by taking unwarranted risks in the knowledge that they would eventually be bailed out. This sort of moral hazard problem, and related possibilities to exploit inside regulatory information, make it difficult to make credible commitments that the euro authorities are 'in control' of European finance.

Yet this ambiguity and uncertainty contributes to nervousness in the financial markets, and to a reluctance to increase exposure to financial markets and instruments that depend on the European regulatory environment. Until these issues are resolved, the global reach of European financial markets will be hamstrung. And resolving these issues requires confronting some potentially serious disagreements among countries, and among groups within and across countries.

On all three of these dimensions, there is likely to be continuing conflict. The short-term direction of exchange rate policy; the longer-term general stance of the monetary authorities, whether they look primarily inward or outward; and the depth and regulation of European financial markets, are all crucial determinants of the euro's international role. And all will in turn be determined in large part by the pulling and hauling of powerful interests in the member states of the euro zone, in a context of great institutional complexity and ambiguity.

Conclusion

I do not mean to imply that these conflicts cannot be overcome, or that EMU will necessarily founder on the shoals of these controversies. There are powerful pressures for European governments and EU institutions to resolve the problems that stand in the way of the euro's realization of its global potential.

However, the euro, like all currencies, is a creature of its society. Domestic—that is, euro zone—political forces will be brought to bear on the EMU policy-making authorities. The future of the euro is complicated by the fact that these political forces, and indeed these policy-making authorities, operate in an environment of great institutional novelty and uncertainty, in which it is not always clear who the relevant forces and authorities are.

Nonetheless, a full understanding of the euro's role in international monetary and financial relations—whether it will act as leader, challenger, partner, or obstacle—depends on the domestic context within which the policies of the ECB and other euro authorities are made. A central task for scholars and observers is to clarify the nature of the conflicting interests and institutions that make up the Economic and Monetary Union, and to understand how they interact in the formation of EMU macroeconomic policy.

Notes

1. An excellent introduction to the issues is Fratianni, Hauskrecht and Maccario (1998).
2. Broz (1997), Krugman (1984), and Tavlas (1991) include excellent surveys and/or examples of this sort of analysis.
3. Another fascinating recent example is the yen, discussed in Rosenbluth (1993).
4. One approach to understanding these conflicts is in Frieden (1994).

References

Broz, J. Lawrence. 1997. *The International Origins of the Federal Reserve System.* Ithaca: Cornell University Press.

Fratianni, Michele, Andreas Hauskrecht, and Aurelio Maccario. 1998. 'Dominant Currencies and the Future of the Euro.' *Open Economies Review,* 9, pp. 467-491.

Fratianni, Michele, and Andreas Hauskrecht. 1998. 'From the Gold Standard to a Bipolar Monetary System.' *Open Economies Review,* 9, pp. 609-635.

Frieden, Jeffry. 1994. 'Exchange rate politics: Contemporary lessons from American History.' *Review of International Political Economy,* no. 1 (Spring).

Green, John, and Phillip Swagel. 1998. 'The Euro Area and the World Economy.' *Finance and Development* (December), pp. 8-11.

Krugman, Paul. 1984. 'The International Role of the Dollar: Theory and Prospect.' In John Bilson and Richard Marston, eds., *Exchange Rate Theory and Practice.* Chicago: University of Chicago, pp. 261-278.

Lohmann, Susanne. 1998. 'The Dark Side of European Monetary Union.' In Ellen Meade, ed., *The European Central Bank: How Decentralized? How Accountable?* Washington, D.C.: American Institute for Contemporary German Studies.

Prati, Alessandro, and Garry Schinasi. 1998. 'Ensuring Financial Stability in the Euro Area.' *Finance and Development* (December), pp. 12-15.

Rosenbluth, Frances. 1993. 'Japan's Response to the Strong Yen: Party Leadership and the Market for Political Favors.' In Gerald Curtis, ed., *Japan's Foreign Policy: After the Cold War.* New York: M. E. Sharpe.

Tavlas, George S. 1991. *On the International Use of Currencies: The Case of the Deutsche Mark.* Princeton Essays in International Finance, no. 181. Princeton: International Finance Section.

13. THE PROSPECT FOR GLOBAL MONETARY BILINGUALISM

Gerhard Michael Ambrosi

Introduction

It is a well-known observation that money is in a certain way comparable to language.[1] As the latter facilitates communication and thus serves as a public good, so does money facilitate exchange and thus it also has a public good function. It lowers the cost of exchange for the whole society. In both cases the beneficial effects are the greatest the most wide-spread the usage. Since the US dollar is 'Still the Lingua Franca', as Frankel (1995) pointed out in an article in the spirit of this analogy, what then could be the role of the euro in a global context? Are not those functions which an international currency could be expected to deliver[2] supplied by the US dollar already?

The answer to this question has several facets—formal definitial ones, substantive economic ones, and institutional political ones—which I will touch upon in this paper. The conclusion will be that there is no economic automatism in sight concerning the future role of the euro. But there is the prospect of a common global interest in establishing a new international monetary order in which the euro and the dollar play cooperative roles in stabilizing the global markets for their respective currencies and for financial assets in general.

Consolidation Effects of the Euro on International Trade and Official Reserves

From an arithmetical point of view, the euro is *bound* to have a diminished international weight in comparison to the international presence of the currencies given up for it, as McCauley (1997, p. 51f) demonstrated at considerable length. This is due to the fact that with the disappearance of the pre-euro currencies, the inter-country transactions which they supported will now be internal 'Euroland' transactions and thus they will lose their former international status. On these grounds, the share of international trade as percentage of the G-10 trade will drop from 55 percent to 32 percent for the euro area. But for the same reason it will increase from 23 percent to 34 percent for the United States. Correspondingly, the percentage of official reserves, international assets, foreign-exchange transactions, denominations of trade—these figures will all drop in euro terms in comparison to their respective values in terms of the former pre-euro currencies. Due to this *definitorial* decrease of inner-European international assets and transactions, the ratio to this decreased denominator will *in*crease if US dollar values are the respective numerators (see McCauley, 1997, p. 52, table 13), since dollar values are not directly affected by such institutional changes.

But let us be clear about the purely formal character of such calculations. They say nothing about the actual supply and demand for the respective currencies. Indeed, as Buira (1995) recently has shown, the ratio of IMF quotas (of potential international credit) to total merchandise trade has dropped dramatically from 1950 to 1993, namely from a value of 6.9 to 1.9 (see ibid., table 3, p. 35).[3] One might argue that then the need for additional international credit and liquidity becomes even greater and that the disappearance of inter-European reserve assets will lead to a shortage of reserves in a global context. But nothing of the above calculations shows that the requirements of additional international liquidity must be met by an increased role of the dollar in the global context. Quite to the contrary, there seems to be wide-spread belief among analysts that as far as the demand for dollars as international reserve is concerned, the least likely direct future consequence of EMU is that there will be an increase in its importance.

This follows first of all from the other side of the coin of this institutional change which, after all, is one of financial consolidation from a fragmented though 'international' European setup to an integrated euro-'inland'-regime of considerably enhanced financial self-sufficiency. A large part of European foreign trade was international but was conducted as intra-EU trade. So long as it was trade between different currency areas it required international finance to back it. This part amounted to about 60 percent of total international EU-trade. Hence the majority of (formerly) foreign trade of the EU henceforth does not *require* the same coverage by international reserves as it did before. McCauley (1997, p. 62ff) discusses this question in quite some detail. It emerges that in the longer run there might well be an *excess* of dollar holdings on this account of about $55 billion.

The length of the time frame which is likely to be required for this excess to become virulent and the relatively small amounts involved in this context suggest, however, that there are no dramatic effects to be expected either way from the fact that much EU internal foreign trade becomes Euroland domestic trade. Indeed, Peter Kenen (1996; p. 24) believes that European countries are not likely to wreck the value of their dollar denominated assets by quickly throwing their excess reserves on the market. They will hold on to them 'as they have no attractive alternative' (ibid.). This indeed is what seems to be happening. While the dollar appreciated considerably over the first months of 1999, the reserve holdings of the EU countries *in*creased in spite of the *de*creased need for them. This shows on the one hand the restrained behavior of the European central bankers. On the other hand: one should not forget the considerable potential for change in US dollar and euro reserve positions, since European reserves are about double the amount of those of the USA while all the indicators for the respective areas where these currencies are / will be legal tender are about the same. Any quick adjustment to comparable levels of reserve holdings certainly will exert a depressing effect on the value of the dollar.

Summing up the arguments considered in this section, we noted that the definitorial consequences of the consolidation of EMU member states to Euroland point towards a diminished presence in some international statistics of the European countries concerned. In particular, the reserve holdings of partner countries' currencies will not count as reserves any more. The substantive outcome of this consolidation might well be contrary to such calculations, however. Many analysts predict an *excess* of dollar reserve holdings in the euro territory. This excess has the potential of depressing the euro-dollar exchange rate. It is not plausible that this potential will be used by the monetary authorities of the EMU, however. In fact, the short-term developments were foreseen by some (Kenen, 1996) to go towards an appreciation of the dollar with respect to the euro. Initial experience after the introduction of the euro does confirm such a view. The long-term perspective is, however, to the opposite. This scenario is not beneficial for monetary stability. It leaves speculators on the alert concerning the shift from short-term pyramiding of speculations to long-term market fundamentals. With a view of a 'bear market' for dollars on the distant horizon, its advent might become an uncomfortably quick reality.

Changes in the Monetary Functions of the Dollar

Further substantive considerations also support a conservative assessment of the international impact of the euro with respect to the dollar in the short run but potentially dramatic changes in the more distant future. Ronald McKinnon (1998) pointed out that there is little reason to expect a diminution of the dollar's role as a vehicle currency, i.e. as a medium of intermediary exchange between two currencies which have a thin market in direct trading.

This view confirms an earlier statement by Bénassy-Quéré et al. (1998) who attribute to the dollar a still prominent role as vehicle currency (p. 12), at least as far as the year 1995 is concerned to which their data in this context refer.

But for several reasons the pre-euro data cannot be a reliable guide to the future. A considerable part of the foreign exchange turnover which the above authors take as indicator for the vehicle function of the dollar was generated within the EU. One of the most curious uses of the dollar as a vehicle currency was its role in creating 'official' ECUs for the EU. These were generated by European central banks through revolving swap transactions involving exclusively gold and dollars. Thus, in spite of the ECU's *definition* as a basket of European currencies, the European central banks' 'official' ECU stood in fact not for a single European currency but predominantly for dollars. This privileged use of the dollar has disappeared with the advent of the euro, of course. But contrary to the findings of the last section, this happened not for statistical reasons but because an explicit change of the monetary constitution in Europe has taken effect with the advent of the euro. This signifies not only a decrease of formal status of the dollar in Europe, but also a decrease in a considerable amount of dollar-denominated transactions there. It is therefore not the whole foreseeable story which McCauley (1997, p. 67) relates when he suggests that the euro 'stands to incorporate most of the currencies for which the mark plays a vehicle role at present' and he therefore suggests that the potential of the euro as a vehicle currency is likely to remain just that—a 'pure' potential. The role of the dollar as a vehicle currency will be considerably reduced in Europe because the statutes of 'EMS I' are not valid any more. In comparison to the dollar, the euro will play a far more prominent role as a vehicle currency than the mark was permitted to play. Indeed, one might see herein one of the rationales for enacting EMU: to overcome the statutory limitations which the DM had to have as one of many national currencies in a communital Europe. The euro can well be the official bench-mark for other currencies in 'EMS II'. The DM could not take a comparable position within 'EMS I'—at least not in the context of an explicit institutional agreement.

Are these statutory changes in Europe of limited and regional relevance and likely to be overcome by global developments? Revival of the Asian economies might make up for the decrease of the relative weight of the dollar as a vehicle currency in Europe. Portes/Rey (1998, p. 310) discuss the vehicle function of the euro in a tripolar context where payments are effected between 'EU-15', USA and Japan either in dollars or in euros.[4] In this scenario, a total shift to the dollar as vehicle currency is imaginable as well as a case where the euro is the global vehicle currency. The final outcome between these extremes will depend on actual transaction costs. These in turn will depend on the degree of integration between the respective areas. Until now the USA has gone much further in this respect than the EU. Therefore there are good economic reasons to predict that not much will change concerning the dollar's vehicle currency position in Asia. But articles like the one of Portes/Rey (1998) are meant to bring this very fact into the public conscience. One of their conclusions is that in order 'to move beyond the *quasi status quo* [of the hegemony of dollars in global transaction, GMA], European authorities will have to introduce structural reforms' (ibid., p. 331). Implicitly, this confirms a conservative assessment of the present impact of the euro on the global role of the dollar as a vehicle currency, but challenges this position for the more distant future.

Another monetary function which the euro might assume from the dollar is that of serving as an invoicing currency. This aspect was given some stress when the Commission (1990, ch. 7) published its arguments for making EMU palpable to the public. In this vein, Bénassy-Quéré et al. (1998, p. 13) note that in the past years already the dollar declined considerably in this particular service (from 56 percent of world trade in 1980 to 48 percent in 1992). This matter is discussed in more detail by McCauley (1997, p. 69f). But he dismisses the quantitative relevance of this debate in 'these days, when world trade turns over in the global foreign-exchange market twice a week' (ibid., p. 69).[5] In essence, McCauley (1997) claims that economists are by and large agnostic about international invoicing: little of it is known for sure, even less of it is well understood, and much of what appears to be well understood might turn out to be *mis*-understood. But in this case, McCauley's earlier point about the relatively minor importance of this function is a consolation for the agnosticism forced upon us in this particular field of monetary functions of currencies.

One of the most important functions of money is the supply of liquidity. Richard Cooper (1998, p. 12) recently pointed out that the high liquidity of the dollar-denominated Treasury Bills due to re-purchasing agreements of the Federal Reserve and due to offmarket transactions is unparalleled in the world and may be expected to stay so in the foreseeable future. With this conviction it is understandable that this author sees little challenge being offered to the dollar by the advent of the euro. But the constancy of the present setup of the world monetary constitution rests on a far larger set of elements, especially when the marketability of financial assets is involved. The specificity of the Fed's re-purchasing agreements may continue. But the lack of liquidity of the eleven and a half[6] former currencies of what is now 'Euroland' will not carry over to the euro. It is, of course, debatable how one is to quantify this change since liquidity is hard to operationalize in numerical terms. But it is an important observation that the mere fact of pooling eleven currency areas itself has a significant liquidity-increasing effect, as Mundell

(1999) points out in this volume. He goes on to warn of potential inflationary pressures from such an increase. But there are other observers—Paul Krugman (1999) in particular-who see the most menacing global economic problem ahead to be posed by deflation[7]—and thus by the opposite of the over-abundance of liquidity. Indeed, Krugman sees herein one of the gravest problems posed by the European Central Bank: it seems to be set to fight the problem of inflation of the past and not the deflation awaiting us in the future.[8] An increase in euro liquidity might therefore be far from being a grave danger for the monetary system of the next few years. Indeed, if an increase in demand for euro reserves should materialize in the future, this demand might well be met by a correspondingly increased supply of euro-denominated liquidity.

The future liquidity of the euro has two aspects: on the one hand the monetary base and the institutionally managed availability of euros; on the other hand the marketability of euro-denominated assets. Of these, only the first aspect is attributable to the workings and the policy of the European Central Bank. The wider aspects of liquidity depend on the general working of the assets markets.

In the latter respect the introduction of the euro seems to be a great success indeed. International bond issues in the first half year of 1999 are about equal in dollar terms ($313bn) and in euro terms (€293bn). Euro-denominated bond issues by corporates and utilities amounted to €70bn during the first five months of 1999 and thus they were then already almost double the amount of the corresponding volume in pre-euro currencies of the total previous year, according to an enthusiastic report in the *Financial Times* (see Luce, 1999)[9]. Such enthusiasm stems in part from the diagnosis of the emergence of an entirely new culture of business finance as a consequence of the introduction of the euro. European companies resort more and more to bonds rather than to direct bank loans. This leads to cheaper finance for the companies, to a larger choice for financial investors, to a better spread of risks and to a larger and more liquid market in euro-denominated bonds. Thus the expectation that the euro could evolve into a highly liquid new potential reserve currency seems to be warranted not least from the side of the private financial markets in Europe. It has not reached that stage yet. Especially in the high yield and high risk section of the financial markets the US is expected to continue to outperform the euro-denominated markets.[10] Nevertheless, the structural change of private financial markets which now already can be seen to take place in Europe gives a solid basis for expecting an attractiveness of the euro which no single pre-euro currency offered.

From the discussion of this section it emerges that in the first few months of its existence already the euro made a strong impact on international financial markets and institutions. Outside observers like the British

Financial Times or the Swiss-based *Bank for International Settlements* diagnose market data which indicate that the euro is not only a *potential* equal of the dollar. Now already it seems to have almost equal attractiveness for borrowers and lenders on international capital markets. The weakness of the euro with respect to the dollar in the early months of 1999 did not reassure commentators that the position of the dollar will remain unchallenged for the foreseeable future. Quite to the contrary, some see a basic lack of sustainability in the present international monetary setup. This reinforces apprehension about potential political conflict and about a dangerous instability in world financial markets.

Regional Interests and the Advent of the Euro

In view of the developments outlined in the last section, it is significant that for quite some time already there are predictions about international conflict associated with the introduction of the euro (Feldstein, 1997). Sources for potential conflict are believed to be, in part, of an intra-European nature resulting, e.g., from incompatible objectives.[11] Conflict could also result from opposition against American 'cultural imperialism'.[12] But these seem to be rather romantic views about conflict. They do not face a potentially well-founded American worry about the loss of substantial seigniorage gains in the event that the euro might establish itself as an alternative key currency. Portes/Rey (1998, p. 329) demonstrate that the welfare ranking between the US and the EMU could be either in favor of the former with a value of 1 to 3, or in favor of Europe with a value of 3 to 1 to the detriment of the US. These alternative outcomes would depend on a maintenance of the predominance of the dollar in the former case or of the euro in the latter. The temptation might be great for each of the two parties to force a decision in the preferred direction. But since money is a shy deer, a conflict strategy might well work to the detriment of both parties.

Bergsten (1997a) saw the political impact of the euro in a far rosier light. But this optimist insisted on the requirement of a 'quantum leap in transatlantic cooperation' (ibid., p. 83). This cooperation will not come forth unless each of the partners feels that it is in his own interest. The USA has, however, a tradition of 'benign neglect' in matters of currency management and it might well be doubted that it will part from such a position. Two reasons can be given for the expectation of the required change in traditional positions on economic policy.

a)   The economic impact of the long-term perspective of a decline in the value of the dollar vis-à-vis the euro—a development which is even more plausible in view of the recent appreciation of the dollar.

b)   The foreseeable problems of the world monetary system and its institutions due to currency and banking crises.

In this section I will deal predominantly with the reasons which can be listed under point a). In the next section I will deal with some considerations concerning point b).

To worry about a decline of the value of the dollar might be considered as rather un-American. After all, the US did fare quite well with the past attitude of benign neglect of questions concerning the external value of the dollar. But this might have been sheer luck. Fate was favorable to the American economy in two respects: commodity prices turned out to be on a long-run decline in spite of the 'oil crises' in the 1970s.[13] There is research by Carruth/Hooker/Oswald (1998) suggesting that real oil prices track the general development of unemployment in the US from 1979 through 1995 quite well. But not only were commodity prices on a real decline on a global scale, they were also mostly denominated in dollars. The more the euro turns out to be a successful alternative key currency, the more it seems to be likely that it might also replace the dollar as invoicing currency for commodities. Although we noted above that economists admit to severe agnosticism with regard to invoicing patterns, this is a potential development which could touch American interests sufficiently strongly to set their monetary authorities thinking how to find orderly procedures for managing these contingencies. This is even more likely because American national welfare may be affected negatively not only by exchange rate induced increases in prices for energy and commodities. To a very large extent the USA by now imports finished products from the rest of the world. The current account with the European Union is notoriously negative for the USA. A constant tendency towards a decline in the value of the dollar with respect to the euro will give a prospect of declining terms of trade with Europe which also will affect American welfare negatively. On the basis of such considerations it is imaginable that the USA might be far more eager in future to explicitly devise a policy for stabilizing the dollar exchange rate than it was in the past. In view of the weight of the euro, such an arrangement must first of all involve the European Union.

In Europe, on the other hand, regional self-interest might well exist to go along with an American intention to stabilize the external value of the dollar on the basis of a formal long-term political commitment. It would give a justification to the ECB for supplying more liquidity to the outside world than without such an arrangement, thereby lowering monetary interest rates. In a global setting of price stability, this will not jeopardize the credibility of the ECB's commitment to price stability. This will be even more so if it is known that much of the new liquidity created in Europe will be used for reserves outside of the euro's territory. This scenario is the more plausible the longer the comparatively high rate of unemployment persists in Europe. Low real interest rates should stimulate interest-dependent-demand for investment goods and for durable goods in Europe. If lax monetary policy in Europe does *not* work in that way, however, because Europe finds herself in a 'liquidity trap' comparable to the one we know presently from Japan, then this could also be in the economic political interest of the Europeans. It will enable a cheap refinancing of the large European government debt, thereby reaping the benefits of seigniorage in the form of lower opportunity costs for debts. There is little indication, however, that the public in Europe is being prepared by its political leaders for this type of global currency arrangement.

Maybe the most compelling reason for contemplating a global cooperative arrangement involving the euro and the dollar, is a widespread apprehension that the present international set-up is not sustainable. In the wake of the Asian financial crises of 1997 there was considerable pamphleteering directed against the present international financial setup. Its tendency ranged from calls for unconditional abandonment of the old institutions inherited from the Bretton Woods system,[14] to plans for an imaginative re-establishment of this system,[15] right to discussions of establishing a World Central Bank.[16] It would lead too far to follow up those discussions in the present context. But one should take note of their existence. They convey an increasing urge for global political action in order to stabilize the world financial system. Beattie/Coggan (1999) use a quote from Paul Volcker, the former chairman of the US Federal Reserve, in order to convey the precariousness of the present global economic situation. He described earlier in 1999 the world economy as depending on the expenditures of the US consumer, whose enormous appetite for consumption—the American savings rate turned negative in 1999—depended on the stock market, which in turn 'was dependent on about 50 stocks, half of which had not shown a profit'. Any sudden decline in the value of the dollar could send asset prices tumbling, the American consumption-led boom collapsing, and the crises in the rest of the world exploding. The authors vividly canvass this vision and attribute the responsibility for future catastrophes of this type to 'policy-makers ... for their failure to curb the economic imbalances before they became so severe' (ibid.). The main imbalance in this view is presently posed by the excessive value of the dollar in relation to the lack of savings and to the size and duration of current account deficits in the USA.

We conclude this section by noting that there are several reasons which urge for a formal arrangement between the euro and the dollar. The basic perspective of such concerns is long-term and stems from the widely held conviction that in 1999 the dollar is overvalued for a number of reasons with respect to the euro. It would be foremost in the interest of both, the US, and the EU, to have some sort of stabilizing agreement. But the concerns about the stability of the euro-dollar exchange rate are of relevance for the world economy in general.

The Scope for a New World Monetary Order

The widespread feeling of unease concerning the present world financial set-up has roots which go deeper than questions of temporary misalignments between individual exchange rates. This unease should be seen in the context of the principal problem that the role of money as a public good is a rather ambiguous one in an international setting. The well-known likening of money to language which was the starting point of this chapter has actually only limited validity.

Contrary to the usage of other public goods like a language for which the non-exclusion principle holds, the amenity of liquidity of money when used as an asset does carry with it economic opportunity cost. This is the interest foregone by not placing the money in less liquid but more remunerative investments. The beneficiaries of these opportunity costs are the suppliers of money. If left to themselves, they will be tempted to overextend their supply. By so doing they eventually call into question the entire institution of money.[17] This problem is obviously so great that virtually every sovereign state made arrangements to monopolize money supply—at least in the sense of making legal arrangements for limiting private money supply. Thus it is not quite correct to regard the monetary authorities in a multi-tier banking system as *lenders* of last resort. If money is to maintain its beneficial societal function, the monetary authorities must be the *limitors* of money supply of last resort. This limiting function must rely on control and coercion in order to be credible.

It is for this close connection between the power of the state to coerce and the necessity of money to be scarce in order to have societal value that money is a legal phenomenon as much as an economic one. But as long as we have no 'world law' and no world government, one important element of a modern monetary system is missing as soon as we leave the individual state.

Followers of Fritz von Hayek's famous scheme for the denationalization of money will totally disagree with the above. But I subscribe to Otmar Issing's (1999, p. 7) recent assessment 'that under the Hayek proposal, we are likely to get either one or other of the following unfavorable outcomes. On the one hand, we could see the emergence of floating exchange rates between different privately issued moneys, resulting in an uncertain discovery process without any guarantee of a stable outcome, along with a deterioration in economic communication and coordination in the economy overall. On the other hand, any attempt by private issuers to pre-empt these outcomes by fixing the exchange rates between their currencies would probably trigger Gresham's Law and result in accelerating inflation.' Speaking as a member of the Executive Board of the European Central Bank, Issing might not be considered an unbiased judge in this question. But the fate of the British 'hard ECU' proposal which was submitted in the spirit of Hayek's scheme may be taken as a historical judgement. The verdict is that confidence in money requires a legal order for supervising the money supply. This framework must go beyond a mere market liberalization. Indeed, it is one of the often-voiced criticisms that the lack of a central government for Europe makes EMU a risky experiment. But if even the institutional framework of the EU which, after all, has its laws, its court and its intricate system of coordinated national legislation, was considered as being insufficient for monetary unification, then the prospect for a convincing world monetary order must appear as utopian. We thus are in a dilemma: there is no prospect that Hayek-type denationalization will bring monetary stability. Nor can we hope that a generally accepted legal system will stabilize the global monetary arrangements in the near future.

The consequence of these considerations is that the envisaged global monetary order can only be one of governmental cooperation in the spirit of enlightened self-interest. The scope for such self-interest was briefly outlined in the previous section. But the requirements for order go beyond the present set-up of proclamations of mutual 'benign neglect'. They call for true guidance in the sense of limiting and directing private and public agents. It would go beyond the scope of this paper to investigate that order in more detail now. But one of its main characteristics must be a mutual acceptance of the roles of the dollar and the euro as they emerge from the interactions of well-guided but self-interested economic actors. In view of the comparability of economic fundamentals of the two currency areas, the most likely outcome of a new international monetary order will be a monetary 'bilingualism' involving the dollar as well as the euro.

Summary and Conclusion

Assessing the prospective international role of the euro, Eichengreen (1997, p. 53) gave three 'reasons why the transition to a world in which the euro rivals the dollar as a reserve currency will be slow (if we get there at all)'. In the present paper I covered these (and some other) reasons and I come to a somewhat different conclusion: the self-interest of the Europeans and of the USA, indeed of the world financial community in general, should work towards an orderly cohabitation of these two currencies. I want to present this conclusion in relation to Eichengreen's three reasons. They were:

a) the historical precedent set by the USA in money becoming a reserve currency;
b) the eclipse of the former reserve currencies: French franc, DM, lira etc. due to monetary consolidation of the euro area;
c) the growth prospects of the Asian economies since these are more likely to use dollars than euros.

Dealing with these reasons in reverse order, we note concerning point c) that a few weeks after Eichengreen's positive assessment of the growth prospects in Asia during the first half of 1997, the economically booming 'tigers' of that region seemed near to extinction due to widely unexpected currency and financial crises. Their onslaught called into question the entire world financial order. This experience should have alerted investors all over the world that financial diversification and risk-spreading will be of increasing importance for international portfolios. Since the euro is fundamentally the only credible and highly liquid alternative to the dollar, this point speaks more *for* than *against* a considerable importance of euro-denominated assets in an international context. The paper by Portes/Rey (1998) which was considered above, addresses the very point of the euro's acceptance in an Asian context and called for appropriate policies by the European authorities.

The technical consequences of the abolition of national currencies and the creation of the euro which are the subject of point b) work in *two* ways as was seen above in section 2). We concluded there that the *net* effect is a considerable overhang of official dollar reserves in Europe. It may be trusted that European monetary authorities will deal sensibly with this problem. But there is a constant potential of an excess flow supply out of excess official dollar holdings in Europe. In addition, the unique status of the dollar as being the main financial basis for the creation of ECUs through revolving swap operations by national central banks has disappeared together with the ECU. All this will amount to considering point b) a reason for *diminishing* the relative importance of the dollar as a reserve currency in a European setting and not for enhancing it.

With regard to the history of the world financial system, Eichengreen (1992, 1996) is a master *sans pareil*. It is with great hesitation that I contradict him concerning his point a). But in section 4 of this paper it appeared that Europe today is far more in the position in which the USA found itself at the time of setting up the Bretton Woods system than is the USA itself. Then, and in the years of World War I and before World War II, the Europeans ran large current account deficits. Although the historical settings are not comparable, it must be recalled that it is now the US which runs large and persistent current account deficits. At the time when the Bretton Woods agreement codified the dollar's monetary pre-eminence, the world was indebted to the US. Now the USA is in a net debtor position. We noted above concerns about the fragility of the present 'equilibrium' of the world economy (Beattie/Cogan, 1999).

Maybe the most appropriate conclusion is an optimistic expectation concerning international cooperation with regard to currency arrangements. Paul Volcker (1997, p. 259), the former chairman of the American Federal Reserve Board, set the right tone for such an expectation by stating that 'the creation of the euro ... could become the impetus for renewed thinking on the international front'. He continued by recollecting that 'the idea of a common European currency germinated almost 20 years ago in dreams of some farsighted leaders'. We may refresh those memories by remembering that the roots of the euro lay not just in dreams which Giscard d'Estaing and Helmut Schmidt might have had when they devised the EMS in 1978. The most tangible roots for the euro are to be found in the results of the committee work done under the guidance of Pierre Werner in 1970. The Werner Plan for European monetary union of that year was the blueprint for the euro of today. The length of time it took to implement the Werner Plan reinforces the validity of Volcker's final appeal (ibid.) concerning world monetary cooperation, namely to 'start the intellectual process now [rather] than wait for the crisis and conflict that, if not inevitable, are all too possible'. This process should start from the working hypothesis that the monetary 'language' of the future is spelled in terms of dollars *and* euros.

Notes

1. See e.g. Tobin (1992), p. 141, where the idiosyncrasies of moneys are likened to those of languages.
2. A discussion of these functions may be found in Bénassy-Quéré et al. (1998), pp. 9-11.
3. Compare also Table 2 in Mundell (1999) which shows that the ratio of reserves to quasi-money declined for most countries worldwide. This shows that there seems to be a general tendency to hold less reserves—an observation which confirms the conclusion of the next paragraph that probably there is a dollar overhang.
4. The yen is not considered as a means of payment in this global setting, but its potential future relevance is acknowledged.
5. Portes/Rey (1998), p. 323, reproduce some relevant turnover data. According to those statistics, total turnover in US$ coming from EU-15 was about 4000bn in April 1995 (BIS data) whereas the average of monthly trade transactions of EU-15 with the US over the year of 1993 was $11bn according to IMF data. On the basis of these data, financial turnover is almost the 400fold of trade turnover. This seems to support McCauley's remarks about the relative

unimportance of commercial turnover. But then there is the open question about the relevance of such figures, collected by different institutions and pertaining to different years.

6. The half stands for the Luxembourg franc which had an only nominal (but visible) existence in the monetary union with Belgium.

7. According to *The Economist* of February 20, 1999, p. 19, fig. 1, the word 'deflation' was almost unknown in newspaper articles at the end of the 1980s. By 1999 more than 600 newspaper articles *per annum* mention this term in their selection.

8. Paul Krugman as quoted by Barber (1999): 'Krugman thinks the European Central Bank is wrongly obsessed with fighting inflation rather than worrying about the threat of deflation. He describes the bank as an institution designed to fight the last war.'

9. Similar data emerge from the June 1999 edition of the *BIS Quarterly Review*. They remark (ibid., p. 15): 'There was an unprecedented volume of international securities issues in the first quarter of 1999.... [T]he single European currency ... had a notable impact on the extent of overall activity and the mix of borrowers. The introduction of the euro accelerated structural transformation in Europe.' From the tables given in that context, it emerges that international securities issues in euro terms rose by 9.47 percent of March 1999 stocks whereas US-denominated issues rose only by 6.56 percent.

10. But even in this field there seem to be significant changes. In its June 1999 *Quarterly Review*, BIS (1999, p. 15f) remarks: '...in their search for higher yields, European institutional investors have accepted a wider range of credit risk. This was illustrated by the strength of demand for corporate issues, subordinated bank debt, asset-backed securities and low-rated sovereign bonds.'

11. Feldstein (1997, p. 69): 'What is clear is that French aspiration for equality and a German expectation of hegemony are not consistent.'

12. Feldstein (1997, p. 72): 'French officials in particular have been outspoken in emphasizing that a primary reason for a European monetary and political union is as a counterweight to the influence of the United States.'

13. The commodity price index of *The Economist,* March 20, 1999, p. 126, showed that in dollar terms the 'all items' index dropped to a value of 82,4 in March 1999 in comparison to a value of 100 in 1990.

14. See Johnson/Schaefer (1997). Actually, their paper predates the Asian crisis but their arguments can be taken as being indicative of a certain fundamental criticism of the IMF.

15. See the pamphlet published by EIR, ed., (1998) for one such voice. See Feldstein (1998) for another.

16. For a discussion of such plans see Isaak (1999).

17. For a fuller analysis of the general problems dealt with in these passages see De Grauwe (1996).

References

Barber, Lionel. 1999. 'Pundit gets his fingers burnt [Lunch with Paul Krugman].' *Financial Times, Weekend FT,* July 10-11, III.

Beattie, Alan, and Philip Coggan. 1999. 'A fragile balance. A sharp fall in the dollar could tip the US into recession, hurt European and Japanese exports and damage global growth prospects.' *Financial Times,* no. 33, 971, July 28, p. 10.

Bénassy-Quéré, Agnès, Benoit Mojon, and Armand-Denis Schor. 1998. *The International Role of the Euro.* Luxembourg: European Parliament, Directorate General for Research.

Bergsten, Fred C. 1997a. 'The Impact of the Euro on Exchange Rates and International Policy Cooperation.' In Masson et al., pp. 17-48.

Bergsten, Fred C. 1997b. 'The Dollar and the Euro.' *Foreign Affairs,* no. 76, pp. 83-95.

BIS, ed. 1999. *Quarterly Review, International Banking and Financial Market Developments.* Basel: Bank for International Settlements, Monetary and Economic Department. BIS website (www.bis.org).

Buira, Ariel. 1995. *Reflections on the International Monetary System.* Princeton: International Finance Section, Department of Economics, Princeton University.

Carruth, Alan A., Mark A. Hooker, and Andrew J. Oswald. 1998. 'Unemployment equilibria and input prices: Theory and evidence from the United States.' *Review of Economics and Statistics,* 80, pp. 621-628.

Commission of the European Communities, ed. 1990. 'One market, one money. Potential benefits and costs of establishing an economic and monetary union—an assessment.' *European Economy,* no. 44. Brussels: Commission of the European Communities.

Cooper, Richard N. 1998. *Key Currencies After the Euro.* Paper no. 98-3. Cambridge: Harvard University, Weatherhead Center for International Affairs.

De Grauwe, Paul. 1996. *International Money. Postwar Trends and Theories.* Oxford: Oxford University Press.

Eichengreen, Barry. 1992. *Golden Fetters. The Gold Standard and the Great Depression, 1919-1939.* New York: Oxford University Press.

Eichengreen, Barry. 1996. *Globalizing Capital. A history of the international monetary system.* Princeton: Princeton University Press.

Eichengreen, Barry. 1997. 'Comments on C. Fred Bergsten.' In Masson et al., pp. 49-57.

EIR, ed. 1998. *Phase II der Weltwirtschaftskrise. Krisenmanagement gescheitert, jetzt Neues Bretton Woods [Phase II of the world economic crisis. Crisis management failed, now New Bretton Woods].* Wiesbaden: EIR-Nachrichtenagentur.

Feldstein, Martin. 1997. 'EMU and International Conflict.' *Foreign Affairs,* no. 76, pp. 60-73.

Frankel, Jeffrey A. 1995. 'Still the Lingua Franca—The Exaggerated Death of the Dollar.' *Foreign Affairs,* no. 74, pp. 9-16.

Isaak, Robert. 1999. 'A World Central Bank: To Be or Not to Be?' In Nölling et al., ed., pp. 255-264.

Issing, Otmar 1999. 'Hayek—currency competition and European monetary union.' Annual Hayek memorial lecture, Institute of Economic Affairs, London, May 27. *BIS Review*, 66, pp. 1-15.

Johnson, Bryan T., and Brett D. Schaefer. 1997. *The International Monetary Fund: Outdated, Ineffective, and Unnecessary.* Washington, D.C.: The Heritage Foundation.

Kenen, Peter B. 1996. *Sorting Out Some EMU Issues.* Princeton: International Finance Section, Department of Economics, Princeton University.

Krugman, Paul. 1999. *The Return of Depression Economics.* Norton; Penguin.

Luce, Edward. 1999. 'Bonded to a bright future. The euro's popularity on the debt markets, where it is already rivalling the dollar's supremacy, holds the key to its prospects as a global reserve currency.' *Financial Times*, no. 33933, June 14, p. 17.

Masson, Paul R., Thomas H. Krueger, and Bart G. Turtelboom, eds. 1997. *EMU and he international monetary system.* Proceedings of a conference held in Washington, D.C. on March 17-18, cosponsered by the Fondation Camille Gutt and the IMF. Washington, D.C.: International Monetary Fund.

McCauley, Robert N. 1997. *The Euro and the Dollar.* Princeton: International Finance Section, Department of Economics, Princeton University.

McKinnon, Ronald I. 1998. *The Euro versus the Dollar as International Money.* Stanford: Stanford University, William D. Eberle Chair of International Economics.

Mundell, Robert. 1999. 'The Euro and the Stability of the International Monetary System'. In Robert Mundell and Armand Clesse, eds., *The Euro as a Stabilizer in the International Economic System.* Boston: Kluwer Academic Publishers.

Nölling, Wilhelm, Karl Albrecht Schachtschneider, and Joachim Starbatty, eds. 1999. *Währungsunion und Weltwirtschaft—Festschrift für Wilhelm Hankel.* Stuttgart: Lucius et Lucius, 1999.

Portes, Richard, and Hélène Rey. 1998. 'The emergence of the euro as an international currency.' *Economic Policy*, 26.

Tobin, James. 1992. 'Money.' In J. Eatwell et al., *The New Palgrave Dictionary of Money and Finance.* Vol. 2. Quoted from Tobin, ed., 1996, pp.139-168. London: Macmillan, pp. 770-779.

Tobin, James, ed. 1996. *Essays in Economics—National and International.* Cambridge and London: MIT Press.

Volcker, Paul A. 1997. 'An American Perspective on EMU.' In Masson et al., pp. 254-259.

14. THE EURO AND THE OUTSIDERS: THE CASE OF THE SWISS FRANC

Jörg Baumberger

The euro has been launched for six purposes:
a) to take advantage of various economies of scale and networks related to the size of a currency area,
b) to simplify accounting, bureaucratic reporting, and statistics,
c) to preclude all temptations for competitive devaluation in the European Union,
d) to break the primacy of the US dollar, at least in Europe,
e) to politically strengthen the union and make it safe for permanent peace in Europe,
f) hopefully to increase the aggregate cake of seigniorage of the EU.

These benefits were deemed to exceed the costs in terms of the benefits of variety that have to be sacrificed, viz.:
a) loss of the money instrument for absorbing macroeconomic shocks,
b) loss of options for diversification,
c) loss of benefits of international currency competition,
d) loss of a national lender of last resort,
e) net loss of seigniorage for at least some countries.

Still, there remain outsiders. The oddest of them no doubt is Switzerland. This country, located in the geographical center of the European Union with extremely close ties to the European Union, has not only opted for an independent currency but also for staying outside the Union itself. Currency-wise, the country is back to questions that have been regarded as settled once and for all since the second half of the 19th century, viz. whether the country should, or should not, have a national currency at all (Halbeisen). This paper explores the meaning, risks, benefits and costs of not joining the European Monetary System. By the same token, so to speak *e contrario*, it sheds some light on what might be in store for Switzerland should the country *join* the Union, or at least unilaterally adopt the Union's currency via some kind of currency board arrangement. Given the small weight Switzerland would have in European Central Bank decision-making,[1] influence-wise Swiss membership in the monetary union would be roughly equivalent to unilaterally adopting the euro via a currency board.

What Does It Mean to Be an 'Out'?

What does it actually mean to be an 'in' or an 'out' with regard to the euro? Superficial talk of ins and outs tends to obscure the complexity of both the insider and the outsider status. After all, neither the in-economies nor the out-economies are closed systems. Both ins and outs are basically capitalist economies. There is private property, and people and firms enjoy a wide range of individual freedom of contract and freedom of organization, domestically and internationally. The outs are very open in many respects. There is virtually free exchange of goods and services, if not under the Treaty of Rome, so at least under World Trade Organization (WTO) rules. Most importantly in the present context, there are free movement of capital and perfect financial openness and freedom to hold and trade foreign assets of whatever denomination and nature. In all respects in which the euro might matter, in-economies and out-economies are extremely open with respect to each other.[2] In part, it is this very openness which gives rise to the specific problems and opportunities related to the out-status.

Being out of Euroland really boils down to a pretty trivial feature, viz. being out of the geographical area where the euro is, or will shortly be, *legal tender*. In Euroland, the euro is legal tender while outside Euroland some local, national, currency is legal tender. This may be much or little. From a purely legal point of view, legal tender regulations constitute a fairly soft constraint (Mann, 42ff). To be sure, the difference in currency *is* an obstacle in terms of risk and transaction costs, but *where and to what extent* exactly the economic agents will encounter this obstacle is less a matter of geographical demarcations than of choice. The fact that at least taxes have to be paid in legal tender invariably creates a bias in favor of the official currency insofar as it involves a risk for every agent who considers, or feels compelled to, write contracts in a foreign currency. Taxes certainly are the last line of defense of a currency. Some observers think it a drawback for outsiders that the European Central Bank will never bail out a bank or banking system located in non-Euroland. But this denial of ECB bailout, is, for all intents and purposes, irrelevant for outsiders since in the event of a *national* banking crisis, they might be better off having a national instead of a European lender of last resort. Greater size of the jurisdiction of a central bank also means greater distance to local difficulties. Thus, the risk of a national liquidity crisis to end up turning into a national system crisis appears to be smaller for countries with a domestic currency than for Euroland countries (Goodhart). *Ceteris paribus*, Euroland banks may, therefore, be more prone to liquidity crises than non-Euroland banks. The downside of this, of course, is that proximity of the central bank may also entail larger moral hazard.

The benefits of operating within a large and uniform currency area mainly accrue only to the insiders. Still, some of the benefits of uniformity are also available to the outsiders. British, or Swiss, traders also benefit from Euroland uniformity in that, at least in their trade with Euroland, they need only one currency instead of many (Baltensperger). Their monetary environment is not as simple as the insiders', but it is simplified as well. This is no trivial aspect for a country, like Switzerland, whose gross current account revenues amount to half of its GDP.

In short, insofar as residents of out-countries find it advantageous to transact, denominate, and price in euros they are free to do so and vice versa for the in-residents. Thus, the extent to which outside economic agents are plugged into, or stay outside, size and intensity of euro and non-euro penetration is in part a matter of choice and contractual agreement. To be sure, they are excluded from the (quasi-automatic) positive network externality that comes with a legal tender statute, but they may, via contractual arrangements, pick up some of the benefits, anyway. It may also be worth mentioning that economists tend to overestimate the lock-in effects arising from network externalities. If the benefits of a particular standard are really significant, agents more often than not find means and ways to overcome lock-in effects (Leibowitz and Margolis).

All Outs Are Not Created Equal

One common assumption is that non-euro European currencies, almost by definition, are weak currencies issued by countries with shaky systems of government finance, i.e. currencies too weak to be admitted to the club of the ins. This assumption has been fostered by the Maastricht Treaty's ambitious convergence criteria which were deliberately designed to keep weak members out so as not to mortgage the ECB with responsibility for insufficiently mature economies. Things turned out differently. Some mature economies opted out of the euro, and constituencies of important in-countries were less than enthusiastic about the prospect of abandoning monetary sovereignty (Gärtner). A more appropriate description, today, would therefore be that the outsiders exhibit greater diversity than the insiders, on both sides of the economic maturity spectrum.

There are at least four kinds of outsiders. With respect to their relationship to the EU and its institutions, we may distinguish:

1. EU members that are not allowed in.
2. EU members that have exercised an opting out clause.
3. Voluntary outsiders economically and territorially eligible for membership in EU, but (so far) unwilling to join.
4. Involuntary outsiders economically non-eligible for membership in EU, but willing to join.

With respect to economic parameters, we find a wide array of extremely different economies:

On the weak side, there are Greece and, further down, the emerging economies of Eastern Europe. Particularly the latter have very weak financial systems and government finances. The United Kingdom is a class of its own. It is a highly sophisticated financial center and has an orderly and efficient system of government finance. The UK is an interesting case insofar as the size of its financial market by far exceeds the importance of its currency, which proves that the local legal tender has no great effect on the location of the financial markets. Except for size and depth of the financial market, the Nordic countries are no less developed.

Table 1: The Different Classes of Outs

	traditionally weak currencies	traditionally non-weak currencies	traditionally strong currencies
non-voluntary outs	Greece, Eastern European membership candidates		
voluntary outs		United Kingdom, Denmark, Sweden, Norway	Switzerland

Switzerland, in this club of unequals, is definitely a league of its own, and not just because it is neither a member nor a candidate for membership[3] in the EU. Switzerland, by any standard, is a highly developed economy, it is well advanced into a service economy, and its currency no doubt commands somewhat more international interest than those of the Nordic and other still more populous and similarly prosperous countries, though far less, of course, than the British pound. The Swiss franc has a solid record of secular appreciation against all currencies of the world. Particularly since World War II, it has significantly appreciated against all Western currencies including the D-mark. Even since January 1, 1999, the problem of the Swiss National Bank has not been the weakness but rather the strength of the Swiss franc against the euro.

Table 2: Exchange Rates Against CHF

	CHF/DM	CHF/FF	CHF/£	CHF/US$
1960	1.05	0.89	12.25	4.37
1970	1.19	0.79	10.50	4.37
1980	0.92	0.39	3.61	1.59
1990	0.90	0.26	2.50	1.51
1999	0.82	0.24	2.29	1.39

Source: OECD[4]

In assessing the 'weight' of Switzerland in various financial dimensions and markets, one has to take care not to confuse domestic weight with international weight. Services, particularly financial services, have long been an export commodity. Switzerland is home to some global players in international financial services. If rough estimates are a guide, it has a major share in international asset management.

Its capital, i.e. its domestic saving, similarly, has been an export 'commodity' for many decades, actually to such an extent that it has now the highest ratio of net foreign assets to GDP in the world (Mauro). Even its currency, to some extent, is an export commodity in that there are indications that sizeable proportion of Swiss base money is circulating abroad. Swiss franc denominated debt and assets are sought after by an audience somewhat larger than the domestic market, and some central banks hold Swiss franc denominated international reserves.

There is a loyal, permanent international clientele for Swiss franc assets and debt and a shifting one that uses the Swiss franc in times of international turmoil only to leave it after the smoke has dissipated. And Swiss financial institutions intermediate large amounts of claims in foreign currencies. In other words, Switzerland has found an international market for a large array of capital and money related 'products'.

Figure 1: Assets Managed by Swiss Banks

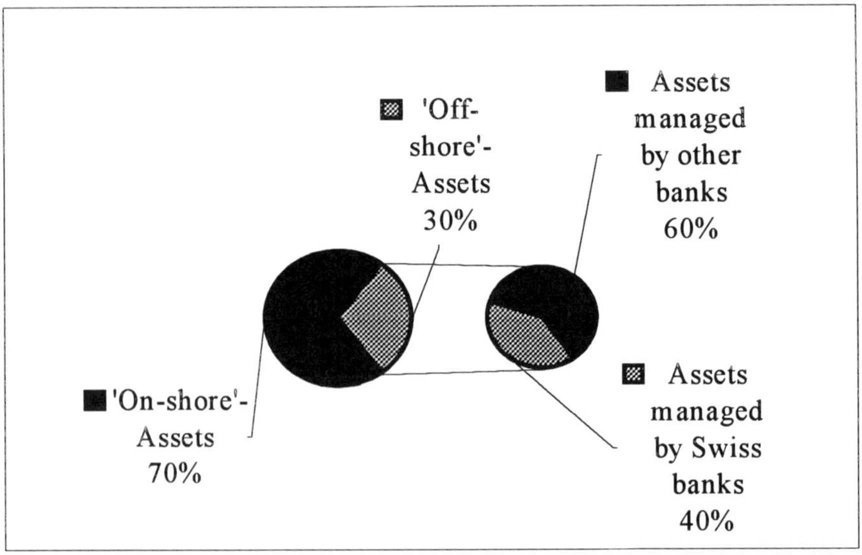

Source: Hagander[5]

All this makes international money and finance very important *for Switzerland* without thereby making Switzerland important for the world at large. Switzerland does not rock the international financial boat, but the maneuvers of the heavier boats do rock the Swiss one, precisely because of its heavy involvement on the international financial scene. The unique set-up of the Swiss economy provides opportunities, but also makes the economy vulnerable.

The euro in this respect is a new and heavy boat in Switzerland's monetary neighborhood that might create new kinds of turbulences. Most Swiss commentators are confident that Switzerland need not expect turbulences from the euro, *provided the euro be 'stable'*. On closer scrutiny, this statement is either tautological or wrong. If by 'stability' is meant exchange rate, or real exchange rate, stability, it is next to tautological. If, on the other hand, it is thought to mean low inflation, it is definitely wrong.

There are at least three aspects of stability: inflation, exchange rate stability, and stability of the financial system. There are good chances that the ECB will manage to keep inflation low, though the reputation remains still to be built. This does not preclude wide and relatively long-lived swings in nominal and real exchange rates against the Swiss franc. This has been amply demonstrated by the path of the Swiss franc-D-mark exchange rate. Neither does it preclude that potential financial trouble in the Euroland might have spillovers into the Swiss franc.

Figure 2: Employment in the Financial Sector (1998)

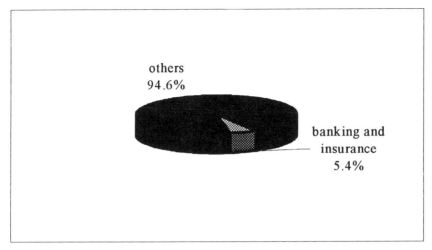

Source: Swiss federal statistical office, Press release

Figure 3: Value Added in the Financial Sector (1996)

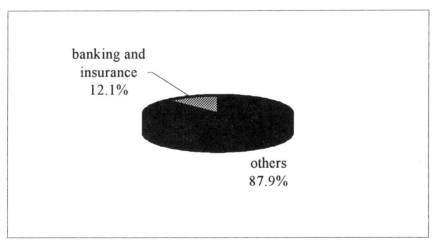

Source: Swiss federal statistical office, National accounts

Inequality of Currencies

The prevailing international monetary system is, and has always been, characterized by hierarchy. Since there is no such thing as an international legal tender, the hierarchy is an emergent property arising spontaneously from the interaction and interests of independent agents. The factors underlying the prevailing hierarchy are, in part, fundamental and in part accidents of economic and political history that gave one currency a headstart which subsequently proved decisive in a competition characterized by aspects of natural monopoly.

Before going into details, it is useful to recall that hierarchy of currencies may mean different things which should not be confused. Currencies are referred to in many different contexts. Not every phenomenon described in terms of a currency unit is the same. We have to distinguish:

a) Things that *are* currencies: money base of a currency. Only a tiny fraction of all the things denominated in a currency *are* currency. Still, the monetary base is not irrelevant. It is the medium whose delivery is promised and can, in principle, be legally enforced. The monetary base of some currencies circulates world-wide while others hardly succeed in holding their own on the home market where they are legal tender.

b) Things, more precisely contractual payment promises, that are *denominated* in terms of a currency and therefore give rise to claims to predefined cash flows in that currency. These include all fixed interest vehicles, deposits and contracts in general denominated in the currency in question including trade contracts and trade credit denominated and invoiced in a currency. Again, some currencies are used for denominating cash flows world-wide while others have a hard time to stay afloat in their countries of origin.

c) Things that are just *measured/valued/priced* in terms of some currency.

d) Currencies to which other currencies are *officially pegged.* Some currencies are pegged to others while others are pegged to it. Occasionally the currency used as a peg is itself in turn pegged to some other currency.

The choice of currencies in the first three roles takes place more or less independently of national legal tender regulations. The rank of a currency in each of these three dimensions need not be the same, though, of course, it may. Currently, it is the dollar that prevails in all four dimensions. Other currencies follow with a considerable distance. The crucial aspect in all this is b: the penetration of a currency in the denomination of cash flow claims. The higher the penetration of a currency in terms of denomination of financial claims the higher will be the demand for the currency in question, and the more frequent its use as a standard of value, price, and economic measurements and comparisons. This is largely due to the presence of network externalities and, hence, of natural monopoly. Uniformity offers public-good-like benefits. But this does not mean that one currency will necessarily take over the whole cake.

Just as most natural monopolies have a fringe of smaller competitors, currency hegemonies, generally, are complemented by an array of monetary niche products that fulfil useful functions for the global system. Indeed, there remain good reasons to deliberately denominate some contracts in terms of a medium *other* than the dominant, or the home, currency. Legal tender regulations do not guarantee but merely create propitious conditions for the emergence of at least some important share of a home market. Good, credibility-enhancing management of a minor currency may, and does, create more or less extensive markets for denomination in currencies other than the dominant one, be it only to provide for an emergency alternative against exploitation by the leading currency of its dominant position, or simply for the purpose of diversification. Such a position, however, hardly goes beyond the store of value function. Secondary currencies, no matter their reputation and prestige, hardly win widespread acceptance as a world-wide competitive transaction and pricing medium. But there has been in history, and likely will always be, a demand for alternative denominations of financial assets. To the extent that the Swiss franc commands attention, it constitutes such an alternative asset denomination. With this role, there comes a foreign demand for its monetary base. It is hard to predict whether this role of the Swiss franc is likely to shrink or expand under the euro. However, since the menu of available denominations shrinks for both EU and non-EU investors, there could conceivably emerge an increased demand for debt and asset denomination in Swiss francs. In a world of everlasting peace and certainty about future monetary policy, currency might indeed constitute a perfect natural monopoly, and insofar as diversification matters it would occur along criteria other than currencies. In a world of intermittent military and economic warfare, and a world in which monetary policies of dominant currencies are hard to predict, however, there is a clientele for diversity of denomination, and a derived demand also for the monetary base of an alternative currency. The Swiss franc is not, has never been, and will never become, an international valuation standard, nor is it likely to ever become a peg for other currencies. But its role, modest as it is, as an alternative asset and liability denomination may well be enhanced by the monetary unification of Europe. Whether this kind of internationality of the currency is an unmitigated blessing for the domestic economy of the country is, of course, another question, exposed as it thereby becomes to the turbulences of the foreign financial markets.

Interest Rate Island

The unique set-up of Switzerland's economy and monetary policy have, in ways not yet completely understood, produced one truly unique result: the interest rate island. Whereas the currencies of the outs have, in history, ranged from non-weak to definitely weak, the Swiss franc has been a strong currency for almost a century. It could even be called anomalously strong. No currency, in or out, save the Swiss franc has a long-run record of interest rates consistently lower than the Deutschmark rates. Insofar as interest rates in the euro area have converged toward levels typical of the D-mark they all converged from above. Swiss franc rates, on the other hand, should they ever converge to the level of the euro, would have to converge from below. The Swiss franc, therefore, has, not inappropriately, been called an *interest rate island.* Curiously, this differential cannot be explained by differences in monetary policies and, consequently, in inflation. Swiss monetary policy, statistically speaking, has no better record than German monetary policy. The nominal difference of, on average, 200 basis points (Figure 4 and Figure 6) reflects, *grosso modo*, a difference in real interest rates (Figure 5 and Figure 7).

In recent years, the differential has, at times, shrunk or even reversed its sign. This has led some economists, particularly Swiss economists, to dismiss the island hypothesis, at least as regards the future, which, of course, is tempting since the straightforward explanations that come to mind, viz. differences in monetary management, seem to fail in the case in question. Obituaries may be premature, though, because the instances of adverse evidence can be explained quite easily. In the early nineties, Swiss interest rates rose to levels similar to D-mark rates. This episode, however, mainly reflects the liquidity impact of an unusually tight and tough Swiss monetary policy. At that time, the Swiss National Bank was faced with a surge of inflation which was the result of institutional changes whose impact on inflation was, at the time, hard to predict. Within a very short time, two institutional innovations occurred on the Swiss money market, one was the drastic reduction of required bank liquidity reserves, and the other the adoption of a new, highly efficient, system of interbank clearing.

This, together with an injudicious monetary target, led to a surge in inflation, a bubble on real estate markets. Once the error became evident, the Swiss National Bank reversed its policy and moved to a fierce policy of disinflation, which could not fail to drive interest rates to levels so far unknown in Switzerland, though by no means unusual by European or American standards. Once monetary policy had returned to normal, the differential also promptly reappeared. More recently, the differential again began to shrink, but, one suspects, for another, also perfectly plausible reason. As D-mark and euro interest rates have been tumbling, Swiss interest rates have fallen to very low levels, indeed. They did not hit the zero percent line but they came pretty close to the nominal interest rate floor, which had the effect of squeezing the interest rate spread.

Figure 4: Short-Term Interest Rate (Nominal)

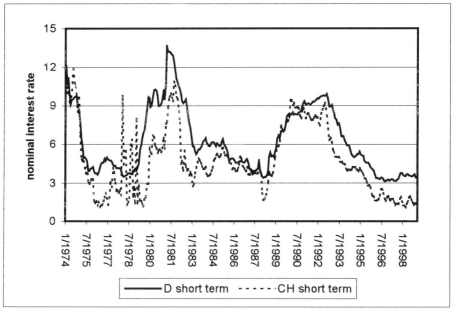

Source: OECD[6]

Figure 5: Short-Term Interest Rate (Real)

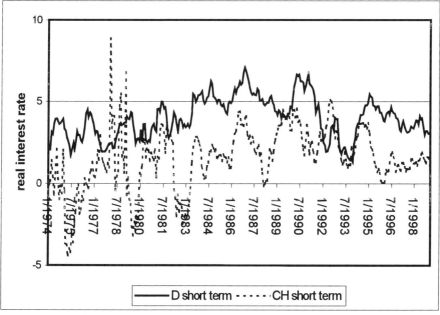

Source: OECD[7]

Figure 6: Long-Term Interest Rate (Nominal)

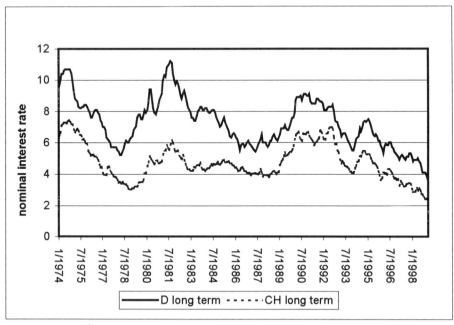

Source: OECD[8]

Figure 7: Long-Term Interest Rate (Real)

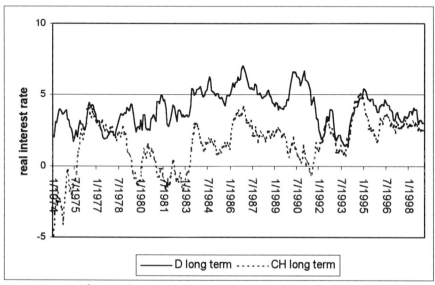

Source: OECD[9]

Will the consolidation of the euro definitely sink the interest rate island? To answer this question requires an answer to the prior question, what are the fundamental determinants of the differential in the first place?

Of course, there is more to expectations than can be detected *a posteriori*. Thus, the differential may, theoretically, be due to a persistent difference in *expectations* regarding Swiss and foreign, particularly German, monetary policy and inflation. To be sure, the Swiss franc's record of stability and convertibility is considerably longer than the D-mark's, be it only for the fact that the Swiss franc has an uninterrupted history that extends well beyond the birth of the D-mark and even beyond the post-great-inflation Reichsmark. However, given the impressive performance of German monetary policy in the postwar period, this is hardly the decisive factor.

A persistent, and possibly more important, factor may have to do with Swiss aloofness in many processes that might be perceived as threats by at least some investors: Swiss aloofness from international armed conflicts and, as far as feasible, from economic sanctions (signaled, among other things, by non-membership in the United Nations), Swiss aloofness from cross-border tax investigation, and banking secrecy.

To some investors, particularly investors trying to take account of financially relevant psychological factors, the disproportionately large amount of central bank international reserves, including a formidable amount of gold, might also appear as an indication of the likelihood of prudent and conservative monetary policy which may justify an interest rate discount.

Some studies (Mauro) attach more importance to a natural home bias in Swiss foreign investments. Switzerland has both a high investment-to-GDP and saving-to-GDP ratio. Saving traditionally exceeds investment by a relatively large amount, so that, for many decades, possibly back to the 18th century, Switzerland has been a net capital exporter. From an institutional point of view, the Swiss financial market is thoroughly integrated with the international financial markets. And there are no institutional obstacles to investing savings abroad and foreign savings domestically. Still, domestic savers may be asking not just compensation for expected depreciation of foreign currencies but also a risk premium for investments abroad. Conversely, the foreign borrowers who issue debt in Swiss francs, or just get short or long-term credits denominated in Swiss francs will ask for a negative risk premium on the interest due on their debt claims (Mauro).

Figure 8: Current Account

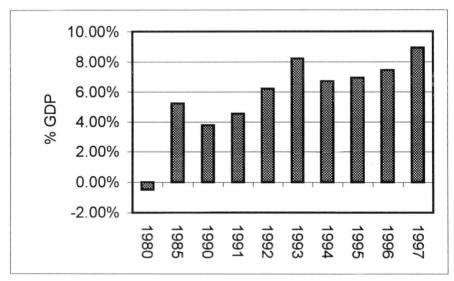

Source: Swiss National Bank, Monthly Bulletin

Finally, there is the hypothesis of the chief economist of the Swiss National Bank (Rich), according to whom the interest discount reflects the price international investors are willing to pay for an alternative currency denomination in a world where the alternatives are legion but where most of them are relatively shaky.

All these hypotheses do not contradict each other, and their relative explanatory power may vary in time. Still the 'technology' of creating an interest rate island remains more or less in the dark. Consequently, it is hard to predict whether the interest rate island still has a long life before it. If any of the above hypotheses is accurate, the anomaly might very well survive even under conditions of a very stable euro. Useless to add that chances for its survival are even better under an inflation-wise unstable euro, or a euro subject to political controversy.

It is definitely easier to find ways sufficient to sink the island, if one so wishes, than it is to define the conditions conducive to permanent survival of the phenomenon. A sufficient condition for the sinking of the island would be the irrevocable commitment of Switzerland to join the European Union. Since membership in the EU, for Switzerland, would inevitably involve the adoption of the euro (a newcomer would not be granted the benefit of an opting-out clause), there would be no room any more for an interest rate differential, except for a, no doubt minor, national solvency bonus.

Figure 9: Capital Account

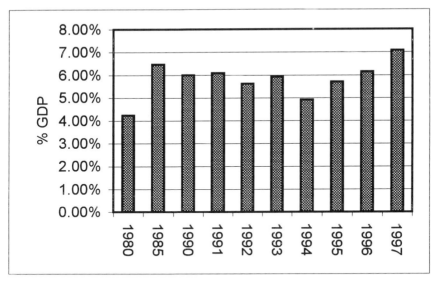

Source: Swiss National Bank, Monthly Bulletin

Figure 10: Saving and Investment

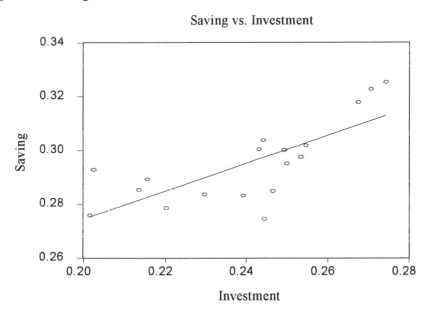

Source: Swiss federal statistical office, National accounts

In that case, the Swiss franc long rates would adjust immediately to the euro rates. And Swiss franc short rates would, depending on the timetable of adhesion, more or less rapidly converge to euro short rates, too. Essentially the same would happen if, without plans to join the EU, the Swiss National Bank would make a credible commitment to freeze the Swiss franc-euro exchange rate. It is an open question what, short of an irrevocable commitment to EU membership, it would take to make such a commitment credible after a long time of independence.

The fact that the Swiss economy, in particular its real estate markets, have in a long process become accustomed to a low level of nominal and real interest rates, makes an alignment with the euro a much more hazardous adventure than the alignment of all the other European currencies to the D-mark, and subsequently to the euro. In all countries, the prospect (via the pegs of the Exchange Rate Mechanism) of a peg to the D-mark had the effect of permanently lowering the interest rate, which did not fail, in each of the countries involved, to unleash a boom of adjustment closely related to this prospect. In the case of the Swiss franc, the effect will be the opposite. The prospect of permanently higher loan and mortgage rates would not fail to have a depressive impact on the economy, an impact which would hardly be compensated by extra growth and the benefits of rising coupon revenues.

At this point, no one knows whether and how long the interest island will survive. Of course, a permanently low real interest rate is not a value in itself, but there can be no doubt about the fact that its disappearance would be a painful process.

Will the Euro Become a Parallel Currency in Switzerland?

Given the extensive freedom of contract enjoyed by domestic economic agents, the merger of eleven, and soon more, currencies in Europe raises the question of whether the euro will end up becoming a parallel currency, or even the dominant currency, in Switzerland. The transition from an environment with many currencies to one with a single currency is bound to have effects on the role of the Swiss franc in Switzerland itself. To sound out these effects, it is useful to recall the various aspects of currency use enumerated in the second section. For some of those aspects, Switzerland's geographical location in the middle of Euroland and the size asymmetry of the home market for goods and services with respect to the Euroland market do matter. Thus, e.g., retailers in Switzerland are more likely than hitherto to express prices in both Swiss francs and euros and to accept payment in euros. This phenomenon, however, should not be overestimated. On the one hand, this is already common practice in border regions and tourist resorts. And on the other hand, as long as the Swiss franc shows no instability and signs of weakness, the exchange rates applied by these retailers are likely to be rather unfavorable to Euroland-clients so that prior purchase of Swiss francs at an exchange office remains advantageous. Nonetheless, there will be inroads of the euro into domestic retail transactions. These inroads might reduce demand for Swiss base money and might pose some intricate, though not insoluble, problems of monetary management. They would also involve a reduction of seigniorage revenue. If this takes place, the Swiss National Bank might have to reconsider the targets of its monetary policy since sticking to a money supply (no matter whether M0, M1 or M anything) rule could turn out to create a systematic inflationary bias, at least for some time. Still, these are technicalities that, in principle, can be solved.

Retail transactions, however, are but a tiny fraction of the transactions taking place in a currency. How about the denomination of other contracts, labor, business transactions of goods and services, and, most importantly, financial claims? Wages are among the last to move to the euro. Cross-border transactions of goods and services by business are more likely to adopt the euro, voluntarily or involuntarily. But it is good to remember that many Swiss exports are already invoiced in foreign currencies today. Thus, cross-border trade credit is already somewhat dominated by currencies other than the Swiss franc. So it is hard to estimate what difference the emergence of an euro environment will really make.

Another story is the denomination of financial contracts. As mentioned earlier, there is no *a priori* reason to assume that the Swiss franc would be competed out of financial uses. Swiss franc-denominated claims might even become more sought after, at least at some moments so that interest rates might remain low while the currency would continue to appreciate, or at least would exhibit higher volatility.

Some economists (Rich) view it as a contradiction that the Swiss franc base money demand might fall while simultaneously the Swiss franc might appreciate on the foreign exchange markets. This is an intricate question. As a first approximation, there is no inconsistency between the two phenomena. After all, financial markets don't demand base money but rather claims denominated in terms of a certain currency. Growth of these claims can take place without any, or with little, increase in base money supply. All it takes for each of these claims is a willing lender and a willing borrower. Of course, these contracts are, legally, claims on cash flows of base money, and therefore some base money holdings remain requisite for the financial system. But it takes very little base money, indeed, to support an immense amount of financial holdings and transactions. So the scenario of a shrinking demand for Swiss franc base money and expanding demand for Swiss franc-denominated assets, of shrinking Swiss franc use in retail trade and increasing demand of

Swiss franc financial vehicles, is no contradiction. The question is less whether such a configuration is conceivable than whether it is likely. Two caveats should be borne in mind. First: In history parallel currencies have tended to emerge only under conditions of serious internal monetary disruption. Second: Increased demand for holdings of Swiss franc-denominated assets need not cause the Swiss franc to appreciate. Much also depends on the supply of such debt by the issuers.

Conclusions

It has been argued in this article that, in a system of open capitalist economies, the status of 'in' and 'out' is endogenous rather than exogenous. Among the countries that are formally 'out', Switzerland is a special case in that it has been thoroughly integrated in the global financial system well before the advent of the euro. Capital and financial services are among its major export 'commodities'. This means that Switzerland will be particularly affected by the fate of the euro.

Two intriguing questions are whether the Swiss interest rate island will survive the consolidation of the euro, and whether the euro will become a parallel currency in Switzerland. Although we are far from completely understanding the interest island phenomenon, there are good chances that it might still survive for a while. As to the question of the parallel currency, we have to admit that institutions do not preclude such a development, but as long as the Swiss National Bank maintains its strict policy of price stability and thereby continues a prestigious tradition, chances are that the inroads will remain limited.

All this should not be construed as a scenario of tranquillity. Even with responsible policies on both sides of the euro divide, bilateral turbulences will not be missing.

Notes

1. Switzerland's potential share in the capital of the ECB is estimated at about 3 percent. And its weight in 'one-country-one-vote' decisions would, for the time being, amount to one-twelfth, with decreasing tendency as new countries join the monetary union (Senti, pp. 50-54).
2. (Institutional) Openness should not be confused with such things as perfect capital mobility which is often interpreted as behavioral indifference of investors between domestic and foreign assets or the domestic and foreign currencies.

3. To be precise, formally speaking, Switzerland *is* a candidate. It has filed an application in 1992. But, for all intents and purposes, the application is dormant.
4. OECD: Main economic Indicators, calculated from 'Exchange rate monthly average' (January data) against US$.
5. Hagander, Nils (1995), pp. 1-11.
6. OECD: Main economic Indicators: 3-month Euro-deposits (Switzerland); 3-month FIBOR (Germany).
7. OECD: Main economic Indicators: 3-month Euro-deposits (Switzerland); 3-month FIBOR (Germany); Inflation calculated out of 'Consumer price index, all items'.
8. OECD: Main economic Indicators: Yield on the secondary market: Public sector bonds (Germany); Yield on the secondary market: Confederation bonds (Switzerland).
9. OECD: Main economic Indicators: Yield on the secondary market: Public sector bonds (Germany); Yield on the secondary market: Confederation bonds (Switzerland); Inflation calculated out of 'Consumer price index, all items'.

References

Baltensperger, Ernst. 1996. 'Die Europäische Währungsunion und ihre Bedeutung aus der Perspektive der Schweiz.' *Aussenwirtschaft*, pp. 197-221.

Gärtner, Manfred. 1997. 'Who wants the euro—and why? Explorations of public attitudes towards a single European Currency.' *Public Choice*, vol. 93, no. 5, pp. 487-510.

Hagander, Nils. 1995. 'Private Banking 2000: Diskontinuitäten und Erfolgspositionen'. In Bruno Gehrig, *Private Banking*. Zurich: Verlag Neue Zürcher Zeitung, pp. 1-11.

Halbeisen, Patrick, and Müller Margrit. 1998. 'Die schrittweise Nationalisierung des Geldes: Von der Einführung der Schweizer Währung (Münzreform 1848) zur nationalen Kontrolle über das Geldwesen (Gründung der Nationalbank 1907).' In Alois Mosser, ed., *Österreichs Weg zum Euro: Aspekte, Perspektiven, Handlungsspielräume*. Vienna: Manz, pp. 63-86.

Goodhart, C. A. E. 1997. 'The two concepts of money, and the future of Europe.' Paper presented at the Konstanz Seminar on Monetary Theory and Monetary Policy, May 27-30.

Laxton, Douglas, and Prasad Eswar. 1997. 'Possible effects of European Monetary Union on Switzerland: A case study of policy dilemmas caused by low inflation and the nominal interest rate floor.' IMF Working Paper, WP/97/23.

Leibowitz, Stan, and Margolis Stephen E. 1995. 'Policy and Path-Dependence: From QWERTY to Windows 95.' *Regulation, The Cato Review of Business and Government*, vol. 18, no. 3 (Fall).

Mann, Fritz A. 1992. The Legal Aspect of Money. 5th edition. Oxford: Clarendon Press.

Mauro, Paolo. 1995. 'Current account surpluses and the interest rate island in Switzerland.' IMF Working Paper, WP/95/24.

Rich, Georg. 1999. 'Der Euro und die schweizerische Geldpolitik.' In Richard Senti and Walter Büsch, eds., *Schweizerfranken oder Euro*. Zurich: Schulthess Polygraphischer Verlag, pp. 73-99.

Senti, Richard. 1999. 'Das Europäische System der Zentralbanken—institutionelle Grundlagen.' In Richard Senti and Walter Büsch, eds., *Schweizerfranken oder Euro*. Zurich: Schulthess Polygraphischer Verlag, pp. 35-55.

15. THE EURO AND THE DOLLAR: CURRENCY COMPETITION, COMPETITIVENESS AND POLICY COORDINATION

Christian de Boissieu

The May 1998 decisions have been decisive for the launching of the euro. After May 1998, the markets *de facto* ratified the basic choices: the grid of intra-European parities, the eleven countries, the time-table of the whole process. The credibility of EMU meant that even before its official launching as of January 1999, the euro was already existing for the investors and had an impact on the international monetary and financial system.

The purpose of this paper is to study some aspects of the competition between the dollar and the single European currency. I will focus on two aspects of the subject :
- currency competition and the competitiveness of the euro not only in the short term but also in the medium and long term;
- the market shares of the euro concerning both financial and commercial transactions: what to expect? What are the implications for the international coordination of domestic policies?

Currency Competition and the Competitiveness of the Euro

The euro has been launched not for six months, but for years, decades, ... Like the dollar since 1950, it will be successively weak-strong-weak... according to the growth and interest rate differential between the United States and Europe and some other determinants. Therefore exchange rate considerations must be distinguished from what is more crucial in the medium and long term, namely the role of the euro as an international reserve currency and Europe. This role is going to be mainly determined by the credibility of the single currency and Europe.

About the Quality of a Currency

For a long period of time, economists have been focusing on the quantity theory of money, one way or another. Currency competition and competitiveness (i.e, the ability to compete) appeal to a quality theory of money. How to envisage the quality concept? I would refer to Hayek (1976), who underlines two 'not wholly unrelated dimensions': the expected behavior of the value of the currency; its acceptability (equivalently, its degree of liquidity).

The first criterion assesses any money by its capacity to post a purchasing power approximately constant in time (the stability condition). In an environment with competing monies, economic agents are going, *ceteris paribus*, to prefer currencies with low inflation variability and low inflation costs. Here the external value of the currency (measured by the exchange rate) has to be considered provided it has a significant effect on its internal value.

The second criterion is somewhat more complex since it relates both to the medium-of-exchange function and the expected liquidity of the currency. In order to be competitive, a reserve currency must rely on domestic capital markets and financial intermediaries that are fully deregulated, deep and resilient (for the markets) and sophisticated enough.

Behind and beside the stability and acceptability criteria, some other determinants of credibility have to be taken into account including the political dimension. Moreover, the Hayekian paradigm must be complemented. For instance, the tension between currency concentration and diversification is as permanent internationally as it is domestically. Concentration is warranted by potential and/or actual economies of scale (in a Baumol-Tobin type of model) and the derived reduction in unit transaction costs with the size. It could also be founded on 'preferred habitat' considerations. Diversification is rational for risk-averse agents facing portfolio decisions under uncertainty.

The Macroeconomic Record of the Euro Zone

The Hayek view rightly focuses on price stability as the main component of monetary competitiveness. Some other macroeconomic variables are relevant, such as growth, the quality of the policy mix and the external position of the zone.

Price Stability

The euro zone posts an impressive record as far as disinflation is concerned. The CPI growth is close to zero in most of the member countries. An asymmetric situation still prevails for Ireland and to a lesser extent for Spain, Finland, the Netherlands... But, in terms of the magnitude of the standard deviation of inflation rates in each country and across countries, the stability condition is fulfilled. The current debate concerning the measurement of inflation, which came from the United States and the Boskin commission, is also a European one. But the correction needed to incorporate the quality effect and related topics is smaller in most EU countries (about 0.3-0.4 percent in annual terms) than in the US.

Growth and the Business Cycle: Convergence and Disparities Among Countries

Despite the single market and the launching of the euro, no euro zone business cycle does exist yet. Considering the 11 member countries, we could group them into three categories by their growth record in 1998-1999 (first semester):

(i) the booming countries, particularly Ireland, to a lesser extent Spain and Portugal (with a catch-up effect vis-à-vis more developed member countries), Finland and the Netherlands;

(ii) the low growth countries, especially Italy and Germany which have been the most exposed to the consequences of the Asian and Russian crises given their international specialization;

(iii) countries posting an intermediate record such as France.

We could assume that the deepening and the effectiveness of the single market and the euro will boost growth convergence. Nevertheless, for some time, several business cycles will continue to be effective not only in the EU but also in the euro zone.

The credibility of the euro, both inside and outside Europe, will be conditioned by the average growth record of the zone and the record of the most important and strategic countries (Germany, France, Italy...). For many investors, it will also depend on the labor market situation and the perception of social risks associated with unemployment. In the medium and long term, the euro would not get an effective credibility if European unemployment were not receding significantly. Since European unemployment combines classical and Keynesian unemployment, structural reforms are needed to reduce the overall cost of labor (especially for the unskilled workers) and improve the general functioning of the labor market.

The External Position of the Euro Zone

The euro zone is posting a dramatic external surplus (about $100 billion for the current account surplus in 1997). This surplus comes from two sources:
-   a significant improvement in the price and non-price competitiveness of many European countries. France is a good example among many others of this phenomenon.
-   the slow pace of investment and growth compared with some other zones (the US, some emerging countries...).

The current account surplus could be a positive factor for the credibility of the euro at the start and for the first years of the single currency. In the long run, a succession of external surpluses and deficits has to be envisaged for the euro zone, hoping that some deficits would derive from the rebound in European growth (and employment) rather than from a loss of competitiveness. This succession of phases could encourage the use of the euro outside the EU, as US deficits have favored the international use of the dollar. At some point, there could be a trade-off between liquidity and credibility considerations. The Triffin dilemma has made this point very clear for the dollar since the end of the 1950's. The euro zone is not at all in the configuration envisaged by the Triffin paradox. Nevertheless, we must keep it in mind when looking at the long-term credibility of the single currency.

Deep Financial Markets and the Competitiveness of the Euro

Capital markets in the euro area are now fully integrated. A euro zone yield curve does exist: nominal interest rates are the same for a given maturity and a given counterparty risk, and real rates have also converged (not to exactly the same level). Before the launching of the euro, capital markets in Continental Europe (not to speak about the City) were fragmented. None was reaching the critical size in terms of volume and liquidity. Due to the integration of national capital markets, particularly of the wholesale business, European markets are definitely above the critical size. They could benefit from economies of scale and economies of scope. Their competitiveness vis-à-vis Wall Street and London (as long as the UK is 'out') has been improving tremendously in many respects: lower unit transaction costs (than before), the insurance of liquidity, etc.

The Main Challenges

When enlarging the discussion beyond the stability and acceptability criteria, we find several factors which will be decisive for the credibility of the euro and its competitiveness vis-à-vis the dollar, the yen, etc.

Progress in Economic Coordination and the Quality of the Policy Mix

Just before and after the launching of the euro, a conflict similar to the prisoner's dilemma has prevailed between the ECB and the national central banks on the one hand, some governments on the other hand. The stake is clear-cut: we need to get the optimal policy mix, i.e the cooperative solution of this prisoner's dilemma. Until now, non-cooperative solutions have been dominant. For example, by dropping its rate to 2.5 percent early April 1999, the ECB initiated a cooperative step towards a better policy mix and handed over to the governments as regards the necessary cuts in public spending and public sector deficits. The answer sent by governments has not been so positive: the Ecofin Council allowed Italy to reach a 2.4 percent deficit for 1999 (instead of the announced 2 percent).

The policy mix debate has both functional and institutional dimensions. For example, some clarification is needed concerning the role of the Euro Council and its articulation with Ecofin.

Another debate crucial for the credibility of the euro relates to tax harmonization. Tax and quasi tax discrepancies across countries are not sustainable, in the medium and long term, with the single currency. They will be reduced. How? Two scenarios are still likely: either some tax convergence through the coordination process in Brussels, or full tax (and quasi tax) competition. As long as the unanimity rule prevails for tax coordination, the second scenario is the most likely, with large implications for the adjustment in tax ratios and public expenditures.

Implementing Structural Reforms

Most EMU member countries are still facing the challenge of structural reforms. One exception among the G-11 is the Netherlands. France and Germany have to adjust their social security and pensions schemes, improve their labor market, adapt their educational system, etc.

Clarification Concerning the ECB

I stress two dimensions which could be crucial for the credibility and competitiveness of the euro.

First, the accountability of the ECB must be better organized. The Maastricht Treaty implements a rather vague concept of ECB accountability. Without any sort of artificial import, the euro zone could draw some interesting lessons from the accountability of the US Fed (the Humphrey-Hawkins procedure, the publication of the FOMC minutes with the usual lag...).

Second, the ECB will fulfil the lender of last resort function in case of a systemic crisis. This function is not explicitly organized by the Treaty. In some circumstances, a trade-off between the goal of price stability (the main ECB objective) and systemic stability could occur. From a purely technical viewpoint, the ECB has been given the instruments (reserve requirements, open-market operations...) which allow sterilization and could alleviate or even discard the trade-off.

Political Support

EMU and euro will not last without a significant progress in political cooperation. The subjects are manifold: the reform of European institutions and procedures, the implementation of a common defense and security policy in the aftermath of the Kosovo war, more convergence about the time-table and the conditions for EU enlargement, etc. EMU could lead to a new institutional category different from a genuine Federal State. We must count on a 'learning by doing' process in order to fix the border between centralized and decentralized instruments.

The Market Shares of the Euro: What to Expect? Implications for International Coordination

Exchange Rates and Market Shares

The role of a currency could be assessed by its market shares. At the international level, the medium-of-exchange function leads to consider the invoicing of world trade flows. The reserve-of-value function could be gauged by the currency structure of private and public portfolios.

Exchange rates and market shares are not fully independent from each other. For example, when the dollar was weak (e.g. 1994-1995), G-7 central banks intervened and increased the market share of the dollar in their official reserves. Moreover, investors are sensitive to actual and expected exchange rates when they choose the currency composition of their portfolio.

Nevertheless the international role of a currency is, up to a certain threshold, quite insensitive to its exchange rate. I appeal to two different examples : 1) When the dollar was weak, its market shares have not dropped significantly, i.e. more than the downward trend observed since the early 1970's would anticipate. 2) Since January 1999, a weaker euro than expected has not jeopardized its role in the international monetary system. Considering the euro-bond market, the euro was currency number one (with a market share of 44 percent) for the issues during the first quarter of 1999.

A Likely Gap Between the Financial Success of the Euro and Trade Inertia

First, we consider financial transactions. Over the period 1980-1997, the market share of the dollar has seen a downward trend, with a low slope for the share in official reserves (IMF data) and a more pronounced slope for the denomination of external bond issues. The Deutschmark and the yen have been the 'winners', and they have increased their market shares significantly at the expense of the dollar. This trend illustrates one important dimension of the multicurrency system which has been developing over the past twenty years.

Since portfolio decisions are volatile and reversible, they could lead to a dramatic increase in the market share of the euro even in the short run. We could anticipate that the euro will benefit from an aggregation effect: its market share will be quickly larger than the sum of the market shares of the participating currencies (after deducting any possible double counting). Many central banks all over the world, including for example the People's Bank of China, have announced their willingness to redeploy their official reserves in favor of the euro. Private investors are also sensitive to the rationality of diversification. The fact that the euro has been weaker than expected since January 1999 could have slowed down the portfolio shift. Nevertheless this shift will work in favor of the single European currency with essential implications: geographic reallocation of seigniorage, gradual development of an external financing constraint for the United States provided that they keep posting a current account deficit, etc.

As far as the invoicing of world trade is concerned, the currency shift will be more gradual since inertia phenomena do exist. Inertia in monetary behavior, which is consistent in the short run with overshooting phenomena and large portfolio shifts, comes from long-term trade relationships and the existence of 'preferred habitats' for many exporters and importers. Due also to network effects and externalities, the leading currency (namely the dollar) benefits from a significant advantage vis-à-vis competing currencies. Moreover each commercial trader tends to favor the denomination of his imports or exports in his national (or regional for the euro) currency in order to remove any exchange rate risk. Such a behavior could slow down the use of the euro by non-European traders.

All in all, the likely development of the euro as a reserve currency could be represented by figure 1.

Figure 1: Proportion Rules on Development of the Euro

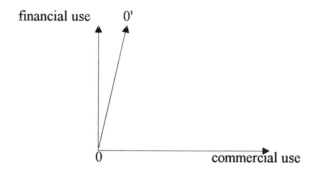

It is very likely that the market shares of the euro will develop along the line 00' illustrating a gap between the financial and the commercial use of the single currency. If this gap were above a certain threshold, there would be a negative feedback on the financial role of the euro. In other words, an excessive gap could jeopardize this financial role unless the adjustment is working the other way with some endogenous forces leading to an extent in the commercial use.

Currency Competition and Policy Coordination

Does a multicurrency system, compared with the more asymmetrical monetary regime of the pure dollar standard, facilitate the adjustment process? There is no clear-cut answer to this question.

Intuitively it is likely that up to a certain point currency diversification could strengthen the stability of the system by better absorbing shocks and distributing risks more widely. But this statement needs to be supported by theoretical models and empirical estimates.

In effect the multicurrency system does not entirely correspond to the so-called monetary triad (dollar, euro, yen). When looking at the international role of the yen (not its exchange rate), it is clear that it has dramatically been reduced with the launching of the euro. At present the international monetary and financial system is closer to a monetary duopoly (dollar, euro) than to an oligopoly. This change is not irreversible yet and the international role of the yen could rebound in the future. The duopoly (dollar, euro) is still very asymmetrical but one of the goals of EMU is to get a more balanced system.

As regards systemic stability, the existence of a hegemon could be required as assumed in the theory of hegemonic stability (see Keohane (1984). We could draw one important conclusion from this controversial theory: more symmetry does not necessarily mean less instability.

With more competition between the dollar and the euro, the international monetary system will have to articulate and balance two logics, the logic of competition and the logic of cooperation. How can two reserve currency areas (the United States, the euro zone) be induced to accept an ex ante coordination of their policies? I think that we will continue to live in a world in which the degree of policy coordination (monetary, budgetary...) is going to lag much behind the degree of financial integration. The outcome, namely financial instability and systemic risks, is somewhat unavoidable. Nevertheless we have to be more ambitious and effective for the G-7 coordination exercises. First, all the functional and institutional implications of the euro have to be drawn for a better working of the G-7. Second, the G-7 goals and instruments must be redefined. The coordination of national prudential policies through the exercises taking place in Basle and Brussels have been much more credible and effective so far than the multilateral surveillance of monetary and fiscal policies through the G-7. We have to be both ambitious and pragmatic since coordination clearly is a 'learning by doing' process. Enlarged international coordination is not a substitute for, but rather a complement to the tough currency competition which will keep developing.

References

de Boissieu, Christian. 1996. 'The SDR in the Light of the Multicurrency System.' In M. Mussa, J. Boughton, and P. Isard, eds., *The Future of the SDR in Light of Changes in the International Financial System*. Washington, D.C.: International Monetary Fund.

Hayek, Friedrich A. 1976. *Denationalisation of Money.* London: Institute of Economic Affairs.
Keohane, Robert O. 1984. *After Hegemony: Cooperation and Discord in the World Political Economy.* Princeton: Princeton University Press.

16. THE IMPACT OF THE EURO ON THE INTERNATIONAL STABILITY: A CHINESE PERSPECTIVE

Mingqi Xu

Evaluating the Current Stability

With the successful launch of the euro, most of the observers of the economic world see the euro as a stabilizer in the international economic system. The fact that the Asian financial crisis struck most of the Asian countries causing a great chaos in international economic activities while the euro zone remained insulated and relatively stable convinced more people that the euro is a stabilizer. It can help maintaining international financial stability and pushing forward the reform of the international monetary system. A few scholars also pointed out the possibility of fluctuation once the euro is introduced.[1] Since the introduction of the euro on January 1, 1999, the exchange rate relative to the US dollar has been floating in a narrow span and the international financial markets, especially European capital markets, maintained a relative stability. Instead of shifting huge funds into euro assets, international investors seemed very cool about the euro event and most of the asset managers have kept watching rather than shifting their portfolios. Until now erratic fluctuations have not happened in the way some observers predicted. This again seems to prove the positive impact of the euro.

Everybody believes that the euro will become the second biggest international currency. Many people, especially Europeans, think that the euro will become a competitor to the US dollar and that the competition will create a more stable situation than what we are experiencing today. This is true only in the sense that the integration of 11 euro-countries will eliminate the fluctuations of all the formerly weak currencies of the members. Integration brought a large strong currency that can strengthen its stabilizing ability to outside shocks as a whole. With the removal of intra-European exchange rate fluctuations, capital flows among European nations will be more stable and free from distortion and frequent speculative attacks.

However, the role of the euro as a stabilizer outside Europe is not certain. The so-called competition between the US dollar and the euro does not really happen in the conventional sense. So the stability at equilibrium point through competition, which is what many economists believe, does not appear to hold in the current situation. At present the relative stability in the international economic system is still maintained by the US dollar dominance. Several factors have contributed to the dominance of the US dollar as a stabilizer.

Firstly, the strong US economic performance and the weak European economy have encouraged international capital to stay in the US capital market. The euro has not attracted as much investment as many anticipated. Although some observers believe that 50 percent of newly issued international bonds were denominated in euro, the stock value of assets remained unchanged. The instability caused by quick flows of international capital did not happen.

Secondly, the uncertainty of the political situation in Europe triggered by the war in the former Yugoslavia made Europe a less attractive place to invest. Nobody knows how this war will affect the European economy and political structures. Many fear that the EU is going to spend more money to deal with the refugee problem and to cover military expenses. This will increase the budget deficit and the target of the Stability Pact is unlikely to be met. So inflation is going to rise and the unemployment problem is not going to be solved very soon. All this in turn helped the US dollar to maintain its dominant position in the international monetary system, which also means that the relative stability depends on the US dollar.

Thirdly, the Asian economic recovery is slow, which also prevents capital from flowing back at a quick pace. This added to the comparative stability of the international financial markets and contributed to a relatively stable US dollar exchange rate. Japan is still in recession and the Japanese yen is less attractive than before. Thus, the yen seems to lose its important position in the international monetary system.

Fourthly, instability in Latin America did not spill over to the rest of the world. The US dollar seemed unaffected by Brazil's crisis.

However, the comparatively stable situation in the international financial system after the Asian financial crisis and since the birth of the euro does not bear relation to the euro. The euro as a stabilizer cannot be understood from the current situation.

According to most European observers, the recent downward floating trend of the euro exchange rate is an advantage for both the euro and the European economy. They also think that this will not affect the prospect of the euro becoming a key international currency.[2] If we believe that the current situation is temporary and if we accept that sooner or later the euro will catch up and become an equal partner to the dollar in the international economic system, will the euro play a stabilizing role in the international economic system? I think we cannot be so sure about this. The only thing we can be sure about is that the two-polar system will phase out the possibility of a triangle system. The Japanese yen will have less and less of a chance to play a key role in the international monetary system as the euro is growing and becoming more stable. But the question is whether a two-polar system is automatically more stable than the current system. Even if we rule out the possible instability in the transitional period towards a two-polar system, the two-polar system itself does not ensure more stability. Without a carefully designed mechanism and international policy coordination, especially the coordination between the US and the EU, the euro cannot be a successful stabilizer in the international economic system.

Stability Under a Two-Polar System

I would like to point out that there is the threat of potential instability if some of the existing problems related to the euro in the international monetary system will not be properly solved. These are problems that occur in a two-polar monetary system without a well-designed international management and policy coordination.

Assume that the euro represents 50 percent of international reserve and that the euro area is as big as the dollar area. About half of the world trade involves the euro and almost the same amount of international financial transactions are denominated in euros. What will be the result? Will there be a stable equilibrium as many suggest? Probably not. For as long as there are differences between Europe and the US in terms of economic growth rates, balance of payments, interest rate and inflation rates etc., there will be fluctuations in the exchange rate between the dollar and the euro. Exchange rates will more or less reflect these economic fundamentals. What is more important is that portfolio flows related to expectations may sometimes exert a powerful pressure so that the euro-dollar exchange rate and other financial prices swing at an unprecedented range and speed. Why could this be possible? Simply because the euro-dollar exchange rate is too important to be neglected under such a two-polar system and everyone may become a speculator if there is not any management or international constraints on transactions.

Under the current dollar-dominated multi-reserve currency system, the US dollar exchange rate with other reserve currencies is important to most of the countries in the world, yet more countries pay attention to their own currency exchange rate with the US dollar rather than the exchange rate among reserve currencies. Many of them have pegged their currencies to the dollar in order to maintain stability. Under a future two-polar system, countries will have to anchor their currencies to both the dollar and the euro. In theory, this will help countries to ease the pressure to adjust their peg from time to time. But in reality, countries will have the pressure to pay more attention to the euro-dollar exchange rate since this rate will affect not only the exchange rate of their own currencies, but also the value of their diversified foreign exchange reserve. As a result, huge portfolio funds will flow between euro assets and dollar assets, which in turn will cause the euro-dollar exchange rate to fluctuate dramatically.

Institutional investors and some international speculators possess huge amounts of funds nowadays. They are inclined to invest and to speculate in the international market in order to reap short-term profits. Financial crises are usually triggered or amplified by this kind of speculative investment. Under a two-polar system, speculations by these players would only be more severe, as there is no significant counterweight. So the role played by the euro is not definitely positive and the stability will not follow automatically with the emergence of a two-polar system. A two-polar system requires more anti-speculative measures by international authorities and the governments concerned.

Many people believe that with the competition brought by the euro, the international monetary system reform will be speeded up and the current unstable financial situation can be changed in the near future. This seems to be merely wishful thinking. Since the launch of phase three of the euro, the US government has repeatedly rejected the call for quick reform of the international monetary system and has denied the need for an international management of exchange rates. Many Americans think that the birth of the euro will not change much of the pattern of the current international monetary system. In the near future, the US dollar will still hold its dominant position. So they do not care about the need for coordination and cooperation in managing the exchange rates and they are opposed to measures against speculative capital flows.

Europeans show the desire to coordinate more closely with the US. Officials from EU member states as well as from the ECB appealed on several occasions that there should be a mechanism for stabilizing the exchange rate between the dollar and the euro.[3] However, these imaginations have not yet received a positive response from the other side of the Atlantic. The US government insists on her traditional exchange rate policy of benign neglect by arguing that there is no need for the dollar to have a specified range of fluctuation as long as the dollar is the number one currency in the world. Other currencies are free to be pegged to the dollar, but the dollar is not to be tied to any measure. Therefore, over a short time horizon, international management on the euro-dollar exchange rate is not likely to happen.

Implication of a Two-Polar System for China

In the absence of close international coordination, changes in the international monetary system brought by the euro could be destabilizing. A two-polar system may emerge through turbulence. Even if the euro grows quickly enough and becomes a similarly important international currency in a short time, we won't have a very stable international monetary order.

What does this prospect mean for a developing country such as China? It means that we have to be more cautious. The euro is a good thing for Europe and it creates a chance to build a fairer and more stable international monetary system. But it does not necessarily provide more opportunities for investment and financial risk management on the part of China. Rather, it brings challenges in foreign exchange reserve management and financial transactions.

Being a big developing country with an open economic policy, China is very sensitive to the international economic situation. International financial crises and fluctuations in the exchange rate between key currencies often impose additional cost upon China's economy. China hopes that a more stable international financial arrangement would replace the current turbulent situation. China also welcomes the euro in the hope that it will add to the demands for reform of the international financial system. Although we pay great attention to a new opportunity of diversifying our foreign exchange reserve, it is not China's first priority. As the euro-dollar exchange rate fluctuates, shifting some of the reserve into euro assets does not change the essence of the matter. If China shifts its $145 billions foreign exchange reserve according to market movements and expectations, it will add to the instability of the foreign exchange market. If it does not, fluctuations will cause a huge loss over time. So China (like many other participants in international financial activities) is very cautious in holding euro assets.

Of course, it could be argued that it is because of exchange rate fluctuations that we need to diversify our foreign exchange reserve. In theory, it is. In reality, it is not that simple. Under the multi-reserve system, diversification means that the principal part of a country's currency reserve is in US dollar assets and the remaining part is in some other currencies such as the D-mark, the Japanese yen, the pound sterling etc. The ratio of the remaining part is changeable according to a country's needs. But the proportion of the assets in US dollars is not adjusted according to the needs created by commercial and financial transactions, but rather according to the fluctuations in the value of the dollar. When the dollar is strong, the share of the dollar in the reserve is growing. When the dollar is declining, its share goes down too. This pattern of compositional change will remain as the euro becomes the second principal currency and perhaps as important as the dollar. Developing countries will adjust their euro holdings according to its real value and changes in the expected euro exchange rate. Their real commercial and financial demand for the euro will be secondary in making decisions regarding the composition of asset holdings. Thus, for developing countries, a two-polar system adds more uncertainties to exchange reserve management rather than providing a good way to manage exchange reserve. This is why the Chinese Government showed its strong intention to shift some of the dollar reserve assets into euro assets since its launch, but it has not made a big step towards this.

If all countries in the world take the same attitude and wait for the right moment to switch reserve assets, turbulence in international capital market and foreign exchange market will be unavoidable. If international speculators deliberately use some of the fluctuations to arouse herd behavior, financial shocks may well happen again. For a developing country like China, this is the last thing we want to see. We want to be sure that there is an internationally coordinated action or management when needed. We hope that a two-polar system will be established based on well-designed international coordination.

Whether this hope will come true or not, I think China is going to anchor its currency RMB to a basket of currencies in which the dollar and the euro each have a substantial weight. Under a two-polar system, it would be costly to stick to the dollar-backed pegging. But as I mentioned above, double-currency backing or a basket of currencies do not really change the essence of the matter. The rationale for pegging the Chinese RMB to the dollar is to maintain the economic stability both at home and for the whole of Asia. Exchange rate pegging itself is not an end in itself. Developing countries adopt a strategy of pegging mainly because they are too weak to sustain the frequent exchange rate fluctuations. If the pegging to double currencies cannot provide stability, countries may either choose to anchor their currencies to the dollar or to the euro. So without a stabilizing mechanism between two poles, a two-polar system is not necessarily a good thing for developing countries' exchange rate management.

Will a two-polar system encourage free floating or managed floating in developing countries? I think this could be the case. Actually the two-polar system will make the pegging regime very difficult to operate. Unless you stick either to the dollar or to the euro, pegging to both or a basket of currencies requires more efforts and skills. The results usually differ relative to pegging to the dollar. If the dollar-euro exchange rate fluctuates frequently, this kind of pegging would only smooth the fluctuations but not exempt a currency from them. In facing this kind of dilemma, developing countries may have to adopt a more flexible exchange rate regime. This effect is neutral. Without taking into account other factors, no one can be sure that it is stabilizing or destabilizing to the international economic system.

In bilateral relations, the euro provides a vehicle for both China and the EU to expand their economic exchanges. China sees the euro as a promoting force for trade with the EU and hopes that the euro will bring more investment to China. Chinese business circles are willing to use the euro as an intermediary in doing business with their European partners. Most of the companies and banks have finished the preparation and transition to open a euro account. Ordinary people are already familiar with the euro. In this sense, the euro is playing a stabilizing role in enhancing bilateral economic relations.

How Could the Euro Play a Stabilizing Role?

A French writer was correct in writing as follows: 'Europe is still in the accounting phase. It has not yet developed an image of itself. It is not yet ready, like a great nation, to face danger and storms. It has not yet reached adulthood. Our adolescence is inscribed in our currency'. (Régis Debray, 1998). Uncertainties in the international economic system brought by the euro have all been attributed to the lack of determination by Europeans. Almost every European scholar would mention the size, population, GDP, trade volume and so on in order to show the strength of the euro zone and assure you of the successful future of the euro. It is true that the euro zone has enough economic strength to match the United States of America. But economic strength alone does not provide sufficient power. Determination is sometimes more important than the economy. The euro represents the EU's vision on the economic integration of Europe. In a globalizing world economy, the EU must develop a sense of leadership before it can compete with the US. If it is not determined to take responsibility, the euro can only be a regional currency. It will not be a stabilizer in the international economic system. Only if the EU is determined to play a decisive role in the international economic system, can the euro be used as a means for competition and can proper international coordination be reached by persisting in one's efforts.

The Europeans have been very careful not to mention the phrase 'challenging the dollar leadership'. The word they used is 'competition'. Whether it is challenge or competition with the dollar leadership, the result is the same. A two-polar system embraced both meanings. If the EU is expecting this, it should take the responsibility from now on. It should change its inward-looking policy. It should also take measures to enhance international cooperation and to push forward the reform of the international financial system. In the group of Seven, the EU has more members than the US. Europeans should learn how to take initiatives. Followers usually don't have any vision of the future. If the EU is going to be a power and the euro is going to be a key international currency, the EU must act like a leader from now on, at least in the international economic domain.

Being a monetary policy-maker, the ECB has independent power to make decisions. But people doubt that the exchange rate level of the euro is under consideration of the Council of Ministers. The ECB shows no interest in adjusting the rate and will not take it as an important factor in making monetary policy. If this is true, there should be a mechanism to amend this weakness when exchange rate adjustment and international coordination are needed. In theory, a reserve currency country can adopt a policy of benign neglect regarding the exchange rate. In fact, only the biggest reserve currency can really act in this way. As the second biggest reserve currency, the euro is bound to be concerned with its exchange rate in terms of the dollar. The reason is very simple. There exists a bigger currency for everybody to choose. The euro will lose its position and even its stability. Only when the two biggest match each other in terms of size, can both neglect their exchange rates fluctuation. But at this time, coordination and cooperation in managing exchange rates would be a better choice. I hope that the EU will create an internal mechanism to allow the ECB to use monetary policy to adjust the exchange rate when it is needed.

In order to create a favorable condition for the euro to be widely used, the EU should be in favor of the suggestion to discourage speculative capital flows. As I mentioned above, speculative capital flows will set off shocks on exchange rate markets. This is one of the main risks that could harm the development of the euro's international role. Although monetary integration gives the EU more strength to combat speculative attacks on its members' currencies, the current international environment has not yet been adjusted to discourage speculation. The risk persists that if there is an opportunity, speculative attacks on the euro could well happen. So creating an international mechanism to discourage speculation is not only good for the Euroland, but also good for the world economy as a whole.

The EU should speed up the integration of internal capital markets. Insufficient and inefficient capital markets are one of the most acute factors of inferiority as compared to the US. Without an efficient capital market that can provide enough attractive financial assets, the euro is not likely to acquire its central position in the international financial system. Many US scholars do not believe in the euro's leading role in the near future mainly because they don't see a challenging capital market.[4] Market development is not a one-day process. It takes time. But policy adjustment plays an important role in it. More open and flexible attitudes should be adopted in order to allow outsiders to be active in euro-based transaction activities.

The EU should also change its attitude towards the balance of international payments. Being a key currency issuer, it has the responsibility to provide the rest of the world with sufficient amounts of euros. If it always keeps a surplus status, the euro cannot be an important international key currency.[5] Other countries can obtain euro assets either through a trade deficit or a capital account deficit. But such a deficit is not a bad thing for the EU. It will bring seigniorage to the euro zone. The Asian countries traditionally belong to the dollar area. This is mainly because we have a trade surplus with the US or we have net capital inflows from the US. If the euro is going to be widely used in Asia, it should invest or lend more money to Asia. It should also expand its trade relations with Asian countries.

Conclusion

The euro is in its adolescence at present. It will become an adult. In its adolescent period, the euro may be a source of instability. The current comparative stability in the international economic system since the birth of the euro is not related to the role played by the euro. It is a reflection of the continuing dominance of the dollar. Even if we have a two-polar system consisting of the dollar and the euro, we may not have the same degree of stability as we imagine. Stability will not be automatic with such a two-polar system. It requires international coordination and cooperation. But we have not seen signs that the US is going to have the same vision as Europeans and the rest of the world would have. Being a big developing country, China hopes to have a more stable international financial situation. We are opposed to international speculations. We welcome the euro and its stabilizing role in the international economic system. We hope that the EU will enhance its demand for reforming the international financial system. The euro will grow up if it is determined to face the future. If the euro zone takes measures to improve its internal strength and at the same time look after external relations, the euro will play an important role in the international economic system as it grows up.

Notes

1. For example, Professor C.F. Bergsten anticipated that after the introduction of the euro, about US $ 500-1000 billions of funds will flow out of US into Europe, causing instability in international financial markets (Bergsten, 1997).
2. Although I believe that this downward trend of the euro exchange rate vis-à-vis the US dollar is not a serious problem for EU and it might be good for EU's export, it certainly does not promote a good international image. It will certainly prolong the transitional period towards a two-polar system in which the euro enjoys a status equal to that of the US dollar.
3. For example, the former German Finance Minister Lafontaine repeatedly expressed his hope that the exchange rate stabilization by the ECB and the Fed be maintained. The president of the ECB, Wim Duisenberg, also showed a willingness to coordinate with the Fed in the area of monetary policy operation.
4. For example, Professor Richard Cooper mentioned this in his paper of 1992. Funke and Kennedy (1997) also found the relation between currency denomination in the capital market and its position in the international financial system to be significant.
5. The President of the German Institute of Economic Research, Professor Hoffmann, once told me that compared to their US brothers, Europeans are provincial regarding the balance of payments. He thought that it would take time for the Europeans to become smart in this area.

References

Bergsten, C. Fred. 1997. 'The Dollar and the Euro.' *Foreign Affairs*, vol. 76 (July/August).

Cooper, Richard N. 1992. 'Will an EC Currency Harm Outsiders?' *Orbis*, vol. 36 (Fall).

Debray, Régis. 1998. 'A Faceless Currency Representing a Virtual Europe.' *International Herald Tribune*, November 28-29.

Fratianni, Michele, and Jürgen von Hagen. 1992. *The European Monetary System and European Monetary Union*. Oxford: Westview Press.

Funke, Norbert, and Mike Kennedy. 1997. 'International Implications of the European Economic and Monetary Union.' OECD Working Papers, no. 174, Paris: OECD.

Gros, Daniel, and Niels Thygesen. 1992. *European Monetary Integration*. London: Longman.

McCauley, Robert N. 1997. 'The Euro and the Dollar.' *Essays in International Finance,* no. 205 (November). International Finance Section, Princeton University.

Tavlas, George S. 1997. 'The International Use of the Dollar: An Optimum Currency Area Perspective.' *The World Economy* (September).

Welfens, Paul J. J., ed. 1996. *European Monetary Integration—EMS Developments and International Post-Maastricht Perspectives*. Berlin: Springer.

PART IV
CONFERENCE SESSIONS

Introductory Remarks

A. Clesse: My name is Armand Clesse, Director of the Luxembourg Institute for European and International Studies, one of the organizers of this conference. The other is, as you know, the Pierre Werner Foundation and its Vice-President is with us, Ambassador Guy de Muyser.

I don't want to go into details about this conference, about the topic 'the future role of the euro as a possible stabilizer in the world economic system'. The title and therefore the origins of this meeting I owe to the man sitting on my left, Professor Kindleberger, who was here in Luxembourg at a much smaller meeting, just over a year ago, on October 18, on the political implications of monetary integration in Europe. And it was at that meeting that he brought up the topic of the euro as a stabilizer in the world economic system. It was then I conceived the idea of holding a larger meeting.

There are quite diverse ideas and thoughts about the future role of the euro as all in this room know and know much better than myself. Some very extreme opinions were voiced in recent years. For example Martin Feldstein has argued that the introduction of the common European currency may lead, he didn't say will lead, but may lead to war between European nations because it would increase not just economic and social tensions between European nations, but also political ones. Others have argued that the euro will become the most important currency in the world before long and will even supplant the dollar as a reserve currency, for example as the main currency in Asia. But that kind of ideas is what our debate should be about.

Session 1: Monetary Leadership and Economic Stability: The Lessons of the Pound and the Dollar

A. Clesse: We start with a historical perspective, looking at what we may have learned from the role of sterling and of the dollar in this century. Under the title 'Monetary leadership and economic stability' we have three main speakers on the list: Professor Kindleberger, Professor Skidelsky and Professor van der Wee. So Professor Kindleberger.

C. Kindleberger: Good morning. I am glad to be back in Luxembourg after my initial visit in 1944 with the troops. It is different. Particularly these buildings did not exist then. But it is nice to be back here with old friends. I have lots of them and I'm delighted to be here. When I say old friends, I mean that we have been friends for a long time. They are not really old.

I will talk more about monetary leadership than about the euro. I want to recur to my view of the 1929 depression and suggest the comparabilities of that time with today. Some of you may be aware that I have a particularly curious view of the 1929 depression. It goes back to Irving Fisher and deflation. I have in mind the fact that the commodities collapsed in October, November and December 1929 after the banks got all tied up in trying to sort out brokers loans and rationed credit. There was a young man named Bernanke who talked about rationed credit. He didn't say whom they would ration credit to. And I say they rationed credit to commodity brokers. In the old days, exporters would sell commodities sent to New York and London and bought by commodity brokers who needed credit. If they couldn't get credit, he commodities got dumped. And you had a decline in world trade of imported commodities, of 12 to 15 percent (not cotton and wheat which were exported by the US), which led to tremendous deflation world-wide.

The commodities had been falling before that, and countries like Uruguay and Australia depreciated their currencies early. But the stock market collapse produced a large impact on the credit system and this, it seems to me, was responsible for the serious deflation. Business sagged quietly until May 1931 when there was the collapse of the Austrian Creditanstalt. Then one needed a lender of last resort. The Bank for International Settlements tried to help with a small amount of money. But lenders of last resort function often get involved in politics and on the eve of the second tranche of this help the French decided that they wanted to impose political conditions on Germany. This, it seems to me, meant that the collapse accelerated enormously from May 1931. The United States which had not been helping up to that time—isolationist, not participating in Versailles, not participating in the League of Nations and insisted on the collection of war debts—didn't help. Britain was rather weaker after stabilizing its currency. But my thesis in general was that there was no leadership in the system, with the British weakening and the United States isolationist. And what I really worry about now is that the United States may be weakening and Europe may be so concerned with its own problems of the euro and the East that there will be a leadership gap. One thing people do, of course, is to attack the IMF. I'll come to that when I'll talk tomorrow. I have in mind that leadership is important. I use the word 'leadership' rather than 'hegemony'. I ran across a historian the other day, Charles Maier at Harvard, who talks about 'consensual hegemony'. That strikes me as being an oxymoron. Oxymorons are popular now, of course. I heard Galbraith the other day, after 'conventional wisdom' of some years ago, which was an oxymoron, he now has 'innocent fraud'. I think he attacks the capitalist system for it. 'Innocent fraud': many economic actors are fraudulent, but not aware of it, so that it is innocent. But 'hegemony' is a word I don't like. It has too much force in it. And I would have thought that 'leadership' is better. The leader should support more and should pay more than others. He is not, as it would be said of a public choice, doing it for *seigniorage*, let's say, or doing it for making more money. But he gets paid in a different coin: prestige. And he is doing it for responsibility or duty. 'Duty' is a word that doesn't resonate today as compared with 'rights'. People talk about their rights, they don't talk about their duties. I was blessed with a mother-in-law who said: 'You have to do it. It is your duty.' And that lesson is not widely shared, I am afraid. Now the United States is weakening in its duty, toward the UN and it was very slow in backing the IMF. I am concerned that there may be a shortage of leadership in the years to come. I will come back to that theme later.

H. van der Wee: As an economic historian not just of Modern Times, but of the Late Medieval and Early Modern Periods, as well, I feel that any remarks about the role played by the British *pound sterling* and the American *dollar* during the 19th and 20th centuries ought necessarily to be preceded by a survey of the leading European currencies from the Late Middle Ages to the French Revolution and an outline—albeit brief—of the role they played in the European economy of the pre-revolutionary period.

During the 13th and 14th centuries, the leading currency in Europe north of the Alps was the French silver *gros tournois*, and the leading money of account was the French *livre de gros tournois*. The 15th and 16th centuries, however, saw monetary leadership in the region shift to the Low Countries—i.e. the 17 provinces of the Northern and Southern Netherlands—the leading currency becoming the Flemish silver *groat* and the leading money of account concurrently the *pound* of 240 Flemish *groats* (which, for the sake of simplicity, I will henceforth call the Flemish *pound*). From the 1520s on, the Flemish-Brabantine gold *Carolusguilder* (soon to become the large, silver *Carolusguilder*) and the silver *double groat* or *stiver* became the leading currencies, while the Flemish-Brabantine *guilder* of 20 *stivers* became the leading money of account for business. The replacement of the Flemish *pound* by the *guilder* and of the *groat* by the *double groat* or *stiver* nevertheless did not imply any fundamental change in the monetary system and in monetary leadership, as the *guilder* was in fact made a satellite money of account of the Flemish *pound*, of which, indeed, it was always to be worth one sixth. The new system was to all intents and purposes a continuation of the old system, except with a new denomination.

It was the Dutch *guilder* (formally a continuation of the Flemish-Brabantine *guilder* of the 16th century) that held sway as the leading money of account of the European business world during the 17th and 18th centuries, the *stiver* remaining the basis of the silver currencies in both the Northern Netherlands (now The Netherlands or Holland) and the Southern Netherlands (now Belgium). To this day, the *guilder* retains its position as the money of account of The Netherlands, though it is no longer the leading money of account of the European economy.

From the 13th-14th centuries on, gold coins began to be struck in increasing numbers in European countries and came to be used increasingly as means of payment in international trade, serving both for payments in cash and as the basis of a commercial money of account. In the countries north of the Alps, however, they were seldom used as a basis for the current money of account. In point of fact, they usually circulated at floating rates expressed in terms of the local or regional money of account, the value of which was in principle determined by the metallic content of the basic silver coins of the area. There were, of course, several exceptions, the most notable in Northwestern Europe being the German *Rhineguilder* and the French *écu*. Originally, both these gold coins were in effective circulation and at the same time were used as money of account in business circles and in the administration of institutions. Subsequently, however, they disappeared from circulation. The *(Rhine)guilder* continued to be used as a commercial and administrative money of account, but not as a money of account with a value determined on the basis of a certain amount of gold. It became a pure multiple—at a fixed rate—of the old current money of account (in the Low Countries, the Flemish *pound*), whose value continued to be determined—as it always had been in the past—by the metallic content of its basic silver coins. The French *écu* also continued to be used as a money of account— inter alia at the Lyons international fairs—but only by way of representing a fixed and immutable weight of gold. In everyday current transactions, this notional *écu de marc* was always valued in terms of the basic silver coins of the *livre de gros tournois*.

In the late 18th century, Great Britain, with the *pound sterling*, took over monetary leadership from the Dutch, holding it until the beginning of the 20th. This time, however, leadership was not limited to Europe, but came to embrace the whole world. Since the Second World War, as we all know, the American *dollar* has superseded *sterling* as the world's dominant currency. Certain monetary economists predict that the *dollar* will come to be challenged by the *euro*, though that challenge is unlikely to emerge in the near future.

I am not a specialist in the history of the French *livre de gros tournois* and therefore do not intend to address that particular subject. What I would like to do, however, is to go in greater detail into the monetary leadership of the Southern Netherlands (Flanders-Brabant) during the Late Middle Ages and the Early Modern Period, and into that of the Northern Netherlands (the Dutch Republic) during the 17th and 18th centuries, before making a comparison with the monetary leadership of Great Britain and the United States.

In looking for factors that determined the transfer of monetary leadership from France to Flanders—i.e. the gradual replacement of the French *livre de gros tournois* by the Flemish *pound* as the dominant, commercial money of account in Europe north of the Alps—both demand and supply have to be taken into account.

Demand for the French money of account and for the silver coins that were its basis fell in the course of the 14th century, because the French economy as a whole was weakening; indeed, it was soon to be faced with full-blown decline. From the beginning of the century, firstly, the long-distance trade between Italy and Northwestern Europe came to be a predominantly maritime affair, conducted via the Strait of Gibraltar and signaling the decay of the fairs of Champagne, which, as a whole, once formed the main staple-market of a flourishing transcontinental trade between North and South. Somewhat later in the century, the Hundred Years War (1337-1453) broke out, and later still the Black Death (1347-1351). War, epidemics and famine were not only to lay waste the country for decades, but also and more particularly to ruin the French economy.

In contrast, there was a continuously growing demand for the Flemish and later the Flemish-Brabantine money of account and for their basic silver coins (the Flemish *groat* and Flemish-Brabantine *stiver*). Bruges and later Antwerp became the main staple-markets of Europe, and the textile and metal industries of Flanders, Brabant and Liège—both urban and rural—became the leading export sectors of Europe. Foreign merchants, attracted to the Low Countries from all over Europe, looked to have a stable commercial money of account (implying a stable basic silver coin) at their disposal, one that could be used as a key-currency system, or that, in other words, would guarantee their being able to contract safely in the area and to obtain easy access to credit should there be a strain on the money market. The local producers, merchants and population were also in favor of a stable money of account and a stable coinage system. Local merchants wanted them for the same reasons as foreign merchants. Producers, both independent artisans and wage-earners, wanted them as a guarantee against price inflation, because artisanal income and wages always lagged behind when prices rose. The urban middle classes and institutions, lastly, wanted them as a guarantee of a stable income from their large-scale investments in life and perpetual annuities, as well as a guarantee against erosion of the value of their hoarded wealth in silver coin.

Factors of supply also favored the stability of the Flemish and Flemish-Brabantine monetary system, and this was in turn to stimulate demand for that system. Although all in constant need of money and credit, the counts of Flanders in the 14th century, the dukes of the Burgundian Netherlands in the 15th and the Habsburg monarchs in the 16th always pursued a policy of maintaining a stable and strong money of account, based on a series of stable, basic silver coins. They also undertook the minting of a substantial quantity of a stable gold coin and—when gold became scarce—of a stable, large silver coin. The only exception was Archduke, later Emperor, Maximilian of Austria who, for a few years in the 1480s until he restored it in 1489, abandoned the traditional policy of his predecessors. The primary goal of these rulers was clearly to provide foreign and local merchants with a stable monetary system for their international and local transactions.

Maintaining a policy of monetary stability was not an easy task in the Late Medieval and Early Modern Periods. The French kings, particularly during the Hundred Years War, continuously debased their silver *gros tournois*, a policy that put great pressure on the Flemish *groat*, which was a direct offspring of the French *gros* and which had for many years been closely connected with the French system. In order to be able better to resist this French pressure, the Count of Flanders attempted to unify the Flemish and Brabantine money of account systems and the silver coins that were their basis. The monetary convention concluded in 1384 between the Count of Flanders and the Duchess of Brabant organized this union and announced the issue of a common, basic silver *groat*. The union nevertheless failed, because Flanders and Brabant were still independent principalities with different sovereigns; they were, indeed, to remain so for some time.

A new attempt at monetary union was made in 1433, when Philip the Good, now Duke of Brabant and Count of Flanders (and now also sovereign of a large part of the Low Countries), announced that the monetary systems of all the territories under his rule had to be unified, and proclaimed the Flemish *groat* as the basic silver coin of the entire unified system. The regional systems of money of account (those of Artois, Flanders, Brabant, Hainault, Zeeland, Holland, Namur and others) were allowed to be used at local level, but the Flemish silver *groat* became the sole and exclusive basic coin of all systems, even for daily local transactions. Via this common coin, thus, all regional monies of account became linked in a fixed relationship to the Flemish money of account, whose value was of old determined by the silver content of the Flemish *groat*.

Under the new circumstances, the Flemish silver *groat* and the Flemish *pound* reinforced their position as respectively the leading silver coin and the leading money of account of the Low Countries as a whole. Furthermore, because of Flanders' dominant position in European trade at that particular time, the Flemish monetary system also became the leading system in Europe. Monetary unification was no doubt a crucial factor in the consolidation of the Flemish monetary system's leadership, but it has to be emphasized that the decisive precondition for the success of the monetary union was the political unification of the region that had taken place in the preceding years.

Although the monetary system of Flanders and of the Low Countries as a whole was based upon a silver standard, it should be emphasized that the dukes also issued a large number of gold coins. When these gold coins were struck, they were always accorded an official rate in terms of the Flemish money of account, which, as already mentioned, was based upon the silver *groat*. The official rate had, of course, to be adjusted regularly. When gold became scarcer, or when the demand for gold coins increased, they circulated in the market at a premium. When it appeared that the premium was definitive, the official rate was adjusted to the market rate. It is not inconceivable that the main goal of the ducal authorities in issuing gold coins was to produce a coin especially suited for international payments and to make it available to local and foreign merchants.

Foreign gold coins were imported, too, in particular from Portugal during the 15th and early 16th centuries, the gold metal in this case coming from Portugal's flourishing trade with the West Coast of Africa. Golden *Rhineguilders* also penetrated into the Low Countries, the gold here probably originating from Africa, too, via Lisbon, though to a greater extent from East-Central Europe and from Italy along the trade route of the Rhine. The *Rhineguilders* were similar to the gold coins of the Low Countries, but, being somewhat lighter and circulating at the same rate, had a comparative advantage. German merchants intensifying their trade relations with Antwerp in Brabant from the second half of the 15th century onwards made their payments increasingly in cash with the *Rhineguilder*, and this German coin proved so popular that it became a money of account for an increasing number of contracts on the Antwerp market and even on other markets in the Low Countries. Charles V in 1521 therefore decided to internalize the phenomenon. He announced the issue of a new gold coin similar to the *Rhineguilder*, but called the *Carolusguilder*, according it an official rate of 20 Flemish silver *double groats* or *stivers*. This was, in fact, an attempt to introduce a bimetallic standard, but the attempt at bimetallism failed and the golden *Carolusguilder* soon disappeared from circulation, as indeed did the golden *Rhineguilder*, because silver from the New World began inundating Europe and because gold, becoming relative scarce on the world market, was undervalued by official rates. However, the *guilder* of 20 *stivers* remained as a money of account. More so, it soon became the leading money of account of Brabant, Flanders and the rest of the Low Countries, and at the same time also the leading commercial money of account of Europe north of the Alps. The Flemish-Brabantine guilder of account was still based in principle upon the Flemish silver *groat* and indeed now for good upon its multiple, the Flemish *double groat* or *stiver*, which was minted mainly at Antwerp in Brabant. This therefore became known as the Brabant guilder system.

The Revolt against Spain, which started in 1568-1570, was gradually to destroy the European primacy of the Antwerp market, in particular by undermining the leading export position of the urban and rural industries of the Southern Netherlands. At the same time, the war weakened European demand for Brabant money of account and for currency circulating in Brabant. The Northern Netherlands now succeeded to the industrial, commercial and monetary leadership of the South. Amsterdam became the commercial successor to Antwerp, i.e. the leading staple-market of Europe, and the Dutch industries became the leading export sectors of Europe. The focus of international demand for a stable, strong money of account and for a stable basic currency system shifted from the Brabant guilder system (i.e.

for its currency and money of account) to the Dutch guilder system, though, as already mentioned above, both guilders belonged fundamentally to the same monetary system, i.e. that created in 1433 and introduced into all the provinces of the Low Countries under Burgundian and later Habsburg rule. However, in consequence of the Revolt, as well as of Dutch independence— *de facto* since c.1600, official since 1648—the Dutch guilder system achieved a still greater degree of autonomy. Because of Dutch successes in international trade and in industrial production for exports, international demand for that system grew continuously.

The Dutch authorities responded to the international demand with an appropriate monetary policy, which they pursued with the explicit intention of further developing the trade potential of the Dutch Republic. The primary aim was to provide merchants, active on international markets, with the means of payment they needed in respect of both coins and bank money. The high-quality, silver trade coins (*negotiepenningen*), struck in large quantities by the Dutch mints, supplied the coins for export; the public Bank of Amsterdam, founded in 1609, supplied stable, trustworthy bank money for merchants and bankers.

Naturally enough, the demand for stable money extended beyond the needs of international trade. There was also a domestic need for stable money, if only for the small, day-to-day commercial transactions. However, the stability of the domestic circulation of coins was far from being as solid as that of Dutch international money (bank money, as well as the high-quality *negotiepenningen*), an important element in the relative weakness of this domestic circulation being that domestic demand in the Republic could not compete with foreign demand. The difference in competitiveness was due to divergent elasticity of demand, in turn caused by the availability of an alternative. In the sector of international trade, precious metals were ultimately indispensable. In principle, this was also true in domestic circulation, except that foreign, old, and otherwise inferior coins could in fact circulate as an acceptable substitute for good coins against a relatively high nominal value.

The alternative could have been avoided by aiming coin production— based on a lower standard—at domestic circulation, although this would only have been possible at the expense of the trade coins, i.e. the much needed *negotiepenningen*. Because the authorities were unwilling to go along that path, the market itself ensured the necessary deterioration in the quality of the coinage in domestic circulation.

Seen in this light, the disordered domestic circulation of coins in the Dutch Republic in the first half of the 17th century was thus not the result of debasement (in the sense of government-induced inflation), as has often been argued, but of the absence of debasement. This hypothesis, proposed by Menno S. Polak, is confirmed and verified by the fact that, at least from the 1640s onwards, the Dutch current guilder of account (i.e. that used in the domestic economy and based upon the coins circulating in that economy) stood in a set relationship to the Dutch Bank guilder of account, which represented a fixed and immutable amount of silver.

What, then, can be learned from the French, Flemish, Brabantine and Dutch experience, in order to obtain a better understanding of the leading position occupied by the *pound sterling* and the *dollar* in the 19th and 20th centuries? That experience shows in the first place how crucial a factor that demand—both domestic and international—is for the rise of a leading monetary system. The factor of demand, in turn, is closely related to the economic primacy of the country in search of monetary leadership. In the past, this factor implied a demand for a stable and strong currency, which last was considered a guarantee for being able to contract and invest safely. However, if demand and economic primacy are necessary conditions for acquiring monetary leadership, they are, to be sure, not sufficient conditions of themselves. Government has also to pursue a monetary policy that is consistent with the expectations of those looking for a safe, leading monetary system.

As far as the leading position of the *pound sterling* is concerned, the model fits. The definitive introduction of the gold standard by the British government in 1774 and again after the French revolutionary period was part of a conscious policy towards achieving a stable and strong monetary system. The Bank Charter Act of 1844, meeting the wishes of the Currency School, reinforced that policy. Banknotes of the Bank of England increasingly became gold certificates, enabling the London money market to attract extra credit from abroad in the event of a liquidity crisis, as Charles P. Kindleberger has illustrated so well. The return to gold in 1925, after the suspension of convertibility during the First World War, was a final attempt to maintain the *pound sterling* as a leading monetary system in the world. Its success was not to last very long, as we all know. Britain went off the gold standard again in September 1931, the main and fundamental factor underlying this being that the British economy had lost its vigor, its primacy. Because the United States did not immediately introduce an appropriate monetary policy, the world was left without monetary leadership during the 1930s.

Did the government of the United States ultimately introduce such a policy? As a matter of fact she did, and was rewarded with the *dollar* acquiring undisputed ascendancy in the world from the 1940s to the early 1970s. However, does the model fit when it comes to explaining the development of monetary leadership after 1971? The gold/dollar standard of the previous decades quickly became purely a dollar standard, notwithstanding the fact that American monetary stability and monetary strength seemed to be on the wane. In my view, the American government did not, in the years thereafter, abandon its basic preference for monetary stability; rather, it looked to adjust its dollar standard to a new international monetary equilibrium, as economic growth policies within the framework of Keynesian doctrine had led to worldwide inflation, with rates differing appreciably from one national economy to another, thereby upsetting the entire international monetary system.

Is the present monetary policy of the American government still consistent with the model, thus explaining the persistence of the dollar standard? The economists in this audience are better qualified than I am to answer that.

R. Skidelsky: The gold standard and the Bretton Woods System were both associated with leader currencies. Under both systems powerful national currencies were linked to a gold base. They did most of the work gold was supposed to do. Did the two systems work because they had leader currencies, or did they just happen to have them?

This is the question posed by Professor Kindleberger. To him we owe the analysis of monetary systems in terms of structural characteristics. He rightly disposes of the argument that the gold standard was self-equilibrating. It worked because Britain managed it; the Bretton Woods system also worked because the United States managed it—managed in the sense that the top currency in both systems, the pound for the gold standard and the dollar for Bretton Woods, lubricated the works. Without this management, or leadership as he calls it, countries would not have accepted the 'rules of the game'. A corollary of the argument is that where there exist several top currencies, they will compete for mastery, centralized management becomes impossible, and a global monetary system will break down. Kindleberger thinks Charles Maier's notion of a 'consensual hegemony' is an oxymoron.

Kindleberger defines the leadership function mainly in relation to certain public goods necessary to the maintenance of an orderly exchange rate, in the absence of which it would collapse. The 'duties' of the leader substitute for those of the absent world government: it provides the world with a market for imports, a flow of investment capital and emergency finance for short-term balance of payments disturbances. These 'services' are like the 'special incentives' identified by Mancur Olson in his classic analysis of public goods. Only the last two are financial, but trade and finance are closely linked, in the sense that countries with a large share of world trade are likely to have internationally acceptable currencies and develop financial facilities geared to maintaining and expanding trade relations. Obviously a leader country has to be of sufficient 'weight' in the world economy to provide such services. The history of the interwar years and the post-Bretton Woods era is said to exemplify the view that a multi-polar currency world is a high unstable one.

But is this true? Was the pre-war gold system a centrally managed one? The first thing which strikes one is that the 'services' which Kindleberger specifies were provided by Germany and France as well as by Britain, though Britain was the major provider. But the three centers were not competitive. You can describe it as 'consensual hegemony' but the 'sharing out' of leadership functions was much more the result of the division of the world into informal, though overlapping, spheres of influence based on economics and politics.

Before 1914, there was already a shadowy 'sterling area' of countries affiliated to Britain, which conducted most of its trade in pounds and was the main recipient of British loans. Germany was the economic locomotive of continental Europe, supplying its neighbors with much of their manufactured goods and capital, and taking most of their imports. France supplied Russia with much of its development capital, for political reasons. Even though London can be reasonably enough described as 'lender of last resort' for the system, the Bank of England needed support from the central banks of both France and Russia in the Barings Crisis of 1890. The economic order is best described as cosmopolitan. It was dominated by bankers and traders, not by governments. Cooperation between central banks was *ad hoc*, but it was real none the less. It was broken up by political, not monetary, competition.

We can approach the historical issue by asking a different kind of question: was sterling a hegemonic currency? Was it privileged above others in the sense of having a power of *seigniorage*? Implicit in the idea of hegemony is the power to exact tribute. In financial terms, this means the ability to derive income from printing money. In the simplest case one gets goods by paying with money rather than by giving equivalent goods in return. It is not clear that sterling had any such privilege before 1914. None of the core gold standard countries held each other's currencies as reserves before 1914. This route to increasing the global money supply was blocked by the gold convertibility requirement. On the other hand, the peripheries of the system were linked to the core currencies through currency boards. There was a possibility of *seigniorage* in these arrangements, and there has been much dispute about whether Britain, even before 1914, was accumulating 'sterling balances' or debts to its trading partners. There is no evidence that sterling in general was being over-supplied. But Britain was able to manipulate its imperial position in India to force on it unwanted goods and services, while using India's foreign currency earnings to offset its deficits with North America and elsewhere. But the limits of sterling's hegemony were set by the bounds of Britain's colonial empire.

After the First World War, there were two hegemonic currencies, the pound and the dollar. Their role as reserve currencies was acknowledged by the Genoa Conference of 1922. Britain now exploited the privileged position of sterling to 'borrow short and lend long' before 1931. This played a part in upholding the restored gold standard for a few years. Much more important was the overseas lending of the United States which was financed by a large trade surplus. The system collapsed in 1931 not through competition between the co-hegemons—there was plenty of cooperation between the Bank of England and the Federal Reserve Bank in the late 1920s—but because of the profound disturbance to trade and capital flows caused by the First World War, and secondarily because France, which had never accepted the gold exchange standard set up by Genoa, started exchanging its sterling holdings for gold.

The years 1931 to 1936 resemble to some extent the years following 1971, when the Bretton Woods system broke down and failed to be restored. In the 1930s there were still two dominant currencies, the pound and the dollar. Twenty or so countries, mostly in the British Empire, though not including Canada, but with some others, pegged their currencies to sterling—we may call it a sterling exchange standard—and held a large part of their monetary reserves in sterling, for reasons of history and trade. There was some build-up of sterling balances in the late 1930s, but they were more or less covered by Britain's gold and dollar reserves, so there was no need to block them. This became a problem only during and after the Second World War.

The relationship between the dollar and sterling was conflictual till 1936. The US refused to sanction sterling's depreciation in 1931. The dollar was on gold. When the pound depreciated against the dollar in 1931, America raised the price of gold from $20 to $35 dollars an ounce, thereby restoring the '5 dollar pound'. The currency war was only ended with the Tripartite Monetary Agreement of 1936, by which Britain, the United States and France agreed to support each others' currencies, at an agreed exchange rate, in the foreign exchange markets. But this currency war resulted from the breakdown of the gold standard: it did not cause it.

The real seigniorial currency in the 1930s was the German mark. The Schachtian system of bilateral payments, as worked in Eastern Europe, enabled Germany to pile up mark balances, or debts, in the bilateral clearings. This was because Germany made long-term purchasing agreements with countries which depended on exporting to Germany. Germany was a regional hegemon. Its financial and economic position would probably have been stabilized and extended had it not been for Hitler's insane political plans.

The post war or Bretton Woods system was much more obviously a Kindlebergian hegemonic system. The dollar alone was convertible into gold, and therefore the major reserve currency of the system—though the sterling area lingered on. Because it was convenient to all, the US was able to get its major allies Germany, France and Japan to accept increasing quantities of dollars in payment for goods. This led to the Triffin paradox: but the paradox became the motive force of the system. However, it collapsed when US foreign liabilities exceeded its gold reserves.

The hegemonic thesis thus needs considerable modification. The gold standard and Bretton Woods were not the same kind of system. We need to distinguish between pre-eminent and hegemonic currencies. The collapse of 1931 was not due mainly to the war of currencies: that followed after the restored gold standard had collapsed.

However, I accept the main point of what I take to be Professor Kindleberger's approach, which is to focus on the structural characteristics of monetary systems, rather than on their supposedly self-equilibrating properties; or to put it another way, to concentrate not on the rules of the game, but what made them possible.

The lessons of history give a modest comfort to those who now look at an emerging global economy with two or possibly three pre-eminent currencies: the dollar, the euro, and the yen. This situation does not have to be a recipe for currency wars. Indeed, it is quite likely that it will lead, in due course, to another Tripartite Monetary Agreement. This would mark a formal recognition that the world is, in fact, divided into major, but overlapping, currency zones, as was the world before 1914.

A. Clesse: Thank you, Robert. So, who would like to take up, comment on, criticize what has been said by the three speakers so far? Professor Giersch.

H. Giersch: I want to express my scepticism vis-à-vis Professor Kindleberger's views about the role of leadership. There is some emotional resistance I have against leadership, which you will understand since Germany had excessive leadership internally after 1933, and expressed itself in a very awkward way in this kind of leadership. But isn't it simply too natural to think that order requires a paternalistic solution, requires hierarchy? As students of the market process we should be equally prepared to understand how order can develop in a spontaneous way, under rules of competition as we observe them in traffic on the roads where we don't have that kind of leadership, but still it works.

My skeptical opinion results from misgivings about leadership and colonialism and imperialism which were practised under dictatorships in Germany, and too much hegemony within Germany and internationally. It refers also to the kind of monetary system which was discussed when I started studying economics during the war. What the Nazis had thought out for Europe was a kind of Reichsmark hegemony for Europe as a whole, as you have described it vis-à-vis South Eastern Europe and Eastern Europe, but it was also thought to be the basis of a system for a dominating Reichsmark in a Nazi-Europe. I think that the conditions for the necessity of leadership and of monopoly instead of currency competition have to be established very carefully because so many people think that competition inevitably leads to chaos. Why should chaos be the normal outcome if there are rules as we have them, in terms of cautious behavior, on the roads:

signaling systems on road are nice substitutes for prices as we know them on market. Why can self organization not be applied to money? Why do we need, so to speak, a monotheistic vision of the world order instead of having oligopoly with cooperation or even competition?

R. McCauley: I have a question for Professor Skidelsky. I am confused at your use of the term *seigniorage*. At one point you seem to apply it to the act of borrowing short and lending long. It may well be, as Marcello DeCecco has argued in *Money and Empire*, that the Indians got a rather pitiful return on the balances that they held in the City of London. In principle, however, the act of borrowing short and lending long, an act we associate with banks, is not what we mean by the term *seigniorage*.

R. Portes: Two points raised by Robert Skidelsky's remarks. The first arises from his observation about the 1920s and 1930s that the key source of the disruption of the international financial system was the wartime debts and the implications that that had for capital flows in the 1920s. I wouldn't myself have seen it that way. It seems to me that that what you saw in the 1920s was the emergence of New York as a major financial center, the double role of London and New York, sterling and the dollar, in lending long-term to a variety of sovereign debtors, and then the breakdown of that lending at the beginning of the 1930s. And the actual disruption of international capital flows really began in 1931 in Latin America, not in Europe, with the wave of defaults starting in January 1931 and proceeding through Latin America a wonderful first example of contagion, by the way. It did not spread to Europe until 1932. And that was on both dollar and sterling debts, of course.

The second point concerns the remarks about the attempt to reconstitute the gold standard in 1933. I would again see a good part of the problem at that time in trying to deal with the consequences of sovereign debt default. And that is an international distributional issue, and the debates in the global monetary conferences of 1933, in particular, foundered on this difficulty of trying to deal with global debt restructuring. That seems to me relevant to the role of the dollar today. It is not the International Monetary Fund that is the international lender of last resort. It is of course the United States. The IMF can't create money unless and in so far as you think that the SDR is IMF money, but that too is under the control in good part of the United States. So it is the United States that is the international lender of last resort. It is the dollar that has that role thrust upon it, in a sense, and it can't fulfil it. The present financial difficulties highlight this problem and suggest that coming out of the Asian crisis and its ramifications, we will have to see, once again, a big write-off of debt over the next ten years. And that is partly because it wasn't possible effectively to stop the defaults. It wasn't possible for the international lender of last resort to do it. All the big financing packages failed, in that respect at least. And the financial crisis of 1997-1998 (along with the creation of the euro) may itself turn out to have laid some of the foundations for a shift in international monetary relations of a very different kind.

J. Baumberger: I think there are two ways of interpreting Charlie Kindleberger's theory of leadership. One may be that he argues in favor of a kind of leadership in exceptional situations, i.e. in emergency situations; the alternative interpretation would be leadership as a kind of permanent institution. Now, as Mr. Clesse said, I come from a country with little central leadership. There are 26 jurisdictions that are very independent, and the Swiss have traditionally been skeptical concerning central leadership. Still, even this thoroughly decentralized country has managed to develop some institutions designed to deal with emergencies. For example, in times of conflict, parliament elects a General (General writ large) who enjoys quite far-reaching powers, in fact almost plenipotentiary powers, and the civil government, too, is given very extensive powers. So far, we have managed to survive in this way. Once the emergency is over, the general is dismissed from his function as general.

I think the real problem emerging with the euro is how we can provide leadership in times of crisis. I would conceive that in times of crisis hierarchical leadership may be called for, but it might be dangerous to make it a permanent institution. The establishment of a permanent hierarchical leadership may interfere with the normal functioning of the markets. In normal times it is desirable that leadership be spontaneous and emerges as a kind of spontaneous order. In principle, the market needs no permanent leadership. The problem will be how we can provide the structures that can deal with crises without ending up in a permanent state of emergency simply because the incumbents come to like their job or are politically expected to make a permanent display of active leadership. After all, there is always some faction that wants to make us believe we are in an emergency. And there are always media that like to see 'powerful action' by whomsoever has the power to wield such power. The euro complicates these things without bringing any solution regarding the adequate balance between emergency powers and fruitful normal market laissez-faire. The rhetoric of countervailing powers with which the euro has been sold to the peoples of Europe does nothing to simplify things.

G. Ross: I don't know whether I'm going to add much to the discussion, but the introduction of the concept of leadership always puzzles the hell out of me. Leadership is something we know is there when everything is going all right, we know is not there when everything is not going all right. But that doesn't tell us very much about leadership. I think we need to know more and I wonder if Charlie or anybody else could say something about what leadership might be, the structural elements of leadership that would be put into the present situation. Because we are facing a setting in which, if the euro flies, which it probably will, we will have to have something that will look quite unprecedented like multicentric leadership. Robert talked a little bit about something like that existing, but not working very well in the pre-1914 period. But multicentric leadership is almost an oxymoron, to use your word.

R. Skidelsky: Could I just reply very briefly to the points in reverse order. Professor Ross asks how I would describe the pre-war gold standard system. It was not so much one of multicentric leadership, as to some extent a spontaneous order in the way Professor Giersch has just said. It consisted of core countries and peripheries, first class countries and second class countries. First class countries were on the gold standard, second class countries had currency boards. That corresponded, to some extent, to imperial centers and imperial dependencies, Latin America being a sort of intermediate zone, was neither quite one nor the other, and that's where most of the defaults and unsteadiness took place.

I agree with Professor Baumberger. If you try to institutionalize permanent leadership through lenders of last resort, rather than surprise interventions, then you are, I think, overwhelmed by the problem of moral hazard.

Two points in reverse order of Richard Portes. I agree that global debt restructuring was a problem in 1933, but the problem that dominated the London Economic Conference of 1933 was the rate at which to refix the two leading currencies, the pound and the dollar. At that point, the pound had suspended gold convertibility. The United States was still on the gold standard at the old rate, and so was the franc. But the United States wanted freedom to allow its exchange rate to fall to eliminate what it saw as Britain's unfairly gained competitive advantage. The United States in the 1930s would only accept what was called a five dollar pound; it refused to accept the British devaluation. And Roosevelt made it absolutely clear that if the British wanted a lower rate for sterling, the president of the United States would use his authority to drive down the dollar. That's what killed any attempt to restore the gold standard in the 1930s.

You say that the problem wasn't due to war debts, I think it was. In one crucial respect, capital flows, the system had altered as a result of the First World War. It is not just that the United State became the major source of overseas capital, but that a great deal of it went to Germany, for the first time. Before the war, the vast majority of the capital went from the core to the peripheries. Now Germany became a huge importer of capital. That was a fundamental source of instability, right at the heart of the system weight because Germany was borrowing to pay dead debt, and municipal programs, not to finance exports. In the 1920s the British were in effect printing money to pay for imports, that is, they were trying to invest more than their current account surplus enabled them to. That's what I mean by *seigniorage*.

R. Portes: Actually, I think you will find that the majority of the capital flows did not go to Germany, they went where the breakdown came. OK, we agree on that. And as I say, historically, in terms of what broke the system, the breakdown first came in the defaults of Latin America, not in Central Europe. They were subsequent to and in part, I believe, caused by the defaults in Latin America.

R. Skidelsky: Unless we get agreement on the dates, we are not going to resolve the argument. This system cracked. It was a big break in the United States and in Europe, in 1929. The Latin American defaults were consequent.

C. Kindleberger: I'm impressed by Herman van der Wee's saying that the big need is for international money. The demand for international money goes way back and accounts not only for the guilder but also later for sterling and the dollar. The world needs international money. International money performs the functions of money in general. And if you have flexible exchange rates, you destroy international money. I happen to be a fixed exchange rate man although I agree it's difficult.

I want to say a word about Professor Baumberger. I completely agree that in stable times, when things are not exciting it is best to be pluralistic, as Professor Giersch would argue. But there are times when the market gets seized up, or there is a war, or there is a volcano, or an earthquake, or some serious trouble and you need to change the system from being one of pluralism to one of authority. And the trouble is it is very hard to move back and forth easily. If you want to see an example of it, look at the Dutch Republic in the 18th century. There is a book by Simon Schama. Most of you have read Simon Schama on art, but he has one on the Dutch Republic—the liberal period from 1760 to 1813. Everyone tried to centralize, but they couldn't because they were so used to decentralization.

Finally, I want to say that when you believe in rules or things organized hierarchically, one of them is the banking system. Banking systems are awful. There are banks which start up everywhere and they move. Where do they move? They move to a financial center, they move to Wall Street, to Berlin, to Paris. One of the most charming stories I know is the chapter in Jean Bouvier's 'Crédit Lyonnais' about how the 'Crédit Lyonnais' moved to Paris. It is hard to say whether the origin was the death of his first wife, after which he married a Parisian. This is an extraordinary process and it is a process that does not only exist, it seems to me, at a national level; it is a process which is international as well. But I agree with Professor Portes, it sometimes leads to trouble because the leader, the consensual hegemon gets too big. His ideas get too big. It is hard to keep him in place.

A. Clesse: Thank you very much. So this first session became quite lively towards its very end.

Session 2: Monetary Leadership and Economic Stability in a Globalizing World

A. Clesse: The topic of session number two is monetary leadership and economic stability in a globalizing world. Professor Mundell, would you take the floor first?

R. Mundell: Thank you very much. It's a great pleasure to be here and to be sitting next to Pierre Werner and Charles Kindleberger. So I have the double pleasure of being here with a pioneer of the euro and one of my old and favorite teachers. I am also proud to see some students here.

The introduction of the euro is a very significant event. We all agree on that. We have to ask how significant it is and what can we compare it with. It is often said that it is the most important event in the international monetary system since the break-up of the fixed exchange rate system in the 1970s. But you could make a case for the possibility that it is more important than that because the break-up of the fixed exchange rate system didn't change the power configuration of the system. Before and after the breakdown, the dollar was the dominant currency. If, however, the euro becomes a currency comparable in status with the dollar, you have to go back to the shift from the pound sterling to the dollar in the 1915-1924 period. Even then you could argue that the shift from the pound to the dollar was less important because in 1914 the United States' economy was already three times as large as either the British economy or the German economy. It was therefore inevitable that size alone would be a dominant factor in making the dollar the important currency. So it may be more important than that. It may be, in fact, that you have to go back to the shift from bimetallism to the gold standard in 1873 to find a historical parallel.

Now in the above I have implicitly assumed the euro is going to be very important, but we have to have something to compare it with. In my accompanying paper there is a list of currencies that have dominated in some sense in the past. It is a great convenience to be able to look back at the thousands of different currencies and denominations that have existed and be able to simplify the historical world, as economists should do, by finding the important currencies that were dominant in the different eras. Professor van der Wee may chide me for not putting in the groat, but I will talk to him about that later. Anyway, in recent history we do get back to Britain in the 19th century and the dollar in the 20th century. And the question is: What will happen to the euro in the next century? What role will it have?

I have listed the main features of great international currencies. I list seven of them.

One is a large transactions area, best measured roughly and crudely by GDP size. On that basis the euro will do fine. The EU-11 is a little bit smaller than the US GDP, but the EU-15 will be considerably larger. We can assume that eventually Europe will be a larger transaction area than the dollar if we discount the special international role of the dollar in foreign exchange reserves.

The second criterion is that a country has to have a stable monetary policy. I don't think that anyone can really argue that over the future—barring some events that are unpredictable and probably tragic—the euro would have an inflationary monetary policy. It will have a stable monetary policy. But compared to what? US monetary policy in the 1990s has been very stable. But that is a short experience. Remember that the US had a very unstable monetary policy in the late 1970s and even in the late 1960s. So Europe wouldn't have to give anything away on that issue.

Absence of controls, number three. This is important. I don't need to say too much about it. We have moved into a muddy world now where the United States imposes exchange controls as sanctions as part of US foreign policy. Maybe Europe will do the same at some point, but I don't think in comparing the euro to the dollar that Europe will give anything away on those grounds.

We come to number four: the strong central state, the strength and continuity of the central state. A state must be able to preserve its existence. That's very important, because if the euro isn't going to be here in 30 years time, who would ever want to buy a bond denominated in euros. So there has to be a sense of continuity, a sense that it is not going to break up, a sense that it will last and continue. But Europe is not a strong central state, there is no political union. And one of the strong reasons why a strong central state is so important is to protect it from invasions from without. Now, Europe may not have itself a great defense posture, but fortunately it is itself part of NATO, the most successful military alliance in history. As long as that 'security area' continues, one can be confident about stability. So NATO compensates for the lack of a strong central state.

Number five is a fall-back value. The euro will be the first potentially strong international dominant currency that has been issued without a gold backing. That doesn't seem strange to modern economists. However, remember that the period when the international monetary system has done without a metallic backing of some kind is only about 25 years old. We don't know whether it is going to survive much in stability in periods of great crisis. This is yet to be known. Nevertheless, Europe has large gold reserves and foreign exchange reserves, far larger than the United States. So reserves will partly compensate for lack of a fall-back value.

The other two factors, I list, are tied up with the other things: sense of permanence and low interest rates. Low interest rates are signs of stability and permanence, and they come together. But all in all, given those qualifications I've made, I see no reason why the euro won't be able to survive and perform well.

Next, we discuss liquidity effects. What is the liquidity impact of the creation of the euro? There is first an efficiency effect. When you replace 11 currencies or 15 currencies with one currency, the liquidity of the European currency, of the euro, is greater than the liquidity of the equivalent aggregate of the other. This will have the effect of a sudden increase in liquidity in the system where 9 euros will now do the work that 10 equivalent different currency units did before. This factor is hard to quantify, but I cannot imagine it would be less then a 10 percent increase in liquidity. So this will be a potential inflationary factor.

Then there is the money multiplier issue. The level of the money multiplier in Europe, the ratio of money supply to the euro backing of it is likely to increase and that will be a force for more inflation, because the euro will now become outside money for the national currencies and the governments here will have a temptation to try to economize in their use for grounds of *seigniorage*. Now I know that *seigniorage* is being given back in proportion to stock in the ECB, but nevertheless this will be a factor. The money multiplier has been increasing in the 1990s in Europe and it will continue to increase even more once the euro is introduced.

The stability of the money multiplier is also a problem, because the money reserve ratio and the money multipliers in the different European countries are different. They are enormously different. The ratio of reserves, central bank money to money, is very different. Now what that means is that when there is a monetary union, when low reserve ratio countries have surpluses, and high reserve countries will have deficits, for example, money will get tighter. What that means is that a pure reliance upon monetary targeting in the early period would be quite risky. Monetary targeting works well only if the *structure* of the system is both constant and known. Whatever is the case for monetary targeting in the long run, it is not a good idea, at least if it is used to the exclusion of *other targets*, in the short run.

Next comes redundant reserves from pooling, that's well known, that will be another inflationary factor, because it will be a temptation to increase spending, as has already been proposed in some countries

Next comes a factor associated with the new power of the euro. The automatic credit comes from the fact that the euro will now be like the dollar. Europe will now have what General de Gaulle criticized the Americans for, having this 'exorbitant privilege' of being able to pay off debts by issuing dollars that other countries continue to hold and use as money. Europe now has that 'exorbitant privilege' and that will make for more fiscal relaxation in Europe. So I have noted four inflationary factors. We now come to two important offsets.

Two types of the international demand for euros could offset the inflationary factors. In the paper I have some back-of-the-envelope-calculations for the year 2010. Foreign exchange reserves are 1.6 trillion today. I assume they will be 3.2 trillion in the year 2010 and that if in the year 2010 Euroland is the same size or larger than the United States, people will want to hold at least an equal quantity of euros compared to dollars. Which means that virtually the whole build-up of new reserves will have to be in euros. This means an increment of something like 100 billion dollars a year for euros for the next 12 years. That will mean that there will be a zero growth in demand for dollars and 1,2 trillion growth in demand for euros. Even if the adjustment is smooth, it would have a big impact, if it were not completely adjusted, by changes in capital movements. It would have a big impact on trade balances, reducing US deficit and reducing European surpluses or increasing their deficits unless it was accompanied by larger capital outflows from Europe. But it probably won't be all that smooth, because once people have decided that they want to have a substantial portion in euros, this will take place rather quickly and then it will happen rather quickly, making the diversification problem, which is the second part of this adjustment, serious. There will be a big problem of managing the dollar-euro rate.

Now on the issue of expansion of the euro area. First, there are the EU-4, the four EU countries that remain outside EMU. Greece is now on track for going in by 2002. I don't have the time to go into it now, but, contrary to what seems to be rather conventional wisdom, I believe that by the year 2002 even Britain as well as Sweden and Denmark will be in the euro area. The CEEEC-5—with which EU eastward enlargement negotiations have already opened—I would assume have a reasonable chance. They could be in, or have close to partial membership at least, in Euroland, by the year 2005. And the other five countries in Eastern Europe, the larger countries—I am excluding here Yugoslavia, Bosnia and Albania; I don't quite know what to do with those countries—could be in by the year 2010. So by the year 2010, there may be an additional ten countries, maybe more. I haven't counted Malta, Cyprus and some others.

Now, nothing stays constant, except the laws of change. And there will be laws of change. The development of the euro will provoke a reaction in the rest of the world and certainly provoke a development, I think, in four, five, six, seven years, of the dollar area in Latin America and in part of Asia. So that will be a factor that will have to be taken into account. If you look now at the stability of currency areas in the system, we know there is the dollar area, we know there is the euro area, the big uncertainty is what will be the nature of the Asian structure. There is no political structure in Asia that would make feasible an Asian currency area that would include both Japan and China. I don't see that happening for political reasons. If that is not the case, then I think the dollar area will expand into much of Asia. Whether Japan mates with the dollar or with the euro will be partly a political question. It will probably be that, because of defense arrangements, Japan will have to be an ally of the dollar, or at least reduce volatility with respect to the dollar.

I have discussed stability in three uses of the term. Exchange rate volatility will be reduced within Europe by definition. It will be increased a little bit for the EU 4 countries that stay outside and that is why, I think, those 4 countries should come in rather quickly. Maybe Switzerland should also come in. And the countries of Eastern Europe, the CEEEC-5 countries, that want to come in, should come in through adopting something like currency boards. That's the best approach to entry. After all a currency board mimics exactly what will happen under a common currency. If a country can't do a currency board, it can't do monetary union. So it should go ahead and try the currency board.

Now I leave aside the dynamic stability question. I have discussed it a little bit in the paper, but I don't think we can say much about that. And that is more or less the last thing I want to say.

I want just to conclude though by coming back to the fascinating discussion this morning about leadership. Barry Eichengreen in his *Golden Fetters* really says that the gold standard system broke down because of lack of cooperation. Charlie Kindleberger, long before that, said, it is lack of leadership. Leadership breaks down. Now those are very close together, but to me both concepts have the problem that they are effects rather than causes. By definition, if something breaks down, there is always a lack of cooperation. Countries go to war because they stop cooperating and start fighting. And there always is an absence of leadership. So I would just want to say here that, moving outside the monetary model to the political model, in the postwar period 1945 to 1990, you didn't have what you could call leadership in the Cold War between the United States on one hand, and the enemy, the Soviet Union on the other hand. You had a highly stable standoff. You get results quite apart from any explicit form of leadership. I don't really believe that it was Britain that held together the system for the gold standard. I agree with Robert Skidelsky the gold standard could and did work as a decentralized system. Now, one country is always going to be the top dog, or the earliest dog, the price leader in the system or the first to put up or down the discount rate. That is always the case, and would have been the case even in the absence of Britain. Leadership is not a necessary condition for success in the system and historically it may well be that leadership has hurt rather than ameliorated adjustment in the system. I do though think that, despite what I have said, there is now a problem with our new bipolar world, and the division of leadership between the United States and Europe. There has to be some management of the dollar-euro rate, because if there is a diversification, a big shift into euro, an appreciation of the euro, this is going to play havoc with Europe's attempts to reduce its unemployment problem. So, I think, there will have to be some form of leadership somehow developing. Maybe Charlie will be the one to provide the solution to that.

R. Henning: I will address three areas: (1) The question of system structure and how it changes, (2) US views on monetary union and (3) the institutions by which external monetary policy will be made and international cooperation will take place.

On the first issue of systemic structure, in *The World in Depression* Professor Kindleberger laid the lion's share of responsibility for the economic disaster of the 1930s at the feet of hegemony lost. Great Britain had lost its position as economic leader or hegemon, and the United States was as yet unwilling to fill the vacuum. This left no major power both willing and able to serve as a source of stable long-term investment, serve as a lender of last resort and absorb distress exports. This thesis inspired a generation of international political economists in their analysis and debates over, what is called within the discipline, structural realism or neorealism which embodies, among other things, the notion that a stable, liberal international economic order requires hegemonic leadership. The creation of the euro represents the first true test of this thesis for the monetary area specifically since Professor Kindleberger's book was first published in the early 1970s. The logic of neorealism, as it has been developed in the literature, suggests that international cooperation will decline. Professor Kindleberger's formulation was far less deterministic.

There is a widespread expectation among economists that the United States and the euro area will pursue policies of mutual benign neglect with regard to exchange rates and international financial crises. This would imply that crises that should be confronted would slip through the cracks or at least not be confronted in a timely matter. My proposition to this group is that this conclusion must take into account the robustness of the institutions of external monetary policy-making in the US and the EU and the international institutions through which cooperation takes place at the systemic level, such as in the G-7 and the IMF. Let me offer a couple of observations about US views towards EMU and then come back to these institutional matters.

There are several currents of thinking in American analysis of EMU, specifically regarding whether it is beneficial or harmful to the United States. I call the first view a 'zero-sum analysis': 'What is good for Europe could be bad for the United States'. It is not the dominant concern in US analysis but it is a subcurrent. This zero-sum view focuses on the role of the euro as a challenger to the dollar and is chiefly concerned with power and relative influence.

The second, a more dominant view, is a 'positive sum analysis': 'What is good for Europe, is good for the United States'. But there are two subgroups within this school of thought. The first subgroup, a minority of American economists, believes the EMU will be good for Europe. The second anticipates that EMU will be bad for Europe. The second view is driven by the theory of optimum currency areas, of which Martin Feldstein is an adherent, but perhaps an extreme one. This theory informs the attitudes of many US policy-makers. The US Treasury and the Federal Reserve's position is that a successful monetary union will be good for the United States, but that structural reforms will be necessary to make monetary union successful. At the top of the list of structural reforms are greater labor market flexibility, deregulation, privatization and fiscal consolidation.

There is a third school which I will label 'geopolitical'. This is the notion that the monetary union, to the extent that it consolidates and gives further impetus to European integration more broadly, helps to provide economic and political stability to Central and Eastern Europe. This would benefit the United States because it would help relieve a burden that the United States might otherwise have to bear. And this reasoning is very much appreciated by US policy-makers.

Institutional analysis helps to answer the question as to what policy the euro area will adopt with respect to the exchange rate and international financial crises and rescues. The answer revolves in part around (1) whether the Council of Ministers will issue general orientations for exchange rate policy, (2) the relationship between the Council of Ministers and the ECB regarding exchange rate policy and (3) the arrangements regarding international representation of the euro area in bilateral relations with the United States, the G-7 and the International Monetary Fund.

Two days prior to our conference, Ecofin decided on the transitional arrangements for external representation of the euro area to be confirmed at the Vienna European Council meeting and proposed to Europe's partners in 1999. The essence of the Ecofin agreement was that, in relations with the G-7 and the IMF, the EU would propose to have a three-member delegation led by the Presidency of the Council of Ministers as long as the Presidency was a euro-area country or, in the case it was not, the chairman of the Euro-11 council. The second member of the delegation would be the Commission offering 'technical support in a secondary supporting role'. The third member would be the European Central Bank. Defining this proposed delegation was a very important step, even though it was not fully accepted by the rest of the G-7 or the membership of the IMF. The presence of the national central bank governors from the euro area in the full G-7 was particularly hard to defend.

The December 1998 Ecofin agreement should be regarded as provisional because it was partial. It was limited in scope to simply answering the question of who goes to international meetings. There was nothing in this agreement, apparently, about what these people should say when they get to such meetings, how that message should be prepared and determined in advance, what will be the latitude of the delegation in responding to American and others' proposals, or how proposals and agreements reached in these forums should be ratified by the rest of the membership of the euro area. It would be wholly unacceptable, from the American standpoint as well as from the European standpoint, for the Euro-11 presidency to read a prepared statement in the name of the monetary union and be unable to respond to proposals for joint action.

In addition to defining the nature of the delegation therefore the EU should, first of all, give the Presidency a mandate to negotiate agreements, both formal and informal, with other political authorities within the G-7, for example, as circumstances such as the Brazilian and Russian crises require. Secondly the Council of Ministers should agree in advance to procedures for quickly ratifying, or perhaps rejecting, any agreement that the presidency, with the assistance of the Commission and in consultation with the ECB, negotiates at these meetings. These provisions are necessary to avoid replicating the pattern that we have seen in transatlantic trade negotiations, which would be particularly damaging in the monetary area because the latter requires quick, decisive and sometimes stealthy responses by policy-makers to crises.

Member states within the monetary union want to retain maximum privileges in these international bodies, perhaps more than the logic of common external monetary policy permits. They want to have their cake (monetary union) and eat it too (maintain national representation in these bodies). This desire prevents, for the moment, the consolidation of the G-7 and the European quota in the IMF, as some of us have proposed for the longer term. But three forces will assert themselves and favor a greater centralization over time. The first is efficiency. The second is European law. And the third is the interest of the international community.

With regard to European law, as soon as two euro-area finance ministers, or perhaps two national central bank governors, contradict one another in an international meeting, there will be grounds for objection, either on the part of the Commission or on the part of other member states, that they have broken their pledge to present a common front on matters of external monetary policy. This dispute might well be justiciable in the Court of Justice. The international community, the United States and the rest of the membership of the IMF have an interest in streamlined representation and quota consolidation in the Fund and those interests will assert themselves with time. These considerations may well force member states of the euro area to face up to the external logic of the Monetary Union in the long run.

A. Clesse: Thank you very much, Randall Henning. The impact on the Asian area was mentioned. We don't have, at this point, participants from Asia. There will be somebody from China tomorrow. But there are many who are experts on Asia. The impact on Central and Eastern Europe was also mentioned and we have here a number of experts: Vaclav Klaus, Andrei Kortunov, Richard Portes and others.

As you notice, these presentations cover quite a wide array of issues, reaching even, in Professor Henning's presentation, into session number five on institutional implications. That is probably unavoidable. Nevertheless I had in mind for this second session the broader implications for monetary leadership and how it is related to world economic stability. There is always a risk of overlapping.

R. Cooper: I want to say two things. These are both partial responses and perhaps they fall under the later session, but since Randy raised the question of the format in which Europeans should organize themselves to deal with the rest of the world in the G-7, I thought I might first tell a story and then make a comment.

The story comes from Richard Holbrooke. He is an American diplomat, a former banker, once editor of *Foreign Policy*. He has had a lot to do with Europeans in the last several years on the questions of Bosnia and now Kosovo. We are concerned here with the EMU aspects of Maastricht, but, as you all know, the Maastricht Treaty also includes provisions on coordination of foreign and defense policy. Europeans have made an effort to coordinate their approach to foreign policy. One of the results of that effort was to have a European spokesman with powers to represent the EU in the Dayton discussions on Bosnia. Holbrooke was the American representative. Before the sessions started, representatives from two of the three largest European countries came to him privately, and separately, and said they wanted him to know that the officially designated European spokesman did not represent the position of their countries. I cite that as a real life example of the problems which Europe will face in getting its act together, particularly when the Presidency is held by one of the smaller countries. But it will be a problem even when the Presidency is held by one of the larger countries.

The comment I want to make is in response to Randy's observation that the Europeans would present a common front. Now a common front can be achieved only by pre-negotiating it. And pre-negotiation of the common front means Europeans come to the party with the Americans, the Canadians and the Japanese with a set position. We have had a lot of experience with this in the world of international economic negotiations with the G-7, in which they have done heavy, intense negotiation among themselves to reach a common position, and once they have negotiated it, it is inflexible because in the name of solidarity, they don't want to deviate from the agreed position. The spokesmen do not have the authority to negotiate. It is not a negotiating session, it is a presentation. I want to give a slightly different twist to what Randy said: what is important is to designate a spokesman not merely to present a common front, but to have some authority to negotiate in circumstances in which rapid action may be required, as in the case of Korea in December 1997 or, as in the case of Russia in August 1998. The European representative needs flexible authority. It is hard for me to imagine that if, say, Portugal is in the Presidency, the Europeans will give the Portuguese Presidency plenipotentiary powers to negotiate on behalf of the EU, or the EMU. So I believe we are all going to have to live with a regime in which the countries that have the financial or military power to act are actually represented in some way. It is untidy, but I take it to be a fact of life if we want action.

A. Clesse: Thank you Richard. We shall come back, above all, in session five, to these specific issues. I think before giving the floor to Andrei Kortunov, perhaps Christian de Boissieu could say a few words.

C. de Boissieu: I would like to comment on the two presentations, by Bob Mundell and by Randy Henning, on monetary policy and exchange rate policy. Bob Mundell spoke of the stability of monetary policy, it figures in his text. I would like us to return to this question: will the shift to the euro enable us to do 'Greenspan without Greenspan'? The problem is knowing whether monetary policy in the euro zone will be pragmatic, which is perhaps more important than it being stable. Will it be transparent? The question of the ECB's accountability should not be dealt with separately from the question of stable prices and of the performance of monetary policy. It is therefore necessary to come back to certain institutional problems. With respect to the exchange rate, it is necessary to evoke institutional problems, but not just those. Will the shift to the euro allow us or not—my question is both positive and normative—to carry out a policy of benign neglect vis-à-vis the euro's exchange rate with the dollar? This concerns the status of the exchange rate, euro against dollar, in conducting monetary policy.

I defend the thesis that taking account of the structures of the euro zone, a degree of commercial openness of 12 percent, which is comparable to that of the US today, is a degree that will decrease over time as new countries join the euro zone—certain lessons on how to conduct monetary policy in the euro zone will have to be drawn. To what extent can we adopt in the euro zone a policy of benign neglect and on the basis of what degree of over- or undervaluation do we have to conduct a more active policy, against the background of the institutional debate caused by the ambiguity in the Treaty of Maastricht with respect to the division of labor between the political decision-makers and the ECB regarding exchange rate policy?

A. Kortunov: As a representative of a country which has probably no chances of getting into the European Union in any foreseeable future, I can afford to be a little bit more philosophic than my predecessors. Let me touch very briefly three issues which, I think, deserve certain consideration. First of all, attitudes in Russia and also in other countries of Eastern Europe to financial and monetary leadership. Second, prospects for Russia's integration, or rather reintegration, into the global financial system, especially after what happened in the country in August of this year. And finally the impact of the euro on the Russian foreign and economic policies.

First of all, I think that although it is banal I would like to say once again that financial leadership is perceived outside of the developed world as probably the most mysterious, the most abstract and the most ambiguous type of leadership. First of all, because this type of leadership is associated not with states, not with state leaders whom we see on our TV screens every day, but with rather technical, rather sophisticated mechanisms as well as with anonymous institutions. The modus of their operation is mostly unclear not only to people in the street, but also to politicians. Their goals are ambiguous at best. Leaders of international financial institutions are not as charismatic as state leaders. So these actors are unknown and quite often this leadership is perceived as a force of nature rather than a manifestation of human logic and human will.

If you take for example how they approach the IMF in Russia, you will see that attitudes to the IMF are a matter of faith rather than a matter of logic and political choice. You can either praise the IMF or you can curse it, and basically the attitude to the IMF is a litmus test which will show the true colors of every politician in the country in question. If you are a pro-IMF politician you would say that financial leadership gives your country access to international finance, it creates healthy pressure on your own financial system and basically it is a path to the club of civilized nations. If you believe that the IMF is an incarnation of eternal evil, you would say that this globalization and this leadership accelerates capital flight from your country, it exposes your country to the vulnerability of international financial markets, it creates too strong pressures on your own financial system and it also leads to the dollarization of your economy. And in both cases you will find a lot of evidence to prove your point.

I think that the same happens on the other side of the barricades. If you look at policies of international financial institutions towards Russia or Ukraine or any other country in this part of the world, you will see that they are also politicized. For me, one of the key problems is the de-politicization of this relationship. How can we make sure that these relationships are perceived as technical rather than political? How can you desacralize the approaches to international financial leadership in countries which are subject to influence from related institutions and organizations?

Now in terms of the prospects for Russia's integration into the international financial system after August 17 of this year, I think, it is evident that the prospects are rather bleak. If you take the short-term future, I would even say the middle-term future, a lot depends on what decisions are going to be made as far as the Russian financial system is concerned. If foreign banks are allowed to operate in Russia and to take over the nearly collapsed Russian financial system, then this process might go faster. If

Russia keeps mostly isolated in terms of its financial institutions from the rest of the world, I see no way how Russia can attract major foreign investments in any foreseeable future. If you take a longer-term perspective, I think that what we will see in Russia and countries like Russia is a very peculiar model of enclave integration. You will see integration which will not depend on political institutions or particular financial structures. It will be a backdoor integration which will be a factor of regimes rather than organizations. I think that it will mean that some regions of the countries in question, some social strata, some professional groups will find it relatively easy to get integrated, but at the expense of the others. That, in turn, will clearly create very serious social and economic constraints, tensions and probably even dangers as far as the integrity of Russia and countries like Russia is concerned.

Speaking of the euro in this framework, as in America, there are two basic opinions about the euro and its potential impact on the Russian position vis-à-vis Europe. If you are a pessimist, you would argue that the euro is bad for Russia because it makes Europe more integrated and it makes the walls between European countries and the rest of the continent even higher. Europe will be closing in, when and if the euro is introduced. Optimists would argue that the euro will create a new center of gravity in the world. It will make Europe more dynamic, and even neighboring countries which have no chances of getting into the European structure would benefit from that. So Russia might, at least, hope that it will be able to exploit new opportunities that will emerge in European energy markets, in European labor markets and that it will be able, in the longer term, to benefit from an expanded financial market in Europe.

In practical terms, I think that the impact of the euro will depend on how strong or how weak the Russian state will be. Generally speaking, I think, that optimists are in a majority. One has just to compare the public reaction in Russia to the enlargement of NATO to the reaction in Russia to the enlargement of the Union. You can see that the attitude to the European Union has always been much more benign than attitudes towards NATO, although in a practical sense, the consequences for Russia in the case of the European Union might be much more important and much more problematic than the consequences of the NATO enlargement. But, depending on how strong or how weak the Russian state might be, I think we can speculate about how closely the Russian currency might be tied to the euro.

If the Russian state is getting stronger and more centralized, then I would envisage a currency board established in Russia with the rouble tied to the euro. And that would reflect a more important and probably a more historic change in the Russian orientation from its global foreign policy agenda to a continental foreign policy agenda. That means that Europe will probably replace the United States as the main foreign policy partner of Russia early in the next century.

Now if the Russian state continues to be weak, if Russia continues to be a no man's land, then I can imagine the territory of Russia being divided between different dominant currencies. It is easy to predict that just as it is now, the Far East will be dominated by the Japanese currency, some of the western parts of the country will be dominated by the Deutschmark and later by the euro. However in that case I believe the dollar will remain as the ultimate reserve currency, as a means of exchange, and the current level of the Russian economy, the dollarization, will probably remain the same.

A. Clesse: Thank you very much, Andrei. Let us try to keep the discussion coherent in terms of topics. It would make sense if somebody would add something on the impact on Eastern Europe in general, not just Russia.

V. Klaus: If I may make a short comment. First, I am not a good person to speak about monetary unions, because as some of you know I was the last Minister of Finance of a dissolved monetary union called Czechoslovakia. And I tried to do my best to keep the monetary union together, but I failed. So I may be a good expert for the future, if European Monetary Union will break down, to suggest how to deal with the breakdown of a monetary union, because it seemed to us as something impossible to achieve. But, as you may know, we did achieve it in a very smooth way and there was almost no political, military, or even economic problem in doing so. So, it seems to me, one experience is, 'Let's try monetary union, because it can be dissolved.' This is one of the theorems I would suggest as almost a crucial one here. No, it is not a joke. It seems to me that it is a very important statement. I was born in a monetary union called Czechoslovakia and it had never come to my mind that it could disappear. But it did and it disappeared relatively easily.

My second experience is that on December 31, 1992 we liquidated the political and fiscal union called Czechoslovakia. We did not liquidate the free trade area and the customs union. Both of them still exist, five years later. We tried to keep the monetary union, but I must say that without the existence of a political and fiscal union, the monetary union lasted just six weeks. On February 13, we separated the currencies. This is the source for my continuing to return to the connection between fiscal, political and monetary union in the European area. And this is the source for my repeated criticism that the inevitable path from monetary to fiscal and political union is not seriously discussed in Europe these days.

As regards the potential future membership of a small, open economy in Central Europe in a European Monetary Union I am rather optimistic, because it seems to me that we have succeeded in having something like six or seven years of a fixed exchange rate with the German mark, during nearly the whole decade of the dramatic changes in the economic structure of the country. The Czech Republic could belong to something like the German monetary currency zone relatively easily, like Austria and the Netherlands.

R. Portes: Václav Klaus has just said so many provocative things that I have to restrain myself. I will say only that I agree with his pessimism. My own pessimism is about the speed at which negotiations with the countries on the accession list are proceeding. They are not proceeding with any real efficacy, any real commitment on the side of the European Union, and I think the target date of 2002/2003 is, regrettably, very optimistic and very unlikely.

I would just pick up one point that actually goes back to what Bob Mundell said relating to the East European countries: 'if a country can't do a currency board, it can't do monetary union'. I don't see that at all, and I would be interested to hear his further reflections on this. It seems to me that if a country is doing a currency board, its currency can be attacked as Argentina's was in 1995. And in that case, the strains on the domestic monetary system can be very considerable. You can't attack a currency that doesn't exist and consequently monetary union is actually easier than a currency board. That is not to say that going into monetary union would be desirable for the Central European countries now, or if they were admitted in 2002, because one can argue that, as part of the economic catching-up process, their real exchange rate will have to appreciate in the long term fairly substantially over a fairly long period. And to constrain that within the context of monetary union would be undesirable for domestic monetary stability, in the limited sense that that can be understood when you are within the monetary union, that is to say that they end up with very substantial inflationary pressures during that period.

So I would not recommend, if they were able to come into the Union in 2002, that they should come into monetary union immediately upon entry.

E.-M. Claassen: I am always impressed by Robert Mundell, but I first of all would like to stress what Václav Klaus said. It is not a single case, the Czech-Slovak disintegration. We have this strange historical fact that we have on the one hand a tendency towards monetary integration, and then, if you look at the Russian rouble, monetary disintegration. And I would say, and that it is a big issue for Asia and Latin America as well, that we go more or less to a floating exchange rate system. So if you look at the world economy, not only Europe, Russia, Eastern Europe, we are in a very strange historical position. On the one hand, we have monetary integration in Europe, but on the other hand, increasingly you will have less and less currency boards and a greater amount of less fixing and more floating. That is a general point. It is a strange historical circumstance.

But I would go back, very shortly, to what Bob Mundell said. The dollar-euro relationship. What is happening with the euro? Now what is very interesting and special, in the context of Russia at the moment, is what Mundell said. In 1914, and now I go back into history, the United States represented three times Britain. And now if you look at all these inflationary European economies, including Russia in 1922, or Germany in 1923, these hyper-inflationary countries after the First World War, they had the dollar. There was dollarization already. People could say: 'Why was it not the pound sterling?' So, this was after the First World War, not after the second. Bob Mundell said the United States were still on the gold standard. Now for the euro, it is not the gold standard, but he said we have sufficient international reserves. That is not irrelevant in comparing history. Bob Mundell said as well that if we have no political unification in Europe, there is NATO. That's an interesting point. After the First World War, the USA was a strong military power. It won the First World War. You should not forget that.

Now two minor points in regard to the euro, about whose exchange rate we will talk later. Now, for the moment, for the next months, what are the main preoccupations? There are two things. First the monetary tools, the instruments. Bob Mundell said what is happening with the money multiplier, its diversion between members of the currency union and, probably with the velocity of money—it will increase. The amount of money will relatively go down in the long run. So that is one point for monetary policy. At the moment they retain the old German target of growth rates. Is that for transition to the full euro standard?

The more important point is: 'What is monetary stability?' This is not discussed. Alan Greenspan discussed it two years ago and then came the Asian crisis and then he had other problems. Now the European Central Bank doesn't know either. Who does know? Is there monetary stability when inflation is less than 2 percent? Greenspan doesn't know either. But to put a number, like the Maastricht criteria, monetary stability is equal to less than 2 percent. Not equal to 2 percent, but less than 2 percent. It could be between 0 and less than 2 percent. This uncertainty certainly is not daunting only for we economists. It is an uncertainty and it provides one possible debate for the future. Where does inflation stop and where does deflation begin?

J. Frieden: I want to build on something that Bob Mundell and Randy Henning both mentioned in somewhat different ways: Mundell in talking about the importance of a central state and Henning in talking about the institutional characteristics of the euro's international role. And I want to make an observation about what I regard as a very important question mark about characteristics of the determinants of the euro's exchange rate policy that have important implications for the topic of the session, that is monetary leadership and the role of the euro in monetary leadership and in monetary stability internationally. Almost everywhere where there is an independent central bank, there is a testy relationship with the finance ministry and the treasury, between the monetary authorities and the government more generally. And my impression is that, generally speaking, this relationship is tenable, tends to move towards some sort of political equilibrium, at least in part because the government and the treasury have fiscal policy in their policy arsenal so that monetary policy from the standpoint of the central bank and fiscal policy from the government are discussed together. Where there is a disagreement over the direction of policy, both sides have tools they can try to use, either for bargaining purposes, or, if it should come to that, to try to achieve their goals. It seems to me that this is a fundamental question about the euro internationally and euro exchange rate policy more generally, because in the EU there is essentially no counterpart on the fiscal side, to the European Central Bank. I put on the table what I presume will be at least part of the discussion in the next session: the question of what the implications of a strong and independent central bank but no counterpart fiscal authority are for the role of the euro in international monetary affairs, in as much as fiscal policy has implications for exchange rate policy. It seems to me that there is the possibility that in the absence of a European fiscal authority there will be national fiscal responses to euro monetary policy which runs the risk of being highly conflictual and certainly uncoordinated, or the possibility, somewhat implausibly, of a genuine European fiscal stance emerging as a counterpart to European monetary policy. This is an issue worth considering in trying to think about the international role of the euro, both in bargaining form—in the context in which Randall Henning was talking about it—and more generally, economically.

A. Clesse: There are a few participants left from this morning on the speakers' list. For example Lord Skidelsky. He resolved his question with Andrei Kortunov, bilaterally, but I encourage him to raise it publicly in the forum. So Robert.

R. Skidelsky: When Mr. Kortunov was making his presentation, he said that from the point of view of Russia, and indeed recipient countries in general, it would be much better if the IMF and other institutions made their loans on technical criteria rather than political criteria. Is this a realistic proposition? Wouldn't Russia have received much less money than it did had decisions been taken on technical criteria alone? Because obviously one of the reasons for the constant flow of IMF loans to Russia is that they are terrified of the break-up of the country and therefore of what would happen to the nuclear arsenal. This is a way of extorting money. But the money does no good. The conditions are cheated on and a lot of it ends up in Swiss bank accounts. What is the answer to that particular dilemma? It seems to me to be a no-win situation. How do you break out of the trap? That was my question. It may be not interesting enough to deserve an answer, because you might say there is no way out of it at the moment.

A. Clesse: Andrei Kortunov, does it deserve an answer?

A. Kortunov: Sure it deserves an answer, but I am not sure that I can provide one. But first of all, I think that the IMF made a number of serious mistakes when it released its money for Russia in the first place, and, indeed there were political considerations. However, these were not separated from economic criteria and I think first of all the IMF should have avoided double standards. It should have avoided floating bench marks which it had, as far as Russia was concerned. In a way, the IMF itself provoked the Russian authorities to launch a policy of money extortion, because it turned out to be the most efficient policy for Mr. Yeltsin and his friends. They found out that they had to scare the IMF, or rather the United States or the international community, in order to get money. And therefore, even before the 1996 elections, these fears and these statements about a possible breakdown of the country and nuclear missiles running loose in Eurasia, were blown up out of all real proportion.

I don't think that the danger of a real decomposition of Russia, or the danger of losing control over the nuclear arsenal was as real as it was portrayed here and in Russia also. We should have probably paid more attention to the example of Gorbachev when he tried to scare the West by showing apocalyptic pictures about what would happen if the Soviet Union was to break apart. Well, the Soviet Union broke apart although it didn't produce 15 nuclear states. And with due management, the problem was resolved.

Now, what is to be done? It is hard to tell right now, because there is a certain degree of inertia and the IMF cannot recognize its failure in Russia, it cannot just retreat from Russia without losing face. And at the same time, I think, Russia is, in a way, on drugs and it will be very difficult to get off the needle. But we discussed possible options. One of the options that I suggest is to include into the package of assistance means a condition that Russia will allow foreign banks to buy out its financial system. The only way to mobilize resources in the country—and there are financial resources in the country, I would even venture to say considerable resources in the country, that can be used—is to involve institutions which might be trusted by the public which has its dollars under mattresses. I don't think that Russian banks are capable of doing that just now, so probably it is foreign banks which will be trusted by Russians to manage their money.

Session 3: The Emergence of the Euro and Its Future Position vis-à-vis Other Leading Currencies

A. Clesse: Session number 3 is 'The emergence of the euro and its future position vis-à-vis other leading currencies'.

S. Collignon: These thoughts developed around Randy's analysis of the way we are organizing and handling our external representation. Those who know me know that I had a lot of faith, having pushed for the euro for over ten years. Maybe this is the moment when I can also start to express that I am somewhat concerned about the way we are handling our internal affairs in the monetary union. Dominique Strauss-Kahn gave a very good speech the other day at the CEPR birthday party where he suggested how to set up our external representation. And then we will have to think what we will do and we will have to talk to our American or other industrialized friends and then we will also talk to our emerging partners. Now that is good, but it isn't certain that it will necessarily work that way. I have been trying to think about what could actually happen. If the worst things of Randy's scenario would happen, which way is it going to go?

First of all, what I observe is that probably in Europe on balance we have a consensus in favor of stabilizing transatlantic exchange rates. But I am not so sure that there is somebody to receive that message on the other side. And if you think that the euro and the dollar will each cover roughly 40 percent of the financial markets, that means 80 percent in total, that means the transatlantic exchange rate will dominate the world. The rest of the world will be simply at the receiving end.

For Asia, this would be of particular importance as it would disturb their whole external trade and, possibly also, their investment strategies. They are still more orientated towards the dollar bloc, but at the same time they have important interests with Europe and they have an important share of inner-Asian trade. If we can't sort out how we are going to take decisions within Europe, and we don't have any machinery that works so that we can negotiate and engage into a constructive dialogue with our American partners, then the consequence for Asia will be that they will become destabilized by the volatility of the transatlantic exchange rate. This destabilization will push them necessarily into looking how to stabilize their regional monetary relations. Then the question is: Who is going to be the anchor around that? Given the way things have been with the Japanese for a long time it is not likely that they will fulfil that function easily. If this does not work, then the natural answer is the Chinese yuan. And we see already within local and regional trade, the Chinese currency does take on a little bit of an anchor currency function there. If that became true, and given the enormous weight and size of China, then we get into a completely different geo-strategic development, because it will probably mean in the long run that Pacific integration, or what I call 'wet integration', might fall apart, and that something more of a dry integration from China to Europe could happen.

Then there would be the question of what would Russia do. If Russia happened to give itself a proper currency, then it is possible that it would be something of a pivot between China and Europe. We would get into some kind of stability zone between Asia and Europe. But if Russia does not have a currency, it is more likely that, let's say Irkutsk, would live on the yuan standard, Moscow on the dollar standard and St. Petersburg on the euro standard.

These are just some thoughts of what could happen and what the long-term strategic consequences would be, if we don't get together between America and Europe to stabilize our own affairs. And I would like to bring that into the discussion as a kind of provocative thought.

G. Ambrosi: My comment is on the contribution of Robert Mundell. I think he showed in an excellent way what we can expect in principle concerning asset demand for the euro as a reserve currency. I could totally agree with that analysis and I do believe there will be a long standing excess demand for euros as a reserve currency in the near future for people who want to switch out of the dollar. Now if that is the long-term situation, and maybe this situation is not really so long-term as he pointed out, it could very well be that there are also some sudden changes. In his presentation he said that the Europeans might be the ones who are interested in that. I think Mr. Collignon believes, similarly, that it is not in the interest of the Europeans that that should happen, because the demand for the euro will increase, the currency will appreciate and we will have less possibility to sell our goods on the world market. The other side of the coin is that the dollar will depreciate, and now comes in the catchword of globalized world, and the one region which really is globalized—Europe is not that much—is America. America is a far more open country than it was before and it has a large balance of trade deficit. So what it means if the dollar depreciates, is that the welfare cost of the imports of the United States will become far larger. So a country which is really disinterested in having that development, in my view, is the United States.

And now to the interesting aspect of Mr. Henning's remarks. He says that from the institutional aspect, Europe will follow a policy of inertia, a non-policy, meaning it will be struck by inertia, that is that in exchange rate matters it will follow the same policy as the United States followed right up until now, namely a policy of benign neglect because they cannot do anything else. Now I think this is an interesting change of roles. The United States might very well be strongly interested in having a management of currency exchange rates whereas previously it was not, and Europe, which generally stands for the idea of managing exchange rates, might not be interested in that.

Now, as far as the third parties are concerned, I think it will be quite interesting, especially for countries like China-Russia is maybe a special case. China, I think, will be very much interested to be in a position to have a choice. The rest of the world did not have a choice, as far as reserve currencies are concerned, until now. Because the most liquid currency was the dollar. The most abundant currency for reserve requirements was the dollar. Now, for the first time in post-world war history, they have an alternative. So I think it will give them liberty to behave far more as a rational investor. Whether that will lead to more volatility or whether that will lead to further structural changes in the portfolios, is open to debate.

R. Mundell: Of the many different subjects that have come up, I think that it would be useful if I comment on two of them.

The first is about the benign neglect of the euro or whatever phrase we use to describe the system in which the ECB would have either monetary targeting or inflation targeting without concern for the exchange rate. I really completely agree that benign neglect is not a good policy for Europe and it would very quickly turn out to be very bad if there are shifts in stocks, portfolio shifts into the euro or, theoretically, in the other direction. A big change in the exchange rate, let's say an appreciation of the euro, which I think is most likely, would bring strains within Europe of the same kind that existed when the mark soared against the dollar in the summer of 1992. It would create pain, and there would be no escape from it, as Italy was able to escape in 1992. Big changes in the exchange rate are going to increase tension inside the Community.

So I think that something other than benign neglect is in order. It is very hard to see exactly what that policy should be. But just imagine a scenario in which the ECB started off with the idea of benign neglect and then the euro did start to soar and it went substantially, 20 or 30 percent, up, definitely exacerbating the unemployment problem in Europe. And then, after a little while of waiting, the Europeans decide: 'Well, we really have to get the euro down.' Or maybe, at that point, if Europe started an independent policy to push down the euro against the dollar, the United States may say: 'Hey, we don't want that. We liked that dollar-euro rate. The rate is half ours.' And you would end up with the same kind of bashing that you get currently between the United States and Japan with the dollar and the yen.

And then what Lord Skidelsky talked about this morning, about the problem after 1934, after the US devaluation of the dollar, when the pound had to settle for a rate around $5 or so. The UK was not a free agent.

So from the very outset, it would be a great mistake for Europe to concede or give away the idea that they are going to benign by neglecting the dollar-euro rate. I think that they will have to stake a claim to their own interest in it. Now, I don't know what the resolution of that is going to be and there is the problem, that Stefan and other people have raised, of the anchor, third currencies, and so on. The euro-dollar rate is not going to be such a big problem for Europe as the dollar-yen rate has been for Japan. I hope it can be done outside a formal institution, but some kind of way of managing the rate is going to be necessary. But I don't have the solution for it.

The other question is what Richard Portes raised—the idea of a currency board. And I had said if you can't do a currency board, you can't do a monetary union. And he didn't like that. And he said, it was almost as if he was turning it around, a currency board might be harder to do than a monetary union. Because in a monetary union you have no choice about the exchange rate, but with a currency board you still have a choice about the exchange rate. And so he thought that a currency board might be harder than a monetary union. I don't believe that is true at all. I think that would be really quite easy, and the optimum policy for all the countries that are going to go into the euro is to establish a currency board. A currency board automatically mimics the monetary policy as if you were in the union. That is what gives it credibility. If you are in the union, and you have an excess supply of money, the money flows out and it is gone, eliminating the excess money. The central bank cannot sterilize. Similarly, if there is an excess demand for money, the money comes in. It goes from one region to another and you get an equalization of the demand and supply of money. Exactly the same thing happens with a currency board, because if there is a balance of payments surplus, you buy reserves, and that increases the money supply domestically. You sell reserves, and that decreases the money supply. The essence of the adjustment mechanism of a currency board is that you don't have any sterilization operations. The central bank cannot neutralize the effects of the balance of payments on the money supply. The market knows that the equilibrating process is there and as long as it is there, they won't speculate against the exchange rate. There is of course a problem if you let some people fool around with the currency board, and start to manipulate it in directions that are not viable. Something like what Hong Kong did, when they decided to have an open market to support the stock market! When they established a national agency for handling the currency board they moved away from the currency board and they got immediately into trouble. A system somewhere in between is Argentina.

Argentina has a kind of currency board with its convertibility law and this system requires a parliamentary vote in order to devalue. Devaluation requires an act of parliament. And that is a barrier. If you don't think that is a big enough barrier, you could require a two thirds majority of parliament. But Argentina was, in fact, very clever, when it decided that in Argentina dollar clauses are not enforcible. The courts would not uphold a dollar contract, in the same way that the courts won't uphold a gold clause in the

United States. What an ingenious clause! If, for example, parliament ever voted for, let's say, a 20 percent devaluation of the peso against the dollar, all those dollar clauses will be null and void and everybody who is a creditor would lose 20 percent, just like that! Parliament will almost never, as long as there is a sufficient weight of creditors against the peso, change the currency board, for that reason.

I think the currency board system is one that is ideal for all the small countries contemplating monetary integration. I would even go further. Not just those countries which are trying to join directly and immediately—and are invited to join—the European Union, but other small countries like Croatia and Slovakia. These countries could not have a better monetary policy than that which a currency board would provide. They get the benefits of the scarcity relationships and transactions convenience in a monetary area as large as Europe and they get the best monetary policy they could possibly have, as long as Europe itself was stable, which, I believe, it would be.

R. Rosecrance: May I ask Professor Mundell how much, in terms of reserves, an Eastern European country would have to have to form an effective currency board with the euro?

R. Mundell: Well, it would depend on what their expected deficits were likely to be. That would depend on confidence, in turn. Ideally and certainly a pure 100 percent currency board would be starting off from scratch, it would be 100 percent of the high-powered money supply. And then, of course, critics would say: 'Oh, but what about confidence in the banking system and so on. The central bank can't then be a lender of last resort.' Well, one solution for that was the Argentine solution. They shifted the lender-of-last-resort function over to the government and the government drew on the International Monetary Fund. The Estonians did something more ingenious: they had more than 100 percent reserves. They had something like 125 percent reserves and that provided a cushion which they could use for support of the banks if they got into trouble. I don't regard the fact that countries need reserves as a very big problem because the amount you need is much smaller than what is needed for a crisis. Look at the size of the bailout that has been going on since Mexico. $40-50 billion for Mexico. More than double what they would have needed for an exchange back-up had they had a currency-board type of adjustment. $ 40 billion or more also for Indonesia and for Korea, much more than they would need for a currency board. The cost to the international community, were they to assist a country with reserves in setting up a currency board, would be a small fraction of what would be needed to bail these countries out of a crisis.

J. Frankel: I did want to make a comment on Mundell's point about currency boards. I have always thought of there being a continuum from fixed exchange rates, to currency boards, to monetary union: an increasingly firm commitment to giving up monetary sovereignty. So that if you didn't have the ability to give up monetary independence sufficiently to achieve a fixed exchange rate, then a currency board would be even harder. And, in case if you didn't have enough for a currency board, monetary union would be even harder. I have recently had some second thoughts about that. It has to do with something we have learned in recent years, how difficult it is to gain and keep the confidence of international investors. Something like a commitment to a currency board, even if you write it in the law, just does not give you 100 percent confidence the way some of our theories seemed to imply. So the question is: If Argentina, Hong Kong or Mexico are willing to seriously peg the exchange rate, is it reasonable to think that they should go all the way to full monetary union, or dollarization?

The main argument against it has always been: what happens if the Federal Reserve Board raises interest rates? They do it in response to domestic needs and monetary conditions in the United States, while a country like Argentina would have to suffer the same increase in interest rates that might not be relevant for its own conditions. But the situation is worse now. Under an exchange rate peg or currency board these countries have interest rates that go up *more* than US interest rates go up when US monetary policy tightens. They don't get any benefits of any residual bit of sovereignty or monetary independence, even a little bit. So there is a certain argument that they might as well just take the dollar as their currency. The interest rates would actually come down rather than go up.

There are other things to be said about the pros and cons of giving up monetary independence. I don't think what I have said fully answers the question. And I am certainly not speaking as a matter of US policy. And I am struck by the fact that, despite all our theories about how the borders of the optimum currency area do not have to coincide perfectly with political borders, it is very striking that the correlation is almost 100 percent. The EMU is almost the first case of different large countries adopting the same currency. There are hardly any cases of a single country, a political unit having different currencies. The overlap on borders is almost 100 percent, by which I infer that there is a strong political desire for people to have their own currency. That may be the answer as to why full monetary union is not right for most countries.

R. Mundell: This is not an answer, because I don't disagree really completely with what you say. You say that there is a problem of establishing confidence when you have a currency board. I agree that this is a very important problem. It requires national leadership. What you had in Argentina was leadership. It was not just Cavallo who agreed, Menem agreed too. You had Carlos Rodriguez, Roque Fernandez, Pedro Pou and a whole group of people who understood what was going on and could back it up, and they had enough force and intellectual power so that when the IMF came down and told them: 'Don't do it that way!', they were able to present all the arguments against it. The leadership and understanding were there.

So a country that doesn't have leadership has a problem with a currency board. I guess Estonia managed to do it somehow, and it seems to be working all right. And Hong Kong managed to do it back in 1983. To me, the great sadness is the weakness in our system. This leadership should not be necessary. Each country should not have to supply its own. In fact, to me this is the job the IMF should be doing. They should be providing leadership in this direction. They should be saying: 'You small country want to have monetary stability. Go for a currency board. We will show you how to set it up.' Then you don't need local leadership.

The great tragedy is that the IMF had maneuvered itself into a difficult position. Remember in the 1951 and 1963 annual reports when they wrote vicious attacks on flexible exchange rates. Read those annual reports. 'The worst kind of exchange rate system is a flexible exchange rate. They always depreciate.' There is an oxymoron, of course; all rates can't depreciate! But now the IMF line is just as arrogant and dogmatic but it is saying exactly the opposite. They turned it around. Any fixed exchange rate is a bad system, it is not going to work out. They seek to undermine it. Anything but a currency board! In my view this is one of the major reasons why it has proved to be such an abysmal failure in Asia. It is not that we don't need the IMF, we do need the IMF, it is extremely important, but we need an IMF that has a mechanism for reassessing its own propaganda.

A. Bénassy-Quéré: I would like to come back to the comments at the start of this session. I would like to say that we can be relatively optimistic with regard to monetary cooperation both on the European and on the US side.

On the US side, as Randall Henning said earlier, the main problem of who the external representation of monetary union is has been solved. On the US side, I share Michael Ambrosi's optimism. I think that once the euro has become an international currency, once investors really have the choice between the dollar and the euro, the US attitude could change. For instance, the Americans will experience the fact that the exchange rate is not only a tool for macroeconomic adjustment, but also the source of speculative shocks. Hence, variations in the exchange rate are not necessarily stabilizing for macroeconomic activity. The other reason is that the US is a heavily indebted country; if investors have the choice between the dollar and the euro, and if the exchange rate between both is highly unstable, they could demand a risk premium, and therefore the US interest rate could be higher.

Hence, I would be a bit more optimistic than Stefan Collignon was at the start of this session. I am also more optimistic on the subject of Asia. I think that for Asia, the euro is a tremendous opportunity to reap benefits from the diversification of external trade. For so far the Asian countries have not reaped these benefits because they were pegged to the dollar. Variations in the dollar were often devastating. The fact that the exchange rate between the euro and the dollar can vary significantly can now be neutralized by an Asian country via more diversified exchange rate reserves. And if Asian economies do not revert to a peg to the dollar, which seems likely, they will be able to manage their exchange rate with a basket of currencies containing the euro and the dollar, for instance, while waiting for a regional currency to emerge. So this is a slightly more optimistic vision than that which was expressed by Stefan Collignon. Thank you.

R. Henning: Let me respond to two points that were raised. Apologies to those of you who have made comments to which, for lack of time, I am unable to respond.

Dick Cooper concluded his comments by saying that we all will have to live with the regime in which all of those with the power to act will be involved in some way in these international meetings, the G-7 in particular. And for the time being, I agree with that. Some have gone so far as to argue that the present configuration of the G-7 is optimal, actually better than consolidating the G-7 into a G-3, for example, because it will give the United States a window into the intra-European negotiations. With the German, French and Italian finance ministers present, the United States will have an opportunity to observe their preferences and differences and be able to either broker a compromise or mould proposals in such a way to attract Community support. This is a compelling consideration, but I am concerned about a couple of things.

First, this configuration leaves too many people in the room for the United States, Japan, and others to be comfortable when discussing very sensitive issues such as exchange rate and monetary coordination. Secondly, not all the members in the monetary union will be present, of course. So, there will still have to be consultation between the large members of the euro area, represented in the G-7, and the rest of the Euro-11 membership. Finally, if the European members are held to their obligation to speak with one voice in these meetings, then the United States may not be able to observe their individual preferences and thus broker or mould proposals in a constructive way.

The second main point to which I wanted to respond was raised by Jeff Frieden and dealt with the policy mix and the exchange rate. I would like to see coordination between monetary and fiscal authorities as a general matter. But the ability of fiscal policy to respond to monetary policy and vice versa has been constrained at the national level by the politics of fiscal policy, which do not render the instrument readily adjustable either to the business cycle or to central bank policy. Speaking to central bank officials, we observe a deep distrust that any bargain that they could conclude with the fiscal authority would be upheld when a change in government takes place or a new legislature is elected. As a result, we see a lot less fiscal-monetary cooperation than is desirable at a national level. The change in the amount of such cooperation that we experience in Europe with the shift to the monetary union, where monetary policy is centralized and fiscal policy is decentralized, will probably be less than we might imagine.

What makes the relationship between finance ministries and central banks manageable as far as exchange rate policy is concerned is societal preferences, something on which both Professor Frieden and I have written. When a societal consensus exists with respect to exchange rates, conflict between finance ministries and central banks is tempered. Where a societal consensus does not exist, or where it is changing and unstable, policy is up for grabs and the relationship between the finance ministry and the central bank is more contentious. So, how societal preferences are configured in the euro zone, particularly the relationship between private banks and industry, will be a critical element in the exchange rate policy-making process for the euro. These preferences as well as the official institutions will determine the euro exchange rate policy.

R. McCauley: I really appreciate the opportunity to sit just down the table from my teacher, Charles Kindleberger. I first took his graduate course in the financial history of Western Europe, and then his undergraduate course in international economics. At the end of the latter class, he asked me whether he would be seeing me in his kindergarten class the next semester. I would have willingly signed up for it!

It is my job today to question the commonplaces not only of this gathering, but also other gatherings of this type. In particular, should we be so certain the introduction of the euro will lead to a weak dollar? Second, should we expect a balanced pair of policies of benign neglect at either side of the Atlantic? Speakers sometimes quote John Connally—probably the worst Secretary of the Treasury since Morgenthau, who wanted to turn postwar Germany into a producer of cuckoo clocks—saying that 'it's our dollar, but your problem', and then look forward to the day when 'it's our euro, but your problem'. Turnabout is fair play, I suppose, but the implied symmetry should be questioned also.

We have heard already several times the usual story of why the dollar will weaken when the euro is introduced. The story employs good arguments; on their own terms they are quite reasonable expectations. The notion is that we should expect portfolio shifts by central banks and by private asset managers from the dollar into the euro. These portfolio shifts will tend to push up the euro against the dollar, turning Euroland's comfortable current account surplus into a deficit. (This is a variation on transfer problem analysis and my argument against it echoes Kindleberger's argument with Triffin.) I agree that we should expect these portfolio shifts to happen as asserted. But the story should not stop there. Now, why are these portfolio shifts going to happen? Usually the story highlights substantial gains in the liquidity, breadth and depth of European financial markets with the euro. I too expect such structural change in European financial markets and agree that it will lead asset managers to shift away from the dollar towards the euro.

What is missing in this is the notion that the same structural changes to the European financial markets can be expected to draw issuers to Europe as well. The liability managers of the world will not be immune to the same, newly enhanced attractions of European bond markets. If Korea and Brazil, for example, borrow more in the euro, they will create the assets that will allow the People's Bank of China, let's say, to invest more in the euro. All of this can happen with the euro necessarily rising, without Europe's trade surplus turning into a deficit and so on as the usual tale postulates.

If you look at the data, the portfolio weight attached to the euro in the official reserves of non-industrial countries exceeds the weight of Euroland currencies in their external debt. So, if you think that there are good reasons for them to shift their official reserves, then the same reasons would suggest *a fortiori* that they shift their liabilities toward the euro. Since Europe runs a current account surplus and has accumulated positive net international wealth, it follows that the rest of the world on balance has accumulated a net debt and thus that its liability management quantitatively makes more difference than its asset management. So, the next time that you hear the story of large shifts by asset managers in favor of the euro pushing up its value against the dollar, ask yourself, 'what about the liability managers?'

In some cases this may be a case of a solution looking for a problem. That is, those who want to manage exchange rates are naturally well-disposed toward a story that suggests the necessity of managing exchange rates. Lop-sided arguments about portfolio shifts serve as the background music to get you in the mood for exchange rate management.

All that said, I think that there are other, better reasons to expect the euro to prove strong against the dollar over some horizon. The relative cyclic positions of the economies on either side of the Atlantic seem to be moving in favor of the euro. Moreover, I note the very close linkage at high frequency of the weakness of the dollar and that of the New York Stock Exchange when the latter is most volatile. So if you entertain doubts about the price of US stocks, you may also entertain doubts about the dollar.

But most fundamentally, what economists really know about exchange rates is that, over time, surpluses and deficits cumulate into positive international wealth and net debts, respectively, and these make a difference to exchange rates. The dollar has traded against the Deutschmark in the course of the 1990s from 1.40 on one side to 1.90 on the other. 1.90 is not far from estimates of purchasing power parity. 1.40 is not far from what analysts like John Williamson take to be the fundamental equilibrium exchange rate of the dollar, which would stabilize the US net debt in relation to its GDP. The variations in the dollar's exchange rate over the cycle in this decade can be regarded as bouncing from one end to the other of these two notions of equilibrium. Over time, however, accumulating US international indebtedness will tend to make McDonald's hamburgers cheaper in New York than in Frankfurt.

Finally, let us consider the widespread idea of balanced benign neglect. There is truth in this view. There is little doubt that policy-makers in Washington will pay more attention to the euro's movement against the dollar than they did to the Deutschmark's movements against the dollar. Why? Because in the past, movements of the Italian lira and Spanish peseta and other European currencies tended to split the difference to some extent between the dollar and the Deutschmark. In 1995, for example, when the dollar was weak against the Deutschmark, so, too, was the Italian lira and other European currencies, so that the dollar's effective exchange rate did not move by as much as it might have without the buffer of the currencies in the middle. Of course, with Monetary Union, the buffer disappears. And the dollar's effective exchange rate will tend to move more for a given change in the dollar-euro exchange rate than it did for the same movement in the dollar-Deutschmark rates. Across the Atlantic, by contrast, the people meeting in a skyscraper in Frankfurt will be able to pay less attention to the dollar than did their suburban predecessors at the Bundesbank. Again, the reason is that a weak dollar would tend to tear apart the bonds among currencies in Europe and that will no longer happen under Monetary Union.

Will the world arrive at a condition of balanced benign neglect, however? Certainly not right away. The dollar-euro rate will, for the foreseeable future, constrain Frankfurt's pursuit of price stability more than Washington's. The differing constraints are grounded in the currency geography ably investigated by Agnès Bénassy. As things stand, the dollar area is at least twice as big as the US economy. So when the dollar moves, it tends to take a very large chunk of the world economy with it. By contrast, Euroland will have a relatively smaller economic mass attached to it. In particular, the currencies of Eastern Europe, some Mediterranean countries and West African countries will tend to move with the euro. But if you add up all of these economies, at present, they are rather small in relation to Euroland proper. So movements in the dollar-euro rate will tend to impress themselves more on policy-makers in Frankfurt than in Washington, even if both of them care only about price stability, because Euroland will enjoy less insulation of its foreign trade than the United States.

A question mark hangs over the dollar area, which into 1997 included not only the Western Hemisphere but also most of Asia outside of Japan. In one of the most interesting developments in exchange markets in 1998, currencies like the Australian dollar, the Singapore dollar, the New Taiwan dollar, all so-called dollars, shared at times quite a bit in the yen's movements against the dollar. How this will settle out is not clear. Note that Dr. Mahatir chose to stabilize the ringget against the dollar, whatever his political differences with the United States. Moreover, the Korean won and the New Taiwan dollar has recently shown some stability against the dollar. But the question remains; going forward in East Asia, what exchange rate regimes will be chosen and how will regional currencies respond to movements in the major exchange rates?

At least for the foreseeable future, however, policy-makers in Washington will continue to enjoy a large dollar area outside the United States. This will tend to make movements of the dollar-euro rate less relevant to them than to their counterparts in Frankfurt.

H. Rey: Richard Portes and I, like many people in the room, have worked on the internationalization of the euro. What we tried to do is to provide a consistent theoretical framework to analyze that issue. What we are going to say today is partly drawn from a paper we wrote for *Economic Policy* in April 1998.

The first question we thought about was whether it actually matters if the euro becomes an international currency or not. There are many reasons why it may matter. The first one on the list is the link between currency hegemony and political power. It is certainly something many political scientists have talked about. We would like to focuse more on the economic implications of currency hegemony. There are several important ones. The first one is the 'unconstrained' balance of payments financing. 'Unconstrained' is probably exaggerated, but there is something to this idea. As Ronald McKinnon says: 'The privilege of going into international debts so heavily in your own currency is open only to the center country in the international monetary system.'

A second obvious item is international seigniorage. There we can be a bit more specific. When we think about *international seigniorage*, at first we think about *seigniorage on cash*. In other words, how many people carry $100 notes in the world economy outside the US. We have a rough figure for that type of seigniorage. It adds up to something like 0.1 percent of the GDP per *annum* This is effectively an interest free loan to the US Federal Reserve Bank. A second kind of seigniorage that Richard and we emphasize is what we call the *liquidity discount*. The liquidity discount comes from the fact that US bonds are very liquid. By liquid we mean that there are lots of people using them. The turnover in US bonds is very high; a lot of institutional investors for example hold US bonds, because they know that the markets are deep and that they can buy and sell these bonds very easily without much change in their prices. This 'liquidity' is priced by the market. We have preliminary estimates of this liquidity discount—an upper bound—which adds up to 0.1 percent of GDP per *annum* as well.

A third item is efficiency benefits. They have to do with transaction costs. If a lot of people use the US dollar in many markets, then if you transact mainly in dollars, it is a benefit for you because you don't have to incur transaction costs most of the time. For these efficiency benefits we also provide something like an upper bound estimate which amounts to 0.2 percent of GDP per *annum*.

Then we come to other types of potential benefits which may matter. The first one has to do with capital markets. It is arguable that today, in the European Union, goods markets are actually more integrated than capital markets and bond markets. The birth of the euro will lead to more integration in the capital markets and bond markets within the euro area. This is another potential economic benefit.

How do we think the international role of a currency shapes up? We argue that in the international environment it is more the demand factors that come into play than the supply factors. Within national boundaries, a lot of the use of a currency is linked to some kind of national legal restrictions. In the international environment, this is not the case any longer. And whether a currency is used or not, depends a lot on what market participants do.

In such a situation, one thing which is an important determinant of the extent to which a currency is used are the so-called *network externalities*. Currencies are media of exchange and when more people use them, they become more useful. It is an intrinsic property they have. So these network externalities, which are some kind of increasing return to scale in currency use translate into lower bid-ask spreads for currencies which are widely traded. If a currency is very widely used, then the transaction costs in this currency are lower, which induces more people to use that currency. This is why such a process may lead to multiple equilibria. In such an environment alternative scenarios may occur. They depend on expectations of agents in the market and history matters.

What we put at the center of our analysis are financial markets. We believe that largely the role of a currency as a reserve currency and as an intervention currency nowadays derives from its private use in financial markets. If a lot of market participants start using one currency, then it will be more attractive for authorities to use it in their reserves and it will also be an intervention currency. Invoicing practices will also adapt to its new environment. We think there are strong synergies between the vehicle currency role, which has to do with foreign exchange markets, and all the other roles of an international currency.

For example, if we have an efficient financial system with low transaction costs, then it will attract capital inflows, which in turn will raise liquidity on foreign exchange markets which will expand the vehicle currency role of a currency and lower transaction costs further. The converse is also true. If a currency is very widely used as a vehicle currency, then it lowers the costs of portfolio substitution and home financial markets will become more efficient. When we take into account these feedback effects from the domestic financial assets market to the foreign exchange market, we have very strong network externalities.

So what does this model say? We made several assumptions. The first one has to do with the credibility of the European Central Bank. We assumed that it will be a credible institution so that liquidity effects will be the main factors driving the potential use of the euro as an international currency.

We divided the world into three blocs: a dollar bloc, a euro bloc and a yen bloc. Then we had a look at all the transactions between these blocs, whether they are transactions in goods, bond flows or equity flows. We got some data on transaction costs and turnover data, both for government bonds and foreign exchange markets and we tested our various scenarios.

In some scenarios, the euro is not much more than a big Deutschmark. In other scenarios, the euro could become something like the dollar. In other scenarios it is something intermediate. We looked at the likelihood of these scenarios based on the actual data coming from transactions in goods and transactions on capital markets and bonds markets.

What came out of the analysis is that the key determining factor of the internationalization of the euro would be how fast and how well financial markets within the euro area would integrate. If integration doesn't succeed very well, if markets remain as segmented as they are today, if government bonds markets in particular remain as segmented as they are now, then the euro won't be much more than a big Deutschmark.

On the other hand, we found that if the European financial markets become really integrated, then the euro could take on some of the significative roles of the US dollar for international transactions. The key is the depth and breadth of the European financial markets.

R. Portes: And in particular, in the bond markets, because as Bob Rubin said, it is the bond markets that run the show. We know that. We are not saying anything different. That is partly because the cross-border trade in bonds is considerably greater than cross-border trade in equities, and that is an order of magnitude greater in terms of total flows of transactions than cross-border trade in goods and services. That is important to remember when you are looking at these issues.

Now I am going to skip some slides because Hélène took some of my time. That is all right. You don't want to hear about whether the European Central Bank really wants to promote the euro as an international currency. You will have to ask Wim Duisenberg and his colleagues. On that issue you remember of course that the Bank of Japan and the Bundesbank, for example, resisted for many years the internationalization of their currencies. But the authorities may not be able to do anything about it. That is part of our story, because financial market integration is already happening. The process of internationalization of the euro is intimately bound up with the integration of European financial markets.

There is a wide range of phenomena to which I want to draw your attention.

First, governments are acting. Governments need to have a full yield curve in their liabilities. They want to sell to institutions, not just individuals. They have all decided to redenominate immediately as from January 1 their existing outstanding stocks of debts. By the way, a high proportion of bank assets are precisely those government debt liabilities. That means that the banks will have an incentive, in terms of matching their own assets and liabilities, to push their depositors into euro-denominated accounts. The process will be market driven. The American investment banks have been very helpful in this. I think the ECB won't be able to hold it back.

An illuminating anecdote from this process, which is indicative of what is going on, is the way that Germany first said: 'No, we can't possibly redenominate the outstanding German bonds. Our pensioners wouldn't accept that their Deutschmark bonds are turning into funny things they don't know about yet.' But the French then decided to redenominate their stock of bonds as from January, and the Germans took maybe a couple of months to realize that the competitive disadvantage that this would cause them in the markets was unsustainable, so that they had to go ahead and do it too.

Competition is there, it is a market. I don't think the authorities, even if they wish to, would be able to hold it back. We know about the various amalgamations of securities markets institutions or different kinds of cross-border combinations. This is happening in derivative markets as well. We are also going to see very quickly much more cross-border banking competition and much more banking amalgamation. That has been possible, of course, since the appropriate banking directive came into place some time ago. Not much has happened. But watch what will happen. You have seen a sign already when BBV took recently a substantial stake in the privatization of *Banca Nazionale del Lavoro*. I suggest to you that that is just the beginning of integration in the banking sector. Until now, the inventory of national domestic government bonds has served as collateral for central bank lending. Now the European System of Central Banks will accept a wide range of collateral. There is no artificial advantage for domestic institutions to make a market in their own government bonds. And institutions will operate, because of that, across the euro zone in a full range of euro securities. Securitization has progressed very slowly overall in Europe until now. But as information grows, as the advantages of the banks in dealing with asymmetric information fall, we will see that accelerate with the coming of a single currency area. Inter-bank operations will be in euros. That is a third of all the total balance sheets of the banking system. That too will promote the euroization of the overall security and financial institutions position in Europe.

Consider junk bonds and venture capital. The attractiveness of a market is in part its liquidity. The reason for the very slow development of junk bonds, venture capital and so forth in Europe is the fragmentation of the markets. Make them integrated and hence much more liquid, and what will you see? You will see a transition towards the position now in the United States, where only 7 percent of corporate bonds outstanding are triple A and double A companies. In Europe, in the euro area it is 69 percent. In the United States 38 percent, on the other hand, of corporate bonds outstanding are single A and 16 percent are sub-investment grade. In Europe, those figures currently are 20 percent and 8 percent respectively. This will change, and guess who is going to move in which direction? Again the European securities markets will become much more attractive, both for asset managers and for liability managers. I will come back to that issue and that distinction in a moment.

How fast will this happen? I would suggest to you that it is going to happen very quickly indeed in the government bond markets. Again, estimates tend to go down month by month in terms of the time that this integration will take. I have given you some guesses, but talk to the market participants out there.

What about the famous portfolio shifts? This capital market unification I talked about is going to accelerate the erosion of the home bias of the American institutions and we will clearly see a big shift by the Japanese institutions. They are already saying that, and the markets are expecting it. I see no reason why the markets should be wrong. And, of course, central banks will shift. The Chinese have already stated their intention to shift significantly. We will see. Anything can happen. These just seem to be likely projections.

Now there are a set of problems here. The transition may be tricky and difficult. We know there are several estimates for the possible size of this portfolio shift: e.g., Randy Henning, Bob McCauley and Bill White. If you take the range of the estimates out there, it is a pretty wide range. But still we are talking clearly here about very large portfolio reallocations.

The disagreement I have with Bob McCauley we have discussed several times. I suppose the paper that I wrote with George Alogoskoufis almost two years ago is one of the sources of that 'conventional wisdom' that he criticized. And the question is indeed whether asset managers will move faster than the liability managers or the opposite. There I make a very simple point. A stock shift is different from a flow shift. The effect that he was talking about will typically operate in the new issues market. And the new issues market is only a small fraction of stocks outstanding. It certainly isn't anywhere near as big as the size of the portfolio shift that one might expect to take place within a relatively small number of years. So even if the entire new issues market will shift over to euro-denominated securities, it seems to me it will take a while to cope with the portfolio stock reallocation that we can expect. If that story is correct, than we do have the pressure for the euro to appreciate and possibly even to overshoot that has been discussed already.

My final slide is called *managing the risks*. How do we cope with all this if there are pressures for appreciation of the euro? The monetary authorities—Bob Mundell referred to this—will have to adjust to that and simply cannot ignore those shifts. I believe that whatever they may say, Dr. Duisenberg and his colleagues are conscious of this and that there is enough flexibility in the monetary strategy of the ECB, in so far as it has been defined for us, to admit that adjustment. We know that these shifts in currency dominance can be associated with instability, historically. We also know that if the euro and euro-denominated securities become a serious alternative to the dollar for international portfolio holders beyond the current status of the individual European currencies, then the environment for American policy-makers will be rather different. In particular, if there are difficulties in the domestic financial system of the United States, or worries about the longer-term US current account and indebtedness position, there will be a serious alternative for investors. That alternative would be euro-denominated securities. And that, to some extent, will change the policy environment for the United States. That means that we should want and expect more international policy coordination, and I am enough of an optimist to believe that that will come.

Finally, one of our previous slides referred to the inertia that is characteristic of these switches between these multiple equilibria going from one major international currency possibly to a bipolar system, possibly even further. When I first was writing about these questions several years ago I was overly influenced by that consideration. The speed with which financial institutions and financial markets react today is so much greater than the speed of reaction that we saw in the 1930s. I referred earlier to the contagion that we observed in the international sovereign debt markets in the early 1930s. There was contagion, no doubt about that. It just went a lot slower than it has done since the Thai crisis. It seems to me that that is a lesson in other dimensions. The transition to the new equilibrium, whatever it is going to be, will move rather faster than the historical considerations suggest.

C. de Boissieu: I was struck by the fact that most of the debate we had is a debate at the articulation of two aspects of our topic.

The first aspect is what I would call the exchange rate problems. Namely the level of the euro-dollar exchange rate, but also the debate about the anchor issue to which I will not come back.

The second aspect, which was raised by Bob and also by Hélène Rey and Richard Portes is a debate about what I call market shares. That is the role of the various currencies at the international level which for me is summarized by their market shares.

At some point there is some connection between the two aspects, but the connection is more complicated than we used to say. It is said in the Rey-Portes paper that one of the most important determinants to explain the evolution of market shares for the euro in the years to come is going to be the liquidity and the resilience of financial markets in the euro zone. I agree with this factor, but I think that we must come back to this issue: how to explain market shares in the short term and also in the medium and long term, if we look at the financial role of the currency and if we look also at the commercial role?

First, I want to say a few words about what I would call the competitiveness of the euro. That refers to the ability of the euro to compete with the dollar, which is different from the competitiveness of the euro zone as such. Second aspect: what to expect? I want to present here some arguments.

If you look at the list of arguments which are going to explain the ability of the euro to compete with other currencies, we put on the table several arguments: growth, price stability records... We come back to the very notion of what it means when speaking of the quality of a currency. I want to refer to Hayek. In Hayek's *Denationalization of Money*, you have some pages which are very nice concerning the way he was explaining, twenty years ago, what he means by the expression *quality of a currency*. For him the *quality of a currency* was based on two arguments: the stability of its value, and also the expected liquidity. Here we come back to the argument of the depth and the resilience of the banking sector and the financial markets.

To add some other factors, I think that the quality of the monetary-fiscal mix is an argument in the competitiveness of any currency. Here we have good news for today: you have heard that the Bundesbank and the other central banks have decided today to drop their leading rates by 30 basis points. In France I was advocating this kind of move for at least two months. I think we were in a kind of prisoner's dilemma as regards the monetary-fiscal mix in Europe. We had over the past months this *dialogue de sourds* as we say in French. Sometimes, French is useful. We had this kind of dialogue of the deaf between the Bundesbank, the ECB and the fiscal authorities in the aftermath of the German elections and the new government in Italy. I was very afraid that this kind of prisoner's dilemma could lead us to a bad situation as regards the monetary-fiscal mix at the start of the euro when we have to try to boost our growth given the impact of the international crisis.

Today's move is not the end of the prisoner's dilemma, but it is a big step towards the possible removal of the prisoner's dilemma at the start of the euro. Now, what is to be expected is a move from the fiscal authorities, especially in Italy, but also in some other countries, including my country, whereby the fiscal authorities must be very clear, very explicit about their willingness to stick to the stability pact, or perhaps to something tougher than the stability pact.

In order not to be exhaustive as regards the list of arguments which could determine the external competitiveness of the euro as a currency, I would add another argument, which was not explicitly discussed yet, which relates to the Hélène Rey-Richard Portes argument. It is very nice to have deep and resilient financial markets. It would be important also, I think, to clarify how to manage a situation of financial crisis in the zone and to anticipate this. A LTCM-type crisis is not going to stay, only a US side-problem. We could not say that an October 1987-type crisis is going to be always dealt with exclusively by Mr. Greenspan or his successor. We have, in order to be credible—and when we talk about financial markets, it is not only a question of quantity, it is also a question of qualitative aspects—to clarify as soon as possible the issue of the lender of last resort activities in the euro zone.

What I am saying here is that we are entering the euro zone with a lot of ambiguities in this respect. If we had in ten years from now a pan-European liquidity crisis in our financial markets in the euro zone, I guess it will not only be a problem for the *Banca d'Italia* or for the *Banque de France*. At some point, some kind of central intervention will have to take place. But when I say this, I am raising a well-known issue: how to reconcile, in the euro zone, price stability with financial stability? We will face a trade-off, as Mr. Greenspan was facing a trade-off during the October 1987 crash. But I think that we have the means to sterilize the monetary consequences of any possible intervention by the ECB acting as a lender of last resort in case of necessity.

We come back here to the discussion about the instruments of the ECB, which is not a purely technical debate. The debate about reserve requirements in the zone, about open market interventions, about collateral and refinancing of commercial banks, is in some way a technical debate. But if you take it also from the point of view that I am putting on the table, that is the possibility to sterilize intervention in case of a big financial or banking liquidity crisis in the euro zone, I think that we have to think now, in order to anticipate what could occur in five, ten or fifteen years from now.

I pass to another aspect of my presentation. What to expect as regards the market shares of the various currencies? Here I come back to the debate about the portfolio shift at the start. We have to make a distinction between the very short-term impact of the introduction of the euro and, I would say, the more permanent effect.

The portfolio shift could be a transitory phenomenon with the issue being overvaluation. I am not so much interested by the debate concerning the hard versus the soft euro, because we are creating the euro not just for six months. We are creating the euro for, I hope, years and possibly decades.

Therefore, I am expecting the euro to be exposed to cycles of overvaluation and undervaluation. As the dollar, since the war, has been exposed to cycles of overvaluation and undervaluation. I cannot forecast the periodicity of those cycles. I think that they will exist in function of the monetary-fiscal mix on the two sides of the Atlantic and some other factors. If we look at market shares, the issue is not whether the euro is going to be a hard currency, too strong or not. The issue has to do with the medium- and long-term credibility of the euro as a currency, that is the possibility for this currency to be used extensively outside the zone. For instance, two thirds of the notes denominated in US dollars are used outside the US, according to Dick Porter and other Federal Reserve Bank people. I was very struck by this figure. Not only in Russia or in Panama, but in the whole of what is called the dollar zone. Could we think at some point that when we introduce euro notes in 2002, a significant proportion of notes denominated in euro are going to be used outside? Not two thirds, but I guess a significant proportion.

I want also to come back to what for me is the substance of the debate. When we look at the market shares of the euro for the future, we have to make a distinction between the financial use and the commercial use of the euro. I think that we agree, that we arrive at some consensus: the euro is going to take big market shares as regards its financial use, due to well-known arguments (diversification, credibility of the zone and deep and resilient financial markets in the zone...). When we look at what could occur as regards the commercial use of the euro, we are less optimistic. Due to inertia, hysteresis—if I want use a complicated word to denominate something which is simple—and the network effect which was already cited, the dollar will continue to prevail for several years.

Here we come back to the Baumol-Tobin argument. If you look at the commercial use, there are some good arguments (economies of scale...) in order to justify concentration. If you look at the financial side, there are good arguments in order to justify diversification. We will see a big gap for several years—I cannot say whether it is going to be three years or ten years, it is difficult to know—between the financial use of the euro and its commercial use. The problem we have here is whether this gap between the two aspects of the international role of the euro will remain rather significant and whether, if it is increasing, at some point there could be a big problem (e.g. a negative feedback effect on the financial use of the euro). I think that such a gap is going to be difficult to sustain in the medium and long term. At some point, either such a gap could jeopardize the financial role of the euro, or, due to the fact that the financial role is going to stay, there will be some kind of endogenous forces which will lead the commercial use of the euro to increase in order to fill the gap. When I was looking at the literature concerning this aspect, I had a concept which I take from Sir John Hicks, namely the distinction between what he called a 'full currency' and a 'partial currency' or 'partial money'. In *The Two Triads* he formulated a nice theory about all these concepts, the complete money versus the partial money. For the euro to become a complete currency, in the sense of Hicks, we have to fill this gap.

When I look at the specific forecasts for the commercial use of the euro at the international level, I think that due to a network effect, it is going to be a step function. There will be some discontinuity in the possibility of the euro increasing its market share as regards its commercial use. That is, whenever the euro reaches a certain threshold—I don't know, 20 percent, 30 percent, 40 percent—there is going to be an acceleration towards the next threshold. We have to think in terms of a step function if we want to anticipate the evolution of the increase of the euro on the commercial side, whereas, if I look at the financial role of the euro, besides the portfolio shift at the start, I anticipate a more progressive, continuous function.

A. Clesse: Merci beaucoup, M. de Boissieu. Perhaps we should take a few minutes for questions or comments following the presentations by Robert McCauley, Hélène Rey, Richard Portes and Christian de Boissieu, before moving on to the impact of the euro on international stability. Mr. Patterson.

G. Patterson: I have a quick question for Professor de Boissieu. He was emphasizing, as indeed did previous speakers, the importance of developing liquid and deep financial markets for the future of the euro. Professor de Boissieu touched on a matter which is at the moment much concerning the European Parliament's monetary subcommittee, namely prudential supervision. There seems to be a gap in the system in that the European Central Bank has no responsibility at all for prudential supervision. On the principle of home country control it is devolved down—or, rather, it remains devolved. But different member states in the euro area, and outside the euro area but in the EU, have very different systems. Does Professor de Boissieu think that we should develop a uniform system of prudential supervision? Does he think that the best model for this would be central bank supervision? Which I have to say Mr. Duisenberg doesn't want. Does he think it ought to be the Commission or does he think we have to have an entirely new organization to manage this?

C. de Boissieu: In order to clarify the debate when looking at banking and financial crises, I need to make a clear distinction between three aspects: prudential policies, deposit insurance schemes and lender of last resort facilities. I was talking in my presentation about the curative aspect (lender of last resort facilities). You are coming back, rightly, to the preventive aspect: prudential policies, including perhaps deposit insurance schemes.

According to the Maastricht Treaty, prudential policy is a matter for national authorities. There is no debate concerning the devolution of power. It is the same for deposit insurance.

Second aspect of my answer. Because it is a question for national authorities, we have perhaps to deepen our coordination in order to limit competitive distortions among member countries. I have no problem when I look at banking commissions. In Germany the banking commission is formally attached to the Ministry of Finance, despite the fact that the Bundesbank employs more than 100 persons in order to implement banking supervision. In France, the banking commission is officially attached to the *Banque de France*. I think that we could live in the euro zone with these kinds of institutional discrepancies.

Nevertheless, we must deepen our coordination through some new European directives. Just two examples. There is no European directive concerning liquidity rules. Perhaps, at some point, it will be necessary if not to come to the same rule in each member country, at least to reduce discrepancies as regards liquidity rules in the banking sector in Europe. Second example: internal control. In the aftermath of the current crisis, internal control is becoming the big topic. It would be crazy to say that we must have the same rule for internal control in France, in Germany or in the UK... I am not saying this. What I am saying is that through some kind of a European directive, we must establish some general guidelines (also at the G-10 level, through the Basle Committee) in order to reduce existing gaps, each member country being free to adjust to this new European directive according to its willingness to do so. If you look at the issue of deposit insurance, we have a 1994 European directive, which is very general. If you look at the current situation in the countries belonging to the euro zone or to the EU zone we see a wide variety of deposit insurance schemes. I am not saying that we must converge to the same solution, but we must reduce some of our discrepancies.

A. Clesse: Thank you very much. I beg you to be brief in your questions or comments.

C. Kindleberger: I have a very brief comment.

A. Clesse: The conference is in your honor, so I can't refuse your request.

C. Kindleberger: I am impressed by the fact that scientific knowledge grows by steps. First David Currie who said that the euro would bring a big wave of reserves to Europe and depreciate the dollar. Then I read McCauley who said that the world would also issue liabilities in Europe to weaken the euro, build back the dollar. Next I hear Portes say that the world would also buy European securities. But I wonder whether we should not also worry whether investment outside Europe would be high or low to determine whether the asset ratio will be more important than the liability ratio?

A. Clesse: Shall we take a few other questions first, very quickly, and then we can react to all this together. Agnès Bénassy-Quéré.

A. Bénassy-Quéré: I wanted to comment on the second part of Christian de Boissieu's intervention. I think he said something very true which is, although there are large externalities between the various functions of an international currency, the development of one function, namely the vehicle function, does not guarantee the development of all other functions and especially the trade invoicing function. However, I think the development of another function could fill the gap he mentioned. This function is the anchor function. The countries in the area around Euroland will have a big incentive to peg their currencies, or loosely peg their currencies, to the euro. Once they have done that, they will have a big incentive to denominate their trade in euros. So this could fill the gap that Christian de Boissieu mentioned. Besides, this makes a bridge between the discussion before and after the coffee break: Robert McCauley was saying this morning that Euroland would be more interested in the euro-dollar exchange rate than would be the US, because a larger share of international trade is done by countries which peg their currencies to the dollar. This could become less true as time goes on, because on the one hand, part of the Asian countries will not find much incentive to peg their currency to the dollar any longer. On the other hand, more and more countries will want to peg their currencies to the euro. This could re-balance cooperation.

G. Ross: I just want to ask a question. At the end of Portes' and Rey's paper, and de Boissieu's as well, there is a whole list of topics about which one worries—about the risk management capacities of the whatever it is, the ECB or the European Union. I would like to have their answers, or some people's answers of how to ameliorate risk management capacities institutionally over time to maximize the possibilities for managing these risks successfully. In other words, what evolution of institutions and maybe even *moeurs* is necessary to raise the barrier maximally to prevent disaster?

K. Deutsch: Two short questions to both Mme Rey and to Mr. McCauley. What do you think are the implications of any adjustments in financial flows and stocks on the interest rate environment in Europe and potentially also on the desirability or feasibility of exchange rate management in the transatlantic context?

A. Clesse: Who wants to answer these different questions? For example, Hélène Rey, you were asked directly. There was the question by Charles Kindleberger also. Would you like to respond, Hélène Rey?

H. Rey: I will reply to the question on interest rates. I have worked a bit on the relations between US and European interests rates over the last 6 years.

Before beginning my work, my intuition was that when the European block would be more integrated on a monetary level, there would be a decrease in the correlation between European and US interest rates. For there would be two big entities face to face, rather than one big block and a smaller one consisting of small countries that follow the big country's leadership.

But when one looks at empirical evidence on interest rates over the last years, one becomes aware of the fact that, except for some episodes and some years, the leadership of US interest rates over the interest rates of the various European countries was not at all manifest. The correlations fluctuate significantly according to the various periods. It is therefore not obvious at all to draw any firm conclusions.

C. de Boissieu: I would like to say a few words on the question by Mr. Ross regarding the institutional aspects. If one wants a better risk management— in my presentation I had financial and bank risk in mind, but others are to be taken into consideration too—one has to bring out the institutional challenge, which is not exclusively related to the advent of the euro. In all the countries you have a challenge, which is to improve the coordination between the regulatory authorities that deal with banks, those that deal with the markets and those that deal with insurance companies. There has been some progress in terms of international coordination between national banking regulations and the Committee of Basel, and with Brussels thanks to the European Commission. I think that there has to be an effort everywhere and this is where perhaps the euro will be the opportunity for us to make some progress regarding the coordination between banking authorities and the authorities that are in charge of the markets. As long as we have not made progress regarding coordination, we will be ill-prepared to manage systemic risks.

As for my comments on the lender of last resort in conjunction with the role of the ECB, the problem does not appear to me to be of an institutional nature. Rather, it is a reflection upon the ECB's role in the years to come and how to manage to combine the objective of price stability with that of financial stability in the euro zone. But I do think nevertheless that Mr. Greenspan has given us over the last 11 years some examples of how these are *grosso modo* compatible and that the response is not predominantly institutional.

R. Portes: Following what Christian just said, unfortunately things moved in the wrong direction in terms of the relationship between the monetary authority and the supervising and regulating authorities. What we have seen with the move to the European Central Bank is another layer added of separation and of informational confusion and distortion between the actual hands on supervision and regulation which are under national authorities (and typically not the national central banks in many cases), and the European Central Bank in Frankfurt, which has no direct relationship to those national supervising authorities at all. This is the situation and the risks involved, and also by the way some of these questions of lender of last resort, are discussed in a very recent CEPR publication called *Monitoring the European Central Bank*, but it seems to me that we have gone exactly in the wrong direction. And sooner I hope rather than later, the trend will be towards more centralized authority for the ECB in dealing with these supervision and regulation issues. I think this is a very dangerous area right now and this was also dealt with, by the way, in the IMF capital market report this last autumn. The authorities, I have to say both the national and the eurotower authorities, are very sensitive on this point and they have a lot to be sensitive about. This is a serious issue and I don't think this has been handled very well.

A. Clesse: I have the feeling that Robert McCauley has something very important to say.

R. McCauley: Klaus Deutsch asked about capital flows and interest rates in Euroland. I expect that changes in US long-term interest rates and shifts in the capital flows between the United States and Europe will exert less influence on long-term interest rates in Europe than they did, for instance, in 1994. The euro bond market will be a great place to borrow, so you will see a lot of foreign issuance in the long term. Perhaps of more importance for European long-term interest rates, however, will be the speed with which the Italian government extends the maturity of its debt and eventually the speed with which the UK household sector shifts its mortgages from floating to fixed rates.

Richard Portes asserted that asset shifts will happen faster than liability shifts. I shall not dwell on the high fraction of short-term debt in the international financial system that Korea's unhappy experience in late 1997 underscored or the use of derivatives to switch currency denomination even before a bond matures. Let me point out, however, that as countries have drawn IMF credit denominated in SDRs to pay off dollar interbank credits, we are already seeing a substitution of the euro, or perhaps proto-euro, for the dollar in the international liability structures of emerging market countries.

Session 4: The Impact of the Euro on International Stability

A. Clesse: The topic of session 4 is the impact of the euro on international stability. Now, there is no pre-established order. The program is an alphabetical one. Looking at the topics proposed, I think perhaps Richard Cooper's one is the widest: *The Impact of EMU on the Rest of the World* and especially on the international role of the dollar. I think Jeffrey Frankel will also cover this topic and in a sense, Hervé Carré. Tomorrow morning also a Chinese scholar will be with us to speak on this. Richard Cooper, please.

R. Cooper: This session is called *The Impact of the Euro on International Stability* and it follows very naturally from the previous panel. I want to start where Rey and Portes left off. I am extremely sympathetic with the framework they laid out, with the factors that they identified. I think that they emphasized the right issues.

I would just like to add one point to what they said—it was implicit in what they said but I would like to make it explicit. When we talk about the euro or the dollar, we are actually speaking in metaphorical terms. Apart from greenbacks, the dollar doesn't exist. Euro notes won't exist until 2002. The Hong Kong Monetary Authority doesn't decide whether to hold dollars or euros or yen, it has to decide whether it wants to hold dollar-denominated somethings, or euro-denominated somethings, or yen-denominated somethings. Therefore when one addresses the international role of the euro, or of the dollar, one has to ask very concretely what is the something that is being held? The point is implicit in the Rey-Portes analysis, but it needs underlining that 'the dollar' is a metaphor, and at the operational level people are dealing in dollar-denominated somethings. Similarly, 'the euro' is a metaphor; economic agents are going to make their decisions about euro-denominated somethings. Therefore, when one talks about the international role of the euro, one has to ask very specifically: what are the somethings that we are talking about? McCauley addressed it in part, and Rey and Portes addressed it in part. I like the Rey-Portes emphasis on network externalities. I differ however with their conclusions. I believe that the process of developing widely acceptable euro-denominated securities is going to take much more time than Portes suggested.

Before I give the reasons, I want to make some distinctions, because currencies have very different international roles. I expect the issuance of euro-denominated securities to rise rapidly. That is McCauley's point. But I also expect the issuance of dollar-denominated securities internationally to rise rapidly. Both are related to the increasing globalization of the world economy.

We are going to see a continuing diversification across currencies. That does not involve a substitution of one for the other. It involves a continuing rapid growth of the share of international issues relative to purely domestic issues.

For concreteness, I will focus on foreign exchange reserve holdings as the leading single proxy for the internationalization of a currency. What monetary authorities hold is closely related to their perceptions of the accessibility of markets and is closely related to the vehicle use of currencies. It is also closely related to the holdings for transaction purposes of large private firms such as Exxon and BP.

I believe that the internationalization of the euro will be a good deal slower than Portes suggested and in my view that makes all the difference in the world. Something that happens over, let's say, ten years has a markedly different dynamic than the same thing happening over twenty-five years. Timing is a critical variable here.

France and Germany have been historically allergic to short-term government debts, and most of their long-term government debt remains in primary placements and does not trade in the secondary market, although France has done a good job over the last decade in developing a secondary market. There is a lot of short-term Italian paper out there. But here is the point: there will not be European paper. There will be Italian paper, there will be German paper, there will be French paper, there will be Dutch paper. If you are the Hong Kong Monetary Authority or the Singapore Monetary Authority or the Reserve Bank of India: what should you hold? I suggest without any aspersion on Italy, that it is going to be some time before monetary authorities will comfortably hold Italian paper, even when it is denominated in euros, in view of past and continuing concerns about Italian government finances.

Ironically, the Stability Pact is an inhibition to the development of the euro as an international currency. The Stability Pact will put sharp limits on the rate of growth of European government paper of all kinds, short-term and long-term.

There is also the question of withholding taxes. Withholding taxes drive foreigners up the wall. There is the question of the secondary market. As I understand it, the European bond market is mainly a primary market. This is changing rapidly, but there is nothing like the secondary market in bonds and particularly government bonds in the United States. The United Kingdom is, of course, an important exception, but British government bonds and bills will still be denominated in pounds, not in euros, for the foreseeable future.

Finally, there is the question of yield. At the moment, the yield on dollar-denominated government securities is higher than the yield on the high quality European government securities. Monetary authorities are not insensitive to yield. So I would argue that habit, liquidity, and yield all argue for continued holding of dollars. The euro will gradually become more important, but I repeat how fast the process takes place makes a big difference. My best guess is that this process will take place much more slowly than Richard Portes suggested.

Suppose that I am wrong. Bob Mundell has supplied us a projection that is illustrative, and it is consistent with an actual projection that Fred Bergsten has made. Mundell shows projections with no increase in dollar balances over the next twelve years and a substantial increase in euros such that by 2010 they will roughly equal holdings of dollars.

This scenario may swell the pride of French Ministry of Finance officials and Brussels officials, but it is close to a disaster scenario. It would really be an extremely turbulent first decade. And it would be even worse if there were some actual switching. As Christian de Boissieu observed, once switching reaches a certain point, sometimes called a tipping point, you can get very rapid movement. Mundell has switching at the margin. All the incremental demand for reserves is in euros. This implies a very substantial deterioration of the current account surplus of Europe, compared with the present situation. It also implies a very substantial reduction of the large US current account deficit currently $200 billion a year, rising to $300 billion as a result of the Asian crisis. What will bring that switch about? The price of the dollar in terms of the euro must drop substantially.

But will that be politically sustainable? It was suggested earlier that that would be a big problem for the United States. To be sure, it would deflate the pride of some of our treasury officials and would hurt people like me who travel a lot, but it would be wholly welcome to American farmers and by American manufacturers, and they are the ones who have the votes. Therefore a depreciation of the dollar brings back John Connally's observation: it is the US currency, but it is the European problem. If the dollar would go down sharply, the yen is likely to go with it, and I ask: how long would European manufacturers and European farmers sit still with an appreciation of the euro relative to the dollar and the yen of the order of 20 percent or more from where we arc now? I picked that number arbitrarily, but markets would think of a change at least that great if there were to be a major switch from dollars to euros. It would create a political crisis. Protectionist pressures would rise sharply in Europe, and anxieties would rise around the world about the viability of the world trading system. We would have a serious management problem. This is not a comfortable scenario. This is a scenario of instability.

How well can we manage such instability, if it were to occur? We touched on that briefly this morning. Portes said he was optimistic about the ability to manage. I am optimistic in terms of the skills and the common sense of the people involved. I am however pessimistic in terms of the institutional set-up. Europe is putting itself into a position to make serious action-orientated international cooperation in the financial area very difficult. This could pose a serious problem, particularly if movement towards the euro goes as rapidly as some think it will. I am not so pessimistic in general, because I think it will go more slowly. So I don't think we will have this crisis scenario.

But if we did, particularly within the next five years, it would reveal the fundamental institutional weaknesses which Randy Henning and others have identified: who in Europe would make the critical decisions, and how quickly?

My forecast would be that the ECB, far from drawing down its now excessive dollar reserves, would add to those reserves in order to keep the euro from appreciating rapidly. We would find ourselves in the same kind of situation that we have had, from time to time, over the last twenty years, because of the impact of exchange rates on the real economy. As long as the ECB could persuade itself that it would not damage price stability, my expectation is we will not see the Mundell scenario because if necessary there would be a substantial increase in European holdings of dollar reserves, which is a paradox.

A. Clesse: Thank you, Richard. Indeed, your forecast would be enough for us to discuss the rest of the afternoon and the whole of tomorrow, but certainly some of the people around this table will support or challenge your forecast and the implications of this scenario. Who would like to follow up? Jeffrey Frankel please.

J. Frankel: Thank you. I am going to speak both about the impact of EMU in general and the impact of the euro *per se*. Let me begin with the observation that some Europeans think that the United States doesn't want EMU to succeed. Maybe this is less of a problem now than it was a year or two ago. I am here in part as a representative of the US administration. So let me just put on the record that I think the progress that was made to meet the Maastricht criteria was very impressive and not entirely forecasted, that EMU is an historic achievement and an inspiring experiment as a large step towards European integration and is welcomed both economically and politically, and we wish it every success. Why has there been this impression at times that Americans don't welcome EMU? I think that Randy Henning said it very well, in addition to stating why we do find it desirable. There are two answers. First with regard to EMU in general. American economists have in the past been skeptical on optimum currency area grounds. And then second, on the euro there is suspicion that it is a negative sum game, that the euro would be a rival for the dollar, which would be bad for the US.

So let me discuss first the effects of EMU on the members of EMU and on the rest of the world and then the effects of the euro on both parties. As far as the effects on the members, my list of criteria for optimum currency areas has got four items on it: trade integration, correlation or symmetry of shocks, labor mobility (which was the original Mundell definition), and fiscal integration. It is a familiar claim that, on these criteria, the EU is less suited for optimum currency areas than are the states of the United States. Let me make a point that might be slightly less familiar. I think there is ground for thinking that as time passes, the European countries will increasingly satisfy the criteria for an optimum currency area. What I have in mind is that, as trade integration goes up, the correlation or the symmetry of shocks goes up. I thought that was an obvious proposition until I read a number of economists, Barry Eichengreen and Paul Krugman in particular, saying the opposite was true, that if countries become more integrated, they specialize more, and shocks will become more asymmetric. But I did some tests with Andy Rose and in our paper just published in the *Economic Journal,* we offer some evidence that the opposite is the case. That is when countries trade more, the correlation goes up, which offers some grounds for thinking that even for some European countries that might be on the margin of satisfying the criteria now, if they are going ahead and join, they may be exposed to higher integration and will satisfy the criteria.

What are the implications of EMU for other countries? There is the question of European countries that hope to join eventually but will have to go through a transition period. I wouldn't rule out the possibility that we would see in the future a repeat of the 1992 crisis in the ERM, or for that matter shades of a currency crisis in other parts of the world more recently, if some country which clearly fails the criteria nonetheless enters a transition towards joining EMU. The overall policy prescription is a very familiar one, I think. If countries are going to give up the monetary independence and if the other criteria can't be accelerated, then what you have to work on is structural reform to reduce market rigidities so that there is less need to adjust to asymmetric shocks in other ways.

What about implications outside of Europe? Assuming that eliminating exchange rate risk and transaction costs promotes trade, one could look at the issue as a case of customs union area theory, of a free trade area theory, that it might be trade averting or trade creating, which would be an important clue as to the effect on the world. But I am optimistic that it will be trade creating, that it will promote growth in Europe and that it will be good for everybody. I think US firms in particular can benefit from the elimination of transaction costs within Europe. There is a sense in which US firms are more experienced than European firms in operating in large markets and benefiting in this way.

Let me now turn to the euro. My list of criteria that qualify a currency to be used as an international currency also has four elements on it, like the earlier list. It has a lot of overlap with Bob Mundell's list and the Portes & Rey list and everyone else's. But let me just go through and give my reading.

1) Size. The US still has a somewhat larger GDP than Euroland. It becomes an approximate tie between the dollar and the euro. This would change if Britain and Sweden and Denmark joined.

2) Historical inertia obviously favors the dollar-network externalities and all that Hélène Rey mentioned.

3) The need for financial markets that are deep and open and liquid and free which Dick Cooper has just mentioned. This criterion, I think, clearly favors the US over the European continent or Japan or just about anywhere else.

4) Confidence in the value of the currency. Here I would say that it is basically a tie. In the 1970s we, in the US, had higher inflation rates certainly than Germany, but I think now, if you look at the recent inflation record in the US and compare it to Europe, I think that is a tie. Any of these criteria could change, but in the way I described them. If you add them up, I still come out with the US dollar ahead. The euro will clearly be the number two as an international reserve currency as of January, immediately ahead of the yen. But I am more with Dick Cooper here. I would say even if there is a tipping phenomenon, so that the consolidation of euro economies has a sort of a disproportionate effect on the use of the euro internationally, I think that tipping wouldn't take place in real time. Tipping doesn't mean it will happen very fast. It will be a very long drawn out process.

What about the impact of all this on home countries and on the rest of the world? We have mostly been talking on the impact on the home countries. My list of benefits is a familiar list here: seigniorage, convenience for one's businessmen, a certain advantage for one's banks.

There are both benefits and costs to have your currency used as an international currency. But beyond that I would say that these are small benefits. Our estimate of US seigniorage from the dollar is about 13 to 16 billion dollars per year (It is a flow per year). It is small, but not nothing.

What about the impact on the world? Now I am coming closer to the assigned topic of the session: the effect of the euro on world stability. Is it in the world's interest to have one international key reserve currency or to have two or more? I can think of good arguments on both sides.

The most obvious argument is on the first side. Why do we have money to begin with? To avoid a double coincidence of wants. Because of network externalities or economies of scale. The reason why we have money to begin with is to cut down the transaction costs. By that logic, it makes sense to have only one. This is certainly in the Kindleberger tradition. Now let me take the occasion and add my name to the list of people who first learned international economics from Charlie Kindleberger. And there is the issue of instability Richard Cooper was just mentioning, a world with two currencies at a stage when they are in competition could be unstable, which is part of the issue for the historical precedent of the pound versus the dollar in the inter-war period.

There is an argument on the other side, however, which is that if there is just one currency, that the host country could abuse its privilege and print too much of this currency, inflate—that is the way many Europeans felt about the US dollar in the 1960s. The idea here is that if you have two or more currencies, you have healthy competition, each keeping the other honest, and a certain discipline, so as to avoid abusing the position.

I don't have a strong feeling as to which is the right answer. I can just say that I think that the US Government is relaxed about our ability to compete. The dollar's international currency status is just one more reason on a list of reasons why one wants to follow sound macroeconomic policies and preserve the stability of one's currency.

Just one final note on the question of three or more. Obviously there are other currencies in the world that are used outside their home country, that have some international currency role, the yen and others. I have not believed in the past and I don't believe now that it is really a three bloc world. I have been writing for some time that the currency of Asia is really the dollar much more than the yen and I still believe that. For example, I don't think the Chinese yuan is a plausible candidate to be a currency of Asia, because it lacks those deep, open, liquid, free financial markets in particular. So I think we are heading towards a bipolar currency world rather than a tripolar one.

A. Clesse: I saw the Ambassador of China in Luxembourg listening with a lot of interest to your last remarks about the possibilities and non-possibilities of the yuan. Should we now move perhaps to Hervé Carré from the European Commission?

H. Carré: In my presentation, I would like to discuss two issues. First, the external stability of the euro and then the international stability which touches on the theme of this afternoon.

Among the various determinants of an exchange rate, I would like to cite some which seem to me to be of particular relevance.

The first and foremost determinant will be inflation expectations prevailing in the area. Given the anti-inflation commitment of the ECB, there should be no particular threat to a stable euro from this perspective.

The second determinant, which is quite important also, is the current account position of the euro area. As you know, the current account is at present in surplus and it will remain in surplus in the near term. This surplus is, in absolute terms, the largest of the three major currency areas. I could also subscribe to the remarks by Jeffrey Frankel. I don't know what the third one is, at the world level at least. This surplus could contribute to broad pressure on the euro exchange rate. However, to the extent that this current account disequilibrium reflects different cyclical positions, or some structural adjustments, which are taking place now, there is no reason to worry about these imbalances as such.

But maybe the most important determinant of the exchange rate of the euro in the future will be the policy mix. In this regard, monetary policy will be supported by the fiscal discipline implied by the operation of the stability and growth pact and an acceleration in supply side reform, which has moved to the top of the EU policy agenda since Cardiff and the UK Presidency. Such an acceleration in economic reform will help to further reduce the counter-inflationary burden on monetary policy. So we see that fundamentals will be strengthened by the policy mix as we can expect it.

I would entirely agree with what Richard Portes and Hélène Rey have said on the capital markets. Europe will have deep, wide and resilient capital markets. Of course, they will differ from the US market because there will be no equivalent to the US Treasury and this is quite important. However, new rules and conventions have been agreed for the bond market, outstanding public debt will be redenominated as from January 4, new issues of public debt will be in euro. We will have as from January 4, 1999 a very efficient capital market. We can expect from the operation of this capital market a more efficient monetary policy and better allocation of resources. That is quite important for the future of Europe.

Let me turn now to the international financial system. For us, in the Commission, the prospects for the euro as an international currency will depend on the quality of economic management in the euro area. I am convinced that the framework of macroeconomic stability and market-based competition in the EMU will ensure that the euro area economy is well managed. On the other hand, nobody can expect international investors to take these assurances on trust. Policy-makers in the euro area will have to deliver. They will have to demonstrate a clear enduring commitment to the principles that they have signed up in the Treaty. But as the strength of this commitment becomes clear, I believe the euro will gradually emerge as a major international currency. Over time, we expect to see the euro used increasingly as a store of value in denominating financial liabilities, as a portfolio currency, as a unit of account in trade, as a means of payment and, of course, as an official reserve currency.

Following the previous speaker's remarks, I personally regret that the international aspects of the EMU are so often discussed in terms of rivalry between the US and Europe, between the euro and the US dollar. It has to be recognized that the introduction of the euro is not motivated by the desire within the European Union to become a global counterweight to the United States. The objective of the EMU and the euro is to create a more efficient, a more dynamic, a more prosperous Europe in order to cut unacceptably high unemployment rates. But, a more dynamic and a more prosperous Europe is good for the US and for the world economy.

It has also to be recognized that the emergence of the euro as a major international currency will alter the structure of the international financial system. The system will become either bipolar with the dollar and the euro as main currencies or multipolar with other major currencies.

The implications of such a new structure for the stability of exchange rates are quite uncertain. Greater exchange rate stability can be expected if sound economic policies are pursued in all of the major currency areas. In these circumstances, market expectations will adjust relatively smoothly to international economic developments implying correspondingly smooth movements in interest rates and exchange rates. However, in the event that economic policies in one or more of the major currency areas were not sound, there would be a clear risk of a destabilizing exchange rate volatility. So, Europe will share an even greater responsibility with the US to guarantee the smooth operation of the international financial system.

To conclude, there is a need for improving the quality of macroeconomic dialogue in the major currency areas. Improvements would include enhanced surveillance by the relevant international organization so as to ensure greater transparency in economic developments and policies in each currency area. With the benefits of greater transparency, policy-makers in the main currency areas could intensify cooperation, and cooperation would include greater and more timely exchange of information and more frequent multilateral discussions in order to identify policy inconsistencies.

I agree with the conclusions drawn by Richard Portes on this issue. These practical improvements are clearly within reach. They would present a good beginning. Whether an improved macroeconomic dialogue would evolve into more concrete forms of international policy coordination is difficult to foresee right now. But there is no doubt that Europe with a single currency and a single voice—this has been achieved two days ago—will be in a better position to fulfil its responsibility in this respect.

J. Frieden: I too want to focus on a broad interpretation of the international position of the euro. That is, not just the use of the euro in invoicing or other commercial and financial matters, but also the potential role of the euro, or more properly the euro zone authorities in international monetary affairs. What kinds of policies might be undertaken? What attempts at macroeconomic coordination might be undertaken? What is the potential for the emergence of currency blocs, the extent to which the euro presages a bipolar monetary order? I want to do it from a somewhat different angle than the other speakers, although most of them have alluded to what I want to focus on, which is the political side of determinants of the euro's international role.

The issues raised and discussed in detail by Portes and Rey, Mundell, and others are important both for the economic, commercial and financial use of the euro, and for its role in international monetary affairs. The economic factors, externalities, portfolio shifts and things of that sort are crucially important. However I want to—given my inherent belief in comparative advantage—emphasize how the euro's international role is also, importantly, a function of euro zone monetary and financial policy, both short-term and long-term. These euro zone policies will be made in the typical and characteristic way of conflicting interests in clashing institutions that characterizes international monetary policy in all countries.

At the core, in the simplest sense, the usual trade-off arises between domestic and international monetary objectives, where one must give either on the domestic front to obtain international objectives, or on the international front to obtain domestic objectives. In the case of the euro, this potential clash of interests has an added level of institutional and political complexity and uncertainty due to the multi-country nature of the euro zone. So we are not just talking about the domestic politics of the euro in a single country. We are talking about domestic politics of the euro in a context in which there are many national domestic politics, there are many national political institutions and some supranational 'domestic' political institutions as well.

So on what policy and political base might we expect the euro's international position to depend, and what conflicts might we expect to develop over them? All three of them, in one way or another, have been mentioned by previous authors. I focus on the domestic—and by domestic I mean euro zone—political aspect of all three of them.

The first is the specific exchange rate stance *per se* in the short term; that is whether the euro will be relatively weaker or relatively stronger. And it may well be, as Christian de Boissieu says, that this is not of particular importance over the long run, because the euro will probably go through typical cycles of over- and undervaluation. But it is of course the case that a euro expected to be relatively weak and expected to weaken in the initial phases is going to be less likely to attract holders. If it is the case that markets perceive euro policy as either aiming at, or leading to a relatively weak euro, there will probably be little desire on the part of monetary authorities to coordinate—one can do that without too much macroeconomic policy coordination. Here the trade-off involves the traditional one between credibility and competitiveness; that is, anti-inflationary credibility, and competitiveness for tradables producers. As a result, there are easily expected differences among important groups in the euro zone and the countries that make it up.

The financial markets tend to be particularly desirous of a relatively strong euro, especially because they look forward to the increased international role of the euro and some of the denomination rents associated with that international currency status.

Obviously import and export competers, the manufacturers that Dick Cooper mentioned prominently, are certain to be very unhappy with a strong and strengthening euro.

So there will be debates over the specific level of the euro's exchange rate and those debates will be important. They may also, in fact, spill over into non-monetary policy areas. A very strong euro, about which nothing is done, is almost certain to lead to protectionist pressures from tradables producers, and that could have detrimental effects, both on European policy and on Europe's relations with the rest of the world.

The second issue is the more general and overall stance of international monetary policy. What I have in mind here is the priority placed on international versus domestic prerogatives, or international versus domestic goals. The kind of trade-off that one thinks of here is that between flexibility and exchange rate stability. Markets often focus on the degree to which monetary authorities target, say, nominal exchange rate stability, or whether there is single-minded concern with responding to domestic monetary and macroeconomic conditions. Again, there are many in the financial markets who are concerned primarily to ensure that euro zone international monetary policy tries to stabilize the euro-dollar and other euro rates. But there are also many inside Europe—from all across the political spectrum—who believe that euro zone monetary policy should be aggressively internally orientated, and we have had some discussion already about how the relative closure of the euro zone with EMU might contribute to this.

Within this, of course, there is the more specific question of particular exchange rate arrangements which obviously would involve subordinating euro domestic policy to international agreements. Again, some will want them, and some will not. There is also institutional uncertainty about how those agreements might be negotiated and enforced, which raises a whole host of other problems. So the second issue is that of the broader stance of priorities involved in international monetary policy, domestic or international.

The third is the depth and predictability of European financial markets and the European financial environment, something that both Christian de Boissieu and others have focused on. Here, I think almost all of us expect a rapid consolidation and even convergence of European financial markets and banking systems. There are many unresolved issues, from the lender of last resort issue through financial regulation to a host of others. I think that their non-resolution would have a dampening effect on the general use of the euro in international trade and payments, simply because they would not provide the depth and breadth of financial markets that holders of international currencies look for.

These issues too, as is implicit in the comments made so far, are very controversial within the euro zone. The assignment of lender of last resort facilities to national authorities or supranational authorities raises very important distributional issues, as well as very important potential coordination issues. There are possible bailout problems, moral hazard and things of that nature. The same is true about regulatory issues. In every other aspect of European regulatory policy, so too in financial markets, there are major disagreements among different national and subnational financial sectors about how regulatory policy should evolve.

So whether with regard to short-term exchange rate policies—a relatively stronger or weaker euro; or longer-term stances to privilege either exchange rate stability or domestic price stability and macroeconomic stability; or with regard to the financial depth and regulatory capacity of the European financial space, there are certainly conflicts of interest over all these policies.

In addition to the conflicts of interest, there is also a great deal of institutional uncertainty. Without going into detail, I want to raise once more a point that I mentioned in response to Randy Henning's remarks, that is the relationship between monetary and fiscal policy. Randy dealt very well with one aspect of it. My point was not so much that the monetary-fiscal mix would be optimal in some sense, but that—as de Boissieu said—typically in national policy making, where you have an independent central bank and a government, there is a complex and often repeated dynamic game played between the government and the monetary authorities over the monetary and fiscal mix. The fact that that game exists does not imply that it will reach Pareto optimality. But where it is successfully institutionalized and routinized, there is some uneasy coexistence in which the monetary authorities know that there are constraints upon their actions imposed by the potential fiscal response of the government and the government knows vice versa. So there is, as I say, a sort of complicated game between monetary and fiscal authorities.

This set of either formal or informal institutional relationships is essentially absent in the euro zone. It is conceivable, and this is what Randy was saying, that it is not necessary. I tend to believe that if monetary policy pursued by the ECB is not to the liking of important groups in European society pressures will be exerted either on national governments or on European institutional authorities to do something about it, whether in trade policy or in fiscal policy at the national level or perhaps at the European level. The institutions of the European Union and of the euro zone will have to find a way to deal with these cross-coming institutional pressures.

My point, simply put, is that as with all international currencies, as indeed with all currencies, domestic political factors are crucial. The interests and the institutions that characterize and lead to pressures on European monetary and other economic policy-making authorities will be powerful. They are predictable in some sense, but unpredictable in others, because we don't exactly know what sort of shocks Europe will face, what sorts of institutional innovations will be undertaken. But I would argue that a true understanding of the euro's international role and of the participation of the euro in international discussions over monetary and macroeconomic stability depend crucially on the political and institutional line-up within the euro zone.

R. Mundell: Just a short comment. A qualification to Dick Cooper's devastating scenario which isn't exactly the same as mine. Because if, as we assume, there is an increasing demand for euros of the order of some 100 billion dollars a year, that doesn't impose an equivalent current account deficit on Europe, unless, as I said in my paper, there are no countervailing capital movements. It is quite conceivable that this build-up of liquid euro liabilities could be offset by long-term lendings. Europe itself becomes a banker in the same way the United States did.

V. Klaus: I have a very short remark to M. Carré. First a comment and then a question.

First, listening to his presentation, I think his presentation was different from the rest of the group. I don't know how to put it politely. His speech was full of normative statements. There was no analysis and no description of the real world if you listen to him carefully. I am oversensitive to that because of my past. He was speaking very often in terms of 'politicians *could* increase cooperation', 'politicians *should* increase the exchange of information', and so on. The whole presentation was done in this framework which is, in my opinion, typical of exponents of the euro. I have problems with such a way of looking at things.

My question: You mentioned a very strange thing. Maybe I am not studying carefully enough the economic literature concerning European Monetary Union. In your presentation I heard, for the first time, in this context, the term 'policy mix'. This is something that I do not fully understand. Of course, I know what we normally mean by policy mix. So I know what I am talking about. But when you speak about European Monetary Union, I am a little puzzled. I can imagine the monetary policy of a European Monetary Union, but I can't imagine the fiscal policy of a European Monetary Union. So my question is: When you talk about policy mix, I would ask: 'Whose policy mix?' Who is the agent maximizing something, some target, some utility function? Who is making the fiscal policy? You mentioned, if I am not wrong, 'fiscal restraint'. What is fiscal restraint? We all know from our own countries that to impose fiscal restraints of up to one percent more or less of the fiscal deficit, of the fiscal surplus, is for governments to lose elections, to go out of power. To repeat, I don't know 'whose' fiscal policy?

H. Carré: I understand that I have been normative. I am not an academic. I do not come from the academic world. I do not come from government circles. I come from the Commission staff. That is very different. The 'policy mix' is the subject of many studies published every year by DG II and I would refer you to those studies. In the case of the external aspects of EMU, we spent some time, three years ago, on a study which was made public two years ago—I am surprised that you have not read it. On fiscal restraint, I have been asked what is the fiscal authority within the European Union? Of course there are 11 fiscal policy-makers within the Union. This is the unique character of EMU. However, the aggregate of 11 fiscal stances makes one fiscal stance. In the future, you can expect that the analysis of that stance will draw increasing attention.

R. Rosecrance: I am really delighted to be here. It is an extremely distinguished gathering and I have certainly learned a lot. And I would like to raise our sights just a little to talk not just about the various particular problems of the change over to the euro but of the impact of the euro upon international stability as a whole. And if you pardon me, I would just like to step back for a moment and consider the general problems of international stability. I am not an economist but rather an international relations type, so I want to bring in some of the political factors as well as the economic ones.

The current international system is at least volatile and perhaps unstable. The reason for that is that the US deficits however large they may become (and for this year they are estimated to be around 300 billion dollars or so) will not be sufficient to absorb over time the production of our friends in Latin America and Eastern Asia. So that there is a tremendous amount of export capacity that does not get taken up by the world markets, however large the American market may be. Now, if this is true then the United States, as an international stabilizer and as a market of last resort, is unable completely to carry the load. So my essential argument is that the US needs a stabilizing partner to carry this task, to somehow recirculate the surpluses that are being earned by certain countries in Eastern Asia.

Now, I think this function is one that has been very effectively discharged by countries in the past. If you look at Britain in the 19th century, the last year in which Britain had a trade surplus, as opposed to an invisible surplus, was 1822. After that it had a balance of payments surplus but it did not have a trade surplus. What it did, that was extremely interesting, was to finance the investments that it had made in other countries and to allow the countries to discharge their indebtedness to the United Kingdom by permitting them to sell in the British home market. So that by 1910-1913 virtually all of the countries that had become indebted to Britain as a result of British investments or loans (the United States, Germany, practically all the Commonwealth countries and so on) had surpluses in the British home market. Only India still had a deficit. So that the UK managed to allow the indebted countries to pay it back. And therefore it recirculated the surpluses in a fairly effective way.

Now, if that was the pattern in the 19th century, I think the problem today is if the United States needs a stabilizing partner, that partner is not going to be Japan. It has not been Japan, and I think it will not be Japan over the long term, at least in economic terms. Perhaps in political and strategic and other terms Japan will still be very important to the United States. But Japan continues to insist on foreign trade surpluses. And, of course, the current deflation that we have in Japan that now looks as if it is going to continue through this year and into next year is going to make this situation of surpluses even worse. And in so far as Japan has coped with the problem of its surpluses, it has done so, I think only by disguising its surpluses through manufacturing in export platforms in East Asian countries which then sell to the United States. The goods seem to be East Asian goods, but they are indirectly part of the Japanese surplus. So, I think that there is a real problem with Japan as an economic stabilizer. It still wishes to advance its position vis-à-vis others rather than to allow others to rise. And there is a famous computer game, which I do not want to spend a lot of time talking about today, called 'Sharks and Fishes'. You can get it on your PC if you wish, and in this game the objective is to get a stable population of sharks and fish. Before this game starts you have to decide certain things (how many sharks, how many fish, what is the breeding time of sharks, what is the breeding time of fish, the life span of sharks and fish and so on) and the assumption in the game is that the fish live on abundant plankton so you do not have to worry much about their food supply, but the sharks, of course, live on the fish. Now, when you start this, you plug in something like 1000 fish and 50 sharks and then you push the button and you see these lines on the computer, as the population of each of them goes up and down. Usually it turns out after about 4000 iterations the sharks eat up all the fish. Now, that is a fairly short-sighted policy because then, of course, the sharks all die. I always tell this parable when I go to Japan because, it seems to me, it is very necessary to point out that if they are eating us they should eat us a little bit less rapaciously so that we have time to regenerate and build-up the food that they need later on. This is a parable to indicate that the Japanese have not succeeded in acting as a stabilizing force in international economics.

Now, the question that I want to raise this morning is: can Europe be a stabilizing partner for the United States if it is true that Japan has not and is not going to perform that function? I think the answer to that is possibly 'yes'. But, this depends very much on the policy Europe decides to follow in the next ten or twenty years. And, I think, it is very important to talk about partners in stability. I have learned a tremendous amount from my colleague, Professor Kindleberger, who talked about leadership which was transmuted in international political economy to the hegemonic stability theory that people deduce from his work. I am not at all arguing that it is not useful to have a single stabilizer or a single leader if that can be attained. But I think there is enough historical evidence, some of that given by Barry

Eichengreen and others and also in an influential paper by Duncan Snidal in 1985, that it is possible to achieve the same sort of results with a group of cooperators in this system, even though a single power can obviously do the job very effectively as well. So, I think the situation that we face today is that there is no single power stabilizer in the international economic system. We are going to have to focus on the three or four, or two or three groupings or powers to serve this purpose. I am speculating now on the possibility that Europe and the United States might be the core of that group. Because if it turns out that one of the functions of the new euro is to really become a world reserve currency, then in order to do that you have to put the euro into other people's hands. There are only two ways in which that can be done: one is by lending abroad and the other by running a deficit in the balance of trade, so that others can acquire the euro and use it for their own purposes. I was very impressed with the statement of Professor Mundell on page 15 of his paper in which he points out, 'as the euro builds up and becomes a reserve currency', perhaps totaling 40 percent of the reserves of the international system, that this massive shift towards the euro, unless it were offset by increasing lending by euro and increased borrowing by the United States, would mean for Europe a massive shift in current account balances, with that of the Europeans turning negative and that of the United States moving into a more positive position.

So, I think this is the kind of question that one faces when one thinks of the euro becoming a major international reserve currency. And I think one should think very carefully about how desirable this is. It may be very desirable from a world perspective, but it is conceivable one can look at it from a purely European, a sort of sectarian perspective, and say it might not be wholly desirable because, how many Korean cars does France want to import? How many Chinese textiles do Germany and Italy wish to see within their economy? So, a high-valued euro would suck in imports in a major way and you need a euro of this kind, I think, to really be an effective reserve currency. If you do achieve this high-valued euro over a period of ten, twenty years, whatever it may be, as a reserve currency competing with the dollar, this would considerably ease the burden the United States faces, because it would allow the United States to depreciate its currency to some degree and to regain some of the economic strength that it has lost in previous years. Now, this prospect, of course, could be very destabilizing. You could have, as Professor Kindleberger hints in his new paper: 'Bipolar conflict between Europe and the United States over economics', something that would succeed the bipolar conflict between the United States or the West as a whole and the Russia of the Cold War. And no one wants that. One wants to have a stabilizing arrangement, not a volatile and destabilizing one. We do not want to get into competitive exchange depreciations again as we did in the 1930s. Therefore, it seems to me, we need a new forum, a transatlantic forum, at least in terms of discussion and perhaps, even further than that, in terms of helping to set exchange rate policy between Europe and the United States. Otherwise, one could have a new economic conflict in world politics and not have this sort of stabilizing arrangement I have been talking about. We want to go behind regional blocks, beyond NAFTA in North America and beyond the EU in Europe.

My own judgement is that we are not going to have a world government in the near future, nor indeed will the United Nations ever develop into a world government. What we have are a whole series of clubs and a club network can be a very destabilizing one, if these clubs are exclusive. But what I see emerging in world economic politics now is what I would call 'overlapping clubs', so that as the clubs get formed there are ways of bringing them back into relationships to one another; even if an East Asian club were to be formed the WTO could become an overlapping club bringing the groups together. And, I think, particularly in regard to Europe and the United States, something better than anything we have now in terms of consultation on monetary questions is really necessary. So, I end my talk with a notion that perhaps we are going to be pressed to avoid conflict between Europe and the United States and to serve these stabilizing functions to create a new transatlantic overlapping club.

A. Clesse: Thank you, Richard. Are there any comments regarding the analysis of Richard Rosecrance? And perhaps also the possible impact of the Euro in Asia. Richard Cooper.

R. Cooper: The shark-fish metaphor is a very colorful one, but metaphors can mislead as well as illuminate. Exactly what food are the Japanese 'sharks' eating? In what sense are the Japanese eating the rest of us up? Rather than leave a group like this with the impression that the Japanese are playing a notorious role in the world economy, we need to be told in what way. That metaphor needs to be clarified. One can argue that the economic problem up until 1997 has been: too few goods, not too many. If we can find people in the world that are willing to accept low rates of return and price their goods accordingly, why should the rest of us worry about that?

C. de Boissieu: I have a question which is the following. I agree with you when you are talking about the necessity to have some cycles in our balance of payments over time. If we want to facilitate the use of the euro outside we could come back to something close to the Triffin dilemma. We could have the feeling that there will be a zero-sum game between the US, Japan and the euro zone as regards the structure of their balance of payments. This would be misleading. We must also take into account the role of emerging countries and the fact that there will not be a zero-sum game between the US, Japan and the euro zone in terms of balance of payments. Other parts of the world will take their part of the adjustment.

K.-H. Paqué: I would briefly add a point which links back to what Richard Cooper said basically. Again the metaphor of the sharks and the fish. And, what Japan has done for years now is that it really has kept back its internal absorption, both in the short term and also in the long term because it does not deregulate its heavily protected service sector. It has an efficient traded goods sector but a vastly inefficient non-traded goods sector, and in macroeconomic terms this leads to very low productivity in investment which then in the end leads to the curious situation that these are extremely low interest rates, with a low level of new investment. So, the country hurts itself dramatically. For the last few years this has become visible. So Japan hurts itself more than the rest of the world. I would completely agree with Richard Cooper on that. The question is, of course, whether this will be a stable situation in the long run because at some point even the Japanese will start thinking about doing something about it. And this is happening, you can observe that in the last two years they are thinking first about more expansion in the short run in macroeconomic policy, in fiscal and also monetary terms. And secondly, they may also start to think in terms of a two-handed approach of fuelling a demand expansion on one side but on the other side also starting to do something about the internal sectors. So I do not agree with the kind of eternal picture that you pointed at, that we have to live perpetually with the situation that the Japanese are not ready to shoulder some responsibility in stabilizing the macroeconomic streams internationally. And even if they are not ready to do so, I do not really see how much of a price we have to pay for that.

But politically, I would say that it may be worth an effort, really, to try again, not to shut the door vis-à-vis the Japanese and say: 'Ok, you do not shoulder your responsibility anyway, we have known that for forty years now and we try to go for macroeconomic coordination between Europe and the United States only.' I think that would be politically not very wise to do. I think it would be much better to bring the Japanese in, not in a bilateral fashion, but in a trilateral or in a multilateral fashion. And that links back to all the trade issues which have unfortunately moved increasingly to the bilateral agenda—the Americans and the Japanese bashing each other. But it should be brought back into a multilateral context.

A. Clesse: Thank you, Karl-Heinz. There is perhaps a slight risk that the debate becomes too wide, too large, moving too much away from the specific issue of the impact of the emergence of the euro on international stability. So, let's keep the discussion focused on that, and then we have to move on to the institutional implications of the emergence of the euro. Robert Skidelsky.

R. Skidelsky: I want to ask a very short question. Is it Professor Rosecrance's thesis that monetary leadership requires that the leader countries run balance of trade deficits with the non-leader parts of the world? Is that what you are really arguing? I can see that is what happened in the 19th century because manufacturing nations were importing foodstuff and raw materials from the developing countries and also lending the money to develop them. But I wonder how good a model that is for thinking of trade relations in a world in which most flows of capital are between developed countries? I would be grateful if you would comment on that.

R. Rosecrance: Well, some of my best friends are Japanese so that I do not feel too bad about attacking them. Perhaps the 'sharks and fishes' analogy as Cooper points out, is a little bit too extreme. But, I think, the main problem that we have, if we are going to develop the world as a whole, is finding markets for emerging countries. And I think, with Europe's Lomé Convention, Europe thought of such things. They would be very helpful to Africa and other countries and, I think, the United States has taken a very large share of the exports of emerging countries for a long period of time. But I believe I am correct in saying the Japanese have not done so and that up until now, at least, have pursued, perhaps excessively, an external trading strategy rather than an internal stimulus strategy. I think, you may well be right that they are beginning to change and I hope that is correct. It is very interesting if you look at the Japanese trade networks in East Asia. I realize this does get us a bit far away from the euro, but the exports that these countries have as a result of Japanese foreign direct investment do not go back into Japan because of *keiretsu* and other arrangements. It is all exported, presumably, to North America and Europe. It is just a reverse of the Ray Vernon product cycle thesis which envisaged that the investment that you make in a new product eventually comes back into your country as imports, as cheaper imports. So, I think, there is an instability involved in this and I do not wish in any way to criticize the Japanese because they obviously have provided us with a profusion of wonderful goods at low prices that we ourselves could not produce or were not willing to produce for one reason or another. So, I am not wishing to make a general statement about Japanese policy. But I do think that it would be very helpful now if they could turn much more to internal stimuli and internal development rather than relying on their export surpluses of the past. And that is essentially my only point.

As far as Lord Skidelsky's point about making the euro available, obviously one does not have to have balance of trade deficits in order to do so. But you have to put it in other people's hands. So you have got to lend abroad or you have got to buy from abroad. And, I think, lending may very well be the most important way of dealing with it now. But even lending, eventually has to be paid back. So, at a certain point you are going to have to find a way for your debtors to pay back, and one way of doing that is a balance of payments deficit.

A. Clesse: Thank you, Richard. Are there some thoughts about the euro and Asia. We have now somebody from Asia. It might be interesting to hear how the Chinese perceive the emergence of the euro. Professor Xu.

M. Xu: I think that I am the only one here from Asia. So, I am very grateful to Dr. Clesse for providing me with this opportunity to hear the opinions of the finest scholars in Europe and the United States. I think that the euro now becomes a hot topic in China and in the Asian countries. The most important thing we are concerned with is the future role that might be played by the euro in the international monetary system. As many scholars already mentioned, the euro will be a sort of partner of the US dollar in stabilizing the international monetary situation. But I think that there is still a kind of danger that if there is no coordination between the United States and the euro countries, the emergence of the euro may create an unstable situation or even more instability. It is already proven that huge amounts of hot money floating between currencies has sometimes caused great fluctuations in foreign exchange rates. Sometimes this kind of fluctuation is not really linked with fundamental economic indicators. So, I think that international stability cannot be reached without some coordination between the United States and the euro countries, even if the euro's internal value is stable. But right now it seems to me that there is no such consensus or even any intention to have this kind of coordination between the European Central Bank and the US Federal Reserve System, and that they will still pursue an inward-looking policy and let the exchange rate float as it is. But if, as I think, the future is a kind—as Professor Kindleberger mentioned in his paper—of bipolar system, then we need this kind of coordination between these two poles.

And the other thing is that, I think, the governments in international society should pay a little bit more attention to the foreign exchange rate fluctuations as we see that huge fluctuations in foreign exchange rates will cause financial crises, although, of course, the financial crisis in Asia was not mainly caused by the external imbalance, but by the foreign exchange rate fluctuations which made things worse. I should say that it was the sudden collapse of the exchange rate which led to the severe financial and economic crisis. So, I think that the European Central Bank and the US Federal Reserve System should prepare to build a kind of mechanism for future monetary cooperation. Because a bipolar system would make it much easier than what we are having right now to reach some kind of stable situation.

I agree with what Professor Rosecrance just mentioned, that if the euro is going to play a kind of key international currency role, the euro countries should prepare to have a more flexible current account. They should not always keep the current account in balance or in surplus. Otherwise other countries such as China and other Asian countries will not have enough euro to hold and to use. I am also considering the possibility that China and some other Asian countries try to shift some of their foreign exchange reserves into euro and if so, the European capital market should also be more flexible. Otherwise we would not have enough attractive financial assets to invest and to manage our foreign exchange reserves. So, there is something that should be done if the euro is really going to play this kind of supplementary international key currency role to the US dollar.

R. Henning: Dr. Xu, I share your concern about instability in this bipolar regime, and I agree that one of the great costs of exchange rate instability will be the impact on third areas and third countries, such as China and the rest of Asia. I also agree that US-EU coordination is desirable. But let's assume that you do not get such coordination, which, frankly, probably is the most likely outcome. My question is, what are the options for China and how would you assess them in an environment of mutual benign neglect between the dollar and the euro area? What are the possibilities of regional integration in Asia? How does this affect the Chinese calculus of the costs and benefits of regional integration? Would instability between the euro and dollar make Chinese cooperation with Japan in particular more desirable?

A. Clesse: Thank you. I think that before giving the floor back to Professor Xu, let's take a few more opinions or views and also some elements of an answer to this very broad question. Professor Norbert Walter.

N. Walter: First. If we just look at trade flows, it is indeed astonishing that Asia has been focused on the dollar to the degree it has been. If we add the trade flows with Europe they are as large as the flows with the United States. So, there would have been already, in the past, an interest of Asia in a more balanced exchange rate orientation. Of course if you look into the trade flows and their development in Asia it is very obvious that intra-Asia trade flows are the largest part and are increasing. And therefore, of course, it would be quite interesting for the region to not be exposed to the vagaries of anyone's external currency. But, I guess, some of us are much more talented than I am in the theory of money. It is very obvious that to have a common currency you need some mutual trust, and you probably need some institutional arrangements. And Asia,-if Europe is heterogeneous, Asia is very heterogeneous. In Europe we are approximately a group of equals, certainly we do not have a clear hegemon. In Asia, I believe, we have real giants or elephants and there is one economic giant of today, ageing however, Japan. This economic giant was never really willing to perform as the provider of a reserve currency, particularly for microeconomic reasons, and I would stress that, microeconomic reasons. There is an emerging political giant, China. And there seems to be an eternally sleeping giant, India. But it is quite obvious that there is a natural tendency for those giants to be dominant. Today it would be Japan, in twenty years' time it may be China. But we have learned in Europe that it takes a number of decades before you build-up some mutual trust, and if you can build institutions that function on that very basis of mutual trust—and money at the end of the day is trust. And therefore, I think, there is a very long way to go before we can expect Asian trade, Asian transactions, to be based on an Asian currency. Of course there are compelling economic arguments for it, but the political analysis does not provide any hope for any early solution of that kind.

I argued that the shares of trade would suggest that Asia does not expose itself uniquely to the vagaries of the dollar because some basket may fit its interest somewhat better. And for many of the non-Japan Asian countries a basket of equals, the yen, the dollar and the euro, may be not an inappropriate theoretical solution to the problem. It could help to reduce some of the risks. And we all have learned the world does not like complicated schemes, neither do the financial markets. And therefore I expect another pegging of Asian currencies to the US dollar. This must not result in as much volatility, if the euro and the US dollar are trading in a narrow range, which in my view is a distinct possibility after the portfolio adjustments out of the US dollar and into the euro have been completed in two or three years. If Asia pegs its currencies to the dollar again at a more reasonable rate probably it would not be in such bad situation as it was over the last two decades or so, particularly, over the last five years. So, my best guess is that the compelling arguments for an Asian monetary union will not be heard throughout the next generation and most probably, some theoretical considerations of having a basket of currencies to orientate and to anchor their currencies to will not be followed, but instead we will move away from the excessive floating that we have had over the last two years, to something that is again a fixing of—hopefully more realistic—parities towards the United States dollar or some form of dirty floating.

R. Cooper: I agree very much with ninety percent of what Norbert Walter said, especially about the importance of trust and confidence. I do not expect the Japanese yen to emerge as a serious international currency, despite the rapid growth of trade in East Asia. The ten percent that I am skeptical about, is that sound management of monetary policy in the United States and in Europe, which I also assume will take place, will by itself lead to greater stability of exchange rates. If we want greater stability of exchange rates we are going to target them and work for them. Good monetary policy alone will not achieve what most people would consider stability of exchange rates. I can easily imagine the dollar-euro exchange rate moving up or down year in and year out by twenty percentage points. That does not sound like much if you are used to hyperinflation, but twenty percentage points is very disturbing to people in the business world whose margins are typically four, five or six percent. So, I still think we have a problem.

G. Ambrosi: I would like to address particularly the point that Professor Xu made, advocating a bipolar system. Now, if we have a bipolar system it is something similar to a two-metal standard. You have two elements in which you could conduct payments. And, as we know from Grecians' law, the bad money drives out the good. In any case you have a constant tendency to have switches from one unit to the other unit. That is really the danger of having two substitutable units in exchange. Whenever the public appreciates a difference between the two units, which are traded at a managed and fixed exchange rate, you will have not less fluctuations but wider fluctuations than you would have otherwise. And so, I think, one must be rather cautious about such a bipolar system where you have a managed exchange rate between the two elements.

Also, as far as the idea of Asian monetary union is concerned and having an inner-Asian unit which emerges as that Asian currency, I would like to remind you of a curious feature of the European monetary system which is that in order to create an inner European unit of account, ECU, we do not use either francs or marks or whatever, we use dollars and gold in order to make, through revolving swap credits, the ECU, which is used for international payments in the European monetary system. So, I do not see really a necessity to have an internal currency emerging as the basic currency for a monetary union in Asia.

C. de Boissieu: In order to get exchange rate stability at the world level, a sound economic policy is necessary but not sufficient. Because as you know speculation and private investor behavior are conditioned not only by the stance of monetary policy and conditions but also by what is going to take place as regards fiscal policies on the two sides of the Atlantic and in some other places and also by structural policies.

A second aspect concerns the basket option. I totally agree with what you said, Norbert Walter. But for me the anchor problem is one thing and the exchange rate regime is another. The lesson that we must learn is the following. The financial crisis in Asia is not only a question mark about the anchor, whether Asia wanted to divorce from the dollar or not or is going to divorce definitively from the dollar. It has also to do with the optimal degree of flexibility of the exchange rate regime. You could have a crawling peg with the wrong anchor. Possibly, in some circumstances, a crawling peg with the wrong anchor is better than a fixed exchange rate regime with the right anchor.

A. Clesse: Thank you. We will have soon to move to the next topic. I do not know whether Andrei Kortunov would like to make a few remarks about how this evolution in Asia is seen from Russia? Andrei Kortunov.

A. Kortunov: Well, I think that what we see right now, given an extremely weak central state in the country, is that particular regions of the Russian federation tend to fall into particular currency zones. If you go to the maritime province of Russia you will see that the basic reserve currency is, of course, the Japanese yen. However, if you get further west then the situation becomes quite different. And already in the Amur region the main trading partner is not Japan but rather China. There are speculations about how the Chinese yuan might at some point become the major reserve currency for a number of Russian regions in that part of the country. However, in view of the volatility of the yuan itself and existing regulations in China, I believe that it is a little premature to argue that the Chinese currency might compete with the dollar as the basis for transborder trade between Russia and China. It is more likely that after a couple of years of barter exchange we will see shift to a more, let's say, hard currency exchange between Russia and China and, of course, the main reserve currency will still be the dollar at least in the foreseeable future, that is how I see the situation there.

A. Clesse: Professor Xu, you may react before we move on to the next topic.

M. Xu: Just one answer. I quite agree with Professor Henning saying that if we do not have what we expect to have, then the Chinese government will cautiously diversify its foreign exchange reserves. And perhaps, as Professor Walter mentioned, we may change the peg to the US dollar. We may change the foreign exchange rate management within the peg into a basket of currencies. But, I think, that even if we are a peg to a basket of currencies, the dollar would still be the most important currency that the Chinese yuan would peg. I think that its weight in the basket will be dominant, at least in the near future.

Session 5: The Institutional Implications of the Euro

A. Clesse: We move now to the institutional implications of the emergence of the euro. Roy Denman.

R. Denman: Well, let me try and offer some observations on two aspects of this. One is some perspective of how the Union is represented externally and the second some consequences for the future construction of Europe of the coming of the euro.

First. The Union is not simply a matter of new clauses added to the treaties. The form the Union has taken and will take, was set out nearly seventy years ago. In the darkest days of the Second World War, someone could have gone to the League of Nations building in Geneva and found in the archives a prophecy. It was in a report on customs unions. The report said that for a customs union to exist you would have to have free movement of goods. For it to be effective, you would have to have free movement of persons and capital. For it to continue you would have to have stable exchange rates. For exchange rates to be stable you cannot have separate economic policies designed to promote employment. For the necessary coordination of economic policies some political mechanism is required, and the greater the interference of the state in the economic affairs, the more extensive the mechanism would have to be. And there, even in 1942, you could have seen the future of Europe in the second half of this century, and the first half of the next. And it has worked out like that. As Walter Hallstein, the first President of the Commission, said in 1958: 'customs union, economic union, political union'.

Now, how has and will the external representation of the Community go? You all know that the Treaty of Rome provided that the Commission should negotiate on trade, subject to a mandate agreed by ministers. I suspect if the Treaty would be written now, it would not say that. It would say that the country of the Chairman of the Council of Ministers would negotiate and the Commission would be in a humble position to say: 'If I may say so Sir the tariff on gravestones is eight percent and not ten.' Well, it did not work out like that. I suspect because the French, who then ran the Six, were quite clear that the Commission would never dare to challenge them. But the Commission began to stir. I remember having lunch in early 1961—when the first GATT negotiations, in which the Community featured, had just started—with the German representative within the six. He said to me one day, he with a voice like a foghorn, (the wine glasses would tinkle at the end of the room when he spoke): 'Something momentous has happened!' I asked: 'What?' He said: 'The Commission has disagreed with the French.' And that was like someone getting up in the Politburo and disagreeing with Stalin.

Trade ministers of the member states were still very suspicious of bureaucrats in the Commission daring to represent them. I remember in the mid-sixties in the Kennedy Round, the Commission representative Theo Hijzen, appearing to see the Americans and later British, flanked by the German, who looked like a major in civilian clothes, and a Frenchman, a good friend of mine, who had a beret and was wearing dark glasses. An American friend of mine said: 'I guess that guy is under close arrest.'

But then the Commission began to spread its wings further and it came to the end of the Kennedy Round. I refer to this because the point was made yesterday, that in coordinating policy among various member states you get a position so inflexible you cannot move. Well, Jean Rey, a great Belgian who was the responsible commissioner, found that he could not get an agreement without exceeding his instructions. He could not summon a Council of Ministers in time. So he rang up Bonn, and spoke to a Staatssekretär without much effect. He rang up Paris, and spoke to the famous Couve de Murville, de Gaulle's Foreign Minister. After he had explained himself Couve said: 'Est-ce que vous voulez vraiment une réponse?' Rey had a vision of Couve going up a mountain and receiving a thunderbolt from an angel. So he exceeded his instructions and got a deal. And from that moment on the Commission had won its spurs. It was able to negotiate with some flexibility. Because you need flexibility and also you need permanence. We did not have to say to ourselves every six months: 'Well, we still have to deal with the Greeks next month or six months later it will be the Portuguese.' That continuity and establishment of authority were very important. So, let me encourage you to think that ultimately the representation of the Union in economic and monetary affairs will end up with two: the President of the European Central Bank and the commissioner responsible for economic and monetary affairs. Now, this drives ministers of finance into a frenzy because if trade ministers thought they were important, finance ministers think they are near God Almighty. But, how long that will last, depends basically on politics and on economics. How quickly Europe will progress towards a political unity.

The third element is political representation of the EU. As Richard Cooper said rightly yesterday: 'Europe is in a mess.' The trouble is that if finance ministers think they are near God Almighty, foreign ministers think they are God Almighty. And they have never read John Jay's contribution to the 'Federalist Papers', which I recommend to all Europeans here. He said what a tragedy it would be if America were split into several confederacies, yet then the English and the French and Spaniards would play us all off against each other and what a pitiful figure we would cut in the world and how badly we would be able to represent our interests.

Then some reflections on what the euro will mean for the future of the Community. I make you four prophecies.

Prophecy number one. Finance ministers now will meet in the Euro-11 next year on a regular basis. At some point they will find they have to refer things upwards. So, Prime Ministers of the Euro-11 will meet. That will cause many perturbations in what I call the 'outer fringe', the Brits and the Swedes and to some extent the Danes and the Greeks.

Prophecy number two. When Prime Ministers meet and start talking among themselves, they will not limit their talk to economics. Economics bores some of them, and stupefies others. They will rather talk about foreign policy where they all feel at home. And that will mean the beginning of a common foreign policy among the Euro-11, essentially a Franco-German policy. That will be much easier to get, I assure you this by consulting the English who will always ask for the Americans permission. The Greeks who are quite maniacal about Macedonia and the Turks, and the Swedes who are good humanitarians and should have stayed with the reindeer.

Prophecy number three. The 11 will find, indeed, that it is easier to agree among themselves without the troublesome Eurofringe. So the integration of Europe will proceed more quickly.

Prophecy number four. This very rapid progress will make it difficult, more and more difficult, for the Brits to enter. Because the price of entry will increase every six months or every year.

Now, this last point goes far beyond what people say in London. My British friends would say: 'Oh, it is quite all right, clever Tony Blair will wait after the election in 2001 before fully backing the euro. He does that because he does not want to annoy Mr. Murdoch, get the press against him and possibly lose the election. After that, we shall have a referendum, we shall win that and we shall soon join the Euro-11. Fireworks will be set off along the French coast, and from Berlin to Lisbon champagne will be opened. Well, it will not be like that. To begin with the Brits, while they do not have to join ERM before entering—that was changed at Amsterdam—they have to have for two years exchange rate stability between sterling and the euro. That will not be easy to get, with sterling bobbing like a dinghy between two liners. But locking sterling to the DM as in the ERM is remembered badly in London. They thought it was a great disaster when they had to leave. Of course it was not the fault of the ERM. The British joined at the wrong time, five years too late, for the wrong reason, to cut interest rates before a Conservative Party Conference, and that at an impossible rate of 2.95 to the DM. Indeed the Germans warned us that it was impossible, but Mr. Major's then Chancellor said that Mrs. Thatcher insisted. That is what you get when you have ministers interfering in things like exchange rates. So, that will be a very difficult condition to swallow.

And the second difficulty is that the British politicians have never explained the truth to the British electorate. They have portrayed the European Community as an affair of free trade in cotton underwear and orange marmalade. Now, they say the issue is banknotes. The question is:

'Will the Queen's head appear on the euro banknotes?' But they have never explained that ever since 1950 and Robert Schuman's declaration, it was made quite clear that the objective was the establishment of a European federation. And my friends in Brussels can never understand why British politicians have not explained this to the public. Well, federation is not part of the English political vocabulary. Sure, we have an arrangement with the Scots, but the Scots were subdued a long time ago. The idea of forming part of a European federation is much more difficult. The Brits have never been defeated and occupied, have never seen the need to restrain national power. And their politicians have never experienced a federation because they have never lived in one. No British politician has ever lived in Germany or Switzerland. If they had lived there they would have noticed the absence of angry crowds in, say, Zürich or Munich, agitating against a centralized tyranny. So, if they do not know what a federation is, it is difficult for them to explain this to the electorate. And then we have the British press, two thirds of it owned by two North American publishers. Every week, every month, you get a torrent of abuse of Europe. I have a friend in the West country, he was a surgeon and was at Cambridge, only some years after me, and he firmly believes that European federation is an evil thing. It is only a slight exaggeration to say that he and his friends believe that police in uniforms, like the SS, will enforce a Brussels regulation. They will stop people and ask: 'Have you had your quantity of frog legs this week?' 'No. Well, into the prison'. Now, picture this happy situation, supposed by Mr. Blair. Victory in the election in 2001, then the referendum. And picture a politician, coming from London, explaining in the village hall why in a certain number of weeks' time, the 'Pig and Whistle', a local pub, will only accept euros and not pound notes. There will be cat calls from the back: 'Why? Why is the Queen's head disappearing?' And then he will say: 'Oh. By the way, we shall be joining in a few months' time a continental federation.' So the House of Commons will become as important as the Bavarian Landtag, and you will have taxes which will not be voted exclusively by you. He would be well advised to get out of the hall quick and start running, otherwise a mob will remove his trousers and throw him into the village pond. So, I think it will take some time before Britain joins. It took us 23 years from 1950 to join the then European Community. I think we might do it in ten this time. Well, I hope I am wrong. I feel I may be right.

X. Larnaudie-Eiffel: I only had one disagreement with the person who intervened so brilliantly before me, regarding the entry conditions to the second wave. I have reacted, and I know that it is something which our British friends like to reiterate; for historical reasons which you very well recalled, it is easier for our British friends to consider a direct entry into the euro, rather than via the European Monetary System (EMS). But for the

United Kingdom, like for Sweden, Denmark, Greece and later the new member states of the EU, there is a treaty, a sum of conditions that have been negotiated and ratified by all and that will be applied with a form of jurisprudence. So, at the European Commission, we are today obviously well incapable of saying how the United Kingdom will fulfil the necessary conditions when the moment has come to join EMU. But suffice it to see how we have applied concretely to countries like Finland, Italy or others the criterion of membership in the EMS and of exchange rate stability—because the criterion is two-fold in the treaty—in order to have an idea of the underlying conception. To be totally clear, I think it would be an illusion to think that the United Kingdom is capable of participating in the EMS for the moment. But this is my only disagreement. Instead, there are many points of convergence with the intervention that preceded me. But I may not be able to benefit—because I do not quite have as much experience and because I have a different institutional position—from the liberty of tone which he has used in the same room where three times a year the ministers of finance meet, and I can tell you, with somewhat less honesty. Except for, and I will come back to this later, when they are in the composition of the Euro-11, that is, between ministers of finance of the countries that participate in the same currency.

I will attempt to show why we at the European Commission think today—to take up the metaphor from earlier on—that the ecosystem, which constitutes the international monetary system or the international economy, cannot be summed up in terms of an opposition between hawks and doves. Instead, it is a system of great complexity and that in the light of such systems, it is like in ecology, solutions that envisage sophisticated institutional or economic organization are sometimes the most intelligent ones. And if I judge on this by their behavior for some years now that the euro is coming closer, and to come back to one of the speakers who preceded me, I think that we can trust the financial markets to know how to decrypt messages that are a bit more complex than simple slogans. This may well seem theoretical, but I will try to explain myself very concretely. In building the euro, I think that in Europe we have learned a number of things that are of interest when thinking of the international monetary system.

The first thing, which I think was examined above by Richard Cooper, is that in order to avoid inflation, it is absolutely necessary to have a monetary policy aimed at stable prices, and an independent and efficient central bank. But, as reminded us Christian de Boissieu above, this is not sufficient to optimize the whole of economic policy. A budgetary aspect has to be added. A structural aspect has to be added. This is what we are trying to put in place at the moment, and it starts to work, the first concerted reduction in interest rates in the euro zone is a first demonstration thereof. Something has been created that did not exist in Community law, which is called Euro-11, which has no proper existence in the treaty, which is a body that cannot take decisions. It is an informal body. Everything that is discussed there has to come before the 15 member states. This is normal, we will not exclude the UK, Greece, Denmark and Sweden. They are members of the EU, they participate in the single market and even if they do not vote on certain decisions that only concern the euro, it is legitimate that they be held informed and that transparency is comprehensive. But within the Euro-11, precisely because no decisions are taken, there is dialogue, which becomes very interesting and very direct between ministers of finance and the president of the ECB. This does not affect the ECB's independence. And it works! It allowed Europe to adopt what is called the Stability and Growth Pact, which is after all an ambitious series of regulations in the long term for budgetary policies. Put simply, there is a federal approach of the budgetary deficit of the euro zone, the evolution of which is under control, and an optimal trajectory. Year after year it is checked that this trajectory is adhered to, and if necessary, though it is dissuasion, sanctions have been envisaged in order to show that there is a collective political determination. And, after all, member states are free to organize their fiscal revenue with a minimum of fiscal harmonization to avoid disloyal competition and expenditure, as this is still member state competence. Therefore, this renders operative something which is intellectually difficult to conceive, that is, a monetary pole of a federal nature, even if it is interesting to see that in the current phase of construction it is still the federal states and not the center which hold real power. Yesterday's gesture was a demonstration thereof, but all this will evolve quickly, and after all, governmental political power is as varied as the components of the European Union. For even if the ultimate goal of all this is, as you recalled it brilliantly, to achieve a form of 'European federation', it is wrong to have in mind that this will bring together another United States of America. The cultural, historical, economic (in the past), social and linguistic determinants are significantly different from what there is on the other side of the Atlantic. The end point will evidently not be the same, even if we think that European integration will make substantial progress. Thus, in terms of the first laboratory, we have found quite a complex system, but which allows to have a collective and efficient approach to a highly complex economy.

The second sense in which the euro has served somewhat as a laboratory regarding the institutional dimension is what is called differentiated integration. Not all the EU member states are automatically part of the euro. They have to fulfil the criteria laid down by the treaty, the famous convergence criteria, in order to enter. And in the cases of the UK and Denmark—because it was obtained in the bilateral negotiations—there has to be a specific declaration of political willingness to do so. Later, for the countries of Central and Eastern Europe, the same mechanism will apply. Hence, there is a considerable risk to have countries which are not part of the zone, but who have *de facto* lost power on the essential part of economic policy, and which therefore face the risk of being disadvantaged because, for instance, they can become less attractive for foreign investors. Yet these countries have to fulfil a host of Community regulations for the functioning of the single market. Thus, there is the need to find a positive exit to this problem. It should of course not lead to an explosion of the EU, which in my view has only been partially constructed. One should not reject what is called 'outs', but, in order to show that they are not rejected, one should refer to them as 'pre-ins'. This is a first way of signaling this. The second way to realize this and to make this understood within the Euro-11 is to associate them. To be concrete I always cite two examples: first, when the scenario of shifting to the euro was first conceived in 1995, not many people thought that it was going to happen. And especially in the UK, the perspective to see the UK give up sterling one day was really far away. At this time, when looking for ways to conceive this scenario, with Yves-Thibault de Silguy, proportionately speaking, we received one French banker, two German bankers and three British bankers. And the latter believed in it, they came to help us. The second example is as follows: when the Euro-11 meets, at the moment participate at all its meetings the president of the Monetary Committee, the MEPs, the directors of the Treasury, and the state secretaries to the Treasury. The president of the Monetary Committee, Sir Nigel Wicks, is also British. At the European Commission, you will be surprised by the number of British high civil servants who work actively on this matter. Yves-Thibault de Silguy's spokesperson is someone from the British Treasury. I could cite examples of the same nature for the other countries that are not part of monetary union. What I want you to understand is there is a political willingness on the part of the European Commission and all its member states, because national public opinion is in the process of shifting, all the governments at least, towards joining the euro quite quickly, and that everything that is necessary on the practical level is in place for them not be cut off in the interim. This too may be of great use later—this is why I have chosen those two examples—when we will tackle the issue of a better cooperative functioning of the global ecosystem, that is, the international monetary system.

I will end with the following two ideas: our hypothesis is that the advent of the euro, and even the evolving and imperfect character of its external representation, is a guarantee which will not be one in the scenario outlined by Randall Henning, of double benign neglect. This is the first idea. The second idea is that—excuse me for not developing the underlying reasoning—in a potentially more stable world, or as some argue less stable because bipolar—here I refer to the works of Professor Kindleberger—we think that the type of association at a differentiated mode which we were forced to invent to achieve the euro without retarding it and without making the EU explode, can bring innovative solutions to international monetary cooperation. I will try to explain myself quickly in two minutes.

On the first point. What will happen in January? Last Tuesday, during the Council of Ministers, a report was prepared that I think the Heads of State and Government will adopt at the European Summit in Vienna on 11-12 December and that explicates how the euro will be represented on the international scene from 1 January onwards. The principle is as follows: it is the 'Holy Trinity' that will represent the euro. It is composed of our member states, of the European Commission, put simply, competent for all things political and economic, and of the ECB, obviously competent in all independence for monetary policy. I will not take up in its entirety everything that Roy Denman said about the predictable evolution of the system. It is a possibility, it is not an objective for us, we will see. And the difference we would make is by comparing to trade policy. What does this concretely mean? It means that at this very moment, Oskar Lafontaine, Dominique Strauss-Kahn, Gordon Brown, Carlo Ciampi are in the process of discussing with Robert Rubin and preparing a meeting of the G-7 that should take place in Frankfurt, if I am not wrong, sometime around 20 February and that will be the first meeting in the presence of the euro. What are they discussing? Obviously not only the number of chairs around the table. That is perhaps not the most important thing. They talk about what they need to have in order to conduct a genuine discussion on 'does talking together about exchange rates mean something?' And I think the answer becomes increasingly clear—yes of course. If there has been a policy of benign neglect so far vis-à-vis the dollar, it was much more on the part of the Americans than on the part of the Europeans. It wasn't a European who said 'The dollar is our currency but your problem', it was Mr. Connally if my memory is correct, in the early 1970s. The Europeans are demanding greater cooperation. For, as Professor Xu put it very well, it is vital. We will not have increasing growth, or growing international trade, if we do not achieve on the international level more exchange rate stability. And that does not go as far as talking about fluctuation margins. I do not know if more or less 15 percent, like in the current European Exchange Rate Mechanism, is a good figure or not, I have no idea, we will see. However, the idea is that less instability is needed. To have less instability, there is a need to coordinate, not only monetary policies, but also budgetary policies, in order to get to the situation where economic cycles are as converging as possible on both sides of the Atlantic. This is why, and I bet this will happen—I cannot allow myself to make prophecies so I will confine myself to bets—the G-7 will effectively end up by being strengthened by the advent of the euro.

This is true of the G-7. I think that it will also be true of international financial organizations because with the Euro-11, with the relations with our 'pre-in' countries, I think that we are inventing, as I have said, differentiated integration. And if the events of recent months have taught us anything, it is that the G-7 in its current composition is not quite sufficient to address the totality of a chain of economic phenomena in some countries, stock markets generally, etc. This is why our American friends have initiated the G-22 or G-26; it is easier to get lost but it is an informal club, as you have noted, and which allows, outside the normal context which should have been that of the interim committee of the International Monetary Fund, to bring together the other countries that have so far not joined discussions of the G-7 finance ministers.

I very much think that there is a future in these formulae, and that on an informal level, differentiated approaches give an idea of what is possible. For instance, it is possible to meet more frequently at 7 and to have an extended meeting from time to time for issues that are genuinely of a wider interest than the transatlantic dialogue. And I think that this will naturally take us further, as is the case in Europe where the euro—I will not elaborate this today—leads us to consider fiscal harmonization, social harmonization, and to lead us to something more federal, something more united. But we are confident that on the international level, this experience of enhanced cooperation on all aspects of economic policy, extension of the discussions to others, will also take us to a purely institutional level. Not to a world government, which we do not believe in at all, but to real organizations as they were conceived of at the Bretton Woods Conference. And the fact that ideas emerge today, conform to what was decided at Bretton Woods at that time, to establish a true Council of the Monetary Fund, is undoubtedly a first sign of such an evolution.

A. Clesse: Thank you very much. I think that this will stimulate the discussions. Perhaps we could spend a few minutes taking questions because unfortunately you will have to leave very soon. You must be extremely busy, very taken these days, even more than usually. So it is very good of you to have come here nevertheless. So let us take some questions rapidly.

R. Cooper: I have short questions, but there are three of them. The first concerns the decision regarding the Trinity that you mentioned. According to the new rule, as I understand it, the Presidency, the Commission and the ECB will be represented at G-7 meetings. Did the discussions that took place address the question as to whether meaningful decisions can be made under those circumstances, especially when the Presidency is held by a non—G-7 country. For example, will Portugal, sitting for the Presidency, have the authority on behalf of the EU-11, in this case, to take decisions regarding foreign exchange rate policy? Or will it just read a pre-agreed brief?

Second, where will a foreign exchange intervention actually take place? The national central banks are reluctant to give up the capacity to intervene in the market, so we have the prospect of ten (not counting Luxembourg) central banks intervening in the market. How is that going to be coordinated, or is there a process envisaged whereby that 'ten' will be reduced as quickly as possible to a sensible 'one'?

Third, I understood your remarks—but I may have misunderstood them—to suggest that coordination of fiscal policy will go beyond the boundaries that are set by the Stability Pact, so that there will be coordination even if countries are well inside the agreed limits. My question, which is easy to ask, hard to answer, is: Why is there any concern whatsoever in the Commission about coordinating fiscal policy among the national member states so long as they stay within the limits set by the Stability Pact?

R. Skidelsky: Well, I am also a friend and I very much enjoyed Denman's very amusing speech. But I have to fight political battles in England and undoubtedly there is lot in the picture of England being paranoid about what is happening in Europe. But one can break down the paranoia a little bit if one could get clear answers to certain questions.

A. Clesse: Robert. I am very sorry to interrupt you. Is it to Xavier?

R. Skidelsky: Yes it is. I just said clear answers.

A. Clesse: Because we come back to Roy Denman later. We have not finished on that. Sorry.

R. Skidelsky: Well, I am just about to ask those questions. First of all, when you say that we are moving towards a federation but it is not like the United States federation, what sort of federation is it? One cannot ever get a clear answer to that question. Secondly, Richard Cooper said we do not have a central treasury. Is a central treasury required in your view to deal with the problem of asymmetric shocks or can they be dealt with, sufficiently, by national fiscal policy? Thirdly, is it your view that in order to make the euro a successful currency we need political unification?

G. Ross: You, Mr. Larnaudie-Eiffel, were very optimistic about transatlantic bipolar coordination. And I have not heard a single thing in our two days that would support that optimism. So far, I hear Jeffrey Frankel and Randall Henning, who basically said: 'We have said nice things about EMU, we are not against it, except that some economists think it does not have the proper currency zone and so on.' But the government officials in Washington are way behind, at least that is how it looks. They have good intentions and they give blessings to what you are up to. But basically they are waiting to see what happens, and they are going to respond incrementally to whatever happens. It seems to me we have got a real issue, it is not a real problem there, of how you generate the kind of coordination that you really want to generate, and probably everyone needs to coordinate with the United States. Transatlantic dialogue, which you mentioned, and more dialogue coming from Europe towards the United States than is coming back, even though everybody tries very hard. How do you generate the resources to create the kind of cooperation, coordination that the international monetary system really will need? Because the Americans have demonstrated no commitment to producing coordination yet.

C. de Boissieu: With respect to the functioning of the two-level rocket, Euro Council at 11 and Ecofin Council at 15, I have well understood why we have got to this. Is this two-level rocket sustainable over the long term? Take fiscal harmonization. If an 'out' country blocks fiscal harmonization, is there not a risk of tension between the two levels of the rocket?

I think that it is audacious or running a risk to speak about federation because I think that we are in the process of inventing, with the ambitions and risks that this contains, a new institutional form that we cannot define as yet. We have not determined the equilibrium point between the core and the periphery. Is it not a bit deceptive to refer to concepts that raise some problems?

R. Henning: Monsieur Larnaudie, if the euro area is to be a force for stability in the global system, the mechanism through which this would occur, in part, would be through the Council of Ministers issuing general orientations on exchange rate policy. Of course, that would happen under article 109, paragraph 2, on the recommendation of the Commission. So, is there anything that you can tell us about your plans to make proposals in this regard?

U. Marani: I will be very short. I think that Mr. Larnaudie is very optimistic about the future of this idea. Because I would like to know, what is the position of the European Commission about the relation between the Ecofin and the ECB. Because I think that there is a technical factor that is a problem, a political problem. I think that it is also very hard to rationalize the heart of a central bank. The ECB announced a strategy of firm control of monetary aggregates instead of inflation targeting rules as indicated by the Bank of England. Well, I think that this system of intermediate control of monetary aggregates (whichever one will be chosen, and I think that the ECB will choose M3 like the Bundesbank) does not have any possibility, except by chance, of being achieved in the ECB if the new exchange rate fixed by the Ecofin institutionally is anterior and exogenous. The system can work only in a situation of absolute agreement on the hierarchy of economic policy final targets and of complete agreement between the Ecofin and the ECB.

Now I think that there are some possibilities of deviating from the Stability Pact. The first one is the Lafontaine proposal, the tendency to a reduction of European unemployment with an increase of national public deficit. The second one is increasing pressure for a more accommodating exchange rate with respect to the US dollar in order to increase the export of the Southern countries. What do you think?

X. Larnaudie-Eiffel: I will try to be extremely brief in my answers. May I be forgiven in advance if I forget a sub-question or something else. An introductory remark nevertheless.

Optimism and federation. Jean Monnet had quite a nice phrase, he said 'I am not optimistic, I am determined'. So, what the European Commission will tell you will always seem to you on the optimistic side, that is normal, we are paid for this. We are there to make the mechanics advance, so we will not demolish them. We are trying to be relatively objective in the analysis of our work. But there is a bias, it has to be admitted, which is that we want more Europe, that we want it to progress and that obviously we want the euro to succeed.

Secondly, with respect to federation, Christian you are absolutely right This word is never used outside some well-informed circles like this one, it should not be mentioned at a public meeting, mainly because it is a concept loaded with many ambiguities and contradictions if applied to the European situation. So, I agree with you and I am convinced that we are inventing— this will certainly take time—something *sui generis*, something completely new on the institutional level. I only used the word to link it to the aspirations, which we evoked earlier, of the great figures of the European construction.

Richard Cooper asked me a number of questions. How will the trinity function? First of all, it is a model in evolution. Who will command authority? Authority will stem from two things: generally speaking from representativeness. That is, a Portuguese minister who outlines the position of the 11 has a more important role on the international scene than a Portuguese minister who has no common position to announce. What matters is the point of view of the 11. And this point of view has to be representative, because what will interest our partners most is not Germany's, the UK's or France's point of view, it is the point of view shared by the euro zone as a whole.

Secondly, it has been envisaged, precisely because of the concern that you report, that one of these ministers already knows well the workings of the G-7. It is a body that has certain practices. Ministers will be in charge at each country's turn, in 1999, it is Oskar Lafontaine, in 2000, it will be the French minister, etc. He will be there as a sort of tutor, like in universities, to help the minister who will have the presidency of the Euro-11 during those periods, that is, for instance, the Finnish for the second half of 1999. And there are also two institutional factors of continuity, the ECB of course, and the European Commission. So, all this seems a bit complex, this is why I said that it wasn't a problem of the number of chairs around the table; what matters is that the Americans or the Japanese face a representative European delegation who has a memory and a certain know-how. And this is the solution that was identified to achieve this objective. As for interventions on the foreign exchange markets, they are decided by the ECB and they are executed on the national exchange markets by the national branches, that is, the former national central banks. So there is a clear division of labor, all this is coordinated and I think it will be efficient if there will be the need to make use of it.

Why are there attempts to coordinate beyond the Stability Pact? No, nothing has been added to the Stability Pact, and the Stability Pact itself adds nothing compared to the treaty. Contrary to the impression that we may have generated over the last years, we are not obsessed by a deficit limit of 3.0 percent. This is not what interests us, this is not the objective. What is the objective then? That over the medium term the budgetary position of the member states is sufficiently healthy so that the ECB is not faced with a responsibility that exceeds it and that the ECB is not obliged to adopt an excessively restrictive monetary policy. This is now very concretely interpreted in terms of an average position of the member states, but with an approximate structural budgetary equilibrium, and margins that leave some room for maneuver, which vary from one country to the other because the elasticity of variations in the overall budget (surplus or deficit) differs across countries. This is what we seek to achieve. If all countries have put order into their public finances, this is the position that avoids disequilibria on the level of the euro zone as a whole. Why should such disequilibria be avoided at the level of the euro zone as a whole? For it is the only way to preserve both savings that are then available for investment, and a monetary policy that is sufficiently accommodating for a greater growth potential than has been the case in the last 20 years.

Beside the issue of federation, Robert Skidelsky was asking whether it would not have been necessary to establish a common Treasury at the European Union level, and notably, so he said, in the light of the problem of asymmetric shocks. Two things in this respect. There is a much greater interpenetration of Community and national administrations than what is said frequently. And thus, a number of bodies are in the process of developing, such as the Monetary Committee, which will become the Economic and Financial Committee at the beginning of next year. Second example: we are in the process of restructuring our Directorate-General of Monetary and Economic Affairs. We have asked each member state to dispatch one of their civil servants who specializes in their budget in order to help us in improving our analysis of national budgets. So, a European administration is emerging around the notions of plurality and coordination of economic policies. As this occurs at the level of civil servants, it is never very spectacular, nor public. But this is growing. If I compare the degree of relations that I have with my colleagues in the various capitals with being totally ignorant about Community issues twenty years ago when I started in the French administration, or when I joined the French Treasury, we do not live in the same administrative world any longer. Something has moved. As for asymmetric shocks, I will not elaborate greatly, but really our position is that the likeliest situation is that there will not be typically national asymmetric shocks. We think that there will be asymmetric sectoral shocks, which will affect countries a bit differently according to the importance of the sector, which can vary from one country to another. But we really see only a very small probability indeed that a shock will hit exclusively one country. And therefore the response of purely national economic policies seems to us in most cases, in the overwhelming majority of cases, to be an inadequate response.

Is a political union necessary for EMU? I would reply 'Yes, but a form of political union, not a federation', to take up the earlier debate. We do not need a federation. Instead, what we do need is a mechanism that ensure a good collective management. And for this, a European government is not inevitably needed, if everyone plays the game. But this goes back to the problem of managing clubs. If one does not assume that the members, which will join the club, really want to participate, one does not create a club in the first place.

Mr. Ross asked me how the issue of some coordination of economic policies could be tackled at the international level. I do not have a ready-made answer. It seems to me that the kind of things that we could reflect upon is the sort of instruments that were used in Europe to achieve gradually a certain degree of convergence of economic policies. This begins with mutual information. And mutual information can be codified. It is possible to request from everyone a certain amount of evidence, on public finances, debt, economic forecasts, etc. This is a first stage. To my knowledge this does not exist so far within the G-7 in a formalized way.

The second possible stage is for every participant to inform the others about their short-term and medium-term objectives. This is already being done on the level of very general economic policies, but neither in this area is there a standardized document, so it is not necessarily comparable. When attending a G-7 meeting of finance ministers, there is a succession of interventions by finance ministers, they all have their own economic culture and talk a bit in a way they would talk about their economic policy before their own parliament. To date we have not created a common idiom on this. So, this kind of ideas, which are still extremely 'low-key' at the moment, would help very concretely, if one was certain of speaking the same language, in assessing the results. You see, this is a whole chain, quite gradual, but concrete measures can be taken.

Christian de Boissieu asked a question about the sustainability of the two-level rocket, between the Euro-11 and the Council of 15. I think that the conception one should adopt is that, firstly, the Euro-11 was created because unfortunately not all 15 countries managed to join the euro. Otherwise one may have had informal or restricted council meetings or Ecofin council meetings, but there would have been no need to separate between 11 and 15. Secondly, when talking about fiscal harmonization, which was taken up here a year ago by the Heads of State and Government, the 4 remaining countries join. The Euro-11 is informal, but there are 15 participants around the table. For talking about fiscal harmonization without the UK being on board obviously makes no sense.

Randall Henning asked me about the recommended exchange rate. There is no final product as yet, our reflections are in the next stage. Such recommendations will not be made every morning, there is no point in repeating the same if there is nothing to say on the markets. Therefore we are already discussing misalignment with our member states, i.e what situations would justify a strong political and public expression by the Council. So this took off more than a year ago. On the basis of this, as soon as there is agreement on the type of situations, we will draft something that resembles a G-7 declaration, or something of the sort, but which will give the markets an indication as to the conception adopted by the monetary authorities. And this is what will be submitted to the Council for approval. But to reiterate, this will not be a daily procedure. It will only happen if there are some real changes.

Finally the last speaker was Ugo Marani. I will like to say the following. I do not share at all his pessimism, not at all, and notably I honestly think that I did not hear Oskar Lafontaine say the same thing as he did. What I heard, last Tuesday at the Euro-11 and the Ecofin council in Brussels, is to the contrary, and they repeated it yesterday, Lafontaine and Strauss-Kahn. There is agreement that there is no better budgetary strategy than the Stability Pact. So now attention has to be paid to growth, and there is a need for a more flexible monetary policy. Of course this debate will evolve as a function of the evolution of the situation and we will come back to this at least within the coming year. But after the polemic statements of the press for three weeks, the last update has been very clear. It is not to question the Stability Pact, nor the strategy for public finances which it implies, because, once again, it is the only way to have a more accommodating monetary policy.

Session 6: What Should Be the Euro's International Role?

A. Clesse: First, we will continue with institutional implications. Niels Thygesen from Denmark, please.

N. Thygesen: The agenda I want to address has already been opened up by some of the interventions yesterday, by the questions of Professor Richard Cooper this morning, and by the exchange yesterday between Mr. Carré and by Minister Klaus. I shall continue the bad habit of addressing the institutional issues for the euro area mainly by looking inwards, though we need in Europe to manage the new currency in an external perspective. My more specific point which was mentioned yesterday, most clearly by Richard Cooper, is that EMU has some institutional weaknesses which may make it difficult for it initially to play a constructive role. I share the long-run optimism of Sir Roy Denman, but some important short-run problems should be recognized.

What are the challenges for those who will manage Europe's common currency? There are really two tasks in the international economy. The first is to manage a major international currency, which is likely to appreciate somewhat over the next 2-3 years. I find it difficult to avoid the conclusion that the shift in portfolios that we can expect could be accommodated without some appreciation of the euro. Since I am closer to the Portes-Rey scenario for competition with the dollar than to that of Richard Cooper, appreciation could well run ahead of the modestly superior inflation performance that the euro area may have relative to the United States. The euro is likely, in addition, to fluctuate quite substantially against the US dollar and other international currencies.

The second task is to act in possible future international financial crises with the mixture—using the philosophic language of Professor Kindleberger—of leadership and sense of duty that is the hallmark of quality in international economic management.

There is arguably a hopeful scenario as regards the first question on managing the euro in a traditional macroeconomic context. Some appreciation will not be unwelcome since it would help the current account adjustments in Europe and in the United States and facilitate the task of the European Central Bank to maintain low interest rates. The euro area can certainly live with some fluctuations in the euro given the small share of trade with the dollar area—even including the countries in Asia that are still closely linked to the dollar. Fluctuations in the dollar can no longer drive the European currencies away from each other once we have the euro; yet different sensitivities in different European countries to the movements vis-à-vis the dollar will no doubt persist and pose problems for a joint monetary policy. So more than benign neglect of external considerations will be needed.

There are two weaknesses in the policy framework for the euro area that I want to discuss. The first is the absence of any explicit framework for dealing with the aggregate policy stance and the policy mix, because of the focus in non-monetary policies, which remains national The second, more neglected in the international debate, is the surprisingly decentralized state of the supposedly one unified actor, the European System of Central Banks.

Regarding the first point, the Stability Pact is a mechanism for limiting divergent individual behavior inside the EMU, not a mechanism for outright coordination. It will no doubt on average improve the policy mix by making it unlikely that we could end up with major deficits in the area as a whole. I sympathize with the mechanisms of the Stability Pact. Something like it was required primarily because EMU itself strengthens incentives to conduct overly expansionary budgetary policies. Let us assume—optimistically— that it will in fact be observed, I think that is more likely than the alternative, so that we will not have a repeat of earlier phases in Europe where good times, most recently in the late 1980s, were used to undermine the underlying budget position. But within the limit (and that comes back to Richard Cooper's question) of 3 percent for the budget deficits, there is certainly still scope and need for discussion of the speed of reducing deficits from the present levels towards the average levels that have been set at a near balance or small surplus, not least in the most important countries: Germany and France. Just as the European System of Central Banks will have to look carefully at the speed at which discrepancies between forecast inflation and the inflation objective of at most 2 percent should be eliminated, the Euro-11 finance ministers will have to develop a framework for looking at the aggregate performance of the 11 to guide their monitoring of the member states behavior inside the limits of the Stability Pact. Maybe this is now beginning to develop; after the initial excesses in statements by the new German Government, there are now suggestions that Germany too will be respectful of the provisions of the Stability Pact, with some more emphasis on coordination of the type I have described.

Let me turn to the second question relating to the ECB or the European System of Central Banks. Some recent academic reports from the Center for Economic Policy Research (CEPR) in London in October, and from the Center for Economic Policy Studies in Brussels in December, has drawn attention to these weaknesses. Somewhat immodestly, may I also draw attention to the book, published with Daniel Gros in 1992, where we discussed in some detail the problem we are now addressing. When the statute for the European Central Bank was drafted in 1991, the formulation proposed by some countries to rely on national central banks (NCBs) for executing policy to 'the maximum extent possible' was rejected. But since then the NCBs have reasserted their position in two dimensions: operations and analysis. When the system was designed, the intention was to centralize some operations, notably foreign-exchange operations, in the European Central Bank. Led by France and Italy there was even a suggestion to pool reserves and have joint management during the transition. Mr. Lamfalussy, who later became more cautious as President of the European Monetary Institute, wanted a jointly owned operational unit to execute both forex and money market operations. However, not only has there been no shared experience during the transition to EMU. When EMU finally starts, there will not be one early thereafter because the ECB will not be present in the markets. All operations will be carried out through the national central banks, both foreign exchange and money market operations. In addition, it was foreseen from the start that dealings with individual banks, discounting and so on, would be decentralized. Decisions will be taken centrally, but implemented in a decentralized way and monitored by the ECB. Obviously, this system is workable but it is not the most efficient. It does not exactly present a clear face to the outside world. Some have said that the ECB is really based on the US model. The Federal Reserve Board does not engage in market operations but delegates them to the New York Federal Bank. But it does not delegate them to all twelve federal reserve banks as now is being done in Europe to the different NCBs. This is clearly potentially inefficient.

An important problem is the question of analysis. The balance between the European Central Bank, the core, and the national central banks is a difficult one apparently. In federal countries such as Germany and the United States, the respective central banks have inherently a national perspective when they prepare decisions and vote on monetary policy. The background material for the Federal Open Market and for the Bundesbank Council is prepared centrally in Washington and Frankfurt. In the euro area it will take a long time for this practice to develop. One problem is, of course, the initial absence of reliable data. National central bank governors will be arriving with their own briefs from their own staffs, their own data with special emphasis on the more familiar national ones and these will at least be an excessive pleading of national circumstances. I may add that, in these circumstances, it is understandable that the European central bankers have resisted the full blast of Anglo-Saxon transparency in decision-making, particularly the publication of voting records, that would clearly be divisive—as would be the frequent appearance at press conferences of national central bankers. Now, this situation can be illustrated by simple figures; the staff of the European Central Bank is an extremely small one, currently about 500 people, while there are currently about one hundred times as many employees in the 11 NCBs and no plans, as far as I can see, to reduce the staff. There will be a fight to retain as much work and as much analysis as possible in the national central banks.

This also has implications for the efficiency with which the European institutions can act internationally. And it is, in my view, aggravated by the recent decisions—or proposals as Mr. Larnaudie-Eiffel was careful to say—about external representation. The G-7 which is a main forum for policy coordination internationally has come under attack as ineffective, not least because there is overrepresentation, numerically, by the Europeans: four out of seven. This argument applies a fortiori for the G-10 where they are seven out of ten, or eight out of eleven if you count Switzerland. This was one major motivation for finding a different forum, where this problem was a little bit less evident, this year with the G-22—the G-7 plus 15 emerging market countries. The G-22 was successfully initiated by the USA in the spring and it reported, in October, on important issues of the international system. Now, in future meetings of the G-7 there will be the President of the European Central Bank and two additional participants: the representative of the European Commission and the President in office of the Euro-11, if he is not already present as one of the participating finance ministers. More than that, the central bankers of the countries that are individually in the G-7, have, to my knowledge, no intention of relinquishing their participation. So there will be even more European faces in the Group of Seven. Whether the United States will find that acceptable is certainly a question. The Europeans, in their eagerness to negotiate a joint position, have probably not paid sufficient attention to outside perceptions of the weakness of the European structure.

There are a couple more illustrations of the reassertion of the influence of the national central banks. The committee that reports to finance ministers, now renamed the Economic and Financial Committee, successor to the Monetary Committee, was meant initially to have been a committee solely for finance ministry officials, though with two representatives from the ECB. But national central banks have now decided—and have had the agreement of the finance ministers—that they will continue to take part. Committees within the ECB, on external representation and some other issues, are still chaired by national central banks representatives. And by way of anecdotal evidence, the more one talks to national central bankers in Europe the more they refer to the ECB as a secretariat more than I, at least, had imagined when the enterprise started.

In short, I find this a troublesome scenario from which to start. Though I sympathize with Sir Roy Denman's view, that there are dynamics inherent in this process, and that things will probably sort themselves out, it will take quite some time, and that will impede the kind of leadership role that Europe could potentially play in the G-7 and elsewhere. You may think this is an unpleasant statement to make on a day when the newspapers are all applauding a joint decision by the NCBs to lower interest rates, but I am afraid that there is some realism in the remarks that I made.

E.-M. Claassen: First I will speak in French. Anyway, I am indifferent between French and English because my mother tongue is German. But as we talk about the common currency, there is also a common language as Bob Mundell has often said, so communication, language as a form of scientific communication. It used to be Latin and now it is English. So it is that which explains Christian de Boissieu's switch to English. But I will keep on speaking French, I like the French language a lot, but that does not mean that I prefer English. As a professor teaching in French universities, whenever I have started a course in international economics in the last two or three years, I always pose the same question, whether I teach in France or Germany, and I put a question to the students that I could also put to my colleagues. I ask under which exchange rate regime France operates until December 31 of this year. This is so because it is important when teaching international economics, above all international macroeconomics, that I introduce the models of fixed exchange rates or flexible exchange rates. It is necessary to make a distinction in the literature. So it is very important that when I start a course on international macroeconomics, that I decide which model I deem applicable to a country like France or Germany. So for the French students, I say that France has a fixed exchange rate regime, and so we will look at the models of fixed exchange rates. In Germany, when asking the same question, unfortunately I am obliged to teach the other part of macroeconomics, because I say that it is necessary to apply floating exchange rates. This may seem mysterious and even banal, but is a fundamental factor in teaching: it is crucial to know under which exchange rate regime countries operate. The marvelous difference is effectively between France and Germany.

But the institutional question that I pose here for the euro is more delicate than the much broader question of the type of exchange rate regimes. When I return from a conference I always ask myself what I recall, what I have learned. And for me, who am personally very attached to questions of exchange rate regimes, Christian de Boissieu too, I was very surprised (I wonder whether I was the only one to pay close attention) by the exchange between Robert Mundell and Jeffrey Frankel about the currency board. This is one system among others for a fixed exchange rate regime. And with what certainty—I never thought that this should be said, but from today on I do—can this occur in the case of the euro, if the euro opts for a fixed exchange rate. Robert Mundell has convinced me that this is conceivable. But consider Argentina, Hong Kong and their interest rates. Robert Mundell's answer was: 'it is the result of an undisciplined macroeconomic policy and of course there is a need to manage the currency board.' In Brazil, interest rates stand at 40-42 percent for Brazilians. But it is not the currency board but instead fixed exchange rates. But these are accidents, as there are of course fixed exchange rate regimes that resemble currency boards.

I will look at what types of fixed changes we have as options for the euro. though I am not a dogmatical fanatic for one or the other exchange rate. I take only two examples, Austria and Switzerland. Two countries, seven million inhabitants. Austria succeeded extremely well since the mid-seventies with fixed exchange rates with respect to the German mark. Do not forget the margin between the schilling and the German mark was not only lower than one percent, it was 0.11 percent. This is amazing, it was not two percent, it was not one percent, it was since the mid-1970s only 0.11 percent. Now that is remarkable. So, the Austrian economy worked excellently, even to some degree better than the German. And then you look at Switzerland, a constantly floating exchange rate. It worked better than the German mark because the Swiss had relatively a higher price stability than Germany. And then I take, because you are so obsessed by Asia, I do not see what is so special about Asia, I take Hong Kong and Singapore. They are comparable, also comparable with Switzerland, a small country with seven million inhabitants. Hong Kong has seven or eight million inhabitants, Singapore three million. Both economies are comparable with Hong Kong. But do not look at the last twelve months with Hong Kong. Now, there has been a currency board since, I think, '83 or '85, and there has been a currency board exchange rate margin between 1 percent up or down in Singapore. So, these two European examples and two Asian examples show us that both exchange rate regimes are survivable over the long run, because that is a long run, twenty years, twenty-five years.

Now, what is the United States doing? This is more fundamental. Now, there is what we could call benign neglect on the one side, benign neglect on the other side, all this is benign neglect. The key issue is certainly that one country has to follow this benign neglect. At least this is what we saw in the past, although we can imagine that the United States might become active. So, what do I mean by 'active'? By active I mean, that it is a European idea, but I do not know how the United States will react. The European idea, that is, I think, the present idea of some governments, not of the Commission, to say that we have to install a type of European monetary system for the euro-dollar rate. But there are the difficulties which have arisen in two concrete cases of fixed exchange rates. One is in the former European Monetary System because when you change the parity level, which was possible in a fixed, but adjustable parity system, then you had to have a mutual agreement about the new parity. That is what I call a bilateral decision. What should be the new central parity in that particular fixed exchange rate system? If you put that system into operation between Europe and the United States and if the Europeans and the Americans certainly say we have to get an agreement about the central parity and about the margin, it could be manageable in a way analogous to the former European Monetary System. If that is what we want, we must decide, in X-years, a new central parity value for this fixed exchange system. Now that has to be one possibility. This bilateral agreement concluded with the Commission that the new parity could act as a basis for a wider fixed exchange rate system, including the Vatican City and

San Marino because you might also imagine the fixed exchange rate regime is a system that I call 'dollar right system' that could take in another currency like those of Panama or San Marino or Monaco, such as Israel wanted twenty years ago to dollarize the broad economy to get a foreign currency. It could be a single world currency or the first step towards it. This is not nonsense actually.

I see difficulties with the United States to get engaged in a bilateral agreement about fixed exchange rates. So we have only two options. You have either a floating exchange rate system as it existed for Germany for more than twenty years with the consequence of an independent monetary policy, independent from exchange rate targets or euro fixing, but that would be a unilateral fix with margins. If Europe thinks that the exchange rate is not appropriate in the future then they come together, the eleven countries without the United States. The United States will then say: 'Well, you changed the parity.' And that would not be analogous to the European Monetary System because now you fix the euro to the dollar. And remember, Germany always had a floating exchange rate. Germany always had a floating exchange rate with respect to the dollar and none of the European countries had any possibility to intervene in the thinking of the German Bundesbank or the Finance Ministry.

K. Deutsch: I have three questions to Professor Thygesen. Do you think that in the setting of international monetary policy of the EMU, qualified majority voting in the Council will have any role to play or will it be de facto consensus as the norm, which is something that has occurred in the common commercial policy of the European Union? Related to that: would there be a need for a functional equivalent of the 113 Committee in trade organizing the political will of the member states so as to facilitate consensus-finding in monetary affairs? And third, what is the role of the Commission in the external representation of the EMU area? I did not quite understand because the functional delegation in that case is to the ECB and not to the Commission. To my mind, it is more of a consultative role than a codecision role and I am confused about it. Maybe you can explain it to me.

R. Cooper: Professor Claassen gave us a spirited analysis of alternative exchange rate regimes but, unless I missed it, he did not express a preference. Of the various alternatives that he put forward, which one would he recommend to the European Union?

E.-M. Claassen: I am both against euro, and also for the euro as a given fix. Now I would like the euro to succeed. You see that is my formal position. Now I will do everything for the euro to succeed and I am very pessimistic about any fixed exchange rate because a central bank cannot satisfy both targets: internal stability of the European Community and exchange rate targets. So that is my German cultural root. And if there is some additional constraint, that was not in the discussion until now, we want to have a fixed exchange rate with respect to the US dollar, that is different from the twenty last years in Europe, when Germany had a floating exchange rate. Now there is a different scenario for the German mark, for the German citizens as well. Now we will get a fixed exchange rate for the euro, that is a completely different monetary regime. To a certain degree, I am very sympathetic with Mundell's proposition, and among the types of fixed exchange rates, and do not exclude the currency board. I did exclude it before the conference. I thought it would be nonsense. It is not nonsense, especially when we have large foreign exchange reserves in Europe.

R. Cooper: You have qualified your view beautifully now. But you told us earlier, and I thought it was very interesting, that judged by performance based on two pairs of countries, one does not have a clear basis for choosing an exchange rate regime. As the Swiss-Austrian and the Hong Kong-Singapore examples suggest it is possible to have perfectly sensible economic management, either under a fixed rate or under a floating rate.

E.-M. Claassen: I will answer immediately. The Swiss and Austrian fixed exchange rates resulted from the dictatorship of the German central bank. You have to take this political point into account. I agree that both the exchange rate systems for Austria and Hong Kong on the one side, Switzerland and Singapore on the other side, succeeded but I tell you with a certain malicious undertone that they succeeded better in Switzerland and Singapore.

R. Mundell: I always have a problem when we are talking about exchange rates because it always is very country specific. And it is such a fundamental difference talking about an exchange rate for the dollar. With students in America, if you talk about fixed or flexible exchange rate systems, they say immediately: 'What should America fix to?' America cannot fix to the Canadian dollar or the Mexican dollar. Currencies have strength in proportion to their size, and little currencies fix to big currencies not the other way around. The answer is always easy for little countries next to stable big ones. It is easy for me to say, as I have always believed, that Mexico and Canada could not do much better than fixing to the US dollar, but I would never say that the United States should fix to the Canadian dollar. Some may know that there is some talk now about North American monetary integration, and some would go so far as to say that we need a North American Monetary Union. I say that is ridiculous because the United States, which is twelve times as large economically as Canada, is never going to share or give up its great world currency for the sake of accommodating the Canadians or the Mexicans. The asymmetry is too great.

So you see, as I have tried to make clear in dozens of places, that as long as the euro is a stable currency, the currencies around the periphery of Europe, should they want to get into the Union, should fix to the euro. I do believe that countries in Latin America would be much better stabilizing to the dollar, and that holds also for a few currencies in Asia. But when we come to the question of important currencies like the dollar, or the euro, you can never say they can fix because you do not know what they can fix to. The euro cannot fix to the US dollar without US assent. You have always in the case of two—more or less—equal countries fixing, who does the fixing? Well, historically, the United States, for instance, has never fixed to any currency in the past. It never had a fixed exchange rate with any currency. When the Bretton Woods Agreement was set up and the fixed exchange rate arrangements were being considered, the Americans saw the limitations of the 1 percent band for the dollar. They started to think about it and said: 'That would be a ridiculous thing for the United States. It would mean that the United States would have to intervene in 40 or 50 countries then in New York to stabilize each other's currency.' So, what was inserted in the Bretton Woods agreement was this article IV-4-b clause, which said that a country that announces to the Fund that it is buying gold freely does not have to keep to the currencies of other members within the exchange rate provisions. That was the asymmetrical part of the Bretton Woods system. We are not in that system now and the US has no option for fixing, and the euro has no option for fixing because, of course, this is half an American show.

Now, I do believe that the dollar-euro rate is the most important price in the world and something will have to be done to manage it. But you have to always have an anchor. There always has to be some third element that is an anchor to determine which country needs to adjust. Historically, it has been gold or silver. That is now out of the way. If today we could be sure that gold were stable, I would recommend a gold standard. I would recommend countries fix to gold, if I thought that the gold-commodity-price ratio would be stable. But I would not recommend that today, and I have never recommended that, unless provisions were first made to make sure that the gold-commodity-price ratio is stable. If you stabilize gold against commodities then gold would make a wonderful stable anchor. But we are not near to even talking about a framework for that. All that we can talk about is ad hoc pragmatic policy. I do not think benign neglect will work. I think it is going to be a dirty float in any case. I think this there is going to have to be something to prevent these big swings of banks, financials going back and forward when they rock the boat one way or the other and you have big swings in the dollar-euro rate. I think the authorities are going to have to stop that.

The very interesting point that Emil Claassen made, this discussion of these little countries is very good, but I do think that you have to make an exception here about the two countries that he chose as the two examples of floating, Switzerland and Singapore. Well, look at those two countries, two of the richest countries in the world, two highly sophisticated countries and both float. But Singapore has got a clear-cut price rule, and so it has a very stable monetary policy. Switzerland of course has not only a stable monetary policy but heavy gold backing for its currency. Those two countries have been successful. But it is much easier for a country that does not have the expertise of those two particular countries to take the easier option of fixing to a big stable neighbor. Estonia is one example. Estonia in 1992 set up the kroon and established the eight kroon per mark, a currency board arrangement. If you look at the history of the kroon, it has had a big spike, a big inflation spike because they set the rate far too low and there was a large inflation, but that low rate had the advantage of letting them build up reserves. The inflation rate is now down and if they do not overshoot, the stabilization will have been a success. The fact is that you need sophisticated monetary managers to manage a flexible exchange rate system properly. Very few developing countries that have flexible exchange rates have managed to preserve monetary stability.

To me the greatest crime of intellectuals in the postwar discussions is to pose a choice between fixed or flexible exchange rates. That is to me a non-economist's way of posing the issue. The problem is always: what is the best approach for monetary stability? Monetary targeting, inflation targeting or foreign currency targeting or even gold targeting? What is the approach to stability? You can not say: 'Let's have floating rates!' without stating what is the alternative target for stability. If a country has a fixed rate and then decides to go off that fix, then what is its new target? What has happened, in fact, is that countries that have opted for floating rates have listened to academics who have pounded on the table saying we have to have a floating exchange rate, but they are not told that they have to adopt some alternative form of stability. Or, if they are told, they do not listen. To me it does not really matter too much whether a country has a fixed exchange rate or a flexible exchange rate; that is not to me the issue. The issue is, does it fix to anything. If one stabilizes the price level, the money supply or the exchange rate, policy is going to be ten times better than having no target at all.

J. Frankel: I just want to make another response to the currency board issue and Professor Claassen's nice example. Bob thinks that Singapore is a special case because it is rich, I think maybe Hong Kong is a special case. Like the other lists I have offered, there is certainly a list of characteristics that make a country appropriate for a currency board. I do not think most countries have it. But one of the characteristics is an almost desperate need to import monetary stability due to an absence of stable institutions or a history of monetary stability. Argentina had a history of hyperinflation. It was first becoming apparent in 1983 that Britain was going to turn Hong

Kong back over to China and there was a real sense of panic and unease and a need to reassure the financial markets, so I think that is in large part why they adopted the currency board. Estonia obviously had a need to create a stable institution where there was none; even Austria maybe (which was not a currency board of course) had a desire to tie itself to the West. Not all countries have such a need, almost desperation, for monetary stability that it is appropriate to give up their monetary independence to that degree.

K.-H. Paqué: Very briefly one remark on the example Austria, Germany, Switzerland. I think one really cannot draw strong conclusions from these examples about the desirability of different exchange rate regimes. And it is precisely because Austria and Switzerland are so similar in many respects. Well, both countries are highly integrated with Germany and share the same anti-inflationary preferences with Germany, and after all in the relevant period there were no strong asymmetric shocks hitting any of these countries. So the question really is, what was the target of the Swiss Central Bank and the crucial experiment would be what the Swiss Central Bank would have done if Switzerland had not been integrated in this sense with the German area. And, I think, basically there was no conflict between external and internal stability during the period in Switzerland. And so Switzerland basically followed, behaved as if it had something close to a fixed rate. So really I think one probably needs different settings, it is precisely the structure differences between countries which makes a rich experiment so as to judge about different exchange rate regimes.

H. Etienne: Professor Cooper asked Professor Claassen: 'What is your preference?' (policy of convergence between the dollar and the euro). The real question is: what will actually happen between the dollar and the euro? Speaking from my own experience, there will be some form of exchange rate system between the three zones of the Triad. In 1978/79 we established the EMS (European Monetary System) while the economic and financial establishment believed only in the virtues of floating currencies. We had to establish the EMS by setting aside that establishment. We then created a very limited nucleus of new people (three in all) who were very close to the actual decision-makers, namely Helmut Schmidt, Valéry Giscard d'Estaing and Roy Jenkins. In some way it was a 'coup d'Etat' against established institutions which were taken by surprise Why did it succeed? It happened just because industry on both sides of the Rhine wanted it to happen. Industry, which may depend for its survival on keeping down two or three percent of its cost, did not want to be any more dependent on erratic moves of the currencies, and especially the movements of the dollar which changed the cost forecasts by a multiple. The same will happen with our euro relationship with the dollar and the yen. Central bankers know that they cannot resist a unanimous pressure of those who are responsible for the economy as a whole. They will by all means prevent parallel behavior between the currencies of the Triad.

I remember delivering a lecture in Cambridge, Mass., in October 1993, at a period when the establishment remained hypnotized by the monetary crisis of August 1, 1993. The talk was entitled 'The end of integration?', the most important being the question mark. I do not remember if Professor Cooper was there, but at least two of the established professors who had previously gone public against EMU were present and did intervene. The trend of the debate was that EMU was bad for Europe and for the world and that anyway it would not happen. My guess was that what had worked in 1978/79 would play again. We would have EMU. The assessment made à propos EMU is valid also for the next step, which is the relationship between the currencies of the Triad. On both sides of the Atlantic the international interests are now as strong as those which existed between countries of the EC in 1978/79, so that the same pressure will lead necessarily to the same result. I leave open the technicalities of this convergence and give no importance at all to theoretical considerations that professors and central bankers may consider fundamental. No professor and no central banker has ever resisted the basic needs of industry.

A. Clesse: Niels Thygesen, do you want to respond?

N. Thygesen: Mr. Deutsch put three questions to me. I think he underestimates the degree of autonomy of the ECB and its way of reaching decisions. Just a simple majority is required on any policy decision as is the case in national central banks, no qualified majority, everybody has one vote.

What is the Commission's role in monetary affairs? A very limited one. The European Central Bank is in charge of monetary policy, the finance ministers in charge of budgetary policy. The Commission analyzes and advises, it does monitor but it really has a strictly advisory role. And I think you suggested that as well. So I trust the Commission will not speak up in G-7.

G. Ross: I am another wondering American political scientist type, I am not a banker, I am not a bank specialist, I am not an economist. But I have really been listening, Armand put me on the program under a question which was not mine, but if I may do something strange and perhaps it will help to prepare our discussion this afternoon, I may ask questions rather than giving answers. The rubric that Armand assigned to me is, what international role is desirable and how to prepare for that role. The first part of the question is pretty easy to answer. We want a euro that is stable, we want a euro that promotes a structural reform; we want a euro that promotes growth, we want a euro that creates satisfactory international cooperation, particularly with the Americans; we want a euro that is capable of productive risk management or multiple risks; we want a euro that is capable of contributing to successful crisis management both internally and externally; we want one that is good for outsiders. In other words, we want a euro that promotes human felicity and human virtue.

So, the first question is really easy to answer. The question is how to get there and that is more complicated. So, I have a rule of life which is that big changes are destabilizing. I think probably North Americans would agree since we are all suffering from jet-lagging that destabilizes, but I think what I want to do is to try to raise four or five problem areas that some other people have raised or that have not been raised. And to pose the question, not to answer it, because I am not an expert: how is it likely to be resolved, can that be resolved, what scenarios has one for resolving them?

The first and most obvious, the one that Professor Thygesen raised, and everyone else has raised, is clearly a major set of coordination problems between the Bank and EMU and member states. I can focus on these things by talking to a couple of issues, one issue that has been raised already many times and another that has not: What happens when you get the predicted appreciation of the euro after January and a depreciation of the dollar and you get the problems of exports and increased unemployment because of the euro or at least attributable to the euro. You are going to have coordination difficulties. How do those difficulties get resolved? And how do you prevent? Is the Stability and Growth Pact enough to prevent member states, enough to give them control over the political reactions against what is going to happen? Is macroeconomic coordination such that it is sufficient? What more needs to be done?

Another scenario. What is going to happen, and this is rather more likely, what happens when the Union faces the quite likely refusal of some member states to undertake serious structural reform? I mean, flexibilizing a labor market and their welfare states. This is politically a bomb as people ought to know. What do you do then? The Luxembourg employment policy is sort of nice, but it has not got any teeth. The Growth and Stability Pact does not focus on these issues, except indirectly. How do you get member state coordination and bank coordination which will not subvert the purposes of the EMU process?

Another area of general coordination which we mentioned earlier which I think is also a very serious issue which we talked about technically, but I think not politically, and I raise the question, is that to make an international role viable for a human, virtuous euro you need the help and understanding of the United States quite obviously. This is Charlie's issue about leadership. And the question is, I mentioned this earlier, the United States administration has only recently given its blessing to EMU, it is quite clearly taking a wait-and-see attitude towards what happens rather than taking any grand positions. Europeans, I am afraid, have expectations of what will come out of this, whether it will be a bipolar situation of leadership or a situation of American hegemony and European followership is an open question. My suspicion is that it will probably be the latter rather than the former and leadership will continue to be provided by us. The Europeans, because they do not have the resources to play and to have it otherwise, will be put into a situation in which they are more pushers than they used to be, but still ultimately takers in these kinds of situations. There will be dollar leadership, and then what, is the question. How do you sell that back here? What are your expectations? How do you play with that? And so on. In other words, international coordination is still a live issue.

A third sort of coordination issues which everyone has mentioned, particularly de Boissieu, crisis management issues. How are you going to resolve the issue of lender of last resort? Who is going to resolve it? Can it be resolved? What do you do in systemic crises of an international kind? There, I think, there is no real problem because coordination with the Americans will not be that hard. But it would be an asymmetrical coordination with the Americans, again you would be more takers than givers although you would be more givers than you used to be. How would you live with that?

And then a fourth set of issues with another set of questions. How does all we have been talking about for two days, intersect with other issues that are on the European Union's plate at the present time? It is all very nice to talk about creating an ideal euro that promotes human happiness, but there are a lot of issues on the EMU's plate at this point. And issues are not automatically, hermetically sealed one from the other. How does the euro play in terms of enlargement? We have talked a lot about what do you do with the outsiders, the four outsiders? Everybody is optimistic about that. I am not so sure. And how do you do, and how does the euro play, in political terms, with the development of issues of institutional reform which have to be faced very soon?

Now, all these questions are not meant to be catastrophe questions at all. Questions are questions and they may have different magnitudes or weight, they may not be so serious and some of them may be very serious. The real issue that I wanted to raise by being such a silly wondering American was to see if we could discuss a little bit more what the plausible pass to confront some of these issues might be? Perhaps there are other key problem areas and we should talk about the proactive pass there as well.

R. Skidelsky: Just one question to Professor Ross, and it is an ignorant one. How will the creation of the euro affect the structure, voting powers, subscriptions to the IMF? Has that all been settled?

G. Ross: I believe there is no effect. This thing has been settled definitively but the conception I am going on is that there will be no change.

R. Cooper: It's governments who are members of the IMF, it's ministers of finance who are governors of the Monetary Fund, the voting structure is determined accordingly and the creation of the euro need not change any of that.

R. Skidelsky: It need not, but it should probably.

G. Patterson: It will. In all the discussions not a single mention has been made of parliaments either national or European. And one of the features of the system is that there is a disjunction between the responsibilities of the ECB, to the European Parliament, and the responsibility of ministers and the national central banks, in one way or another, to national parliaments. Now this may not make any difference at all to the operation of the system except as indicated by one remark made by Professor Ross, namely: what is going to happen if public opinion becomes disenchanted with the management of the system? Parliaments may not have much power; but they are the safety valve for public opinion. And if national parliaments become disaffected with the system, or for that matter if the European Parliament does that could have certain grave consequences. Now I am glad there is a political scientist answering this point rather than an economist because he will appreciate the dangers in neglecting the democratic deficit.

J. Baumberger: I would like to make two points at the end of this conference.

I was glad to notice that there is widespread consensus about the fact that the success of the euro in terms of inflation need not necessarily mean success in terms of stability of exchange rates, nor in terms of stability of the global financial system. At least here we are aware of the problems.

The second point is this: the source of concern to me about the euro is the amount of sophistication and coordination that apparently this currency will require. A system that requires this incredible amount of sophistication, coordination and flexibility on the part of the policy- and decision-makers is quite likely to be extremely information-sensitive. Flexibility, as we all know, is a two-edged sword, one edge being the amount of discretion and unpredictability. Of course, we hope that flexibility will be exercised with the utmost wisdom, but whose wisdom in a world with many wisdoms? This information sensitivity might well have a disruptive effect on the proper and stable operation of the system. I would expect this sensitivity to create problems especially in the early phases of implementation. All in all, I draw the conclusion not to expect any significant improvement in international stability from the introduction of the euro.

A. Clesse: I think it makes sense to close this discussion with somebody from a neutral country.

PART V
KEYNOTE SESSION

Charles Ruppert: It will be very difficult to find my name anywhere in the accompanying documentation of this conference. I am Charles Ruppert, President of the Pierre Werner Foundation. On behalf of the Foundation as well as the Luxembourg Institute for European and International Studies, I have great pleasure in welcoming you here today to this keynote session under the auspices of the Government of Luxembourg, with the support of the European Commission, and held in honor of two pioneers, Pierre Werner and Charles Kindleberger.

I am especially grateful that ambassadors, ministers, members of Parliament and the Council of State have been able to attend. A special welcome to the invited students who as future leaders will have to know what the euro is about.

It is fine to hold a conference but somebody has to pay and as a banker I know what that feels like. The contribution of the banks was necessary to enable this conference to take place. In your invitation leaflet, you can identify the 24 companies, which gave financial support, and the other sponsors who provided good food and technical support, as well as the press. We are equally grateful to the interpreters, whom we do not see, and without whom we would be lost.

If you glance briefly at the list of participants of the seminar, you will be amazed, as I am, by the outstanding attendance from all over the world. It is astonishing that these brilliant people spotted Luxembourg on the map and found the time to share their vast experience and knowledge with us. That is due to one man and his team, Armand Clesse of the Institute who has a lifetime's experience of building up relationships at this level.

Now, why this conference? Small is beautiful, but Luxembourg is tiny therefore vulnerable. So we have to cope with the challenges and turn to the future. There is a Chinese proverb which says that a man who looks over his shoulder will bump into a tree. We do not want to do that. We have shown this in having launched the first euro bond issue in 1993, pioneered the first ECU denominated bond issue in 1981, which many people considered a foolish even exotic thing to do, especially people from the other side of the Moselle and the Channel. That did not stop us. In 1988, we were the first EU country to enact a European directive on investment funds. I will not let the cat out of the bag concerning our next steps but if I say pension funds, that could be a clue. Luxembourg has always been and always will be much more than the tax haven that some see in us.

Luxembourg is tiny but has the fortune to have had and to have great politicians. One of them, very young in political terms and also in mind is Prime Minister Jean-Claude Juncker, born in 1954. We have the privilege to have him with us today. He became a member of the Luxembourg Government in 1982 and is still there. He has covered a lot of areas: social affairs, labor, employment, budget and finance. He has contributed to great achievements in the construction of Europe and remains strongly dedicated to this cause. He is very busy, often abroad, so it is astonishing to have him here today to address us, even if only briefly. We thank you for that, Prime Minister. But before giving him the floor, I must stress that we have a very tight schedule: Mr. Tietmeyer will have to catch his flight. But he was kind enough to catch it this morning to come here despite the snowstorm over Frankfurt. So, Prime Minister, you have the floor.

Jean-Claude Juncker:[*] Monsieur le Président, Mesdames, Messieurs. Le scénario, en fait, est toujours le même. Il y a quelques mois j'acceptais, je dois dire avec plaisir, l'intervention de cet après-midi, ne me préoccupant pas trop de l'actualité qui pourrait être celle d'aujourd'hui. Or, elle vient de me rejoindre puisque je dois recevoir d'ici une heure et demie le Premier Ministre albanais. Et je dois voir mes collègues belge et néerlandais ce soir et demain matin à Bruxelles. Ce qui fait, heureusement pour vous, que mon propos devra être bref.

J'ai accepté cette invitation avec le plaisir que je vous ai dit, parce que j'étais sensibilisé par le fait que ce colloque est organisé en l'honneur de qui vous savez. Depuis de longues années, des décennies en fait, au moins pour certains d'entre vous, nous suivons les travaux du Professeur Kindleberger qui est non seulement bien connu dans son pays natal, mais dont la doctrine n'a pas manqué de produire ses effets, et théoriques et pratiques, dans nos pays.

Et ce colloque est organisé en l'honneur de mon prédécesseur Monsieur Pierre Werner que l'on décrit très souvent dans une formule qui nous est devenue familière comme un des pères de l'euro. Par conséquent, comment ne pas répondre présent lorsque sont présents les deux éminents spécialistes que je viens de citer.

S'y ajoute que la panoplie de ceux qui les assisteront aujourd'hui est impressionnante et je suis très honoré de pouvoir tourner le dos, si j'ose dire, à mon ancien collègue le premier ministre tchèque, Monsieur Václav Klaus, qui continue à occuper d'importantes responsabilités dans son pays.

Et je salue avec le respect et l'indépendance qui s'impose, le président de la Bundesbank, Monsieur Hans Tietmeyer, que j'ai connu lorsqu'il n'occupait pas encore les fonctions qui sont les siennes aujourd'hui, mais lorsque à deux nous nous attachions à doter l'Europe, une année après l'autre, d'un budget communautaire dont l'établissement à l'époque était plus difficile qu'il ne l'est aujourd'hui. Je dis souvent que je suis le seul premier ministre à avoir passé des nuits ensemble avec Monsieur Tietmeyer, mais à Bruxelles. Et donc je suis heureux qu'il soit des nôtres aujourd'hui.

En fait, le séminaire qui se déroule dans notre ville, ville dans laquelle je me permettrai de saluer très cordialement tous ceux qui ne sont que

---

[*] discours prononcé sans texte préparé

passagèrement les hôtes de notre pays, est consacré au sujet gravitant autour du rôle et de la dimension stabilisatrice internationale de l'euro.

Très certainement ne commettrai-je pas l'impair, ni le faux pas, de décrire devant vous quelles peuvent être les conséquences de l'euro sur l'architecture du système financier international. Très certainement ne décrirai-je pas quel impact l'euro risque de produire, et très certainement va produire, sur les relations financières internationales. Spécialistes que vous êtes, vous n'avez pas besoin d'une pédagogie dans la matière où vous êtes coutumiers et familiers.

Je me permettrai de concentrer mon propos sur quelques considérations qui trouveraient place sur le glacis de la dimension internationale de l'euro. Je veux dire par là quelles sont les politiques internes, quelles sont les prémisses internes que nous devons conduire et auxquelles nous devons répondre pour que l'euro puisse développer une quelconque influence positive au plan international. Quel sera, le jour où l'euro sera définitivement arrivé, son impact sur le système financier international?

Je crois que cet impact, de par son ampleur et de par son volume, résulte très nécessairement de la description que l'on peut donner de la force qu'il va développer. Les pays de l'euro aujourd'hui représentent environ 35 pour cent des moyens de paiement internationaux. La zone de l'euro représente 20 pour cent du PIB mondial et 20 pour cent du commerce international. L'euro très certainement sera appelé, à côté du dollar, à se positionner en tant que monnaie de réserve internationale. Tous ces effets—certains entre eux très certainement seront très bénéfiques—se produiront.

Mais pour que l'euro puisse développer une force, puisse devenir une force influente et un facteur d'influence dans le monde, il faudra qu'au niveau des différents pays de l'Union européenne, et surtout de la zone euro, nous mettions en place les politiques qui conviennent. Et je voudrais donc traiter certains de ces aspects.

Tout d'abord je voudrais dire la satisfaction qui est la mienne de voir que les ministres des finances de l'Union européenne au début de la semaine en cours ont été à même de se mettre d'accord sur la représentation extérieure de l'euro. La proposition que les ministres des finances feront parvenir aux chefs d'Etat et de gouvernement qui se réuniront à la fin de la semaine prochaine à Vienne très certainement sera avalisée par les chefs d'Etat et de gouvernement. Et donc pour le premier janvier 1999 nous aurons mis en place un système qui permettra aux Européens d'abord, mais au reste du monde surtout, de savoir à qui s'adresser lorsqu'il s'agit de nouer un contact avec la zone euro. Je suis content de voir que les trois membres de la zone euro qui aujourd'hui sont membres du G-7 ont été d'accord à partager le fardeau de leur tâche avec les autres participants de la zone euro et qu'une place importante a été réservée au président de l'Euro 11 ou au président de l'Ecofin étant entendu qu'il n'y avait jamais de différence de vue entre nous quant au point de savoir s'il fallait oui ou non associer à la représentation extérieure la Banque centrale européenne.

Il est évident qu'une place prépondérante reviendra à l'autorité monétaire européenne. Mais j'ai pu mesurer à l'aune des âpres débats qui ont précédé l'accord que nous avons trouvé que certains d'entre nous, sinon tous, devront apprendre les lois qui désormais vont régir la gestion collective et solidaire de la monnaie commune. Il n'est pas pensable que lorsque 11 pays abandonnent leur souveraineté monétaire—pour l'accroître en fait en se dotant d'une souveraineté monétaire européenne—que nous continuons à regarder le monde comme si nous étions toujours seuls ou juxtaposés dans une même Union européenne. Non, toutes les analyses que nous devons faire, nous devons les faire à l'aune de la zone euro et nous devrons donc faire en sorte que tous ceux qui la composent trouvent leur place, et leur bonne place, dans l'architecture monétaire européenne.

Nous avons assisté au cours des mois et semaines écoulés à quelques âpres débats qui n'ont cessé de me surprendre. Très soudainement est surgi comme un nouveau débat sur une vieille question qui concerne l'indépendance de la Banque centrale et le *policy mix* entre politique économique et politique monétaire. C'est un débat qui m'a surpris dans la mesure où certains pays membres de l'euro ont eu le débat lorsqu'il s'agissait de ratifier le traité de Maastricht, alors que d'autres ont découvert le débat quelques semaines avant l'entrée définitive de l'Europe dans l'atmosphère et la réalité de l'euro.

J'étais surpris sans doute parce que ma longévité fait que j'en ai vu d'autres. Je suis en effet—je vous suis reconnaissant de remarquer qu'on ne le voit pas—le doyen d'âge des ministres des finances d'Europe. Et je suis le seul survivant des signataires du traité de Maastricht. Il n'y a plus aucun ministre des finances à être resté en fonction depuis que le 7 février 1992 nous ayons signé le traité de Maastricht. Cela me pousse parfois à des réflexions philosophiques, mais le plus souvent à des réactions irritées, sinon intempestives, parce qu'on ne peut pas en Europe, ni ailleurs, reproduire à chaque fois qu'un nouveau gouvernement se pointe à l'horizon d'un quelconque parlement, faire revivre les vieux débats et donc les vieux démons que nous avions pensé avoir jugulés lorsque nous avions signé le traité de Maastricht. Il devrait y avoir en Europe la transposition du précepte national qui veut qu'il y ait une certaine continuité du service public. Nous sommes tellement habitués à transposer dans nos droits nationaux des règles qu'édicte la Communauté européenne que nous avons totalement omis de cultiver le respect des vieux principes qui régissaient nos vieilles nations européennes jusqu'à ce que l'Union européenne ne vienne, mais en partie seulement, les relayer.

Je crois que ce débat—indépendance de la Banque centrale d'une part, prise d'influence des décideurs publics sur les décisions de la Banque centrale d'autre part—est un faux débat. Le principe de l'indépendance des banques centrales est un principe qui fut contesté un peu partout à travers le monde jusqu'il y a trente années. Depuis, et sous l'égide, il faut le reconnaître, de la Bundesbank allemande, les vertus de l'indépendance se sont imposées partout. Et lorsque nous avons négocié le traité de Maastricht pendant une présidence luxembourgeoise au premier semestre 1991 et sous une présidence néerlandaise pendant le deuxième semestre 1991, nous tombions non sans difficultés d'accord sur le fait qu'il faudrait accorder à cette Banque centrale européenne au moins le même statut d'indépendance que celui qui caractérisa la success-story de la Bundesbank allemande. On ne peut pas donc contester l'indépendance de la banque puisqu'elle figure en tant que principe directeur dans le traité sur l'Union européenne.

Mais le fait que cette Banque centrale européenne serait indépendante, signifie-t-il que les gouvernements très soudainement auraient disparu, auraient tous démissionné, enrichiraient le paysage européen par des gestes de démission à gogo, que les hommes politiques n'auraient plus le droit de dire leur mot. Non, je ne crois pas que indépendance de la Banque centrale voudrait dire suppression du pouvoir politique et élimination de la pensée politique. Là encore, le traité de Maastricht peut nous servir de guide. Le traité de Maastricht dans les articles y afférents précise bien que les politiques économiques qui sont du ressort commun doivent être mieux coordonnées en Europe. Et qui dit coordination des politiques économiques en fait dit qu'il doit y avoir entre nous, et entre nous et la Banque centrale européenne, un débat vertueux sur les voies et chemins à suivre.

Les hommes politiques se sont habitués à recevoir, en intervalles reguliers—cela commence même dans ce pays—des leçons publiques administrées par les présidents des banques centrales et par les gouverneurs. Je trouve ce phénomène non pas inquiétant mais normal, rassurant. Les banquiers ne sont—contrairement à certains récits de presse qui sont consacrés à leur psychologie interne—nullement gênés de voir les gouvernements et les hommes politiques exprimer leur point de vue.

Il est évident que la Banque centrale européenne n'évolue pas dans un système déresponsabilisé, mais que la Banque centrale européenne a des comptes à rendre. A l'époque quand nous avons conclu le traité, nous avions appelé cela la *democratic accountability* de la Banque centrale. Il est évident que le président de la Banque centrale participera aux réunions du Conseil des ministres des finances et aux réunions du Euro 11, qui regroupe les 11 pays participants de l'euro. Il est normal que le président de l'Ecofin, j'ai pu le faire en septembre de l'année passée, participe activement aux réunions de la Banque centrale européenne. Il est normal que le président de la Banque centrale européenne s'adresse à trois reprises par année aux parlementaires européens.

Cela n'enlève en rien des éléments centraux à l'indépendance de la Banque centrale et le fait que les gouvernements articulent parfois publiquement des positions qui touchent à la politique monétaire qui devra être mise en place et exclusivement par la Banque centrale européenne est un phénomène qui caractérise les sociétés démocratiques et n'est pas une ingérence dans le secteur protégé que nous appelons indépendance de la Banque centrale européenne. Que nous discutions entre nous de la coordination des politiques économiques n'est pas un pouvoir que nous nous serions arrogés, mais en fait constitue l'exécution d'une disposition afférente du traité de Maastricht. Il n'est pas pensable que sur un continent dont une bonne partie est organisée sous forme de marché intérieur et d'union monétaire les ministres des finances, les chefs d'Etats et de gouvernement ne discutent pas entre eux des bonnes politiques économiques à mettre en place. Nous avons adopté lors du Conseil européen de Luxembourg de décembre 1997 une résolution du Conseil européen sur le renforcement des politiques économiques, sur le renforcement de la coordination des politiques économiques, et nous étions tombés d'accord pour dire que nous devrions discuter entre nous des politiques budgétaires nationales, des politiques fiscales nationales, des politiques structurelles nationales et des politiques salariales nationales pour pouvoir les ajuster les unes sur les autres. Pour éviter que certains pays tirent à gauche et que d'autres pays tirent à droite.

Il ne faut pas des rappels un peu pénibles, parce que trop répétitifs de certains ministres des finances qui se retrouvent du côté de la gauche de l'échiquier politique pour nous rappeler sans cesse qu'il faut coordonner les politiques économiques. Nous le savons depuis que nous nous sommes mis d'accord sur le traité de Maastricht puisque c'est une disposition du traité qui nous y invite. Nous nous sommes mis d'accord sur les grands axes de cette coordination lors du Conseil européen de Luxembourg. Par conséquent il ne s'agit pas de revendiquer ce qui déjà a été agréé. Il s'agit de faire sur quoi nous nous sommes mis d'accord. J'observe que les présidences britannique et autrichienne s'y sont employées mais avec un dynamisme que j'aurais pu m'imaginer avoir plus d'élan qu'il ne l'avait.

Nous assistons au déferlement des crises asiatiques, russes, partiellement latino-américaines. Nous sommes à nous interroger sur les conséquences que ces déséquilibres ne manqueront pas de produire dans les différents pays de la zone euro. Nous disons à forte répétition que nos politiques économiques doivent être mieux coordonnées et nous ne les coordonnons pas suffisamment. Il faudrait que parmi les ministres des finances de la zone de l'euro nous nous mettions d'accord sur les bonnes politiques économiques à mettre en place, celles qui devront être réactives aux crises financières qui sont les nôtres, celles qui doivent être pro-actives pour faire en sorte que la zone de l'euro reste une région à croissance économique durable et pour que cet euro devienne un élément de croissance internationale. Par conséquent il s'agira maintenant de nous mettre d'accord. Je proposerai que nous le fassions lors du Conseil européen de Vienne, sur les bonnes politiques macro-économiques à mettre en place, sur le bon *policy mix* et ensuite fortifier et revigorer par une même analyse et par une même intention actionnelle le débat avec la Banque centrale européenne sur les conséquences que la banque, elle, pourrait tirer de la mise en place de ces politiques économiques mieux coordonnées.

Il est évident que nous avons besoin en Europe d'un bon *policy mix* entre politique économique d'une part et politique monétaire d'autre part. Mais j'observe avec une certaine inquiétude—parfois elle va croissante—que certains estiment que la politique monétaire serait le seul domaine politique où des actions en faveur de la reprise conjoncturelle et de la reprise des marchés de l'emploi seraient possibles.

Si la réalité était ainsi faite que la politique monétaire à elle pourrait faire en sorte que des reprises conjoncturelles s'installent, que des affaissements conjoncturels n'aient pas lieu et que les politiques de l'emploi repartent, il y aurait longtemps déjà que toutes les banques centrales européennes et tous les gouvernements européens se seraient mis d'accord sur une action poussée, si j'ose dire, dans le domaine de la politique monétaire.

Or le monétaire ne peut pas remplacer le politique. On ne peut pas d'une part revendiquer une meilleure coordination des politiques économiques et d'autre part surcharger de responsabilités la politique monétaire. Nous avons une division du travail claire en Europe depuis l'adoption du traité qui veut que les gouvernements soient responsables des politiques économiques et que la Banque centrale, indépendante, soit responsable de la politique monétaire. On ne peut donc pas s'attendre à ce que la Banque centrale fasse le travail, très souvent domestique, des gouvernements qui composent la zone euro.

Mais il est non moins évident qu'il doit y avoir un dialogue permanent entre l'autorité monétaire et les instances politiques en Europe pour accorder nos vues, ou pour pouvoir mettre en place un *mix* qui serve avec des conséquences positives les marchés de l'emploi en Europe.

Mais il ne faut pas oublier, c'est une disposition du traité, que la Banque centrale européenne doit d'abord défendre la stabilité des prix en Europe. Ce concept que la stabilité des prix doit être un des principes directeurs de l'Union européenne ne doit pas être mise en cause. Et je persiste à croire que la stabilité des prix est la condition essentielle, sinon la précondition, pour permettre à l'Europe de voir s'articuler sur son territoire des marchés de l'emploi efficaces et fertiles en emploi.

Je ne crois pas que nous devrions réassister de façon un peu muette à un débat que j'avais cru être derrière nous et qui consiste à créditer la thèse que vous pouvez avoir des succès en matière de politique de l'emploi à condition d'endetter les Etats et les budgets nationaux. Si nous avions eu au cours des dernières décennies moins de déficits en Europe, nous aurions aujourd'hui une situation en matière d'emploi qui serait autrement plus avantageuse que celle que nous avons aujourd'hui. Il est un fait que les déficits accumulés au cours de certains replis conjoncturels ont empêché les gouvernements d'employer l'arme fiscale pour revigorer la croissance économique dans leur pays. A quelques exceptions d'ailleurs, comme celle du Luxembourg qui au creux de la vague conjoncturelle a pu alléger le poids fiscal qui pénalisait l'activité économique et qui ainsi a permis à l'économie luxembourgeoise de connaître des taux de croissance qui ne portaient jamais le signe de la décroissance qui caractérisa bien des situations économiques en Europe.

Je me répète en me résumant pour vous dire que la coordination des politiques économiques reste importante, elle est du ressort des gouvernements. Qu'ils fassent leur travail. La politique monétaire est du ressort de la Banque centrale européenne et indépendante. Elle fera son travail tout comme les banques centrales nationales ont fait leur travail jusque dans les dernières heures. Il doit y avoir un dialogue fructueux et fertile entre les deux pôles de l'architecture européenne pour que nous arrivions à dégager le bon *policy mix* qui conviendra à la situation interne de l'Europe et à la situation que l'Europe devra affronter dans ses échanges avec le reste du monde.

Bien sûr, on ne peut pas se cacher l'évidence que la mise en place de l'euro—qui déjà aujourd'hui produit des effets bénéfiques dans tous les pays membres participant à l'euro—nous conduira à des corollaires qu'il ne faut pas sous-estimer. J'ai toujours estimé, et je l'ai dit souvent non seulement à l'étranger, mais également dans mon propre pays, que vous ne pouvez mettre en place un marché intérieur et une union monétaire sans vous occuper de l'évolution, parfois trop divergente, des systèmes fiscaux dans les pays qui composent la zone de l'euro. Je ne parle pas seulement de la nécessaire harmonisation de la fiscalité de l'épargne en Europe, je veux également parler de la non moins nécessaire coordination des autres politiques fiscales relatives à d'autres matières fiscales.

Nous avons toujours estimé, enfin toujours depuis deux ou trois années, que bien sûr la fiscalité de l'épargne en Europe ne pourrait pas continuer à produire des effets concurrentiels néfastes, mais qu'il faudrait également, après l'avoir harmonisée, mettre, mais parallèlement, en place un système qui s'inscrirait en faux contre cette nouvelle vague qui déferle sur l'Europe et qui consiste en une défiscalisation compétitive de certaines branches entières des économies européennes. En matière de fiscalité des entreprises, la concurrence déloyale entre les différents pays de l'Union européenne est au moins aussi vive qu'en matière de fiscalité de l'épargne. Par conséquent on ne peut pas exclure du champ de réflexion et d'action de la coordination des politiques fiscales le domaine de la fiscalité des entreprises.

Pour le reste, nous pensons, nous, que la concurrence fiscale en Europe n'est pas un péché mortel, mais que l'Europe se ferait le plus grand tort si nous abandonnions la compétitivité fiscale entre nous. Il y a à travers le monde des unions monétaires qui fonctionnent avec des régimes fiscaux divergents au plan interne. Il n'y a pas la même règle fiscale partout dans toutes les unions monétaires à travers le monde. Il n'y a pas les mêmes taux d'imposition sur tout le territoire de toutes les unions monétaires qui existent à travers la planète. Il ne faut pas croire que l'Union européenne, la zone euro deviendrait plus forte en faisant en sorte que tous les taux d'imposition seraient exactement les mêmes partout dans les différentes régions de la zone euro. Nous disons donc oui à la concurrence fiscale interne à l'Europe, nous disons oui à la lutte contre la concurrence fiscale déloyale tout comme nous devons applaudir des deux mains les efforts de tous ceux qui voudraient doter l'Union européenne et l'union monétaire européenne d'une dimension sociale autrement plus prononcée que celle que nous pouvons admirer aujourd'hui.

Il est évident que sur un marché intérieur et dans une union monétaire vous avez besoin de quelques règles sociales fondamentales qui constituent des minima pour tous les pays membres de l'Union européenne et de la zone euro. Je n'aime pas trop l'expression 'union sociale' parce qu'elle conduit certains à considérer qu'il s'agirait d'harmoniser les systèmes de sécurité sociale en Europe. C'est strictement impossible. Mais je revendique pour l'Europe la mise en place d'un socle de droits sociaux minima pour les travailleurs. Il nous faudra des règles communes, mais minimales, en matière de licenciements et en bien d'autres domaines du droit du travail pour faire en sorte que cette Union européenne et cette union monétaire européenne ne soit pas vécue par ceux qui travaillent en Europe comme une expérience qui ne leur serait pas destinée. Par conséquent, politique fiscale et politique sociale dans leur partie harmonisatrice et dans les descriptions et définitions que je viens de vous livrer vont ensemble. Je suis comme Pascal en France: j'aime les choses qui vont ensemble. Et je voudrais donc que ceux qui revendiquent avec une frénésie un peu gênante l'harmonisation fiscale redoublent d'efforts lorsqu'il s'agira d'harmoniser le droit du travail en Europe pour le doter de quelques dispositions minimales qui seraient les mêmes partout.

Je suis un peu inquiet de voir notamment dans le domaine du débat fiscal la notion d'intérêt national resurgir. J'observe avec incompréhension un débat hystérique au Royaume-Uni sur l'harmonisation fiscale. Il n'est dans l'intention de personne d'unifier le droit fiscal en Europe. Il est de l'intention de certains d'entre nous, et de l'intention de celui qui vous parle, de mettre en place des règles fiscales minimales pour lutter contre la concurrence fiscale déloyale. Le Luxembourg devra opérer un certain nombre de changements, tout comme ses partenaires d'ailleurs, en matière de fiscalité de l'épargne. D'autres devront opérer de non moins grands changements dans d'autres domaines fiscaux.

La Commission vient de rassembler, de collecter 80 exemples de concurrence fiscale déloyale et j'observe avec un plaisir, qui lui alors va grandissant, que le Luxembourg n'est qu'un petit joueur dans la cour des grands concurrents fiscaux que sont les Etats membres de l'Union européenne. Tous doivent donc faire des efforts pour lutter contre la concurrence fiscale déloyale. Mais si certains grands Etats membres, pour empêcher la coordination des politiques fiscales, nous disent que leur intérêt national veut que cela ne se fasse pas, comment voulez vous que des Etats membres de l'Union européenne à taille plus réduite et à démographie moins pesante puissent convaincre leur opinion publique que dans leur pays un certain nombre de changements doivent être opérés, si ceux qui en prétendant au rôle dirigeant en Europe nous accablent de références à leur intérêt national.

Si nous mettons en place l'euro, nous devons apprendre à raisonner à l'échelle de l'Union européenne et à l'échelle de la zone euro. Par conséquent tous les problèmes qui sont devant nous ont été bien vus par ceux qui ont négocié le traité de Maastricht. Tous les problèmes qui se poseront à nous ont été, et à temps, examinés par ceux qui depuis le début de l'année 1992 se sont chargés de réussir la marche de l'Europe vers l'euro.

L'union monétaire constitue la dernière grande ambition européenne de ce siècle. Il est évident que cette grande entreprise que constitue le passage de 11 pays membres de l'Union européenne à la monnaie unique n'aura de succès que si à terme nous réussirons à sous-tendre cette union monétaire qui se mettra en place par une union politique qui mérite son nom. L'union politique en Europe va de pair avec l'union monétaire. Il n'y a pas d'exemple au monde où une union monétaire aurait survécu en l'absence d'union politique. Et par conséquent, fort de ces exemples historiques, nous devrons nous employer à doter l'Europe d'une véritable architecture politique qui lui permettra de jouer à travers la planète entière le rôle auquel elle peut prétendre suite à la force nouvelle que l'euro lui permettra de se découvrir.

L'union politique, cela veut dire coordination des politiques fiscales, cela veut dire harmonisation sociale, cela voudra dire que nous devrons mettre en place un véritable système de politique extérieure et de sécurité commune, cela voudra dire qu'un jour nous doterons l'Europe d'une dimension de défense qui aujourd'hui lui fait cruellement défaut.

Mais il ne faudrait pas que certains fassent la lourde erreur d'appréciation d'empêcher ce processus de se faire en surchargeant la barque par des considérations d'ordre institutionnel qui aura pour conséquence que certains de nos partenaires en Europe prendront leur distance par rapport au nécessaire complément politique dont l'union monétaire doit être complétée. Provoquer aujourd'hui un débat sur l'abandon du principe de l'unanimité en matière fiscale n'est pas une contribution argumentative à la mise en place d'une union politique parce qu'elle aura des répercussions prohibitives auprès de tous ceux qui ne veulent pas entendre parler de ce principe nouveau qui désormais deviendrait notre règle en matière fiscale. Le Luxembourg, tout comme beaucoup de ses partenaires, reste opposé à l'introduction du système de la majorité qualifiée lorsqu'il s'agira pour l'Europe de se prononcer sur un élément essentiel, non seulement des souverainetés nationales, mais des possibilités de façonnage des paysages socio-économiques dans nos pays que constitue la fiscalité.

Pour le reste je reste convaincu que les conditions pour le lancement de l'euro sont optimales. Je suis impressionné par l'excellente préparation qualitative qui a été faite par les banques centrales en Europe. Je reste un peu sur ma faim en ce qui concerne la substance dans le domaine de la coordination des politiques économiques et je continuerai à travailler avec les modestes moyens que sont ceux de la diplomatie luxembourgeoise à la mise en place d'une union politique plus parfaite. Je persiste à croire que même le traité d'Amsterdam nous permettrait de faire des avancées plus ambitieuses et plus concrètes en matière de politique extérieure et de sécurité commune, en matière de politique de défense, en matière de politique d'asile et d'immigration. Les traités parfaits peuvent conduire à des résultats imparfaits si la volonté de ceux qui sont chargés de les exécuter est imparfaite. Mais des traités imparfaits comme celui d'Amsterdam peuvent conduire à des résultats parfaits si la volonté de ceux qui ont pour charge de les exécuter est elle parfaite. Je vous remercie de votre attention.

Charles Ruppert: Mr. Armand Clesse will now present you the results of the seminar of one and a half days of very intensive discussion.

Armand Clesse: Thank you Mr. Chairman. Don't be afraid, I will not present them myself. There are two rapporteurs, but first I would like to thank those who have supported this event. First and foremost, of course, the co-organizer of the event, the Pierre Werner Foundation and its President Charles Ruppert, then the Prime Minister and the Luxembourg Government, the banks, companies and other organizations which have supported this conference which I think has been a success so far.

The discussions were intense, substantive, and controversial. There was a great diversity of views and the biggest problem for me was to bring the discussions to an end yesterday evening and today, because participants wanted to go on. Now it seems, if I look around, that those who were in the working sessions are somewhat exhausted. These debates took their toll.

So, there are two rapporteurs, one in English and one in French, to try to achieve a linguistic balance which we did not find during the meeting itself. Most participants, even the French, expressed themselves in English, which seems to be the language of economic science, of science *tout court,* but one of the rapporteurs, the French one, promised to give his summing up in French, so we will see.

I can give the floor to the first rapporteur, who is Richard Cooper, from the Kennedy School of Government at Harvard University. I hope the rapporteurs will only talk for ten minutes. Richard Cooper was under the

Carter administration Under Secretary of State for Economic Affairs, and more recently Chairman of the Federal Reserve Bank of Boston.

Richard Cooper: Thank you Mr. Chairman. I don't know how many of you have had the pleasure to go to a conference of the type that we have had during the last day and a half. It was very much an academic conference, designed to exchange analysis, views and opinions, but not to reach consensus or conclusions. No doubt the academics went away from the conference largely with the views that they brought to it, although hopefully at a higher level of sophistication as a result of the discussion. In saying that I don't mean to exclude the possibility that some may actually have changed their views as a result of what was said. In any case, I will not try to summarize the conference in any comprehensive sense, but just give my impressions of the main points of the discussion and the main thrust of arguments as they impressed me. The discussion itself was wide ranging and there are many points that I won't even try to cover.

The first point is that the euro will succeed. This was hardly discussed; it is noteworthy that it was simply taken for granted. The transition to a new European currency will be a successful one, not only in a technical sense of getting started, but in a more general sense that we will see from now on a common currency for Europe and that the principal objective of price stability embodied in the Maastricht Treaty will also be achieved. As I say, these issues were taken for granted. That would not have been true in a conference on this topic one, two or three years ago.

The second point I want to make, however, is that this success will not by itself assure stability of the euro in the world economy and in particular will not assure the stability of exchange rates between the euro and other currencies of which the leading one is the United States dollar. There was, I think, general agreement that over time the euro, a successful euro, as I have said will become established as an international currency in the various dimensions of that term. It is not in fact a well-defined concept. But securities outside of Europe will be issued in euros; securities denominated in euros will be held in pension funds by corporate treasurers, even by central banks around the world; the euro will become increasingly a currency of denomination. So in various dimensions, the euro will over time become an international currency.

There was, however, an important disagreement about how rapidly that process will take place. Some of the participants believe that it will be a gradual process, that hinges, among other things, on the evolution of European capital markets, the evolution of an effective secondary market, increased liquidity in European markets and so on. That process in institutional development itself will take some time. Other participants felt, without disagreeing with the substance of that point, that the evolution would be a relatively rapid one.

An important point: the time it takes for the euro to become a significant international currency itself, becomes an important factor. If as some Europeans both hope and believe, that process is a rapid one, it is more likely to foster world financial instability than if the process is a more gradual and a slower one.

One source of the instability will be the substitution of the euro for the currency that is most widely used today as an international currency, the US dollar. With serious competition from the euro the USA will lose some of the foreign investment that now takes place, and that supports the large US current account deficit. If that investment were to diminish substantially and quickly, it would lead to a sharp depreciation of the dollar relative to the euro. Under those circumstances, the dollar would probably carry the Japanese yen with it. That in turn would lead to serious problems of the competitiveness for those European enterprises that are engaged in world competition. Thus perhaps paradoxically, a rapid development of the euro in its external role is conducive to greater world financial instability. If that were to occur—and I don't want to leave the impression that there was anything like a forecast that it would occur—it would in turn lead around the world to calls for closer financial economic cooperation between EMU Europe and the rest of the world and of course, in particular, closer cooperation with the United States.

I think it is fair to say that there was a general agreement, although again with nuanced differences, that in installing the euro Europeans have given too little attention to the issue of cooperation with the rest of the world. There are still important institutional imperfections and ambiguities with respect to financial decision-making in Euroland: imperfections and ambiguities about the balance of decision-making between the new ECB and national finance ministries, which will continue to be important even after the introduction of a new currency; and between the ECB executive board and the constituent national currency banks, which will continue to exist and indeed will be the operating arms of the ECB in its domestic and, I assume also, in its international operations. There are important ambiguities about how coordination will take place in the formulation of economic policy among all these three groups, and with the European Parliament. So there are a lot of loose ends. Those loose ends will become especially manifest in an environment in which international financial turmoil results from the creation of the euro.

This discussion was particular to the current European circumstance, but as academics we generalized, and had some discussion about the nature of international systems and what configurations tend to be stable and what tend to be unstable. We considered transition from the British pound to the US dollar as an international currency, and whether it is possible to have two financial leaders in the world. I'm sure you will hear some of that from our panel so I won't dwell on it. The key questions are: will Europe have a policy toward the rest of the world and if so what will it be and how will it be decided?

Before closing, I want to touch on an issue that was not discussed directly in the conference but that I believe is important to convey to this group. A number of American economists, of which I am a representative example, have written papers on the euro. The papers have typically raised questions, sometimes serious questions, about the viability of the euro under certain circumstances. The general feedback I have received from Europeans is that these papers are interpreted as being hostile to the euro. I want to take this occasion to make an important distinction between serious analysis on the one hand, and hostile opinion on the other.

Serious analysis, which economists are paid to do in the United States, does not imply a view on the overall merits of a particular proposal. I myself have favored a European common currency for over 25 years, since the early 1970s. But that does not keep me from commenting analytically and critically on this or that particular proposal or aspect of the complicated process of introducing a common currency into many countries. I believe that the Maastricht Treaty was seriously flawed in several respects, that it imposed unnecessary economic burdens on Europe, but that is now water over the dam.

I mention this because I detect a tendency to interpret critical American comments, analytical comments, as hostility to the euro; I want to register the point that in many instances that is an incorrect interpretation.

Some Americans are in fact hostile to the euro. But as some of the American participants in the conference said, the balance of informed opinion in the United States is favorable to the euro, not hostile. In any case, the creation of the euro and the pooling of ten currencies into one is a grand experiment in the annals of monetary history, and we will all be watching it with tremendous interest, and at least in my case with sympathy. Thank you very much.

Armand Clesse: Thank you Richard. Je donne la parole alors à Christian de Boissieu, professeur d'économie à Paris-Dauphine, qui, je l'espère, va s'exprimer en français.

Christian de Boissieu: Monsieur le Premier Ministre, Messieurs les Présidents, Mesdames, Messieurs.

Vous l'avez déjà compris à travers la présentation de Dick Cooper, cette conférence a été plutôt consensuelle. Le consensus est-il bon signe?

Souvent en économie le consensus est dangereux. On l'a bien vu à propos de l'analyse de la conjoncture. Quand tout le monde est d'accord, cela se passe rarement comme prévu. Là il me semble, et je crois que Dick l'a parfaitement exprimé, que le consensus que nous avons eu des deux côtés de l'Atlantique a été constructif et positif. Au fond cette conférence a dégagé un sentiment relativement optimiste sur les perspectives de l'euro et plus inquiet sur le contexte mondial. Ça change un peu parce que pendant tellement d'années on a eu l'habitude inverse d'être plus inquiet sur l'Europe et plus rassuré sur la situation internationale. Pour une fois les rôles sont un peu inversés, j'allais dire que c'est le jeu des chaises musicales. Et la tonalité générale m'a paru plutôt optimiste.

Si j'avais à résumer, je dirais que nos débats se sont situés à l'articulation de deux thèmes qui sont évidemment très reliés. D'abord, le thème de la concurrence entre les monnaies: euro et dollar, mais bien sûr nous avons parlé des autres monnaies, même si l'attention a été portée principalement sur ce duopole asymétrique, et qui va sans doute le rester quelque temps, constitué du dollar et de l'euro. Par-delà le thème de la concurrence entre les monnaies, nous avons évidemment touché au sujet que vous avez abordé vous-même, Monsieur le Premier Ministre, c'est-à-dire la coordination des politiques économiques.

Concurrence des monnaies et coordination des politiques. Je pense que là on est vraiment à l'articulation du rôle des marchés et de ce qu'on doit attendre du côté des décideurs publics.

Ayant dit cela, je vais revenir sur deux thèmes qui ont été au coeur de nos débats. Je vais toucher à des points déjà évoqués par Dick Cooper. Première question: A quoi s'attendre? Et deuxième question: Qu'est-ce qu'il faut faire?

Première question: A quoi s'attendre raisonnablement? Il y a eu un consensus pour au fond évoquer plusieurs idées sur le 'à quoi s'attendre?' Les réponses ne sont pas les mêmes selon que l'on raisonne à court terme ou pour les dix à quinze ans qui viennent. A quoi s'attendre tout d'abord en matière de taux de change? Une crainte a été exprimée pour le court terme que l'euro soit victime de son succès. L'euro peut être en effet victime de son succès et c'est tout le débat qui a donné lieu à des échanges sur le *portfolio shift*, le redéploiement des portefeuilles lié à l'événement que constitue l'avènement de l'euro. L'attractivité de l'euro en tant que tel, l'attractivité de l'Europe par des marchés financiers qui vont enfin atteindre et dépasser la taille critique, qui vont enfin devenir liquides, profonds, crédibles sont des éléments à prendre en considération.

A plus long terme, l'euro fluctuera. En tant que tel, un système monétaire international plus symétrique, ou moins asymétrique, ne sera pas par définition un système monétaire international plus stable. D'autres conditions relatives à la diminution des déséquilibres internationaux (déficits extérieurs américains, excédents courants du Japon et de la zone euro) et aux progrès de la coordination devront être satisfaites.

Pendant ces deux jours le concept de *target zone* n'a pas été évoqué. Je pense que c'est par prudence. Ou par diplomatie. Ou les deux. Et même si le thème n'a pas été évoqué, la question a été indirectement posée. Un quasi consensus a consisté à dire qu'au fond dans dix ans, dans quinze ans, le système monétaire international malgré l'euro ne sera pas très différent du point de vue de son régime de change (changes flottants) entre les différentes zones de ce qu'il est aujourd'hui.

A quoi s'attendre, deuxième aspect, en ce qui concerne le rôle international de l'euro? Dick a déjà évoqué le débat entre ceux qui pensent que le rééquilibrage des parts de marché en faveur de l'euro peut intervenir assez vite et d'autres qui estiment que le rééquilibrage des parts de marché sera plus lent. Nous avons eu un débat sur l'équilibre qui va se faire concrètement. Ce sont les marchés qui vont trancher entre ces deux forces antagonistes, la flexibilité et l'inertie.

Il est clair que le dollar a l'avantage de faire la course en tête, comme on dit en Formule 1. Il y a des circuits automobiles dans lesquels quand on fait la course en tête on ne peut pas se faire doubler. On pourrait dire que sur certains aspects il va être sans doute plus difficile pour l'euro d'affirmer son rôle que sur d'autres. L'euro devrait rapidement gagner des parts de marché dans le domaine des opérations financières, mais dans le domaine commercial il va gagner des parts de marchés sans doute plus lentement. Et donc il faudra articuler tout cela en ayant également en tête la question des autres monnaies. Parce que le débat n'est pas bilatéral entre les Etats-Unis et l'Europe. Il faut réintroduire dans le débat non seulement, à un moment donné, le Japon, mais aussi réfléchir à l'articulation des pays émergents par rapport à ce duopole dollar-euro que j'évoquais tout à l'heure qui risque de rester asymétrique pendant un certain temps. Nous avons abordé à ce sujet la question de l'attitude des pays émergents après l'arrivée de l'euro, non seulement pour le choix de l'ancrage, mais également par rapport à des problèmes de volatilité des changes.

Je vais terminer en évoquant rapidement quelques thèmes autour du deuxième grand point. Que faire? A partir de là l'optique est plus normative. Au fond on peut aborder cette question à deux niveaux. Au plan mondial il y a eu pas mal de scepticisme—que je partage personnellement—sur le fait qu'au plan mondial on peut toujours rêver, c'est-à-dire essayer de mettre en place de nouveaux forums de concertation transatlantique, de relancer le G-7 sur de nouvelles bases a l'occasion de l'arrivée de l'euro... L'idée c'est qu'a priori il faudra du temps pour atteindre dans ce domaine là des résultats concrets. Et donc la question du 'que faire?' est peut-être plus une question pour nous Européens. Je retrouve ici des aspects qui sont vraiment à l'articulation des aspects fonctionnels et des aspects institutionnels. Quand on parle par exemple de la communication entre la Banque centrale européenne et son environnement, à mes yeux c'est à la fois du fonctionnel, une manière d'améliorer la qualité de notre *policy mix*, et cela peut déboucher sur des aspects institutionnels. Donc, je ne crois pas qu'il faille pousser trop loin la distinction entre le fonctionnel et l'institutionnel. Pour que l'euro réussisse, s'affiche non pas comme une monnaie forte—ce qui est un attribut volatile—mais comme une monnaie durablement crédible, il faudra progresser sur les dossiers politiques et institutionnels. Alors on peut aborder ces questions de vide à combler de manière pessimiste ou optimiste. Si l'on est pessimiste, ce qui n'est pas mon cas, on dira: Aujourd'hui l'Europe a le choix entre deux peurs; la peur pour certains du fédéralisme et la peur pour les mêmes, ou pour d'autres, de la précarité sociale. Et à l'articulation de ces deux peurs, la peur du fédéralisme ou la peur de la précarité sociale, on retrouve le débat technique sur la gestion des chocs asymétriques. Il y aura des chocs asymétriques bien sûr dans la zone euro et il faudra les gérer à l'articulation de ces deux peurs, hypothétiques ou réelles. Je préfère aborder la même question sous un angle plus constructif, plus optimiste, en évoquant d'autres aspects.

Nous sommes en train de vivre, à travers l'euro et de ce qui va avec, un processus d'apprentissage (*learning by doing*). Les exemples historiques sont utiles mais ne doivent pas complètement nous bloquer dans un sens ou dans l'autre. Nous sommes en train, je le crois, de mettre en place une innovation, une forme institutionnelle nouvelle, avec des équilibres à trouver entre centralisation et décentralisation, entre coordination des politiques et application du principe de subsidiarité. Cet équilibre ne sera pas facile à trouver, mais ce sont à la fois les événements et le volontarisme collectif qui nous permettront de le fixer.

Ma deuxième remarque est la suivante. A travers l'euro, l'Europe affiche une très sérieuse ambition qui n'est pas que technique, mais qui est également politique. L'euro c'est quand même un projet extrêmement ambitieux et qui légitime notre attention. Je pense qu'il faudra en tirer toutes les conséquences dans la durée et qu'en particulier il faudra que l'Europe en cas de crise financière internationale dans dix ans, dans vingt ans—je ne les souhaite pas ces crises financières, mais elles existeront forcément d'une manière ou d'une autre—tire toutes les conséquences de son ambition qu'elle a par l'euro et pour l'euro pour participer avec les Etats-Unis, avec éventuellement d'autres zones, à la gestion de l'économie mondiale. Au fond à travers l'euro nous aspirons, d'une certaine façon, à la fonction de copilote de l'économie mondiale, fonction que nous avons longtemps revendiquée. D'une certaine façon ce n'est pas au moment où nous allons sans doute pouvoir exercer ce rôle qu'il faudrait prendre le risque, nous Européens, de nous dérober.

Armand Clesse: Merci beaucoup Monsieur Christian de Boissieu. Je rends la parole au Président de la Fondation Pierre Werner, Charles Ruppert.

Charles Ruppert: Our guest speaker today, born in 1931, studied economics and social sciences and obtained his doctorate from the University of Cologne. From 1962 until 1982, he took increasing responsibilities at the Federal Ministry of Economics. It should be remembered that in 1970 in the EC he was a member of the so-called

Werner Group. From 1982 until 1989, he was Permanent Secretary in the Ministry of Finance. Then, from 1990 onwards he was a member of the Deutsche Bundesbank and of the Central Banking Council. Since 1993, he has been the President of the Deutsche Bundesbank, and since 1994 of the G-10 Central Bank governors. We are all very grateful that Dr. Tietmeyer managed to fly in to address us today, despite the awful weather conditions.

Hans Tietmeyer: There are just 28 days left until the start of the monetary union, which is perhaps the most important monetary development since the end of the Bretton Woods system.

Some people may be thinking: 'Just another 28 days, and then we've done it!' before having a sigh of relief as they relax in the armchair.

That is a very human reaction, especially when one considers the great efforts and obstacles, all the advances but all the reverses as well on the way to greater monetary cooperation in Europe.

Thirty years ago the subject of monetary union was already a topic on the agenda of the European Community, which in those days consisted of just six member countries. It was at that time that the road to monetary union was first jointly mapped out by you, Pierre Werner, and the Werner Group, named after you—in which I myself had the honor of working.

Luxembourg and its political representatives were always advocates of progress towards the further-reaching but clearly stability-oriented integration.

Important insights which were gained at that time are still highly relevant today. For example, the currencies of the participating states can be welded together to form a permanently stable monetary union only

- if there is an adequate degree of ongoing economic convergence between the countries,
- if there are common preferred structures in monetary policy and the same priorities prevail, and
- if there is broad agreement on the basic political stance.

The way forward proposed at that time was clearly different to some extent than the path actually charted in Maastricht. It was envisaged that political integration would develop parallel to economic integration.

However, the consultations following the submission of the so-called Werner Plan showed clearly that the politicians at that time were not prepared to abandon national sovereignty on the quite considerable scale demanded. So the first attempt to launch the monetary union fell at this hurdle.

On January 1, 1999 monetary union will therefore be launched at the second attempt. A number of conditions have changed in the meantime:

- Eleven countries will be taking part, as opposed to just six at the time of the first attempt.

- These eleven countries are only part of the overall European Union. Hence there will be differences in the level of monetary integration within the EU.

- And the political framework for integrating the single currency is a rather loose structure.

The euro will have to cope with this as best as it can.

For the goal is not merely to ensure that the euro is stable at the beginning. The goal is to ensure that the euro remains stable over the long term. And in the long term it is highly probable that the euro will need a stronger political underpinning.

It is gratifying that the financial markets already seem to have largely accepted the euro.

At any rate, the euro has passed its first test.

The markets apparently have confidence in the pre-announced exchange rates. So far there have been no marked tensions between the exchange rates of the future participating currencies.

And the euro has already begun to experience the first benefits. In the context of problematical developments in the financial markets which in some cases reached crisis-like proportions, the euro acquired the reputation of a safe haven—even before the actual launching of monetary union—which has led to correspondingly low capital market rates in the future Euroland.

None of these things should be taken for granted. They are the result of
- the rigorous stability orientation of the Maastricht Treaty,
- the large degree of convergence that has already been achieved in the monetary stability policies of the central banks,
- the careful preparatory work, and
- the determined efforts that have been made to date to achieve greater convergence in fiscal policy, too.

The function of a safe haven which the euro area has performed so far clearly demonstrates that the introduction of the new currency is undoubtedly a 'global event'. And a lot of hopes are being placed on the future international role of the euro.

Clearly, the enlarged financial markets in Euroland will result in a wider range of products and a broader choice of investment opportunities.

To what extent these greater opportunities will actually be used—especially by enterprises—depends on other conditions as well.

These include the legal framework laid down by the EU and by the national parliaments of the countries concerned, the different traditions in respect of financial market structures and also questions of taxation.

It remains to be seen just how quickly traditional financial market structures move closer together.

And another thing which remains to be seen is the use to which enterprises will put enlarged capital market. For example, will there be a tendency towards greater concentration as firms seek to exploit 'economies of scale' in Euroland?

And what about the other question which central bankers are often asked in connection with the international role of the euro: How fast and to what extent will the euro become a major international investment and reserve currency? Can the euro take over the D-mark's role as the second most important investment and reserve currency today?

Naturally, the euro will play a significant international role as an investment and reserve currency. If this does not turn out to be the case, it would be an enormous—scarcely conceivable—surprise as well as a bitter disappointment.

The fact that the euro area is already regarded as a safe haven confirms this assumption. It is simply a fact of life that major international currencies are used by investors from time to time as a safe haven.

However, this can also be a problem in certain situations, especially for the exchange rate.

But it is the *future* stability of the euro that will determine its actual role in the concert of world currencies. And the two key criteria for this will be

- sensible monetary policy decisions by the ECB Governing Council, and

- stability-oriented behavior in those aspects of economic policy which remain a national responsibility, especially fiscal and wage policies.

Given such a policy mix, the euro can, and in my view will, assume a major international role—in line with the size and economic importance of Euroland—and also make its contribution to global stability.

And that brings me to the subject of this conference: 'The euro as a stabilizer in the international economic system.'

This title expresses great expectations of the future single currency.

- In what sense—if at all—does the international economic system need a stabilizer?

- And if it needs one, how can a currency help to meet such a need?

Let me begin with the second question: as a general principle, currencies cannot solve structural problems relating to the real global economy.

And as far as the first question is concerned, it must be said that—while the world economic setting is difficult at the moment—there is certainly no cause to talk of a fundamental instability.

In recent weeks the financial markets have at least calmed down a little. The world financial crisis which many people predicted looks unlikely to occur at the moment.

It is true that a number of countries are currently suffering crises entailing considerable local growth losses:

- In the South-East Asian countries this is a direct consequence of the financial crisis. But at the moment there are some encouraging signs of an improvement in certain countries.

- Japan continues to suffer, in particular from the structural problems which have accumulated in its financial sector. Happily it has now taken steps to put its financial sector in order. These now need to be implemented resolutely.

- In Russia the transformation of the centrally planned economy into a market economy has virtually come to a halt.

- And in Latin America contagion effects manifested themselves in the wake of the uncertainty in the financial markets. Fortunately, the financial markets are showing renewed confidence and are tending more to reward the marked structural advances made in a number of countries.

Nevertheless, these regional crises have clearly left their mark on the global economic growth process.

On the one hand, that does not mean that an overall world economic crisis is looming. The robust state of the US and the European economies clearly contradicts such gloomy views.

On the other hand, it is becoming more apparent that the international setting has created some extraordinary risks and uncertainties which are beginning to retard the pace of economic expansion in the industrial countries.

There are some indications that the euro area, too, cannot fully escape the global downward pressure.

Fortunately, this comes at a time when the internal monetary conditions in Europe are rather favorable. The goal of price stability has largely been achieved. Moreover, there seems to be no obvious threat to maintaining price stability in the foreseeable future.

That has given European monetary policy the opportunity for a further round of cuts in the central bank interest rates.

As you know, for some weeks now the euro area as a whole has already experienced a period of considerable decline in the average interest rate. This is the result of the so-called process of convergence of central bank interest rates.

At the beginning of this week, the Council of the European Central Bank made a comprehensive assessment of the monetary and economic situation in the euro area. This very thorough analysis on the ECB Governing Council, as well as yesterday's discussion on the Bundesbank's Central Bank Council, came to the same conclusion: an additional coordinated rate cut is appropriate which clears the horizon for a level of 3 percent for the start and the first stage of the euro.

Therefore, this cut also has to include those currencies whose interest rate already lies at the bottom of the current range. The Bundesbank's decision to cut the repo rate by 30 base points is our contribution to that coordinated action.

The decision is compatible with both the monetary situation and the overall economic conditions. The early announcement of the interest rate level for the launch of the euro may help to stabilize expectations in the financial markets. But of course, the rate cut cannot solve the severe structural problems in most of the euro countries. This is particularly true of the structural problems on the labor markets.

Naturally, it is not only Europe that is suffering structural problems and, therefore, facing tough challenges.

To a large extent, it was structural problems occurring in the monetary and banking sector which played a major calamitous role in the outbreak and course of the regional crises.

- Many of the countries affected had excessively rigid exchange rate pegs.

- Many of the countries affected placed their own monetary policy too much at the service of these problematical exchange rate pegs.

- Many of the countries affected have structural deficiencies in the area of financial market supervision, in particular.

These structural problems in the monetary sector and the banking sector have to be solved first and foremost through suitable policy measures in these countries themselves.

How else could these internal structural problems be solved than

- through a confidence-building economic policy,

- through a greater measure of realism in the exchange rate pegs,

- through a stability-oriented central bank policy,

- through an overhaul of the financial sector and an improvement of banking supervision?

Naturally, international cooperation can also help—but not so much through currency arrangements like the euro as through strengthening the overall functioning and viability of the financial markets. This entails above all

- improving international cooperation in the field of supervision,

- involving private-sector creditors in the task of overcoming crisis, and

- improving the transparency of the financial markets.

All this will sharpen the markets' risk awareness and strengthen their functioning and viability.

But considerable structural problems exist in the industrial countries, too.

In the USA the already low private saving ratio has fallen further in recent years—actually showing a negative ratio of late. Despite the country's balanced budget the imbalances in foreign trade have therefore not been reduced.

And in most of the euro countries unemployment remains too high. The euro will not be able to solve this problem on its own. Instead the euro requires flexibility and competitiveness in the real economy.

It is the politicians who must tackle these internal structural problems. In the longer run this is the best contribution that can be made towards achieving sound financial markets and a prospering world economy.

Boldly undertaking the necessary reforms in the euro area will at the same time prepare the ground for sustained favorable growth and employment prospects.

Given more flexible structures in the markets, a lastingly stable euro will be able to fully exploit the undoubtedly large potential for economic benefits, and then it will be able to foster political integration.

To sum up: the euro is not the final aim of European integration. Even in 28 days' time it will remain a future-oriented project.

For it is not just a question of introducing the euro. The euro also requires ongoing monetary stability. And the euro requires a sufficient degree of political consensus on the basis of economic dynamism and flexibility. Only in this way can potentially dangerous conflicts be avoided in the long run.

We are investing great hopes and expectations in this future-oriented project associated with the euro. All those involved are responsible for doing what is necessary to ensure that these hopes and expectations are fulfilled.

Charles Ruppert: On behalf of the audience, I thank you very much for your outstanding contribution. It is not as easy as you may think to assemble a panel of this quality and what could have happened if we had done it wrong? And to relax a little let me tell you a story:

An English acquaintance of mine, a university professor, was asked to stand in at the very last minute to replace a British official who had to make a speech in the States, somewhere in Texas. The flight was first class, the drinks too. At the end of a heavy day and under the effects of jet lag, our British professor experienced some difficulty in giving a decent speech. The audience became nervous and he realized that his performance was indeed poor. A big Texan directly opposite him was staring at him, his hands slid in his pocket and he pulled out a gun, and placed it quietly on the table. Noticing the fear of the speaker, the Texan said: 'Don't worry, it's not for you. It's for the guy who recommended you.'

Now, let me introduce Professor Dr. Václav Klaus. He was born in 1941, and graduated from the Prague School of Economics. After working as a researcher at the Institute of Economics, he was forced to leave for political reasons. From 1971-1986, he joined the Czechoslovak State Bank and was Professor of Finance at the Prague School of Economics. He played a decisive role in civic and democratic movements. After more than 40 years of communist rule, he was the first non-communist finance minister. From 1992, until he resigned in November 1997, he was Prime Minister and he is now President of the Chamber of Deputies of the Czech Parliament. Professor Klaus has had the great merit of repositioning his country orientating it towards a modern market economy. As a leader he can provide us with some insights from an Eastern European point of view.

Václav Klaus: Ladies and gentlemen, it's a great pleasure to be here.

I didn't expect to be the first speaker of the panel and I don't dare to give you the Eastern European view on these issues. That would be too ambitious. I can give you the view of Václav Klaus only.

There are many topics to be discussed during our two days' conference, and I am sure our panelists will talk about other topics. I am a very special person to have to talk here about monetary union, because I am well-known for dismantling one monetary union called Czechoslovakia. So I am here from the negative side. Not building anything, but liquidating something. It gives me, however, a very special perspective and a very special sensitivity to some of the issues discussed here and elsewhere. I will pick up just one topic. For me, it is the question of the economic and political inter dependence of consequences of the European Monetary Union.

As a politician and a former economist, I have a frustrating feeling that everything about EMU has already been said, that there is nothing to add, that there is definitely no lack of knowledge. The problem is whether we use sufficiently the existing knowledge. Famous economists—some of them are here with us today—Professor Kindleberger, Professor Mundell, Professor Cooper, Professor Frankel and others—repeatedly tried to explain basic, more or less textbook arguments about both optimum currency areas and monetary unions, but I am afraid the architects of EMU didn't listen carefully or sufficiently.

The economists continued to remind us that the conditions for a successful monetary union are microeconomic, which means that they have nothing to do with the macroeconomic conditions specified at Maastricht.

It was repeatedly emphasized that the benefits of free trade are connected with the European Economic Community (which means with a free-trade area and a customs union), and that they are independent of a monetary union.

It was argued that the appeal of getting something for nothing is wrong. It was stressed that it is not possible to convert a variable into a constant without paying an inevitable price, without including movements of some other variable or variables.

We could go on with similar arguments, but it seems to me that it's not sufficient because we usually talk about the benefits of a monetary union and not about its costs. I know that the euro will start in 28 days from now and I am sure the introduction will be very successful. Our task remains to analyze and forecast its consequences inside the European Union, outside the European Union, vis-à-vis the future member countries, vis-à-vis the United States, vis-à-vis Asian countries.

Undoubtedly, there will be costs and not just benefits. We will be confronted with substantial costs, tangible costs as well as non-tangible costs. I will concentrate on one issue only. It seems to me that the architects of the euro must be—to use labels well-known in the economic profession—new classicals or at least elasticity optimists. They have to assume that prices and wages in Europe are so flexible that exchange rate adjustment is not, and will never be, needed. Additionally, they have to assume that labor mobility is very high. The empirical data do not, as I see them, support these assumptions. In such a situation, something else must become flexible and mobile. This variable, of course, exists and we call it fiscal transfers among individual member countries of the EMU. It seems to me to be a mistake that their potential size and frequency have not been sufficiently or openly discussed. All of us know that the size of those fiscal transfers in a recently created monetary union called Germany was and is enormous. I am aware of the size and frequency of fiscal transfers in a monetary union which used to be called Czechoslovakia. I was its last Minister of Finance who was sending the fiscal transfers from one part of the monetary union to another and I know that it was impossible to continue.

There is another problem. It was probably implicitly or subconsciously assumed that the currency domain (monetary union) can be greater than the fiscal domain (fiscal union). As far as I know, it has never been proved that this can create a viable institutional arrangement. I am convinced of the inevitability of the one-way street, of the inevitability of the path: monetary union—fiscal union—political union. Therefore, one of the consequences, and I include it on the side of costs, will be the emergence of a fiscal and political union. And the justified question is: Do we really want it? Do we really want a political union? It seems to me that we shouldn't be guilty of a deadful sin when we raise that question or even give a qualified answer to that.

The existence of a monetary union without political union means that states delegate monetary policy to a supranational agency. It can be neutral in my understanding only on condition that there is a unified economic interest. It is, however, a very problematic assumption to expect anything like that when we look at the current European heterogeneity. I'm afraid, therefore, that the costs and benefits of European monetary union will not be equally distributed among its members which will put the newly created European Central Bank under tremendous pressure.

Recently, I had the opportunity to discuss the euro with an influential European parliamentarian. After a while, he couldn't find enough arguments in favor of EMU and the debate forced him to reveal his deeper thoughts. I understood that he didn't care about the lack of arguments *for* EMU because he had a strong argument *against* something else. He explicitly stated that EMU is against something or someone. And I feel that this is something which must be discussed at a symposium like this one. I feel that the danger is an undeniable undertone of anti-Americanism and anti-Asiatism in his arguments. He hopes to check the assumed global dominance of the US and the assumed economic strength of Japan and other South-East Asian countries through the vehicle of a united Europe. It seems to me that he doesn't know that competitiveness has no connection with size. He forgot that the economic power of Singapore or Hong Kong is not based on a common currency or a political union. We should not underestimate such a way of thinking. I am afraid that the echo of an old French adage 'Le défi américain' is with us again, and this is something that I do not like to hear.

This brings me to my last point. The euro, it seems to me, is a chosen, a very ambitious project—and I agree it is the most important change in the international monetary architecture since Bretton Woods in 1944—as an alternative to something else instead of redefining European integration along classical liberal ideas. The idea of EMU was brought to the fore. I am convinced that Europe doesn't need unification but a liberal order. The relevant question is whether EMU brings us closer to such a goal or keeps us preoccupied with an alternative endeavor. I hope that we will concentrate on the second task with the same determination as on the first one.

Charles Ruppert: Thank you very much Professor Klaus. The second speaker is Professor Jeffrey Frankel, born in 1952. He received his Ph.D. from MIT in 1978. He was Professor of Economics at the University of California, Berkeley, and was active in economic research. In 1988 and 1989 he was a visiting professor at Harvard University and he is also a visiting scholar at the IMF and the Federal Reserve Board. So, it is no surprise that such a specialist in international economics, finance and macroeconomics has attracted the attention of top politicians. Indeed, Professor Frankel has been, since 1997, member of the Council of Economic Advisers of the White House and thus to President Clinton. He can give us an American point of view on topics we are interested in today.

Jeffrey A. Frankel: Thank you. At the end of two days, I want to take this opportunity to say that I think this has been a truly excellent conference and accordingly I want to thank Armand Clesse and the Luxembourg Institute for European and International Studies, the Pierre Werner Foundation, the Government of Luxembourg and the other sponsors of this conference. It has also been a pleasure to honor Pierre Werner and Charles Kindleberger and in the latter case it has especially been an honor for me since I was one of his students at MIT.

With four weeks to go and speaking in part as a representative of the US Government, I also want to take the opportunity to offer congratulations to the citizens of Euroland, of the EMU, on the birth of the euro. To be honest, many American economists even a short time ago did not expect so many of the EU members to meet the Maastricht criteria, particularly the fiscal criteria. Beyond that, the EMU is a historic achievement. It is an inspiring experiment, as others have said. The United States has a favorable attitude towards the EMU and the euro because we think that European integration is desirable, both in an economic sense and in a political sense.

The primary implications of European integration lie with the European people. The implications for the United States and the rest of the world are not as great. Nevertheless those implications are positively related. In other words, what is good for Europe, to a first approximation is good for the United States and for the rest of the world. It is especially true that when European growth is domestically generated, that is good for the United States and for the rest of the world. Let me just note parenthetically that the rising current account deficit in the United States is a result not so much of a falling saving rate—in fact the overall national saving rate is increasing—but rather is the result of a rising investment rate and the investment-led boom we have experienced for the last six years.

I want to devote most of my remarks to explaining or elaborating a bit on what Dick Cooper said, some of the analytical musings that American economists have had about EMU in the past, which could be characterized as doubts, but I think could not be characterized as hostile, as he said. So now I am going to speak a little more as a professor and a little less as a representative of the US Government. It involves of course the timeless debate between fixed and floating exchange rates. Which is the superior exchange rate regime? This is a settled question for members of Euroland but not a settled question for other European countries or for everyone else.

The advantages of fixed exchange rates are many but I think they can be succinctly summarized in two categories: First that they reduce or eliminate transaction costs and exchange rate risk and thereby stimulate international trade and investment, which is a good thing. Second, fixed exchange rates provide a nominal anchor for monetary policy. The advantage of floating exchange rates can be summarized equally, succinctly, namely they give a country the ability to pursue an independent monetary policy. Which should dominate? Which are more important, the advantages of fixed rates or the advantages of floating rates? I think it is a real mistake to think that there is one answer, one right answer to that question that is the right answer for all countries at all times. The answer depends on the circumstances and the country in question, on characteristics of that country. It especially depends on the size and openness of the country and this leads us to the question of the optimum currency area theory.

Luxembourg has long been my favorite example. A sort of textbook example of a small open economy that is well integrated with its neighbors and therefore is too small and too open for it to make sense to have an independent currency and a completely independent monetary policy. But how big and how self-sufficient does a country or a group of countries have to be before it is appropriate to have its own currency and its own monetary policy? And why does this criterion depend on openness at all? The advantages of fixed rates that I named I think are greater for an open economy, one with tradable goods as a high percentage of the economy.

On the other side, the advantages of floating, which I identified as an independent monetary policy, are weaker for an economy that is highly integrated with its neighbors. The reason for that is that there exist other ways to adjust to adverse circumstances. If you are highly integrated with your neighbors you do not need an independent monetary policy as much. I will just quickly run through the four different criteria, ways of characterizing openness or integration. Four different criteria that are on economists' lists to determine whether a given set of regions or countries qualify to be an optimum currency area. The first one is trade, as measured for example by the marginal propensity to import. One argument here is that under fixed exchange rates, openness operates as an automatic stabilizer, that if there is a fluctuation in domestic income, and you are a highly open economy, most of the fluctuation under fixed rates gets passed off to the rest of the world.

The second criterion is what has been called the symmetry of shocks across the set of countries, as measured for example by the correlation in income. The idea here is that if regions or countries tend to always be in the same situation economically, in the same stage of the business cycle, then they can share the same monetary policy and don't require the separate monetary policies to respond to their separate situations.

The third kind of integration or the third criterion for evaluating optimum currency is labor mobility, and this is the one that Bob Mundell originally had in mind when he coined this phrase and started this line of research. The idea is that when a region suffers from a recession, and labor mobility is high, the workers can move to other regions where the economy is in stronger shape. That doesn't sound like a very desirable way of adjusting but the fact is that studies for the United States economy find that the mechanism of equilibration across states that works the fastest—not that it is that fast, but it is faster than various alternatives such as wage adjustment—is in fact workers moving. If there is a boom in New England and a recession in the South, then workers tend to move to where the jobs are.

Fourth is fiscal federalism, the criterion that Václav Klaus was mentioning which also operates pretty strongly in the United States as measured for example by transfers, working to cushion the effect of a downturn in a particular state or particular region. Thirty percent is the size of the US cushioning effect. Thus states of the United States meet these criteria quite well. Luxembourg, or the Benelux countries, also meet the criteria quite well. The EU does not meet the criteria as well as the other examples that I just mentioned. That is the basis for the skepticism that some American economists have long had. Does it mean that the EMU is a mistake? I would say not necessarily, for two reasons. The first one is that there is nothing that says that the United States is the relevant bench mark. The second one is that these criteria that I have been describing evolve over time. We can call them parameters but they are not unchanging parameters for all time. They are endogenous with respect to various things, including with respect to decisions that countries, such as members of the EMU, make regarding their policies vis-à-vis each other. In particular the reduction in regional barriers to trade, that was crystallized especially around 1992 and the increase in labor mobility, which is still much lower than in the United States but is perhaps increasing, make the countries increasingly good candidates for optimum currency area as time goes by.

There is an interesting question about the correlation of income. There are some economists who have said that as Europe becomes more integrated that income correlations will go down. Different countries will become specialized in different products as the amount of trade goes up, and that means that they become less synchronized and some shocks will become less symmetric. That is the basis for the claim that the correlation will go down. I do not believe this is correct. I believe, and I think that there is evidence of this, that the correlation tends to go up when trade is greater. We can say that for the United States, one of the reasons why the correlation across states is so great, and these other criteria hold pretty well, is in part a result of the fact that the States have all been on a common currency for the last 200 years and the structure of the economy has adapted to that. So this is a pretty optimistic conclusion. It says that even for a country that has been only on the verge of qualifying by this criterion, let's say the United Kingdom or Sweden, as time passes will progressively meet the criterion to a greater extent.

In the meantime I think it is important that EMU not distract Europeans from what should be a high policy priority, which is structural reform to reduce market rigidities, for example labor market rigidities, the sort of thing Mr. Tietmeyer was referring to. Indeed it is more important now than ever to increase flexibility in European markets, precisely because the countries are losing this ability to respond with independent monetary policies. Since you are losing that adjustment mechanism, it is more important than ever that this kind of flexibility increase.

I have spent most of my time on the question of the optimum currency area and not much on the euro per se. I won't go into detail there because others have said it. Dick Cooper and Christian de Boissieu have done a good job of summarizing the discussion that we had on that. Except, let me just close by considering the issue of whether it is good for the world monetary system to have a second or more international currencies to rival the dollar, which obviously is to some extent going to be the outcome of what takes place on January 1. One view which is associated with Charlie Kindleberger is that it is more efficient to have a single currency around which the world is oriented. After all the advantage of having a money at all, is to avoid the 'double coincidence of wants'. When you want to sell your product, you don't want to have to find somebody else who is selling exactly the product you want, and is willing to buy your product. Rather, you want to sell your product and take the money and buy another product. That is what makes money convenient.

Then there is this nice analogy with language. The reason that our host has had such a hard time convincing people to speak French is not because English is a nicer language or a more efficient language. It is certainly not a more attractive language, that is for sure. There are advantages to people speaking the same language at each other. It is an accident of history, or it has to do with home-country size, as to which language is chosen. Economies of scale, or network externalities, to use a current term, explain why more and more people speak English around the world. It also explains the advantages of a single currency.

But on the other hand there is also a case the other way, which is that there may be a fear that if there is a single international currency, the country that produces it will abuse the privilege and print too much of it. So there is an argument that having a second currency gives healthy competition and the discipline keeps the monetary authorities in both places honest. Speaking for the United States either one is fine with us. We are not worried about the ability of the dollar to compete and it would just be one more reason on the list of reasons for pursuing sound macroeconomic policies, which we want to do in any case. Let me conclude by trying to answer a question which is often asked: After January, will the euro be the strong currency or will the dollar be strong? My answer to this is that both currencies will be strong. That may sound like a contradiction but it isn't, if you think of strength in terms of purchasing power. Both regions, I believe, will pursue sound money and both regions' currencies will thus be strong. Thank you.

Charles Ruppert: Thank you Professor Frankel. Our next speaker, Mr. Mersch, born in 1949, obtained two graduate degrees in law and in political science in Paris. He is a Luxembourger, one of the very few. After one year as an assistant in public law at the University of Paris, fortunately for us he returned to Luxembourg where he started his career at the Ministry of Finance. He obtained valuable experience at the International Monetary Fund in Washington as well as at the Permanent Representation to the UN in New York. Since 1981 he took on increasing responsibilities in the Ministry of Finance and went on to become the Director of Treasury in 1989. He is now the recently designated President of the recently created Luxembourg Central Bank.

Yves Mersch: Ladies and gentlemen. Paul Volcker once said: 'Six months a central banker, always a central banker.' Well, this barely qualifies me to speak here as a central banker because it's just six months that I have been appointed. And that's why I will also certainly heed the advice that I received from my senior colleague Hans Tietmeyer who cautioned against rhetorical flamboyance.

I looked at what you were discussing over the last one and a half days and I tried to have a fresh look at the question of the euro and stability. I have heard some arguments about internal stability, consistent or compatible with external stability, and vice versa. Other questions are the nuances between competition of policies, coordination and the single monetary policy.

But in order to keep your attention for a couple of minutes after so many speeches I wish to ask: Would the euro not be on the one hand an economic stabilizer and on the other hand a political destabilizer? Let me give you just some personal remarks.

The euro in my opinion will stabilize the European economies. As we have experienced, the single market that we tried to establish with a bunch of regulations, has nevertheless not been fully operational. It will only become a truly transparent market when the price differences are apparent to consumers through the establishment of the euro.

Exchange rates have been sometimes misused as a weapon in our countries; the fees that have been noted inside the European Union in terms of foreign exchange fees can add up to some 0.25 percent of the total GDP of the European Union, according to European Commission statistics.

The euro has been a stabilizer in so far as it has established some preconditions on the fiscal side. As a central banker I am not very satisfied with the degree of structural fiscal consolidation that we have achieved in Europe, but one has nevertheless to acknowledge that considerable progress in fiscal consolidation has been made throughout the European area. This is particularly true if you have a longer term perspective over the last 20 or 30 years.

Let me now quickly turn to why I believe that the euro as a project could also be viewed to some extent as a political destabilizer. And I do not refer here to the change in government colors in 14 out of 15 countries since the Treaty of Maastricht has been voted into law in all our countries. No, I refer here to the fact that the euro has an institutional aspect because of the establishment of a single institution that is responsible for euro-wide policy-making, even though the execution of this single policy will be done through national institutions.

But the euro is especially destabilizing for the nation-state which has so much overdetermined the fate and the history not only of Europe over this century but of most of the world. We have tried to limit the aggressiveness of the nation-state, the inherent aggressiveness I am tempted to say, by resorting to free trade. But we have seen that free trade was not sufficient and we had to go beyond it even to clip the wings of the nation-state in some areas in order to prevent countries from beggar-their-neighbor policies or from policies using exchange rate adjustments as an easy way out rather than making the internal adjustments required.

The Treaty of Maastricht by setting up a single institution for euro-wide policy-making has been criticized for being too ambitious; it was said that the differences of cultures between the different European nations are so wide that it is not possible to carry through anything else than a project based on a Europe of the nations.

If we look at the financial cultures, also very different between the different European nations, one could have had the same doubts whether it would be workable to have a single monetary policy. In some countries most of the financing is done very short-term or linked to short-term interest rates like for example mortgage rates that in some countries are linked to the monetary rates and other countries have a culture and a tradition of very long-term financing. In many countries there exists a tradition of very centralized policy-making in the monetary field, in other countries we have traditionally a very decentralized kind of policy-making. The instruments of monetary policy have been very different from one country to another and even the tradition and the perception of inflation have been very different from one country to another. And nevertheless over the last ten years we have managed to establish a single corps of rules and policy issues and instruments able to run a euro-wide zone. And that is of course a forceful example how we can overcome cultural differences.

I wish also to add another example that is put forward in discussions about us having insufficient labor mobility in Europe. It is true that only 40 percent of Germans understand French and that only 20 percent of French understand German. It is also true that 60 percent and 80 percent of each of these peoples understand English. Further the language issue is not the only reason why you would not move from one country to another. It is true that mobility will probably start both at the lower scale of remuneration where the need is greatest and also at the higher scale of experience and of professionalism and education. Broader regions round Luxembourg are already a good example of great labor mobility. And such regions will multiply throughout Europe, as the true rules of a single market are adopted, which will be encouraged by the establishment and successful management of a single currency.

I fully agree that we cannot stop. The dynamics of European integration will only be spurred on by the euro project and that is why the 'project euro' is such a subversive element in the eyes of the more aggressive proponents of the nation-state and has also been attacked and opposed so much by the same people. The other areas of integration in Europe are the European defense and tax regimes. About tax regimes we also hear the argument that there are cultural differences. It is certainly true. We will start by first talking, cooperating, coordinating, maybe then approximating, maybe then harmonizing, and finally, to some extent unifying if that is necessary, or arriving at reciprocal recognition. We have some experience. To conclude, let me simply say that for me Europe and the euro is one single fight and that the euro is a vector of dynamics for the European project. It will create a new balance, it really is a future-oriented prospect. Thank you.

Charles Ruppert: Professor Norbert Walter, born in 1944, obtained his Ph.D. at the Goethe University in Frankfurt. After a period of active research in Frankfurt, as well as at the Kiel Institute of World Economics, he went on to lecture at the Christian Albrecht University on currency problems and the international capital market. In 1978, Dr. Walter became Professor, and Scientific Director of the Kiel Institute. Since 1987, Professor Walter has worked with the Deutsche Bank, Frankfurt, where he is Managing Director of Deutsche Bank Research and Chief Economist of the Deutsche Bank Group. His face should be familiar to you as he is frequently called upon by the media to give his opinion, especially on financial and monetary topics.

Norbert Walter: Ladies and gentlemen. At this late hour I do not propose to offer additional scholarly remarks, probably more a presentation in the mode of a caricature.

First I'd like to say a few words on the change from the flexible exchange rate scheme to the single currency in Europe. This is a tale told time and time again, but there is little truth in it. Over the last decade or so there has been only one monetary authority in Europe. Its representative in Euro-11-land is sitting behind me: Dr. Tietmeyer, the President of the Deutsche Bundesbank. There has been no national interest rate policy, no national exchange rate policy. Ten countries gave that up a good ten years ago. There is nothing to be given up in 1999!

Second, such a talented man as Václav Klaus is arguing that size doesn't matter in terms of competition. As long as we Europeans tried to compete with Boeing through Fokker, we were not particularly successful. Airbus had a difficult start, but it finally worked. Airbus is now a formidable challenger of Boeing in civil aircraft. Imagine for a second that the United States had invented GSM. Would you believe that the two most important countries of the world would still stay out of GSM? Size does matter. Not in everything, but in a number of fields. And we Europeans should not shy away from stating it occasionally.

Third: coming from a bank and speaking in favor of the euro reveals either complete stupidity or masochism. Why? It's so very obvious. We, the banks, the financial sector, have to spend a fortune—on preparations for the euro—only to reduce our revenues. On top of this, we significantly increase competition in our industry. We kill a number of our businesses completely:

foreign exchange transactions within Europe, the currency risk hedging businesses within Europe. Then we lose margin in payment systems. Why are we doing this? We must be stupid, completely stupid. The only reason for some of us to be positive about the euro must be that we want to eat up others, and feel sure that we are capable of doing so. Otherwise we should not argue in favor of the new currency. And those least in favor of the euro should be the central banks, i.e. the national central banks. They will lose their sovereignty and even more jobs than the private banks. And they know it, or certainly will do after the next or the next-but-one review by McKinsey.

So much for that. The euro is a very interesting experiment and much more pervasive than Europeans think at this time. As of next year we will have Euroland benchmarking. The pension funds, the life-insurance companies of Europe will have the possibility, under the same type of regulation that exists at present, to invest in eleven European countries rather than just their home country. Shareholder-value will truly be adopted as a concept. There is no way to avoid it because pension managers and the life-insurance companies will look at the European benchmark rather than the national benchmark. So there will be a challenge for European management not seen before, and in that process we will see quite some turmoil. Some companies will default, some will merge. To think only in terms of competition between European countries, however, is rubbish. Euroland is an excellent platform for firms that are used to platforms of Euroland size. This holds true for American companies. They will make use of this Euroland platform much earlier than those Europeans who are not yet Europeans but still Belgians, or Italians or Germans, and are not open to a Euroland strategy because they still are confined to their national culture.

A word on the European Central Bank and its statute. Believe me, if the European heads of state and finance ministers had understood what they were creating when they created the European Central Bank, they would not have done it. It is the most powerful institution not just for monetary policy but also for economic policy in Europe, and will be for a long time. Because political union will remain out of reach for a long time. There will be no counterpart to the ECB on the political level. The Euro-11 Council is a marvelous club, changing permanently and agreeing on hardly anything, while the corporate spirit and the continuity in the European Central Bank will be overwhelming. The ECB will publish monthly reports assessing monetary and economic policy throughout Europe. Nobody else will analyze Euroland as well as the European Central Bank. It will be the most eminent institution. The number to call from the United States for economic issues is Wim Duisenberg. Nobody else. That will be understood quite soon, not just by Alan Greenspan. He has already understood this. The strength of the ECB will be a real surprise and I guess a disappointment for those politicians who believe that they are emperors of the world, or at least of Europe.

A word on the accountability of the ECB. The word 'accountability' is constantly used very strangely in this debate. Why do we not interpret the accountability of the ECB as achieving its targets, namely a stable price level? That's what it was created for. And I know some economists would of course welcome it if central bankers were to suffer from a reduction of their income if they failed to achieve price stability. I'm not a believer in such a simple utility function of central bankers. Therefore I'm not in favor of that approach, but it at least gives an idea of a reasonable interpretation of accountability. Accountability must not mean that the Central Bank is exposed to the vagaries of daily opinions of politicians or a euro electorate. We probably should therefore be a bit more specific when we speak of accountability.

Orientation towards price stability—it seems—is again out of fashion. This is particularly true if you listen to political analysts. I think they are now victims of defunct economists, because they still believe in the permanent trade-off between unemployment and inflation. In terms of the quality of the debate I believe we are back to square one. Didn't western societies learn from the seventies and the eighties? While there is a trade-off in the short run, this does not mean it exists in the medium and long run. Thus, why shouldn't we embark upon therapies that are based on evidence?

There is a fully developed debate about the risk that the euro won't last. An exit from the euro bears high costs—asymmetrically high costs. Just think what would happen if Italy considered leaving the club. Just think what this would do to its government deficit at that very moment: something it would never forget. A considerable risk premium would be added to its large government debt, thus multiplying servicing costs. And Italy knows it. And therefore it won't exit.

If there is a risk to the euro, it is the Franco-German axis of socialists. It would be a real threat to the euro if we were to embark upon a policy that is not in line with the Maastricht Treaty and the Stability Pact. This of course could be a risk. However, I do not believe it is a probable outcome.

The euro to me is a fitness program for Europe which should lead at least to the possibility of us playing an international role. But we should not try to perform our international role by maximizing the number of Europeans in international institutions. That doesn't help our case. We should instead opt for one vote for Europe in a G-4, a G-4 that includes the one superpower, the United States, the second most important economic power, Japan, Europe, and the emerging power, China. And in order to demonstrate that we are on our way to embarking upon an international role worth mentioning, why don't we start, after enlarging Europe to the east, by letting the United States know that Europe has a considerably larger quota in the IMF, and that we therefore want to relocate the IMF to Paris in order to demonstrate that Europe, at least in one institution, is taking up a leading role, not just for itself, but for the world at large. Thank you for your attention.

Charles Ruppert: Thank you Professor Walter. Different people, different opinions. The next two interventions will be made by the pioneers, Mr. Pierre Werner and Professor Charles Kindleberger.

Armand Clesse: These two last interventions will be very short. I will just say a few words about Professor Charles Kindleberger, who was born on October 12, four years before the war, and received his Ph.D. from Columbia. He was, soon after, at the New York Federal Reserve Bank, then at the Federal Reserve Bank in the early 1940's and at the Office of Strategic Services during the war. After the war, he was Department of State Adviser and then became professor at MIT. Among his books, I just cite a few: 'The World in Depression, 1929-1939', 'Manias, Panics and Crashes', a very famous book, 'A Financial History of Western Europe', and then a book he wrote for our Institute, of which we are particularly proud, 'World Economic Primacy, 1500-1990'. We held a conference on the manuscript of this book a few years ago at Harvard. If some of you are interested in it, we have some copies left: we may offer it. I was not a student of Charles Kindleberger but I have been very close to him during the past ten years and in fact we took the title for this meeting from him. He was here more than a year ago at a very small workshop on the political implications of monetary integration in Europe, and that is where he spoke about the euro as a possible stabilizer in the world economic system.

Charles Kindleberger: Mr. President, distinguished panel, I am delighted to be back in Luxembourg. I used to be an economist, before I became an economic historian, or historical economist, and I am going to spend my time, which will be short, on economic history.

Let me add one point to the economic analysis which has been put forward. I did not hear much in the last day and a half about automatic stabilizers. A common market such as the European Union, typically has a common budget, with a single system of taxes which is progressive, and a common system of welfare, assisting the poor and not the rich. In these circumstances when part of the total has an asymmetric shock, with lower income, it pays lower taxes and receives higher welfare payments. I think of this particularly because a New York Senator, Patrick Moynihan, was recently quoted in a newspaper that New York State was getting a bad deal from Washington: it pays more in taxes than it receives in federal expenditures. I know Senator Moynihan slightly and wrote him a letter, which he will probably never see, saying: 'Come on, Professor Moynihan, learn a little. We have automatic stabilizers. New York is rich and

Mississippi is poor. It is entirely appropriate when New York gets richer, or Mississippi poorer from some shock or even in tranquil times, that New York pays more in taxes than Mississippi, and receives less welfare. As a former political scientist, you should understand this.'

There is no economic or social justification for balancing local expenditure and tax receipts for part of an economic union. An historical example comes from the German Zollverein of 1835. When it was established, Prussia reduced its share of taxes from those collected on tariffs on imports in its many ports, as compared with Bavaria, Baden-Württemberg, Hesse and so on. Income was shared by population, not collection.

In his summary of the earlier discussion, Richard Cooper started each sentence, it seems, with the word 'Hopefully'. It is important to observe, however, that there are dangers ahead as well as hopes. I again turn to history. In 1925, Winston Churchill said on the return of the pound to gold: 'We want the pound to look the dollar in the eye.' I did not know that currencies had vision. What is clear is that the British were concerned with status. A French analyst, perhaps Alfred Sauvy, even said that the return to gold was more a matter of religion than economics. For the comparative status of the euro and the dollar, one has to bear in mind Gresham's law. If the euro becomes strong, and hopefully it will, it is important that the United States does not take the view that, let's say, Secretary of the Treasury John Connally did: 'We want the dollar to rule the world.' Sensible economic historians or historical economists do not want a competitive struggle between the euro and the dollar. We want the system to work, and not be subject to financial crises.

My third and final point concerns the worry of many about the world financial system, and the scores of proposals put forward to fix it. Almost every financial economist in the United States has a proposal to reconstruct the system. The IMF is criticized excessively. I take a more positive view, partly perhaps because some of my students help to run it, but more deeply, I think, because of the extreme position of those who attack economic globalization, who say, like the Siena Declaration recently, let's get rid of the WTO, the IMF, the World Bank and so on. Even a very sensible Harvard economist, Jeffrey Sachs, wants to reorganize the G-7, adding Russia which makes eight, and then eight developing countries to produce a G-16 to supervise world financial institutions, this despite the fact that UNCTAD, the United Nations Conference on Trade and Development, seems not to have been doing a very good job lately. I urge something that most of you will dislike, 'muddling through', that is, taking up problems one at a time as they come up, rather than all at once, through a new Bretton Woods, a new World Economic Conference, as in 1933, discovering a new Keynes, as an article in *The New Yorker* recently advocated. We should recall that the IMF did very little between 1944 and 1958, and that problems were tackled pragmatically—though in the spirit of the Atlantic Charter—by such measures as UNRRA, the British loan, the Marshall Plan. The World Bank and the IMF worked until 1958 largely on the periphery. This was muddling through, and it worked. What I am trying to say is: 'Please no more world plans. Let us take problems as they come up and solve them.' Thank you.

Charles Ruppert: Professor Kindleberger, we are very thankful for your excellent contribution. Now the last pioneer, Mr. Pierre Werner. Born in 1913, he studied law and political science in Paris and started his career as a lawyer and then as a banker. He was with the Ministry of Finance since 1945, and was banking commissioner for seven years before becoming Minister of Finance in 1953 at the age of forty. He became Prime Minister for the first time in 1959, and stayed in office until 1974. Despite his merits, he had to give way to the opposition for five years until he was re-elected Prime Minister in 1979. He was actively involved at the European level as a politician, especially in monetary affairs as witnessed by the so-called Werner Report. After leaving the political scene, Mr. Werner assumed responsibilities in different Luxembourg and international companies, notably the media. Mr. Werner should be considered as one of the founders of the Luxembourg financial center as well as of the Luxembourg satellite communication industry. We can learn a great deal from his experience.

Mr. Werner intended to make his speech in French. As there is no more interpretation, he will be kind enough to address you in English so as to permit more general understanding. Thank you very much Mr. Werner.

Pierre Werner: Mr. President, ladies and gentlemen. I hope that you are not yet too tired to hear a few words from my side. I could understand that after some controversial discussions, those who are not familiar with the problems might be concerned or even confused about the discussions which have taken place here.

At this stage I shall not enter into details about the aims, about the structures, not even about the stabilizing effect of the euro of which I am personally convinced. Many years ago, in 1971, I took part in a panel discussion in Paris where one of the participants was the Secretary of the Treasury of the United States. I developed, already at this early stage, the aims of European monetary integration. I raised also the question of the appropriate size of an integrated Europe. We were at that time only six countries facing the rest of the world. I asked the Secretary of the Treasury a question and he answered it in his intervention. I said: 'Would it not be good for the United States to have a European competitor?' He agreed that it could have advantages for the United States. He pointed to the experience that if you worked only on the external front of monetary policy, you might forget the internal financial consequences for your own country.

That is only to say that, generations come and go, and it is always difficult for a new generation to draw conclusions from earlier events. Professor Kindleberger and myself are from a generation that can remember why all this happened.

Why did the European belligerents start a kind of European unification? We know, from our own experience, that there was a common need behind the new political thinking. It was simply to end the periodical world wars which started in Europe. And how could you make peace, and how could you keep peace, in Europe for a longer time? Fortunately there were men and women who, at that time, thought that there should be no more war, at least in Western Europe. They believed in particularly that the classical, historical clash between the Germanic and the Romanic states should be brought to an end.

So that's the larger frame in which I would set the conclusions of this colloquium. Remember the reasons why I consider, even if there may be difficulties, even if all our wishes cannot be fulfilled, it is necessary to drive home the political impact of monetary union and that of a single currency.

There have been voices claiming that it would be outrageous to give up sovereign rights. But I could enumerate all the important sovereign rights which already have been pooled, in the common interest since 1950. Or do you think that starting a common agricultural policy would have been possible if the unilateral right to fix the prices and the income of the farmers had not been given up?

There is also a logic to the whole structure of the common market. The Treaty of Rome already had laid down as a final aim that the Common Market completely free the circulation of goods, services and labor with the further goal of complete liberalization of the flow of capital.

We have now to face the euro. And the euro is simply the consequence of a chain of agreements which have been made over the years, step by step, never going back, never in the bad direction, always moving forward to achieve final economic peace in Europe. Because, and I experienced that as a young man, economic wars can be as disastrous as military wars. I can look back to the thirties of this century when nearly all nations practiced competitive devaluations in chaotic ways to gain export markets. Now, step by step, we have brought about, culminating in the Treaty of Maastricht, the economic and monetary integration of the European Community.

I am convinced that the euro is good for Europe and that it is good for the world. I think that, with the economic potential of the 15 European countries which are now members of the Union, and which could be a greater number soon, the euro should be beneficial to the EU members. It gives the Union's members and their representatives an impact on world affairs.

With these achievements we have kept peace in Western Europe for 50 years. It will be up to future generations to maintain and to strengthen this record in the years to come. It is in view of that perspective that we have been discussing these two days the need for the European economy and the European currency to live harmoniously together.

During some forty years I followed closely all negotiations that took place within the Community. I would like to testify my own experience that both the way and the spirit in which international affairs among the members of the European Union are conducted have completely changed. We have learned not only to defend the interest of our own country, of our own government, of our own people, but also to understand from the outset, before entering into discussion, what are the problems of the other countries. This has had a psychological effect on the minds of negotiators. In Europe all those who are working in this for their governments, have understood that there is now a different type of negotiation. It's no longer *Realpolitik*. In the Union you have to take into account not only your own interests, but also those of the partner with whom you have to discuss. And it has worked! It worked concerning very difficult policies such as agricultural policy, such as common customs tariffs, all those things which we have struggled for over years. It worked! In future it can be extended to other nations who share the same ideas of greater understanding, solidarity and democracy.

Charles Ruppert: Thank you very much Mr. Werner. As I am chairing this keynote session, there are just three things which remain to be said: First, Professor Kindleberger is not only committed to economics and monetary affairs, he is also committed to our country. For three months he was fighting in the Battle of the Bulge—Bataille des Ardennes—around the village of Houffalize. We thank him for that. Second, I think that all of us have benefited from this intense debate. Third, I thank all of you. Those who contributed to the colloquium, those who contributed to the keynote session and those who have been listening to it.

Conference Participants

I. Participants in the Working Sessions

Serge Allegrezza, Chargé de Direction, Ministry of Economy, Luxembourg

Gerhard Michael Ambrosi, Professor, European Economic Policy, University of Trier

William Andrews, Professor, Department of Political Science, State University of New York

Michèle Bailly, Senior Counsellor, World Bank European Office, Paris

Jörg Baumberger, Professor, Volkswirtschaftliche Abteilung, University of St. Gallen

Agnès Bénassy-Quéré, CEPII, Paris

Christian de Boissieu, Professor, University of Paris I, Centre d'Economie Bancaire Internationale, Paris

Fernand Braun, Special Counsellor of the European Commission, Brussels

Francis Carpenter, Secretary General, European Investment Bank, Luxembourg

Hervé Carré, Director of Monetary Affairs, European Commission, Brussels

Herbert Christie, Director-General, Directorate for Economic and Financial Studies, European Investment Bank, Luxembourg

Jul Christophory, Director of the Luxembourg Office of the European Commission

Emil-Maria Claassen, Professor, University of Paris-Dauphine

Armand Clesse, Director, Luxembourg Institute for European and International Studies

Stefan Collignon, Research Director, Association for the Monetary Union of Europe, Paris

Richard N. Cooper, Professor, Center for International Affairs, Harvard University

Roy Denman, Consultant, former Ambassador of the European Communities to Washington, Brussels

Klaus Günter Deutsch, Deutsche Bank Research, Frankfurt

Winfried Didzoleit, European Correspondent, Der Spiegel, Brussels

Archie Epps, Dean of Students, Harvard College

Henri Etienne, former Director at the European Commission, Luxembourg

Jeffrey A. Frankel, Professor, Member of the Council of Economic Advisers, Executive Office of the President, Washington, D.C.

Jeffry A. Frieden, Professor, Department of Government, Harvard University

Herbert Giersch, Professor (emer.), Institut für Weltwirtschaft, Kiel

Dieter Hartwich, honorary Secretary General, European Investment Bank, Luxembourg

C. Randall Henning, Professor, Visiting Fellow, Institute for International Economics, Washington, D.C.

Mario Hirsch, Editor in chief, d'Lëtzebuerger Land, Luxembourg

Christopher Hurst, Head of Division, Chief Economist's Department, European Investment Bank, Luxembourg

Charles P. Kindleberger, Professor (emer.), Massachusetts Institute of Technology

Václav Klaus, Professor, President of the Czech Parliament, former Prime Minister of the Czech Republic, Prague

Andrei Kortunov, Chairman, Moscow Public Science Foundation

Norbert von Kunitzki, honorary President of the Board of Directors, SIDMAR S.A., Gand

Xavier Larnaudie-Eiffel, Chef de Cabinet of Mr. Yves-Thibault de Silguy, Member of the European Commission, Brussels

Ugo Marani, Professor, Department of Economic and Social Sciences, University of Naples

Robert N. McCauley, Senior Economic and Financial Representative, Representative Office for Asia and the Pacific, Bank for International Settlements, Hong Kong

Gilbert E. McNeill, Director, American Chamber of Commerce, Luxembourg

Wolfgang Munchau, Economics Writer, Financial Times, Frankfurt

Robert Mundell, Professor, Department of Economics, Columbia University, New York

Susanne Mundschenk, Research Assistant, Association for the Monetary Union of Europe, Paris

Guy de Muyser, Vice-President, Pierre Werner Foundation, Luxembourg

Karl-Heinz Paqué, Professor, Department of Economics, University of Magdeburg

George Patterson, Principal Administrator, European Parliament, Task Force on EMU, Luxembourg

Richard Portes, Professor, London Business School

Hélène Rey, Professor, London School of Economics

Richard Rosecrance, Director, Center for International Relations, University of California, Los Angeles

George Ross, Acting Director, Center for European Studies, Harvard University

Charles Ruppert, President, Pierre Werner Foundation, Luxembourg

Jean-Pierre Schoder, Conseiller de Direction, Central Bank of Luxembourg

Robert Skidelsky, Professor, Department of Economics, Warwick University; Chairman, The Social Market Foundation, London

Niels Thygesen, Professor, Institute of Economics, University of Copenhagen

Norbert Walter, Professor, Chief Economist, Deutsche Bank Group, Frankfurt

Herman van der Wee, Professor, Center for Economic Studies, Katholieke Universiteit Leuven

Pierre Werner, former Prime Minister of Luxembourg, Member of the Council of the Central Bank of Luxembourg

Mingqi Xu, Professor, Assistant Director, Institute of World Economy, Shanghai Academy of Social Sciences

II. Participants in the Keynote Session

Jeffrey A. Frankel, Professor, Member of the Council of Economic Advisers, Executive Office of the President, Washington, D.C.

Jean-Claude Juncker, Prime Minister, Minister of State, Luxembourg

Charles P. Kindleberger, Professor (emer.), Massachusetts Institute of Technology

Václav Klaus, Professor, President of the Czech Parliament, former Prime Minister of the Czech Republic, Prague

Yves Mersch, President, Central Bank of Luxembourg

Hans Tietmeyer, President, Deutsche Bundesbank, Frankfurt

Norbert Walter, Professor, Chief Economist, Deutsche Bank Group, Frankfurt

Pierre Werner, former Prime Minister of Luxembourg, Member of the Council of the Central Bank of Luxembourg

Pictures Taken at the Conference

Charles P. Kindleberger
Professor, Massachusetts Institute
of Technology

Pierre Werner
Former Prime Minister of
Luxembourg

From left to right: **Hans Tietmeyer,** President of the Deutsche Bundesbank; **Jean-Claude Juncker**, Prime Minister of Luxembourg; **Václav Klaus**, President of the Czech Parliament, former Prime Minister of the Czech Republic

Christian de Boissieu
Professor, Centre d'Economie
Bancaire Internationale

Richard N. Cooper
Professor, Harvard University

Jeffrey A. Frankel
Professor, Member of the
US President's Council of
Economic Advisers

Yves Mersch
President of the Central Bank of
Luxembourg

Robert Mundell
Professor, Columbia University

Norbert Walter
Professor, Deutsche Bank Group

Charles Ruppert
President of the Pierre Werner
Foundation

Armand Clesse
Director of the Luxembourg
Institute for European and
International Studies

Index of Contributors

Ambrosi, G., 215-30, 310-11, 357
Baumberger, J., 231-50, 287, 389
Bénassy-Quéré, A., 315-16, 331
de Boissieu, C., 251-60, 300, 325-30, 332, 351, 357, 369, 406-9
Carré, H., 341-43, 347-48
Claassen, E.-M., 157-73, 304-5, 378-82
Collignon, S., 309-10
Cooper, R., 177-201, 299-300, 335-38, 351, 356, 367-68, 381, 382, 389, 404-6
Denman, R., 359-62
Deutsch, K., 111-33, 331, 381
Etienne, H., 385-86
Frankel, J., 93-109, 314, 338-41, 384-85, 418-22
Frieden, J., 203-13, 305-6, 343-47
Giersch, H., 285-86
Henning, R., 35-46, 296-98, 316-17, 355, 369
Juncker, J.-C., 394-403
Kindleberger, C., 3-20, 273-75, 289-90, 330-31, 428-30
Klaus, V., 303-4, 347, 416-18
Kortunov, A., 300-3, 307, 358
Larnaudie-Eiffel, X., 362-67, 370-73
Maillet, P., 135-56
Marani, U., 369-70
McCauley, R., 286, 317-20, 333
Mersch, Y., 423-25
Mundell, R., 57-84, 291-296, 311-13, 314-15, 347, 382-84
Nikolov, K., 21-33
Paqué, K.-H., 352, 385
Patterson, G., 329, 389

Portes, R., 286-87, 289, 304, 322-25, 333
Rey, H., 320-22, 332
Rosecrance, R., 47-56, 313, 348-51, 353
Ross, G., 287-88, 331, 368-69, 386-88
Ruppert, C., 393-94, 403, 409-10, 415-16, 418, 422, 425, 428, 430, 432
Skidelsky, R., 21-33, 282-85, 288-89, 306-7, 352-53, 368, 388, 389
Thygesen, N., 375-78, 386
Tietmeyer, H., 410-15
Walter, N., 87-92, 355-56, 425-28
van der Wee, H., 275-82
Werner, P., 430-32
Xu, M., 261-70, 354-55, 358

Date Due